PROCEEDINGS OF THE BLACK STATE CONVENTIONS, 1840-1865

Vol. I

Proceedings of the Black State Conventions, 1840–1865

Volume I:
New York
Pennsylvania
Indiana
Michigan
Ohio

Edited by

Philip S. Foner *and*
George E. Walker

Temple University Press
Philadelphia

Temple University Press, Philadelphia 19122
ⓒ by Temple University. All rights reserved
Published 1979
Printed in the United States of America

Library of Congress Cataloging in Publication Data
Main entry under title:

Proceedings of the Black State conventions, 1840-1865.

Includes bibliographical references and index.
1. Afro-Americans--Congresses. 2. Afro-Americans--
History--To 1865--Sources. 3. Slavery in the United
States--Anti-slavery movements--Sources. 4. Afro-
Americans--Colonization--Sources. I. Foner, Philip
Sheldon, 1910-   II. Walker, George Elizur, 1947-
E184.5.P75   973'.04'96073   78-10841
ISBN 0-87722-145-6 (v. 1)
ISBN 0-87722-149-9 (v. 2)

To Rosyln Foner for
Heroic Tolerance

and

To the Memory of
DWIGHT CARROLL MINER
Late Professor of History at
Columbia University
A Great Teacher and Friend

TABLE OF CONTENTS

Introduction to the Black State Conventions   xi
  Reference Notes   xix

PROCEEDINGS OF THE NEW YORK CONVENTIONS

Introduction   1

Convention of the Colored Inhabitants of the State of New York,
    Albany, August 18-20, 1840   5
    Reference Notes   23

New York State Convention of Colored Citizens, Troy,
    August 25-27, 1841   27
    Reference Notes   30

Minutes of the Fifth Annual Convention of the Colored Citizens
    of the State of New York, Schenectady, September 18-20, 1844   31
    Reference Notes   36

New York State Free Suffrage Convention, September 8, 1845   37
    Reference Notes   41

Cazenovia Fugitive Slave Law Convention, August 22, 1850   43
    Reference Notes   50

Proceedings of the State Convention of Colored People Held at
    Albany, New-York, On the 22d, 23d and 24th of July, 1851   54
    Reference Notes   75

Proceedings of the New York State Council of Colored People,
    January 2, 1854   79
    Reference Notes   84

State Convention of the Colored Citizens of New York, Albany,
    January 20, 1855   86
    Reference Notes   87

Colored Men's State Convention of New York, Troy,
    September 4, 1855   88
    Reference Notes   97

Suffrage Convention of the Colored Citizens of New York, Troy,
   September 14, 1858   99
   Reference Notes   101

PROCEEDINGS OF THE PENNSYLVANIA CONVENTIONS

Introduction   104

Proceedings of the State Convention of the Colored Freemen of
   Pennsylvania, Held in Pittsburgh, on the 23d, 24th and
   25th of August, 1841, for the Purpose of Considering Their
   Condition, and the Means of Its Improvement   106
   Reference Notes   117

Minutes of the State Convention of the Colored Citizens of
   Pennsylvania, Convened at Harrisburg, December 13th and
   14th, 1848   119
   Reference Notes   135

Proceedings of the State Equal Rights' Convention, of the
   Colored People of Pennsylvania, Held in the City of
   Harrisburg, February 8th, 9th, and 10th, 1865, Together
   With a Few Arguments Presented Suggesting the Necessity for
   Holding the Convention, and an Address of the Colored State
   Convention to the People of Pennsylvania   139
   Reference Notes   166

PROCEEDINGS OF THE INDIANA CONVENTIONS

Introduction   172

Report of a Meeting of the Colored Citizens of Indiana,
   January 17, 1842   173
   Reference Notes   175

State Convention of the People of Color of the State of
   Indiana, August 9, 1851   176
   Reference Notes   177

PROCEEDINGS OF THE MICHIGAN CONVENTIONS

Introduction   180

Minutes of the State Convention, of the Colored Citizens of
   the State of Michigan, Held in the City of Detroit on
   the 26th & 27th of October, 1843, for the Purpose of
   Considering Their Moral & Political Condition, as
   Citizens of the State   181
   Reference Notes   195

Proceedings of the Colored Men's Convention of the State of
   Michigan, Held in the City of Detroit, Tuesday and
   Wednesday, Sept. 12th and 13th, '65, With Accompanying
   Documents. Also, the Constitution of the Equal Rights
   League of the State of Michigan   198
   Reference Notes   211

PROCEEDINGS OF THE OHIO CONVENTIONS

Introduction 214
Reference Notes 217

Minutes and Address of the State Convention of the Colored
    Citizens of Ohio, Convened at Columbus, January 10th,
    11th, 12th, & 13th, 1849 218
    Reference Notes 238

Minutes of the State Convention, of the Colored Citizens of
    Ohio, Convened at Columbus, January 9th, 10th, 11th, and
    12th, 1850 241
    Reference Notes 256

Minutes of the State Convention of the Colored Citizens of
    Ohio, Convened at Columbus, Jan. 15th, 16th, 17th, and
    18th, 1851 257
    Reference Notes 272

Proceedings of the Convention, of the Colored Freemen of Ohio,
    Held in Cincinnati, January 14, 15, 16, 17 and 19, 1852 274
    Reference Notes 294

Memorial of John Mercer Langston for Colored People of Ohio to
    General Assembly of the State of Ohio, June, 1854 297
    Reference Notes 303

Proceedings of the State Convention of Colored Men, Held in the
    City of Columbus, Ohio, Jan. 16th, 17th & 18th, 1856 305
    Reference Notes 316

Proceedings of the State Convention of the Colored Men of the
    State of Ohio, Held in the City of Columbus, January 21st,
    22d & 23d, 1857 318
    Reference Notes 330

Proceedings of a Convention of the Colored Men of Ohio. Held in
    the City of Cincinnati, on the 23d, 24th, 25th and 26th days
    of November, 1858 332
    Reference Notes 341

Proceedings of a Convention of the Colored Men of Ohio, Held in
    Xenia, on the 10th, 11th and 12th days of January, 1865;
    With the Constitution of the Ohio Equal Rights League 342
    Reference Notes 353

INDEX 355

INTRODUCTION TO THE BLACK STATE CONVENTIONS

Beginning in 1817, local and state-wide meetings of black Americans were held in many northern communities in protest against the American Colonization Society.[1] The agitation increased during the 1820's, when the Colonization Society purchased Liberia and began the propaganda campaign throughout the nation to rid the United States of free blacks, who were judged to be a menace to society and for whom there was no hope, according to the Society, of their ever achieving equality in American life.[2] Through this agitation against the racist policy of the Colonization Society, thousands of American Negroes for the first time felt a sense of communication with groups from other sections of the nation. It was inevitable that this development would lead to a realization among the Negro people that their ultimate victory lay in an integrated program representing a national viewpoint.

Events during the late 1820's hastened the movement for a national organization of black Americans. In 1829, the Ohio courts declared that the Black Laws adopted in that state in 1804-1807 were still constitutional. These laws restricted the freedom of the Negro people and demanded of each a $500 bond for good behavior. Unwilling to wait for officials to enforce the decisions, groups of white citizens in the northern part of the state, egged on by the Colonization Society and by a desire to eliminate black labor competition, took matters into their own hands and gave notice that the Negro people either post the bond within a limited time or get out of the state. When blacks disregarded these warnings or were slow to act, mobs fell upon them; on one occasion killing a number and destroying the property of the others. Overnight Negro communities in Ohio were emptied as the Negro people fled into Canada, into western Pennsylvania or into states in the Great Lakes region.[3]

Fearing that legislators and mobsters in the east would follow the pattern set by Ohio, Negro leaders decided to plan concerted action on a nation-wide scale to stem the tide of repression. A circular issued by five black leaders in Philadelphia called for a convention of Negro delegates from the several states "to meet on the 20th Day of September, 1830, to devise plans and means for the establishment of a colony in upper Canada, under the patronage of the General convention." Forty delegates met under President Richard Allen,[4] organizer and first bishop of the African Methodist Episcopal Church, and concurred in a proposal to buy extensive Canadian land with a view to establishing a colony of free Negroes. But their most significant achievement was the recommendation that a parent society be formed, to be called the National Negro Convention, with auxiliaries in different towns and cities.

In the six years following 1830, the National Negro Convention met annually and adopted programs for the security and elevation of the Negro people.[5] In addition, the Convention founded a series of organizations, known as the Phoenix Societies, in the urban areas of the North. Under the direction of Rev. Christopher Rush, Rev. Theodore S. Wright, and Rev. Peter

Williams, Jr., these local societies made proposals to improve the moral welfare of blacks and to instruct them in literature and the mechanical arts.[6]

A series of dissensions which had been brewing since 1831 split the National Convention after its 1836 meeting. Some of the delegates were convinced that Canadian colonization was still the most urgent business at hand. Others felt that it was necessary to concentrate upon building a better social order in the United States. Some were beginning to support political action while others clung to the Garrisonian doctrine of moral suasion. One group doubted the efficacy of associating with any set of white abolitionists, and advocated restricting the Convention to Negro membership. Another group, convinced that blacks could not achieve equality in existing institutions, favored the establishment of separate schools and churches for the Negro people. The latter was opposed by a group of Pennsylvania Negroes under the influence of the wealthy Robert Purvis, William Whipper, and James Forten, Sr., who refused to recognize any special needs and problems of the Negro people requiring separate organizations, and called for their immediate and complete integration into American life.

In 1836 the Pennsylvania-dominated American Moral Reform Society, organized a year before to extend the work of the Phoenix Societies, withdrew from the National Convention, set up its own constitution, and published its official organ, The *National Reformer*, edited by William Whipper. Meeting annually from 1836 through the early 1840's, the society endorsed the platform of Garrisonianism--the doctrines of followers of William Lloyd Garrison, who, in the struggle for immediate emancipation, advocated moral suasion, passive resistance to violence, anti-political action, disunion (separation of the North from the South)--and proclaimed that the Negro people attend only those schools and churches open to both races. The Garrisonians, through the *Liberator* and the *National Anti-Slavery Standard*, supported this point of view.

Opposition to the Moral Reformists grew as it became clear to many of the 500,000 free blacks in the United States that white people were not anxious to share their institutions. In 1840 a demand arose for the holding of a new National Negro Convention, and Committees of Correspondence and local and regional bodies were established. In September, 1840, the National Reformed Convention of the Colored People met in New Haven, under the leadership of David Ruggles. The delegates emphasized two points in their proceedings: the importance of Negro initiative in "extricating themselves from the tyrants' yoke," and the degrading influence of slavery upon the free Negro population. Through the efforts of Ruggles, William C. Nell, Reverend J. W. C. Pennington, and John B. Vashon, the American Reform Board of Disfranchised Commissioners was organized and met in New York City in 1841.[7]

Although the American Moral Reform Society and the Reformed Convention were short-lived, the state conventions and local auxiliary societies progressed rapidly during the 1830's and early 1840's--despite the unfortunate factionalism. Societies of free blacks appeared in New England and the Middle States and in the great western centers of Detroit, Chicago, and Cincinnati. State conventions were held annually in the western states of Ohio, Illinois, Michigan, Indiana.[8]

After a lapse of seven years, the National Negro Conventions reconvened in Buffalo in 1843. Fifty-eight delegates were present, thirty-six of whom were from New York State; ten states, including Virginia, North Carolina, and Georgia, were represented. By a narrow majority of one vote, the delegates voted down a proposal by Henry Highland Garnet, pastor of the Liberty Street Negro Presbyterian Church, urging the slaves to rise up and overthrow slavery.[9] They voted to send capable Negro speakers into northern communities to inform whites and Negroes about "the claims, disabilities, sentiments and wishes of the colored people," to impress the free blacks with the importance of education, of improvement in science and literature, and of applying themselves to the mechanical arts. The Convention also went on record as favoring the circulation of petitions to Congress for the abolition of slavery in the territories and opposing the annexation of Texas.[10]

Meeting in Troy, New York, in 1847, the National Colored Convention was attended by sixty-eight delegates from nine states, forty-six of whom were from New York and fourteen from Massachusetts. A report was adopted on the best means of abolishing slavery and destroying caste in the United States. It condemned "any attempt to lead our people to confide in brute force as a reformatory instrumentality," and endorsed moral suasion--"a faithful, earnest, and persevering enforcement of the great principles of justice and morality, religion, and humanity"--as the "only invincible and infallible means within our reach to overthrow this foul system of blood and ruin."[11] The delegates also voted to establish a national Negro press, "wholly controlled by colored men . . . towards which the strong and the weak amongst us, would look with confidence and hope."[12]

Nothing came of the plan to establish a national Negro press, but the National Convention movement continued. In September, 1848, between sixty and seventy delegates met in Cleveland, and they represented a cross-section of the free black people--printers, carpenters, blacksmiths, shoemakers, engineers, dentists, gunsmiths, editors, tailors, merchants, wheelwrights, painters, farmers, physicians, plasterers, masons, clergymen, barbers, hairdressers, coopers, livery stable keepers, bath-house keepers, and grocers. Committees were appointed in different states to organize vigilante groups "so as to enable them to measure arms with assailants without and invaders within." At the suggestion of Frederick Douglass, a resolution was amended to read that the word "persons" used in the resolution designation of delegates be understood "to include *women*."[13]

For five years after the Cleveland convention, the National Convention movement lay dormant. Following the passage of the Fugitive Slave Act of 1850, many Negroes were too terrified to attend public gatherings. Any black who was unable to produce satisfactorily proof of his freedom was in danger of being returned to slavery. Hundreds of Negro families from Ohio, Pennsylvania, and New York fled to Canada, abandoning their homes and work. Professor Fred Landon estimates that approximately twenty thousand Negroes, the greater proportion of whom were probably former slaves, fled to Canada during the decade 1850-1860.[14]

The very intensity of the drive against the Negro population in the North compelled the revival of the National Convention. In July, 1853, a hundred and forty delegates from nine states gathered in Rochester, New York, in what was the most important of all the National Negro Conventions. The call for the gathering indicated some of the major problems which made the reconvening of the National Convention necessary:

> The Fugitive Slave Acts, . . . the proscriptive legislation of several States with a view to drive our people from their borders--the exclusion of our children from schools supported by our money--the prohibition of the exercise of the franchise--the exclusion of colored citizens from the jury box--the social barriers erected against our learning trades--the wily and vigorous efforts of the American Colonization Society to employ the arm of the government to expel us from our native land--and withal the propitious awakening to the fact of our condition at home and abroad, which has followed the publication of 'Uncle Tom's Cabin'--calls trumpet-tongued for our union, cooperation, and action.[15]

The 1853 Convention adopted the "Address of the Colored Convention to the People of the United States," drawn up by Frederick Douglass. This remarkable "Address" set forth the basic demands of the Negro people for justice and equality. The "Address" demanded that "the doors of the schoolhouse, the work-shop, the church, the college, shall be thrown open as freely to our children as to the children of other members of the community"; that "the white and black may stand upon an equal footing before the laws of the land"; that "colored men shall not be either by custom or enactment excluded from the jury box"; that "the complete and unrestricted right of suffrage, which is essential to the dignity even of the white man, be extended to the Free Colored Man also"; and that laws, "flagrantly unjust to the man of color . . . ought to be repealed." These demands were justified on the simple principle that the Negro people were American citizens "asserting their rights on their own native soil."[16]

To implement its program and provide for its operation before the next annual meeting, the Rochester Convention organized a National Council of the Colored People consisting of two members from each of ten northern states.

Aided by state councils, the popularly elected members of which were to have direct control of local affairs, the National Council set up four committees; the Committee on a Manual Training School, which was to procure funds, select the location and establish the school complete with dormitories and a farm; the Committee on Business Relationships, which was to establish a large-scale employment office; the Committee on Publication, which was to compile records, statistics, and the history of every phase of Negro life, a collection which was to be made available to the public; and the Committee of Protective Union, which was to establish a kind of co-operative at which Negroes could buy and sell staples.17

Thoroughly satisfied with their work, the delegates left Rochester determined to translate their deliberations into action. They had reason for feeling elated. The Convention had received favorable comments from a large section of the press. A citizen of Rochester, who had never before attended an anti-slavery meeting, wrote a glowing letter to the New York *Tribune* describing his reactions to the sessions:

> Throughout, it has been conducted by colored men, and their debates as well as proceedings generally have been equal to any of the white men who have heretofore espoused their cause as abolitionists or philanthropists of any kind. . . . I have never heard more chaste and refined dictum from any class of men, neither have I seen better oratorical powers displayed. . . . I have never seen delegates come in cleaner apparel, and more dignified manner than the colored men.18

Unfortunately, many of the plans laid down at Rochester and ratified at local conventions never went beyond the paper stage. At the first meeting of the National Council in January, 1854, not enough delegates were present to constitute a quorum. The second, the last meeting, at Cleveland, was disrupted by factional disputes shortly after it got under way.19

The collapse of the program for the elevation of the Negro people outlined at the Rochester Convention practically spelled the end of the antebellum Negro Convention movement. On October 16, 1855, one hundred and twenty-four delegates representing six states and Canada met in Philadelphia and conferred for three days. After a heated debate on the subject of the manual labor question, the plan for such an institution was rejected as being designed to further separate the Negro youth from the population, and a substitute plan was adopted which called for the establishment of industrial associations in communities with large Negro populations. The associations were to correspond and cooperate with one another, and hold a national convention in October, 1857.20

Despite the spirited discussion, the delegates had few illusions concerning the possibility of continuing the National Convention. When they left Franklin Hall on October 18, 1855, the majority knew that they had participated in the last National Convention for years to come. Indeed, not until almost a decade later was such a convention again held. On September 22, 1864, the National Convention of Colored Men gathered in Syracuse, New York. One hundred and forty-four delegates from eighteen states, including seven slave states, were present. After several speakers, including a black woman from Syracuse, had addressed the delegates, the convention proceeded to organize the National Equal Rights League. In the declaration announcing its formation, the delegates petitioned Congress to remove "invidious distinctions, based upon color, as to pay, labor, and promotion" among Negro soldiers. They thanked the President and Congress for abolishing slavery in the District of Columbia, for the recognition of the Negro republics, Liberia and Haiti, and for the retaliatory military order invoked because of "barbarous treatment of colored soldiers of the Union army by the rebels." A special resolution expressed the delegates' gratitude to Senator Charles Sumner and General Benjamin Butler for their activities in behalf of the Negro people.21 With the adjournment of the Syracuse Convention, the National Negro Convention movement of the pre-Civil War and Civil War era came to an end.

Factional disputes, the absence of a truly functioning organization between Conventions,22 personal jealousies, fears of disclosure, lack of finances, the exodus of blacks to Canada and Europe after the passage of the

Fugitive slave Act were among the major reasons for the failure of the Negro Convention movement to maintain a stable existence and to convert large parts of its program into reality. Yet the movement was one of great significance for the Negro people. The auxiliary conventions directed by officers of the National Convention were able to improve conditions of Negro people living in northern rural sections and remote villages. Throughout all the northern cities, the local Negro meetings organized benevolent societies to provide essentials for needy persons, to create mutual insurance funds for their members, to provide teachers and social workers for the communities, to extend loans, and to furnish jobs and markets for goods. Sponsoring itinerant speakers, the National Convention emphasized the importance of rudimentary education and advanced study in arts and sciences even where public education facilities were restricted. Particularly did the convention address itself to the courage, the self-reliance of the Negro people to counteract the propaganda of white newspapers and speakers. It urged the Negro to apply himself to trades and to respectable daily tasks. At the same time, the convention exposed merchants and industrialists, including white abolitionist employers, who refused to hire Negro help or insisted on placing them only as porters. The Convention's opposition to emigration was influential in dooming the colonization movement to failure. The efforts and accomplishments of the Convention stimulated the frank praise of incredulous whites and did more than any agent to refute the widespread theory of Negro inferiority.

The National Convention and its state and local auxiliary societies created among the Negro people a feeling of confidence and self-reliance. It was to these groups that the free Negro turned to voice his opinions. For these bodies were his own organizations; he spoke, wrote, petitioned not as an individual but as a member of the Convention of American Negroes. The Convention brought northern Negroes together as no other body did and provided them with an opportunity to conduct an organized struggle for a meaningful freedom. Through the Convention, as through the general anti-slavery movement, Northern blacks sought to end slavery and achieve full equality with free men and women.

The history of the National Negro Conventions is fairly well known and the proceedings of the pre-Civil War Conventions have been reprinted in an edition by Howard H. Bell.[23] (Unfortunately, the poor quality of the reproduction and the almost complete lack of editorial annotations and introductory information considerably reduces the value of the publication.) But little has thus far appeared on the state black conventions of the ante-bellum and Civil War years, and none of the proceedings have heretofore been reprinted. Yet, in several ways, the state colored conventions were perhaps even more significant than the national gatherings. For one thing, they reflect more accurately and in greater detail the grass-roots thinking of the free black community--mainly, of course, in the North--and for another, representation at the state conventions more completely reflected a cross-section of this community than did most of the national conventions. This is not to say that these state conventions insulated themselves from the national concerns of the larger black community. On the contrary, they frequently underscored and crystallized these issues and, on several occasions, served as spring-boards for the calling of national conventions. Moreover, there are similarities between the national and state conventions, for like the national, the state conventions were concerned with the twin struggle against slavery and for equality for the free Negro community. But virtually all the state conventions had as their main objective the general improvement of the Negro people within their respective localities.

Among the many-sided issues around which the black state conventions revolved, at least five assumed controlling influence throughout the period. These were colonization, the battle to obtain the suffrage, education, abolitionism, and the struggle for equality. Other issues, too, received a hearing, such as the establishment of farms and manual labor schools, support for black organizations (such as the church and literary and benevolent institutions), along with the black press. Economic concerns loomed high on the agenda of the state conventions. The increasing limitations of economic opportunities for blacks in the North, the "organized conspiracy" to remove black workers from skilled occupations, and the competition in the unskilled arena from Irish immigrants[24] were pointed to at many of the conventions. But the overwhelming theme, reaffirmed again and again, was the demand for basic American rights, rights deemed inviolable, such as personal freedom and the suffrage. This demand became the watchword for the overwhelming majority of the state conventions.

The state conventions of this period generally followed the same format. A call would be issued; delegates would respond from various parts of the states, the most numerous from the large urban areas; the conventions would begin with an opening address; resolutions touching upon a broad range of black concerns would then be introduced and vigorously debated. Education for their children, for example, appeared frequently as a question which blacks were earnestly asked to support. Resolutions were also frequently introduced calling attention to the need to support or read newspapers, especially those organs, whether white or black, which championed their cause. Other resolutions, dealing with slavery and anti-slavery, colonization, the evils of intemperance and vice, all figured in the proceedings of most of these conventions.

Following the presentation and approval of resolutions, the official *Address* of the convention, setting forth its claims and sentiments, was sent forth to the general public. It was not unusual to have at least three addresses, one directed to the state legislature, another to the white people of the state, and a third to the blacks. For keen analyses of the issues outlined and for breadth of research and argument, these addresses are among the outstanding political documents of the period. Some were unusually long and repetitive at times, but most presented their arguments in clear, detailed, and masterly fashion. Together with the addresses of the National Negro Conventions, these documents of the black state conventions, with their arguments in support of black rights, compare favorably with the major legal and constitutional treatises in American history. And for eloquence they have few superiors. Take, for example, the "Address" of the very first convention included in this collection, that of the Colored Inhabitants of the State of New York, August 18-20, 1840:

> We base our claim upon the possession of the common and yet exalted faculties of manhood. . . . WE ARE MEN. 1. Those sympathies which find their natural channel, and legitimate and healthy exercise in civil and political relations, have the same being and nature in us that they have in the rest of the human family. 2. Those yearnings and longings for for the exercise of political prerogatives, that are the product of the adaptedness of man's social nature to political arrangements, strive with irrepressible potency within us, from the fact of our disfranchised condition, a prevalent and unreasonable state of caste, and the operation of laws and statutes not proceeding from, yet operating upon us. 3. Those indignities and wrongs which naturally become the portion of a disfranchised class, and gather accumulated potency from an increase and intenseness of proscription, naturally and legitimately revert to us.

Or take the following from "A Letter to the American Slaves from Those Who Have Fled from American Slavery," adopted by the Cazenovia (New York) Fugitive Slave Law Convention, August 21-22, 1850:

> You are taught to respect the rights of property. But, no such right belongs to the slaveholder. His right to property is but the robber-right. In every slaveholding community, the rights of property all center in them, whose coerced and unrequited toil has created the wealth in which their oppressors riot. Moreover, if your oppressors have rights of property, you, at least, are exempt from all obligations to respect them. For you are prisoners of war, in an enemy's country.

And there are the following in the Addresses of the Pennsylvania State Conventions dealing with the constitutional ban of 1838 depriving blacks of the right to vote:

> It is impolitic for the state thus to restrict any portion of her inhabitants, because it degrades them, and in so far detracts from the honor and respectability of the state. It deprives them of one of the most powerful stimulants to a virtuous and upright life; paralyzes their efforts to attain wealth and respectability; and thus lessens the general wealth of the state, and the amount of taxes which would otherwise be paid into the state treasury. It is oppressive, because we are required to pay the same homage and obedience to the laws as other citizens, and the same taxes, and are yet denied the same equivalent. It also deprives us of political defence. Our worst adversary may be a candidate for an office, the salary of which is in part made up of taxes paid out of our own pockets, and yet we have not the power of casting a single vote to prevent his triumph. It tears away the bulwark, the very citadel of our liberties, and leaves us exposed on every side. It is wrong, because it inflicts punishment upon the innocent. The elective franchise is the highest privilege known to republicans; it is the foundation and only safeguard of all political rights; and to deprive one of it, is to inflict the highest political punishment.
>
> . . . It has been argued that we were disfranchised on the grounds of *condition*. This we deny. The *reasons* urged for our disfranchisement were *founded* on *condition*. Those who laboured to disfranchise us, *dared* not to make *condition* the *standard*. While they asserted our inferiority, they were too cowardly to give us a fair field to become competitors for the *prize of merit*. They were cunning logicians, and well knew no argument founded on *condition* would meet the *false prejudice* of *their constituents*. They knew that the period had long since passed when it would be *possible* to *frame* a standard of *condition* that would separate the *white* from the *colored* people.
> So they disfranchised us by *extinguishing justice--disqualifying merit*, assuming *condition* as their *reason*, and *complexion* as the *standard*. By refusing to make their *standard* the basis of their reasons, they have admitted its injustice; and by refusing to make their *reasons* their *standard* of disqualification, they have denied *their* validity.

Then there is the blunt but eloquent statement in the Address of the Colored Convention to the Citizens of Kansas in 1863: "The Tree of American Liberty, whose spreading branches now overshadow a continent, germinated in a soil watered with the blood of black as well as white men. That black men do not now enjoy the rights for which their ancestors in common with yours fought, is their misfortune, but your reproach."

There is also the irrefutable statement in the Address of the Colored People of Missouri to the Friends of Equal Rights, October 12, 1865:

> We are told that we are weak; hence we ask for those rights which make free men strong; and are ever deemed essential to the white man's confidence and courage.
> We are told that we are ignorant; hence we ask for those lessons of experience in governing ourselves which, also, is ever deemed essential to the white man's advancement.
> We are told that we are poor; hence we ask that by our own votes we may encourage our own industry, make corporations for our capital, may charter our enterprises and give laws to our commerce, and, with the white men, be permitted to illus-

trate the axiomatic truth "that no man is so reliable as he who is entrusted with the welfare of his country," and is ever "'more responsible when he goes to the ballot box. . . .'"

We ask for a citizenship based upon a principle so broad and solid that upon it black men, white men and every American born can equally, safely and eternally stand.

That "principle" was spelled out by the 1857 Ohio State Convention of Colored Men when it noted that the "Declaration of Independence, and the American definition of human freedom, declared that *all* men are created equal--that is, that all are equally endowed with natural and inherent rights. These rights are not *created* by *Constitutions*, nor are they *uncreated by Constitutions*. Their existence is not dependent upon the curl of a man's hair, the projection of his lips, the color of his skin, or the clime in which he had his birth. They are a constituent element of manhood--whether that manhood be encased in ebony or ivory."

On the assumption that the authors of this statement, following the lead of Frederick Douglass, meant to include womanhood within the word "manhood," we can assert that like nearly every sentence in the documents of the state black conventions now published for the first time below, it has lost none of its significance today.

The state conventions that follow have been arranged by state and chronologically within the state. Since the number of conventions varied from state to state, the introductions to each state's conventions vary in size. Reference notes for each convention have been placed at the end of that convention. Unless otherwise indicated, all conventions listed in this volume are in pamphlet form.

In preparing this collection of proceedings of black state conventions, we have had the assistance of many libraries, historical societies, and repositories. We wish particularly to thank the staffs of the Schomburg Division of the New York Public Library, the Moorland-Spingarn Research Center (Howard University Library), the Cincinnati Historical Society, the San Francisco African American Historical and Cultural Society, the Indiana State Library, the Indiana Historical Society, the Beinecke Rare Book and Manuscript Library (Yale University), the Harvard University Library, the Pennsylvania State University Library, the Library Company of Philadelphia, the Historical Society of Pennsylvania, the New-York Historical Society, the Burton Historical Collection (Detroit Public Library), the New Jersey Historical Society, the Library of Congress, the California Historical Society, the Oberlin College Library, the Chicago Historical Society, the New York Public Library, the Columbia University Library. The library of Lincoln University, Pennsylvania, was very helpful in obtaining materials through interlibrary loan. Special thanks are owing to Mrs. Charlene Calder, secretary in the History Department at George Mason University. She devoted an enormous amount of time in making telephone calls and typing our correspondence with scores of libraries and historical societies throughout the United States.

Philip S. Foner
Lincoln University,
Pennsylvania

George E. Walker
George Mason University
Fairfax, Virginia

REFERENCE NOTES

1. For the origins of the American Colonization Society, see Philip S. Foner, *History of Black Americans: From Africa to the Emergence of the Cotton Kingdom* (Westport, Conn., 1975), pp. 584-593.
2. *Ibid.*, pp. 592-593.
3. "Banishment of the People of Color from Cincinatti," *Journal of Negro History*, VIII (July 1923), 331-332.
4. Eighteen delegates were from Pennsylvania, four from New York, one from Connecticut, two from Rhode Island, seven from Maryland, three from Delaware, three from Virginia, and one each from New Jersey and Ohio.
5. Sixteen delegates met in Philadelphia in June, 1831; 29 delegates met again in Philadelphia in June, 1832; 56 delegates convened in Philadelphia in June, 1833; 40 delegates from seven states met in New York City in June, 1834; the 1835 convention met in June in Philadelphia, and the next convention met in June, 1836, in New York City.
6. Bella Gross, *Clarion Call: The History and Development of the Negro Convention Movement in the United States from 1817 to 1840* (New York, 1947), pp. 34-36.
7. *Ibid.*, pp. 40-41.
8. Philip S. Foner, *Frederick Douglass* (New York, 1969), p. 110.
9. Frederick Douglass, still under the influence of Garrisonian principles of non-resistance and moral suasion, led the opposition to Garnet. See Philip S. Foner, *Life and Writings of Frederick Douglass*, II (New York, 1950), 22-23. For Garnet's speech in favor of his resolution, see Philip S. Foner, *The Voice of Black America: Major Speeches by Blacks in the United States, 1797-1973* (New York, 1975), I, 103-111.
10. *Minutes of the National Convention of Colored Citizens, Buffalo, New York, August, 1843* (Buffalo, 1843), pp. 24, 37-39.
11. *Proceedings of the National Convention of Colored People, and Their Friends Held in Troy, N.Y. . . . , October, 1847* (Troy, 1847), pp. 31-32; *The North Star*, Jan. 14, 1848.
12. At the convention, Gerrit Smith presented the delegates with 120,000 acres of New York State farming and timber land on which 3,000 Negro people of that state, if they wished to settle upon the property, could put small farms into operation. See Zita Dyson, "Gerrit Smith's Efforts in Behalf of Negroes in New York," *Journal of Negro History*, III (Oct., 1918), 354-359.
13. *Report of the Proceedings of Colored National Convention, Held at Cleveland, Ohio, on Wednesday, September 6, 1848* (Rochester, 1848), pp. 8, 12; *The North Star*, Sept. 19, 1848; *Liberator*, Oct. 20, 1848. For Douglass's position as a pioneer male champion of woman's rights, see Philip S. Foner, *Frederick Douglass and Women's Rights* (Westport, Conn., 1977).
14. Fred Landon, "The Negro Migration to Canada after 1850," *Journal of Negro History*, V (Jan., 1920), 22.
15. *Proceedings of the Colored National Convention Held in Rochester, July, 1853* (Rochester, 1853), p. 4. *Uncle Tom's Cabin; or, Life Among the Lowly* (Cleveland, 1852) was so popular that it was translated into at least 23 languages.
16. *Ibid.*, pp. 6-8.
17. *Ibid.*, pp. 17-22.
18. *New York Tribune*, July 12, 1853.
19. *Frederick Douglass' Paper*, Feb. 5, 1854.
20. *Proceedings of the Colored Convention Held in Franklin Hall, Sixth Street Below Arch, Philadelphia, October 16th, 17th and 18th, 1855* (Salem, N.J., 1856).
21. *Proceedings of the National Convention of Colored Men Held in Syracuse, New York, October 4-7, 1864* (New York, 1864), pp. 44-62.
22. To give the National Convention movement a permanent organizational structure, Frederick Douglass proposed the idea of a National League of Colored People. The object of the League was the abolition of slavery and improvement of the free black population of the United States. It would seek to achieve these goals by means of lectures and the press, "and all other means within their power, consistent with Christian morality." The League would have a president, secretary, treasurer, and a council of nine. (*The*

North Star, Aug. 10, 1849.) The League never was created due to the cool response from the Negro people. (Foner, *Life and Writings of Douglass*, II, 27-28.

23. Howard Holman Bell, ed., *Minutes of the Proceedings of the National Negro Conventions, 1830-1865* (New York, 1969). The volume includes reprints of proceedings of twelve conventions. Bell is also the author of *A Survey of the Negro Convention Movement, 1830-1861* (New York, 1969).

24. For a discussion of this development, see Philip S. Foner, *Organized Labor and the Black Worker, 1619-1973* (New York, 1974), pp. 6-11.

PROCEEDINGS OF THE NEW YORK CONVENTIONS

INTRODUCTION

As far as is known, the Convention of the Colored Inhabitants of the State of New York, August 18-20, 1840, was probably the first state-wide gathering of blacks in the United States. It assembled for the specific purpose of agitating for the right of suffrage. Blacks in New York were denied the franchise, under the provisions of the state constitution of 1821, unless they owned property valued at $250. (Up to 1821, most blacks had exercised the vote; the effect of the new requirement was summarily to exclude the majority of the free Negro population from exercising this right.) This convention represented by far the most concerted effort on the part of blacks up to that time to regain the suffrage. It was reported to have attracted a large audience, with sessions ranging from 40 to 140 delegates and supporters.

On the third day the delegates passed a series of resolutions outlining the strategy blacks should take with reference to the franchise. Continued reliance upon petitioning was a major element in this program. One resolution urged that a committee of seven be set up, consisting of four members from Albany and three from Troy, whose duty "it shall be to correspond with other committees throughout the state, appointed for the same purpose." Another, issued by the Business Committee, requested the establishment of a committee of five from each county in the state "except from New York," which would be allowed ten members. These committees were to be known officially as "County Committees." The last resolution provided that the County Committees forward their petitions to the Central Committee, which body was then to forward them to the appropriate legislative committee at the capital in Albany.

The second state-wide meeting of New York blacks (November 18-20, 1844) also had as its central objective the extension of the elective franchise. At this convention, a faction, headed by Ulysses S. Vidal and James McCune Smith, delegates from New York City, drew up a protest condemning the action of the Rochester convention (August, 1843), which had met for the specific purpose of discussing ways and means of obtaining the elective franchise, had passed a series of resolutions extremely critical of the Whig and Democratic parties as proslavery in character, and had urged blacks in New York not to lend them support. There was also an indirect endorsement of the principles of the Liberty Party, which did take a pro-suffrage position in favor of blacks. The Smith-Vidal faction at the 1844 convention contended that the Rochester Convention lacked the right to adopt "resolutions extraneous or detrimental to that object." The protest further noted that the Convention had made the extension of the franchise an issue dependent on "the success of a party which must ever comprise but a portion of the people, instead of relying on the will and magnanimity of the whole people."

On August 21-22, 1850, a black convention assembled at Cazenovia, in up-state New York, to protest the imprisonment of abolitionist William L. Chaplin, who had been arrested by Washington police, on Maryland soil, for having participated in the escape of two slaves, the property of Robert Toombs and Alexander H. Stephens. The convention also made public "A Letter to the American Slaves from those who have fled from American Slavery." This was one of the most militant and moving appeals to the slaves to throw off the shackles of bondage since Garnet's famous appeal at the 1843 National Negro Convention.

Like the earlier ones held in 1840, 1841, and 1845, the New York State Convention of Colored People of July 22-24, 1851, dealt with the struggle to obtain the suffrage (although opposition to the program of the American Colonization Society figured in the convention). The convention also adopted a resolution approving the recommendation of the Business Committee calling for the investment of monies in public stocks, as being "feasible, safe, and promising much toward the amelioration of the condition of the colored people."

The third convention of the Negro people of New York reiterated its opposition to the program of the American Colonization Society and noted the miserable failure of the Society to effect its objective, pointing to the fact that in its thirty years of existence, only 7,000 blacks had actually emigrated to Liberia. Yet, despite this poor showing, the organization continued its evil activities, hoping to influence the state legislatures and the general public to support its program through appeals directed against the rights of blacks to remain in this country. It noted with much chagrin that Virginia had appropriated $30,000 for the scheme in 1849 while Maryland had a similar fund for the same purpose. But it was quite pleased to note that the New York legislature had not yet succumbed to such a proposal. The convention also condemned the effort by Liberia to seek recognition by the government of the United States and, strangely, found reassurance in the fact that the American government "has refused to recognize the independence of Hayti, and she will refuse to recognize the independence of Liberia." The Report of the Committee on Colonization concluded on a most emphatic note, insisting that if the question of emigration were put to the entire colored population of the United States for their consideration, "we would hear, by way of response, one long, loud acclamation, rising up simultaneously from the city, the village, the valley, the mountain side, No! No!!! Never!!!"

The Report of the Committee on Education stressed the need to acquire education as a means of overcoming a condition of "self-degradation in which ignorance and vice has engulfed a large proportion of the race." Yet for education to have any lasting impact for good, blacks would have to foster three all-controlling qualities in the human condition--man's intellectual, moral and physical attributes--and all three were mutually dependent on each other for the full development of human character. Hence blacks should not only pursue those avocations associated with menial occupations such as porters, waiters, barbers, domestic workers, etc., but should diversify their work activities, where they could, to embrace the mechanical and agricultural pursuits and business, along with such fields as law, medicine, dentistry, writing, editing, engineering, engraving. Only by proving their capacity and competence in these areas would they be in a position to disprove the widely held notion of their inferiority.

The New York State Council of Colored People, which met on January 2, 1854, grew out of the National Council of Colored People, the body set up at the National Negro Convention in Rochester, July, 1853. The Colored Men's State Convention which met in Troy, September 4, 1855, assembled to discuss ways of attaining the suffrage, a perennial issue facing blacks in New York since 1821. In addition to encouraging the Negro population statewide to continue petitioning the legislature for the removal of suffrage restrictions, it urged the formation of "suffrage and political leagues in every city or town where colored persons reside" to secure this objective. As if to prove that the denial of the suffrage did not diminish the political aspirations of black New Yorkers, the convention recommended to the twenty-seventh senatorial district of New York (Rochester) the nomination of Frederick Douglass for the office of state senator.

The final New York convention in this collection was the Suffrage Convention of the Colored Citizens of New York, Troy, September 14, 1858. Meeting several months after the Dred Scott decision had been handed down, the convention denounced the decision as a "foul and infamous lie. . . . It is a bold, impudent and atrocious attempt to extend and perpetuate the blasting curse of human bondage." Blacks then debated the *propriety* of supporting the newly formed Republican Party even though it was not an abolitionist party. Reaching the conclusion that any hope of gaining the suffrage under the Democratic Party--"our most inveterate enemy"--was an illusion, the delegates urged the "defeat and ruin of the so-called Democratic party," and agreed that "the Republican Party, all things considered, as more likely than any other to effect this desirable end." Hence the convention voted to "advise the eleven thousand colored voters of this State to concentrate their strength upon the Republican ticket for Governor, &c., now before the people."

This position was not reached without considerable debate and controversy. Quite a few of the delegates had grave misgivings as to the reliability of the Republican Party, but while this point of view commanded considerable support among New York blacks, it did not prevail. Debate was cut off and the resolution endorsing the Republican Party was carried.

CONVENTION OF THE COLORED INHABITANTS OF THE STATE OF NEW YORK
AUGUST 18-20, 1840

Dear Zuille,[1]--As you are aware, we left at 5 o'clock, to attend the State Convention at this place. Five of us took passage in the majestic steamer, Rochester, in preference to the cheap boat. We regarded the business before us too important, and of too lofty a character, to justify us in taking a barge of a boat, though at the lower price, to linger away we knew not how many hours, and hazard the chance of being in season for the opening of the Convention, as we should not as the sequel proved. We therefore came along in great speed, and were all treated like gentlemen, and arrived at half past four o'clock A.M.

Upon arriving, we found A. Crummell,[2] and C. L. Reason,[3] in waiting, having stepped on board the North America as she passed, and arrived just ahead of us. We also found here, the noble spirited J. W. Duffin, of Geneva, who arrived on Friday evening, determined to be in season, and the dignified and noble minded A. Steward,[4] of Rochester, both full of the spirit of the objects which brought us together.

At ten o'clock, the Rev. Theodore S. Wright[5] called the Convention together--there being about 40 delegates present--by appointing our humble self, as Chairman. After a few remarks from the chair, prayer was offered by Rev. J. T. Raymond.[6] Frederick Olney, and Charles Morton, were appointed Secretaries. A committee was appointed to make out the roll of delegates, and a committee appointed to nominate officers for the Convention, who, after having retired, returned and reported Austin Steward of Rochester, for President, R. P. G. Wright, of Schenectady, J. T. Raymond, of Albany, and Wm. P. Johnson, of New York, Vice Presidents. C. L. Reason, New York, H. H. Garnet,[7] Troy, and Wm. Topp,[8] of Albany, Secretaries. A business committee of ten was then appointed, through whose hands all business proper for the Convention should pass, consisting of Theo. S. Wright, F. Olney, P. H. Reason,[9] C. B. Ray,[10] J. W. Duffin, E. P. Rogers, Rev. Mr. Archer, C. Morton, J. Wencell, and George Baltimore. Mr. A. H. Francis, subsequently arriving from Buffalo, was added to the committee. There were four from New York, and the whole state was represented in committee. It was thought best to make it thus large. A committee of two was appointed to draft rules to govern the Convention. The Convention was adjourned to meet at two o'clock.

During the morning session, the delegates poured in from all directions, and when we assembled at two o'clock, we found the body of the house nearly filled.

The committee on rules to govern the Convention, reported a list, which were adopted. The business committee reported a set of resolutions, which were read, taken up separately, which, after some very harmonious and happy discussions, were disposed of by adopting some, and referring others to committees to report upon the subjects upon which they treat. The afternoon session continued in until six o'clock, during which time we transacted a large amount of business, beyond all expectation; we should think as much and as well as our anti-slavery annual meetings for the two years past, transacted in two days, speaking I should think within proper limits.

This evening was taken up with a public meeting in which the subject of education, and prejudice were the principal subjects. E. P. Rodgers, our worthy President, Wm. P. Johnson, and others speaking upon the first, and H. H. Garnet upon the last--one of his happiest efforts.

Our Convention has been conducted thus far in a most excellent spirit; the great harmony that has prevailed is almost without parallel, and yet all our discussions are characterized with the deepest feeling, the great interest manifested indicates that we are in the way of our duty. We have upwards of one hundred delegates upon our list. To-morrow morning at 8 o'clock, is a season set apart for an hour of prayer on behalf of the Convention. It is now late and I must close.

Colored American, August 22, 1840.

NEW YORK STATE CONVENTION

We were nearly all of last week attending our State Convention, which commenced its session in Albany on Tuesday morning, the 18th inst., and closed on Thursday evening, at 6 o'clock. Our readers will therefore excuse the errors which appeared in our last. We had two sessions per day, from nine until twelve, and from two until six o'clock. The evenings were occupied in public meetings, in public speeches from different speakers, and upon various subjects, embodying our moral and political duties.

There were present on Wednesday, as we were informed by the roll committee, upwards of one hundred and forty delegates from different parts of the State, from Flushing on Long Island, to Buffalo. If the Convention was a fair representation of our people in the State, then we are a more talented, a better educated, more improved and elevated people than we had any anticipation we were, and we have always been very sanguine that we were a noble people. For in point of talent, wisdom and piety, it was second to none perhaps we have ever attended. Another feature in the Convention--it was made up of a large majority of young men, though there were enough old men present to give it weight and stability, the business being principally done by the former.

We have never attended a Convention, or any meeting for public business, where there seemed to be so much deep feeling and intense interest in the subjects that come before them, accompanied with so much harmony of feeling, esteem and love for each other, and conducted with such a spirit of kindness, as were all the discussions of this Convention. Not an angry debate had we, and all the questions that came before us, whether we agreed or disagreed upon all points, were settled amicably and yet without compromise. The spectators, numerous as they were, both of male and female, from Troy and other places, as well as of Albany, and in attendance morning, afternoon and evening, manifested no less interest than the delegates themselves, and were ready to applaud debates, which excited their deep interest. We had in attendance also, upon all our meetings, morning, afternoon and evening, many of the leading men in Albany of the Whig political party, and of public matters, who gave us the most respectful attention, and looked on with grave and dignified respect, and appeared as though they were in the presence of those who know whereof they affirmed, and well what they were about, and the effect as one of their own class said to us, cannot but be salutary upon their minds.

The business of the Convention was of a respectable and noble character, as well as conducted in the kindest spirit, as the proceedings when published will show. The principal points at which we arrived were, first an address to our people upon their duties in relation to our rights. An address to the people of the State in general, in relation to our rights and their duties and interests as connected, and the appointment of a central committee, located in Albany and Troy, and of county committees throughout the State, with power to appoint town committees, and to fill vacancies, the special duties of which, are to attend to the matter of petitioning, and to other matters in connection with our rights.

But little other business was attended to excepting that which bore directly upon the main question which brought us together, viz., the extension of the elective franchise to us, as to other men.[11] Some collateral matters were attended to.

The third party measure came up in a resolution presented by the business committee, after some discussion by them, which, had it been adopted, would have committed the Convention to that measure.[12] But was, after some warm discussions, withdrawn. The third party as some call it, had in the Convention warm friends, and some of its ablest men; it had also some dissenters, and also some not opposed, but opposed to identifying the Convention with that measure. We think the measure might have been carried through if it had been thought advisable. But as we had assembled to adopt measures, to obtain the right to vote, and not to strike upon a measure, as to how we should exercise a right, we did not possess, we thought, therefore, that it was work extraordinary, over much, for a body of disfranchised men to adopt a measure which identified them with a voting party, and to carry out which, voting was necessary, when we had not those votes to exercise. Under these circumstances in part the resolution was withdrawn.

We repeat what we have already stated, that the talent, the improvement, the religion and the interest felt among our people were represented at the Convention. We anxiously wanted one good opportunity in the state, to get the unbiased and uninfluenced embodied views, and feelings of our people before the community, as in the Providence of God we now shall. We were strongly opposed, although defeat was impossible, by the *National Anti-Slavery Standard*,[13] if whose measures had succeeded, would in the opinon of many have proved exceedingly detrimental to our people of the state and through them to our people at large. For one in writing from Albany to this city says, "that the Convention will advance the colored people of the state twenty years," we will allow one half, and say ten.

The Convention can but have a happy and lasting influence upon our people in Albany. Never had they before, a measure with which they felt themselves so identified, and which awaked up to such an extent their interest. And those of them who had it in their power, were exceedingly hospitable, and their kindness will long be remembered by the delegates.

Our paper formed no part of the proceedings of the Convention, a number wanted to bring it forward, but we prevented. It however occupied a prominent part of two of the public meetings and there were found on its side warmer and more friends then we looked for. It goes well in this state, and with a steady hand, will be made to go better.

We have written more than we should, had we not been disappointed in receiving a *synopsis* of the proceedings from the Secretary, who, absent from home, has been unable to furnish us with an abridgment. The whole proceedings will be published in this paper, and in pamphlet from at an early day.

Colored American, August 29, 1840.

FROM THE MINUTES OF THE ALBANY CONVENTION OF COLORED CITIZENS

An abstract of the proceedings of the Convention appeared in this paper soon after the Convention was held. We now give our readers everything in the proceedings of that important body, which has not already appeared, excepting rules of order, and some other incidental matter, &c. The whole would have appeared sooner, but as it was intended to publish the minutes in pamphlet form, it was thought best to wait until they had so appeared, and the pamphlets nearly disposed of. Those of our readers who have not done themselves the great favor by purchasing the pamphlet, will here be put in possession of the proceedings.--*Ed. Col. Am.*

After the President had taken his seat, and declared the Convention open for regular business, it was, on motion of Charles B. Ray,

Resolved, That all persons favorable to the call for this Convention, and who have come under that call to deliberate in the doings of these meetings, be requested to hand in their names to the standing committee, as delegates to this Convention.

Resolved, That a committee of two, consisting of Charles L. Reason, of New York, and Rev. Eli N. Hall, of Albany, be appointed to draft rules for the government of this Convention.

Resolved, That a committee of ten be appointed, to suggest, in a becoming form, business for this Convention. Adopted.

The following gentlemen were appointed as a business committee:

>Charles B. Ray, of New York, Chairman
>James W. Duffin, Geneva
>Charles S. Morton, Albany
>Elimus P. Rodgers, Whitesboro
>John Wendell, Schenectady
>Armstrong Archer, Williamsburgh
>Theodore S. Wright, New York
>Patrick H. Reason,   "
>Frederick Olney,   "
>George Baltimore, Troy
>Abner H. Francis, Buffalo

After adopting these preliminary arrangements, at 12 o'clock the Convention adjourned, to meet at 2 o'clock P.M.

Tuesday Afternoon.--The business committee reported, by their chairman, the following preamble and resolutions:

Whereas, We have assembled together here in convention, to devise means, and deliberately to act, and to call upon all who are willing, to assist us in acting, that we may remove that proscriptive clause in our State Constitution, contained in these words: "No man of color, unless he shall have been for three years a citizen of this State, and for one year next preceding any election, shall be seized and possessed of a freehold estate of the value of two hundred and fifty dollars, over and above all debts and incumbrances charged thereon, and shall have been actually rated and paid a tax thereon, shall be entitled to vote at any election"--we think it our place here to declare, that we hold all distinctions between native-born citizens growing out of complexion, as unjust--not because it restricts us socially with respect to the rest of the community, but because it unwarrantably withholds rights inherent to us as men, and farther guaranteed by the noble charter of our country's liberty; it therefore becomes us, as the objects of this proscription, directly to state the ground of our grievances, to protest against the unrighteous discrimination, and to appeal to the reason, and nobler sentiments of the power holding majority, for its peaceable but thorough overthrow:--therefore be it

Resolved, That all laws established for human government, and all systems, of whatever kind, founded in the spirit of complexional cast, are in violation of the fundamental principles of Divine law, evil in their tendencies, and should therefore be effectually destroyed.

Resolved, That the toleration of complexional difference in the State of New York, is a stain upon its Constitution, and attaches it to the great system of oppression in the land, so vital to our national character--since it is upheld, not only in direct opposition to the common rights of humanity, but also runs counter to those very political principles asserted by the framers of our republican government.

Resolved, That the Acts of the Convention of 1821, which amended the State Constitution so as to extend the right of suffrage to one portion of the citizens of the State, unrestricted, and demand for its exercise a property qualification of another portion, was a violation of every principle of justice, anti-republican, and repugnant to the assertion of man's equality upon which our government is founded.

Resolved, That the discrimination introduced by the adoption of the above mentioned article was a violation of justice, because it deprived us of those rights which should have been enjoyed in common by all native born citizens, because it guaranteed to foreigners naturalized, advantages over denizens of the soil; because it oppressed those who fought and bled for their country's freedom, and thereby were entitled to the unrestricted enjoyment of its political institutions.

Resolved, That we look upon it as anti-republican, and repugnant to the assertion of man's equality, upon which our government is founded; first, because 45,000 of the inhabitants of this State are excluded from the basis of representation; and secondly, because the proscription, merely on account of color, denies the declaration, that "all men are created free and equal," results in the limitation of our liberties, and consequently in the curtailment of our means of "pursuing happiness."

Resolved, That the exclusion of colored men from a free exercise of the elective franchise, gave a falsity to the high ground which the State had taken on the subject of slavery, tore down the principles of its own profession, and was an evidence to slaveholders of their triumph, degrading to a State calling itself free, and holding liberal principles.

Resolved, That we hold the elective franchise as a mighty lever for elevating in the scale of society any people, and feel sensible, that without it, we are but nominally free, the vital means of our improvement being paralyzed; we do therefore, believe it obligatory upon us, and do hereby pledge ourselves to each other, to use all just means in our power, by devoting a portion of our time, talent, and substance, to agitate this question, until we obtain a restoration of this inestimable boon.

Resolved, That a committee of three be appointed to draw up an address to our people, setting forth our duties in relation to the foregoing resolution, and to the cause of human rights in general.

Resolved, That the committee consist of Henry H. Garnet, Charles B. Ray, and Theodore S. Wright.

Resolved, That the government of our country having made provision for those aggrieved, to petition for a redress of grievances; and we, the people of color in this State, being sorely aggrieved by that clause of the Constitution, heretofore cited, which deprives us of the right of suffrage upon a property qualification; we do, therefore, call upon our people throughout the State, extensively to petition the Legislature on this subject.

Resolved, That a Committee of three be appointed to report on the above resolution.

Alexander Crummell, J. W. Duffin, and Rev. J. N. Marrs, were the committee. On motion,

Resolved, That a committee of three be appointed to collect from the delegates statistics of our people.

Resolved, That Abner H. Francis, Michael Dougee, and Uriah Boston, be said committee.

Resolved, That a committee of three be appointed on incidental expenditures. Rev. Thomas James, Rev. John Chester, and Henry R. Crummell, were appointed.

Resolved, That a committee of three be appointed on printing. It was made up of P. H. Reason, C. B. Ray, and A. Crummell.

Resolved, That H. H. Garnet, E. P. Rodgers, and Rev. Eli N. Hall, be a Committee to draft resolutions and appoint public speakers for a meeting this evening. Adjourned.

Wednesday Morning, Aug. 19. On motion,

Resolved, That the Convention go into a committee of the whole, this afternoon, immediately upon organizing, to hear statistical statements from the delegates.

Resolved, That a committee of six be appointed to draw up an address to the people of the State of New York, upon the political condition of our people. Adopted.

A. Crummell, Rev. J. Sharp, T. S. Wright, P. H. Reason, C. B. Ray, and C. L. Reason, were appointed that committee.

On motion,

Resolved, That a committee of two be appointed to draft a form of petition, praying to the next legislature for the right of suffrage; the said petition to be signed by the President, Vice Presidents and Secretaries, as well as the entire delegation assembled here in behalf of the colored people in this State.

Resolved, That P. H. Reason, and A. Crummell be the committee.

The following resolution was then submitted.

Resolved, That inasmuch as the possession of a freehold estate, to the amount of $250, secures to us the elective franchise, we do, therefore, strongly recommend to our people throughout the State to become possessors of the soil, inasmuch as that not only elevates them to the rights of freemen, but increases the political power in the State, in favor of our political and social elevation.

A very spirited debate arose on this resolution, owing to the exception taken to that part of it which asserted that the obtainment of a certain amount of property, "*elevates us to the rights of freemen.*" The resolution was supported in the affirmative by C. B. Ray, T. S. Wright, E. P. Rodgers, chiefly, and opposed by H. H. Garnet, U. Boston, A. Crummell, and others. The discussion on the resolution, continued till near the close of the session, when Mr. Ray introduced an amendment, which was strongly opposed, owing to its containing, as was contended the same objectionable feature as the original resolution. While yet the question was pending, the Convention adjourned at half past 12 o'clock.

Wednesday Afternoon. The minutes were read and approved.

The Convention went into a committee of the whole, to receive statistical statements; Austin Stewart in the chair. A number of very important facts respecting the real and personal estate owned in the represented places and their vicinities--the state of schools, churches, &c., were made known--statistics of many places removed from the seats of representation, were communicated by the delegates who had made it their duty to procure such general information. The committee sat in very pleasant meeting, for one hour and forty-five minutes, when it rose and reported progress, the facts obtained being handed over to the committee on statistics, to be kept by them for the further use of the committee on address.

Mr. Ray's amendment, which was under consideration at the close of the morning session, was called up, and after some further discussion, was laid indefintely upon the table.

On motion,

Resolved, That a committee of eight, one from each senatorial district, be appointed by the house, to form plans and suggestions, by which we can effectually and harmoniously proceed in our future efforts to obtain the right of suffrage.

Resolved, That P. H. Reason, U. Boston, Wm. H. Topp, E. P. Rodgers, A. H. Francis, A. Dunbar, J. Sharp, James W. Duffin be that committee.

To be continued.

The committee appointed on Wednesday morning to report a form of petition for special signatures of the Convention, reported through P. H. Reason, chairman, the following, which was adopted.

Form of Petition

The State Convention of colored citizens assembled at Albany, on the 18th, 19th and 20th, to consider their political condition, in behalf of their brethren throughout the State, would respectfully represent:

That although by the nature of the government we are taught, that an equality, not of property or favor, but of rights, is the firmest foundation of liberty, and that on which democracy is founded--yet, by Art. II, Sec. 1, State Constitution, a distinction is made with regard to them of the most serious nature--which, while it acknowledges them as citizens, denies them the rights which all others possess as attached to that honorable appellation.

They would submit it to your honorable body, whether it can be for the benefit of the community, that a part should be depressed and degraded; whether humanity and policy do not alike suggest the propriety of elevating the character of the humblest members of the State, by not debarring them from the most efficient instrument of their elevation, simply on account of complexional difference.

In view, therefore, of the injustice and levelling policy of this act, they would respectfully ask, that by an amendment, the enjoyment of equal political rights and privileges, may be extended to them as to foreigners. In fine, they would respectfully pray for the abolition of that part of the State Constitution which imposes upon them unequally a property qualification for the use of the franchise.   Signed, &c.

The committee appointed on Wednesday morning to draw up certain instructions or recommendations to the people on petitioning, in behalf of the convention, submitted through the chairman, Alexander Crummell, the following:

The committee on the resolution which has reference to petitioning, would beg leave most respectfully to

Report

Prayer is one of the earliest and most spontaneous of all human exercises. Man is a creature of wants, which are ever presented in continuous succession. From his imperfect and dependent nature, petitionary addresses are ever attendant upon him, from the dawn of existence to the last slow lingering descent and appearance of life.

In this feature of human character, man meets with sympathy and instruction in entire universal being. In proportion to the extent of want, and the intenseness of desire, so is the depth and fervor of the petition, the earnestness of its tone, and the frequency of its presentation.

The colored people of this State are, from the non-possession of the right of suffrage, the proscribed class. This proscription is the fountain Marah, from whence proceed those bitter waters that run through all the various ramifications of society, connecting themselves with all our relations, tainting and embittering the fresh streams of existence in their pure and healthy flow. The consciousness of want in this matter, is deep, strong, and universal--and so should the expression of it be.

The mode of giving an adequate and natural development of the sense of wrong and want, is for the aggrieved class, in a community where rights have been wrested from them, to appeal to the better principles, the fundamental sentiments of our common humanity, and make a continual and earnest entreaty for their restoration.

In making such appeals and entreaties, we have much to expect. Oppression, prejudice, and injustice, although they have made sad and dire work with man's better nature; although they have withered many of the best affections and noble sentiments of the human heart, and impaired much of the clearness of man's mental vision and the moral beauty of his spiritual nature; yet reason is not wholly destroyed; the image of God is not yet entirely effaced from the nature of man. There are yet remaining to him, high sentiments and gentle sympathies, and deep laid principles, which create a fellow feeling between man and man--which constitute a bond connecting and binding together the heart of universal humanity. The principle of rectitude is as universal among men as the light of the sun. Conscience, well described as

> God's most intimate presence in the soul,
> And his most perfect image in the world,

still remains, exerting her power over the thoughts, and words, and actions of men.

To these sentiments we can yet appeal. From our own human consciousness can we make our most earnest and effectual entreaties to our fellow men in power. Such an appeal cannot but be heard. It will receive deference from its very nature. It will bring forth sympathy by reason of the source from whence it proceeds. It will meet with favor, from being in accordance with the spirit of the age. It will command respect, from its consonance with universal justice. It will secure its success and triumph, from the light of reason, the principles of Christianity, and the dictates of living and eternal right. The committee would therefore recommend the following resolutions:

Resolved, That it is a solemn duty of the free colored people, in city, town, village, and hamlet, continually and earnestly TO PETITION the Legislature for an equal and impartial exercise of the elective franchise, until they effect a consummation of their desires.

Resolved, That the petition which has been used in various places in the State, and copies of which we have at hand, be recommended to our people for the purpose of petitioning.[14]

       Respectfully submitted,
         Alex Crummell, Ch'n.

James W. Duffin, } Committee
Rev. J. N. Mars,

The business committee reported the following resolution:

On motion,

Resolved, That the report of the Committee be accepted and adopted.

On motion,

Resolved, That we recommend to our people to become possessors of the soil within the limits of this State, if possible, as a means to their becoming more permanent residents, happier in their circumstances, and elevated in their condition.

Resolved, That in recommending our people to possess themselves of the soil, we no less protest against that clause in the Constitution of the State, which requires a property qualification of us, in order to exercise the elective franchise--considering it wrong in principle, sapping the foundation of self government, and contrary to all notions of natural justice.

Resolved, That each delegate be assessed the sum of 25 cents, to defray in part the expense of publishing the proceedings of this convention, and that a committee of three be appointed to attend to this business forthwith.

Henry R. Crummell, U. Boston, and J. W. Loguen,[15] were appointed the committee, who occupied the rest of the session in performing the duty assigned, bring in a report before adjournment, of $27.47 cts. collected.

The convention adjourned at a quarter past 5 o'clock.

Thursday Morning, Aug. 20.--The business committee reported the following resolutions:

Resolved, That the idea contained in the Declaration of Independence, that men should inherit rights aside from accidental circumstances or factitious arrangements, it is a sentiment set forth, not merely in that document, but one that is also consonant universally with reason and revelation.

Resolved, That the framers of the State Constitution, in practically embodying the principles contained in the above resolution, formed the government of the State fundamentally republican.

Resolved, That one of the distinctive and peculiar features of republicanism, is, that rights are to be guaranteed and extended, without arbitrary or unnatural distinctions.

Resolved, That whenever, in the administration of such government, a portion of its citizens are deprived (from any such invidious,) of an equal participation of the privileges and prerogatives of citizenship, the principles of republicanism are manifestly violated.

That, That to the non-possession of the elective franchise may be traced most of the degradation to which we, as a people, have been for years subjected, and is the fruitful source of unnumbered and unmitigated civil, literary, and religious wrongs.

Resolved, That in proportion as we are treated with disrespect, contumely, and neglect, in our political, literary, and ecclesiastical relations, from the want of the elective franchise--so would we command respect and influence in these different relations by the possession of it.

Resolved, That there is great hope for the politically oppressed in their own exertions, relying upon the favor of heaven, and appealing to the just sentiments of those in political power.

Resolved, That the way to obtain rights that have been wrested from a depressed people, is, by the continual presentation of the first principles of political freedom, truth, and justice, accompanied by corresponding efforts on the part of the proscribed.

The following report was handed in by Patrick H. Reason, chairman of the committee:

Report

The committee of eight, one from each senatorial district, appointed to suggest a plan by which we can effectually and harmoniously proceed in our future efforts for the right of suffrage, respectfully report the following resolutions:

1. Resolved, That a committee of seven be appointed, consisting of four members from Albany and three from Troy, whose duty it shall be to procure signatures to petitions, and to correspond with other committees throughout the State, appointed for the same purpose.

2. Resolved, That a committee of five from each county in the State, except New York, where there shall be a committee of ten, be appointed in accordance with the last clause of the above resolution--said committees to be termed "county committees."

3. Resolved, That it shall be the duty of the county committees to forward their petitions, when prepared, to the central committee, postage paid, and at as early a date as possible; and the chairman of the central committee to present the same in person to some member or committee of the legislature.

The committee would recommend the house to go immediately into a committee of the whole, to appoint the several county committees.

Respectfully submitted,
Patrick H. Reason,
Uriah Boston,
William H. Topp,
Elimus P. Rodgers,
Abner H. Francis, } *Committee.*
Ambrose Dunbar,
James Sharp,
James W. Duffin,

On motion,
Resolved, That the report of the committee be accepted.
Resolved, That the first resolution of the committee be adopted.
Resolved, That the central committee of seven consist of the following members: H. H. Garnet, Troy, chairman; C. S. Morton, M. Dougee, John P. Anthony, S. Myers, Albany; G. H. Baltimore, and Daniel Jones, of Troy.
Resolved, That we go immediately into a committee of the whole, to appoint county committees.

The convention went into committee of the whole, R. P. G. Wright in the chair.

On motion,
Resolved, That the third resolution of the committee be adopted.
Resolved, That the committee be discharged with thanks.

Mr. Henry H. Garnet, as chairman of the committee on the address to the colored people, submitted. On motion,
Resolved, That the report of the committee on the address be adopted.

Mr. Alexander Crummell, from the committee on the address, reported an address.

On motion of Charles L. Reason,
Resolved, That the report of the committee on the address to the people of the State, be accepted and adopted; the committee continued, and empowered to embody facts and statistics, as furnished by the appropriate committee; and that it be published with the signatures of the President and secretaries, after having received the careful revision and sanction of this same committee in New York.

Adjourned at half past twelve o'clock.

Thursday Afternoon. The committee on expenditures reported as follows, and were discharged.

Report

The committee on expenditures beg leave to report:
For lights for public meetings, $1.50
Sexton's services, 3 days at $1, 3.00
Quills and paper, 37½
$4.87½

Moved, That William H. Topp pay the above bills.
The business committee reported the following resolutions: On motion,
Resolved, That while we deem it our imperious duty to co-operate with our friends in all lawful measures for the promotion of every great work, and especially for the cause of human rights, we maintain it to be important, also, in view of our peculiar circumstances, and of the importance to our cause of embodying the unbiassed sentiments of our people, that we assemble together, as occasion may require, in public conventions.
On motion,
Resolved, That a National Convention of our people is a movement of great magnitude, inasmuch as it imports to embody the representatives of 500,000 of the people scattered throughout our extended country; a movement, therefore, to be entered upon, not hastily, but only after mature, extensive and harmonious deliberation by the whole people; therefore, we disapprove of the national moral reform convention, to be held by call in New Haven, on the 10th September, because entered upon too hastily--too limited and indefinite in its objects--and located by no means to accommodate the majority of our spreading people.[16]
On motion,
Resolved, That this convention exceedingly deprecate any system of general emigration offered to our people, as calculated to throw us into a state of restlessness, to break up all those settled habits which would otherwise attach us to the soil, and to furnish our enemies with arguments to urge our removal from the land of our birth.
The above resolution gave rise to somewhat of a debate, owing to the opposition of Messrs. Charles L. Reason and Alexander Crummell, who contended that it was introduced in opposition to the object of the convention, as set forth in its call. They were overruled, however, and the resolution adopted.
On motion,
Resolved, That this country is our country; its liberties and privileges were purchased by the exertions and blood of our fathers, as much as by the exertions and blood of other men; the language of the people is our language; their education our education; the free institutions they love, we love; the soil to which they are wedded, we are wedded; their hopes are our hopes; their God is our God; we were born among them; our lot is to live among them, and be of them; where they die, we will die; and where they are buried, there will we be buried also.
On motion,
Resolved, That a publishing committee of four of the city of New York, be appointed to publish the proceedings of this convention in the most convenient manner, and the earliest possible day.
Mr. Wm. H. Topp, from the committee on expenditures, reported a balance of $27.00, expenses deducted, now in his hands, which was, by motion, placed in the hands of Mr. Charles B. Ray, as chairman of the publishing committee.
Mr. Alexander Crummell having made some becoming remarks on the unanimity of feeling that had pervaded the meetings, which he in a great measure attributed to the calm judgment and dignity of the presiding officer --moved, that the thanks of the convention be presented to our worthy President, Mr. Austin Stewart, for the patient and dignified manner in which he has presided over the deliberations of this convention, and that the members rise as they respond to the motion.
The motion was affirmed unanimously, the whole house standing.
The President made a reply, the members again rising, in which he said that he was really thankful that it was his happiness to take part in the doings of a body which had assembled for so great an object; he was pleased

to see the earnest and willing spirit that had brought each individual
brother here, kept up in so friendly a manner; he reciprocated the patient
manner in which they had yielded to his frequent opposing decisions, and
hoped and trusted that the work which they had accomplished, would tell for
much good on our whole people.

On motion of Uriah Boston, it was

Resolved, That the thanks of the convention be tendered to the secretaries, for the willing manner in which they have performed their duties.

The Vice President, Rev. John T. Raymond, here presented to the
President, and through him to the delegates generally, sentiments expressive
of the cordial feeling of the people of Albany toward them, in whose behalf
he spoke, and expressed their entire approval of the measures and spirit
adopted by the convention, and their thanks in anticipation of the probable
good influence that would follow from the views that from day to day had been
thrown out in the meetings.

A short reply was again made by the President.

A hymn was sung, and the closing prayer made by the Rev. Theodore S.
Wright. Adjourned.

Colored American, October 31, 1840, January 2, 9, 1841.

ADDRESS OF THE NEW YORK STATE CONVENTION TO THEIR COLORED FELLOW CITIZENS

"Hereditary bondsmen, know ye not,
Who would be free, themselves must strike the blow!"

Brethren:--The Convention has been held. The sentiments and determination of our people are before the public. We have taken our position. You
are now called upon for exertions of such strength and peculiarity of
character as never before distinguished the colored people of this State
--exertions in behalf of one of the most cherished and precious rights of
freemen.

The mind of our people is fixed and determined; and the course of events
and the arrangements of His providence, make manifest the will of God, that
here on this continent we are to remain, citizens of this republic, inhabitants of the soil, till the latest periods of time. How--in what condition--
shall we and our posterity live here? We are not satisfied with our present
condition in the state. If we look into the past, we behold nothing inviting
there. We see nothing but "chains and slavery." Our lot for the last two
centuries, has been oppression, of a severe and unmitigated character. From
this state, we have been but a few years relieved. During this time, we have
been working our way up, with steady perseverance, to respectability and
intelligence. Improvement and elevation, then, for the future, is the
universal sentiment among us. The man who is willing that we should remain in
the sad and unfortunate circumstances in which we now are, is unworthy the
exalted privileges of a freeman.

It is the nature of man, and his destiny, to be ever progressive. In
this feature of character, we sympathize with the rest of our fellow-creatures.
We cannot escape from it. Society is all alive about us. It is pressing
onward toward higher excellence, laying new plans for increased social happiness, carrying out divers modes for a purer, and more elevated, and more
general enjoyment of civil and political rights and prerogatives. The deep
foundations of political injustice are now being broken up. Political disfranchisement is becoming more and more odious. Mankind, in the mass, are
putting forth just and reasonable exertions for rights--are intent upon
escaping from the slough of political wrong, injustice, and oppression, in
which they have been kept from a free and healthy exercise of their best
powers. And shall we remain inactive?--we, who have and are now suffering
so much from political wrong, from legal proscription!

Colored men of New York! Are you willing that your people should
longer constitute the proscribed class? Are you willing ever to be deprived
of one of the dearest rights of freemen? Are you willing to remain quietly
and inactively, political slaves? Are you willing to leave your children

no better public inheritance than to be among the disfranchised--the politically oppressed? O no! And let the mechanic at his toil, answer no! and those who ply the broad rivers and noble lakes, answer no! and the farmer, amid the rich fields and abundant harvests of the West, let him answer no! and those who live in the inland towns, on the rivers, and our farming brethren of Long Island, and the thousands who throng the crowded city; from all these, let the universal, unanimous reply come, no! Let the opinion of people, of all ages, in all circumstances, in all relations be fixed upon this matter. Aye, and when the pure incense of prayer goes up, let it bear the gentle burden--No!

My brethren, the possession of the franchise right is the life blood of political existence. It runs through all the convolutions of our civil state. It connects itself with our literary immunities, enters into our ecclesiastical associations, and blends with our social and domestic relations. If it have pure, uninterrupted, and general exercise, it is found instinct with life and vitality. It is strengthening in its effects, and revivifying in its influences, To be deprived of it, is like extracting the living principle from the blood of the system. Is it any wonder, then, that our energies have been relapsed, that our powers have been crippled, our purposes nerveless, our determinations dead and lifeless? Is it any wonder that we have been the poor and persecuted ones, outraged and degraded, unable to obtain commisseration from the church, or even humanity from the world?

Brethren, from this has proceeded our degradation. This has been the source of our suffering and oppression. And in all this, is there not enough to rouse the soul, and awaken the latent energies of every man of us? But a redeeming spirit is abroad, and new purposes have been decided upon among ourselves.

Brethren, by united, vigorous, and judicious and manly effort, we can redeem ourselves. But we must put forth our own exertions. We must exert our own powers. Our political enfranchisement cometh *not* from afar.

The history of the world is replete with instruction upon this point. Where rights have been wrested from a people, the restoration of them by those in power, as a matter of favor can never be expected. They are to be otained only by continual presentation of the great truths pertaining to their specific wrongs, accompanied by corresponding energy and activity on the part of the aggrieved.

We call upon you, then, for effort; nor for effort alone. We call upon you for *sacrifice*. Examine the annals of the human race, look over the face of the universe, and you will find, that whenever anything was of great worth to be achieved for man, men have been needed, and men have been willing to sacrifice their every thing--their all--yea, to give up life, for the good of their oppressed people. How full of such glorious reminiscences is the history of our own country! But we--we are not called upon to make sacrifices of such character. But, we ask, if in all ages of the world, men, in view of the prostrate condition of their compatriots, and the inevitable heritage of posterity, have been willing to sacrifice everything of dear and sacred nature for the good of man; is there not enough of public spirit, of patriotic feeling, among us, peeled, stricken and smitten, fleeced and flayed, as we have been, as we now are, to induce, *impel* us to some sacrifice of time, and money, and labor, in our own behalf? We hope, we trust we do not say to much for the character of Colored Americans, New Yorkers, when we confidently say, "There is!"

Let every man in the state arouse himself. Let every city, and town, and village, bestir itself to action. Let associations be immediately formed; and where families are few, let there be an organization in every hamlet. Let the chief objects of these associations be, to obtain the name of every man to a petition, to be presented by the State Central Committee to to the Legislature, until all traces of proscription are stricken from the statute book. Let petitions be scattered in every quarter. Let every man send in his remonstrance.

Brethren, we call upon you to make this great effort. We call for the exertion of the entire people. We call upon age, with its wisdom and sage experience; upon youth, with its freshness, and zeal, and eloquence. We call

upon that portion of the people whose influence is tender, gentle, and
benign--we call upon the women. We invoke the entire people, in their
strength and manliness, to put forth intelligent, and well directed effort in
this matter.

We respectfully solicit the efforts and influence of the clergy. This
is a rational struggle, in which it becomes them to participate, inasmuch as
our ecclesiastical disabilities originate in political degradation, and because the clergy of the power-holding body are generally against us. Let the
prayer of the fervid saint go up for the people. We need that influence that
can nerve the arm--that can move the universe.

That we shall eventually triumph is sure and certain. Whether the day
of success shall be near or remote, depends measurably upon whether we put
forth efforts characterised for their strength and straight-forwardness. Ours
is the cause of truth. For its success we have the pledge of God himself.
And truth is full of His mightiness. We have no fear of truth and principle
in any circumstances, among wicked men or malignant fiends. It matters not
how hard the times, how evil the day--onward she goes, conquering and to
conquest:--

The eternal years of God are hers.

Through all the vicissitudes of time, amid all the revolutions of earth, hers
is a triumphant, a heavenly career.

Let these convictions seize upon and color the minutest portions of our
souls. Let them be characteristic of our efforts in this matter.

Thus, brethren, we shall achieve the great object upon which we are
intent. Thus shall we further the cause of man. Thus shall we secure to ourselves great and important privileges of civil and religious liberty.

Signed, &c.

Colored American, November 21, 1840.

ADDRESS OF THE NEW YORK STATE CONVENTION
OF COLORED CITIZENS, TO THE PEOPLE OF THE STATE

Fellow Citizens:--The State Convention of Colored Citizens assembled in
Albany, August 18th, 19th and 20th, to consider their political condition, in
behalf of their people in this state, would respectfully address you on a subject to them of the most vital import. They would call your earnest and un-
prejudiced attention to the unjust and withering policy that in 1821 led to
the endorsing of an anti-republican enactment, (Art. II, Sec. 1, State Constitution,) by which a portion of the citizens of this State were restricted in
the exercise of a natural right, and refused an equal participation in its
political arrangements. And they would also solemnly desire you to look
around, and witness the multiplied evils that have for years weighed, and do
now weigh heavily upon them, from not being allowed to use, on liberal and
worthy terms, the all-important privilege of the elective franchise.

The patriotic framers of our State Constitution, in view of the then
recent unwarrantableness of British jurisdiction, and pondering on the self-
evident truths that had been made the solemn charter of their country's
liberties, did, in 1777, (by declarations as were calculated most efficiently
to secure the rights and liberties of the good people of this State--most
conducive to the happiness and safety of their constituents in particular, and
of America in general.

Basing themselves upon the avowed principle of the democratic colonies,
that taxation and representation should go together, and that governments
receive their just power from the consent of the governed--they established in
the Constitution, as a foundation guard to the plainest rights of the people,
such provisions as were best designed to keep inviolate their undeniable prerogative to select their rulers--this being the first article of belief in
their republican faith.

In so doing, they did not think it consistent with the principles they
professed, to divide freemen; those who had shared with them the dangers of

war; who had ever been willing to aid them in achieving their independence; we say, they did not divide these, their fellow citizens, into castes, and in the face of justice, confer privileges on one class that were refused to another. Every freeman, according to Art. VII of this firstly adopted instrument, who paid taxes, and hired a tenement worth forty shillings a year, was entitled to exercise the common right of voting.

In 1821, in opposition to the intellect, the philanthropy, and consistent republicanism of many noble men, who dignifiedly stood up and contended against the unprovoked intolerance that urged forward the measure, an act was passed, which, while it protected liberally others in the exercise of the franchise, made it incumbent upon every colored citizen to possess $250 freehold estate, in order to use the before common privilege. This requirement, as we have before declared, resulted most disadvantageously to us.

We now find ourselves existing in the chief division of the government, with no marks of criminality attached to our names, as a class; no spots of immorality staining our characters; no charges of disloyalty dishonoring our birthright; yet prevented (by an invidious complexional proscription) from being participants in those free born rights and sympathies that are bountifully guaranteed, not only to common humanity of this State, but also to foreigners, of whatever clime or language. We find ourselves the subjects and not the objects of legislation, because we are prevented from giving an assenting or opposing voice in the periodic appointments of all laws, just or unjust, that may be enacted, to which we are bound to subscribe, even while we have no instrumentality, either in their formation or adoption.

We find ourselves crippled and crushed in soul and ability, because with all the longing that our spirits may possess to drink deeply of those pure waters that mentally and morally refresh and invigorate, we are thrust from the fountain with the cold treatment of aliens, having even that self-protecting instrument taken from us, which is the primary assurance and safeguard of citizenship.

We find ourselves shut out by the secondary influence of a monied restriction, from a right which is the basis of a people's liberties and prosperity; and by the withering influence of this, we are virtually and manifestly shut out from the obtainment of those resources of pecuniary and possessional emolument, which an unshackled citizenship does always ensure, and which very resources are held up before us as requirements for the use of a privilege, that, in accordance with the spirit of the government, should be the freest and most sacred.

This unequal participation in the privileges of the state, we consider invidious and proscriptive. It proceeds from no principles of justice; it is not predicable either from the position or character of the people upon whom it so unequally operates. The causes which were supposed to justify its enactment, or warrant its continuance, have either no existence, or are equally applicable to a large body of respectable voters of the state.

What are we, as a people, in the state? What is our condition? What is the character we have? What the reputation we sustain? We are native born citizens of the state--immediate descendants of men, held, not long since, as slaves. From this state we were *translated* into the partial enjoyment and limited possession of freedom. Cut off from the sympathies of our fellow citizens, almost abject in poverty, allowed, in many places, but a scanty, and inadequate participation in the privileges of education, and deprived almost entirely of the elective franchise, we have nevertheless, by the practical operation of common sense, by habits of industry, and the cultivation of the religious sentiments, been enabled to elevate ourselves above abasement, and possess ourselves of many of the advantages of RELIGION, INTELLIGENCE and PROPERTY.

We present the curious and acknowledged creditable spectacle of a people, bending under the weight of proscription, who yet will not suffer by a comparison with their more privileged fellow citizens of the same rank, in either religion, virtue or industry.

Although from arbitrary distinctions that prevail throughout the community, we have been debarred entirely from collegiate education; although, to a considerable extent, we have been excluded from the advantages of the common school system, yet we have been enabled, not only to sustain them from among ourselves, but likewise, in many instances, select schools of our own. A spirit of intelligence pervades our entire people. Keeping pace with the progressive spirit of the age, and the continual intellectual progress of the nation, there are but few families in which books are not a common and necessary commodity.

In all parts of the state, from Montauk to Buffalo, literary and debating societies and clubs exist among our people, in city, town, and village. In some instances, these societies are adorned and made more useful by libraries and reading rooms. Our schools and associations are continually sending forth a host of youth, with strong determination and purpose of subserving the best and highest interests of their proscribed race. And not an inconsiderable number of the rising hope of our people, have sought, in some of the higher institutions of learning, either in this or a foreign land, the privileges of a classical education.

We have scattered, as bright spots all along the State, a number of young men, aspirants for the ministry, preparing for academical instruction; or entering, once in a while, the medical profession; with cultivated minds, and hearts devoted to the interests of man, and the great purposes of truth. The causes that have thrown a damp upon our literary ardor, have operated disadvantageously in our ecclesiastical relations. The prejudice against us in the community, has been more potent than the dictates of Christian equality. Not only are we debarred from the rightful exercise of ecclesiatical privileges, but we also meet with indignities and hindrances in the simplest forms of religious communion. We have often been driven from the quiet and peaceable enjoyment of those rights with which the death of a common Saviour invested us, in common with the rest of our fellow creatures of the human family.

Of necessity, then, have we been often forced to form relgious societies of our own. Throughout the State, we have upwards of forty independent religious congregations, of the Presbyterian, Episcopal, Methodist and Baptist denomination; each with a temple erected to the worship of the Almighty; most with settled pastors under a regular yearly stipend; in connection with which there are about 6000 communicants, who, with the respective congregations in attendance with them, average in the aggregate not less than 15,000 of our people who statedly are under the influence of religion, in connection with our own churches, besides those in attendance elsewhere.

The amount of energy and intellect brought out by these various projects, may be justly regarded as bespeaking much for the virtue and character of a disfranchised and oppressed people. Aside from this, a large body of our people are in partial communion with the various Christian communities throughout the State. From these sources, streams of religious influence and blessings are in continual flow, refreshing and invigorating our entire body.

An undue and disproportionate development of powers, produces unnatural effects. A continual enlargement of certain capacities, to the entire neglect of others, of equal, or it may be of more importance, produces deformity. In order to develope symmetry of either form or character, a full, general, healthy and vigorous exercise of *all* the powers, is absolutely necessary. In bringing forth the character of a people, this is clear and manifest. The history of the serfs, under the feudal system, the character of the same class in Russia, and the prominent traits of the disfranchised class in all communities at the present day, and especially the condition of enslaved men throughout the universe, give strong verity to the sentiment herein expressed. Human nature is complex in its formation. In proportion as the various powers of man are harmoniously educed, so is the nobleness and vastness of its capacity manifested. Free scope and ample verge given for the exercise of the physical and mental powers, to the detriment of the moral, an hideousness of character is evinced. And so if the moral alone is cultivated, to the neglect of the mental and physical, the character is not symmetrical.

In a community, man sustains various relations, and possesses powers adapted to them--which, if not permitted a natural and legitimate exercise, are turned upon himself and follows with augmented and fearful capacity for evil, from the fact of having been diverted from a natural channel. It is thus with the possession or non-possession of the franchise in any state of society. Man is a creature of law--his nature adapted to government and its various functions. He sympathizes with its modes, and forms, and operations; and this, from the fact that there is not a single shade of revolution in the political aspect of a country, but it is felt to the extreme limits of the body politic; operating upon the individual being of all its subjects.

The deprivation of our people of the elective franchise, and a participation in the various rounds of public duty, shows the evil here spoken of. The powers that should have been thus employed, have not lain dormant. A trait which we possess in common with our common humanity, has been manifested in us. Powers will have exercise, either healthy or unhealthy. The impartial and proscriptive non-suffrage act, has been to us hurtful in the extreme. The powers that should naturally have been thus exercised, were wrested from their legitimate employment. It has been the source of evil, unmitigated, unalleviated; without even an approach to an adequate benefit. It is true we might become possessed of the immunities of citizens and voters by the property qualification. But this spur, this incitement as it is regarded by some, lost all its zest, in the bitter reflection, in the searing conviction, that we were made aliens and strangers in the country of our birth; a disfranchised class in the very land whose liberties they helped achieve by patriotic service, and whose soil is enriched by their purest and noblest blood!

But this is not all. When we were deprived of the elective franchise, the blow given which severed that hold, by which respect, deference, and consideration is obtained by the poorest and humblest citizen. Our fellow citizens saw they had nothing to expect from us. We became a proscribed, depressed class. We felt everywhere we went, in all our relations, that we had been made separate from the rest of our fellow citizens.

The pure and refreshing waters of literary excellence, were not allowed to flow by us, to quench the burning thirst of an eager and longing people. In the various religious bodies, they have not found their purity of Christian feeling powerful and universal enough to treat man, aside from arbitrary distinctions, "without respect to persons." In short, the means and facilities-- the ways and avenues to wealth and influence were shut against us.

We ask, what might be expected of any people in such circumstances? What might be anticipated as legitimate results from such a condition?

Under like disabilities we perceive the sufferings of the Irish in Ireland, the degradation of the Greek, the besotted stupidity of the lower castes in India, and the abasement and continual decrease of the aborigines of our own country. So in this State; under like sufferings, under like injustice, the greater amount of crime and sufferings among our people, have proceeded from a non-participation in the prerogatives of citizenship. Notwithstanding all these difficulties and depressions, calculated as they are to sicken the heart to a great extent, and make the soul give up, we have nevertheless been enabled to live above them.

We have been deprived of the elective franchise during the last twenty years. In a free country, this is ever a stimulant to enterprise, a means of influence and a source of respect. The possession of it sends life, vigor and energy through the entire heart of a people. The want of it in a community, is the cause of carelessness, intellectual inertness, and indolence springing above all these depressing circumstances, and exerting ourselves with unwonted alacrity, by native industry, by the accumulation of property, we have helped contribute, to a considerable extent, not only the means of the state, but likewise to its character and respectability.

We claim, that there is no consideration whatever in existence, on account of which, the odious proscription of which we complain, should be continued. The want of intelligence, our misfortunes and the *crimes* of others, which was once urged against us, does not now exist. Again: *we are the descendants of some of the earliest settlers of the State.* We can trace our ancestry back to those who first pierced the almost impenetrable forests that then lifted their high and stately heads in silent grandeur to the skies. When the vast and trackless wilderness, that had alone answered to the fierce roar of the roaming beast, or the whoop of the wild native, spread itself before the earlier settlers, our fathers were among those, who, with sinewy frame and muscular arm, went forth to humble that wilderness in its native pride. Since that time, our fathers, and we ourselves, have lent our best strength in cultivating

the soil, in developing its vast resources, and contributing to its wealth
and importance. Those who are the least acquainted with the history of the
State, cannot but grant, that in this respect, we have contributed more than
our proportionate part.

In times when patient toil and hardy industry were demanded, it will
thus be seen, we have ever been present and active. Not only so. *In times
of peril has our aid been called for, and our services as promptly given.*
When the country, its interests, its best and most cherished rights and institutions, have been assailed, not unavailingly have we been looked to.
When the shrill trumpet call of freedom was heard amid the mountains and the
rocks, and along the rivers of the north, and a reverberating reply was heard
from the broad fields and pine forests of the South; when the whole country,
aroused by the injustice of British policy, arose as one man, for the maintenance of natural and unprescriptable rights; the dark browed man stood side
by side with his fairer fellow citizen, with firm determination and indomitable spirit. During that memorable conflict, in severe and trying service, did
they contend for those principles of liberty set forth in the Declaration of
Independence, which are not of partial or local applicability, but which
pertain alike to every being possessed of those high and exalted endowments
that distinguish humanity.

Their blood is mingled with the soil of every battle field, made
glorious by revolutionary reminiscence; and their bones have enriched the
most productive lands of the country. In the late war of 1812, our people
were again called upon to defend their country. The splendid naval achievements on Lake Erie and Champlain,[17] were owing mostly to the skill and prowess
of colored men. The fame of Perry[18] was gained at the expense of our disfranchised people. Not inconsiderably is it owing to them, that Americans of
the present day can recur with pleasurable emotions, and pride of country, to
the battle fields of Plattsburgh and Sacketts Harbor.

We are Americans. We were born in no foreign clime. Here, where we
behold the noble rivers, and the rich fields, and the healthful skies, that
may be called American; here, amid the institutions that now surround us, we
first beheld the light of the impartial sun. We have not been brought up under
the influence of other strange, aristocratic, and uncongenial political
relations. In this respect, we profess to be American and republican. With
the nature, features and operations of our government, we have been familiarized from youth; and its democratic character is accordant with the flow of our
feelings, and the current of our thoughts.

We have thus laid before you, fellow citizens, some considerations why we
should never have been deprived of an equal suffrage, and why a just and impartial guarantee of this right, should soon be made.

But bating all these, we lay our claim on still higher ground. We *do*
regard the right of our birthdom, our service in behalf of the country, contributing to its importance, and developing its resources, as favorable considerations--considerations adapted to banish all thought of proscription and
injustice, from the power holding body of the country, and to lead them to a
hearty and practical acknowledgment of the claims and rights of a disfranchised
people.

Yet for these alone, we do not ask for the extension of the elective
franchise. We would not, we do not predicate any right to it from any such
basis. We would not fall into the error of basing rights upon grounds so
untenable. We object to others placing our rights upon complexion. We ourselves would not lay our claims to consideration on this or any similar ground.

We can find no system of moral or political ethics in which rights are
based upon the confirmation of the body, or the color of the skin. We can
find no nation that has the temerity to insult the common sense of mankind, by
promulgating such a sentiment as part of its creed. However individuals or
nations may act, however they may assail the rights of man, or wrest from him
his liberties, they all equally and all *profess* regard for natural rights,
the protection and security of which they claim as the object of the formation
of their respective systems.

Rights have an existence, aside from conventional arrangements or unnatural partialities. They are of higher origin and of purer birth. They
are inferrable from the settled and primary sentiments of man's nature. The

high dignities and exalted tendencies of our common humanity are the original grounds from which they may be deduced. Wherever a being may be found endowed with the light of reason, and in the exercise of its various exalted attributes, that being is possessed of certain peculiar rights, on the ground of his nature.

We base our claim upon the possession of those common and yet exalted faculties of manhood. WE ARE MEN. 1. Those sympathies which find their natural channel, and legitimate and healthy exercise in civil and political relations, have the same being and nature in us that they have in the rest of the human family. 2. Those yearnings and longings for the exercise of political prerogatives, that are the product of the adaptedness of man's social nature to political arrangements, strive with irrepressible potency within us, from the fact of our disfranchised condition, a prevalent and unreasonable state of caste, and the operation of laws and statutes not proceeding from, yet operating upon us. 3. Those indignities and wrongs which naturally become the portion of a disfranchised class, and gather accumulated potency from an increase and intenseness of proscription, naturally and legitimately revert to us. From possessing like sympathies for civil and political operations with others, and like susceptibilites for evil, when nature is hindered in any of its legitimate exercises--on the ground of our *common humanity*, do we claim equal and entire rights with the rest of our fellow citizens. All that we say here, meets with full sympathy from all connected with the history of the country, the nature of its institutions, the spirit of its Constitution, and the designs and purposes of its great originators.

We have no reason to think that the framers of the Declaration of Independence, in setting forth the doctrines it contains, regarded them as dogmas or idle theories. We believe they put full faith in them, as actual truths and living verities. This they evinced, by pledging to each other their lives, their fortunes, and their sacred honors. This they manifested, by an unswerving opposition to injustice and oppression.

It was in accordance with the views of that great charter of American freedom, that they framed the Constitution of the country. Setting aside the stale primogenital fallacies of the blood-dyed political institutions of the old world; repudiating the unnatural assumptions of the feudal system, and exploding the aged and destructive sophism of natural inequalities in the family of man, they clung with undying tenacity to the connecting chain that runs through the whole mighty mass of humanity, recognized the common sympathies and wants of the race, and framed a political edifice of such a nature and character as was congenial with the natural and indestructible principles of man, and as was adapted to secure to all under its broad AEGIS, the purest liberty God ever conferred upon him.

That Declaration, and that Constitution, we think, may be considered as more fully developing the primary ideas of American republicanism, than any other documents. In these, individuals are regarded distinctly and respectively--each and every one as men, fully capacitated by the Creator for government and progressive advancement--which capacities, in a natural exercise, are not to be interfered with by government.

Republicanism, in these two documents, has an eye to individual freedom, without lets or hindrances. In her operations, she is impartial. She regards man--all men; and is indifferent to all arbitrary and conventional considerations. This we deem to be the character of the Constitution after which it was modelled. Republicanism was to be the distinguishing feature in its operations.

The Constitution of our own State, as it sprung from the clear head and pure heart of that incomparable patriot, JOHN JAY,[19] in its preamble and several sections, was, in spirit, concordant with it. By this we mean, that although the qualifications for voting, *in general*, were higher than those prevailing at the present, yet the ground of the suffrage enactment was not based upon national peculiarities, or complexional distinctions. It is said that *any* man possessed of such and such qualifications should be a political denizen of the State.

As the State advanced in age, intelligence and population, augumented in wealth, and extended in resources, the call went forth for the extension of the franchise right. In accordance with the will of the people thus expressed, a convention was held in the city of Albany in 1821-2.

We beg that it may be remembered, that the convention was called for the purpose of *extending* the suffrage right. We would also call your attention to the fact, that the votes by which many of the delegates were elected to that convention, were cast by colored voters. And more especially would we remind you, that during the proceedings of that convention, in its reports, addresses, &c., a peculiar deference is ever paid to the republican features of our common country, and its democratic tendencies. Yet in that convention, that portion of the citizens of the State whom we here represent, were shut out from an equal and common participation in the prerogatives of citizenship, in the operations of both State and National Governments, and thus placed under the operation of laws and statutes without our agency, and to which we are subjected without acquiescence.

We, the Colored Citizens of the State, in Convention assembled, representing 50,000 of the population, do ask your earnest attention, your deep reflection, your unbiassed and conscientious judgment in this matter. We ask you, as a matter in which YOU are deeply concerned, to come forward and restore the fountains of political justice in this State to their pristine purity. We ask you to secure to us our political rights. We call upon you to return to the pure faith of your republican fathers. We lift up our voices for the restored spirit of the first days of the republic--for the great principles that then maintained, and that regard for man which revered the characteristic features of his nature, as of more honor and worth than the form and color of the body in which they dwell.

For no vested rights, for no peculiar privileges, for no extraordinary prerogatives, do we ask. We merely put forth our appeal for a republican birth-right. We wish to be something more than political serfs and slaves. We fully believe in the fundamental doctrines set forth in the Declaration of Independence. We acquiesce in the sentiment that "governments derive their just power from the consent of the governed." And we say it is injustice of the most aggrieved character, either to deprive us of a just and legitimate participation in the rights of the state, or to make us bear the burdens, and submit to its enactments, when all its arrangements, plans, and purposes, are framed and put into operation utterly regardless of us, in their incipient state, than if we were nonentities; but which, in their practical operation, act upon us with destructive tendency, eat away our soul, and destroy our life. We ask for a living manifestation of belief in the above doctrine; we know already too much of its dead letter.

Fellow citizens! the Colored Citizens of this State, through us their representatives, respectfully and earnestly ask at your hands, the speedy adoption of such plans, and the formation of such measures, as may soon lead to the erasure of the odious proscriptive act of which we complain--be secured an equal suffrage, and the State freed from a stain upon its character.

A. Steward, Pres.

C. L. Reason,
H. H. Garnet, } Secretaries
Wm. H. Topp,

Colored American, December 19, 1840.

REFERENCE NOTES

1. John J. Zuille was a prominent Negro leader in New York City, active both in the convention movement and in the struggle by blacks to regain the suffrage.

2. Alexander Crummell (1819-1898), grandson of an African prince, was born free in New York, where he attended the African Free School. After graduation from Oneida Institute, he was refused admission to New York's General Theological Seminary because he was black. He completed his studies

in Cambridge, England, and afterwards spent twenty years in Africa as minister and teacher. On his return to the United States, he became a noted black scholar and founder of the American Negro Academy.

3. Born in New York City, Charles L. Reason received his education in the African Free Schools of New York City. In 1852, Reason became head of the Institute for Colored Youth in Philadelphia. He was also one of the first blacks in the United States (William G. Allen was another) to teach at a predominantly white school, becoming professor of belles lettres at Central College in McGrawville, New York. Reason was highly active in the political, social and educational activities of his people.

4. Austin Steward (1793-?) was born in Prince William County, Virginia. His master, Captain William Helm, later sold his plantation and moved his remaining slaves to New York State. In the town of Bath, where Helms settled, Steward was hired out by his master. But with the passage, in 1799 of the state's gradual emancipation law, however, along with a series of statutes passed in 1807, which prohibited the removal of the slaves from the state and guaranteed their freedom if their master had promised in writing to free them, Steward's liberty seemed certain. In 1815, he achieved his release from bondage and hired his services in his own right. Steward later became a prosperous grocer in Rochester during the 1820's.

In the early 1830's, Steward was instrumental in organizing and directing a settlement of American free blacks and escaped slaves in Canada. The Wilberforce Settlement, as it became known, was located near London, Ontario (then Upper Canada). In 1837, however, Steward left Wilberforce, returned to Rochester, and reentered business. He met with little success and gave up the enterprise altogether after fire destroyed his premises. In later years he engaged in school-teaching in Canandaigua, New York, and for a time served as agent of the *National Anti-Slavery Standard*. While little is known about him after 1850, Steward was an active participant in the Negro Convention Movement, having achieved the high distinction of being elected president of the New York State Convention of Colored Citizens in 1840.

5. Theodore S. Wright (1797-1847) was born in New York City. After completing his formal education, Wright entered Princeton Theological Seminary, where he received his degree. In 1828, Wright became pastor of the First Colored Presbyterian Church (generally known as Shiloh Presbyterian), founded in 1823. Here, he ministered until his death. Wright was an active member of the New York Vigilance Committee, founded in 1837 by David Ruggles, which aided fugitive slaves. Wright also served on the Executive Committee of the American Anti-Slavery Society from its founding until 1840. He was also a member of the Board of Managers for New York State from 1834-1836. When the American and Foreign Anti-Slavery Society was organized in 1840, Wright became an active supporter of this organization. Throughout this period Wright remained intimately involved in the many-sided struggles and campaigns of his people.

6. The Reverend J. T. Raymond was pastor of Zion Baptist Church in New York City. The church, founded in 1832, was located on Spring Street, between Varick and Hudson Streets. Raymond ministered to the congregation until 1839. From 1848 to about 1854 Raymond served as minister of the Abyssinian Baptist Church of New York City. From 1840 to 1848, he pastored a church in Boston. John Daniels, in *In Freedom's Birthplace: A Study of the Boston Negroes* (Boston and New York, 1914), p. 452, noted that Raymond was "a man of high character, and an active worker for anti-slavery and many of the principal reforms of the day."

7. Henry Highland Garnet (1815-1881) was born a slave in Maryland, the son of an African chief who had been kidnapped and sold into slavery. He escaped with his parents in 1824 and settled in New York City. He was educated at New York's African Free School, Canaan Academy in New Hampshire (until local farmers destroyed the school), and Oneida Institute. Licensed to preach, he became one of the foremost ministers in New York City. At the National Negro Convention in 1843, he called for slave rebellions as the surest way to end slavery. In the 1850's, Garnet was a leader in the African emigration movement.

8. William H. Topp (1812-1857) was a noted black abolitionist and a tailor by profession. Long active as a leader of his people in Albany and in

New York State, Topp played a significant role in the black suffrage struggle in New York. A very good friend of William Lloyd Garrison, Topp's death on December 11, 1857, caused Aaron M. Powell, a well known abolitionist and former editor of the *National Anti-Slavery Standard,* to pen the following comments which appeared in the *Liberator,* dated December 18, 1857: "He was a devoted philanthropist, a fond husband and parent, a beloved friend, a truly good and noble man. Few there are whose lives have been characterized by a more steadfast devotion to the interests of humanity,--especially to the wellbeing of the outraged American bondsmen, and the nominally free, but persecuted and proscribed colored people of this country. . . . I mourn his loss from our immediate circle, as a dearly beloved personal friend."

9. Patrick H. Reason was the brother of Charles L. Reason. A gifted portraitist and engraver by profession, Reason on one occasion was paid $70 by Lewis Tappan, a wealthy New York merchant and abolitionist, to do a steel engraving of Tappan's brother, Benjamin. Although somewhat eclipsed in prominence by his more famous brother, Reason was a frequent participant in the numerous conventions and antislavery activities of his people.

10. Charles Bennett Ray (1807-1886) a leading black journalist and clergyman was born in Falmouth, Massachusetts. It was his boast that the blood of the aboriginal Indians, of English white settlers, and of the first blacks brought to New England mingled in his veins. Ray was the eldest of seven children and received his education at the schools and academies of his native town. Ray studied at Wesleyan Seminary, Wilbraham, Massachusetts, and later attended Wesleyan University. In 1832, he went to New York and opened a boot and shoe store and in the following year joined the American Anti-Slavery Society. Active in the New York City Vigilance Committee, on which he served as corresponding secretary, Ray used his home on many occasions to hide escaping slaves.

In 1837, Ray was appointed general agent for the *Colored American,* a recently established Negro weekly and the second of its kind to be published in the United States. Three years later, Ray became sole owner and editor of the paper, until it ceased publication in 1842. In 1846, Ray assumed the pastorship of the Bethesda Congregational Church in New York City and ministered there for many years.

11. In 1821, a constitutional convention was called in New York State to revise the earlier state constitution of 1777. At this convention, all free blacks in New York who did not own a freehold estate of at least $250 were summarily barred from voting. Up to this period, blacks had generally voted here. The irony is that this virtual disfranchisement occurred at a time when most property-based qualifications had passed out of existence and a greater democratization of the ballot appeared possible. For a greater discussion of this whole issue, see George Walker's, "The Afro-American in New York City, 1827-1860" (unpub. Ph.D. diss.), Columbia University, 1975, pp. 157-187.

12. The reference is to the Liberty Party formed in April 1840. Up to this period, blacks had generally supported the Whig Party, notwithstanding the fact that it frequently hedged on the extension of black rights. Now the view obtained among some that neither the Whigs nor the Democrats could strike a blow at slavery because their memberships included hundreds of thousands of slaveowners. In its platform of principles, the Liberty Party pledged itself not only to the "overthrow of slavery" within the limits of national jurisdiction, but also to the "restoration of equality of rights among men in every state where that party exists or may exist."

13. The *National Anti-Slavery Standard,* founded in 1840, was the official organ of the American Anti-Slavery Society. That newspaper generally opposed any convention called by blacks for the *exclusive* purpose of advancing their rights fearing that such distinct and separate meetings would merely confirm in the public mind the idea of black inferiority. Unfortunately, the *Standard* failed to recognize the lamentable fact that as a proscribed class in American society, blacks had special and peculiar needs which had to be addressed by conventions of this type.

Perhaps the *Colored American* aptly expressed this position by noting that "no people ever succeeded in establishing their principles, or regaining their rights without 'exclusive action' on their part, where they had power so to act. . . . Would not the Americans still have remained under the sovereignty of Great Britain if they had not acted exclusively." It concluded by making this penetrating observation: "Our friends of the *Standard* are at fault: we cannot follow them through all their devious wanderings. They must either admit that there may be, under some circumstances necessity, for exclusive action, or else abandon their first position. If admitted, show us where and how the necessity may exist if it does not now. You would not have us remain passive 'dumb dogs' and open not our mouth when the iron enters our soul. You would have us speak with 'angels trumpet-tongued,' sound the alarm, cry aloud, and make our wrongs known. How are we to do it? How act? How speak? How call for redress? If we wait till Providence interposes we may wait till the 'crack of doom.' If we act with our white friends, as we said before, the words we utter will be considered theirs, or their echo. . . . We cannot in future waste our time in combatting shadows. The *Standard* must either abandon their first position, or explain what they mean by 'exclusive action.'" (See the *Colored American,* reprinted in the *National Anti-Slavery Standard,* July 16, 1840.)

14. The form of each petition was as follows: "To the Honorable the Legislature of the State of New York: "We, the undersigned, colored citizens of the town of _____ Country of _____ and State of New York do most respectfully pray your honorable body to take measures for so amending the Constitution of the State, that the Elective Franchise may be extended to us on the same terms as enjoyed by other citizens." (See the *Colored American,* Dec. 5, 1840.)

15. Jermain W. Loguen (c. 1813-1872) was born near Mancoe's Creek in Davidson County, Tennessee, the natural son of a planter whose slave, named Cherry, was for many years his mistress and bore him several children. Tradition has it that Cherry, in turn, was a freeborn "pure" African, who had been kidnapped during her childhood in Ohio and sold into slavery.

Loguen escaped from slavery in 1834 and settled at first in Canada and later in Rochester, New York. In Rochester, he became a porter and was able to study at Oneida Institute, Whitesboro, where he received the only schooling he had. Settling finally in Syracuse, Loguen became active as an abolitionist and a leader of the Underground Railroad. When the Fugitive Slave Bill of 1850 was passed by Congress, Loguen militantly vowed that he would not obey it. A minister by profession, Loguen later became a bishop of the African Methodist Episcopal Zion Church. See his autobiography, *The Reverend Jermain W. Loguen, as a Slave and as a Freeman: A Narrative of Real Life* (Syracuse, N. Y., 1859).

16. The proposed national convention had been sponsored by David Ruggles, leader of the New York Vigilance Committee. It drew sharp disapproval from such prominent blacks as William Whipper and Robert Purvis, leaders of the predominantly Negro, American Moral Reform Society because it was charged as being "exclusive in character." In other words, the gathering was to be a *distinctly* black convention. As noted above, the *National Anti-Slavery Standard* had criticized such meetings, and some blacks concurred in its reasoning, fearing that such separate meetings would serve only to reinforce discrimination and segregation against them. This attitude, however, was effectively rebutted by other blacks.

17. Lake Erie and Champlain were among the most important naval engagements of the War of 1812, the former having been fought in September 1813 and the latter in September 1814.

18. Oliver Hazard Perry (1785-1818) was the famed American naval officer whose ships, the *Niagra* and the *Lawrence,* figured in the decisive battle engagements with the British on Lake Erie in September 1813.

19. John Jay (1745-1829) was the first chief justice of the United States Supreme Court. He was also author of the famous Jay Treaty with England in 1795. Upon leaving the high court, he served as governor of New York State (1795-1801). Throughout his career, Jay opposed slavery and as governor he signed New York's liberal Gradual Emancipation Act of 1799, which looked toward the eventual abolishment of slavery in the Empire State.

NEW-YORK STATE CONVENTION OF COLORED CITIZENS, TROY,
AUGUST 25-27, 1841

At the New-York State Convention of Colored Citizens, held in Troy, August 25th, 26th and 27th, 1841, the following address was prepared and adopted:

To the Electors of the State of New-York

Fellow Citizens--Deeply sensible of the dignified and responsible position which you occupy, as the source of all political power in the greatest State of the American Union, we would respectfully but earnestly solicit your attention to a subject which greatly concerns our common weal. Great, as unquestionably is our Empire State, it is evident that her hitherto rapid improvement, her present preeminence and her future welfare, are all dependent on the energy, the intelligence and patriotism of the people--the whole people.

True, New-York has not been wanting in Clintons,[1] Jays,[2] Fultons[3] and Livingstons,[4] and other bright stars in every department of human greatness--but these eminent men might have fretted away their lofty abilities, and "died without a sign," had they not fallen upon the congenial and fostering soil of a people of whose genius they respectively became the impersonation.

It is not only true that to whatever of greatness our State may have claim, she is entirely indebted to her people; but it is also true, that, considered in relation to their common welfare and common rights, nothing can affect a part of the people which does not equally affect the whole people. If crime, great or small, be perpetrated, the whole people being injured, the forms, as well as the practice of our laws, seek out the offender, and inflict condign punishment upon him in the name and in behalf of the whole people. If an injury be suffered by any one of the people, the cause of that *one* is taken up, and redress is afforded by the *whole* people, who are injured through that one, and who maintain the administration of justice in each and every case. And if laws be passed, whether affecting the whole, or a small portion, or even one of the people, these laws are alike passed in the name and with the consent of the people.

The people of our State, then, are a whole, made up of individuals, whose relations to each other and to the whole people are indestructibly equal. And herein lies the very essence of the republican form of government; that it is impossible to separate an individual from the mass, and inflict on him personal wrong or degradation for no fault on his part, without virtually and in fact destroying the peculiar nature of this form of government; for that moment such wrong or degradation is done, the government is changed from a republic into an oligarchy, or tyranny of many masters. And furthermore, any circumstance, whether a law of the land, or a local abuse, or time-honored grievance, which affects disastrously the rights of any, however small a portion, of the people, is of necessity a grievance and an evil to the whole people: since the prosperity of the whole is made up of the sums of individual welfare, and whatever injures the welfare of an individual must detract from the prosperity of the whole.

If you combine equals with unequals, the whole must be unequal; if you combined affranchised with disfranchised, free with slave labor, the result must be disastrous to the whole community. Yet such is the present condition of the state of New-York.

This being true, how enormously extensive must be the evil, in what light soever we may view it, which is the result of that arrangement in the State Constitution, by which 50,000 of her citizens are bereft of all political power? How great a loss is not this to the State? Here is not an unit, but a *fiftieth part* of the entire body politic, consuming, in their due proportion, the products of the State--dependent, in the same proportion, upon the resources of the State--the subjects of legislation, equally in that proportion, with the other 49-50ths of the people--looking up also to the State as their guardian, and throwing themselves equally upon her laws and her magistracy for protection and defence. The State, in her legislation and arrangements for her own prosperity, and the benefit of her whole people, makes these arrangements proportionably for this portion as for the rest of her people, because they constitute a part of the whole. And yet they are not able to render back their due proportion, because crippled in their energies by that arrangement which deprives them of that right, the possession and free use of which is the living principle, the main-spring of a government. The State, by this policy, inflicts a wound upon herself, and detracts from her real strength; because government is a system having its foundation in the real strength and powers of the whole people; and any arrangement, therefore, in the policy of the State, which paralyzes the energies of any portion of the people, breaks in upon the general order, and sends, in so far, confusion and disorder into the whole system.

This arrangement of our State Constitution is a blow directly crushing the native energies of him whom it directly affects; the full development of all of whose powers is essential for his healthy existence, whether we regard him in his intellectual, moral or physical being. It is as true in the two former, as in the latter, that if "one member suffers, the whole suffer with it;" and it is true also, that if he suffers as a moral being, he suffers, in consequence, in his intellectual and physical being. In which light soever, then, you may view it, whether by any law of the land, local abuse, or the common consent of the people, man is crippled in any of the powers of his being, he is crippled in his whole being; and himself, and all dependent upon him, and all the relations he sustains, whether to social or to public life, to his family or the body politic, suffers in due proportion.

May we not, then, in behalf of that class among us who feel the evil inflicted upon them, and who labor under all the consequent disadvantages, address you upon this long-continued grievance, to them more than to all others? Nay, more, ought we not to do so? And will *you* not, where rests the power to create, renew or change any arrangement in the Constitution and the laws, listen to us, if for no other reasons, for the multiplied energies which it will call forth in the service of the State? And while so much of real power is lost to the State, and which ought to be regarded as a misfortune, a great calamity is inflicted upon the disfranchised themselves. And what deepens the misfortune which the State has inflicted upon herself, and converts it into an enormity, is these 50,000 people are disfranchised for the commission of no crime.

For what crime can be alleged against the colored population of this State, unless it be criminal in them to love the soil which gave them birth.

The annals of crime in our State do show that, in proportion to their number, they commit a greater number of smaller offences than the whites. (It must be borne in mind, that the police officers arrest colored persons for the slightest faults, and often for no fault at all; because they have not the fear of colored men's votes. The writer of this saw, in December, 1840, eighty colored persons, chiefly women, arrested in one police office, 100 West Broadway, New-York city. All the whites present, with the exception of the proprietor, who demanded to be arrested, were let go scot free. The annals of the Court of Sessions show, that 8 white to 1 colored person,

forfeit their recognizances; these facts, bing taken into account, would
greatly alter the annals of crime.) Granted. But why is this? Inquire of
the Constitution of the State, and it will appear that this population are
degraded from the rank of citizenship; and it is the very nature of republicanism to prove, that if you degrade a man from the rank of citizenship for
no fault of his, you force him upon the road to crime and deliquency. Else,
what would be the value of citizenship of republicanism? It is an absurdity
in terms to say that you can degrade a man without a manifestation of the
same on his part. If, then, the colored population be chargeable with a disproportionate number of small offences, let the charge be laid to the right
source--the defect in the Constitution of the State; and if that be the source
of the evil, in the name of the peace, prosperity, and the fair fame of our
republic, let the source be removed that the evil may perish.

But, fellow citizens, a question of this kind may occur to you--that,
although the State may suffer harm from the disfranchisement of her colored
population, would it not be a greater evil to make them equal with the whites;
and would it not degrade the latter to associate with the former?

This is a fair statement of a popular objection, and we will meet it in
candor and sincerity.

We answer the objection by saying, that men may be *politically* equal,
and yet remain socially distinct: this grand problem it has been the glory of
American institutions to demonstrate. The Jews, for example, down-trodden in
every European nation, in our State enjoy *political* equality, and yet maintain their separate social identity. And the same is true of the Society of
Friends. But there is a living and complete confutation of this objection in
the State of Massachusetts, which, rather than tax colored men without granting them votes, so long ago as 1792 enfranchised her colored population; and
no one can point to that State as *peculiar* for confounding what our objectors
term social distinctions.

Another objection may occur to you. You may say that if the elective
franchise be granted to the colored population, they may, "en masse," join one
of the parties which politically divide the State, and thus fatally prejudice
the interests of the others.

Such an occurrence, we solemnly assure you, fellow citizens, in the nature
of things, can never happen: for, from an extensive knowledge of them, we can
assert, that they are divided in their views with respect to the politics of
our country, the same as other classes of the community; and are now found
connected with the different parties which divide the State; and under any
circumstances, we have reason to believe that they would still be found
mingling with the different parties, as now found. But we are not appealing
to parties in this matter; it is no party measure. Ours is a most just
cause, a righteous claim--to consider which, belongs to no party, but the
whole people.

Another objection may possibly be urged, namely: that the colored population are too ignorant and degraded, rightly to exercise the precious boon of
the elective franchise. Freemen of New-York, can you patiently listen to this
wily, threadbare argument? Unfit to vote? Is there any thing in our institutions which has a greater power to unfit men to vote, than there is in the
tyrannical despotisms of Europe? Have the colored population who have lived
under the glorious institutions of the State of New-York had less opportunity
rightly to appreciate the value, and exercise the privilege of voting, than
the ten thousand per annum who swarm our genial shores, from the besotted and
deadening sway of European kings? What a compliment to the monarchical form
of government.

But we are able to appeal to facts which entirely overthrow this
objection. During 49 years, the colored population of Massachusetts have
voted on an equality with the whites; and we triumphantly appeal to the long
list of able men selected by the people of the Bay State, to show that the
equal privilege of voting, as manifested in the choice of her electors, shows
them all to be men of sound judgment in selecting public servants; and corruption at the polls is an offence never yet alleged against the colored voters
of the Bay State.

Another fact we boldly assert: that in proportion to their number, the
colored population of the State of New-York are not more ignorant of reading
and writing than their fairer fellow citizens. And further: in the city of

New-York, whilst the colored population is to the white as 1 to 18 and a fraction, there is 1 colored to 17 white children attending public schools; in other words, there are upwards of five per cent, more of colored than of white children enjoying the benefits of education afforded by the State fund. (See 36th Annual Report of the Public School Society of the City of New-York.) We ask you, then, fellow citizens, if people who are thus careful to educate their children, manifest a want of intelligence which should exclude them from the polls?

Finally, it may occur to you, that as the colored population are allowed to vote on possessing a freehold of $250, and are freed from personal tax, that they should be satisfied--because they are represented when taxed. But are they not taxed for their *tea*, clothing, and household utensils, imported from abroad? And if they hold $249 worth of real estate, are thy not taxed for *that*, without representation? But you may say, the colored people are exempt from fire and military duty, and therefore they should not be permitted to vote. If the colored population had asked and persisted in maintaining an exemption from these duties, then this might be an argument; but as they have never asked such exemption, but on the contrary, have ever been found in the fore front of the battle in defence of their natal soil, it is beneath the dignity of the people of this State to prevent men from performing duties which they have executed, and would gladly execute, and make that prevention on the part of the people a reason why the said persons should be denied a precious, unbought, priceless right, the right to vote.

Fellow citizens, in conclusion, we beg that you will earnestly ponder this matter, in its simple relation to the welfare and prosperity of our commonwealth. It is your duty to do whatever you can to advance the republic, to fire her energies, exalt her children, and place them on an equality with the inhabitants of the first republic in the Union, in the world. Fellow citizens, we beseech you to do right in this matter, for righteousness exalteth a nation.

National Anti-Slavery Standard, September 23, 1841.

REFERENCE NOTES

1. Dewitt Clinton (1769-1828) was elected governor of New York in 1817. He gained fame as a result of his plans for the Erie Canal, which was completed in 1825.

2. John Jay (1745-1829), as mentioned above, was the first chief justice of the United States. Jay had two sons. Peter Augustus Jay (1776-1843), a noted lawyer and a member of the New York State Assembly, had voted unsuccessfully in 1821 against the efforts of a special constitutional convention held that year to place limits on the suffrage rights of blacks. His brother William Jay (1789-1859) was a prominent judge, author and social reformer, active in the growing struggle against slavery, and William's son John (1817-1894) was a brilliant lawyer, author, diplomat and a staunch defender of black rights.

3. Robert Fulton (1765-1815), the accomplished civil engineer, invented the steamboat in 1803. After several earlier attempts had failed, he successfully sailed up the Hudson River from New York City to Albany on August 17, 1807.

4. Robert Livingston (1746-1813) was a prominent New York political leader. He graduated from King's College (now Columbia University) in 1765 and three years later entered the practice of law. A member of the Continental Congress, Livingston also served on the committee to draft the Declaration of Independence. As Thomas Jefferson's minister to France in 1801, Livingston figured in the delicate negotiations which acquired the Louisiana Territory for the United States in 1803. Long an avid enthusiast of steam navigation, Livingston worked with Robert Fulton in designing the *Clermont*, the first successful steamboat.

MINUTES OF THE FIFTH ANNUAL CONVENTION OF THE COLORED CITIZENS OF THE
STATE OF NEW YORK, SCHENECTADY, SEPTEMBER 18-20, 1844

Whereas, in a republic its great and distinctive feature is the "consent of the people," they signifying their approbation *for* or their dissent *from* such rules and laws as have being by the exercise of their voting power,--and whereas a numerous minority of the people of the State of New York (viz: the colored portion thereof) are not permitted fairly to vote and are as a consequence governed without their consent, therefore

Resolved, That for the completion of that feature of Republicanism in our state government hereabove instanced, we are called upon by every motive of self political emancipation to adopt all lawful and energetic means to secure an equally free exercise of the suffrage; and the majority of the people of the state are bound, in order to be consistent with their professions, to alter that Anti-Republican clause in our constitution which restricts us in the exercise of the franchise, and thereby render the state just and impartial in this essential feature of Democratic governments.

Resolved, That our brethren throughout the State be requested to commence immediately circulating petitions, praying the Legislature to extend to the colored citizens of New York the right of equal suffrage.

Resolved, That the delegates from each county be a committee to circulate petitions in their districts, and that they forward them to the Legislature at an early period of their session, or to the Central Committee[*] by the first of January next.

[*]On the central committee were: Henry H. Garnet and William Rich of Troy; Stephen Myers and Richard Thompson of Albany; and John Wendell of Schenectady.

Herbert Aptheker (ed.), *A Documentary History of the Negro People in the United States*, 2 vols. (New York, 1951), I, pp. 244-245.

STATE CONVENTION OF THE COLORED CITIZENS OF NEW YORK,
HELD AT SCHENECTADY, SEPTEMBER 18-20, 1844

<u>Report of the New-York Delegates</u>

The Report of the undersigned, delegates from the City and
County of New-York, to the Convention for the
extension of Elective Franchise, held at
Schenectady, September 18th, 1844,
respectfully sheweth,

That in obedience to instructions received at an ajourned meeting of the citizens of the city and county of New-York, held September 16th, 1844, at Union Hall, 101 Anthony street, and furnished with funds placed by that meeting in the hands of the Chairman of the delegation, your delegates proceeded to Schenectady, and on the morning of the 18th of September went to the Baptist Church; in which, at 10 o'clock A.M. the Convention was opened, without prayer, and having elected R. Francis, of Rochester, Chairman, it proceeded to business.

The morning session was occupied by the adoption of one Resolution (relating to the Franchise) and the discussion of a second Resolution of like character.

The afternoon session was opened without prayer; two letters, by a vote of the House, were read to the Convention: the first, from Rev. T. S. Wright, of New-York, urging the Convention, if it took sides with any party, to go for the Liberty Party; the second was from Rev. C. B. Ray, of New-York, who, calling himself as delegate elect (which was not true) urged the same course upon the Convention; both the letter writers deprecated any party movement by the Convention. Appended to the last letter was a Protest,* which, after some debate on the propriety of its being read, was referred to the Business Committee.

The Chairman of the Business Committee announced as next in order the following:

The Protest

Of the undersigned colored citizens of the city and county of New-York, assembled on the 16th of September, 1844, to send Delegates to the Convention of the citizens of New-York, to be held at Schenectady, September 18th, for the purpose of obtaining an extension of the elective franchise; respectfully Sheweth; that

Whereas, at the State Convention held at Rochester, August 22d, 1843, for the purpose of obtaining the same object, the following Resolutions were adopted:

"Resolved, That the Whig party, and the Democratic party, so called, the latter having positively refused, the other neglected to go to the extent of their ability to place those they had unrighteously proscribed upon a common level, politically, with other citizens, have both showed themselves unworthy the countenances and suffrages of the true friends of equal liberty, and the proscribed class themselves cannot vote with either without directly giving their own power and influence against themselves and their brethren universally.

"Resolved, That in going to the polls to vote, we will in no case whatever, vote with either of the pro-slavery parties of the land, since that would be, in our judgment, giving our suffrages against ourselves."

We do solemnly protest against the adoption of the above Resolutions by the Convention of 1843, and also against the adoption of any resolutions of kindred spirit, by the Convention about to assemble at Schenectady--

1st. Because the Convention of 1843 having assembled to take measures to obtain an extension of the elective franchise--a specific object--had no right to adopt resolutions extraneous, or detrimental to that object.

2d. Because the constituents of that Convention, being attached to no *one* political party, and therefore opposed to no other *one* political party, the Convention had no right, without previous notice to its constituents, to pass resolutions which, directly or indirectly, identify its constituents with any political party.

*We, the undersigned, feel called upon to enter our protest against the doings, in any shape, of the Convention of last year, having been informed that a resolution was passed at a very small meeting in this city, last night, with the view of moving the Convention to such a step.

Respectfully yours, truly,
(Signed)   Theo. Sedgwick Wright,
            Charles B. Ray

3d. Because the above resolutions place the success of the attempts to obtain an extension of the franchise on the sucess of a *party* which must ever comprise but a portion of the people, instead of relying upon the will and magnanimity of the whole people.

4th. Because the Convention, by assuming an attitude hostile to two political parties, thereby places itself, and those whom it assumed in this matter to represent, in the position of men asking from two political parties the power, to enable them to overthrow those parties--whilst the truth is, we seek the elective franchise, not for the purpose of upholding one party and prostrating another, but we ask it in good faith, as good citizens, feeling our capacity to enjoy that great privilege, and our determination to exercise it for the best interests of the *whole people*, without regard to sect or party.

Resolved, That the above Protest be signed by the Chairman and Secretary on behalf of this meeting, and that the delegates from this city be requested to present the above protest to the Convention with the request that it may be recorded upon the minutes of the Convention.

In behalf of the meeting,
Jeremiah Powers, Chairman[1]
James M'Cune Smith, Secretary

The Protest having been read to the Convention, James M'Cune Smith, of the city of New-York, moved, "That the Protest be accepted, and recorded upon the minutes of the Convention." In support of this motion, he stated the facts in the case, to wit: "That the minutes of the Rochester Convention had not been read before any meeting of the citizens of New-York, until the evening of September 16th, 1844: that at the meetings held in that city, immediately after the adjournment of the Convention held at Rochester, the people of New-York city had, by a large majority, negatived a resolution of the same import with those objected to in the Protest; and that the earliest meeting at which the Rochester resolutions were read, had now protested against them: the protesters firmly believing that the said resolutions were not relevant to the franchise, took this means of recording their sentiments --sentiments which did not affect the inherent truth or falsehood of the Resolutions, but simply their relevancy."

Rev. H. H. Garnet, of Troy, opposed the Resolution to accept and record the Protest: first, because the Resolutions protested against were, in themselves true; secondly, because, according to the statement of the mover, the Protest had been adopted at a small meeting; thirdly, because the Convention at Schenectady had no connection whatever with the Convention at Rochester, each Convention being independent and finishing its own work without appeal. He further said, that if the Protest had been signed by two individuals, he would have permitted it to be recorded.

Mr. Thompson, of Albany, advocated the reception and record of the Protest; because, the colored people seeing the franchise, as a boon, from the whole people, not from any party or portion of the people. He illustrated the absurdity of a contrary course, by the following fact which was not denied, viz: That the Convention at Rochester had passed a Resolution, instructing the General Committee to wait on the Governor, and request him to make favorable mention of the extension of the franchise to the people of color, in his annual message: that when the Central Committee waited on Governor Bouck, his Excellency stated his willingness to comply with their request, in case he found sufficient reason in the *minutes of the Convention*, which he requested the committee to bring to him. But the Chairman of the Central Committee (Rev. Mr. Garnet of Troy) could not be prevailed on to carry the minutes to the Governor, although frequently urged to do so. "And why?" said Mr. Thompson, "because those very minutes denounced the party to which Governor Bouck belonged."

William P. Johnson, of New-York, opposed the motion, and hoped that the Protest would be crushed beneath the feet of the Convention, because it was an unrighteous proceeding: the meeting which adopted it, was an illegal meeting, having been made an adjourned meeting at the end of the previous one, when everybody, almost, had gone away.

Ulysses B. Vidal, of New-York, urged the reception and record of the Protest; because New-York city having been misrepresented at the Rochester Convention, had undoubted right to record her sentiments in regard to the resolutions against which she protested, at this the very first and most fitting opportunity; he further (after eliciting from Mr. Johnson that his statement in regard to the adjournment was made upon hearsay) stated that he (Mr. V.) had been Chairman of the meeting in question, and that the adjournment had been legally made while the body of the meeting was yet in session: he further held, that this Convention having been appointed to be held at Schenectady by the Rochester Convention, was, therefore, the creation of the Rochester Convention, was in strict connection with it, and had a right to review its doings.

Mr. Moulton, of Troy, objected to the Resolution to accept the Protest; because this Convention had no right to review the proceedings of the previous Convention.

William P. Powell,[2] of New-York, advocated the reception of the Protest, on the ground that it would enable this Convention to regain the confidence lost and thrown away by the last, in the false step which it had taken. He dwelt upon the inconsistency of the colored people in identifying themselves with a political party to obtain the Elective Franchise in 1844, when they had already lost the Franchise, by a similar false movement in 1821.

J. M'Cune Smith,[3] of New-York, said that the debate had taken too wide a range. The question before the Convention was, shall we grant the request of the citizens of New-York, and record their Protest, or shall we not? If the Convention accepted the Protest, it did not adopt its sentiments, it simply granted to the people of New-York the right to be heard, granted their respectful request--their petition. If the Convention rejected the Protest, it rejected the request of the people of New-York, denied their their right to be heard, violated the sacred right of petition and remonstrance.

Rev. H. H. Garnet, of Troy, moved that the Convention do adjourn, to meet at 7 o'clock, P.M. which was carried.

During this debate, the number of delegates present did not exceed twenty-five.

During the interval, at the invitation of Mr. Rich, of Troy, your delegates partook at a splendid *Soiree*, at which were present about one hundred ladies from that city.

The session having been opened with prayer, Rev. H. H. Garnet, of Troy, again opposed the reception of the Protest; he admitted the strength of the proposition that a rejection of the Protest would be a violation of the Right of Petition: but held that to be a false statement of the present case, and a statement which had been assumed by the cunning of the delegates from New-York, (he was here called to order and retracted the word cunning); he insisted that the Protest was not a fair issue and that it must be rejected.

J. M'Cune Smith, of New-York, said that the opposition having admitted the strength of the position occupied by those who urged the reception of the Protest, it was useless to debate the question further: it remained with the Convention to admit or reject the right of the citizens of New-York to record their sentiments respectfully expressed--"to admit or deny the right of petition."

The question being put, the Convention by a vote of 11 ayes and 38 noes, refused to accept or record the Protest.

Of the 49 votes cast, about 33 were from Schenectady and Troy, nearly all in the negative: thus these two places with a joint total colored population of less than 1,000 rejected the petition of New-York, containing 20,000 free colored people.

Immediately upon the announcement of this vote, U. B. Vidal, W. B. Powell, and James M'Cune Smith, of New-York, rose--the first two tendered their resignations as members of the Business Committee, and all tendered their resignations as members of the Convention, each giving his reasons for taking this step; the resignations were accepted by the Convention.

In taking the very decided step of withdrawing from the deliberations of the convention, your delegates respectfully submit, that they were fully warranted by the facts in the case. Having been honored, fellow-citizens, with your appointment of us as your representatives in the State Convention, we accepted this distinguished trust with a full sense of its importance and responsibility; with a firm determination to present to the convention such matter as you in your judgment should think proper to trust to our care, to express what we firmly believed to be your sentiments, and to maintain for you that unyielding regard for your rights which has ever distinguished the people of the city of New-York.

Fellow citizens! you had entrusted us with a document, a Protest, respectfully worded, and accompanied with a respectful request that it might be recorded upon the minutes of the Convention. This request was rejected by the Convention! Had it been a request to reject or adopt the sentiments of the Protest, it would have been another matter; for then, the Convention would have been urged to adopt the sentiments of a meeting of the citizens of New-York; and a refusal to adopt would have been an expression of a difference of opinion. But a refusal to *accept* and record the Protest, was a refusal to record the sentiments of that meeting. It was a denial of the right of the people of New-York, assembled at a public meeting, to record their sentiments upon the minutes of the Convention--sentiments which were expressed in regard to the only object which the Convention had in view. This right being denied by the Convention, your delegates felt that a primary and inalienable right of their constituents had been violated. They felt that their constituency was thereby outraged and insulted, and they could not any longer remain a part and party of the Convention which had, deliberately and wantonly, done this insult.

Your delegates had been told, openly, in Convention, before the Protest had been read, that it would be rejected--but they, incredulous that so great an insult had been already premeditated, performed their duty and presented the Protest--the result showed that the fate of the Protest from New-York had been determined by some combination of the delegates from other places before they had even heard the Protest read!

Other facts might be related to show the unfair means by which this deliberate, premeditated insult was consummated, but they are in themselves irrelevant to the issue which alone remains before the people of New-York.

Your delegates might have borne with indignity and insult in the hope that by remaining at the Convention they might yet, in their humble way, have contributed to the great object--the extension of the Elective Franchise, for the attainment of which they were sent to labor. But your delegates were now convinced that by the rejection of the Protest from New-York the Convention deprived itself of the only means by which it could continue to labor for the franchise. *So long as the Resolutions adopted at Rochester,* (against which the city of New-York had protested,) *remains recorded as the sentiments of the colored people of the State of New-York, so long will it be utterly useless for the people of color to strive for the extension to them, on equal terms, of the Elective Franchise!* Because the Rochester Convention's Resolutions identify the people of color with one political party, they promise the votes of people of color to that party, and that party only: they therefore change the ground of our effort, instead of asking for a *right* based upon the highest principles of general good, they ask for a *means* by which to help into power certain political aspirants who have made specious promises, thus confirming the charge which has been urged against the people of color, that their votes could be bought for a price.

Believing, that, by a refusal to second your Protest, the Convention had not only poured insult upon you, but had also destroyed the only mode by which it could effect anything towards extension of the Franchise, your delegates knew that their opportunity for successful labor had passed away, and they resigned their membership of the Convention.

Fellow-citizens! believing that you are unwilling that your sentiments in regard to the propriety of keeping aloof from political partisanship the great question of the Franchise, shall be misrepresented at one Convention, and that your right to be heard shall be denied by another Convention; believing that you are unwilling that you shall be handed over, bound hand and foot, to one political party, no matter which; believing that you are unwilling that your ancient and unwavering determination to be heard in whatever concerns your welfare, shall at this late day be crushed and trampled upon--we respectfully, but fearlessly submit our conduct in this matter, to your decision; assured, whatever the decision may be, that we will continue to labor along with you to obtain that priceless boon, that glorious privilege, that last, best RIGHT OF FREEMEN, the enjoyment of the Elective Franchise! A right, our only safe claim to which can be based upon our bringing to the altar of the Empire State, and of our common country, an independence in thought, an intelligence in opinion, a devotedness in patriotism, a sternness of integrity, which shall be above, or at least, equal to, the standard occupied by those of our fellow-citizens who now do vote.

                    With great respect,
                      Ulysses B. Vidal,
                      James M'Cune Smith,
        Delegates from the city of N.Y. to the State
        Convention, held at Schenectady, Sept. 18th, 1844

National Anti-Slavery Standard, October 24, 1844.

REFERENCE NOTES

    1. Jeremiah Powers was one of New York City's leading black abolitionists who served as chairman of its famous Committee of Thirteen and as a vigorous spokesman in the campaign of his people to regain the suffrage in the state.

    2. Born free in New York State, William P. Powell (1806-1875) spent his early years at sea as a cook. In October 1833, he helped form an anti-slavery society in New Bedford. A staunch Garrisonian during these years, he became both a subscriber and an occasional contributor to the *Liberator*. For a time, he conducted a boarding house for sailors in New Bedford and married an Indian girl at Plymouth, Massachusetts.

    In 1839, Powell moved to New York and opened a sailor' home, first at 10 John Street, then at 33 Pearl Street in lower Manhattan. He conducted his business under the auspices of the American Seamen's Friends Society, with an employment bureau as adjunct until 1851. During this time, Powell was prominent in antislavery meetings. He greatly assisted fugitive slaves and his home provided hospitality to many antislavery leaders. Owing to the increasing proscription of his people in the United States, however, he sailed with his family to England, arriving in December 1851. While there, Powell resided at Liverpool and secured a job in the British Custom Service, remaining for about ten years. He returned to the United States with his family in 1861 and continued his association with the sailors' home in both New Bedford and New York. The latter was virtually destroyed during the violent Draft Riots of 1863, with Powell and his family barely escaping with their lives. He died while on a trip west in 1875 en route to Honolulu. For a study of Powell, see Philip S. Foner, "William P. Powell: Militant Champion of Black Seamen," in Philip S. Foner, *Essays in Afro-American History* (Philadelphia, 1978), pp. 88-111.

    3. James McCune Smith (1813-1865) was born in New York City of free parents. He was educated at the African Free School and privately under a tutor in the classics. After having been rejected by the medical school of Columbia College, Smith sailed for Scotland, where he remained for five years to complete his studies at the University of Glasgow, receiving the B.A., M.A., and M.D. Upon returning to the United States, Smith engaged in a lucrative medical practice and ran an apothecary shop. His patients were both black and white. Although a full qualified physician, he was not admitted to the New York County Medical Society. A prolific writer of both private and public letters, Smith lectured extensively and wrote essays. Between 1840 and 1841, Smith served as co-editor of the *Colored American*, and in the fifties he wrote a column for *Frederick Douglass' Paper* under the pseudonym Communipaw. Highly active in both the educational and political affairs of his people, Smith served for a time as president of the Radical Abolitionist Convention in 1855. He also served on the Executive Committee of the American and Foreign Anti-Slavery Society. Smith was a long-time correspondent and friend of Gerrit Smith, the philanthropist.

NEW YORK STATE FREE SUFFRAGE CONVENTION, SEPTEMBER 8, 1845

We mentioned last week that such a meeting of the colored was held in Geneva, on the 8th instant. The following is an abstract of their proceedings:
The following persons were chosen officers of the Convention:

President--Austin Stewart, of Canandaigua.
1st Vice President--H. K. Thomas, of Buffalo.
2d Vice President--T. E. Grant, of Oswego.
Secretary--J. W. Duffin, of Geneva.

The correspondence which follows, was read, and ordered to be printed, with the minutes.

Farmington, N. Y. Sept. 12, 1845.
Dear Sir: --The colored citizens of Western New York, have called a Suffrage Convention, to be held at Geneva, on Wednesday, Oct. 8th, 1845, to adopt measures to secure for them the elective franchise.
Your known love of liberty, and hatred to oppression, have induced the committee to extend to you an invitation to be present at that Convention. And I hope, Sir, you will believe me, when I assure you that your decision in the Virginia controversy, while Governor of this State, together with your advocacy of the right of the colored citizens of this State to right of suffrage, have secured for you a home in the heart of every colored American.
I am, Sir, with respect,
Your obedient servant,
William W. Brown,[1]
In behalf of Committee.
To Hon. Wm. H. Seward.[2]

Auburn, Sept. 22, 1845.
Dear Sir: --Your letter in behalf of the colored citizens of Western New-York, inviting me to attend a convention of the friends of equal and universal suffrage, at Geneva, has been received.
Absorbing professional engagements oblige me to be content with the part of an observer, rather than an actor in public affairs. Therefore, I cannot promise myself the pleasure of accepting your invitation; but I tender you assurances of my hearty sympathy and co-operation.
The prejudices of white men in our country against your race, so groundless in reason, and nurtured so long, and so ungenerously, have produced just, and at last, intolerable self-punishment.
The free white laborer trembles, at the approach of every session of Congress, lest the planters of the South, voting for slaves, may deprive him

of protection against the competition of half-paid and half-starved industry in Europe. The poor man of the North is denied liberty of speech in the House of Representatives, and the liberty of addressing citizens of the South on a common evil, through a free press. The commerce of the country, and all its vast interests of improvement, by railroads and canals, have been hazarded in the danger of a war for Slavery; and finally, that institution has secured a preponderating power in the Senate of the United States, by breaking down its high and glorious prerogative of making treaties with foreign States.

These are the alarms, the injuries, and the dangers which perplex the white men of the North. None of them could have happened if the freed men of the North had enjoyed and exercised their inalienable right of suffrage. Their instinctive sympathies could not have been misled. When the white man reproaches you with your complexion, you may safely tell him that a dark skin never covered a dough-face.

I confess, I look impatiently for the restoration of your right of suffrage. I see in its consequences not merely the elevation of a large portion of may fellowmen, to higher social virtues and enjoyments, in our own State, but also an influence which will strengthen public opinion, and direct it to the banishment of human Slavery from the face of the earth.

Be assured, then, that the votes I shall cast for a Convention and a Constitution, wich will be harbingers of such results, will be the most cheerful exercise of the elective franchise in my life.

I am, dear Sir, with many thanks for the great kindness expressed in you letter,

Very respectfully,
Your obedient servant,
William H. Seward.

Mr. Wm. W. Brown, Farmington, Ontario Co.

The business committee then reported the following resolutions, which were taken up, discussed separately, and adopted:

Resolved, That the only thing for which a Government and laws are wanted is, for the protection of man in the rights which God has given him.

Resolved, That equality in the use of the elective franchise is the only true basis of a Democratic Government.

Resolved, That the extension of this right to one portion of the citizens of this State, and the withholding it from another, however small, is a shameful denial of the fundamental doctrines of genuine Republicanism.

Resolved, That the disfranchisement of the colored citizens of New-York was altogether uncalled for, and unjust, as forty-five years of equal suffrage full prove.

Resolved, That the majority, by imposing a property qualification upon colored voters, who are greatly in the minority, while they will not observe the same qualifications among themselves, betrays a spirit of despotism and oppression, which we can find only in the most tyrannical and despotic Governments.

Resolved, That it is hypocritical for the people of this State to complain of oppression in foreign lands, while they are tolerating an invidious constitutional distinction in regard to the fundamental principles of the Government, which holds that all men are created equal.

Resolved, That we find no fault with the laws of the land, which welcome the oppressed of other nations (if they are white) to the benefits of our institutions, and which furnish a safe asylum; but we complain that we, native-born citizens, are denied the same rights which are so largely and freely extended to foreigners.

Resolved, That the town Board of the several towns in this State, upon which is devolved, by the statute, the duty of selecting from the tax lists, suitable jurors for the courts of record of the respective counties, in uniformly rejecting persons of color, without regard to their qualifications or moral worth, have added greatly to the oppressions under which the colored people labor, and have thus given a semi-official sanction to the prevalent wicked prejudice against color, and gratuitously multiplied the disabilities of an injured people.

Resolved, That the property qualification required of colored voters, is unreasonable, unjustifiable, and unnecessary; draws one line of caste between blacks and whites, and another between colored men; and virtually says to the freeholders--Property, not intelligence, integrity, and patriotism, is the measure of the man.

Resolved, That we demand the restoration of our rights, at the hands of the people of the State of New-York, who, without any cause, took them from us, and have persisted in the wrong for the last twenty-four years.

Resolved, That to the non-possession of the elective franchise may be traced most of the degradation to which we, as a people, have been subjected, and is the fruitful source of unnumbered and unmitigated civil, literary, and religious wrongs.

Resolved, That in proportion as we are treated with disrespect, contumely, and neglect, in our political, literary, and ecclesiastical relations, from the want of the elective franchise; so would we command respect and influence, in these different relations, by the possession of it.

Resolved, That there is great hope for the politically oppressed, in their own exertions, relying upon the favor of Heaven, and appealing to the just sentiments of those in political power.

Resolved, That we hold the elective franchise as a mighty lever for elevating, in the scale of society, any people, and feel sensible that without it, we are but nominally free, the vital means of our improvement being paralyzed: we do therefore believe it obligatory on us, and do hereby pledge ourselves to each other, to use all just means in our power, by devoting a portion of our time, talent, and substance, to agitate this question, until we obtain a restoration of this inestimable boon.

Resolved, That in case a Convention should be called, it is the duty of every friend of equal suffrage to vote for those delegates, in the Whig or Democratic parties, that are in favor of extending to the colored people of this State, equal suffrage.

The following address was adopted by the Convention, and some arrangements were made for future meetings:

Address to the People of the State of New York

Fellow-Citizens of the State of New-York, we appeal to you to restore to us the elective franchise which you have withheld from us for the last twenty-four years; we honor New-York and her noble institutions, but we cannot honor that spirit which actuates the majority, to take away the rights of the minority. To all her citizens the right of suffrage is valuable in proportion as she is free, but surely there are none who can so ill afford to spare it as ourselves; to deprive us of "equal suffrage," is a denial of the fundamental principles of genuine democracy. By depriving us of our rights you deny "that all men are born free, that they are endowed by their Creator with certain inalienable rights;" when you have taken away an individual's right to vote, you have made the Government a despotism to him; to foreigners the want of the right may be tolerable, because a little time or labor will make it theirs; they look forward to the day when they can enjoy it, and hence they enjoy its benefits, but when a distinct class of the community, already sufficiently the objects of prejudice, are wholly and forever disfranchised and excluded to the remotest posterity, from the possibility of a voice in regard to the laws under which they are to live, it is the same thing as if their abode was transferred to the deserts of Arabia; they have lost their check upon oppression, their wherewith to buy friends, their panoply of manhood--in short, they are thrown upon the mercy of a despotic majority. Like every other despot, this despot, majority, will believe in the mildness of its own sway, but who will the more willingly submit to it for that?

We love our native country, much as it has wronged us, and in the peaceable exercise of our inalienable rights, we will cling to it.

We are citizens; this we believe would never have been denied, had it not been for the subserviency of the people of the free States to Slavery; but as our citizenship has been doubted by some who are not altogether unfriendly to us, we beg leave to submit some proofs which we think you will not hastily set aside.

We were regarded as citizens by those who drew up the Articles of Confederation between the States in 1778; the fourth of the said articles contains the following language: "The free inhabitants of each of these States, paupers, vagabonds, and fugitives from justice excepted, shall be entitled to all privileges and immunities of free citizens in the several States." That we were not excluded under the phrase "paupers, vagabonds, and fugitives from justice," any more than our white countrymen, is plain from the debate that preceded the adoption of the article, for, on the 25th of June, 1778, the delegate from South Carolina moved the following amendment in behalf of their State:

In article 4th, between the words free inhabitants, insert "white." Decided in the negative--ayes, two States--nays, eight--one State divided. Such was the solemn decision of the Revolutionary Congress. On the adoption of the present Constitution of the United States no change was made as to the rights of citizenship. This is explicitly proved by the Journal of Congress. Take for example the following resolution, passed in the House of Representatives, December 21, 1803:

> On motion, resolved, that the committee appointed to inquire and report whether any further provisions are necessary for the effectual protection of American seamen, do inquire into the expediency of granting protection to such American seamen, citizens of the United States, as are free persons of color, and that they report by bill, or otherwise.
> *Journal House of Representatives, 1st session, 28th Congress.*

Proofs might be multiplied; in almost every State we have been spoken of, either expressly or by implication, as citizens.

What have we done, fellow-citizens, to forfeit the right of the elective franchise? Why should tax-paying colored men, any more than other tax-payers, be deprived of the right of voting for their representatives?

We ask your attention to facts and testimonies which go to show that, considering the circumstances in which we have been placed, our country has no reason to be ashamed of us. Our fathers shared with yours the trials and perils of the Revolutionary, and the last war; when our common country has been invaded by a foreign foe, colored men have hazarded their lives in its defence, our fathers fought by the side of yours in the struggle which made us an independent nation, we offer the following testimonies:

Hon. Mr. Burgess, of Rhode Island, said on the floor of Congress, January 28th, 1828, that "at the commencement of the Revolutionary war, Rhode Island had a number of this description of people; (slaves,) a regiment were enlisted into the continental service, and no braver men met the enemy in battle; but not one of them was permitted to be a soldier until he had first been made a freeman."

Said the Hon. Charles Miner,[3] of Pennsylvania, in Congress, February 7, 1828: "The African race make excellent soldiers, large numbers of them were with Perry, and aided to gain the brilliant victory on Lake Erie, a whole battalion of them was distinguished for its soldierly appearance."

The Hon. Mr. Clark, in the Convention which revised the Constitution of New-York, in 1821, said in regard to the right of suffrage of colored men: "In the war of the Revolution these people helped to fight your battles by land and by sea. Some of your States were glad to turn out corps of colored men, and to stand shoulder to shoulder with them; some of your most splendid victories, on Lake Erie and Champlain, where your fleets triumphed over a foe superior in numbers and engines of death; they were manned in a large proportion with men of color; and in this very house, in the fall of 1914, a bill passed, receiving the approbation of all the branches of your Government, authorizing the Governor to accept the services of 2,000 free people of color."

Said the Hon. Mr. Martindale, of New-York, in Congress, January 22, 1828: "Slaves or Negroes who had been slaves, were enlisted as soldiers in the war of the Revolution; and I, myself, saw a battalion of them, as fine, martial-looking men as I ever saw attached to the northern army, in the last war, on its march from Plattsburg to Sacketts Harbor."

On the 20th of March, 1779, it was recommended by Congress to the States of Georgia and South Carolina to raise three thousand colored troops who were to be rewarded for their service by their freedom. The delegation from those States informed Congress that such a body of troops would be not only "formidable to the enemy, but would lessen the danger of revolts and desertions" among the slaves themselves.--See secret *Journal of the old Congress, volume 1, pages 105-107.*

During the last war the free colored people were called to the defence of the country by General Jackson, and received the following testimony to the value of their services:

> Soldiers! when on the banks of the Mobile, I called you to take up arms, inviting you to partake the perils and glory of your white fellow-citizens, I expected much from you, for I was not ignorant that you possessed qualities most formidable to an invading enemy; I knew with what fortitude you could endure hunger, and thirst, and all the fatigues of a campaign; I knew well how you loved your native country, and that you had, as well as ourselves, to defend what man holds most dear, his parents, wife, children, and property; you have done more than I expected. In addition to the qualities which I previously knew you to possess; I found moreover, among you a noble enthusiasm, which leads you to the performance of great things.
>
> Soldiers! the President of the United States shall hear how praiseworthy was your conduct in the hour of danger, and the representatives of the American people will, I doubt not, give you the praise which your deeds deserve. Your General anticipates them in applauding your noble ardor, &c.   By order, (signed)
>
> Thomas Butler, Aid-de-Camp.

Are we to be thus looked to, for assistance in the "hour of danger," but trampled under foot in the time of peace? Did our fathers fight for American liberty that their children might be disfranchised and loaded with insults? Can the people of New-York justify themselves in wrenching from us the birth-right, civil liberty. We would respectfully ask you to look at the fact, that, while you deprive the colored American citizens, of the benefit of the elective franchise, you at the same time extend it to the foreigner, who may land upon our shores ignorant of our constitution and laws.

We lay hold of the principles which New-York asserted in the hour which tried men's souls, and which they pledged their lives, their fortunes, and their sacred honor to sustain. We take our stand upon that solemn declaration, that to protect inalienable rights, "governments are instituted among men, deriving their just powers from the consent of the governed," and proclaim that a government which tears away from us and our posterity the very power of consent, is a tyrannical usurpation which we will never cease to oppose.

National Anti-Slavery Standard, October 30, 1845.

<u>REFERENCE NOTES</u>

    1. Born a slave in Kentucky, William Wells Brown (1815-1884) escaped to the North and became an effective antislavery speaker, playwright, historian and novelist (author of *Clotel, or the President's Daughter,* the first novel published by an American Negro). In 1854, years after he had escaped from slavery, his English friends, worried for his safety under the Fugitive Slave Act of 1850, purchased Brown's freedom for three hundred dollars. Besides being one of the most active abolitionist lecturers, Brown was deeply involved in the temperance, woman-suffrage, prison-reform and peace movements.

    2. William H. Seward (1801-1872), a leader in the Whig Party and one-time governor of New York, was a strong supporter of black rights. The views of the Negro people in western New York were paralleled by their brethren in New York City three years earlier. For on December 19, 1842, the

Negro people of New York met at Union Hall and drew up an address, along with resolutions for the purpose of "expressing the high consideration which they entertain for his excellency Governor William H. Seward, for his noble and generous acts since he has filled the office of governor--especially towards the colored citizens." In that year, Seward had declined renomination by his party for a third term, and blacks felt it incumbent upon themselves to show their appreciation of his wise and just administration. The Address, drawn up by the meeting, noted in part: ". . . The undersigned would add, that they are not moved to it by a preference for any political creed; but on the contrary, isolated from the ferment of political strife, they have calmly viewed the course of your excellency in relation to certain great principles, laid down, but which until the occurrence of your executive career, had long remained as a dead letter; principles, towards the carrying out of which, your excellency has done so much; principles, the full practice of which, by making New York a free state, indeed--no portion of her inhabitants being proscribed for physical peculiarity, or for cherished views--would enable her to advance with unfettered strides in her glorious career." (See the *New York Tribune,* reprinted in the *National Anti-Slavery Standard*, Jan. 26, 1843.)

3. Charles Miner (1780-1865) was a well-known Pennsylvania editor and congressman. He was opposed to slavery and on May 13, 1836, offered a series of resolutions in the House of Representatives in favor of its abolition in the District of Columbia and its eventual extinction in the United States.

CAZENOVIA FUGITIVE SLAVE LAW CONVENTION, AUGUST 21-22, 1850

The meeting of fugitives from Slavery and their friends held in Cazenovia, New York, 21st and 22d day of August, 1850, commenced by appointing Samuel J. May,[1] as temporary Chairman, and Samuel Thomas, Jr., as temporary Secretary.

Samuel Wells, J. W. Loguen, Charles B. Ray were appointed a Committee to nominate officers for the Convention.

Gerrit Smith,[2] Mary Springstead, James Baker, Fordyce Rice, Caroline Brown were appointed the Business Committee.

The following resolution, offered by James C. Jackson, was adopted.

"Whereas William L. Chaplin[3] is, contrary to the laws of God and man, suffering imprisonment, and whereas the litigation, and various measures, which, we trust will result in his liberation, and in the establishment of righteous principles, will require the expenditure of large sums of money: Resolved, therefore, that this Convention proceed to appoint a Committee, to be entitled "The Chaplin Committee," whose business it shall be to adopt such measures, as they shall judge fit to effect his liberation, and promote the cause of law and justice; and that, for the purpose of applying themselves with means for accomplishing these objects, we advise them to raise, within thirty days, twenty thousand dollars."

The following persons were appointed to nominate a "Chaplin Committee," Joseph C. Hathaway, William R. Smith, Eleazer Seymour, James C. Jackson.

Mrs. F. Rice, Phebe Hathaway, and Louisa Burnett were appointed to nominate a committee of females, whose duty it should be to obtain by contributions of ten cents each sufficient means to purchase a silver pitcher and a pair of silver goblets and a gold medal with appropriate inscriptions therein--to obtain the same, and to present them to William L. Chaplin, as a testimonial of the high regard of the friends of the slave for his distinguished services in the cause of humanity. (The names of the persons composing this Committee will appear in our next.)

The following persons, being nominated for the officers of the Convention, were appointed.

Frederick Douglass, President.
Joseph C. Hathaway,[4] Francis Hawley, Chas. B. Ray, Chas. A. Wheaton, Vice Presidents.
Charles D. Miller, and Anne V. Adams, Secretaries.
Letters from S. R. Ward,[5] Wm. Goodell,[6] and Wm. H. Burleigh were read.
On motion of Mr. Loguen, a Committee were appointed to report an address or addresses from the fugitive slaves. This Committee consisted of J. W. Loguen, James Baker and E. L. Platt.

Joseph C. Hathaway gave a deeply interesting account of his and Miss Theodosia Gilbert's late interview with Mr. Chaplin in the jail of the city of Washington. Mr. Chaplin was not armed, and had no suspicion, that the persons in his carriage were armed.

Mr. Loguen reported two addresses from the fugitive slaves--one to the slaves, and the other to the Liberty Party. After an extended discussion upon the former, they were both adopted.

The following persons, being nominated, were appointed to constitute the Chaplin committee: James C. Jackson,[7] Joseph C. Hathaway, Samuel J. May, Charles A. Wheaton, G. W. Clark, Wm. R. Smith, George W. Lawson, Cyrus P. Grosvenor, G. W. Johnson of N. Y.: Francis Jackson,[8] John G. Whittier[9] of Mass.: Silas Cornell, Thomas Davis[10] of R. I., C. D. Cleveland, E. M. Davis,[11] of Pa., C. C. Foote[12] of Mich.; Hon J. R. Giddings of Ohio; Hon. G. W. Julian[13] Ind.: Hon. C. Durkee, Wis.

The series of 17 resolutions, reported by Gerrit Smith as Chairman of the Business Committee were after much discussion adopted.

A contribution was then called for to meet the expenses incurred in visiting Mr. Chaplin, and in other matters connected with his [case]. The sum of $168.79 was raised in answer to this call.

Vote of thanks to Mrs. Wilson for the use of her grove.

Each session of the Convention was opened with prayer and George W. Clark and the Edmonson sisters, who were once in slavery, favored the Convention with occasional songs.

Convention adjourned.

A Letter to the American Slaves from those who have fled from American Slavery

Afflicted and Beloved Brothers:--The meeting which sends you this letter, is a meeting of runaway slaves. We thought it well, that they, who had once suffered, as you still suffer, that they, who had once drank of that bitterest of all bitter cups, which you are still compelled to drink of, should come together for the purpose of making a communication to you.

The chief object of this meeting is, to tell you what circumstances we find ourselves in--that, so, you may be able for yourselves, whether the prize we have obtained is worth the peril of the attempt to obtain it.

The heartless pirates, who compelled us to call them "master," sought to persuade us, as such pirates seek to persuade you, that the condition of those, who escape from their clutches, is thereby made worse, instead of better. We confess, that we had our fears, that this might be so. Indeed, so great was our ignorance, that we could not be sure that the abolitionists were not the friends, which our masters represented them to be. When they told us, that the abolitionists, could they lay hands upon us would buy and sell us, we could not certainly know, that they spoke falsely; and whey they told us, that abolitionists are in the habit of skinning the black man for leather, and of regaling their cannibalism on his flesh, even such enormities seemed to us to be possible. But owing to the happy change in our circumstances, we are not as ignorant and credulous now, as we once were; and if we did not know it before, we know it now, that the slaveholders are as great liars, as they are great tyrants.

The abolitionists act the part of friends and brothers to us; and our only complaint against them is, that there are so few of them. The abolitionists, on whom it is safe to rely, are, almost all of them, members of the American Anti-Slavery Society, or of the Liberty Party. There are other abolitionists: but most of them are grossly inconsistent, and, hence, not entirely trustworthy abolitionists. So inconsistent are they, as to vote for anti-abolitionists for civil rulers, and to acknowledge the obligation of laws, which they themselves interpret to be pro-slavery.

We get wages for our labor. We have schools for our children. We have opportunities to hear and to learn to read the Bible--that blessed book, which is all for freedom, notwithstanding the lying slaveholders who say it is all for slavery. Some of us take part in the election of civil rulers. Indeed, but for the priests and politicians, the influence of most of whom is against us, our condition would be every way eligible. The priests and churches of the North, are, with comparatively few exceptions, in league with the priests and churches of the South; and this, of itself, is sufficient to account for the fact, that a caste-religion and a Negro-pew are found at the North, as well as at the South. The politicians and political parties of the North are connected with the politicians and political parties of the South; and hence, the political arrangements and interests of the North, as well as the ecclesiastical arrangements and interests, are adverse to the colored population. But, we rejoice to know, that all this political and ecclesiastical power is on the wane. The callousness of American religion and American democracy has become glaring: and, every year, multitudes, once deluded by them, come to repudiate them. The credit of this repudiation is due, in a great measure, to the American Anti-Slavery Society, to the Liberty Party, and to anti-sectarian meetings, and conventions. The purest sect on earth is the rival of, instead of one with, Christianity. It deserves not to be trusted with a deep and honest and earnest reform. The temptations which beset the pathway of such a reform, are too mighty for it to resist. Instead of going forward for God, it will slant off for itself. Heaven grant, that, soon, not a shred of sectarianism, not a shred of the current religion, not a shred of the current politics of this land, may remain. Then will follow, aye, that will itself be, the triumph of Christianity: and, then, white men will love black men and gladly acknowledge that all men have equal rights. Come, blessed day--come quickly.

Including our children, we number in Canada, at least, twenty thousand. The total of our population in the free States far exceeds this. Nevertheless, we are poor, we can do little more to promote your deliverance than pray for it to the God of the oppressed. We will do what we can to supply you with pocket compasses. In dark nights, when his good guiding star is hidden from the flying slave, a pocket compass greatly facilitates his exodus. Candor requires the admission, that some of us would not furnish them, if we could; for some of us have become non-resistants, and have discarded the use of these weapons and would say to you: "love your enemies; do good to them, which hate you; bless them that curse you; and pray for them, which despitefully use you." Such of us would be glad to be able to say, that all the colored men of the North are non-resistants. But, in point of fact, it is only a handful of them, who are. When the insurrection of the Southern slaves shall take place, as take place it will unless speedily prevented by voluntary emancipation, the great majority of the colored men of the North, however much to the grief of any of us, will be found by your side, with deep-stored and long-accumulated revenge in their hearts, and with death-dealing weapons in their hands. It is not to be disguised, that a colored man is as much disposed, as a white man, to resist, even unto death, those who oppress him. The colored American, for the sake of relieving his colored brethren, would no more hesitate to shoot an American slaveholder, than would a white American, for the sake of delivering his white brother, hesitate to shoot an Algerine slaveholder. The State motto of Virginia: "Death to Tyrants;" is as well the black man's, as the white man's motto. We tell you these things not to encourage, or justify, your resort to physical force, but, simply, that you may know, be it to your joy or sorrow to know it, what your Northern colored brethren are, in these important respects. This truth you are entitled to know, however the knowledge of it may affect you, and however you may act, in view of it.

We have said, that some of us are non-resistants. But, while such would dissuade you from all violence toward the slaveholder, let it not be supposed, that they regard it as guiltier than those strifes, which even good men are wont to justify. If the American revolutionists had excuse for shedding but one drop of blood, then have the American slaves excuse for making blood to flow "even unto the horse-bridles."

Numerous as are the escapes from slavery, they would be far more so, were you not embarrassed by your misinterpretations of the rights of property. You hesitate to take even the dullest of your masters horses--whereas it is your duty to take the fleetest. Your consciences suggest doubts, whether in quitting your bondage, you are at liberty to put in your packs what you need of food and clothing. But were you better informed, you would not scruple to break your master's locks and take all their money. You are taught to respect the rights of property. But, no such right belongs to the slaveholder. His right to property is but the robber-right. In every slaveholding community, the rights of property all center in them, whose coerced and unrequited toil has created the wealth in which their oppressors riot. Moreover, if your oppressors have rights of property, you, at least, are exempt from all obligations to respect them. For you are prisoners of war, in an enemy's country--of a war, too, that is unrivalled for its injustice, cruelty, meanness--and therefore, by all the rules of war, you have the fullest liberty to plunder, burn, and kill, as you may have occasion to do to promote your escape.

We regret to be obliged to say to you, that it is not everyone of the Free States, which offers you an asylum. Even within the last year, fugitive slaves have been arrested in some of the Free States, and replunged into slavery. But, make your way to New York or New England, and you will be safe. It is true, that even in New York and New England, there are individuals, who would rejoice to see the poor flying slave cast back into the horrors of slavery. But, even these are restrained by public sentiment. It is questionable whether even Daniel Webster,[14] or Moses Stuart,[15] would give chase to a fugitive slave; and if they would not, who would?--for the one is chief-politician and the other chief-priest.

We do not forget the industrous efforts, which are now in making to get new facilities at the hands of Congress for re-enslaving those, who have escaped from slavery. But we can assure you, that as to the State of New York and the New England States, such efforts must prove fruitless. Against all such devilism--against all kidnappers--the colored people of these States will not stand against them. A regenerated public sentiment has, forever, removed these States beyond the limits of the slaveholders' hunting ground. Defeat--disgrace--and, it may be, death--will be their only reward for pursuing their prey into this *abolitionized* portion of our country.

A special reason why you should not stop in that part of the Nation which comes within the bounds of John McLean's judicial district, is, that he is a great man in one of the religious sects, and an aspirant for the Presidency. Fugitive slaves and their friends fare hard in the hands of this Judge.[16] He not only puts a pro-slavery construction on the Federal Constitution, and holds, that law can make property of man--a marketable commodity of the image of God but, in various other ways, he shows that his sympathies are with the oppressor. Shun Judge McLean, then, even as you would the Reverend Moses Stuart. The law of the one is as deadly an enemy to you, as is the religion of the other.

There are three points in your conduct, when you shall have become inhabitants of the North, on which we cannot refrain from admonishing you.

1st. If you will join a sectarian church, let it not be one which approves of the Negro-pew, and which refuses to treat slaveholding as a high crime against God and man. It were better, that you sacrifice your lives than that by going into the Negro-pew, you invade your self-respect--debase your souls--play the traitor to your race--and crucify afresh Him who died for the one brotherhood of man.

2d. Join no political party, which refuses to commit itself fully, openly, and heartfully, in its newspapers, meetings, and nominations, to the doctrine, that slavery is the grossest of all absurdities, as well as the guiltiest of all abominations, and that there can no more be a law for the enslavement of man, made in the image of God, than for the enslavement of God himself. Vote for no man for civil office, who makes your complexion a bar to political, ecclesiastic or social equality. Better die than insult yourself and insult our social equality. Better die than insult yourself and insult every person of African blood, and insult your Maker, by contributing to elevate to civil office he who refuses to eat with you, to sit by your side in the House of Worship, or to let his children sit in the school by the side of your children.

3d. Send not your children to the school which the malignant and murderous prejudice of white people has gotten up exclusively for colored people. Valuable as learning is, it is too costly, if it is acquired at the expense of such self-degradation.

The self-sacrificing, and heroic, and martyr-spirit, which would impel the colored men of the North to turn their backs on pro-slavery churches and pro-slavery politics, and pro-slavery schools, would exert a far mightier influence against slavery, than could all their learning, however great, if purchased by concessions of their manhood, and surrenders of their rights, and coupled, as it then would be, by characteristic meanness and servility.

And now, brethren, we close this letter with assuring you, that we do not, cannot, forget you. You are ever in our minds, our hearts, our prayers. Perhaps, you are fearing, that the free colored people of the United States will suffer themselves to be carried away from you by the American Colonization Society.[17] Fear it not. In vain is it, that this greatest and most malignant enemy of the African race is now busy in devising new plans, and in seeking the aid of Government, to perpetuate your enslavement. It wants us away from your side, that you may be kept in ignorance. But we will remain by your side to enlighten you. It wants us away from your side, that you may be contented. But we will remain by your side, to keep you, and make you more, discontented. It wants us away from your side to the end, that your unsuccored and conscious helplessness may make you the easier and surer prey of your oppressors: But we will remain by your side to sympathize with you, and cheer you, and give you the help of our rapidly swelling members. The land of our enslaved brethren is our land, and death alone shall part us.

We cannot forget you, brethren, for we know your sufferings and we know your sufferings because we know from experience, what it is to be an American slave. So galling was our bondage, that, to escape from it, we suffered the loss of all things, and braved every peril, and endured every hardship. Some of us left parents, some wives, some children. Some of us were wounded with guns and dogs, as we fled. Some of us, to make good our escape, suffered ourselves to be nailed up in boxes, and to pass for merchandise. Some of us secreted ourselves in the suffocating holds of ships. Nothing was so dreadful to us, as slavery; and hence, it is almost literally true, that we dreaded nothing, which could befall us, in our attempt to get clear of it. Our condition could be made no worse, for we were already in the lowest depths of earthly woe. Even should we be overtaken, and resubjected to slavery, this would be but to return to our old sufferings and sorrows and should death itself prove to be the price of our endeavor after freedom, what would that be but a welcome release to men, who had, all their lifetime, been killed every day, and "killed all the day long."

We have referred to our perils and hardships in escaping from slavery. We are happy to be able to say, that every year is multiplying the facilities for leaving the Southern prison house. The Liberty Party, the Vigilance Committee of New York,[18] individuals, and companies of individuals in various parts of the country, are doing all they can, and it is much to afford you a safe and a cheap passage from slavery to liberty. They do this however, not only at great expense of property, but at great peril of liberty and life. Thousands of you have heard, ere this, that, within the last fortnight, the precious name of William L. Chaplin has been added to the list of those, who, in helping you gain your liberty, have lost their own. Here is a man, whose wisdom, cultivation, moral worth, bring him into the highest and best class of men--and, yet, he becomes a willing martyr for the poor, despised, forgotten slave's sake. Your remembrance of one such fact is enough to shed light and hope upon your darkest and most desponding moments.

Brethren, our last word to you is to bid you be of good cheer, and not to despair of your deliverance. Do not abandon yourselves, as have many thousands of American slaves, to the crime of suicide. Live! live to escape from slavery, live to serve God! Live till He shall Himself call you into eternity! Be prayful--be brave--be hopeful. "Lift up your heads, for your redemption draweth nigh."

To the Liberty Party:--The fugitive slaves, who are, assembled in Cazenovia, N. Y. come to you with a very earnest petition.

The National Convention, which you are to hold in the city of Oswego, the second day of next October, is to nominate a candidate for President of the United States. Your petitioners are aware, that F. Julius LeMoyne,[19] William Goodell, and Gerrit Smith, are each spoken of as such candidate.

As to Mr. Smith, we know, that he always refuses nominations to office; and that he, now, goes so far, as to refuse to admit, that he would accept of the office, however elevated or important, to which he might be elected. As to Mr. LeMoyne and Mr. Goodell, we cannot deny their competency to fill the highest offices in the gift of the people--they are wise and true hearted men, an honor to their age, their nation, their race. But, notwithstanding all this richly deserved praise of these men, we are bold to say, that there is another man in this nation, who is not their inferior in the qualifications for President of the United States--Nay, where, in the whole length and breadth of this Nation, can a man be found more competent than WILLIAM L. CHAPLIN to administer its Government? He is emphatically a scholar, a statesman, a philanthropist, a gentleman, and a Christian Job, who was the supreme magistrate in the community, in which he dwelt, numbers among his own qualifications for office, "I WAS FATHER TO THE POOR." --Beautiful, precious, indispensable qualification is this! and who has it more abundantly than William L. Chaplin.

But, we confess it is not because of Mr. Chaplin's ability to fill and adorn the office of President of the United States, that we ask you to nominate him to the office. It is because he is a prisoner!--and a prisoner for such a cause!! It is true, that we would not, for this reason, ask for his nomination, were it not also, that he is fit for it. But, being fit for it, we find in the fact of his imprisonment, good cause why he, among all, who have such fitness, should be singled out for the nomination.

In our esteem, however it may be in the esteem of others, who have not, like ourselves, had personal experience of the woes of slavery, the greatest of all the questions of human rights, which agitate this age, is Slavery. Now, to the just and merciful solution of this question, Mr. Chaplin has devoted himself, with an ability, a zeal, and a self-denial, which none of his fellow laborers and fellow sufferers have surpassed. And, whilst, in return for all this Heaven will reward, and does now reward, him with its love, men have deprived him of his personal liberty. Of all the men in this land, who are fit for President, he is the only one, who, for devotion's sake to the cause of the slave, is suffering this severe deprivation. And is not his imprisonment, taking all the circumstances into account, a very clear and certain providential indication, that he is the man for your candidate? And would not your nomination of him, besides being a merited tribute to his excellent worth, and a soothing and beautiful expression of your sympathy with his sufferings, and of your affliction in his afflictions, and, besides being in your thus openly, and without shame identifying yourselves with his self-sacrificing but [illegible] principles, are most honored evidence of your magnanimity--would it not, also, be an unambiguous and impressive acknowledgement of the transcendent importance of the anti-slavery cause?

Distinguished, however, as is Mr. Chaplin [illegible], we could not have urged him in nomination for President of the United States, did he not, in other respects, also represent and honor the principles of the Liberty party. Your party is devoted to the cause of the landless, as well as to the cause of the enslaved. So is his. Free trade, [illegible] position to National Wars, and National debts and secret societies, are among your principles. So are they among his, also. By why need we go into these particulars? Mr. Chaplin is himself a member of the Liberty Party:--ay, he is, at this moment, the Liberty Party candidate for Governor of the State of New York. Happy party in being thus honored with such a candidate! His new honors--the honors of his prison--are not confined to his own brow. The Party which put him in nomination, shares in them and thus is it, already rewarded for the sagacity and soul, which governed it, in selecting its candidate. A greater reward will follow its nomination of him to a higher office--and it will be all the greater, because of his present circumstances.

Nominate, then, we beseech you, for President of the United States, William L. Chaplin. The news of his nomination will be the most welcome and cheering of all news to the free colored people of this nation. And this glad news will reach many a poor slave, and thrill with joy his now desolate heart. It will astonish all christendom to learn, that the Government of a Nation holds in prison the man nominated to the chief magistracy of that Nation--and holds him there for no other offence than helping his fellow-men, and these too his fellow-countrymen, out of slavery, and does this, too, notwithstanding, the basic principle of that Nation is, that ALL MEN ARE CREATED EQUAL. The slaveholders will stand aghast at this nomination. They will regret, that they provoked it;--and they will strive, in vain, to lay the mighty influences, which proceed from it. Another great benefit which will attend this nomination, is that it will test the religion of those who esteem it to be their duty to vote under the Constitution of the United States. Hitherto, the great mass of professing christians in this land have voted for slaveholders--even for this meanest and cruellest class of pirates, and have

yet been called christians. But, will they be called christians--nay, will
they so much as make themselves believe, that they are christians--if, when
the question before them is, whether on the one hand, to vote for the
followers of Christ, who, for Christ's sake and the sake of His poor, lies
in prison, or, on the other, to vote for the heartless candidate who will
keep that follower of Christ in prison, they shall decide to vote for that
heartless candidate? Again, we beseech you to nominate William L. Chaplin.
That nomination will try the temper of the people--the spirit of the church.
To the bosom of every voter it will bring home the question: "WILL YOU VOTE
FOR THE INNOCENT AND BELOVED PRISONER, OR FOR HIM WHO WILL HOLD HIM A
PRISONER?" Nominate William L. Chaplin, and you will thereby, send to the
polls the great question: "FOR THE PRISONER OR AGAINST THE PRISONER?" And,
remember, too, that, in the trying of this great question, the question of
slavery, of humanity, of religion, will be tried--and tried too, more
officially than they have ever yet been tried in this guilty land.

Our petition and our reasons for it are now before you. In disposing
of them, may you have the Divine guidance.

The Resolutions are as follows:

1st. *Resolved,* That Slavery is the curse of curses; the robbery of
robberies, and the crime of crimes.

2d. *Resolved,* That inasmuch as it is the duty of every man to serve God
with all his power, it follows that no man has the right to curtail his
powers by going into Slavery; but that every man who is in that condition, is
bound to get out of it, if he can; and futhermore, that, on the principle of
the brotherhood and identity of men, he is no more bound to get out of it, if
he can, than others are to help him out of it, if they can.

3d. *Resolved,* That our hearts are in the cell of Wm. L. Chaplin, and
that whilst his enemies deride his condition and his false friends are
ashamed of his chains, he will ever be in our eyes, and that, too, whether he
die in the dungeon or on the scaffold, a scholar, a statesman, a philanthropist, a gentleman and a christian.

4th. *Resolved,* That in that day when the slaveholder shall find, in each
slave he has retained in Slavery, a millstone around the neck of his soul,
Charles T. Torrey[20] and William L. Chaplin will find in each slave, whom they
may have delivered, a welcome remembrancer of their faith in God and love to
man.

5th. *Resolved,* That, odious in the sight of the American people as is
the "slave-stealing," which is charged upon William L. Chaplin, that is,
nevertheless, a sham republicanism, and a sham christianity, which does not
endorse it.

6th. Whereas, whatever may be said of Slavery in the States, it is
admitted by all the intelligent and candid, that the Federal Constitution can
authorize, can suffer, no Slavery in the District of Columbia; and that the
Slavery which exists there, exists simply out of comity to the slaveholding
portion of the country; Resolved, therefore; that William L. Chaplin, and
they who occupied the carriage with him, the evening of the 8th instant, were
a company of innocent freemen; and that they who stopped it were guilty of the
insolence and violence of highwaymen, and should be, and, if this were a
land of law and justice, *would be,* promptly punished as highwaymen.

7th. *Resolved,* That there is not in the Congress of the United States
one liberty-loving and law-loving man who can consent that its present
session shall close until Drayton, Sayre,[21] Harris and Chaplin have been
released from prison, and Slavery expelled from the District of Columbia.

8th. *Resolved,* That Slavery in the District of Columbia is a fearful
precedent, which cannot be too speedily overthrown; for, if Congress can make
slaves of some persons there, it can make slaves of all persons there; and
the like power can it exercise wherever, in any State, there are National
"forts, magazines, arsenals, dock-yards, and other needful buildings," and
upon whatever persons may visit them, or enter a Post Office, or a Custom
House, or a Federal Court House.

9th. *Resolved,* That, whether there is or is not Constitutional Slavery
in the States, the Federal Government should see to it, that all the slaves,
and the posterity of all the female slaves who have ever been, though but for
a moment, and though with or without the consent of their masters, within the
limits of the District of Columbia, be immediately restored to liberty: for

it is too plain to require argument that whoever, whether slaves or freemen, be the fugitives from service and labor, referred to in the Constitution, they are fugitives from one State *into another State*.[22]

10th. *Resolved,* That, much as the Free Soil Party[22] has said of its purpose "to divorce the Federal Government from the support of Slavery," it is now, and has long been, abundantly demonstrated, that this purpose cannot be accomplished without either disbanding that Government or wielding it for the overthrow of Slavery in every part of the Nation.

11th. *Resolved,* That he dishonors both Republicanism and Christianity who acknowledges any law of Slavery, or who acknowledges that such an abomination as Slavery is capable of legalization.

12th. *Resolved,* That slaveholders are the cruellest and meanest of all pirates; and that, instead of being fit to be civil rulers, no Government is just, which does not make them the subjects of its severest punishment.

13th. *Resolved,* That, in the arrest and imprisonment of William L. Chaplin, for no offence but that of loving his neighbor as himself, and of practically maintaining the confessedly self-evident and inalienable right of man to "life, liberty, and the pursuit of happiness," we see not only that the Federal District, which was placed by the Constitution under the "exclusive" control of Congress, is completely in the hands of the slave power, but we see another illustration of the truth, that the struggle in this country between Slavery and Freedom involves the liberties of the free white citizen, as well as of the colored slave--that it is, in short, a life and death struggle, which must result in liberty to all, or in the liability of Slavery to all.

14th. *Resolved,* That, instead of going down into a Free Soil party, or any other sham abolition party, or of identifying themselves with any scheme whatever of "Anti-Slavery made easy," abolitionists are summoned by the thickening of the Anti-Slavery battle, and the multiplying trials of their Anti-Slavery integrity--by the voice of Torrey from his grave and of Chaplin from his prison--to put forth more and more emphatic and self-denying evidences of the sincerity and depth of their sense of the immeasurable and horrid wickedness of Slavery.

15th. *Resolved,* That among the evidences of our devotion to the cause of the slave should be,

1st. No connection with, and no worshipping with, a church which has a negro-pew, or which is associated, directly or indirectly, closely or remotely, with churches, North or South, that have it.

2d. No voting for any man, for any civil office, who makes complexion a bar to either social or political equality; or who will admit that there is the least obligation to obey, or honor, any form or pretense of law, or any judicial decision, which is on the side of Slavery.

3d. No consuming, unless in cases of absolute necessity, any of the products of slave labor--any of the cotton, rice, sugar, which are wet with the tears and sweat, and red with the blood, and heavy with the groans, of the poor, weary and desolate victims of the slave power.

16th. *Resolved,* That, in the names of God and Humanity, Religion and the Constitution, we demand the liberation, not only of Drayton and Sayre, and Harris and Chaplin, but of the slaves of the District of Columbia; and that, in these names do we, also, demand that the American people shall regard the refusal to liberate these victims of the slave power as just cause for Revolution.

17th. *Resolved,* That we call on every man in the Free States, who shall go to the polls, at the approaching Elections, to go with this motto burning in his heart and bursting from his lips: "CHAPLIN'S RELEASE, OR CIVIL REVOLUTION."

The North Star, September 5, 1850; National Anti-Slavery Standard, September 5, 1850.

REFERENCE NOTES

1. Samuel Joseph May (1797-1871), noted antislavery figure of Syracuse, New York, was also famous for favoring woman's rights and educational reform.

2. Gerrit Smith (1797-1874) was a well-known New York philanthropist, reformer and political abolitionist. His home at Peterboro, in upstate New York, became a mecca for men and women seeking financial support for their various reform causes. Perhaps his greatest benefaction was to black Americans when, in 1846, Smith set aside, from his huge private holdings 120,000 acres of land to be distributed among New York State's black population. See Theodore S. Wright, *An Address to the three Thousand Colored Citizens of New York Who are Owners of One Hundred and Twenty Thousand Acres of land in the State of New York, Given to Them by Gerrit Smith Esq. of Peterboro* (New York, 1846), *passim*.

3. In August 1850, William L. Chaplin and others were arrested by Washington police, on Maryland soil, for taking part in the escape of two slaves, the property of Robert Toombs and Alexander H. Stephens. Chaplin was kept in jail at Rockville, Maryland, until December. He was subsequently indicted in the District of Columbia on a charge of assault with intent to kill, and in Maryland he was indicted on seven counts: three for assault with intent to murder, two for assisting slaves to escape, and two for larceny of slaves. Bail was fixed at $6,000 in the District and $19,000 in Maryland. With the aid of Gerrit Smith, Lewis Tappan, W. H. Seward, and others, Chaplin's bail was secured, and he was released from jail. Smith served as treasurer of the Chaplin fund and contributed $10,000 to the movement to free Chaplin.

4. Joseph Comstock Hathaway (1810-1873) was an influential Quaker farmer and abolitionist of Waterloo, New York.

5. Samuel Ringgold Ward (1817-c 1864) was brought to New York at the age of three by his parents, who escaped from slavery in Maryland. Ward received an education, taught school, became a preacher and a leading antislavery agent.

6. William Goodell (1792-1878), an ardent reformer and abolitionist, was also active as a minister, lecturer, author and editor. He helped to organize the American Anti-Slavery Society in 1833, and the following year became editor of the *Emancipator*, its first official organ. Unlike Garrison, Goodell thought it possible to use the Constitution to abolish slavery and was a strong believer in both the Constitution and the Union. An organizer of the Liberty Party in 1840, he later founded the Liberty League, a more radical group and from 1854 to the end of the Civil War edited a well-known newspaper entitled the *Radical Abolitionist*.

7. James Caleb Jackson (1811-1895), a noted abolitionist and physician, ran a water-cure establishment at Glen Haven, New York. Along with Nathaniel P. Rogers, he edited the *National Anti-Slavery Standard* for a year beginning in 1840. In 1847, he joined with William Goodell in the formation of the Liberty League, a fourth-party movement growing out of the Liberty Party.

8. Francis Jackson (1789-1861), a prominent abolitionist, was a close friend and co-worker of William Lloyd Garrison throughout the antislavery crusade. A man of considerable means, he gave strong financial backing to the *Liberator* and on one occasion, in October 1835, during a riot in Boston when Garrison himself came close to being lynched by a mob, held a meeting of the Boston Female Anti-Slavery Society at his home, firmly upholding the right of free speech. Jackson served for many years as president of the Massachusetts Anti-Slavery Society and the New England Anti-Slavery Conventions and was a vice-president of the American Anti-Slavery Society. At his death, he willed $10,000 to aid black freedmen and $5,000 in support of the Women's Rights movement.

9. John Greenleaf Whittier (1807-1892), the celebrated American poet, was a close friend of William Lloyd Garrison. An ardent worker in the antislavery struggle, Whittier frequently penned some of the most moving and eloquent verses in an effort to engender strong antislavery feeling throughout the North.

10. Thomas Davis was a wealthy jewelry manufacturer in Providence, Rhode Island, who was also active in politics, serving as an antislavery Democrat in Congress from 1853 to 1855.

11. Edward M. Davis (1811-1887), a noted Pennsylvania abolitionist, was also an active participant in the non-resistance movement. In 1846, for example, he paid for the publication of Adin Ballou's non-resistance pamphlet, *Christian Non-Resistance in All its Important Bearings*, in Philadelphia.

Davis married Maria, the daughter of Lucretia Mott, the famous women's rights advocate. Despite his Quaker antecedents and non-resistance proclivities, Davis served as an officer in the Union Army during the Civil War.

12. Charles C. Foote ran as the vice-presidential nominee of the Liberty Party in 1852.

13. George W. Julian (1817-1899), antislavery Whig from Indiana, became a leader of the radical wing of the Republican Party. Julian was a member of Congress in 1849-1852 and 1861-1871.

14. Daniel Webster (1782-1852), the noted American statesman and senator from Massachusetts, came out in support of the Compromise measures of 1850, which provided, in part, for the return of fugitive slaves. In his famous speech of March 7, 1850, he admitted that Northerners had not lived up to their obligations to return fugitive slaves and pledged his efforts to see that they did. Webster was highly praised by conservatives throughout the North, but was roundly condemned in antislavery circles.

15. Moses Stuart (1780-1852), a leading clergyman and biblical scholar in New England, upheld the constitutionality of the Fugitive Slave Law.

16. Judge McLean was an associate justice of the United States Circuit Court of Appeals. A man of determined bias and strong pro-slavery tendencies, he handed down several decisions upholding the Fugitive Slave Law of 1850 and ordering the return of fugitives to slavery.

17. On December 28, 1816, the American Society for Colonizing the Free People of Colour, commonly called the American Colonization Society, was organized. Its declared purpose was "to promote and execute a plan for colonizing (with their consent) the free people of color, residing in our country, in Africa, or such other place as Congress shall deem most expedient."

While the Society failed to win the financial backing of the federal government to carry out its program, it did gain the support of many influential groups which sympathized with its objectives. Overall, however, the new Society was dominated by Southerners, for the president and eight of the thirteen vice-presidents were from the South.

From its inception, however, the Society engendered the active opposition of most free blacks in the United States. They were convinced that the colonization scheme was but a means of ridding the nation of the free Negro in order to make slavery more secure. Then, too, since the Society viewed the Negro as an innately inferior and degraded class incapable of progress within American society, blacks rightly charged its sponsors with aiding in the spread of racial prejudice and deprivation of rights they already enjoyed.

18. The New York Vigilance Committee was founded in November 1835 by a group of white and Negro "Friends of Human Rights" to assist any colored person who might be arrested under pretense of being an escaped slave. But much of its work was to feed and clothe runaways and send them on to points of safety outside of New York with money and letters of introduction to friends. David Ruggles, who at one time had been a traveling agent for the *Emancipator,* a New York antislavery newspaper, became secretary of the Committee. For a study of Ruggles, see Dorothy B. Porter, "David B. Ruggles, An Apostle for Human Freedom," *Journal of Negro History,* XXVIII (Jan. 1943), 23-50. Ruggles estimated that during the five years he was secretary of the Vigilance Committee, he aided over six-hundred slaves to escape (*The North Star,* April 14, 1848).

19. Francis Julius LeMoyne (1798-1879) was a noted physician and abolitionist and the first prominent advocate of the process of cremation in the United States. His father, John Julius LeMoyne de Villiers, came to America with French colonists and settled at Gallipolis, Ohio. Later, he moved to Washington, Pennsylvania, where Francis was born. LeMoyne was a candidate of the Liberty Party for the vice-presidency of the United States in 1840, and in 1841, 1844, and 1847 was the candidate of the abolitionists for the governorship of Pennsylvania. His house at Washington, Pennsylvania, became one of the leading stations on the "Underground Railroad" to aid escaping slaves.

20. Charles T. Torrey (1813-1846) was a Boston abolitionist and clergyman. While unsuccessful as a minister and pastor, he soon found his calling as an antislavery lecturer and organizer. An early supporter of William Lloyd Garrison, he later took exception to this man's unorthodox

views on such issues regarding Sabbath observance, civil government and women's rights. He organized the conservative abolitionists of Massachusetts in a revolt against Garrison's leadership. Then, in the fall of 1838, the conservatives founded the *Massachusetts Abolitionist,* with Torrey as editor. Not long after, they seceded from Garrison's Society and organized the Massachusetts Abolition Society.

Torrey gained considerable notoriety in January 1842, when he was arrested at Annapolis, Maryland, after being identified as an abolitionist. Freed after a brief stay in jail, he moved to Washington to engage in newspaper work. Having failed as an editor, he settled in Baltimore, hoping to make a success in business and at the same time assisting escaping slaves from Virginia and Maryland across the border. Arrested in November 1844, his trial attracted nationwide attention. Although ably defended by the distinguished attorney Reverdy Johnson, he was, nevertheless, convicted and sentenced to six years at hard labor in the Maryland State Penitentiary. While in jail, his mind gave way and soon he contracted tuberculosis, which caused his death a little more than a year after his imprisonment. His body was removed to Boston, where at a huge public funeral he was honored as a martyr to the antislavery cause.

21. In the spring of 1848 the schooner *Pearl,* with seventy-seven slaves aboard, was captured at the mouth of the Potomac River and brought back to Washington. The slaves and their white rescuers, Daniel Drayton, Captain Sayres, and Chester English, were imprisoned. The Negroes were turned over to slavedealers to be sold in the lower South, and the white men were brought to trial. During the excitement of this event, a mob attempted to destroy the office of the *National Era* in Washington and to force Dr. Bailey, its editor, to leave the district. Drayton and Sayres were found guilty of transporting slaves and were sentenced to life imprisonment. Exceptions were taken to the judge's rulings and a new trial was ordered, which took place in May 1849. Once again the men were convicted and returned to the district jail, remaining there until 1852, when Charles Sumner, who had just been elected to the United States Senate, began a campaign for their release. Sumner submitted to the attorney-general an elaborate treatise on the injustice of the sentence, and President Fillmore granted the men an unconditional pardon. When it was learned that the governor of Virginia intended to arrest them at their release, Drayton and Sayres were taken by night to Baltimore, and then sent to Harrisburg and Philadelphia. See Philip S. Foner, *The Life and Writings of Frederick Douglass* (New York, 1950), I, 442; Benjamin Quarles, *Black Abolitionists* (New York, 1972), pp. 163, 164, 211.

22. After the decline of the Liberty Party, founded in 1840, Democrats and Whigs who opposed the extension of slavery in the territories met in Buffalo in the summer of 1848 and organized a new party with the proclaimed goals of free soil, free speech, free labor, and free men.

PROCEEDINGS OF THE STATE CONVENTION OF COLORED PEOPLE
HELD AT ALBANY, NEW-YORK,
ON THE 22d, 23d AND 24th OF JULY, 1851

To the People of the State of New-York:

Be it hereby known, that the undersigned Committee, by the expressed wish of the citizens of Troy and Albany, publish and apprize the citizens and inhabitants of the State, that a Convention is called and will assemble in the city of Albany on the 22d day of July, 1851.

The paramount object of this Convention is, to assemble the disfranchised and aggrieved portion of the people of the State of New-York, to deliberate upon, and propose, then and there, the course to be pursued in the future and onward prosecution of our interests and rights.

We are not insensible to the fact that the public mind has been deeply aroused throughout the length and breadth of this great country, and that those important and agitating questions comprehend and involve our interests and the perpetuity of the government.

And most solemnly are we impressed with this truth also, that the denial of our rights is the overthrow of the rock foundation principles of the country; for the Declaration of Independence, in the language of the late and lamented John Quincy Adams,[1] recognizes no despotism, monarchial, aristocratic, or democratic, declares that individual man is possessed of rights of which no government can deprive him.

With this view and understanding, two great questions present themselves for adjustment, the first of which is the recent edict enacted and sent forth by Congress, called the "Fugitive Slave Law;"[2] and the second in character, is the coercive and barbarous Colonization Scheme; either of which questions is characterized with infamy sufficient to libel christianity or sink a nation. There are other questions of local and State character that demand our immediate attention, viz: "the School Question;" a system or law of the State for the general education of all classes of children, without distinction or proscription. This philanthropic and far-seeing law has been suspended in its natural and defined course, and hundreds of children are thereby violently ejected from schools, and this in open violation of the law, and for no reason save that of God's giving them a different complexion from those in power.

A second subject for consideration, but first in importance, is the "Suffrage Question." A special law of the State requires every colored voter to be in possession of two hundred and fifty dollars worth of real estate as a qualification. These local and general subjects require the people to act with promptness, union and energy, to effect the desired ends.

Therefore, fellow citizens, in consideration of these important subjects, however remote from the Capital, or humble and secluded in your position, we ask you, in the name of humanity, posterity and freedom, to stop and consider the importance of your presence and co-operation. Let it not be said that ye are insensible and dead to all the interests and motives that stimulate and enhance life; but come up in your sturdy simplicity from the cultivated fields, from the workshops, and from all your different avocations, and make one

great heart, whose pulse has the life and force of the whole people. Thus inseparably bound in interests, and standing upon the vantage ground of the declared principles of the government, we have nothing to fear; "and are doubly armed, for our cause is just." Look forth upon the green and luxuriant fields, the umbrageous forests, and mountains that aspire to arrest the sun in his downward effulgence, and then say will you forsake these glories and blessings, hearth-stone and roof-tree, and deliberately give up yourselves as unworthy of these blessings? If not, then let there be but one expression coming in multiplied force--omnipotent, because ye are resolved; and let it be this:
NO PROSCRIPTION--NO SLAVES--UNION--FREEDOM AND EQUALITY!!

       Wm. P. McIntyre,
       Edward Freeman,
       Wm. Rich,
       C. Edward Seth,
       Hiram Johnson.

PROCEEDINGS

Thursday, July 22d, 1851.

Pursuant to a call, the Convention assembled in the room of the Court of Appeals, on the morning of the 22d of July, at 9 o'clock. The house was called to order by Mr. Stephen Myers,[3] who moved the appointment of Richard Wright, Esq., of Albany, as chairman pro tem., and H. Hicks, of Catskill, as Secretary pro tem.

By invitation, the Rev. E. N. Hall, of Brooklyn, N. Y., addressed the Throne of Grace.

On motion of Wm. P. McIntyre, of Albany, the call for the Convention was read by the Secretary, after which the Convention proceeded to enroll the names and residences of delegates, as follows:

Albany.--Stephen Myers, Wm. P. McIntyre, Hiram Johnson, William H. Topp, Francis Douge, Charles E. Seth, Wm. C. Gardiner, Benjamin Cutler, Richard Wright, James P. Johnson, John Springsteel, Abr'm Johnson, James M. Williams, Henry Johnson, Primus Robinson, James Youngs, F. Van Vranken, Peter Vandeveer, Jacob Ennis.

Troy.--Wm. Rich, Edward H. Bishop, Wm. Jones, Abraham Stanley, Daniel Hall, Lloyd Hasper.

Catskill.--Henry Hicks, Martin Cross.

Brooklyn.--Eli N. Hall, John N. Stiles.

Whitehall.--Henry Williams.

Ithaca.--Wm. F. Johnson.

New Haven, Ct.--Amos G. Beman.

Mr. C. E. Seth, of Albany, offered the following resolution, seconded by Hiram Johnson, of Albany.

Resolved, That all persons present, who have come from those places where no regular delegation to the Convention is appointed--who concur with the spirit of the call of said Convention, and are desirous of participating in its proceedings, shall, by having their names enrolled, be considered as delegates.

This resolution created a spirited and protracted discussion, which was participated in by Messrs. Wm. H. Topp, Hiram Johnson, Charles E. Seth, Henry Hicks, John N. Still, Wm. P. McIntyre, and others, when after an expression from the Convention, the resolution was declared lost.

After which, W. H. Topp offered the following resolution, seconded by S. Myers:

Resolved, That all persons present, who are really the aggrieved, and identically the disfranchised, and are desirous of participating in the proceedings of this Convention, may, after enrolling their names, be considered delegates. And all such other persons, who wish to participate, may do so by invitation from the Convention.

After a short discussion, the question was taken on this resolution, and declared adopted.

By motion of Mr. S. Myers, seconded by Mr. Seth, it was

Resolved, That a committee of three be appointed to nominate permanent officers of the Convention.

The following gentlemen were appointed nominating committee: C. E. Seth, Francis Douge, and Stephen Myers; who, upon their return, reported the following lists:--

For President, William H. Topp, of Albany.

For Vice-Presidents, Amos G. Beman,[4] of New-Haven, William Rich, of Troy, and James Morris Williams, of Albany, recently from Coxsackie.

For Secretaries, Rev. Henry Hicks, of Catskill, Greene Co., and Charles E. Seth, Esq., of Albany.

Finance Committee--Wm. P. McIntyre, S. Myers, and F. Douge.

Business Committee--Hiram Johnson, Stephen Myers, Richard Wright, William P. McIntyre, C. E. Seth, Henry Hicks, and John N. Still, and Eli N. Hall.

The President was conducted to his seat by Mr. John N. Still, of Brooklyn, and W. P. McIntyre, of Albany.

President Topp, on being conducted to his chair, arose and addressed the Convention, in a brief and happy manner, referring to the main objects for which the Convention was called, and concluded by hoping that good order, harmony, and disinterested humanity might characterize all its deliberations. He resumed his seat amidst the spirited applause of the Convention.

After which, a motion prevailed, that a committee of three be appointed to draft rules for the government of the Convention. The following gentlemen were appointed: C. E. Seth, Francis Douge, and John N. Still, who retired, and on their return, reported the following rules:

Rules

1. *Resolved,* That each session of the Convention be opened by addressing the Throne of Grace.
2. At the time appointed for the assembling of each session of the Convention, the President shall take the chair and call the Convention to order.
3. The minutes of the preceding session shall be read at the opening of each session, at which time all mistakes, if there be any, shall be corrected.
4. The President shall decide all questions of order subject to an appeal of the Convention.
5. All motions and addresses shall be made to the President, the member rising from his seat.
6. All motions, except those of reference, shall be submitted in writing.
7. All committees shall be appointed by the chair unless otherwise ordered by the Convention.
8. The previous question shall always be in order, and until decided shall preclude all amendment and debate of the main question, and shall be put in this form, "Shall the main question be now put?"
9. No member shall be interrupted while speaking except when out of order, when he shall be called to order by or through the chair.
10. A motion to adjourn shall always be in order, and shall be decided without debate.
11. No member shall speak more than twice on the same question, without the consent of the Convention, nor more than fifteen minutes at each time.
12. No resolution, except of reference, shall be offered to the Convention, except it come through the business committee; but all resolutions rejected by the committee may be presented directly to the Convention if the maker of such wishes to do so.
13. Rule as amended. Sessions of the Convention shall commence at half-past 9 o'clock, A.M., and shall close at 1 o'clock, P.M.; to commence at half-past 2 o'clock, P.M., and close at 6 P.M. Evening session shall commence at half-past 7 o'clock, and close at the discretion of the Convention.

On motion of Mr. McIntyre, seconded by Mr. Hicks, the report of the committee on rules was received. The hour for adjournment having arrived, a motion prevailed that they be laid over for the consideration of the Convention at its next session. By motion, the Convention was adjourned until the hour of half-past 2 P.M.

NEW YORK, 1851

Afternoon Session.

The Convention assembled pursuant to adjournment. President in the chair. Prayer by the Rev. James M. Williams. After which the minutes were read and approved.

The President announced, as the first business in order, the rules reported by the committee at the previous session, which were read by the Secretary, and a motion proposed, that they be adopted; pending which Mr. William P. McIntyre made some slight objection to the 11th rule, proposing that it be so amended as to allow members debating *thirty* minutes instead of *fifteen*, as the rule directs; a brief discussion revealed the merits of the rule, and the question was taken on the amendment and lost.

Mr. McIntyre also proposed that the thirteenth rule be so amended, so as to direct that the sessions shall open at half-past 9 A.M., and close at 1 P.M.: and at half-past 2 P.M., and close at 6 P.M.: and at half-past 7 P.M., and close at the discretion of the Convention. After which the question was taken as amended, and adopted. Main question was then called for, and without discussion the rules were declared adopted.

Whereupon Mr. Wm. P. McIntyre introduced the following resolution:

Resolved, That all motions or resolutions voted upon and lost, shall not be recorded upon the minutes of the Convention, unless so agreed upon at the time. A brief discussion ensued, and the question taken, and declared lost. A recess of five minutes was granted, and by solicitation Mr. Wm. F. Johnson, of Ithaca, (who it may not be amiss to remark, is totally blind,) favored the Convention with a song, entitled the "Fugitive Slave." After which, the business committee returned, and reported a series of resolutions, which was, by motion of Mr. Myers, seconded by H. Hicks, received.

Resolutions

1. *Resolved,* That the colored citizens and inhabitants of the State of New-York will support all law that comprehends the interest of the people, and the welfare of the State, without regard to condition or complexion.

2. *Resolved,* That the exercise of the rights of franchise is a duty incumbent upon, and appertaining to every freeman, and any and every violation of a uniform rule or law, is inimical to the rights of the people.

3. *Resolved,* That the imposed conditions which are required of every colored citizen or voter, is an imposition in consequence of its proscriptive character, and unwise distinctions, generating contempt for those who are thus imposed upon, and leaving them no escape from degradation.

4. *Resolved,* That for the purposes of elevating the masses, a proper system of education is of paramount importance, and that any system of common or high school education, which teaches superiority of races, or creates distinctions based upon complexional differences, is opposed to the true interest of all classes by inflating the one with the false notions of their greatness, and crushing the other by such influences, as teaches them submission and inferiority.

5. *Resolved,* That it is the duty of every good citizen, and especially every colored person, to discountenance, in every practical way, the erection or maintenance of separate schools for colored children.

6. *Resolved,* That we regard the common school law of this State with the most profound interest, conceiving it to be a great means for the Christian and civil advancement of the State, in consequence of the uniform character in the education of all classes of children.

7. *Resolved,* That the trustees or commissioners in usurping the right to wrest this wholesome law in its natural tendency and just course, exhibit a morbid prejudice moving in a sphere far beneath the enlightened policy that clothes them with limited power.

A motion upon the second reading of the committee's report prevailed, that these resolutions be taken up by numbers for adoption.

Resolution 1st was then called for, read, and a motion proposed for adoption; pending which, the following gentlemen engaged in a spirited discussion: Messrs. Wm. P. McIntyre, Hiram Johnson, both of Albany, and Mr. Wm. F. Johnson, of Tompkins county, also Mr. Cutler, of Albany. After which the yeas and nays were called for, and resolution 1st declared adopted.

Resolution 2d was then called, read and submitted to the pleasure of the Convention, which was freely discussed by Messrs. Still, of Brooklyn, Myers, of Albany, and J. P. Johnson, of Albany. Question was then taken, and the 2d resolution adopted.

Resolution 3d was then called for, read, and by motion submitted to the pleasure of the house, which without discussion, was adopted unanimously. After its adoption Mr. A. G. Beman, of New Haven, proposed its reconsideration. A motion being stated to that effect, was overruled by the house.

Resolution 4th was then taken up, and a motion offered that it be adopted; pending which the following gentlemen engaged in a warm and interesting discussion: Messrs. Wright, of Albany, and Wm. F. Johnson, of Ithaca, opposing; and Wm. H. Topp, Wm. P. McIntyre, S. Myers, of Albany, and H. Hicks, of Catskill, sustaining. Hour for adjournment having arrived, a motion prevailed that the session be extended fifteen minutes. Discussion was resumed by Mr. Still and Cutler opposing, and Hiram Johnson and Myers sustaining. After which the Convention adjourned until $7\frac{1}{2}$ P.M.

Evening Session.

The Convention assembled pursuant to adjournment. Prayer by the Rev. E. N. Hall. After which the minutes of the previous session were read and approved. The president announced as the first business in order, the consideration of the 4th resolution, which was under discussion at the time of adjournment, which resolution was discussed with increased warmth and ability, by Messrs. Topp sustaining, and R. Wright and others opposing. Yeas and nays were then called for, and the resolution declared adopted.

Resolution 5th was then called, and by motion submitted to the house, which, without much discussion, was adopted, by Messrs. R. Wright of Albany, W. F. Johnson of Ithaca, and J. N. Stills of Brooklyn, dissenting.

Resolution 6th was read, and a motion being proposed for its adoption, the question was taken without debate, and unanimously adopted.

Resolution 7th was taken up, and by motion submitted to the pleasure of the house, which resolution created a spirited and lucid debate, in which the following gentlemen freely participated: Mr. Richard Wright and Benjamin Cutler opposing and W. H. Topp, C. E. Seth, S. Myers, Wm. P. McIntyre and J. W. Williams, sustaining. Pending which, a motion was proposed to adjourn, which was overruled by a second motion to extend the session fifteen minutes. After a short discussion the yeas and nays were called for on resolution 7th, and it was adopted.

Rev. Amos G. Beman then offered the following resolution:

Resolved, That there be a committee appointed, to report upon the following questions, viz: three on Colonization, three on Elective Franchise, three on Schools, and three on the Fugitive Slave Bill. The following gentlemen were appointed:

C. E. Seth,	A. G. Beman,
B. F. Cutler,	J. N. Still,
W. C. Gardner,	J. P. Johnson,
Colonization.	*Fugitive Slave Bill.*
Wm. H. Topp,	H. Johnson,
S. Myers,	R. Wright,
E. N. Hall,	Wm. Rich,
Schools.	*Suffrage Question.*

The fifteen minutes extension of the session having expired, on motion the Convention adjourned.

SECOND DAY

Wednesday Morning, July 23d, 1851.

The Convention assembled agreeable to adjournment. President in the chair. Prayer by H. Hicks. After which the minutes of the last meeting were read and approved. The President announced as the first business in order, the consideration of the remaining part of the series of resolutions reported by the business committee, or the reconsideration of resolution seventh which was pending at the time of adjournment. Seventh resolution was then read, and Mr. McIntyre arose and sustained the resolution in a very happy and able manner. He was opposed, however, by Mr. R. Wright. Mr. Hiram Johnson also sustained the resolution in an eloquent address of fourteen minutes, showing the injustice and usurpation of the course of those to whom the resolution refers, and hoped that the gentlemen seeing it in the light it had been represented would give that resolution their unanimous and uncompromising support.

Mr. J. N. Still arose and begged leave to correct an opinion that grew out of a remark he made yesterday during the discussion on resolution fifth. He stated that he acquiesced with the spirit and principle of the resolution, but was compelled to dissent from the opinions of gentlemen who considered it practicable. The vote was then taken on the resolution and declared adopted.

At this stage the business committee reported resolutions, to wit: 8, 9, 10, 11, 12, 13, 14, 15, 16. By motion of Mr. Wright, seconded by Mr. Hicks, the report of the committee was accepted, and a motion prevailed that they be taken up separately for adoption.

Resolutions

8. *Resolved,* That we look with the same feelings of abhorrence and contempt now as ever upon the scheme of the American Colonization Society in their efforts to expatriate the free colored people of this country, as a scheme fraught with incalculable evils to them as a people, and we record our unalterable protest and condemnation against the project, as unjust and impracticable.

9. *Resolved,* That we regard with solemn interest the admonition of Marquis de La Fayette[5] in his farewell address before Congress, 1783, and recommend a serious contemplation of the same to all true Americans. "May this great monument raised to liberty serve as a lesson to the oppressor and an example to the oppressed."

10. *Resolved,* That we believe it to be the determined policy and premeditated intention of a large portion of the people of this country to keep us debased and dependent, making our condition as unhappy and us to appear unworthy, with the view of forcing upon us one of two alternatives--emigration or alienation.

11. *Resolved,* That this Convention views with deep sorrow and regret the many evils that flow through society from the use of intoxicating liquors as a common beverage, and that it urges upon all in the most earnest manner the importance of discountenancing intemperance in all practicable ways.

12. *Resolved,* That it is the duty of this Convention to urge and encourage with all their power the occupation of the Gerrit Smith grants as one of the most safe and speedy means of alleviating our condition in this state, and also of giving character and respectability to our people throughout the United States.

13. *Resolved,* That this Convention appoint a committee of three to investigate and report on this subject.

14. *Resolved,* That the delegates will encourage the investigation and report of this committee in their respective vicinities.

15. *Resolved,* That this Convention recommend as worthy of the patronage and important as auxiliaries in the attainment of the rights of the colored people, and of their moral improvement, the efficient support of the *Impartial Citizen*,[6] edited by Rev. S. R. Ward, in Boston, Mass., and of the *Telegraph*, edited and published in Albany, N. Y., by Stephen Myers, agent of the Delavan State Temperance Union, and *Frederick Douglass' Paper*,[7] published at Rochester, N. Y.

Resolution No. 8 was then called for, read, and a motion being stated for its adoption, Mr. Wm. F. Johnson arose and sustained it elaborately, but made some slight objections to the incongruity of the term "impracticable." Mr. R. Wright thought that this word expressed too much, for with his understanding of the right application of this word it was "practicable" for man to emigrate to all most any part, and therefore he would prefer as a substitute the word proposed by Mr. Wm. F. Johnson *"contemptible."*

Mr. Wm H. Topp sustained the resolution as originally offered, also Mr. McIntyre. The amendment was overruled and the question taken on the main resolution, and adopted.

9th resolution was then read, and by motion submitted to the pleasure of the house. The question was then taken without debate and adopted.

10th resolution was then read, and a motion proposed for its adoption, pending which Mr. Still arose to make some explanations of its merits, which explanation created a lengthy and spirited debate, which drew out many interesting observations on both sides, all agreeing in repudiating the principle at which the resolution aimed, but differing in modes as to the surest way of success. The question was taken, however, and it was adopted.

11th resolution was then read, and by motion submitted to the pleasure of the house. Mr. Wm. F. Johnson thought that a resolution of this character was rather uncalled for, in consideration of the main object of the Convention. This remark aroused the *native* talents, and latent eloquence of S. Myers, who in a speech of 15 minutes, detained the convention agreeably. Yeas and nays were called for, and the resolution declared adopted.

At this stage, a motion prevailed that the 8th resolution be reconsidered; at which point Mr. R. Wright arose and desired to speak, but was objected to, on the ground of having twice spoken upon the same question. Whereupon, a motion was entertained that he be allowed five minutes, but by an expression from the house, was declared lost. Mr. Wm. H. Topp then spoke with great interest upon the question. Mr. Cutler, and Mr. Jones, of Troy, each warmly sustaining the resolution.

Mr. McIntyre said he would, by permission from the chair, correct what he conceived to be a wrong impression entertained by some of the delegates, in the use and application of the term "impracticable." Mr. Hiram Johnson spoke to this effect, upon the reconsideration of the resolution: "That by an unceasing discussion of the nefarious American colonization scheme, invested the subject with an unwarrantable importance, that the practical effect of the scheme does not justify; and the love of home in the colored man repudiates. Therefore," he said "by constant discussion of the subject, made it appear feasible to the minds of many of our people, when it deserves nothing more than an expression of silent or sovereign contempt." Therefore he recommended that to remove the shadow of the practicability of this unchristian scheme, it was only necessary to engage in the business pursuits of the day.

Hour to adjourn having arrived, Convention adjourned until half-past 2 P.M.

Afternoon Session.

Convention assembled as per adjournment. President called the house to order, and by invitation, the Rev. P. Vandivere addressed the Throne of Grace. Minutes of the morning session were read and approved.

The President announced that the business first in order was the resolution 1st, as pending when the morning session adjourned. Mr. Hicks hoped the question would be taken on this resolution without further discussion, for he was of the opinion that to argue it, was to attach importance to it. Mr. Myers, and Wm. F. Johnson, however, thought to the contrary. Mr. Still said the subject of colonization was increasing in interest in his vicinity, and referred to a communication published in the *N. Y. Tribune*,[8] by Augustus Washington, which article was justly censured by the Convention. The question was then taken, and the resolution adopted.

The 12th resolution was then called for, and read, and by motion, submitted to the pleasure of the Convention. Mr. Still sustained this resolution lucidly, and without further discussion, by an expression of the house, it was adopted unanimously.

The 13th resolution was read, and by motion, submitted to the house. Upon which, Mr. McIntyre enquired the duty of the committee referred to in resolutions 12 and 13. After a satisfactory explanation given by J. N. Still, the question was taken, and it was declared adopted.

J. N. Still, Hiram Johnson, and Henry Hicks,
Committee referred to in resolution 13th.

Resolution 14 read, and a motion being proposed, was adopted without debate.

The business committee reported a resolution recommending the investment of monies in public stocks, as being feasible, safe, and promising much towards the amelioration of the condition of the colored people. After a protracted and spirited debate upon the preamble that preceded the resolution, as well as the resolution, a motion was offered and carried to the effect, that the resolution be returned to the committee for their further consideration of its merits, and report again.

On motion, a recess of five minutes was granted. During this short interval, Wm. F. Johnson sang, by invitation, an anti-slavery song, at the conclusion of which, Mr. E. Edward Seth, in accordance with a previous notice he gave to the Convention during the morning session, reported elaborately in behalf of the committee on colonization. He also availed himself of the opportunity to proclaim his dissent in toto from the opinions of some of the gentlemen advanced this morning, during the debate on the colonization resolution--of treating the subject with "silence," studied silence. "Why," he asked, "should we treat it with silence any more than we would slavery!" On motion of Mr. Stephen Myers, the report was accepted. After thrilling, forcible, and eloquent speeches from Messrs. Myers and William H. Topp, of Albany, and Wm. T. Johnson, of Ithaca, commendatory of the report, the question on its adoption was called for, and carried unanimously, to be printed in full, in the proceedings of the Convention.

The committee on finance lifted a collection, and report the result of $1.25.

A motion was then offered by Mr. McIntyre, seconded by S. Myers, that the final adjournment of the Convention shall take place on Thursday afternoon, at 4 o'clock. Carried.

On motion, the Convention adjourned.

Evening Session.

The Convention assembled as per adjournment, president in the chair. Prayer by Rev. E. N. Hall. Minutes of the previous session read and adopted; after which Mr. Hiram Johnson arose and reported in behalf of the committee on the Suffrage question. A motion then prevailed that the report be received; also, on a motion being proposed for its adoption, upon stating the question, Mr. Wm. F. Johnson arose and sustained the report in a most lucid and argumentative address of fifteen minutes. After which the question was taken for the adoption of the report and it was carried unanimously.

A letter at this stage was introduced, from Junius C. Morell, Esq., of Brooklyn, L. I., and read in the audience of the Convention; also one from Mr. A. Williams, of Salem, Mass., and passed to the file. After which, J. N. Still, Esq., reported in behalf of the committee on the Fugitive Slave bill. A motion prevailed that the report be received; also a motion being stated for its adoption, Mr. Still arose and supported the report in a brief and interesting address of fourteen minutes. Mr. C. E. Seth, also in a very feeling manner sustained the remarks of Mr. Still, accompanied with an interesting speech of fifteen minutes, condemnatory of the Fugitive Slave enactment. Mr. W. F. Johnson sustained the report in an eloquent address of thirty minutes; after which the question was taken on its adoption, and it was declared unanimously.

Mr. Hiram Johnson then reported, in behalf of the business committee, the following resolution:

Resolved, That there be a committee of three appointed to draw up a petition, signed by the officers of this Convention, and submitted to the Governor of the State, with a request that he transmit the same to the Legislature, to so amend the Constitution of the State of New-York as to extend equal suffrage to colored men.

It was voted that this resolution be received, and on the question being stated for its adoption, Mr. Hicks proposed that it be so amended so as to read, send it to the Legislature, instead of the Governor. This proposition created a lengthy debate, in which the following gentlemen freely participated: Messrs. McIntyre, Myers, Seth, Jones, and W. F. Johnson, each sustaining their parts with great credit and good feeling. Mr. McIntyre and Mr. Hiram Johnson sustained the resolution as reported, and the other gentlemen as amended.

After which the question was taken on the amendment and lost.

Mr. Topp begged leave to renew the amendment, and by motion his proposition was entertained. Mr. Topp showed clearly his reasons for repeating this amendment; he believed such a course to be without precedent, to send a petition to the Governor for him to bear to the Legislature, and feared that adopting such a resolution would excite ridicule. Without further discussion the question was taken on the amendment to the amendment, and declared adopted: reading thus, That there be a committee of three appointed to draw up a petition signed by the officers of this Convention, and submitted to the Legislature of this State with a request that they so amend the Constitution, &c. &c. &c.

Main question was then taken and the resolution declared adopted.

Wm. P. McIntyre,
J. N. Still,
H. Hicks,
Committee on Petition.

At this stage the finance committee lifted the collection and reported as the result the sum of $2.11. A motion to adjourn prevailed, to meet Thursday morning 9 o'clock.

The Convention adjourned harmoniously.

THIRD DAY

Thursday Morning Session, July 24th.

The Convention assemble as per adjournment; the house was called to order by Vice-President Williams. Prayer by Vice-President Rev. A. G. Beman. Minutes of the previous session read and adopted. After which Mr. J. N. Still moved that resolution 10th be reconsidered. This resolution aimed at the refutation of a libel published in the *Express* of N. Y.,[10] and republished in the *Express* of Albany, reflecting upon the moral and social charcter of the colored people. This resolution called out a warm and elaborate discussion. Mr. Seth hoped that the Convention would give attention to the observations of Mr. Still, in reference to the libellous communication referred to, for, said he, this Convention should give it its just and merited rebuke. Mr. McIntyre thought the best method of rebuke would be to treat it with silent contempt, and he hoped the Convention would not consume time in discussing it, while there were matters of greater moment that claimed the consideration of the house, in view of its final adjournment at the hour of 4 P.M. Mr. W. F. Johnson thought that silence upon that subject would tend to confirm and strengthen the prejudices of those who are really ignorant of the condition of the colored people in the cities, &c.; he would therefore give it an elaborate consideration. Mr. Myers also sustained the remarks of Mr. Johnson, and pertinently referred to a number of circumstances, that would inevitably refute the communication in the *Express*. Mr. Hicks moved that the resolution be laid over, and all further debate relating to it, until the hour of half past 2 o'clock, P.M. The question was taken, and the resolution was laid over.

Mr. Topp gave notice that the committee on Schools and Education was ready to report. He (Mr. Topp) then reported in behalf of the committee. It was voted that the report be received. On a motion being proposed that the report be adopted, Mr. Topp gave an interesting narrative of the principles and condition of the McGrawville College,[11] which was recommended in the report as worthy the patronage of all the friends of equality, and especially the colored people. Also Mr. W. F. Johnson warmly recommended that institution as being all that it professes to be, to all intents and purposes, and he could cheerfully endorse the sentiments of the gentlemen (Mr. Topp) in commending it to the patronage of the colored people. The question was then taken on the adoption of the report, and carried.

Mr. W. P. McIntyre gave notice that he was ready to report in behalf of the committee appointed to draft a petition to the Legislature. He then came forward and reported; and a motion prevailed that the report be received; and on motion the report was unanimously adopted.

Mr. Hicks moved that the Convention take a recess of thirty minutes, at the hour of 12; carried.

Rev. A. G. Beman then moved that the rule be suspended for the time being, which relates to the report of resolutions through the business committee; carried. Mr. Still then by resolution, made reference to the Gerrit Smith's lands. Hour of recess having arrived, the Convention was suspended until 12½ [o'clock].

Thursday, half-past 12 P.M.

The Convention reassembled as per suspension. Mr. Still resumed his remarks on the Smith grants in a happy manner, showing why the colored people should occupy them, which drew out remarks from several gentlemen, among which was Mr. McIntyre, W. F. Johnson and others. President Topp then gave notice that the hour had arrived to consider the suspended resolution, to wit, resolution 11th. After a brief but spirited discussion on this subject, the resolution was declared adopted.

Mr. J. N. Still offered the following resolution, which was entertained by the house:

Resolved, That upon the colored people depends, under God, the important duty of preserving the Christian church from idolatry, and the entire people from infidelity, and the republic from destruction.

Mr. Cutler said he could not go for this resolution, indeed he was opposed to it all together; he could not see the propriety of introducing it in this Convention; the subject to which it relates seems "begged;" besides that, the Convention had not time to consider such grave subjects at this time.

Mr. Hicks observed that if he was sure the discussion upon this resolution would end here, he would reserve his remarks; but he saw a disposition to extend the discussion, and he feared to the overthrow of the resolution, and disrespect to the principle involved; he could not agree with Mr. Cutler, that the Convention had not time to consider this "grave subject," for in his opinion, if the Convention had not time to consider a subject of such vital interest to the people of color, as that of guarding them from skepticism or infidelity, or in other words, saving men's souls, he was at a loss to determine what they had time to consider. He hoped this resolution would pass with an overwhelming vote.

Mr. W. F. Johnson said he felt pained to hear gentlemen on this floor argue as did Mr. Cutler; if the gentlemen could not see the merits of this resolution--if he could not appreciate its spirit, he must say he deeply sympathized with him, for he feared he was bordering to one of the principles wich threatens the destruction of the church and people.

Mr. McIntyre said he regretted the necessity of detaining the Convention at this late stage, but he felt called upon to speak, even at the expense of being classed with Mr. Cutler, who has so warmly opposed the passage of this resolution. He would enquire if we would not be arrogating too much to the colored people, by endorsing the sentiments of that resolution; he thought we did, and he hoped before gentlemen voted on it, they would calmly consider what the resolution assumes.

Mr. Topp said the resolution met his approbation at once, and experience and observation combined to convince him that there was more truth than fiction in the resolution. He therefore hoped it would be adopted.

Mr. Hall said he saw clearly the providence of God in preserving the religion of Jesus Christ pure among his persecuted people, and those very persecutions were a means to that end.

The question was then taken on the resolution, and declared adopted.

At this period, the committee reported through Mr. Hiram Johnson, a series of resolutions, to wit: Nos. 16, 17, 18, 19, 20, 21, 22, 23. A motion prevailed that the report be received; and also it was voted, that they be taken up by numbers for adoption.

At this point, the finance committee raised the collection, and reported 87 cents.

Resolution 16th was then called for and read as follows:

Resolved, That we recommend to all colored voters to cast their votes and to wield their political influence in favor of those men who in their public course have given the best proof of being in favor of universal and impartial freedom. Question taken, and it was declared adopted:

Resolution 17th was called for and read as follows:

Resolved, That there be a State Central Committee of nine appointed, whose duty it shall be to call a State Convention at such time and place as they shall judge expedient. Question taken and declared adopted.

State Central Committee

W. H. Topp, S. Myers, Albany; Wm. F. Johnson, Ithaca, Tompkins co.; Wm. McIntyre, Albany; H. Hicks, Catskill, Greene co.; Wm. Rich, Troy; Hiram Johnson, Albany; George Weir, Jr., Buffalo; Charles B. Ray, New-York.

Resolution 18th was amended to read as follows:

Resolved, That W. H. Topp, C. E. Seth and H. Hicks be a committee to publish the doings of this Convention, and are hereby authorized to collect the necessary means, and that W. P. McIntyre and J. P. Johnson be added to the committee for the purpose of soliciting funds, said committee to furnish each member of the Legislature with a copy at its next session. Adopted.

19. *Resolved,* That this Convention return hearty thanks to the Governor and Trustees of the Capitol for the use of the same for the sitting of this Convention. Carried.

20. *Resolved,* That this Convention return thanks to Mr. Jenkins, the Superintendent of the Capitol, for the politeness and attention he has shown to the members of this Convention. Carried.

21. *Resolved,* That we the delegates tender our thanks to the President of this Convention for the able, dignified and impartial manner in which he has presided over its deliberations. Carried.

22. *Resolved,* That a vote of the thanks of this Convention be presented to the Secretaries, Mr. Seth and Hicks, for their valuable services during the sitting of the Convention. Question taken and carried.

At this juncture the committee on finance reported as follows:

Received by collections,	$5.91
Paid for circulars, ... $2.25	
Paid for stationery, ... 38	
Paid for postage, ... 1.00	
Paid for sweeping hall, ... 1.25	
	4.88
Balance on hand, ...	$1.03

W. P. McIntyre,
F. H. Douge,
S. Myers,
  Finance Committee.

A motion prevailed that the balance in the hands of the committee of finance be paid to the publishing committee. A motion prevailed that the minutes be read, which was complied with, and by motion adopted. After which it was resolved that the Convention adjourn *sine die*. The Convention was adjourned by singing the doxology "Praise God from whom," &c., and by prayer from the Rev. E. N. Hall, and then dismissed in the most harmonious manner.

Signed,   W. H. Topp,
       President.
     A. G. Beman,
     W. Rich,
     J. W. Williams,
       Vice Presidents.
     C. E. Seth,
     H. Hicks,
       Secretaries.

Albany, July 24, 1851.

NEW YORK, 1851   65

Report on Colonization

The advancement which the Colonization Society has made in late years, though *haud passibus aequis*, through bequeathed legacies, through life contributions, and through the strenuous efforts of collective bodies, prove conclusively, though not alarmingly, the hold it has gained on the public mind; and of the paramount necessity of our calling the attention not only of the free colored people of this State, but of every state in the union where they can act individually, and collectively, to the detriment and discomfiture of the institution.

In the formation of this society, in the earliest period of its existence, when the principles, and objects of its organization and government were promulgated, when its Proudfits,[12] its Buchanans,[13] its Ashmuns,[14] its Clays,[15] its Cressons,[16] its Gurleys,[17] its Pinneys,[18] and a host of others were sent into the field as pioneers, as Governors, as Lecturers, as Orators, and as Presidents, under the pretext as we know, and as we ever have and still believe, of ameliorating the condition of the colored people--of promoting their general welfare, by striving to send the nominally free portion of them to Liberia; but whose sole purpose in fact was, and is still, the accomplishment of a "happy riddance" of us, from this our native land, to be transported to the burning deserts of Africa.

This project for our removal, wholesale and retail, created in the mind and heart of every man and woman of us, a bitter contempt, and animosity toward such an institution, and all those who associated themselves with it.

The scheme was derided and mocked and repelled by the people of color and their friends, at every step diligently for a season, until, in the minds of some, the success of such an object seemed too impossible to give cause for any real apprehension of its working evil in the future; and the people appear to have folded their arms, and consigned their hitherto assiduous opposition to the keeping of a *"masterly inactivity,"* tacitly watching the movements of these pretended philanthropists.

But in the progress of time; through the diligent and unremitting efforts and untiring zeal of the colonizationists for the success of their "daring scheme," we find at this stage of the society's existence, of more than a quarter of a century, a resuscitation of life, still vigorous; still growing; strengthening in its strength; accumulating in numbers; gaining in resources; and with a spirit of determination to effect the desire of its purposes, if possible, in the end. To facilitate the completion of this work, the "powers that be" have been invoked to engage in the mean calling--a calling adverse to the wishes and dispositions of nine hundred and ninety-nine colored persons out of every thousand; of urging them by gaudy pictures, to seek a new home in a foreign land, no more peculiar to their natures, (and assuredly repugnant to their inclinations,) than it is adapted to any other portion of the American people, or the European nations.

Through the will of an all-wise Providence we were born in this country; consequently by virtue of that birth, this *is* our country, and the only one we claim as our own, and is in every respect suited to our natures wholly.

That on the color of a man, or of a nation, depends the civilization and evangelization of the same, is not only absurd but libellous of reason.

Not African complexion, or the descendants of Africa alone, but through the hazard of acclimation, foreigners of all complexions may, out of the unhewn material of the native intellect, by the process of civilization, education and evangelization, based upon God's laws--the precept and practice of his religion, not man's, work out that country's ultimate redemption and salvation from ignorance, and place her on the road to national eminence.

And we avail ourselves of the convenience here, to assert that it is not from any feeling of malignance, in the slightest degree whatever, towards Africa, and her rescue from darkness and oblivion, or any other country of heathenism and idolatry, (although the Liberians have suggested some infamous offers to this government in their eagerness to be nationally recognized,[19] and which we shall allude to in the conclusion of this report,) that we denounce the American Colonization scheme; but from the fact, notwithstanding it ostensibly bears upon its face a kind of philanthropy; such skin-deep philanthropy we spurn--that its primary and ending object is our complete removal to Africa, without the expressed application originally emanating from the intelligent colored people directly, themselves.

Then why should they assume a responsibility, unmooted and unauthorized by those whom it is calculated to affect injuriously; a scheme, the very essence of which is so palpably a wrong, and so impracticable, that it can *never* be accomplished. The intelligence, the spirit of humanity, the progressive moral sentiment of the age is averse to it. It is folly's foil to urge it. It is madness to contemplate its success.

And to tell us that we cannot rise to a standard of high, moral, social, and intellectual elevation with the white man of this country, throws no damper of timidity over our all exertions, and resolute perseverance, to pursue the attainment of these objects, with the indomitable spirit of Americans struggling for American rights.

Have we not many things to encourage us? Have we not even amid all deprivations and degradations slowly, yet steadily made advances in the improvement of our moral condition and mental acquirements? The darkness of the past; the dawning light and developments of the present; and the bright hopeful future, all inspire us with confidence to go onward, aiming upward, trusting in the will of Providence, and the growing moral sentiment of the people, that the withheld rights of one portion of the American people will yet, sooner or later, be bestowed upon them.

The opposite of this, no man whose mind is freed and unfettered from the corroding effects of color-prejudice believes.

All our interests are indissolubly identified with the country through weal or woe. And it matters not if colossal impediments obstruct the way, they are but temporary, and we, by the help of God, intend to remain and work out our elevation, and the disenthrallment of our brethren from slavery.

The slow movement of the emigration of free colored people, only 7,000 in 30 years, throws a gloom over the desired speedy accomplishment of the object of the society, and hence the effort made to increase its capacities, and extend its powers for operating more effectually. They have appealed to State legislatures, and have succeeded in getting several of these authorities to move in the matter, by passing resolutions commendatory of the scheme, and recommending the national government to undertake the expense of colonizing all who will go. Some of the most prominent statesmen have given it their approbation. One particularly, who indicates his willingness that the Land Fund should be so appropriated as to facilitate the *peaceable conclusion* of this project, to wit, *our banishment*. Virginia by a law enacted in 1849, appropriates $30,000 for the benefit of this nefarious scheme. Maryland has too a fund of long standing for the same purpose. But we must express our happy pleasure at the failure of the Colonization Society of this State, to obtain at the recent session of the Legislature, an appropriation of $10,000 yearly, for two years, for the malicious purposes of sending the colored people from this State to Africa, and to procure the broad seal of approval of the Commonwealth to such a measure. We entertain no fears however, should such a measure pass the Legislature. We have too much confidence in the good sense and love of home of the people.

We give below the result of the operations of the society, from its earliest state down to the year 1850. Not very flattering, surely, in view of the ratio of increase of the colored population in the United States. The entire number of emigrants sent to Liberia by the American Colonization Society, and its auxiliaries from each State, from 1820 to 1850, inclusive.

```
Massachusetts, . . . . . . . . . . . . . . . . . . . . . . . .        1
Connecticut, . . . . . . . . . . . . . . . . . . . . . . . . .       10
Rhode Island, . . . . . . . . . . . . . . . . . . . . . . . .       32
New-York, . . . . . . . . . . . . . . . . . . . . . . . . . .      107
New Jersey, . . . . . . . . . . . . . . . . . . . . . . . . .        1
Pennsylvania, . . . . . . . . . . . . . . . . . . . . . . . .      101
Delaware, . . . . . . . . . . . . . . . . . . . . . . . . . .        4
Maryland, . . . . . . . . . . . . . . . . . . . . . . . . . .      415
District of Columbia, . . . . . . . . . . . . . . . . . . . .      101
Virginia, . . . . . . . . . . . . . . . . . . . . . . . . . .    2,258
North Carolina, . . . . . . . . . . . . . . . . . . . . . . .      846
South Carolina, . . . . . . . . . . . . . . . . . . . . . . .      344
```

Georgia, ... 551
Alabama, ... 46
Mississippi, ... 505
Louisiana, ... 177
Tennessee, ... 244
Kentucky, ... 255
Ohio, ... 45
Indiana, ... 22
Illinois, ... 26
Missouri, ... 21
Michigan, ... 1
Iowa, ... 3
    Total number sent by the Society, ... 6,116

RECAPITULATION

Number born free, ... 2,315
Number that purchased their freedom, ... 165
Number emancipated in view of emigrating to Liberia, ... 3,636
Number of liberated Africans sent by the U. S. Government,
   Including 756 by the Slave Ship, "Pons," 1,044
    Total number sent by the Society and U. S. Government, . . 7,160

Your committee invite your attention to the bold move of our adversaries, in the presentation of their "Briant" scheme, and "Stanton"[20] report to the last Congress, in order to secure the co-operation of the General Government, which, (through such a compact,) shall become the chief colonizer, in sending from her shores to an uncongenial and unwelcomed clime, her native born citizens; citizens as loyal to the general interests and liberties of the country in '51, as their ancestors in '76; equally as faithful in their allegiance to the government under a just, impartial administration of its constitutional laws now, as were their patriotic sires, whose blood moistened Bunker Hill, Red Bank, Valley Forge, on the lakes Erie and Champlain, and other noted memorable battle grounds, of the revolutionary and the last war.

In this last rally of the colonizationists, the gigantic proposition above mentioned, it is proposed that the government should build large mail steamers, (subject to be converted into war steamers,) to ply between the United States and the west coast of Africa, touching at intermediate maritime ports, to carry out emigrants at $10 per head, just one-fifth of what the society now carries them for. Nothing said, of course, about bringing them back, should they be disappointed in the country, or finding the hot climate disagreeable and injurious to their health and life; for once there, there you must remain.

Let it not be said that none desire to return. We have proof to the contrary of this. The object is to get you out of this country by suasion and possibility, if it can be done; but not to bring you back under any circumstances whatever.

And for the completion of this, all kinds of chicanery and stratagem will be employed to allure the people thitherward; the eternal summer, and the earth's enduring verdancy; the salubrious climate, and the double crops of its fertile soil; its growing marketable productions, and the independence of its inhabitants; the enjoyments and privileges of its citizens, will be pictured forth in glowing colors, to deceive you.

We implore you, fellow countrymen, by reason of the association that cling around you; by virtue of the interests that endear your attachment to your native land; because of the holy ties of consanguinity, identification, and the obligations of brotherhood, and humanity, you owe those in bonds, as bound with them, to let none of these delusive mirrors confound and entrap you.

Yet in the face of all this, we have noticed recently, movements among the people in Ohio, and Maryland, of a disposition, to organize, themselves into societies, (to their shame be it recorded,) for the purpose of emigrating to Liberia, under the auspices of the American Colonization Society. Pray what are the reasons assigned for deserting so cowardly, not only their nativity, but four millions of their countrymen, ground to the earth in the galling chains of slavery?

Is it because their faint hearts despair of ever seeing a brighter morn--of beholding the dawning era when the goddess of universal liberty shall proclaim equal rights to all men; or is it a disinterestedness in the welfare of Liberia?

If it is in sincerity the former, in view of their *modus operandi*, we cannot commend their course and action, because it exhibits such gross imbecility, and the extinguishment of that genius of freedom, which has struggled so long unparalleled in the breasts of colored Americans, from the days of the oppressed colonial settlements down to the present hour. If the latter, we cannot, without giving the falsehood and semblance of indifference to our earnest professions, and appeals for our rightful claims as American born citizens, sanction such pusillanimous proceedings; but on the contrary, knowing as we do, the real motives of the colonizationists, brand their conduct as infamous and contemptible.

Is it not worthy of us as citizens of New-York State; as we would war against slavery and intemperance or any other question, that locally and nationally affected the social, moral, political and religious concern of the people, alike keep pace with the renewed actions and efforts of the Colonizationists, and anew stamp this growing ill design and attack upon our domestic happiness, our hearth side, and our interests universally, with a burning reprobation, and contempt, commensurate with that in spirit and action which characterized the early laborers in this cause of humanity and right, against wrong and injustice? Ought we not the more so when colored men turn "pliant minions," and insufferable dupes, at the bidding of a class of men who professedly are our friends, yet whose very system of philanthropy, were it possible to be put into operation successfully, would, our peace and harmony and felicity destroy; particularly ought we record our dissent, firm and utter condemnation, having not a particle of sympathy with the spirit and letters of a colored man, recently published in the *New-York Tribune*, in favor of "African Colonization," based upon spasmodic ebullition, a seeming panic and phrenzy of despair of the colored people ever securing their legitimate rights of enfranchisement, immunities, &c., in this country; which in every line of said communications, the observer will detect the egotist's proud disappointments, traitorous tendencies and the aspirations of unmerited political distinctions.

The inconsiderate hearer and reader must not wilfully deceive himself with regard to any apprehension we entertain, or at any time previously entertained, of the success of the colonization scheme; for we believe, as truly as we believe in the God of Heaven, the creator of the universe, that ere this object is gained, the clarion-tones of the Arch-angel will note the end of *all* time.

Our professed friends too, as some of them have done, may stigmatize our declarations of attachment to our native land as much as they choose, to their heart's tire content, as sentiments fictitious and imaginary; nevertheless, reason being our guide, and our judgment a responsible dispenser, and accountant of all our expressions and deeds, we will ever claim this land as our home--our own native home; that we are deeply attached to it, and will labor on only to the end for the overthrow of slavery, and for the rights of colored Americans and their posterity.

Fellow citizens, let us resolve, and

"Re-resolve in all the magnanimity of thought," combined with action, that we will never by any consent of our own, voluntarily and shamefully relinquish our birth-right by fleeing the country singly or in legions under the protection of such an institution.

With respect to the repeated assertion that it is morally, religiously, and politically a delusive idea we cherish, in looking forward to the future, for a hope of obtaining respectable and prominent positions in this land, in common with others of capability and merit, by virtue of the development of those holy and noble *triune characters*; but that we must remain as drudges upon society--as hewers of wood and drawers of water evermore, we consider, as all candid, honest men are bound to admit, the most impotent argument advanced for our extermination from these shores, and hyperbolical because unsubstantiated by evidence, practicable and conclusive.

Were it actually necessary--more than that, were it desirable here--we could enter into a statistical review, and instance several localities of colored people, and example very many individuals, (even though surrounded by disadvantageous embarrassments,) who have made and are still making rapid improvement in the highest development of their moral and mental capacities.

Fellow citizens, let no fascinating inducements--no eloquent rhetoric--no eulogistic encomiums of Liberia, draw you into the snares of your dear, philanthropic, and expatriating friends. But by every renewed means in your power, while you will do nothing intentionally and directly detrimental to the development, civilization, and evangelization of Africa, by opposing any man, or a body of men, who choose to emigrate there or elsewhere, under other influences than the Colonization Society of this country, battle against this hydra-head of iniquity--this subtle scheme and corruption, at all times, and under all circumstances, now, henceforth, and forever.

We now call your attention as members of this Convention, as brothers, as citizens, as countrymen, to a fact, though not generally known, is too true. We ask you, can you right heartily sanction the course proposed to be pursued by the Liberians in their solicitude to be recognized by the government of the United States? They are willing, in the language of Mr. Gurley's report, "in view of the peculiarities of the condition of the free colored people, and others of the African race" (meaning the slaves) "in this country, they well know and have no wish by any relations which may be established between their government and the United States, to cause *inconvenience* or *embarrassment*."

They are willing, in substance, to bow slavishly to the worst sense, feelings, and views of the American government, by offering to clothe the white citizens of the United States with full diplomatic power to act as ambassadors, minister plenipotentiary, &c., &c., for Liberia, thus virtually remaining unrepresented, providing the United States confides to the citizens of that republic any business it might desire transacted in Africa with the authorities of said republic.

Was there ever such a treaty formed and ratified in the history of civilized nations? Has the United States government ever placed the nation's seal of honor and fidelity to such a negotiation? But she has refused to recognize the independence of Hayti, and she will refuse to recognize the independence of Liberia,[21] according to the universal mode and manner of recognizing free and independent nations; the power of locomotion; the protection of citizens of each country, at home or abroad; the mutual interchange of ministers, counsellors; security to commerce, &c., &c.

No, fellow-citizens, we do not believe that you would as Americans, endorse such an inglorious negotiation. We believe, if the question were put to the entire colored people of the United States, for their consideration, we would hear, by way of response, one long, loud acclamation, rising up simultaneously from the city, the village, the valley, the mountain side, No! No!! Never!!! Never!!!

C. Edward Seth,
Benjamin F. Cutler,
William Gardener.

Report of the Committee on Elective Franchise

To the People of the State of New-York:

Most sovereign citizens of the State of New-York, your motto is "excelsior," higher and still more high; inspiring as this sentiment must be to every intelligent inhabitant, you will therefore not be surprised at being addressed on the practical application of the principle contained in the above sentiment, though it should come from the most humble of its inhabitants. We, the colored citizens and inhabitants of the State, appeal to you in view of your supreme power, and the intelligence with which you are possessed, in behalf of our rights; a boon that must be ever sacred to men raised under a Democratic and Christian form of government. In the year 1821, unfortunately for us and unwisely for the State, the colored citizens of the State were left trammelled and humbled by the convention of the above date. For forty-five years the colored citizens enjoyed the rights of franchise in common with the white inhabitants of the State. But at this advanced and progressive period of the State's history, the wise and liberal portion of the citizens of the State realized a necessity for an alteration of the State Constitution, wishing thereby to have for an elective basis, the virtue and intelligence of the people in preference to *property* bases or qualification which was then a constitutional requirement. A convention was called for this important object, each county sending delegates to represent its interest, and those delegates receiving their election in part at the hands of the colored electors, met in convention to extend the area of freedom. But alas, fellow citizens, what was the result; the poor who stood in the greatest need of a stimulus to emerge from the condition in which they had suffered so grievously, were still left to struggle with the superincumbent embarrassment, while their white fellow citizens open up a political highway through which all might pass without the least obstruction, save that of a small minority designated by the external complexion which God gave them. This providence of God was used to condemn and fix upon them, to the extent of the circumstance, a disgrace, thus heaping wrong upon wrong, forgetting the many years that they stood side by side as the children of paternal ancestry; at Bunker Hill, Concord and Lexington, the colored man's blood was shed, Lake Erie and Lake Champlain, poured out, for the establishment of those sentiments that are contained in the herald of the country's freedom: "We hold these truths to be self-evident that all men are created free and equal, and are endowed by their Creator with certain inalienable rights, among which are life, liberty and the pursuit of happiness." The ark of the covenant was grounded and settled on these indestructible principles, and moreover, in after years, guaranteed by the adoption of the Constitution of the United States, art. 4, sec. 2, clause 1, wherein it is declared "that the citizens of each of the states shall be entitled to all privileges and immunities as citizens of the several states." The colored man's constitutional rights as a citizen have never been questioned until recently, and that by those whose cupidity prompted them to make an effort to injure him in his strongest position, in the *unquestionable* and *avowed* protection that the United States Constitution throws around and extends to the whole free representative mass. The colored man's rights are not peculiar or extrenuous, but are in common with those of the whole people, and *incontestable* evidence to this effect may be found in the circumstances of the admission of Missouri into the Union in 1821.

The people of Missouri made overtures to Congress for admission into the Union as a sovereign, independent State, and at the same time submitted the Constitution they had framed. But their admission into the Union was resisted by a majority in Congress, on the ground that a clause of the 26th sec. of the 3d art. of the proposed Constitution, made it a duty of the General Assembly to pass laws such as might be necessary to prevent free Negroes or mulattoes from coming to or settling in the State under any pretext whatever; which it was maintained was a violation of the Constitution of the United States, art. 4, sec. 2, clause 1, wherein it is declared "that the citizens of each State shall be entitled to all the privileges and immunities of the citizens in the several States." Hereupon a debate arose of great interest, which agitated the Union to the remotest extremity. The issue of this was as follows: the refusal to admit Missouri into the Union was not withdrawn until the General Assemble of that State, in conformity to a fundamental condition imposed by Congress had, by an act passed for that purpose, solemnly enacted and declared that this State, Missouri has assented and does assent that the 4th clause of 26th section of the 3d article of their Constitution should not be construed to authorize the passage of any law, and that no law shall be passed in conformity thereto, by which any citizen of either of the States shall be excluded from the enjoyment of any of the privileges and immunities to which such citizens are entitled to under the Constitution of the United States. (Ref. to *Niles' Congressional Reg.*, August 18th, vol. 22, pp. 338 and 339.) And Missouri, after having manifested her assent to the fundamental condition imposed by Congress, and having officially communicated the fact to James Monroe, President of the United States, he, in pursuance and under the authority of the resolution of Congress, prescribing the condition aforesaid by his proclamation, dated August 10th, 1821, declared the admission of

Missouri into the Union to be complete. Here then is incontestable proof of
a common proprietary interest in the government and liberties of the country,
colored with the white citizens. We need not be told after the above statement and proof, that the Convention of 1821, of the State of New-York, which
altered or introduced into the Constitution the word "white," making the
clause read "every white male citizen of the age of twenty-one years" should,
on certain conditions specified, be entitled to vote, was an infraction of
the rights of colored citizens. The elective basis of the State was not
property, that being supplanted by the alteration, therefore all the male
inhabitants of the State, by virtue of their locality and the alteration of
the State Constitution, became citizens presumptive, and when in conformity
with the amended conditions, were citizens in fact, no state being invested
with the power to advance the interest and exalt one portion of the people
over that of the other. Congress not being empowered to pass a bill of
attainder, or ex post facto law, it is not reasonable to suppose or logical
to admit that any one State could assume such authority. The resolution
produced a change in all the free inhabitants of the United States; all the
citizens of the several states became citizens of the United States. They
were *subjects* of Great Britain; they became citizens of the United States
from the very nature of our government. In the case of McIlvain v. Cox's
lessees, Cranch 293, it is asserted without contradiction, "It was therefore,
a political revolution, involving in the change all the inhabitants of
America, rendering them all members of the new society, standing on one
common basis as citizens of the new states." *Chan. Kent.*[22]

The elective or representative basis of the general government is then
the free people; each State an independent sovereignty as long as its laws
and regulations do not conflict with the general government. Therefore in
view of the foundation principles of the State and United States governments,
we have sufficient reason to declare our united and uncompromising hostility
to a mal-administration of the laws, whether it is of the State in which we
are residents or of the several States of the Union, for every innovation upon
the rights of the American people is fraught with destruction to the harmony
which binds the several States. The objects of the confederation were to have
a more perfect union, whereby and wherein the rights of the people might be
more securely protected, and those rights are promised in the language of the
Declaration of Independence, "life, liberty and pursuit of happiness." These
are the ground principles of the country's stability; undermine or remove
these and the light of her glory is quenched and all are merged into the
condition of dupes and slaves. Caste or titles were no moving motives to the
uprising and attainment of American liberties, but are at variance with the
genius of the government.

The elective franchise is the birthright and blessing of every American,
of which he can never be legally deprived, unless he involves his right to
the enjoyment of it by the commission of some penal offence against the laws
of his country; and nearly 600 years have elapsed since the barons of England
compelled their king to subscribe to the magna charta, which embraced and
guaranteed to every Englishman an unqualified protection in the possession of
his life, liberty and property; therefore, inasmuch as the advantages and
true principles of the common laws of England were introduced into the United
States when in their Colonial condition; received and adopted as standard
principles and laws, they became the bularks of the American people's
liberties. Property in man being denied and rejected by Lord Mansfield,
1772, from the king's bench,[23] the highest authority in England, a monarchial
government and the one from whence this emerged, set forth boldly and sustained two great principles, a trial by jury, and the right of every man to
himself. The establishment of these principles by the mother country, and
their re-adoption by this, made them the organic law of the nation, the
natural right of every American. It was for these principles and more, that
three million people started up as voluntary offerings to be sacrificed on the
altar of Liberty, to be ever venerated and loved for their successful triumph
in the maintenance of right over wrong; the whole land is consecrated to
freedom with a deep libation of freemen's blood; each and all were patriots
and Americans in that day, who opposed their breasts to the foe, and secured
successfully the triumph of these principles.

And now, has it come to this, that the descendants of those whose hearts beat true to their country, even unto death, that they, their offspring, are compelled to prove a claim to a common interest and right in those ever glorious achievements; that the man with a swarthy brow or black complexion is compelled to protest against the usurpations of his fairer brother, of the most flagrant and gross wrongs; and the mother cannot successfully vindicate her maternal and unalterable interest in the infant on her breast against the unchristian and inhuman laws of this degenerate land and people. It is enough to startle every christian American with a trembling apprehension that God has given the nation over to their abominations and pride, and that the hand writing of their overthrow is apparent. Mene mene tekel upharsin.[24]

Hiram Johnson,
Richard Wright,
William Rich,
Committee.

Report of Committee on Fugitive Slave Bill

The undersigned appointed a committee to report on the FUGITIVE SLAVE LAW, beg leave to submit the following preamble and resolutions:

That we the colored citizens of the State of New-York believing that the dearest rights and liberties, belonging to us as freemen, are fearfully endangered by the *Fugitive Slave Law* recently enacted by our National Legislature, and having a tender sympathy with our brethren who escape from slavery--being assembled in convention to consider said law--do deliberately and seriously *resolve*,

1. That this law, in requiring the freemen of the north to deliver up fugitives from slavery to the iniquitous and oppressive bondage from which they have heroically escaped, is in direct and impious opposition to the command of the Supreme Law Giver--a command, like the moral law, obligatory in all ages from its very nature--*"Thou shalt not deliver unto his master the servant which is escaped from his master unto thee; he shall dwell with thee, even among you in that place which he shall choose, in one of thy gates where it liketh him best; thou shalt not oppress him."* That this law, in forbidding men under the penalty of heavy fines and imprisonment to harbor or assist fugitives from slavery, is in direct and impious opposition to those laws of God which command deeds of humanity and mercy;--that in both these respects this law is in direct and impious opposition to the essence and sum of "the law and the prophets," declared by the divine Redeemer, *"all things whatsoever you would that men should do to you, do ye even so to them,"*--and therefore that no man can, in these respects, obey this law, without palpable and flagrant *disobedience* to God.

2. That this law is plainly and essentially opposed to that self-evident truth in the Declaration of Independence by these United States, "that *all men* are endowed by their Creator with certain inalienable rights; that among these are life, *liberty*, and the pursuit of happiness;" and that no man can approve or obey this law without contradicting this united declaration of the people of this Republic.

3. That this law directly and palpably violates those fundamental provisions of the Constitution of the United States which secure to "every person" the right of trial by jury, and in cases occurring under the laws of the United States, the right of trial by a Court of the United States, (which a Commissioner under this law is not) and the privilege of the *habeas corpus* act, and of counsel when accused, and therefore all citizens of the United States are bound by their obligations under the Constitution, not to obey, but to disobey, this law.

4. That the duties of men towards fugitives from oppression are plain--the duties dictated by humanity and mercy--the bestowment of comfort, sympathy, and needful aid; and we call, therefore, on the inhabitants of the state of New-York to imitate the noble example of the people of New Haven, Ct., who, in the days of the hunted and fugitive judges, who condemned to death an oppressive King of England, obeyed the exhortation of their pious pastor, the reverend John Davenport,[25] founded on the Divine command, *Hide the outcast; betray not him that wandereth; be thou a covert to them from the face of the spoiler."*

5. That we feel ourselves to be weak, needing help; and we earnestly ask of our white friends to give us their aid in our distress, and to show not only in private, but in public, that they have feeling hearts and willing hands.

6. That we believe that public opinion is the bulwark of all law, and that this ODIOUS AND CRUEL LAW will be entirely inoperative, if the moral sense of this community speaks; and therefore we ask of this community; with the voice of our oppressed people, that they will give such an expression of their sentiments respecting this law as will protect this place from the cries and tears of his victims.

7. That we are fully determined, here in our places, to wait the issue; to rest our cause upon God, upon the friends of religion and humanity, and upon our own manhood; to bear ourselves so as to prove that we are worthy, not only of liberty, but of the full privileges of citizens, some of which are now denied us; and to surrender life rather than to be taken into slavery.

8. *Resolved,* That the fugitive slave law is the law of tyrants.
9. *Resolved,* That disobedience to tyrants is obedience to God.
10. *Resolved,* That we will obey God.

Amos Gerry Beman,
John Nelson Still,
J. P. Johnson,
Committee.

Report of the Committee on Education

Your committee cannot hope to embrace in this report, suggestions that will meet every case connected with the subject of Education; we can only deal with general principles.

First, in order that the general welfare of the *colored* people be improved--that the influence of vice and immorality be overcome--that they may become elevated from that condition of *self*-degradation in which ignorance and vice has engulphed a large proportion of the race, it's all important that *they* become educated; without education we cannot hope to be emancipated from the bondage of involuntary degradation, which we are placed under by the cruel and malicious system of prejudice and caste. By education must be effected the full developments of those hidden and important truths, which when brought to bear upon the hearts and consciences of mankind, shine forth in the beauty of their nature and illumine their minds, to the end that all members of the great human family shall have accorded to them their full and complete rank as such, regardless of any outward circumstances as denote birth or country.

Education here must be considered intellectually, morally and physically. There can be no harmonious development of character where attention is given only to the growth and strengthening of particular divisions of capacity, without reference to the entire man. A system of discipline which tends simply to improve the physical nature, or even the physical and moral without regard to the intellectual, produces at best but gigantic strength, the lowest type of man's excellency. And a superstitious religion is always debasing and even dangerous in proportion as it is removed from the light of reason and mental culture. This is not more philosophically true, than proven in the general history of the human race.

Education then, properly understood, has to do with all the laws and principles that regulate our progress in this life, and only answers its legitimate duty when it seeks to elevate, to liberalize, to christianize. To this end, it gives to its subjects a clearer vision and a greater power to bring out hidden virtues and to combat those errors and prejudices that only live as they are able to pervert men's minds and to make them low and groveling.

These truths are clearly seen in the facts that surround us on every side, in the great struggle now being waged between the oppressor and the oppressed. In the community about us, we are realizing daily the bitter evidence, that an education given in a one-sided direction, and continued for a series of years from father to child, grows up into a system all powerful in the accomplishment of its ends, and subduing to its aims well nigh every mind that receives it. Dictated by that self-love that delights to claim superiority and to exercise rule, we see the social and school education of the land fattening upon the hideous error that God has created a noble and an ignoble race, and that by virtue of this he has given a right to the strong to tyrannize over the weak--to load his body with chains and shut him up from the revelations of light and love guaranteed to him in the very ground work of his being.

The history of slavery and caste in this country is so palpable that it needs no recapitulation here. It is a history written in blood and black with enormities and crimes. That it owes its origin and continuance to misdirected views is made evident in the fact that where a different system of culture has been adopted, the so-called antagonistic races have grown up in terms of amity, and have moved on an equal platform, basking under a common civilization, and raching out to a common destiny.

The fact made glaring by the education adopted, that there is a vast disparity in the standard of culture of the two classes involved in the argument, has been made a justifying cause for tyrannizing over those whose only crime has been, that where no food has been given them, they have not grown fat, and where light has been shut from them, their sight has become dim and obscure.

Time, therefore, having sanctioned the erroneous doctrine that because there is a difference in development, the truth is evident that there is a difference in capacity. It rests with us to counteract the perverted teachings of the land, by filling up as soon as possible the chasm of mind that has separated us, and to bring to our mental storehouse those rich freights of thought and intelligence that really make eminent any people, and the want of which makes us yield too readily to such influences as cause us to remain the vassals and slaves of a more powerful clan, and pliant subjects to a system of education highly improper of itself, and which serves to render us less fitted to appreciate the advantages of a true system, and makes us willing instruments to embarrass and postpone the prospects of securing such as is proper.

The system of education most conducive to our advancement seems to be that which will most readily annihilate in us that weakening acknowledgement, that our means of elevation are to be ever distinct and separate from those educational appliances that end so rapidly to push onward the great American people. In other words, we must partake, as far as is practicable, in the advantages of those literary and religious institutions, where *common* rights are respected, and where manhood is acknowledged as an equal inheritance! Schools established by caste, while they may not be contemned where better reliances are not to be had, are depressing in their influences, and unfitted to prepare our children to assume an equality of position in the after severe lessons of life. We never may expect to claim, or our opponents to grant, full freedom in carrying out the great aims of life, where we are educated in acknowledgment of the fitness of that spirit of colonization that shuts us out from enjoying the advantages of the better schools of the land. This being our conviction, let us give good attention to securing for our children a liberal education, remaining steadfast in the determination to unceasing efforts to uproot the evil of proscription on account of color, wherever it is to be met with, either in school houses or in churches, ever maintaining perseverance in the right direction, and a dignity of demeanor that will characterize us as a people knowing our rights, willing to assert them, and to make sacrifices of present convenience to the end of securing their permanent possession.

In addition your committee recommend the passage of the following resolutions:

Resolved, That the character of Central College, in its principles, its ability and appointments, is such as we can cheerfully recommend to the support of the colored people.

Resolved, That the renewed evidence of firm adherence to the principle of the universal brotherhood of man, as given by the noble position maintained by that institution of learning known as "Central College," at McGrawville, Cortland county, which institution spurned the bribe held out to it by way of pecuniary aid from the State, on condition of the departure from its principles, entitles it to the full confidence and zealous support of every friend of impartial freedom.

         Wm. H. Topp,
         S. Myers,
         E. N. Hall,
           Committee.

Petition

To the Legislature of the State of New-York:

  Honorable Sirs,--A State Convention of the colored citizens of this State assembled at the Capitol in the city of Albany, on the 22d, 23d and 24th of July, 1851; respectfully represent to your honorable body, that the Constitution of this State, in article 2d, sec. 1, burdens us with political inequalities, and deprives us of rights which the declared principles of our government hold to be natural and inalienable.

  These invidious distinctions are unjust, and oppressive on the few that edure them,--ungenerous and anti-democratic in the masses that enforce them; as exhibited by the popular vote on the suffrage question in 1846.[26]

  We would further represent, that the colored citizens have ever been loyal to the government, and in the perilous times of 1812, when to shoulder a musket was to bare the breast to the weapon of an enemy; thought placed by partial legislation beyond the compulsory power of the State, did with becoming promptness volunteer their services to defend our common country from the invasions and depredations of a ruthless and vindictive foe, and while by a mistaken stroke of political economy, the children of these volunteers are spurned and degraded, the successors of the very men who met them in mortal combat by sea and by land, you receive with open arms.

  We submit gentlemen, that our proscription is unjust, and we appeal to your generosity as Americans--and your honor as men to do us justice in this matter.

  By the reform convention of 1821, virtue and intelligence was made the elective basis to all white men, while the colored citizens in addition to being trammeled with the requirements of the old system, are doubly injured by the proscriptive character of the new, which impliedly places us beneath this elective basis,--encourages the baser feelings of the more favored class to be arrayed in opposition to us, and closes against us most of the avenues to emolument and honor.

  The Constitution, in Article 13, sec. 1, provides for its amendment or alteration by the Legislature; we therefore respectfully, but earnestly pray your honorable body to repeal these anti-republican and proscriptive clauses of our State Constitution, and all others subjecting us to unequal restrictions, and as in duty we will ever pray.

         W. P. McIntyre,
         J. N. Still,   *Committee.*
         H. Hicks,

Copy in the Moorland-Spingarn Research Center, Howard University Library, Washington, D. C.

REFERENCE NOTES

  1. John Quincy Adams (1767-1848), sixth president of the United States, secretary of state during the administration of James Monroe, and later a member of the House of Representatives (1831-48), where he vigorously supported the right of petition, especially with respect to the passage in Congress of the famous "gag-rule" in 1836, which barred the reception of abolition petitions. His eloquent and persistent opposition secured the repeal of that rule in 1844.

  2. The Fugitve Slave Law of 1850, approved by Congress on September 18, 1850, provided for the appointment of special federal commissioners to facilitate the reclaiming of runaways. These commissioners could appoint marshals to arrest fugitives, and these marshals could, in turn, "call to their aid" any bystanders at the scene of an arrest, who were "commanded" to

"assist in the prompt and efficient execution of the law. . . ." Slave owners could "pursue and reclaim" fugitives with or without a warrant; the commissioner would judge the case without a jury. In addition, "in no trial or hearing under this act shall the testimony of such alleged fugitive be admitted in evidence." Satisfactory written or oral "proof" being offered that the person arrested was the sought-for fugitive, the commissioner would issue a certificate. The slave owner was authorized to use all "reasonable force" necessary to take a fugitive back to the place of his or her escape. If a slave owner feared "that such fugitive will be rescued by force," it was the duty of the officer involved to employ any number of persons necessary "to overcome such force" and deliver the fugitive back to the fugitive's owner. Any marshal who failed to execute the fugitive law properly was to be fined $100; the marshal was also liable for the full value of any fugitive escaping from his custody. Finally, an officer was "entitled to a fee of ten dollars" if he delivered a fugitive to a slave owner, but only five dollars if he freed the black claimed. For a greater discussion of this whole issue see George Walker's, "Black Resistance to the Fugitive Slave Law of 1850, 1850-1856" (unpub. M.A. thesis), Columbia University, 1971. passim.

3. Stephen Myers was perhaps the leading black abolitionist in upstate New York. While he was chairman of the Albany Vigilance Committee, his home frequently served as an overnight sanctuary for black runaways on the last leg of their northward journey. Myers was also active in the suffrage struggle among his brethren in the Empire State, having been appointed the official lobbyist for the New York State Suffrage Association, an organization formed in 1855 to facilitate the acquisition of the vote by the state's largely disfranchised black population. A vigorous foe of colonization, he opposed Governor Washington Hunt's scheme, in the early 1850's, for a legislative appropriation of state funds looking toward the voluntary removal of New York's black population.

An early supporter among his people for the Republican Party, he came out strongly for the election in 1858 of Edwin D. Morgan in his quest for the governership of New York, over the candidacy of Gerrit Smith, a long-time friend and benefactor of blacks who was running on an independent third-party ticket. Myers feared that Smith, who had no chance of winning, would merely split the Negro vote and catapult a pro-slavery Democrat into power. As editor of the Albany *Voice of Freedom*, he played no small role in the subsequent victory of Morgan.

4. Amos Gerry Beman (1803-1874), son of Jehiel C. Beman, was born in Connecticut and tutored at Wesleyan University until students forced him to leave the campus. Beman taught school and became a minister and Underground Railroad stationmaster in New Haven. Beman contributed several letters to Douglass' paper as well as to the abolitionist press. He was a specialist on the history of Africa.

5. Marquis de Lafayette (1757-1834), French general and statesman, came to America during the Revolution to join General Washington's army. He distinguished himself for his tenacious defense of the American cause, having been wounded at Brandywine and sharing the hardships at Valley Forge.

6. The *Impartial Citizen* appeared sporadically from 1848 to 1850.

7. *Frederick Douglass' Paper*, the successor to the *North Star*, appeared in 1851 and continued publication to the eve of the Civil War, when a new publication, *Douglass' Monthly*, appeared.

8. Founded in 1841, by Horace Greeley, the *Tribune* later became an influential antislavery newspaper.

9. Junius C. Morel, also spelled Morell, was a leader in the early Negro Convention movement. He served as secretary of the National Convention of the Free People of Colour, which met at Philadelphia in September 1830. He also served on the committee which drew up its *Address*. Morel was an able speaker and an effective writer. For an example of his writing see the *Emancipator*, Nov. 16, 1837.

10. The *New York Express* was a conservative commercial daily, well known for its pro-slavery sympathies.

11. Established at McGrawville, New York, around the early 1840's by Gerrit Smith and others, Central College, a predominantly white institution,

did welcome blacks as students. It broke a long-standing tradition, however, when it invited the distinguished Negro educator Charles L. Reason (identified above) to the professorship of belles lettres in 1852, a post which was subsequently assumed by his successor, William G. Allen, another noted black man.

12. The Reverend Alexander Proudfit, D.D., was a corresponding secretary and field agent of the New York City Colonization Society during the 1830's.

13. The reference is to Thomas Buchanan. In 1837 he was listed by the New York City Colonization Society as a "patron" who had "contributed a thousand dollars or more." In addition, he was cited by this auxiliary "for distinguished services rendered to the Society in this country and Africa." See *Fifth Annual Report of the Colonization Society of the City of New York, With the Constitution of the Society* (New York, 1837), p. 5.

14. Jehudi Ashmun (1794-1828) was an early exponent of African colonization, most notable for his heroic and vital connection with the colonizing of Liberia. During the early 1820's, while serving as the official representative of the United States government to the colony, he helped save if from collapse after numerous deaths from fevers and desertions by agents sent out by the American Colonization Society. In 1826 he published his *History of the Colony in Liberia from December, 1821 to 1823*. Failing health prompted him to sail to the West Indies for relief, where he died on August 25, 1828.

15. The reference is to Henry Clay (1777-1852), congressman, senator, and secretary of state, was also fourth president of the American Colonization Society.

16. The reference is to Elliott Cresson (1796-1854), a noted Philadelphia Quaker merchant and philanthropist. Early taking an interest in the oppressed of all races, he thought at one time of becoming a missionary among the Seminole Indians. Most of his efforts, however, revolved around the cause of colonization. He was one of the organizers of the Young Men's Colonization Society of Pennsylvania and a life member of the American Colonization Society. In addition to his liberal gifts to the cause, he lectured widely in New England and made several visits to the South and to England in support of his program.

17. Ralph Randolph Gurley (1797-1872) was a philanthropist and lifelong supporter of the American Colonization Society. In 1822, he became an agent of the Society and was successively agent, secretary, vice-president, and life director. For twenty-five years he edited the *African Repository*, official organ of the Society, and lectured widely in the North, West and South in support of this movement.

18. The Reverend John B. Pinney was an officer of the New York auxiliary of the American Colonization Society.

19. Established in 1822, under the auspices of the American Colonization Society, Liberia, with the exception of Canada, served as the chief outlet for black emigration to the African continent before the Civil War.

20. Frederick Perry Stanton (1814-1894) was a lawyer, congressman, and acting governor of Kansas Territory during 1857. Elected to Congress in 1845, he served until 1855, representing a district in Memphis, Tennessee. He opposed the admission of California as a free state and upheld the Kansas-Nebraska Bill.

21. Neither Haiti nor Liberia were recognized by the United States until 1862, during the Lincoln Administration.

22. James Kent (1763-1847) was an American jurist and legal commentator whose reputation for wide learning established him as the first professor of law at Columbia College, serving from 1794 to 1798. In 1798, he received an appointment as judge of the New York State Supreme Court. He was made chief judge in 1804 and from 1814 until his retirement in 1823 presided over the state court of chancery. Kent's written opinions as chancellor did much in reviving Equity, which had largely lapsed in the United States after the American Revolution. His *Commentaries on the American Law* (4 vols., 1826-1830), treating such subjects as international law, American constitutional law, the sources of state law, and the law of personal rights and of property, was considered his most brilliant achievement. The work was highly praised within the legal profession and went through six editions during Kent's own lifetime.

23. In 1772, in the case of the Negro slave James Sommerset, the British court, with Judge Manfield reading the decision, abolished domestic slavery in England, using the argument that liberty was "commensurate with, and inseparable from British soil."

24. In the Bible (Daniel v, 1-31), it is recorded, "In the same hour came forth fingers of a man's hand, and wrote over against the candlestick upon the plaister of the wall of the king's palace." *Mene mene teke upharsin* were the prophetic words in question, observed by Belshazzar, King of Babylon, while entertaining guests during a famous feast. Daniel, an exiled Jew, interpreted the meaning of the mysterious words. The fateful "handwriting on the wall," as revealed by the prophet, told Belshazzar that the days of his kingdom were numbered, that he had been found wanting, and that his kingdom would be divided and assigned to others.

25. John Davenport (1597-1669), clergyman and author, was born in England and later emigrated to America, where he helped found New Haven, Connecticut, in 1638. Davenport is remembered most particularly for his role in 1661 in protecting two regicide judges, Edward Whalley (d. 1674 or 1675) and William Goffe (d. 1679?), both of whom had fled to the colony after the restoration of the Stuarts, who sought vengeance because of the role these two men played while members of the High Court of Justice, empaneled to try the case of Charles I (1600-1649). Both men had signed the King's death warrant.

Davenport had generously paved the way for them at New Haven by a series of sermons and there they found refuge temporarily while the royal officers searched for them. It is said that for a month they remained hid in Davenport's own house. When inquired of, he, however, disclaimed all knowledge of their whereabouts.

26. The reference is to the New York State Constitutional Convention of 1846. The convention itself, after extended debate, refused to approve an equal suffrage clause in the new constitution, but agreed to submit the issue, by way of referendum, to the people. The new constitution was approved by the people on November 3, 1846, by a vote of 221,528 to 96,436, and the proposed amendment granting equal suffrage to black persons was rejected by nearly the same vote--85,306 to 223,834. See George Walker, "The Afro-American in New York City, 1827-1860." See also Charles Z. Lincoln, *The Constitutional History of New York from the Beginnings of the Colonial Period to 1905, Showing the Origin, Development and Judicial Construction of the Constitution* (5 vols.; Rochester, N.Y., 1906), II, 212-213.

PROCEEDINGS OF THE NEW YORK STATE COUNCIL OF COLORED PEOPLE,
JANUARY 2, 1854

In obedience to the order, creating State Councils, the New York State Council met in the city of Albany on the 2d day of Jan. 1854, and assembled at the City Hall, in the County Court Room, at 3 o'clock P.M., when the Rev. J. W. Loguen of Syracuse was appointed Chairman *pro tem.*, and William H. Topp of Albany, Secretary.

The Constitution of the National Council being called for, was read.

Suggestions were made in reference to the word *Free States* in the preamble, to amend word *Free States* in the preamble, to amend so as to include all the States and Canada.

The question as to how many members in the National Council this State is entitled to, whether we are to take the U. S. census as our guide, being a fraction less than 500,000, or claim ten members as being nearer the present number of inhabitants, was discussed.

On motion, Messrs. Topp, Rich and Duffins were appointed a Committee to prepare Rules for the government of the Council.

On motion, adjourned until 9 o'clock tomorrow morning, (Tuesday.)

Tuesday Morning, Nine O'clock

Council met. J. W. Loguen in the Chair. Minutes of the last meeting read and adopted.

On the roll being called, the following named gentlemen answered to their names:

Wm. H. Topp,	Albany
J. W. Loguen,	Syracuse
J. C. Morrel,	Brooklyn
J. W. Duffins,	Geneva
W. J. Wilson,	Brooklyn
Wm. Rice,	Troy
D. K. McDonough,	New York
J. W. B. Smith,	" "

On motion, that a Committee of three be appointed to nominate officers for the permanent organization of the State Council. Messr. Rich, Smith and Duffins were so appointed. The Committee reported

Wm. H. Topp for *President.*
J. W. Loguen " *Vice President.*
J. C. Morrel " *Rec. Secretary.*
J. W. Duffins " *Cor. Secretary.*
Wm. Rich " *Treasurer.*

On motion, the gentlemen so nominated and reported, were declared to be duly elected officers of the Council.

The President elect, Mr. Wm. H. Topp, on taking the chair, in haste and appropriate manner returned his thanks to the members of the Council for the honor conferred on him by their unanimous decision in selecting him to preside over the New York State Council. The remarks of the President were listened to with marked attention by the members and audience present.

On the Council coming to order, considerable discussion arose on a motion by Mr. McDonough to appoint a Committee to nominate the additional members to the National Council. Mr. Morrel opposed the motion, because he hoped for, and desired a fuller attendance of the members of the Council, particularly as he considered the motion to be one of more than common importance.

On motion, Mr. McDonough's motion was laid for the present.

The Committee on Rules and Regulations, appointed yesterday, reported through their Chairman. The report being received was read and adopted as the Rules of the State Council.

Rules

1. Each session of the Council shall be opened by addressing the Throne of Grace.
2. At the time appointed for the assembling of the Council, the President shall take the Chair and call the Council to order.
3. The minutes of the preceding session shall be read at the opening of each session, at which time all errors, if any, shall be corrected.
4. The President shall decide all questions of order, subject, however, in all cases to an appeal to the Council.
5. All motions shall be made by addressing the President, the member rising from his seat.
6. Every motion, except those of reference, shall be submitted in writing.
7. The President shall appoint all Committees, unless otherwise ordered by the Council.
8. The previous question shall always be in order, and until decided, shall preclude all amendment and debate of the main question, and shall be put in this form--"Shall the main question be now put."
9. No member shall be interrupted while speaking, except he be out of order, when he shall be called to order by or through the presiding officer.
10. A motion to adjourn shall always be in order, and shall be put and taken without debate.
11. No member shall speak more than twice on the same question, nor more than fifteen minutes at each time, unless by consent of the Council.
12. All resolutions shall be presented to the Council through the Business Committee, except those of reference; but all resolutions rejected by the Committee may be presented to the Council if the make wishes to do so.
13. Sessions of the Council shall commence at half-past nine o'clock A.M., and shall close at one P.M., to commence at half-past two o'clock P.M., and close at 6 P.M., evening session to commence at half-past seven o'clock, and close at the discretion of the Council.

Signed,
Wm. H. Topp,
Wm. Rich,   } *Committee.*
J. W. Duffins,

On motion of Mr. J. B. Smith, the President appointed Messrs. Duffin, Smith, and Wm. J. Wilson, a Committee to prepare business for the action of the Council. Adjourned.

Tuesday Afternoon, Jan. 3d.

Council met at half-past 3 o'clock. Prayer by the Rev. J. W. Loguen. The President in the Chair. Minutes of the morning session read and approved. Communication by letters from Messrs. George Weir of Buffalo, and Uriah Boston of Poughkeepsie, members elect, were read and ordered on file. In the absence of the Business Committee, Rev. Mr. Lougen, made an interesting speech on "Woman's Rights," which was earnestly objected to, as being irrelevant to the business of the Council, by Mr. Rich of Troy. Mr. Morrel, the Secretary, warmly approved of the speech of Mr. Loguen, and desired, if possible, to go even farther than Mr. Loguen had advanced, as he felt and believed that Human Rights were not to be defined either by sex or complexion.

The Business Committee reported through Mr. J. B. Smith, which on being read, was accepted for consideration:

Report

Whereas, The Census taken in 1850, states the Colored Population of the State of New York, to be a fraction less than 50,000, but we have unmistakable reasons for believing that statement erroneous, and that we exceed the number stated; therefore,

1st. Be it Resolved, That the State of New York is entitled to at least ten additional members in the National Council. Adopted.

2d. Resolved, That a Committee of three members be appointed on Statistics, whose duty shall be to obtain as [soon] as practicable, a correct Census of the Colored Population of the State of New York, with the number of Farmers, quantity of Land owned, the number of Mechanics, and amount of Capital invested, and that said Committee report at our next meeting. Adopted.

Messrs. Duffins, of Geneva, Boston, of Poughkeepsie, and H. M. Wilson, of New York City, were appointed the Committee.

3d. Resolved, That a Committee of three members be appointed to divide the State into 20 Districts, and that each District be allowed two members, and that the Districts be numbered 1, 2, 3, 4, 5, 6, 7, 8, 9, 10, 11, 12, 13, 14, 15, 16, 17, 18, 19, 20, State Council Districts. Laid on the table.

4th. That a Standing Committee be appointed to be located at or near Albany, whose duties shall be to Petition the Legislature for the right of suffrage to attend to the publication of all matters relating to the people of color, to receive the nominations of the several Council Districts, and when received, to publish the same as the regular State Council Ticket. Rejected.

5th. Resolved, That an Agent, or Agents be appointed, to travel the State, and Lecture to the people, explaining the objects of the New York State Council. Adopted.

6th. Resolved, That it shall be the duty of the President of the State Council to make a Report to the Council at each General Meeting of the same, making such suggestions for further improvement, and action, as he may consider best, and proper. Adopted.

7th. Resolved, That a Committee of three on Ways and Means, and a Committee of three on School Privileges, be appointed by the President of the State Council, both of said Committee to report at our next meeting in August.

The President appointed on Ways and Means, Messrs. William J. Wilson, Brooklyn, J. W. Loguen, Syracuse, Charles B. Ray, New York. On School Privileges, Messrs. J. C. Morrel, Brooklyn, J. W. C. Pennington,[1] New York, George Weir, Buffalo.

8th. Resolved, That the State Council have full power to fill all vacancies which may occur in the New York delegation, either in the State or National Council. Adopted.

9th. Resolved, That the establishment of an "Industrial School," on the manual labor principle, meets our hearty concurrence, and shall have our earnest, and united support, and that our desire is that it be located in the State of New York. Adopted.

Signed,
J. W. Duffins,
J. W. B. Smith,   *Committee.*
Wm. J. Wilson,

The motion of D. K. McDonough to appoint a Committee of five to nominate the additional members of the National Council, was taken up for consideration.

A motion to adjourn to half-past 7 o'clock, was lost.

A motion to adjourn until Wednesday morning, at 9 o'clock, was now made and lost.

The Council then proceeded with the consideration of the motion of Mr. McDonough, which after a protracted debate, was adopted.

Mr. Morrel begged to be left off from the Committee, and the President appointed Messrs. McDonough, Duffins, Loguen, Wilson and J. W. B. Smith, the Committee.

Resolution No. 3, from the Business Committee on "Districting the State," was taken up and being under consideration, when on motion, the same was laid over until nine o'clock Wednesday morning.

Mr. Morrel presented the following resolution, which he prefaced with a few remarks:

Resolved, That the New York State Council have learned with deep regret, of the sudden and melancholy death of John B. Vashon, Esq., of Pittsburgh, Penn., long known and endeared to his brethren, as the earnest, faithful, consistent and well-tried friend of the Slave, as well as the able, unceasing and fearless advocate of the rights of humanity, and that this Council truly sympathizes with his bereaved family in their affliction; that a copy of this Resolution signed by the President and Secretary, be transmitted to the family of our deceased brother, and to the *"Frederick Douglass' Paper,"* for publication.

Which Resolution was unanimously adopted, each member rising from his seat. When on motion Council adjourned.

Wednesday Morning, Jan. 4th.

Council met. Prayer by the Rev. J. W. Loguen. President in the Chair. Proceeded to business by reading the minutes of the last meeting, which on motion were adopted.

Resolution No. 3, on "Districting the State," and increasing the number of the New York State Council to forty members, being under consideration elicited, quite an animated discussion. The President, Mr. Wm. H. Topp, considered the resolution to be in opposition to the spirit and intention of the Constitution of the National Council, and therefore earnestly opposed its passage; he admitted the necessity of increasing the Council, but inclined to the opinion that we ought to address the National Council in the matter. On the other side, the advocates for the increase contended that we have the sole and entire control of all matters relating to our State affairs; that the National Council have no authority to interfere in any of our local arrangements, nor can the National Council operate in the State of New York, but by and through the State Council.

The resolution being put was voted down. A motion to reconsider was declared out of order by the President. An appeal from the decision of the President was demanded, but finally it was withdrawn.

The Rules were suspended, so far as to limit each speaker to five minutes, and not to speak more than twice on the same subject.

Mr. McDonough presented the following:

Resolved, That all local Treasuries holding Funds, the result of our State Elections, are hereby requested to forward the same to the Council's Treasurer, Mr. William Rich, Troy, New York, which was adopted, and the Council adjourned to dinner.

Wednesday Afternoon, Jan. 4th.

Council met. Prayer by the Rev. J. W. Loguen. Proceeded to business by reading the minutes of the moring session, which were approved and all adopted.

A motion to reconsider the resolution increasing the State Council being in order, was made and voted; and on the reconsideration the Yeas and Nays being called for, were as follows:

Yeas--Messrs. Loguen, Wilson, Morrel, Duffins, Rich and Smith, 6.

Nays--Messrs. Topp and McDonough, 2; and the resolution increasing the number of members in the State Council, was passed.

Mr. Lewis H. Nelson, a member from Williamburgh, L. I., arrived, and being introduced to the Council, took his seat.

The following resolution presented by Mr. Morrel, was adopted, to wit:

Resolved, That on the 15th day of November, 1854, an election be held throughout the State, for the election of 20 additional members to the State Council; the said election shall be held, and conducted, under the same Rules and Regulations, as were enforced at the election of the members of the present Council, and the said additional members when so elected, shall serve the full term of 2 years from the time of their election.

Mr. Lewis H. Nelson presented a paper marked (A.,) containing two resolutions, which were read and referred to the Committee on "Ways" and "Means."

Mr. Morrel presented the following resolution, which was adopted:
Resolved, That on the election of any member of the New York State Council to the National Council, his seat in the State Council shall be declared vacant.

Mr. Duffins presented the following:
Resolved, That this Council do recommend to the Council Districts to hold nominating conventions, and report the result of their doings to the Secretary of the Council.

A communication from the Rev. Charles B. Ray, of New York City, was received, read, and ordered on file.

The Committee on Nominations reported the following named gentlemen as their selection for members to the National Council, viz.: P. A. Bell[2] and E. V. Clark,[3] New York; J. E. Brown, Chemung; A. B. Platt, Ontario county; W. H. Storum, Chautauque; James Hall, Lansinburgh; Stephen Meyers, Albany; W. J. Wilson and J. N. Still, Brooklyn; and Wm. Tyson, of New York City.

Mr. Duffins presented a written objection against one of the gentlemen nominated, and submitted the name of the Rev. Amos A. Freeman instead. On motion, the reports were read and accepted. When Mr. Smith moved that the report of the majority be adopted, and that the nominees be declared elected to the National Council, strong opposition was manifested thereto. Mr. Wilson moved that they be balloted for; objected to and motion withdrawn.

Mr. Loguen moved to take up the names individually; not agreed to.

Mr. McDonough moved that the ticket be considered elected, and called for the previous question. Some excitement and considerable debate ensuing, when Mr. Morrel moved that we go into Committee of the Whole, on the report of the Committee, which motion prevailed, although Mr. McDonough still claimed his "previous question."

The Council then went into Committee of the Whole. Mr. Morrel in the Chair, and proceeded on motion to ballot for nominees to the National Council. Messrs. Rich and Wilson were appointed tellers; and as the roll was called, each member advanced and deposited his vote. On counting the ballots the result was as follows:

```
        P. A. Bell, 7,            A. B. Slater, 9,
        E. V. Clark, 9,           Jas. Hall, 8,
        W. W. Mathews, 6,         J. N. Still, 9,
        J. E. Brown, 9,           J. H. Storum, 9,
        Charles Pain, 8,          Stephen Meyers, 5,
                    George Morse, 5.
```

There being a tie between Messrs. Meyers and Morse, the Committee proceeded to ballot for the remaining nominee. When on counting the ballots, Mr. Meyers was declared to be the choice of a majority of the Committee; and the ticket nominated in Committee of the Whole was as follows:

```
        New York City,        Philip A. Bell
           do.  do.           Edward V. Clark
        Albany,               Stephen Meyers
           do.                Wm. W. Mathews
        Brooklyn,             J. N. Still
        Newburgh,             Charles Paine
        Lansinburgh,          James Hall
        Chemung,              J. E. Brown
        Chautauqua,           William H. Storum
        Canandaigua,          A. B. Slater
```

And the ticket, as nominated, was reported to the Council, and on motion, accepted and read. When on motion, the nominees were voted upon, and declared duly elected members of the National Council, for the term of two years.

Mr. Wilson presented the following resolution, and demanded the yeas and nays:

Resolved, That no member of the State Council shall be eligible to office in the National Council.

Yeas--Messrs. J. W. Loguen, Morrel, Nelson, Topp, 4; nays, Wilson, Smith, Rich, and McDonough, 4. Mr. Duffins refused to vote on the resolution; and there being a tie, the President gave the casting vote in favor of the resolution, and it was carried.

On motion, Resolved, That the gentlemen elected to the National Council, by this State Council, be informed of their election by the Secretary of the Council. Carried.

Mr. Morrel, offered the following resolution which was adopted:

Resolved, That when this Council adjourns, that we adjourn to meet on the second Tuesday in August next, at the city of Syracuse.

Mr. Wilson presented the following resolution:

Resolved, That this Council for themselves and in the name of their constituents, do most earnestly, and determinedly, oppose every system of Colonization of the people of color from these United States, whether by the "American Colonization Society," or the more dangerous and equally destestable scheme, the emigration Convention intended to convene at Cleveland, in July next. Carried unanimously.

A motion here prevailed, that the Council take a recess for twenty-five minutes. On coming to order the following resolution was offered:

Resolved, That the thanks of the Council are due, and the same are hereby tendered, to the Recorder of the City of Albany, for his kindness in granting to the State Council the use of comfortable rooms in the City Hall, for the purpose of holding its meetings.

Resolved, That the thanks of this Council are respectfully tendered to the City Marshal, for his gentlemanly conduct towards us, and his endeavors to make us comfortable.

A motion to appoint an Agent or Agents, by the Council, was made, and withdrawn.

On motion, Resolved, That the Secretary cause the proceedings of this Council to be published in the *"Frederick Douglass' Paper*," Carried.

Resolved, That this Council return thanks to the officers of the Council for the very able and impartial manner in which they have discharged their duty. Carried.

Committee appointed by the President to District the State: Messr. J. C. Holly, Rochester, J. W. B. Smith, New York, and Wm. Rich, Troy.

On motion, the Council adjourned to meet at Syracuse, on the second Tuesday in August next.

Wm. H. Topp, *President.*
James C. Morrel, *Secretary.*
Albany, Jan. 4th, 1854.

Frederick Douglass' Paper, February 3, 1854.

REFERENCE NOTES

1. James William Charles Pennington (1809-1870), an escaped slave, received an honorary degree of Doctor of Divinity in 1849 from the University of Heidelberg and became a minister in New York City.

2. Philip A. Bell was one of the outstanding Negro leaders of New York City. No matter what the issue, if it touched upon the vital and controlling interests of his people, Bell's voice and pen became powerful tribunes in their defense.

In 1832, Bell was appointed secretary of the second annual National Negro Convention, held at Philadelphia. In January 1837, Bell was listed as proprietor of the *Weekly Advocate* (subsequently the *Colored American*), the third black newspaper to be published in the United States. Bell was active in the antislavery movement and played an influential role in the struggle of blacks to regain the suffrage in New York, frequently canvassing the state for support. During the 1850's, Bell migrated to California and became a leading figure of the Negro community there. At San Francisco, in 1862, he edited the *Pacific Appeal*. After the Civil War, he was publisher of a newspaper known as the *Elevator*.

3. Edward V. Clark was a well-known black New York City businessman active in its social and political life. He conducted a prosperous jewelry establishment. His name, had, morever, a respectable standing even among the dealers on Wall Street.

STATE CONVENTION OF THE COLORED CITIZENS OF NEW YORK, ALBANY,
JANUARY 20, 1855

COLORED PEOPLE OF NEW YORK

Gov. Hunt, in his late annual message, took occasion to recommend a liberal appropriation by the Legislature, for the removal of the free colored people of the State, under the auspices of the Colonization Society.[1] He also presents the inseparable accompaniment of all Colonization recommendations, viz: slander of the colored population. He talks of their 'inferiority'--of their 'life of servility and drudgery'--says 'their anomalous position forms one of the most serious obstacles to the emancipation of the slave,' &c.

The colored people, in an address to the people of New York, vindicate themselves from these charges with an ability which renders their inferiority to Gov. Hunt quite questionable, whether we consider their rhetoric, their logic, or their morals. In conclusion, they protest against the adoption of his recommendation to appropriate funds for their removal to Africa, or anywhere else, for the following reasons:

First--Because the appropriation is unconstitutional. The 10th section of the 7th article of the Constitution states that 'the credit of the State shall not in any manner be given or loaned to, or in aid of any individual association or incorporation.' The American Colonization Society is an 'association' foreign to the State, and unknown to its laws. By granting no matter what sum to that Society, the good faith of the State would be pledged to the cruel and monstrous doctrines on which that Society is founded--that a man has no right to live in the land of his birth.

Secondly--Because such an appropriation is entirely unnecessary. Of the colored population of this State, there are not fifty persons, all told, who desire to emigrate to Africa. Even the New York and Liberia Agricultural Association,[2] no longer held together by the cohesive power of eleemosynary plunder, is organized to send other persons to Africa--other persons having been conjured up for the purpose of lining the pockets of the members of the association.

We need no State appropriation. Should it ever occur that we should be called upon to leave our native State, having means of our own, we shall not burden the public fund in our departure any more than we do while remaining at home. In consulting the mysteries of Providence, touching such departure, and with his face turned toward the East, our worthy Chief Magistrate has not been vouchsafed the true reading of the auguries: *Intonuit laevum*: the road is short to Canada; from whose fertile fields and equal institutions, we might be permitted to witness the prosperity of that State, which, in giving us birth, has entwined in its commonweal every fibre of our being; this would take away half the bitterness of exile, and would leave us the privilege, should peril come to her, of baring the breasts of black men as a shield to whatever may be aimed against the heart of the Empire State.

Thirdly--We protest against such appropriation, because the American Colonization Society is a gigantic fraud, professing to love, while it systematically encourages hate among mankind; professing to liberate the slave, while it binds more firmly the chains of the enthralled; professing to give peace, while it is the last stronghold of the organized disturbance of the entire Union; professing to evangelize Africa, while it hurries to its shores a population which has the best reason to hate Christianity which sends them there; with no other merit than that of a cold, crafty, implacable hater of the colored Americans; it pushes it Jesuit head among high and low; a moulder of, and a profiter by a diseased public opinion, it keeps alive an army of agents who live by plundering us of our good name.

And lastly--We protest against this appropriation, because 'we remember those that are in bonds as bound with them;' bone of our bone, and flesh of our flesh, may evil betide us when the hope of gain, or the fear of oppression, shall compel or persuade us to forsake them to the rayless gloom of perpetual slavery.

Adopted by the State Convention of Colored Citizens in the City Hall, Albany, Jan. 20th, 1855.

J. W. C. Pennington, *President.*

Henry Hicks,
William Mathews, } *Secretaries.*

Liberator, March 5, 1855.

REFERENCE NOTES

1. Washington Hunt (1811-1867) was a Whig member of Congress (1842-1849) and governor of New York State from 1850 to 1852. In his Annual Message to the New York State legislature in January 1852, Hunt called upon that body to make a "liberal appropriation" to help in colonizing those blacks in New York who were desirous of emigrating. Blacks in New York City and elsewhere in the state vehemently opposed his plan. They had supported with enthusiasm his candidacy in 1850 because he had made friendly overtures toward them. His seeming embrace of the colonization program, however, prompted Jeremiah Powers, a leading New York City black, to vow that "in the future we will vote for no man that will not vote for us and the cause of humanity. We will vote Gov. Hunt out next time. He was elected by only two-hundred and fifty of a majority and these were the votes of the colored population." Hunt was defeated for re-election in 1852 by Democratic candidate Horatio Seymour. The full text of Governor Hunt's Message on the "Expatriation of the Free Coloured People" can be found in the *National Anti-Slavery Standard*, Jan. 22, 1852. For Powers' remarks see *Frederick Douglass' Paper*, Feb. 5, 1852.

2. In 1851, Lewis H. Putnam, a New York City Negro, along with other blacks, founded the Liberian Agricultural and Emigration Society. This organization was simply a black version of the American Colonization Society. Hence, at a public meeting held by blacks in the city on October 6, 1851, Putnam and his co-workers came under sharp attack. Among those present at the gathering were Samuel E. Cornish and George T. Downing, prominent New York blacks.

Under their leadership a series of resolutions was passed. One made clear the fixed determination of blacks to oppose all colonization schemes and declared their "abhorrence" for its designs, whether "promulgated by the American Colonization Society or by renegade colored men, made under the guise of an emigration society." Another asked Putnam to "disconnect himself from the Negroes of New York . . . seeing that he has found it to his interests to connect himself with the American Colonization Society, our enemy and villifier." A final resolution called upon blacks in the city to refrain from contributing funds toward the "so-called Liberia Emigration Society, as the colored citizens of New York have no connection or sympathy with it." See *Frederick Douglass' Paper*, Nov. 13, 1851. See also George Walker, "The Afro-American in New York City, 1827-1860," p. 220.

COLORED MEN'S STATE CONVENTION OF NEW YORK, TROY, SEPTEMBER 4, 1855

CALL FOR A STATE CONVENTION OF THE COLORED PEOPLE OF
THE STATE OF NEW YORK
SEPTEMBER, 1855

The undersigned, regarding the present as a favorable time for pressing the claims of the colored citizens of this State upon the consideration of our State Government, with a view to the removal of the odious and invidious disabilities imposed therein, and to gain equal political rights, take the liberty to invite their colored fellow-citizens to assemble, in State Convention, in the city of TROY, on the FIRST TUESDAY of SEPTEMBER, 1855. There is a sacred obligation resting upon the colored citizens of this State, to give the ear of our Legislature no rest till every legal and political disability, with all its depressing and degrading tendencies, shall be swept from the Empire State. The undersigned express the hope that measures will be early taken to have every part of the State represented in the Convention.

P. A. Bell, New York
Thomas L. Jennings, "
Edward V. Clark, "
Rev. Charles B. Ray, "
Dr. Jas. McCune Smith, "
John J. Zuille, "
J. J. Simons, "
Jacob Gibbs, "
Joseph Smith, "
Dr. McDonald, "
Dr. J. W. Pennington "
Dr. Peter Ray, Williamsburgh
Lewis Nelson, "
Wm. J. Wilson, Brooklyn
J. N. Still, "
Martin Cross, Catskill
Jacob Schermerhorn, Kingston
Joseph Dell, Hudson
Chauncy Van Hussen "
Peter Van De Zee New Baltimore
Lewis Jackson, "
John Jones, Sandy Lake
Francis Thompson, Schenectady
Peter Hornbeck, Utica
George Brown, "
James Collins, Ithaca
James Lewis, "
Rev. J. W. Loguen, Syracuse

James W. Randolph,	Albany
Wm. Gardiner,	"
Richard Wright,	"
Stephen Myers,	"
Joseph Newit,	"
Benj. Bourman,	Troy
Wm. Rich,	"
Jonathan C. Gibbs,	"
James H. Davis,	"
Uriah Boston,	Poughkeepsie
Frederick Douglass,	Rochester
Wm. J. Watkins,	"

Frederick Douglass' Paper, July 27, 1855.

PROCEEDINGS

We publish the resolutions which had passed the Convention up to adjournment, at noon, yesterday together. The remainder of the resolutions passed will be found in our report of the proceedings in the afternoon and evening.

The Following is the adopted platform:

Resolved, That this Convention of the colored citizens of the State of New York, September 4th, 1855, specifically to promote their own complete and equal enfranchisement, confess themselves to be unable to find a more solid platform of principles, looking to this vital and highly important end, than is furnished in the Declaration of Independence and the Constitution of the United States.

Resolved, That we hold these truths to be self evident; all men are created with the right to life, liberty, and the pursuit of happiness, and that to protect and preserve these rights, governments are instituted among them, deriving their power and authority from the just consent of the governed.

Resolved, That true liberty, as a tangible idea, precious to the universal heart, has a basis no less broad and indestructible than the inherent capacity of man to discriminate between right and wrong, good and evil, and the power of choice of self-government.

Resolved, That in the colored citizens of the State of New York, this basis for the exercise of freedom is as conspicuous as in that of any other class of the American people.

Resolved, That as taxation and representation should go together; as the strength of every nation and government is in proportion to the love binding its individuals and classes to the common centre, it is alike the dictate of wisdom, as of justice, that the colored citizens of New York should have equal reason with other citizens to respect her laws and cling to her institutions.

Resolved, That the imposition of a property qualification upon the colored citizens of the State of New York, as a condition to the exercise by them of the elective franchise--thus casting upon them a burden imposed upon no other class of the American people--is partial, in that it discriminates where no discrimination should be made; is unjust, in that it inflicts punishment or injury where none is deserved; is unmagnanimous, because it is an imposition by the strong against the weak; is bad policy, because it serves to weaken the attachment of one class of citizens to the political institutions which should be made as precious to them as to any other class; and that, therefore, the statute containing this odious provision should be repealed without delay.

Resolved, That regarding the elective franchise as a grand safeguard against oppression, and the right to exercise it is as essential to the respectability and well-being of every citizen; and further, believing that next to the dignity of being in actual possession of rights, is the honor of making manly efforts to secure them, we solemnly pledge ourselves to give the ear of our Legislature, and our fellow citizens generally, no peace until they shall wipe from the statute book the anti-Republican discrimination against us.

Resolved, That five persons be appointed by this Convention, to lecture in different parts of the State, with particular reference to the Elective Franchise, and that they appoint two of their number to attend the sittings of the Legislature at Albany, to urge upon the members of that body the justice of our claims, and the adoption of immediate measures to secure equal extension of the suffrage right.

Resolved, That this Convention recommend to the colored voters, the formation of political associations throughout the State, with a view to keeping themselves informed of the precise position of parties and candidates which solicit their votes, and to enable them to cast their votes intelligently on the suffrage question.

Resolved, That this Convention earnestly request clergymen having charge of colored congregations throughout the State to embrace every favorable opportunity to impress upon their congregations the duty of using every means in their power to secure their political rights.

Afternoon Session--Wednesday, 2½ o'clock.

Mr. Hodges moved to strike out the word "colored" before clergymen in the last resolution, published above, which was under discussion at the adjournment, and accompanied his motion with some excellent remarks in defence of colored clergymen.

Capt. J. J. Simonds, of New York, followed on the other side.

Mr. Mathews also argued in favor of retaining the word colored.

Mr. Gibbs wished the word colored stricken out.

Mr. Hodges modified his amendment to "clergymen having charge of colored congregations," and it was adopted, and the resolutions as it now stands was passed.

Mr. Bell introduced resolutions relating to Slavery and suffrage. [Laid on the table.]

Mr. Douglass, from the Business Committee, reported a resolution pledging the Convention to support none but free suffrage. [Laid on the table.]

Capt. J. J. Simonds introduced the following resolutions:

Resolved, That a committee be appointed to report a plan for securing mechanical trades for youth and their support in business.

Resolved, That a State Grand Council be established for the purpose of considering the wants and situation of our people, and that auxiliary Councils be authorized in each county.

Resolved, That it is important that two sailing vessels, owned by the Grand Council of this State, be fitted out to reach the grievances of our deluded brethren who have emigrated to Africa or any other unhealthy clime, to give them an opportunity to return at any reasonable expense.

Resolved, That this Convention urge with all its influence, the immediate formation of suffrage and political leagues in every city or town where colored persons reside, to be composed of colored citizens of the State, (as well as all other persons not entitled to vote,) to act together politically or otherwise, to secure a free extension of the suffrage, and a wider recognition of the Democratic principle in our State Constitution. [Read and laid on the table.]

Mr. Douglass read the following resolution which was handed him by a delegate:

Resolved, That we recommend the formation of political associations in every Senatorial District in the State, previous to the coming election in order that both candidates and electors may fully understand that we want our political rights. [Laid on the table.]

Mr. Kelly, of New York, offered the following:

Resolved, That we recommend to the colored voters of the State, wherever there can be found a competent colored person to nominate them to any and all the different offices in the gift of the people, and to use all honorable means in their power to secure their election.

Read and laid on the table. Afterwards taken up and rejected.

Mr. Douglass also read the following resolution, which was laid on the table:

Resolved, That righteousness exalteth a nation, but sin is a reproach in any people. Therefore, it is morally binding on political bodies, as well as on individuals, to have all their deliberations and movements guided and governed by [illegible].

A general discussion here sprung up in regard to a plan of political organization.

The roll was then read. The name of Miss Barbary Anna Stewart was stricken out from the roll, several gentlemen objecting to it on the ground that this is not a Woman's Rights Convention.

A resolution providing that a committee of three should be appointed to draft a Constitution for a Suffrage Society was passed.

The Chair appointed Frederick Douglass of Rochester, J. C. Gibbs, of Troy, and Dr. Ray, of Williamsburgh, said committee.

Messrs. Joseph Bell, of Hudson, R. A. Griffin, of Poughkeepsie, and Mr. Bowen, of Rome, made some interesting remarks, which were well received by the Convention. The latter gentleman gave an exceedingly graphic account of his experience while a slave and since his deliverance from bondage. He closed by saying that he was going to claim all the rights the State of New York granted and as many more as he could get.

Mr. Bell, from the Committee on Lecturers, reported the names as Lecturers to labor in the respective Districts assigned as follows:

Mr. Wm. J. Watkins for the counties west of and including Wayne, Seneca, Tompkins and Tioga.[1]

Rev. J. W. Loguen for the counties of Cayuga, Cortland, Broome, Chenango, Onondaga, Oswego, Oneida, Madison, Otsego, Sullivan, Delaware, Schoharie, Montgomery and Schenectady.

Mr. G. F. Iverson for the counties of Jefferson, Lewis, Herkimer, Fulton, Saratoga, Hamilton, Warren, Washington, Essex, Franklin, Clinton and St. Lawrence.

Mr. Stephen Myers for the counties of Albany, Rensselaer, Greene, Columbia, Ulster, Dutchess, Orange, Putnam, Rockland and Westchester.

Rev. C. B. Ray for New York, Long Island and Staten Island.

Report read, accepted, and, after discussion, adopted.

Dr. Ray, from the committee on plan of political organization, made a report which was read, accepted and laid on the table.

The Convention then adjourned to meet at 7 P.M.

Evening Session--7 o'clock

The Convention met. Prayer by Rev. Mr. Mathews.

The following resolutions, laid upon the table at the afternoon session, were taken up and adopted:

Resolved, That the right of suffrage with us is a primary right--fundamental in our political creed, and that we will in no contingency support any man for civil office who is not in favor--and known to be in favor--of extending to the colored citizens of this State the complete right of suffrage.

Resolved, That this Convention strongly recommend to the colored citizens to withhold their support directly and indirectly from all public journals that make it a point to misrepresent us as a people before the country and the world but to use all means in their power to aid in circulating such papers as are ready and willing to do us justice--to extenuate nothing nor set down aught in malice against us--but give us a fair field and no favors.

The following resolution, offered by Mr. Bell, and laid on the table, was taken up, read by Mr. Bell, and unanimously adopted:

Resolved, That this Convention, while maintaining the Republican doctrine of equal rights of all men, adhere to the principles and opinions heretofore enunciated, and present the following: Slavery being the cause of our degradation in this country, hence of our political disfranchisement in this State, we hereby reaffirm our adherence to anti-slavery principles and that as slavery is a social, moral, political and religious evil, it should be immediately abolished. Our political rights being next in importance, we hereby pledge ourselves to use untiring efforts to effect a restoration of our political rights in this State, and never to cease until our end is accomplished.

Mr. Stephen Myers offered the following:

Resolved, That this Convention recommend to the twenty-seventh Senatorial district to nominate Frederick Douglass of Rochester, for the office of State

Senator,[2] and the friends of freedom in the city of Rochester, and the Senatorial district give him their warm support, and his election is sure. No action.

Constitution

1. This association shall be known as the New York State Suffrage Association.
2. The object of this Association shall be to obtain the equal right of suffrage for the colored citizens of the State of New York.
3. The officers of this Society shall consist of a President, four Vice Presidents, Secretary, Assistant Secretary, Treasurer, and a Board of Managers composed of seven members.
4. It shall be the duty of the President, and in his absence, the Vice President, to preside at all the meetings of this Association. The Secretaries shall keep a record of all the proceedings--and perform all the necessary correspondence in behalf of the Association; and the Treasurer shall faithfully keep all funds belonging to the Association. The Board of Managers shall attend to all the business incident to the prosecution of the one great object set forth in the second article of this Constitution--such as appointing agents--collecting funds--paying out monies--and directing the measures of the Association--and shall make annual reports of all the doings of the Board.
5. The officers of this Society shall be elected at its regular annual meeting which shall be held in the month of September in each year, at such time and place as shall be determined upon by the Board of Managers.
6. All meetings of this Association shall be summoned by a call from the Board, signed by the President and Secretary, and the call published at least six weeks previous to said meetings in shuch public journals as may be willing to publish.
7. Any person may become a member of this Association by signing the Constitution and contributing to its funds.
8. This Constitution shall go into effect this, the fifth day of September, A.D. 1855.

Report read and accepted; and the Constitution unanimously adopted.

On motion, a committee of five were appointed to nominate the officers provided for in the above Constitution, viz.: J. W. Duffin, E. H. Mathews, P. W. Ray, S. Myers, R. D. Kerndey.

Speech of Frederick Douglass

Gentlemen and Ladies: It is with no little embarrassment that I rise on this occasion, and under the circumstances in which I am placed, to address you. This has been a long laborious, fatiguing day with me, and I have had no repose, no retirement, no opportunity to fling together such thoughts as the intelligence of the audience which I now see before me leads me to believe necessary, and proper to enforce on this occasion. I never, perhaps, felt a profounder desire to say something worthy of the great cause to which we are engaged, than I do now, and at the same time, I never felt more incapable of doing so. But since I have been called upon to speak, I will try, if you will be patient and forbearing towards me, to say a few words.

It is very evident that the great question now before the American people--the question upon which the nation will soon be called to decide--is Slavery. Or in other words, the question now before this nation is whether Southern oppression, and Southern slaveholding institutions, shall be allowed to prevail in every part of this great Republic--or whether the institutions of equity, honor and human brotherhood [shall prevail] upon the American people, and each party is marshaling its adherents for the grand conflict. In the Southern States there is no institution, no party, save the slaveholding institution and party. By this institution, 3,700,000 of the human family are stripped of every right, robbed of all justice, whipped, outraged, and compelled to be marketable chattels. Fifteen hundred millions of dollars are said to be invested in this species of property at the South,--fifteen hundred millions of dollars is said to be the money representation of this enslaved portion of the human race. This vast accumulation of wealth--this immense conglomeration of interest--has made the South a unit on the Slavery question --bound them together in every action. So overshadowing has it become as to eclipse, and swallow up every other consideration. In the Southern States of our Union, the non-slaveholder is almost a cypher--literally a nonentity. This is the case with him, even more than with the colored population of this State. One fact alone will illustrate this fact. At the recent State Convention, in Kentucky, notwithstanding the non-slaveholding power of that State embraces a population of over 700,000, and the slaveholding interest a population of only 30,000, the slaveholding interest was so powerful, so all-pervading, that not a single delegate appeared in the Convention as a representative of the 700,000 people embraced in that non-slaveholding population. This fact will show you the tremendous power of this institution in the Southern States. In South Carolina no man, no free, white American citizen, is eligible to a seat in the Legislature of the State, unless he is the holder of ten slaves--unless he can call ten human beings his property. Thus, this institution rules everything at the South. It has given to the South its laws, its morals, its social code, its interpretation of the Bible, its definition of the Declaration of Independence, its understanding of the Constitution of the United States. The non-slaveholding citizens have thus become a mere cypher, and we scarcely ever speak of the South, without speaking of the slaveholders as the South. This Southern institution has also given it a peculiar style of religion. It has so materially changed the religion of that section from what it was in the primitive days of the Quakers and others, who opposed the principle of human oppression, as to give it what may be termed a slaveholding religion--a religion which can be practiced in perfect conformity with the whip, the gag, the fetters, the thumb-screw, and all the horrid, hellish paraphernalia of the slave system.

The South has also given us its own peculiar interpretation of the laws. The system and practice formerly was this: That every man was presumed to be free until he was proved to be otherwise. But this principle is found to be incompatible with the great Southern institution; so they have established one diametrically opposite, and they call upon the North to endorse and sustain it in the fugitive slave bill. This new principle is, that every man is presumed to be a slave until he proves himself to be otherwise. This is what the South is demanding and will continue to demand of the North. There are two principles in this country--Slavery and Liberty. One of these kings is bound to reign in this country. The question for the North to answer is--"Under which king?--Bezzoni. Under which king?" There is in this Northern country what may be styled a Slavery party. Its members are distributed through every other political organization, save perhaps the Liberty Party and the Free Soil Party of the North. This Slavery party will sink every other policy and lose sight of every other consideration in order to advance the interests of the South. For this purpose, its members will become Whigs or Democrats, or *neither* Whigs nor Democrats. It entered the political caucuses of 1852, in the city of Baltimore, and demanded the incorporation of its principles into the platform of the Whig and Democratic organizations. And both parties bowed themselves before this gigantic interest, and consented to take upon themselves the "mark of the beast." They then and there abandoned all other issues to give way to the Slave policy of the South. There was no living issue between the Whig and Democratic party in the election of 1852. It has been asserted that the Whig party was in favor of the improvement of Rivers and Harbors, and so forth, while the Democratic party was not--and that this constituted the issue. What are the facts? The Platform of the Whig Party said--"We are opposed to the *unconstitutional* improvement of Rivers and Harbors." And that was no issue. Both parties endorsed, will all their hell-black etceteras, the Compromises of 1850. Both parties endorsed the Southern interpretation of all these questions which divided the North and South on the subject of Slavery. What were those questions? What was the standard taken by the South? Let us see. It has been said that the North is opposed to Slavery. But the South has discovered that the chain on the negro slave will not cut, and fasten, and fester securely in the flesh, unless the other end of that chain is held by a padlock in the lips of the North.

It is one of the compensating laws of Providence that a wrong done by one section of the nation against the other cannot go unpunished. A man cannot build his mansion on a hill-top, be it ever so fair and lovely, if its base be reeking with nuisance and corruption, without suffering the baneful influences of that deadly corruption. So you of the North, free men and non-slaveholding citizens, cannot sit idly by, and see 3,700,000 of your fellow-beings wronged, robbed of their rights, whipped, outraged, and driven to toil by day and by night, without the shadow of right or justice, without the consolation and revivifying influences of intelligence and of the gospel, and not suffer from the baneful effects of this hideous wrong. You at the North cannot suffer this dark enormity to be perpetrated, without suffering the consequences. And one of the consequences will be that your limbs will be stricken down at your side, your thoughts fettered, yourselves deprived of the freedom of action. No man is really free south of Mason & Dixon's Line but the slaveholder. And soon no man north of Mason & Dixon's Line will be free but he who will succumb to the demands of the slaveholders.

I speak rather by sight than by hearing. The objects of the slaveholding party are becoming open to the sight. They are five in number. The first is, the suppression of all anti-slavery discussion. The second, the extension of Slavery over all the Territories of the United States. Every one of my hearers who is a political reader knows that I have facts to bear me out in asserting this to be the policy of the South. The third is, the nationalization of Slavery in every State of the Union, so as to do away with all Conventions, Associations and discussions of an anti-slavery character, and abolish everything tending to disturb the relations between the master and the slave. The fourth is, the expatriation of every free citizen of color in the United States. Ten millions of dollars is the amount of money which is to be devoted to bringing this result. The fifth and grand object is, the absorption by the United States of Mexico, Southern California, Cuba, the Sandwich Islands, all the islands of the Caribbean Sea, and Nicaragua, bringing them into the Confederacy of our Union, and placing their black population, fourteen millions in number, under the banner of the slave power. Let us look this in the face. What is necessary to secure all their aims and objects? Why, first, this anti-slavery agitation must be put down. And unfortunately, most unfortunately for the ends of right, liberty and justice, both the Whig Party and the Democratic Party have lent themselves to the Slave Power, to engage in putting it down. This was the determination of these parties on that point, as expressed in the Platforms put forth by them at Baltimore. They would resist agitation. They would read out Horace Greeley,[3] that champion of the rights of free men, to accomplish this end. The Democratic Party proposes to go as far or a little farther than the Whig party on this point. It is strong and nervous in its declarations, and strong as thunder in its action. It says it will not only resist agitation, but it will assist in putting down agitation. That is the decision of the Democratic National Party. Now, what does putting down agitation mean? It means putting down the right of speech on a particular subject in this Republic. It means closing the mouth of all those who utter principles designed to operate to the injury of the slave power. Remember, this was a political, not an individual declaration. A political declaration differs from an individual declaration in this:—that it is supposed to be capable at some time of being crystalized, of being moulded into a law of the land. *They mean to put down agitation*. How will they put it down? How have they put it down already in the Southern States? By making every statement uttered in opposition to the slave power an incendiary sentiment. These parties, then acted in obedience to the law of the South when they said they intended to put down agitation. The question now is fellow-citizens, are you quite ready to give up to the South your right of speech? Are you quite ready to relinquish to any particular political subject? For if you give up the right in regard to slavery to-day, you may have to give it up for something else to-morrow. Experience has taught us that the Southern slaveholders are capable of any action, and you know not what they may next demand of you.

This right of speech was once regarded as a very precious institution in our country. It was looked upon as the sentinel on the outer bulwarks of Liberty. Daniel Webster so regarded it in a speech made by him in Congress in 1814, when he declared that it was a principle he should assert to the last—that he should relinquish it only when he relinquished his life—that living he should assert the right, or dying, he should transmit to posterity the honor of a brave defence. He had not then forgotten that this right is sacredly guaranteed in the Constitution of the United States, in the Constitution of every State in our Union.

Well, the two great political parties have found that the free exercise of the right of speech is incompatible with Southern feelings and interest --that it disturbs our Southern brethren. So they have, therefore, in their kindness attempted to give peace to the slaveholders. They have endeavored to do what God in his infinite wisdom has decreed that it shall be impossible to do. "There shall be no peace to the wicked, saith my God."

This is a confession that the exercise of free speech is incompatible with the relations of master and slave. It is a tacit admission of guilt. Innocence has nothing to fear from discussion. It folds its arms and throws itself open to the severest scrutiny. It is only the dark wing of iniquity that seeks to burrow out of sight--to hide itself from the observation of man. It was said by Junius of Lord Granville that his character would only pass without censure so long as it passed without observation. Such is the case with Slavery. With it, observation and censure are synonymous. Therefore, they aim to put down all discussion. If it were possible for the South to do so, it would disband every anti-Slavery organization in the land. Still, the slaveholders would have no peace. For down in the heart of every one of them, God has planted an abolition lecturer, which is continually saying to him, "Thou art verily guilty in regard to thy brother." Cowper was quite right, after all, in regard to slavery, when he said:

> I would not have a slave to till my ground.
> To fan me when I sleep.
> My heart would throb at every sound.

I have experienced slavery in my own person. Before I formed a part of this living, breathing world, the scourge was plaited for my back, and the fetter forged for my limb. By though my blood still burns, and my heart bounds as I look back to those dark days of slavery, I would rather at this moment exchange places with the veriest whipped slave of the South, than the wealthiest slaveholder of that region. He can have no peace. His mind must be constantly casting up mire and dirt. You can see him gather up his bowie-knife and revolver and place them under his pillow at night. That bowie-knife is intended to pierce the heart of the slave, and that revolver to scatter his brains to the four winds of Heaven. But they first pierce the heart of the slave owner's happiness, and scatter his peace to the winds, ere they reach the poor slave. The slaveholder can know no peace. There is no safeguard for the South save in the preservation of the relations of master and slave. Just let it be rumored that ten slaves have been overheard to say that they are tired of being flogged, and they mean to fight, and the whole South is in a tremor. This is why the South wish you to give up the right of free speech.

Let us view the encroachments of the slave power in another light. The Constitution of the United States provides that in all cases at law where the value of the property concerned is more than twenty dollars, trials by jury shall be provided. The South has found that this will not do. It has found that there is a species of property in the South which must not come under this jury definition. Congress passed such a law in 1850, in the shape of the fugitive slave bill. The writ of *habeas corpus* was formerly regarded as the most valuable provision. It provided for the delivery from imprisonment of any person, unless good cause was shown for his detention. The Constitution provides that this writ of *habeas corpus* shall not be suspended, unless when, in cases of rebellion or riot, the public good require it. But it has been found to be in opposition to the designs of the slave power, and the two grand parties have united together, and declared that it shall be nullified. The presumption of the law formerly was that every man is free until he is proven to be otherwise. But now, the slave power, bold and arrogant, has asserted the contrary principle. Every colored man, under the Fugitive Slave Bill, is presumed to be a slave unless he proves himself to be otherwise.

A pure and unbribed judiciary used to be thought something of here in the North. But Slavery demands something else. And in the Fugitive Slave enactment it has secured its demands. It demands and provides that when a judge shall convict any prisoner of being a slave, or in other words, of being worthy of imprisonment for life, he shall receive the sum of $10. But if, on the contrary, he acquits the prisoner, he is to receive only $5. Isn't that a "Hail, Columbia, happy land," provision?

Mr. Douglass then proceeded to establish the position that the Slave States demand that the North shall execute their laws and cited the case of Passmore Williamson[4] in proof. He contended that Mr. W. had committed no crime. He had broken no law of Pennsylvania, but was incarcerated for breaking the laws of Virginia. He dwelt upon the provisions of the Fugitive enactment, which decrees that there shall be "no refuge for the stricken slave through the length and breadth of this fair land--no spot upon which he can plant his foot and say, "Here, by the blessing of God's Providence, and my own right, I am a free man." He contended that the nation is at present in a state of anarchy--that the government of the United States has resigned its functions to three thousand lawless border ruffians of Missouri.[5] A struggle has gone on in that territory [Kansas] and it has resigned its ballot-boxes and its liberties with an ease which puts to shame the fighting before Sebastopol. The reason is obvious. The walls at Sebastopol are of granite.[6] The walls of Kansas are of *dough!* [Illegible]. He says they do not mean to go to Liberia, if they can avoid it. On this point we are somewhat in the position of the boy John when he was going to visit his Uncle Robert. Said he, "I am going to Uncle Robert's. I am going to stay six weeks. And I am going to do just as I please--that is, if Uncle Robert will let me." We intend to remain in this country--*if you will let us*. And although there is physical force enough here to drive us out, I do not think there is *moral force* enough to do it. So we may embody our sentiments in the old song which they used to sing at camp meetings:

> Bredren, we hab been wif you,
> And still is wif you,
> And mean to be wif you to the end!

He argued at some length upon the ground that prejudice against color was not natural, but conventional, and quoted many happy anecdotes to strengthen his position. On retiring he said: "I am thankful for your kindness in listening to me, and beg you not to forget, in the playfulness of my last remarks, the sober earnestness of the first."

The committee appointed to nominate officers for the New York State Suffrage Association would respectfully report as follows:

President--Frederick Douglass, of Rochester.
Vice Presidents--Wm. Rich, Troy; Francis Thompson, Schenectady; Wm. J. Hodges, Williamsburgh; J. W. Loguen, Syracuse.
Secretaries--Jas. McCune Smith, A.M., M.D., New York; J. C. Gibbs, A.B., D.D., Troy.
Treasurer--Richard Wright, of Albany.
Board of Managers--Philip A. Bell, New York; E. H. Mathews, Troy; Wm. J. Wilson, Brooklyn; J. W. Duffin, Geneva; Peter W. Ray, M.D., Williamsburgh.
[Signed by all the members.]
Moved and seconded that the report be adopted. [Carried, and the Officers elected.]

Morning Session--Thursday, 10 o'clock

Convention assembled. Prayer by Rev. U. C. Farlen.

On motion, the thanks of the Convention were tendered to the white citizens of Troy for their favorable expression in favor of the suffrage question, last evening.

On motion the thanks of the Convention were tendered to Mr. Rand for cheerfully and generously giving them the opportunity to occupy the very best Hall in the city for public assemblies and public speaking.

Votes of thanks to the citizens of Troy and the Press of Troy were also adopted.

Resolutions approving of the call for a National Convention to be held in Philadelphia on the 16th of October next, and recommending to the favorable consideration of that body the subjects of mechanical trades, education and a Central College, were passed.

A vote of thanks to the officers was passed. President Rich responded in a neat and appropriate speech when after singing and prayer, the Convention adjourned *sine die*.

Frederick Douglass' Paper, September 14, 1855.

REFERENCE NOTES

1. William J. Watkins (1828-?), a native of Maryland, was a noted black abolitionist who was also active in the Underground Railroad. Between 1855 and 1856 Watkins was associate editor of *Frederick Douglass' Paper*. In 1853, Watkins, along with Robert Morris, another influential Negro, presented a petition, signed by sixty-five blacks, to the Massachusetts legislature, praying that body for a charter to form an independent military company since blacks were barred from the state militias. In support of this position, Watkins also delivered a brilliant speech before the legislative committee on the militia, February 24, 1853, in which he recited the role played by black men in the American Revolution and the War of 1812 and demolished the arguments advanced against granting the Negroes' request. But his appeal brought no action.

Watkins soon became active in politics. During the 1850's he supported the Free Soil Party and urged his people to follow suit. Later, he became an ardent spokesman and campaigner for the Republican Party.

2. It is interesting to note that in 1854, there was talk of nominating Frederick Douglass for Congress on the Liberty Party ticket to succeed Gerrit Smith, the noted philanthropist and abolitionist, who had recently resigned his seat. Commenting on this occasion, Douglass wrote: "The possibility of electing a Negro to the American Congress, is a modern suggestion. The idea is a new one, as little hoped for by the despised colored people, as dreamed of by their white friends. We accept it simply as an indication of a slightly altered state of mind in the country, but without the slightest belief that the idea will ever be realized in our person, tho' we do hope and expect to see it realized in some competent colored man before we shall have done with the journey of life. The thing is in itself reasonable, and, therefore, probable. It is consistent with all the elementary principles of the American government, though it is in conflict with our national prejudices and practices. . . ."

In spite of the fact that black did enjoy the right to the ballot to some degree before Radical Reconstruction, only one Negro, John Mercer Langston, was elected to public office in this period. In 1855 he was elected on the Liberal Party ticket to the post of township clerk in Brownhelm, Ohio. See Philip S. Foner, *The Life and Writings of Frederick Douglass* (New York, 1950), II, 78-79. See also Philip S. Foner, *The Voice of Black America: Major Speeches by Negroes in the United States* (New York, 1971), p. 410.

3. Horace Greeley (1811-1872), founder of the *New York Tribune*, a successful and influential antislavery organ and later one of the foremost of Republican editors.

4. In July 1855, John H. Wheeler, United States minister to Nicaragua, was about to embark from Philadelphia to New York. He had brought along with him a Negro woman named Jane Johnson and her two children, Daniel and Isaiah. Shortly after boarding the boat, Wheeler and his three servants retired to the deck, whereupon Passmore Williamson, secretary of the Pennsylvania Antislavery Society, approached Wheeler and asked permission to speak to his servants. Wheeler refused, but Williamson pushed past him and asked Jane if she were a slave. When she admitted as such, Williamson informed her that since she had been brought into free territory by her master she could be freed. Soon an argument followed and in the excitement which followed a group of blacks who had accompanied Williamson seized the woman and her children and carried them off the boat. The slaves were then loaded into a waiting carriage and carried away.

Williamson, who had taken no actual part in assisting the slaves, was nevertheless implicated. For Wheeler petitioned the United States District Court for a writ of *habeas corpus* in an attempt to force Williamson to produce the slaves before the court. Williamson protested that the slaves had never been in his custody, and failing to produce, he was held in contempt by Judge John K. Kane. With Williamson behind bars, the case soon attracted nationwide attention. Hundreds of letters and scores of visitors poured in on him, including a delegation from the Colored National Convention, which was meeting in Philadelphia in mid-October 1855.

Jane Johnson, in the meantime, had escaped to Massachusetts. She returned voluntarily and appeared before Judge Kane with her counsel and informed him that neither she nor her children had ever been in the custody of Williamson. In fact, she denied ever having seen Williamson once she left the boat.

The case had dragged on for several months, but finally, in view of Johnson's testimony, Williamson was released from federal custody on November 3, 1855. Jane Johnson and her children remained free, since Wheeler had left the country and was in no position to press the issue before the fugitive slave tribunals.

5. After the passage of the Kansas-Nebraska Act, settlers from the North and South poured into Kansas. The slaveowners organized bands of ruffians recruited from the riff-raff elements of western Missouri to invade Kansas and assist in establishing slavery in the territory. In elections for a delegate to Congress in November 1854 and for a territorial legislature in March 1855, the pro-slavery forces through the use of illegal voting and the terroristic tactics of the "Border Ruffians" from Missouri carried both contests. The free-soil element refused to recognize the legislature friendly to the slave power, established their own assembly, drew up a constitution and asked for admission into the Union. By 1856 actual civil war existed in Kansas as the "Border Ruffians" raided Lawrence and other towns, stole horses, and in general molested free-state families. The free soil men retaliated in kind.

6. During the Crimean War (1853-1856) Sebastopol, a Russian military fortress at the inlet of the Black Sea, resisted the beseiging British, French, Turks and Sardinians for 349 days (1854-1855). The hero of the land defense was G. I. Totlebein; the Russian fleet was sunk to block the entrance to the harbor. In September 1855, the French successfully stormed the fortress of Malakhov, on the south shore of the bay, and three days later the Russians were forced to abandon Sebastopol.

SUFFRAGE CONVENTION OF THE COLORED CITIZENS OF NEW YORK, TROY,
SEPTEMBER 14, 1858

A Convention of colored people, consisting of thirty-seven delegates, (instead of four hundred, as a Troy Republican paper states,) met on Tuesday, the 14th inst., at Concert Hall, in the city of Troy, and organized by the appointment of the following officers:

President--Wm. Rich, of Troy.
Vice Presidents--F. Thompson, Rev. Wm. Butler, of Poughkeepsie; E. C. Sippens, of Utica.
Secretaries--J. H. Townsend, of New York; G. C. Levere, Brooklyn; W. Dietz, Albany.

A Business Committee was then appointed, consisting of W. J. Watkins, Rochester; J. C. Gibbs, Troy; J. J. Symonds, New York; W. F. Mowers, Poughkeepsie; W. W. Matthews, Albany; W. Johnson, Hudson; J. W. Duffin, Geneva; W. P. McIntyre, Albany; William Hodges, Brooklyn.

After the organization was effected, the Convention took a recess until 2½ o'clock.

The ladies, in the meantime, arranged, in an adjoining hall, a table loaded with the most palatable refreshments, which were eaten during the recess with a relish.

At 2½ o'clock, the Convention reassembled, and after prayer, as the Business Committee were not ready to report, speechifying commenced, and continued until the Committee came in, when the Chairman's hammer brought all to their seats and restored quiet, when Mr. Watkins, formerly associate editor of *Frederick Douglass' Paper*, but now the 'mouthpiece' of this Convention, made the following report from the Business Committee:--

1. Resolved, That we are more than ever convinced of the necessity of intelligent and consolidated action on the part of the colored men themselves, for the security of the rights guaranteed to them, as a part of *'the people,'* in the Constitution of the United States. We have a great work to perform in the conflict being waged between liberty and despotism; and, duly appreciating the duties and responsibilities devolving upon us, we should so act that our influence, as a political power, should be felt among the ranks of the people.

2. Resolved, That the Dred Scott decision[1] is a foul and infamous lie, which neither black men nor white men are bound to respect. It is a bold, impudent and atrocious attempt to extend and perpetuate the blasting curse of human bondage. We look upon it as an utterance of individual political opinions in striking contrast with the sacred guarantees for liberty with which the Constitution abounds. In order to satiate the wolfish appetite of the oligarchy, Judge Taney[2] and his concurring confederates were obliged to assume that the once revered signers of the Declaration of Independence, and the framers of the Constitution, were a band of hypocritical scoundrels and

selfish tyrants, tearing off the shackles by which they were themselves enslaved, and forging fetters more galling for the comparatively defenceless inhabitants among them--fetters which were to be riveted upon them while the Republic should endure. This venal Court was also obliged to set aside as a worthless parchment the Ordinance of '87, to trample upon former judicial decisions made in favor of liberty, and decide against 'State Sovereignty,' the pet lamb of the tyrant's flock. By this blast of the judiciary, compacts, constitutions, decisions and ordinances were not only driven out of Court, but struck utterly dumb--annihilated!

3. Resolved, That this deadly thrust is aimed not simply at the rights of the colored citizens of the Republic, but as slavery is the common enemy of man, and as its political supremacy has been authoritatively proclaimed by the majority of the Supreme Court, the natural rights of all who form a part of the nation are impudently invaded. We, therefore, call upon all who subscribe to the theory of human rights set forth in the Declaration of American Independence, to trample, in self-defence, the dicta of Judge Taney beneath their feet, as of no binding authority.

4. Resolved, That we *are* citizens of the State of New York, and, consequently, of the United States, and should enjoy all the rights and immunities of other citizens, the edict of Judge Taney to the contrary notwithstanding.

5. Resolved, That we will never cease our efforts to procure the repeal of the property qualification clause in our State Constitution, until success shall crown our labors.

6. Resolved, That in the even of the assembling of a Convention to revise the Constitution, in accordance with the act passed at the last session of the Legislature, we urge upon the members the justice and necessity of redeeming said Constitution from the disgrace now attached to it, in consequence of the unjust, anti-republican and odious restriction upon the exercise of the elective franchise.

7. Resolved, That in the ensuing gubernatorial election, it becomes us to act with special reference to securing the elective franchise. We can accomplish nothing in this direction save over the defeat and ruin of the so-called Democratic party, our most inveterate enemy. In order to secure this defeat, it is absolutely necessary to consolidate the strength of the opposition to said party.[3] And we regard the Republican party, all things considered, as more likely than any other to effect this desirable end, and advise the eleven thousand colored voters of this State to concentrate their strength upon the Republican ticket for Governor, &c., now before the people.

8. Resolved, That in so doing, we do not for a moment endorse all the political tenets of that party; we are Radical Abolitionists, and shall ever remain so; but we regard the nomination made by them at Syracuse as calculated to give aid and comfort to the enemy, by electing the Democratic candidate.

These resolutions were taken up seriatim, and formed the basis of a most exciting debate for three sessions of the Convention.

Messrs. Watkins, Symonds, Deyo, Hodges, Myers, Thompson, Townsend, Rich, Williams, Wright, Smith, Duffin, Garnet and others, took part in the debate.

The equal right of suffrage--the disfranchisement of the colored people--the property qualification--the oppression of the negro race--the best mode of obtaining a redress of their grievances--their determination to assert, maintain and secure their rights--the propriety of voting for the party which promised them the most present good--the comparative merits and demerits, the pro-slavery and anti-slavery character of the different parties--were subjects of discussion.

The seventh resolution, recommending the eleven thousand colored voters of this State to go for the Republican party, was the great bone of contention.

A majority of the members, coming from two or three of the large cities in the eastern part of the State--where they live under the influence of Republican profession and promises--had been made to believe the Republicans would give them their rights, and were, therefore, in favor of the resolutions; while the more intelligent portion of the Convention--such men as Garnet, Duffin, Smith, Williams, and others--opposed it. These gentlemen spoke with great ability and earnestness against the inconsistent and unwise course of the majority, but to no effect. Under the previous question, they shut off discussion, and passed the resolution.

The evening meetings were full of both black and white, and very able speeches were made by Mr. Watkins and Mr. Garnet. Mr. Garnet's speech on Tuesday evening exhibited rare points of analysis, logic, wit and eloquence, and was listened to with the greatest pleasure and applause. We have seldom, if ever, heard Mr. Garnet when he was more happy. We were greatly disappointed at the course of Mr. Watkins; we have known him for a long time, and know he has no confidence in the Republican party--that he has no sympathy with their principles, politics or actions. We have heard him denounce the party in the strongest terms. He is a *radical* abolitionist, as all the colored men of the Convention declared themselves to be. He is no mere *non-extensionist*, but a *prohibitionist*. He knows no law for slavery. The Republican party, on the other hand, repudiate both abolition and prohibition. They acknowledge law and Constitution for slavery, and would to-day surrender the very members of that Convention, were they fugitives from slavery, into hopeless bondage. We were still more surprised to hear Mr. Watkins misrepresent Mr. Smith's views on two or three important points, the result of which would be, whether intended or not, to prejudice Mr. S. in the minds of the colored people.

Mr. Garnet and Mr. Duffin wish it distinctly understood that they have no sympathy with this movement, and do not wish to have their names identified with it.

We are informed that there will soon be a general Convention of the colored people of this State, perhaps at Rochester, or some central place, to take more considerate action on this subject.--[*Correspondent of the N. Y. 'Hour and the Man,' a Gerrit Smith paper.*]

The Liberator, October 1, 1858.

REFERENCE NOTES

1. The Dred Scott Decision was rendered by the Supreme Court on March 6, 1857. Dred Scott, a slave, had been brought by his master into Louisiana Territory north of the line above which slavery was prohibited by law. After he was returned to the slave state of Missouri, he sued for his freedom. Chief Justice Roger B. Taney, writing the majority opinion, held that Dred Scott could never be a citizen within the meaning of the Constitution and therefore had no right to sue in a federal court. The Negro, Taney insisted, possessed "no rights that a white man is bound to respect." Taney also went on to declare that the Missouri Compromise was unconstitutional when it forbade slavery above 36° 30' north latitude.

2. Roger B. Taney (1774-1864), chief justice of the United States Supreme Court (1836-1864), handed down the Dred Scott Decision of 1857.

3. During the gubernatorial campaign of 1858, blacks in New York State were confronted with a dilemma. In that year, Gerrit Smith, candidate of the Radical Abolitionist Party, a group formed at Syracuse, New York, in June 1855, was running against the Republican, Edwin D. Morgan and a Democrat. Blacks had to decide whether to vote for Smith, their longtime friend and benefactor, or the Republican Morgan. Since the Democratic Party was divided and it was conceded by nearly all blacks that Smith had no chance to win, the Republicans under Morgan seemed the more likely choice. But, if too many votes were given Smith, the Republicans would very possibly go down to defeat. Hence it seemed imperative that the black vote not be divided.

As many had hoped, Morgan was elected. Gerrit Smith received only 5,033 votes. See the *New York Tribune*, Nov. 20, 1858. See also George Walker, "The Afro-American in New York City, 1827-1860," pp. 205-207.

PROCEEDINGS OF THE PENNSYLVANIA CONVENTIONS

INTRODUCTION

The State Convention of the Colored Freemen of Pennsylvania, Pittsburgh, August 23-25, 1841, assembled for the specific purpose of calling attention to the recent disfranchisement of blacks within the state and to suggest means of regaining the suffrage. Unlike New York, which required a property test before a black could vote, Pennsylvania barred all blacks from the ballot box by adding the word "white" to male in the revised constitution of 1838.
Delegates from virtually every county of any significance in Pennsylvania were represented. While debate on the suffrage issues consumed most of the time of the gathering, other significant resolutions were also passed. One (resolution 14) called upon each delegate on arriving home "to make out a statistical report of the District, including the Churches, Schools, Benevolent Societies, amount of Property, Taxes, Paupers, &c., and forward the same to the Publishing Committee immediately."
The second black state convention to assemble in Pennsylvania met in Harrisburg, December 13 and 14, 1848. Prominent in its proceedings were such well-known Pennsylvania blacks as Robert Purvis, Isaiah C. Weir, Dr. David J. Peck, Reverend Stephen Smith, J. J. G. Bias, James McCrummell, and John B. Vashon. The convention assembled primarily to focus attention on the continued denial of the franchise, and once again the delegates appealed firmly and logically for restoration of the suffrage.
The largest Pennsylvania black state convention was the State Equal Rights Convention, held in Harrisburg, February 8-10, 1865, with nearly one hundred delegates in attendance. Like its predecessors, this gathering condemned the continued denial of the franchise to the Negro people of Pennsylvania, but now strengthened the condemnation by pointing out that this deprivation continued even though many blacks had come to the rescue of a nation and government torn by a Civil War. It did note, however, in its second resolution "that the Emancipation of the District of Columbia, Maryland, Louisiana, Missouri and Tennessee; the amendment of the Federal Constitution [abolishing slavery], and its endorsement by various State Legislatures, including that of Pennsylvania; the admission of John S. Rock to the Supreme Court of the United States; and the progress of liberal sentiments everywhere manifest, are auspicious signs of the times, and demand our earnest and united efforts for the improvement of our moral, social and political condition."
In the Appendix of the Proceedings, the Convention expressed elation that the institution of slavery had been extirpated from American soil, but was chagrined to note that prejudice, its twin monster, continued to cast its shadow, a "prejudice barring against us the doors of your public libraries, of your colleges of science, of your popular lecture rooms, of your military academies, of your jury boxes, of your ballot boxes, of your churches, of your theatres, and even of your common street cars." It concluded by saying "and knowing all this to be the direct result of the defunct system of barbarism --American slavery--we now ask that, as you have slain the cause with the re-

bellion, you give us security against the continuance of the effect, as manifested in the existence of these inhuman prejudices and prohibitions."

PROCEEDINGS OF THE STATE CONVENTION OF THE COLORED FREEMEN OF PENNSYLVANIA, HELD IN PITTSBURGH, ON THE 23d, 24th AND 25th OF AUGUST, 1841, FOR THE PURPOSE OF CONSIDERING THEIR CONDITION, AND THE MEANS OF ITS IMPROVEMENT

CIRCULAR

TO THE COLORED FREEMEN OF THE COMMONWEALTH
OF PENNSYLVANIA

Agreeably to previous notice, a large and respectable meeting of the Colored People of Pittsburgh was held, in the public School-Room, on Tuesday evening, Jan. 12th, 1841. The meeting was organized by appointing John Peck,[1] President; George Gardner and J. B. Vashon,[2] Vice Presidents; T. A. Brown and John N. Templeton, Secretaries.

The object of the meeting was stated by the President to be, the consideration of the present disfranchisement of the Colored People of the Commonwealth of Pennsylvania, and of measures for obtaining the exercise of that sacred right.

On motion, a resolution was adopted, approving of the holding of a STATE CONVENTION.

The hour growing late, and the meeting having greatly increased in interest as well as in numbers, it was, on motion, resolved, that the meeting adjourn to meet again on next Tuesday evening, and that a Committee of seven be appointed to draft a proper Preamble and Resolutions for the consideration of the next meeting.

On this Committee the meeting appointed Lewis Woodson, Martin R. Delaney,[3] P. Jackson, Thomas Norris, J. B. Vashon, George Galbreath, and Daniel Carney.

Tuesday Evening, January 19, 1841.

Public meeting of the Colored People of Pittsburgh, in Bethel Church, in Front Street, according to adjournment. The officers of the previous meeting were present, and in their seats. The meeting was opened for the dispatch of business with prayer.

The proceedings of the previous meeting were read, and remarks explanatory of its object were made by the President, and one of the Vice Presidents.

The Chairman of the Committee to draft a Preamble and Resolutions for the consideration of the meeting was then called on for his report, which was read by him, as follows:

The Committee appointed by a public meeting of the Colored Citizens of Pittsburgh, on the 12th day of January, 1841, to draft a Preamble and Resolutions expressive of their views on the subject of holding a State Convention, to consider measures for obtaining the exercise of the right of the elective franchise, beg leave to submit the following:[4]

REPORT.--Whereas, among all the rights of a Republic none are so sacred, and among all the safeguards of the liberties of freemen none are so powerful, as the right of suffrage--a right, indeed, which gives political existence to those who possess it, and is political annihilation to those who are deprived of it--a right paramount in vitality and importance to all political rights; and to obtain which when deprived of it, no labor should be counted too severe, no sacrifice too great--and, Whereas, the Colored Citizens of the Commonwealth of Pennsylvania are, by her present Constitution, deprived of the exercise of this sacred right, for no other cause than that it has pleased the Almighty Creator to clothe them with a dark hue, a circumstance over which they had no control, and for which no just tribunal can or will hold them accountable, and to punish them for which, with the highest political privation, is not only doing violence to nature herself, but is offering insult and mockery to the Almighty Creator of all things and Judge of all men--and, Whereas, the history of the past, the observation of the present, and the word and providence of God, show, that those who exert themselves most are the most successful in the attainment of the object of their lawful pursuit; and that those who will exert themselves none, even lose that which they have; and that no honest condition is so hopeless, but that it may be improved and elevated, by the use of just and honorable means--and, Whereas, in opposition to this just and wholesome maxim, the Colored People of the Commonwealth of Pennsylvania have hitherto maintained an apathy and indifference, not only to the exercise of the elective franchise, but to other collateral rights of high importance to them as freemen; an apathy and indifference highly criminal, and for which it is feared they are not prepared to give a satisfactory account, neither to God, their own consciences, nor posterity; and to maintain which apathy and indifference longer, would degrade them still lower in the eyes of all enlightened and good men. Therefore,

Gentlemen:--We are assembled, for the first time, in Pennsylvania, in State Convention; and it is matter of high gratification to witness the presence of so many Delegates on the first day of our meeting. It is strong evidence of the deep interest which we feel in the great object which has brought us together. The object of our Convention is, to consider the condition of our people in this Commonwealth, and to devise means for its improvement. The various grievances which we suffer will be brought to your notice in the progress of the business of the Convention; and it is not, therefore, necessary that I should now stop to mention them. Our Convention will be organized, and our business transacted, in the usual manner; and I hope that all may be done in a manner creditable to ourselves, our immediate constituents, and the Commonwealth of Pennsylvania.

The Delegates then presented their credentials; and those who had come without any, gave in their names to the Secretary.

On motion of Thomas A. Brown, seconded by A. D. Lewis,

Resolved, That a Committee of nine be appointed by the chair, to nominate officers for this Convention.

On this Committee the chair appointed Thomas A. Brown, John N. Templeton, J. Curtis, Thomas Norris, Halson Vashon, Joseph H. Mahorney, P. L. Jackson, Samuel Williams, Thomas S. Robinson.

On motion of Thomas Norris, seconded by John B. Vashon,

Resolved, That a Committee of five be appointed to draft rules for the government of this Convention.

On this Committee the Convention appointed Thomas Norris, A. D. Lewis, John B. Vashon, Edward R. Parker, John Peck.

On motion of John B. Vashon, seconded by Thomas A. Brown,

Resolved, That the officers of this Convention shall be one President, three Vice Presidents, and three Secretaries.

And then the Convention adjourned until half past two in the afternoon.

Monday Afternoon, half past two o'clock.

The Convention assembled pursuant to adjournment, and was opened with prayer by Rev. Leonard Collins.

The committee to nominate officers for the Convention made the following report, which was accepted; and the persons named therein declared duly elected officers of this Convention.

John Peck, of Allegheny, *President*.

William Portor, of Cambria,
Thomas S. Robinson, of Washington, } *Vice Presidents*.
Nathaniel M'Curdy, of Greene,

Lewis Woodson, of Pittsburgh,
John Templeton, of Pittsburgh, } *Secretaries*.
Wm. L. Barns, of Allegheny,

On taking his seat, the President addressed the Convention in a brief and appropriate manner; thanking them for the honor conferred by electing him to preside over their deliberations; noticing the object which had brought them together; and asking their co-operation and support in the performance of the duties of his office.

On motion of Lewis Woodson, seconded by T. A. Brown,

Resolved, That a committee of seven be appointed, whose duty it shall be to prepare business for this Convention.

On this committee the Convention appointed John B. Vashon, Lewis Woodson, Martin R. Delaney, Thomas A. Brown, A. D. Lewis, Halson Vashon, Leonard Collins.

On motion of M. R. Delaney, seconded by Samuel Bruce,

Resolved, That the Committee of Arrangements, appointed by the Corresponding Committee of Allegheny county, to receive and attend to the accommodation of Delegates to this Convention, be continued; and that they attend to the accommodation of ladies and gentlemen visiting this Convention, and to the preservation of order.

The committee on rules for the government of the Convention made their report, which, after undergoing sundry amendments, was adopted, as follows:

1. The President shall take the chair at the hour to which the Convention adjourned, and call the Convention to order.

2. The minutes of the preceding session shall be read, when errors, if any, shall be corrected.

3. The President shall decide all questions of order, subject to an appeal to the Convention.

4. All motions and addresses shall be made to the President, the member rising from his seat.

5. All motions, except those of reference, shall be submitted in writing.

6. All committees shall be nominated by the President, unless otherwise ordered by the Convention.

7. The previous question shall always be in order, and, until decided, shall preclude all amendments and debate of the main question; and shall be put in this form, "shall the main question be now put?"

8. No member shall be interrupted while speaking, except when out of order, when he shall be called to order by the President.

9. A motion to adjourn shall always be in order, and shall be decided without debate.

10. No member shall speak more than twice on the same question; nor longer than thirty minutes at any one time.

11. A motion to reconsider can only be made by one who voted in the majority, and at a session succeeding the one in which the question was decided.

12. No resolution, except to amend, to refer, to postpone, to lay on the table, or to adjourn, shall be offered to the Convention, except it come through the business committee.

13. The sessions of the Convention shall commence at ten o'clock in the forenoon, and at half past two in the afternoon.

14. Each session shall open and close with prayer.

And then the Convention adjourned until ten o'clock to-morrow morning. Prayer by Rev. A. D. Lewis.

Tuesday Morning, August 24th, 1841.

The Convention assembled pursuant to adjournment, and was opened with prayer by Rev. Samuel Williams, of Cambria.

The minutes of the preceding session were read and corrected. The rules of the Convention were also read, for the information of such Delegates as had arrived since the afternoon session of yesterday.

All new Delegates were requested to hand in their credentials or their names to the third Secretary, whose business it was to attend to the roll.

The business committee then reported the following preamble and resolutions:

Whereas, a call for a State Convention of the Colored Freemen of the Commonwealth of Pennsylvania, to be held in the City of Pittsburgh, on Monday, the 23d, day of August, 1841, signed by numerous freemen of said Commonwealth, was issued by the Corresponding Committee of Allegheny county, on the 17th of July, 1841, to consider measures for the elevation of said freemen in said Commonwealth: *And*, *whereas*, said call has been responded to by the assembling of a large number of Delegates, elected in pursuance thereof, and at the time and place expressed therein: *And*, *whereas*, the Convention thus assembled owe it to themselves, their immediate constituents, and the public generally, to make an expression of their wishes and sentiments: Therefore,

1. *Resolved,* By the COLORED FREEMEN of the Commonwealth of Pennsylvania, in STATE CONVENTION assembled, That we love the Commonwealth of Pennsylvania, and feel an inseparable attachment to her institutions and just laws; and deem it alike our duty and our privilege, at all times, to sustain and uphold them.

2. *Resolved,* That as we ever have performed, and ever intend to perform, all duties imposed upon us, as good citizens of the Commonwealth of Pennsylvania, we deem it but just that we should, in common with others, enjoy all the privileges and immunities of citizens; and therefore view with deepest regret that restriction in the third article of her Constitution, which deprives us, as colored men, of the right of suffrage.

3. *Resolved,* That all restrictions in our State Constitution founded upon complexion are impolitic, oppressive, and wrong; and that we will use, and continue to use, all lawful and honorable means to have them abolished.

4. *Resolved,* That we will petition our State Legislature, so to amend the Constitution of this Commonwealth, as to remove all restrictions on account of color; and that we will continue to petition until our prayer is granted.

The preamble and resolutions were each taken up and considered separately, and were discussed at length, by gentlemen, Peck, Vashon, A. D. Lewis, Woodson, and Brown. When the discussion was arrested, by a motion to adjourn until half past two o'clock in the afternoon.

Tuesday Afternoon, half past two o'clock.
The Convention assembled pursuant to adjournment. The President called the Convention to order, and opened with prayer by Rev. Samuel Johnson.

The minutes of the forenoon session were read and approved.

The discussion on the resolutions of the business committee was resumed, and further remarks were made by gentlemen, Delany, and Collins, of Franklin. After which the whole were unanimously adopted.

The business committee further reported the following resolutions:

5. *Resolved,* That we recommend to our people EDUCATION as a powerful means of their elevation; and that we especially advise them to educate their children, and have them instructed in some useful trade, without which they never can attain to any respectable rank in society.

6. *Resolved,* That as newspapers contain, beside the ordinary news of the day, much useful knowledge, which tends to enlighten the understanding and improve the character, we therefore recommend that every family, who can possibly afford it, take one or more well conducted newspapers.

7. *Resolved,* That as Intemperance is a great source of degradation, misery, and crime, rendering its victims a curse to themselves, their families, and society; we therefore recommend our people, as they love themselves and their posterity, and the esteem of all wise and virtuous men, and as they love their rights and hope to obtain them, to abstain TOTALLY from the use of all intoxicating liquors; and that wherever there is a sufficient number in one place, they form societies on the plan of TOTAL ABSTINENCE.

8. *Resolved,* That in the opinion of this Convention, no calling is more honorable, independent, and virtuous, than farming; and that, as there now is, and must continue to be, much competition among common laborers in all our large towns and cities; and that according to common usage, it may be expected

that the most favored class will generally be preferred; we therefore recommend all our people, who are not successful mechanics, to become cultivators of the soil.

9. *Resolved,* That this Convention advise the people of color throughout this state, to discontinue public processions on any day, as being highly prejudicial to their interest as a people.

The resolutions were taken up and considered separately. Remarks upon them were made by gentlemen, Lewis, Norris, Jackson, Hilton, Chidester, Delaney, Collins of Franklin, Vashon, and Woodson; and the whole were unanimously adopted.

On motion of L. Woodson, seconded by S. Williams,

Resolved, That a committee of five be appointed to draft an address to the people of color in this state, to accompany the proceedings of this Convention.

On this committee the President appointed Lewis Woodson, N. M'Curdy, Richard Chidester, J. B. Vashon, Samuel Williams.

And then the Convention adjourned, to meet again on to-morrow morning at ten o'clock. Prayer by Rev. A. D. Lewis.

Wednesday Morning, August 25, 1841.

The Convention assembled pursuant to adjournment. The President being absent, the second Vice President took the chair, and called the Convention to order. Prayer by the first Secretary.

The minutes of the previous meetings were read and approved.

The business committee further reported the following resolutions:

10. *Resolved,* That until we can establish a newspaper of our own in this state, the COLORED AMERICAN be considered our general public organ.[5]

11. *Resolved,* That in the opinion of this Convention, a newspaper conducted by the colored people, and adapted to their wants, is much needed in this state; and that we request their general co-operation, especially in the east, in establishing such a paper.

12. *Resolved,* That there be a State Corresponding Committee of twenty appointed, whose duty it shall be, to carry out the measures of this Convention in regard to the elevation of our people in this Commonwealth.

On this committee the President nominated the following persons, and the Convention confirmed the nomination, viz:

Lewis Woodson, John B. Vashon, Abraham D. Lewis, Richard Bryans, John N. Templeton, Lewis McAlfrey, Charles Richards, Samuel Bruce, Jr., Thomas A. Brown, Samuel Williams, Henry Anderson, Nathaniel M'Curdy, A. D. Shadd,[6] C. T. Clayton, Stephen Smith,[7] James Needham, Robert Gordon, William Webb, Charles Dorris, Leonard Collins.

The Convention then appointed Thomas Norris and Thomas A. Brown, a committee to receive statistical reports; and went into committee of the whole, R. Bryans of Fayette in the chair, to hear and receive such reports from Delegates.

After spending some time in hearing and receiving reports, the committee arose, and the President resumed the chair.

On motion, *Resolved,* That a committee of five, on Publication, be appointed. On this committee the President appointed, Lewis Woodson, John N. Templeton, J. B. Vashon, Thomas Norris, A. D. Lewis.

On motion, The statistics in the hands of the committee appointed to receive them, were referred to the committee on publication.

And then the Convention adjourned, to meet again at half past two in the afternoon. Prayer by Rev. S. Johnson.

Wednesday Afternoon, half past two o'clock.

The Convention assembled pursuant to adjournment. The President called the Convention to order, and opened with prayer by the Rev. Leonard Collins.

The minutes of the previous session were read and approved.

The business committee further reported the following resolutions, which were considered separately, and adopted:

13. *Resolved,* That this Convention authorize the State Corresponding Committee to employ a suitable Agent, to travel through the State, deliver lectures to our people, and perform such other duties as may be assigned him, in carrying out the measures of this Convention.

14. *Resolved,* That it shall be the duty of each Delegation, on their return home, to make out a statistical report of their District, including the Churches, Schools, Benevolent Societies, amount of Property, Taxes, Paupers, &c., and forward the same to the Publishing Committee immediately.

15. *Resolved,* That this Convention recommend to our people generally, and to the Delegates here assembled in particular, to call COUNTY CONVENTIONS, and form associations for raising moneys, to defray the expenses of such Agent as may be appointed to visit them, and to assist in carrying out the measures of this Convention.

16. *Resolved,* That we recommend the holding of another State Convention, east of the mountains, some time during the summer of 1842.

The Convention then went into committee of the whole, to raise funds for defraying the expenses of printing, &c. After spending a short time, $30.52 were collected. The committee arose, and the President resumed the chair.

On motion, The moneys collected in committee of the whole were handed over to J. B. Vashon, Treasurer of the Conventional Fund for Allegheny county, to be held in trust by him for the publishing and corresponding committees of this Convention.

The business committee further reported the following resolutions:

17. *Resolved,* That we respectfully tender our thanks to His Honor, the Mayor of this city, and his efficient and gentlemanly Police, for the protection which they have afforded this Convention during its sitting.

18. *Resolved,* That the thanks of this Convention be tendered to the good citizens of Pittsburgh, for the kind and hospitable manner in which they have entertained us during our sitting.

19. *Resolved,* That the special thanks of this Convention be tendered to the gentlemanly and accomplished Police Officer, who has waited upon us during our sitting, to preserve order among spectators and others, for the faithful manner in which he has performed his duty; and that with our thanks he also be presented with the sum of $5.

20. *Resolved,* That the thanks of this Convention be tendered to the ladies, for their presence during its sitting.

21. *Resolved,* That our thanks be returned to the Trustees, for the use of this Church for the sitting of this Convention.

The third Secretary, whose business it was to attend to the credentials and names of Delegates was called upon, and reported that he had collected and enrolled the names of all the Delegates. The roll was called over, corrected, and approved.

A letter from a great meeting of the City and County of Philadelphia, approving of the Convention, and containing the names of fifteen Delegates elected to represent them therein; together with a request that they should be remembered in the proceedings of the Convention, was received by the publishing committee; and they have agreed that the names of the Philadelphia Delegates shall be added to the roll, although they did not in person attend the Convention.

The whole minutes of the Convention, from the commencement to the close, were read over, corrected, and approved.

On motion, The Publishing Committee were authorized to make such corrections and amendments in the minutes, as may be necessary, to fit them for publication; provided they preserve their spirit and intention.

The business committee then reported their final resolution, which was unanimously adopted:

22. *Resolved,* That the proceedings of this Convention, together with the address, be signed by its officers, printed in pamphlet form, and published.

The venerable and Rev. Samuel Collins then arose, and briefly addressed the Convention; expressing his high gratification at having witnessed the excellent spirit which pervaded it from the commencement to the close; its good order, and the correct and statesman like manner in which it had transacted its business; and concluded by solemnly invoking the blessing of Almighty God upon each member, and upon the doings of the Convention.

The President then addressed the Convention, noticing in a brief and appropriate manner its various doings, and their happy results if properly carried out; the responsibility of each member, and of every individual in the

Commonwealth, in regard to carrying them out; the pleasing fact that so large a Delegation had been together for three days, had transacted much deeply interesting business, without a single unpleasant occurrence; and that we were now about to separate with the blessing of a good man, whose head was whited with the frosts of eighty winters, upon each member, and upon the doings of the Convention.

The whole assembly then united in singing that beautify and impressive hymn, beginning with "Before Jehovah's awful throne," to Old Hundred, with indescribable fervor and pathos; the voices of the ladies, who crowded the gallery, uniting with those of the men from below, producing an effect, which to be appreciated must have been heard. The Rev. Lewis Woodson then led in a solemn and appropriate prayer.

And then, on motion, the Convention adjourned, *sine die*.

John Peck, President.

William Porter,
Thomas S. Robinson, } Vice Presidents.
Nathaniel M'Curdy,

Lewis Woodson,
John N. Templeton, } Secretaries.
William L. Barns,

In pursuance of the duty assigned them by a resolution of the Convention, the undersigned Committee respectfully present to the Colored Freemen of the Commonwealth of Pennsylvania the following

ADDRESS

You have doubtless read the foregoing Proceedings of our Convention, with that attention and interest which their importance demands. Were they the proceedings of any similar meeting, they would be read with attention and interest, on account of their intrinsic merit; but how much more, when it is remembered that they are the exclusive production of the first State Convention ever held in Pennsylvania, by us, as an oppressed people, to consider our condition, and the means of its improvement.

Excellent as the proceedings are, it will be matter of high gratification to you to know, that the spirit in which they were conducted was equal in excellence with themselves. The good order of the Convention, and the correct and prudent manner in which it transacted its business, was matter of admiration to all who visited it. Indeed, it was considered next to a miracle, that such a large number of men could be together for three days, and transact so much important business, without a single unpleasant occurrence.

But, creditable as our Convention has been to all who were in any way concerned in it, and happy as its influence has been, alike upon its members and its numerous visitors and spectators, it is by no means to be considered as the end of the great work of our elevation in this Commonwealth. On the contrary, it should be considered, as it really is, only a happy beginning. He who supposest that meeting together and passing resolutions, however wise and excellent in themselves, will attain our end, is mistaken. And if he builds his hope of success upon such a foundation, let him know assuredly that he builds upon sand.

The resolutions must be carried out; their spirit must be lived up to, and their instructions practiced; otherwise we may look in vain for their happy result. They were drawn up with great care, and strict reference to all the circumstances and relations of our present condition. Their principles are founded in truth, and will prove, to all who embrace them, a foundation which cannot be shaken. The experience and close observation of many years teach us that they are wisely adapted to our best interests, and, if carried out in the spirit and design of the Convention, will unquestionably raise us in society far above our present level.

Our purpose, in this address, is to notice the various resolutions of the Convention; the considerations which induced them; the means by which their objects are to be accomplished; and their result, if properly carried out. We

shall arrange our address under as many heads as it naturally contains, and
consider the several resolutions under their appropriate heads. By pursuing
this course, we believe that each part may be better remembered, and better
understood.--We begin with

The Right of Suffrage

A restriction in the third article of the Constitution of Pennsylvania
deprives us, as colored men, of the right of suffrage; and a resolution of
the Convention declares this restriction to be impolitic, oppressive, and
wrong. It is impolitic for the state thus to restrict any portion of her
inhabitants, because it degrades them, and in so far detracts from the honor
and respectability of the state. It deprives them of one of the most powerful
stimulants to a virtuous and upright life; paralyzes their efforts to attain
wealth and respectability; and thus lessens the general wealth of the state,
and the amount of taxes which would otherwise be paid into the state treasury.
It is oppressive, because we are required to pay the same homage and obedience
to the laws as other citizens, and the same taxes, and are yet denied the
same equivalent. It also deprives us of political defence. Our worst
adversary may be a candidate for an office, the salary of which is in part
made up of taxes paid out of our own pockets, and yet we have not the power
of casting a single vote to prevent his triumph. It tears away the bulwark,
the very citadel of our liberties, and leaves us exposed on every side. It
is wrong, because it inflicts punishment upon the innocent. The elective
franchise is the highest privilege known to republicans; it is the foundation
and only safeguard of all political rights; and to deprive one of it, is to
inflict the highest political punishment.

But what is our crime, that such excessive punishment should be inflicted
upon us? What abuse have we ever made of this privilege? What is there in
our past history to show, that in so far as our number or influence is concerned, the interests of the state, and of the nation, may not be safely
trusted in our hands? Under all circumstances, and upon all occasions, we
have been faithful to our country and obedient to her laws; and in so far as
we have been permitted, have contributed our share to its happiness and
prosperity; and we deem it but simple justice that we should, in common with
others, share its privileges.

Before dismissing this part of our address, permit us to say a few words
in regard to the payment of

Taxes

Some have supposed, that because we are not allowed to vote, we ought not
to pay taxes; but this is in part a mistake. Taxation was in use, long before
voting, as it is practised in this country, was known; and the equivalent
which men in those days received for their taxes was protection. The subject
paid into the treasury of the king so much taxes; and the king granted the
subject, as an equivalent, so much protection. Such is the case in many
powerful kingdoms even at the present day; such as Russia, Austria, Turkey,
&c. The power that receives taxes is always bound to protect; and the
Commonwealth of Pennsylvania, by receiving into her treasury our taxes,
guarantees to us the protection of her laws. We pay our taxes, then, not the
less for our vote, but the more for the protection of the laws.

The important subject of

Education

next claims our attention; and we cannot too much commend to your attention
and practice, the resolution of the Convention on this subject. Considered in
itself, education is a matter of the first importance, on account of the
moral pleasure and elevation which it imparts to its possessor; but when, in
addition to this, it is remembered that it qualifies for every thing useful,
good, and great, its importance is infinite. But the education which we
recommend is that which qualifies for usefulness in its best and most extensive sense; and is not finished, until its subject has learned some trade,
by which he may decently maintain himself in society. Labor is the natural

source of wealth, and is not only right in the sight of God, but honorable in the eyes of all good men; and those who give their children a good education and a trade, give them the best of all fortunes; one infinitely better than silver and gold, because it can neither be squandered nor lost. We therefore most earnestly entreat you, as you love your children, and desire their future usefulness and respectability in society, the happiness of your own declining days, and the general good of your country, to make every possible exertion and every necessary sacrifice, to give them a good education and a trade. We would pursue this important subject more in detail, but deem it unnecessary, because the moment you become rightly interested in it, you will find numerous friends around you, ready to give all necessary advice and assistance.

Newspapers and the Press

next claim our attention. The utility of newspapers is two-fold: 1, to impart intelligence, and, 2, to unite. They are the present history of the world; and he who does not read them is almost as though he were shut up in prison. They tend to inspire public spirit and enterprise, especially in the young, and on that account no family should be without them: it were better that our children should eat plainer diet, and dress in coarser apparel, than to be deprived of the use of a well conducted newspaper. But, in addition to their intelligence, newspapers tend to impart the same sentiments and the same views to all who read them. They bring as it were into the society of each other, the most distant places and kingdoms of the earth. We imagine the day not far distant, when, by the influence of the press, shall be united in one, the whole family of man.

But circumstances make it absolutely necessary, that we should have a press of our own. It is just as absurd to imagine, that we can become intelligent and enterprising, by others speaking and writing for us, as that we can become fat by their eating and drinking for us. It is true that kind friends may persuade the master to unrivet the fetters of the slave, and the Legislature to repeal all unjust and unwholesome laws; but here their kind offices measurably end; the balance of the work is chiefly ours.

To purchase a press and its accompanying apparatus, would cost from five to seven hundred dollars; and to print an ordinary sheet, such as our case would require, would cost perhaps a little upwards of thirty-five dollars a week; amounting in a year say to two thousand dollars. And what are our resources for sustaining this expense? Our population is near fifty thousand; and although the statistical returns to our Convention were very imperfect, yet they were sufficient to show that we own at least two million dollars' worth of property. And will any one presume that one thousand subscribers, able to pay two dollars a year each for a good paper, cannot be found in all those numbers, and all this wealth?

We next call your attention to the subject of

Temperance

And although highly important, we shall not dwell upon it at any length; because it has been so generally agitated throughout the state, you must understand all its consequences as well as ourselves. Temperate as we fondly hope we generally are, yet it is feared more is squandered for ardent spirits, than would furnish us with a newspaper, educate our children, and support our churches. We exhort you, by every consideration, to do all in your power to banish from society this scourge and curse of our race, by promoting every where the popular and unfailing principle of TOTAL ABSTINENCE.

The resolution of the Convention on

Farming

contains the reasons which induced its adoption; and we can not too earnestly recommend it to your careful attention. We have been too long, and too justly, we are sorry to admit, charged with crowding into the large towns and cities, where it is impossible for us to find honorable or profitable employment. So long as we pursue this most pernicious practice, we must expect to remain degraded and despised. Its evils are innumerable, only a few of which can be noticed here.

1. The want of constant and profitable employment must forever keep us poor.

2. Poverty exposes us to insult and abuse from others, without the proper means of defending ourselves; and it also creates strong temptation to the commission of crime.

3. It prevents parents from bringing up their children in an orderly and proper manner, rendering them unfit for anything honorable or useful in future life.

4. It compels them to put their children out at service, to perform the most degrading drudgery, for a bare subsistence, which often proves alike fatal to their health and their morals. This is most lamentably true as it regards our females. The very heart sickens even to think of the insults and miseries which they suffer in large towns and cities; it is enough to extinguish every delicate and virtuous feeling peculiar to the sex.

5. The inevitable poverty of our people, in the cities, crowds them into dwellings, and places, distinguished for any thing but comfort and health; and every one knows that the consequence of inhabiting such dwellings is disease and death. Within the last ten years, causes which we shall not stop here to notice, have either prevented or destroyed the lives of more than two hundred thousand of our people in the United States; and will we lay to, with our own self-murdering hands, and help on this work of death?

6. By settling in the country, and becoming independent farmers, we would escape almost entirely that prejudice which operates so injuriously against us in the cities. It is a mistake to suppose that there is any prejudice against mere *color*. Gentlemen and ladies, distinguished alike for their learning, their virtues, and their taste, have articles of dress, furniture, and equipage, of black, and every variety of color. Indeed, a full suit of black is universally considered the most rich and magnificent that can possibly be worn. Hence prejudice is not against *color*, but against *condition;* therefore improve the condition, and you destroy the prejudice.

We can pursue this part of our address no further; but again must earnestly entreat all our people, who are not successful mechanics, to settle in the country, and become cultivators of the soil.

The last resolution of the Convention to which we shall invite your particular attention, is that in regard to holding

County Conventions

We recommend this measure to you in the confidence of experience. It has been tried in several counties, with the most eminent success. In many places the people knew nothing of their resources or ability to help themselves, until they called one of these general meetings. There are no means like it, for stirring up the feelings, creating public spirit, and bringing about the important results. Hold your County Conventions, and out of them will grow your Temperance, Education, Literary, and Benevolent Societies. And in them you can devise means for raising the funds mentioned in the resolution of the Convention. To carry out the measures of the Convention will require much labor and some funds; more perhaps than any one district can well bear; and it would be unjust to expect that one district should bear all the burthen, when the whole are to share in the benefit. Each district, and each individual, will therefore come forward cheerfully, and contribute their share.

We have thus briefly called your attention to the principal general resolutions of the Convention, the considerations which induced them, the means of accomplishing their objects; and it only remains for us to speak briefly of their result, if carried out in the spirit and intention of the Convention.

We wish to impress most distinctly upon your minds, what we mentioned in the outstart, that the Convention never intended the passage of the resolutions to be the end of our labor, but rather only the beginning. It was well aware that we have been too long, and too justly, charged with beginning every thing, and accomplishing nothing; but it was believed that the time has come, when we are prepared to put this charge to silence; when we will not only begin, but accomplish our designs. It passed them under the full expectation that every individual in the Commonwealth would heartily respond to them, and cheerfully assist in carrying them out. And if thus responded to, and thus carried out, just as sure as the rays of the sun warm the frozen earth, and cause it to produce its fruit in its season, or as the rivers run from the mountains to the ocean, we will be raised to the rank of a wealth, intelligent, and virtuous people.

In conclusion, it is true, that in this Commonwealth we suffer some grievances; but at the same time we enjoy many privileges; and let us not abuse one of them, but use all to the best advantage. Thus we will show, that although we do not enjoy all our rights, we at least deserve them.

The present is a most important crisis in our history. The whole country is more or less agitated on our account, and all eyes are upon us. Every one must therefore feel the necessity of the utmost circumspection in all our conduct, whether private or public. We owe this to God, if we hope for His blessings; to ourselves, if we wish to obtain our rights, and to our posterity, if we wish them to rise up and call us blessed.

> Lewis Woodson, of Allegheny,
> Richard Chidester, of Fayette,
> Samuel Williams, of Cambria,   *Committee.*
> Nathaniel M'Curdy, of Greene,
> John B. Vashon, of Allegheny,

ROLL

Thomas Norris,
Rev. Samuel Collins,
Rev. A. D. Lewis,
Charles Richards,
Rev. Lewis Woodson,
John B. Vashon,
Solomon Norris,
John Peck, of P.,
Samuel Bruce, Sr.,
George W. Parker,
John N. Templeton,
Martin R. Delaney,
George Gardner,
Robert L. Hawkins,
John Curtis,
John Mitchell, Sr.,
Benjamin P. Calder,
Matthew Jones,
Halson Vashon,
William M. Austin,
David Dickens,
Isaiah Watson,
Henry Burton,
Samuel Bailey,
Alfred Gibson,
Robert Smith, Sr.,
Henry Anderson,
Alfred Smith,
John Marshall,
George M. Baker,
Rev. Samuel Johnson,
Samuel Robinson,
Owen A. Barrett,
Rev. G. W. Boler,
Benjamin Richards,
James Benford,
Young Reed,
John Peck, of A.,
Amos Siscoe,
Samuel Venable,
John Auford,
Henry Jackson,
Vincent A. Johnson,
William Wilder,
Jesse Halestock,
Nathaniel Dixon,
Edward R. Parker,
Joseph H. Mahorney,
Robert Bailey,
David Bodey,
James M. Holley,
Samuel J. Wilkison,
Henderson H. Nicholson,
James H. Butler,
David Turbin,
Henry Williams,
William E. Harris,
Moses Howard,
Parker Soil,
Rev. Leonard Collins,
John H. Butler,
Samuel Delaney,
John Lewis,
Frederick A. Hinton,
Joshua E. Campbell,
George A. Collins,
James M'Crummell,
William Nickens,
Zedekiah J. Purnel,
George Butler,
Alexander Ferguson,
Orange Lewis,
Charles Henry,
John H. Butler,
Samuel Collins, Jr.,
Daniel Mahorney,
Bernard Mahorney, Sr.,
Charles Jones,
William M. Jones,
Thomas A. Brown,
James Morgan,
George Duncan,
Rev. Thos. Lawrence,
James Anderson,
Robert Bowie,
William L. Barns,
Juba Newton,
Washington Hunter,
George Spears,
William Murray,
Thomas Timms,
Thomas Knox,
John Williams,
Daniel Carney,
Nathan Moore,
Lewis M'Alfrey,
Henry M. Collins,
Charles Dockens,
Larkin Graves,
Charles Beno,
Obadiah Maloney,
Charles Wedley,
Daniel Johnson,
Jonathan Green,
Bernard Mahorney, Jr.,
George Austin,
Samuel Williams,
William Porter,
Thomas S. Robinson,
Elias Johnson,
Jonathan Willis,
Samuel Adley,
Henry Fields,
Jeremiah Fisher,

Henry Dabney,
James Hardin,
Richard Chidester,
Nathaniel M'Curdy,
William M'Curdy,
Rev. George Hilton,
Edward Minnis,
Thomas Johnson,
William Lewis,
A. D. Shadd,
Charles T. Clayton,
Samuel Stewart,
William Harris,
William Burley,
Richard Bryans,
George W. Graves,
Alfred Powell,
George Richardson,
Oliver Highgate,
Benjamin Stanley,
James Needham,
Saml. Van Brackel,
John C. Bowers,
James Bird,
R. C. Gordon, Jr.,
John Nelson,
James M. White,
Samuel Bruce, Jr.,
P. L. Jackson.

Copy in the Historical Society of Pennsylvania and the Library Company of Philadelphia

REFERENCE NOTES

1. John Peck was an active spokesman for Pennsylvania's Negro community. A wigmaker by trade, Peck worked untiringly to secure his people equal educational opportunities and the right to vote and hold office.

2. John B. Vashon (c. 1789-1854) was an influential black abolitionist. He ran a lucrative barber shop in his native Pittsburgh and later became the owner of the City Baths in the same metropolis. Vashon was active in the Negro Convention Movement, a vigorous anti-colonizationist, and a long-time friend of William Lloyd Garrison, the abolitionist.

3. Martin Robinson Delany (1812-1885) was born in Charles Town, Virginia (now West Virginia), the grandson of slaves and the son of free Negroes. His father's father was supposed to have been an African chieftain of the Golah tribe, captured with his family in battle, sold as a slave and brought to America. His mother's father was said to have been an African prince of the Mandingo line in the Niger Valley, also captured in war, enslaved, sold and transported to America.

Delany received his first instruction in reading from peddlers of books, continued his studies under the Reverend Lewis Woodson in Pittsburgh, and went on to study medicine at Harvard, becoming a doctor in 1852. In 1843, Delany founded a black antislavery newspaper published in Pittsburgh entitled *The Mystery*. Three years later, he became co-editor with Frederick Douglass of the *North Star*. During the Civil War, Delany served as one of seventy-five black officers in the Union Army. In 1852, he published his controversial little book, *The Condition, Elevation, Emigration, and Destiny of the Colored People of the United States, Politically Considered*. This work argued for the establishment in Africa or elsewhere of an independent black nationality.

4. In 1837 the constitution of Pennsylvania was amended to grant the suffrage to many poor whites, but at the same time blacks were excluded from the suffrage by inclusion of the word *white*. Unlike New York State, where

under the provisions of the revised constitution, blacks had to meet a $250 qualification, the effect of the Pennsylvania action was to eliminate *all* black male voters whether or not they owned property.

5. The *Colored American*, founded in January 1837, was the second black newspaper published in the United States. Originally known as the *Weekly Advocate*, its name was changed to the *Colored American* shortly after being established. The Reverend Samuel E. Cornish was the first editor, followed by the Reverend Charles B. Ray, who became editor and proprietor in 1840.

6. Abraham D. Shadd was a leading Pennsylvania black abolitionist and a shoemaker by trade. Active in the Negro Convention Movement of the early 1830's, Shadd became one of the five blacks to serve on the Board of Managers of the American Anti-Slavery Society at its founding meeting in 1833. For a time, he served as agent of the *Emancipator*, which was the official organ of the American Anti-Slavery Society until 1840. A vigorous supporter of the Underground Railroad, Shadd used his Wilmington, Delaware, and later West Chester County, Pennsylvania, homes to aid escaping slaves. During the 1850's, he moved to Canada West and, while there, became the only black to hold elective office prior to the Civil War. His daughter, the militant and indefatigable Mary Ann Shadd Cary, was an outspoken advocate of Canadian emigration.

7. Stephen Smith was a noted black abolitionist, clergyman, and co-owner with William Whipper of a lucrative lumber establishment in Columbia, Pennsylvania. Wilbur H. Siebert, author of the *Underground Railroad*, has a section in his study entitled, "Directory of the Names of Underground Railroad Operators," of which Smith is listed along with 143 other blacks. When Douglass issued his famous "Men of Color to Arms" appeal during the early part of the Civil War, calling upon black Americans to join the Union Army, Smith was listed as one of the signers.

MINUTES OF THE STATE CONVENTION OF THE COLOURED CITIZENS OF PENNSYLVANIA,
CONVENED AT HARRISBURG, DECEMBER 13th and 14th, 1848

MEMBERS OF THE CONVENTIONAL BOARD AT PHILADELPHIA

President
ROBERT PURVIS

Vice President
ISAIAH C. WEIR

Corresponding Secretary
DR. PECK*

Recording Secretary
J. C. BOWERS

Treasurer
REV. STEPHEN SMITH

Board of Managers
DR. J. J. G. BIAS,   GEORGE W. GOINES,
M. W. GIBBS,   WILLIAM WHIPPER,
SAMUEL VAN BRAKLE,   ABRAM D. SHADD,
BENJAMIN MOORE

*All communications must be addressed to Dr. D. J. Peck, (post paid) Lombard street above Seventh, Philadelphia

MINUTES OF THE CONVENTION

Pursuant to a call for a State Convention of the colored citizens of Pennsylvania, for the purpose of devising the most efficient method to petition the Legislature for the elective franchise, the Convention assembled at Harrisburg, Dauphin County, on Wednesday morning, Dec. 13th, 1848.

An informal meeting was held at the Wesleyan Methodist Church, and the Rev. George Galbraith appointed Chairman, and Francis A. Duterte, Secretary.

A motion was made by Dr. Peck, that the delegates present give their credentials into the hands of the Secretary. When the following delegates from the several different counties were enrolled as members of the Convention.

Allegheny County--John B. Vashon.
Berks County--Joseph E. Gardner, Joseph Murry, George C. Anderson.
Blair County--Daniel Williams.
Cumberland County--Wm. Webb, Edward Hawkins, Richard Johnson, Joseph Johnson, Jacob Stratton.
Centre County--Joseph St. Clair.
Chester Country--Abraham D. Shadd, John N. Bond, Charles E. Clayton, Wm. Lewis.
Columbia County--Wm. Thomson.
Dauphin County--John Wolf, Henry H. Price, John F. Williams, Thomas Earley, Aquilla Amos, John Gray, Andrew Gorden, William Spence, Joseph Popel, Charles I. Dorris, Edward Thomason, George Adley, Henry Johnson, Richard C. Brown, James Popel, James Reese, Wm. H. Davis, Charles L. Robertson, Daniel Jackson, Valentine Brown.
Franklin County--Nelson H. Turpen, Jesse Bolden.
Huntington County--Isaac J. Dickson.
Juniata County--Samuel Molston, John L. Griffith.
Lycoming Country--Philip Roderic.
Lancaster County--William Whipper, Leonard A. Williams, Wm. H. Wilson, Washington Webster, Robert Boston.
Mifflin County--David Roach, Jonathan Graham.
Philadelphia County--Stephen Smith, George Galbraith, James J. G. Bias, David B. Bowser, John C. Bowers, James D. Knight, Mifflin W. Gibbs, Robert Purvis, Francis A. Duterte, Isaiah Ware, James McCrummel, Samuel Van Brakle, David J. Peck, Henry Cooper, Joshua P. B. Eddy, Benjamin Moore, Robert Brown, Wm. Marten, Wm. Jackson, Perry Miller.
Schuylkill County--John Lee.
York County--Wm. Stanford, Wm. Cupit.

Resolved, That there be a committee of one from each county present to nominate officers for this Convention. The following persons compose that committee:

Allegheny County,	John B. Vashon
Berks	"	Joseph E. Gardiner
Blair	"	Daniel Williams
Chester	"	Charles E. Clayton
Columbia	"	Wm. Thomson
Dauphin	"	John F. Williams
Franklin	"	Nelson Turpin
Juniata	"	Samuel Molston
Huntington	"	Isaac J. Dickson
Lycoming	"	Philip Roderic
Lancaster	"	Wm. Whipper
Mifflin	"	David Roach
Philadelphia	"	Isaiah C. Weir
Schuylkill	"	John Lee
York	"	Wm. Stanford

On motion Rev. Stephen Smith, J. G. Wolf and H. H. Price were appointed as a committee to obtain a more suitable place for the holding of the Convention.

The committee on officers reported as follows:
President--John B. Vashon.
Vice Presidents--James McCrummell,[1] George Galbraith, John F. Williams, Isaac J. Dickson, Wm. Thomson, Samuel Molston.
Secretaries--F. A. Duterte, John G. Wolf, and Wm. Whipper.
Business Committee--Wm. Whipper,[2] Robert Purvis,[3] David J. Peck, M.D., Mifflin W. Gibbs, J. J. G. Bias.[4]
Finance Committee--Stephen Smith, John C. Bowers, Thomas Early, John Wolf, Samuel Van Brakle.

It was on motion resolved that the committee's report be adopted.

Mr. Vashon, the President elect, was conducted to the chair, at which time, in a short and able manner, he thanked the convention for the honor bestowed upon him.

When a motion to adjourn prevailed, to meet again at 2 o'clock.

Afternoon Session.

The Convention assembled at 2 o'clock, pursuant to adjournment. Mr. Vashon, President, in the chair. Prayers by the Rev. George Galbraith. Roll called. Minutes of the morning session read and adopted.

Mr. Charles Lenox Remond,[5] of Mass., was introduced to the Convention, after which he made a short, but powerful address, on the subject for which we had assembled.

Resolved, That Mr. Martin R. Delany, of Rochester New York, and Mr. Remond, of Mass., be received as honorary members of this Convention.

Mr. Purvis presented a communication from Mr. Woodson, of Allegheny County, which was referred to the business committee.

Resolved, That a committee of three be appointed to prepare rules for this Convention, when the following named gentlemen were appointed: John C. Bowers, Isaiah Ware, and Wm. Spence.

The committee on business reported as follows:

Resolved, That the legitimate object of this Convention, is to petition the Legislature for a repeal of the word "white," from the third article of the Constitution of Pennsylvania.

Resolved, That the people of Pennsylvania, by sanctioning the disfranchisement of her colored citizens, have violated the creed of their republican faith, and brought dishonor on their principles, and degradation, privation, and wrong on those whom they have victimized.

The motion for the adoption of the first resolution, was supported by M. R. Delany, C. L. Remond, and Dr. J. J. G. Bias, M. W. Gibbs, D. J. Peck, M.D., J. C. Bowers, Robert Purvis, A. D. Shadd, and Wm. Whipper, after which a motion was made to adjourn to meet at 7 o'clock.

Evening Session.

The Convention met at 7 o'clock, Mr. Vashon, President, in the chair. Prayer by the Rev. Wm. Jones.

Roll called, and the minutes of the afternoon session read and approved.

The committee appointed to obtain a more suitable place to hold this convention, reported that they were unable to obtain the Court house, on account of it being under repairs, but that the Shakespeare saloon could be obtained.

Resolved, That the report of the committee be adopted, and they be instructed to secure the Shakespeare saloon, and have placards struck off, publishing the same throughout the Borough.

The chairman then stated that the resolution from the afternoon session was in order, when on motion of Mr. Isaiah Ware the resolution was laid on the table, for the purpose of hearing the report of the committee on rules, which were read and adopted.

The resolution which was previously laid on the table was taken up, read, and finally passed.

When on motion, the second resolution was adopted, when a motion to adjourn prevailed, to meet at the Shakespeare saloon to-morrow morning at 9 o'clock.

Morning Session.

The Convention met according to adjournment in the Shakespeare saloon at half past 9 o'clock. An appropriate prayer was offered by the Rev. Mr. Turpin.

The minutes of the last meeting were read, corrected and adopted.

The resolution pending at the adjournment, was, by the president declared to be the first business in order, when, after being discussed by the following gentlemen, Messrs. Bowser, Peck, Gibbs, Smith, and Eddy, were finally passed.

The business committee then submitted the following resolution:

Resolved, That the successful prosecution of our cause, depends much on the form and manner of our advocacy, the character and wisdom of our measures, the zeal and energy of individual action; and demands that we issue an address to the voters of Pennsylvania. Also an address to the coloured citizens, requesting them to make their rule of conduct such as shall successfully vindicate their right to the enjoyment of citizenship.

A motion was made by Mr. Stephen Smith to lay the resolution on the table, to attend to the financial concerns of the Convention, after which he offered the following resolution.

Resolved, That each member of this Convention pay the sum of one dollar, for the purpose of assisting in defraying the expenses of this Convention. Before an action, the Convention adjourned to meet at half past 2 o'clock.

Afternoon Session.

The Convention met pursuant to adjournment at half past 2 o'clock. Prayer by the Rev. Mr. Sanford. President in the chair; roll called; minutes of the morning session read, corrected, and approved.

When the resolutions submitted to the business committee prior to the adjournment was brought up and discussed by the following gentlemen: Messrs. Whipper, Shadd, Bowser, Bowers, Gibbs, Weir, Remond, Delany, Bias, Dickson, Purvis, Gardiner, Eddy, Smith, Van Brakle, and Amos, after which it was read and finally passed.

The business committee presented the form of a constitution to form a State Union Society, to be called the Citizens' Union of the State of Pennsylvania, which was read and adopted.

On motion *Resolved*, That the parent society be located in the City of Philadelphia.

The following gentlemen were elected officers of the Conventional Board: President, Robt. Purvis; Vice President, Isaiah C. Weir; Treasurer, Stephen Smith; Secretary, John C. Bowers; Corresponding Secretary, D. J. Peck, M.D.: Board, J. J. G. Bias, M. W. Gibbs, S. Van Brakle, G. W. Goines, Wm. Whipper, Abraham D. Shadd, and Benjamin Moore.

Resolved, That this Convention recommend that each delegation be instructed to proceed to the formation of auxiliaries, upon their arrival at home.

The following resolution was offered by Mr. Smith.

Resolved, That the thanks of this Convention be tendered to the citizens of Harrisburg, and to Mr. J. F. Markley for the kind accommodation we have received during the sittings of this Convention, in connection with the minister and trustees of Wesley Church.

Resolved, That this Convention recommend to the Board to appoint a committee of three, to convey the petition, &c., to the members of the Legislature.

Resolved, That the Governor, and heads of department be furnished with a copy of the minutes of this Convention.

Resolved, That the business committee be, and are hereby requested to prepare a form of petition for presentation forthwith.

Resolved, That the proceedings of this Convention be printed in the *North Star*, *Daily Republic*, and all other papers friendly; also published in pamphlet form.

Resolved, That there be a committee of five, to prepare addresses; the following gentlemen compose that committee, Wm. Whipper, A. D. Shadd, I. J. Dickson, J. J. G. Bias, Robert Purvis, M. W. Gibbs, and Samuel Van Brakle.

Resolved, That the unfinished business be referred to the Conventional Board, after which the Convention adjourned *sine die.*

John B. Vashon, *President.*

F. A. Duterte,
John Wolf,   } Secretaries.
Edward M. Davis,

APPEAL TO THE VOTERS OF THE COMMONWEALTH OF PENNSYLVANIA

Sirs:--We recognize you as arbiters of our political destiny, and your sovereignty as the source of power from which the fundamental Laws of this Commonwealth must derive their origin, power and sustenance,--and while we admit the justice and force of your national maxims, as penned by the illustrious Jefferson, "that governments long established should not be changed for slight and transient causes," and all experience has proved, that as a people, we are disposed to suffer present evils "rather than fly to others we know not of," yet we are constrained to believe that the object for which we claim your attention is founded on established precedents, coeval with civil government, and rendered necessary as a safeguard to individual liberty and security to the privileges of the citizen.

We, therefore, address you, as the representatives of the Colored Citizens of this Commonwealth, assembled in Convention from various Counties, for the purpose of petitioning the Legislature for a repeal of the word "white" from the 1st section of the 3d Article of the Constitution of Pennsylvania, which reads as follows:--

"In elections by the citizens every white freeman of the age of twenty-one years, having resided in this State one year, and in the election district where he offers to vote, ten days immediately preceding such election, and within two years paid a State or County tax, which shall have been assessed at least ten days before the election, shall enjoy the rights of an elector," &c.

We rejoice that we are relieved from the task of depicting our grievances before you, for the causes which impel us to the present undertaking, are so legibly written on your Constitutional code, and embodied in your political faith, that neither revelation can enlighten nor argument embellish.

We therefore claim the exalted privilege of appealing to you from the seat of the law making power, on a subject that cannot, but be deeply interesting to you, as it is of vital importance to *us*. Because whatever has a tendency to develop the natural, intellectual and physical resources of a state or nation, augments her strength and perpetuates her power.

The constitutional provision you have made for the annual assemblage of your representatives from the various districts throughout the State for the purpose of legislating for the protection of your present and future interests affords us an illustrious example that we should not be unmindful of ours. If you, who have received and enjoyed, not only the blessings of science and civilization, but a representative form of government for three quarters of a century, still need its fostering care to lead you to a higher destiny, surely we, who have occupied the humblest positions, and from whom these blessings and privileges have been measurably withheld, may reasonably claim the possession of their invigorating strength to inspire us in the pursuit of a laudable ambition.

We need not search among the antiquated records of the past for a successful vindication of our claims to impartial laws. These emblems, of our State's humanity are imperishably recorded in the sublime appeals of her distinguished statesmen.

We do not appear before you as the supplicants for any new form of government which is opposed to the foundation principles of republicanism; we only ask the favor of the application of your own principles to your civil code.

We can conceive of no just reason why our present action should not only enlist your sympathies, but merit your warmest approbation. You have hailed, with deafening shouts, the victorious march of republicanism from the battle fields of your own Washington to the heights of Buena Vista, the plains of Cerro Gordo, and the Halls of the Montezumas, though to attain it, armies in the spirit of conquest should rush through rivers of blood and hecatombs of human victims.

You claim that your own Independence Hall is the sacred spot where your republicanism was born, cradled and received a national baptism, and from whence the same vestal fire of freedom is encompassing the globe. You have hailed with joyful acclamation the accession of liberal France to the great family of republics, because it thrust the keystone from the arch of monarchical governments throughout Europe.[6]

We have been witnesses to those soul stirring appeals in behalf of republicanism, in foreign lands; and the conviction forces itself upon our minds that however much you may admire and extol the progress of free principles in other states, that of your own dearest Pennsylvania must occupy the highest seat in your affections.

We do not make our appeal to you as christian sects, or political parties, but as men--christians and republicans--beseeching you to apply the same principles and practice to us as your religion and republicanism dictates should belong to others who have not forfeited their rights by crime.

The barrier that deprives us of the rights which you enjoy finds no palliative in merit--no consolation in piety--no hope in intellectual and moral pursuits--no reward in industry and enterprise. Our ships may fill every port--our commerce float on every sea, and our canvass be wafted by every breeze;--we may exhaust our midnight lamps in the prosecution of study, and be denied the privileges of the forum--we may be embellishing the nation's literature by our pursuits in science--the preceptors of a Newton in astronomy[7]--the dictators of Philosophy to a Locke[8] or a Bacon[9]--the masters of a Montesquieu[10] or a Blackstone[11] on civil and international law--or could we equal the founder of christianity in the purity of our lives, and the power and truth of our precepts and the extent of our morals, yet with all these exalted virtues we could not possess the privileges you enjoy in Pennsylvania, because we are not "white." Is this light of the 19th century! Gracious God! is it possible, that in the absence of crime thy Providence is made a party to our disfranchisement. Humiliating as it may be to contemplate the fact, it is written in the fundamental laws of your government, and must there remain until you, by the exercise of your prerogative, choose to remove it, the principles of your religion and republicanism to the contrary notwithstanding. We appeal to you as a body in whom are deposited the power of state sovereignty for weal or for woe--and to each of you individually desiring that if you feel that the obstruction of which we complain ought not to exist, that you will use your influence to obtain its repeal.

Our object in assembling is not only to petition the Legislature *ourselves*, but also to solicit *you to petition*. We hope that petitions on this subject will be sent to the Legislature from every City, Town, County, and Township in this Commonwealth.

We feel encouraged to petition from a prevalent belief that the position we are forced to occupy is contrary to the spirit and genius of the people of this State,--our petitions can only reach the humanity of the Legislator, while yours will instruct him in a course of action.

We can conceive of no just reason why Pennsylvania should not occupy the highest position among her sister republics. Her early history and position in this confederacy, the principles and measures of her early fathers and law-givers, as well as the circumstances of the American Revolution, have placed her on an eminence to give laws to the world. Her soil has been the theatre of as illustrious events as ever moved the historic pen, or fired the imagination of the orator. Beneath her soil lies the ashes of the immortal dead whose fame is as imperishable as her mineral mountains. She has been the favoured child of fortune, cradled in success. Providence became her nursing mother, by throwing into her lap, with boundless profusion, not only peace and plenty, but a host of intellectual giants, to guide her during her infant pilgrimage through the rocks and quicksands of despotism. Her time-honoured sons have occupied that proud pinnacle of fame upon which the nations of the earth have gazed with awe and admiration; and now when the revolutions of time light the pathway of posterity. When the last scroll of time shall be wound up on the great windlass of eternity it will present the indestructible names of your Penns,[12] Franklins, Rushes, Wistars, Benezets, Woolmans,[13] Morrises,[14]

Wilson,[15] Taylors,[16] and a host of others whose highest aim was justice to mankind. These men were the master builders of your Republican Edifice. If the spirits of the departed are permitted by Providence to take a survey of the scenes of their earthly glory, shall these transcendent spirits look down from their peaceful abode on your amended Constitution, and there behold a *barrier* against the exercise of civil rights, more potent than is to be found in any despotic government on the globe? We know that when adversity overshadows your prosperity, it is only of ephemeral duration--and we humbly trust that you will not suffer the GREAT SUN of your republican Eden to be long eclipsed by a scintillating planet from *exploding monarchies*. To you has been bequeathed the important duty of preserving this government from the fate of the ancient republics. If you protect its principles, and pass them down to posterity unimpaired, you will have completed the noble structure whose corner stone was laid by your fathers; and when future generations shall be surrounded by republics like our planetary system around the great Orb of Day, the traditionary historian will point to YOUR republican model, as the *political* SUN in the great firmament of nations, from whence they derive their light and heat.

No other suitable trophy can be erected to the memory of your revolutionary sires. Then, and not until then, will the martyred blood that washed your virgin soil have produced trees of liberty, from which mankind may, without distinction of complexion, pluck the heaven-born fruit. Their appeal to the Supreme Judge of the world from the rectitude of their intentions was in behalf of *mankind*, and the true mission of republics, can never be achieved until mankind, without distinction of nation or complexion are embraced within its folds.

When your Independence Hall, on the fourth day of July, 1776, was made sacred by a consecration to the great cause of human liberty, your Morris, Rush, Franklin, Wilson, and Ross[17] pledged themselves--their fortunes and sacred honors--for the purpose of establishing a republican form of government, with the representatives from Massachusetts, through her Adams,[18] Paine,[19] and Gerry[20]--with Rhode Island through her Hopkins[21] and Ellery,[22] and although Vermont was not represented in that illustrious body, she may now be added to the list of those States that have succeeded in establishing universal suffrage.

After having finished the duties assigned them by their constituents, they severally returned to their homes, and commenced spreading the live coals from the altar of freedom until the electric sparks galvanized the dead corpse of political liberty, and the people rushed in masses to their standards, while posterity caught the flame, and the proud and ever-glorious result is realized in the fact that each of these States have succeeded in establishing a republican form of government where men of all complexions enjoy an equality of rights.

It is now left for you to decide whether Pennsylvania shall be less fortunate. Must the arduous labours of your great men fail to be consummated, while those of their confederates have been crowned with triumphant success?

We make no foreign issue with you--we place ourselves on your own declaration of rights and principles. On these hang our future hope, and with them we will stand or fall. We will now leave the subject with the hope that no collateral issue may affect the justice of our claims; it being solely a question of rights springing from your own republican creed.

In soliciting an extensive circulation for this appeal, we must draft on the benevolence and liberality of the *press*; for without its favourable influence, no cause, however pure, may hope to succeed, and with it truth and justice must prove invincible.

We shall live and labour in the glorious anticipation of success; but if it should prove otherwise, and you should not consent to repeal the sentence you have passed on Providence, we shall derive the rich consolation that in making this appeal we have discharged a duty we owed to *ourselves*, to freedom, and republicanism--to posterity and to God.

            Wm. Whipper,
            Abram D. Shadd,
            J. F. Dickson,
            J. J. G. Bias,

Robert Purvis,
M. W. Gibbes,
Samuel Van Brakle,
Committee.

Harrisbury, Dec. 14th 1848.

AN APPEAL TO THE COLORED CITIZENS OF PENNSYLVANIA

Fellow Citizens,--Being impressed with the spirit of that great law of progress which directs mankind to seek for liberty and happiness under the protection of free institutions, we have assembled in Convention, for the purpose of exchanging our views with each other on the best method of obtaining it. And in pursuance of the object of said Convention, we have been appointed to address you on the subject of our future action.

You will discover in the report of our proceedings, that we have recommended that petitions be sent to the Legislature, praying for a repeal of the word "white" from the Constitution of this State.

The footprints of every step we have trod, are stamped with success. The unanimity of sentiment that prevailed in the Convention, swelled the harmonious notes which announce the proud future. Our favorable reception by the citizens of Harrisburg, and the respectful attention we received in going and returning from the Convention, proclaimed that the people were pleased with our object, and prepared to second our movements.

We have issued an address to the voters of this state, beseeching them to apply their republican principles to our cause, and blot from their Constitution the last remnants of monarchy.

We assume for our basis and corner stone, "that all just governments derive their powers from the consent of the governed," and that, as we have long been numbered with the latter, every principle of republican justice we maintain vindicates our right to be invested with the same sovereignty exercised by others.

We have launched into a new position. Our fathers sought personal freedom--we now contend for political freedom.

The Constitution, by disfranchising us, while it claims to be republican, has stricken a blow at our manhood, and not only ours, but a majority of those who people this globe.

We intend suing for our rights as *men*; where the Executive and Legislative branches of the government is the Court, and 400,000 legal voters the jury, our own conduct being the witnesses, and true republican principles the law.

No case, of equal importance, can ever be tried in this commonwealth, whether we regard the elevated character and position of the court, the number, intelligence, and power of the jury, or the incalculable interests at stake, pending on the decision. It stands on an undisputed pre-eminence, far beyond any parallel in history.

The justly celebrated Somersett case, that was tried in England, in the King's Bench before Lord Mansfield, on the 7th of February, 1772, when all established usages and precedents were broken down by the promulgation of a decision from the learned bench, declaring that "slaves cannot breathe in England," was but a very faint daguerreotype likeness of our own.

It is true, that if we succeed, a portion of our jurors, like Lord Mansfield, may reverse their previous decisions. It is also true, that the opinions of many of the jury, like their numbers, have undergone a change in ten years, which is favorable to our claims; either from having the question stripped from foreign issues, or causes unknown to us. Of one thing we are certain, that a large empanelment has been added to the jury, since our case was before the people, from those who were deprived by minority, from exercising the prerogative of voters. These have never had the subject placed before them, in a manner and form requiring their study and investigation. It was a wise forecast in the Convention to embody a proviso, that all future amendments to the Constitution should pass two successive Legislatures, before they were presented to the people for ratification. This measure allows all those favorable to the said amendments, a sufficient time to urge their claims on the attention of the people.

It may seem to many, as being too slow in our case, to satisfy the demands of justice; yet it is nevertheless an important safeguard to the rights, privileges, and interests of the people.

Now fellow citizens, we should feel a deep interest in this cause, and hasten its onward march, by every means in our power. For over us, and our children, its preganant consequences, to our future welfare, hangs like a mighty incubus; shall we longer fold our arms with stoic indifference, and falter before this judgment of power, which, like some great Andes, is crushing us and our children beneath its ponderous weight; rather than rise like men possessing the spirit of freemen, and petition those in authority for its removal? In vain has been our acquaintance with letters, if we remain blind to the teachings of history.

Shall the spirit of liberty continue to inspire every nation--rock every government, and freight every breeze, and leave us like some unnatural excrescence, or motionless adamant unmoved by its power.

Shall we read, not only in books, but in the examples of those who surround us, the inestimable value that others place on the free exercise of their political rights, and long remain indifferent to our own. If we do, a more powerful argument cannot be urged for withholding them. It was wielded with great effect on a former occasion, and will remain a standing obstruction to us, unless we by a bold and energetic action, cast it to the four winds.

The old adage, that "the price of liberty is eternal vigilance," is as true now, as when it was first uttered. Others will be induced to advocate our rights, just in proportion, as they discover that we set a just value on them ourselves.

Slaves have learned to lick the dust, and stifle the voice of free inquiry; but we are not slaves--our right to natural liberty, and a qualified citizenship, is guaranteed to us by the Constitution. Full, civil, and political liberty, is regarded by the ablest writers on government, as the only true safeguard to individual liberty--so that, their presence is vindicated by *necessity*.

There are many points of difference between the celebrated Somersett case, and ours. He was separated by water from those influences prejudicial to his case, and it was managed by able counsel, learned in the law, while the decision was wrung from noble Lords, after a patient investigation of the principles proclaimed in the Magna Charta of Great Britain. We are situated in the midst of our jurors, where every possible opportunity is presented for prejudging our cause. Our jurors are men from all creeds of christians, all political parties, possessing minds of every shade of thought, from the most exalted intelligence, to unpardonable ignorance; of every classification of sympathy, and every quality of prejudice, with no other standard before them, than their own ideas of republicanism, which they are not bound by oaths to support, and such is the equal distribution of power among them, that our worst enemy can nullify the act of our best friend.

The evidence that was required in the Somersett case was *language*, in our case it will be *actions*. We should resist on the very threshold of the court this distinction in evidence, as having no foundation in established precedents, in the Judicial and Legislative branches of our government.

You may clearly discover, fellow citizens, the narrow path on which we must tread; every juryman will be a living witness against us, if this rule of evidence be admitted, the least departure from the ground of moral rectitude, will be magnified into a base attempt to overthrow the law, and disturb the peace of society. Our petty jealousies and bickerings, will be regarded as lawless invasions. Even drunkenness that is often characterized as the essence of fashionable folly, among the whites, will be ascribed to degeneracy in us. The tide of our vices, will not be considered to rise and fall by temptation, like those of other men, but as springing from an inherent quality of our nature.

They will describe us as being too *low* in the scale of creation to be reached by the *heavenly light*, and then denounce us for being *immoral*. They will assert our *inferiority* in the scale of creation, and then taunt us with not having established our equality, by the *overthrow* of *nature's laws*. In short, we will be required to perform impossibilities, and denounced for not surmounting them.

These are a portion of the difficulties that must be met and overcome, and every argument that we furnish by our conduct, that militates against our cause, procrastinates the period when we must finally triumph.

But let no one be mistaken from what we have said respecting *condition*, or that we would make it a *standard*; it is only a *means*. If *it* could be made a *standard*, there would not be the remotest possibility of success by rallying under *it*.

But let no man falter under the supposition, that the path marked out is so narrow, that we cannot walk in it. Even if *condition* were the *standard*, the path has been trodden by one, whose life and character was a shining ornament among us for upwards of *three score* years, a *model* man, one of *nature's noblemen*. If integrity of character, connected with all the characteristics which render men good and great, could not preserve him from the ban of proscription, then it must be admitted that condition can present no qualifications, capable of being a passport of admission into the rights and privileges of citizenship in this state. It has been argued that we were disfranchised on the grounds of *condition*. This we deny. The *reasons* urged for our disfranchisement were *founded* on *condition*. Those who laboured to disfranchise us, *dared* not to make *condition* the *standard*. While they asserted our inferiority, they were too cowardly to give us a fair field to become competitors for the *prize* of *merit*. They were cunning logicians, and well knew that no argument founded on *condition* would meet the *false prejudices* of *their* constituents. They knew that the period had long since passed when it would be *possible* to *frame* a standard of *condition* that would separate the *white* from the *colored* people.

So they disfranchised us by *extinguishing justice--disqualifying merit*, assuming *condition* as their *reason*, and *complexion* as the *standard*. By refusing to make their *standard* the basis of their *reasons*, they have admitted its injustice; and by refusing to make their *reasons* their *standard* of disqualification, they have denied *their* validity. As our Constitution has not prescribed any *standard* of religious, moral or intellectual qualifications, we could not have been disfranchised if misfortune had not placed them in our possession. So no amendment could have passed the Convention, and been adopted by the people, having *pecuniary* qualification, that would have wholly disfranchised us. *Condition* was but the *pretext*--the *capital* on which to furnish *arguments*--a *passport* to power, and that *point* being gained, they were determined to disfranchise us, as a body, on *account of complexion*; they did not need *reasons*, because they were prepared to vote on the ground of prejudices. And if their power had been co-extensive with their *wills*, many of them would not only have *disfranchised us*, but the *poor* of *every nation*, and whole *political* parties, that were opposed to them in the bargain.

Therefore, our only hope of effecting a change, in the fundamental laws of this State, is through a successful appeal to the voters thereof, whose sovereign will must direct her future destiny.

We have not only shown, that they did not disfranchise us on account of our *condition*, but that they COULD *not*. And if further testimony be needed, we will bring to the stand, Mr. Martin, of Philadelphia county, the member of the Convention who bears the distinguished honor of having introduced the word "white" into the Constitution. He says in a speech on that subject, "Much has been done for these people--schools have been kept up--they have been instructed in all the sciences, and in the rudiments of religion, and I haved known but one solitary instance of a good result, although I have lived forty years on the same spot, and have been well acquainted with all that has been done. There is a BLACK *gentlemen* in Philadelphia county, JAMES FORTEN, a sail maker, who is an exception.[23] What is his situation? He has accumulated property, obtained a respectable standing, and in *consequence of his colour*, is noticed more than a white man would be in the same situation. I will say, therefore, that all these attempts are fallacious, and that nothing can be done to place the coloured race by the side of the whites."

We leave you after reading the above extract to decide for yourselves, whether Mr. Martin was induced to insert the word "white" from the view that our people had failed to reach that high position contemplated by their benefactors, or from a *spirit* of *jealousy* at the *notoriety* that followed their success, in "*consequence of their colour*." It could not have been the former, because he represents them as having "obtained the rudiments of religion, and as being in possession of ALL the *sciences*."

Such qualifications endorsed by such high authority ought not disfranchise us on *account* of *condition*. If he was moved by *jealousy* not arising from any act of James Forten, but from the distinguished notice he received from others in "*consequence of his colour*," then the argument against our *inferiority* because *exploded*. He says "he has no hatred for these people." If he means that his course towards us is friendship, we pity his enemies. But let us examine his *sense* of *justice*, so that we may be able to comprehend what he would *require* of *us*. Now, he says that James Forten, was a *black* gentleman, and the only exception among a standing population of 20,000, which of course must have doubled itself in the forty years of Mr. Martin's residence and surveillance. Does Mr. Martin make any effort, to *protect* James Forten, from the doon of all those who are *recognized* by the *same complexion*. No, after endorsing his character for "*Prosperity*, *reputation*, and *gentlemanship*," he too must be *immolated*, not on *account* of his *condition*, but mark ye! it is his *complexion*. The *reason*, for the omission perhaps lies in the fact that he prefaced the term gentleman with *black*, and as he expresses a *jealousy* for the fear of *coloured* men's *popularity*, and in case they shall be permitted to vote, would have the power of *distributing offices* in the different wards." There is great reason for the impression, that Mr. Forten was a SHINING MARK, and that Mr. Martin's object was more achieved in effecting *his disfranchisement* than in the very worst sample that could have been presented. Now when Mr. Martin's own endorsement of the condition and character of *James Forten*, would not induce him to make exception in his favour; it most clearly proves that *no condition*, however exalted, possesses a protecting influence. James Forten might have been the MOSES of the *Israelites*--the CHRIST of the *Gentiles*--the WASHINGTON of AMERICA, and he would have been disfranchised, so far as Mr. Martin's vote and influence was concerned.

But, let no one suppose that we undervalue any effort, for the improvement of our condition. We know that it will be capable of exerting a powerful influence on future decisions as well as it did on the past. Our object in using the names of James Forten and Mr. Martin, is to make a strong case for the purpose of *disabusing* your minds of the *false* views that have been circulated, that we were disfranchised on *account* of our *condition*. It would have been unfortunate for Mr. Martin if the forty thousand coloured people in the State could each have represented the same character and influence of James Forten, he would have been without a *conditional basis* on which to erect his *complexional* ISSUE. This would be requiring too much, for *he* was a *model man*, and no nation in the whole tide of time, from the twelve tribes of Israel down to the Liberian republic, ever presented a front where the mass possessed such unsullied purity. In taking leave of Mr. Martin we are unable to say whether his views have undergone any change, but as we understand that he is still living, we are willing the public shall have the benefit of his arguments. His whole course has impressed us with the belief that he did not make the name of James Forten an exception out of respect to the *man* or his *virtues*. The exception was necessary to characterize *his own* intelligence and establish his veracity. JAMES FORTEN, though dead, his example still lives in the memory and affections of those who knew him. If we imitate his virtues, our influence will dissolve mountains of prejudice. He loved to make friends, while too many of us create enemies. The examples of all such will be like millstones around our cause, and if we fail to succeed it will be their fault.

Every man should consider that from this time forward the eyes of his jurors will be upon him, and if we would avoid any unjust cause of offence, in a case involving dollars and cents, how much more careful ought we to be where the great stake is our rights and privileges as citizens. Each one should be careful to win friends to our cause.

We should be careful to present a manly bearing by the exercise of politeness and good manners, and avoid all unnecessary display and ostentation --also profane language and invidious expressions, either in favour of or agains political parties. For, if we obtain the right of citizenship it will not be through the influence of any one party; we must look to the *justice* of the people without distinction of *party*, *creed*, or *sect*. Let us ever bear in mind that "money is the sinew of war," and that to carry this question to a successful issue, you will not only have to act with circumspection, but you will have to tax yourselves for its support. Remember, we can make no sacrifices in this cause which will not produce an equivalent reward. Should we not obtain our enfranchisement at once, we will gain in the consolidation of our people on the great subject of our rights. The dismembered factions of sects and parties will lose their identity in the union of discordant elements. Our wasteful contributions, folly and fancy will seek a channel for investment in an exchequer from which we may draw honor, wealth, intelligence and power. Our superfluous trappings will be substituted for plain and useful apparel. Our science of music and signs will be more fully displayed in the science of letters of economy. In the dissolution of our local and affiliated societies, a base will be discovered on which to erect institutions from whose gigantic structure, national themes can be proclaimed. The seed of revolution once successfully planted, only needs the application of right instrumentalities to carry it into successful operation. With a proper direction of our resources we have within us the elements that will make us a great people.

But, if we would succeed, we must erect our standard on the *rock of principle*--and our measures should always be guided by the *highest expediency*. We must not forget from whence we started, and like the children of Israel keep our eyes directed towards the promised land; ever watchfully surveying the difficulties to be surmounted, and make our attacks on the most pregnable points. We should never waste our ammunition in skirmishing and sound, nor direct our artillery in the air. We must make the history of oppressed nations our light-houses--and never relax our efforts until we have passed the *Rubicon of Caste*, and landed safely on Pisgah's top.

We must ever keep the fact in view that we are disfranchised because we are *not* "white." We must endeavor to influence the voters of this State to repeal this *complexional standard*. Our cause is analogous to those which have been the foundation of revolutions for upwards of two hundred years, excepting those that had their foundation in the *religious intolerance*, while ours is *complexional*.

The Protestant reformation of the 16th century had its foundation in the *religious intolerance* of the *catholics*. Look at the history of Ireland under George III[24]--at a period when she was furnishing England with a generation of patriots, who were weaving laurels for the brow of the British Crown, both at home and abroad--in the field and in the camp--at the bar and in the forum --while in the Parliament the Catholic religion was stricken down by Protestant power, and its devoted worshippers made to suffer in their persons and privileges because they would not consent to abandon the idol of their faith. Look at the history of the Quakers, the Catholics and Jews of this country, have they too not been *hanged, scourged, disfranchised*, and persecuted on account of their religious faith! Have they not been obliged to seek their title to the privilege of citizenship through the dire fogs of persecution that became so tangible, that like Egyptian darkness they "*felt it*," and mark the results. Their talents have been devoted to improvement; faithful to their creed, they have rode triumphantly over the billows of the storm. They might have knelt before the Moloch of power, renounced their faith, and by bowing at the shrine of hypocrisy have purchased a pardon with the price of their conscience. With us it is otherwise, we must suffer the "altars and Gods" to sink together.

The charge upon which we are arraigned, is a debt which hypocrisy cannot liquidate. The *divinity* that debars us from the *privileges* of Citizenship, is more DURABLE than REVELATION inscribed on *parchment*, the intuitions of prophecy *embodied* in *creeds*, or the unwritten evidences of our faith streaming from the fountain of our consciences. It is *emblazoned on our cheeks* by the IMPRESS OF DEITY. Light from heaven irradiates it, and darkness alone can obscure it.

Others by becoming traitors to their principles, might have forsaken their faith, but we cannot abandon our *complexion*. We are forced to meet the issue, and that on *complexional* grounds. The same foe to liberty is in the field that persecuted Luther[25] at the "Diet of Worms," and burned Michael Servetus[26] at the stake--executed Emmet[27] and his colleagues in Ireland--that hung the Quakers in the land of the Pilgrims--that disfranchised the Jews, and in more modern times, mobbed the Catholics. They boldly went to battle with a foe whose Godlike power shook the whole earth. They girded themselves with the weapons of truth and justice, and became invincible. The contest was long and severe, but the *great* DAGON of power and oppression fell and crumbled at the feet of a revolutionary power, that has poured more blessings into the lap of nations than any event recorded in the world's history. It is the scattered fragments of that enemy to mankind, that relentless foe to civil and religious liberty which had spent its force in wars of religious despotism that is now again resuscitated and consolidated for the purpose of executing *complexional intolerance*. It is this power, so often foiled and beaten that has stricken down our rights, privileges, and citizenship in Pennsylvania. And the most humiliating part in the whole drama, is, the contemplation that we are obliged to contend for our rights with the sons of those conquerors who shed their blood in battling with the same enemy and in defence of the same glorious principles, and whose ashes have produced trees of liberty, under which their posterity may not only be protected from the storms of despotism, but may repose in peaceful security beneath their branches. We regret that we are forced to appeal to those sects and parties that are fresh from the fires of persecution, and whose parental history is scarred with the wounds and bruises of the conquered and slain. But, we will appeal to them; they are but men, and have hearts, feelings and sympathies as other men, therefore we will appeal to them, as men whose origin and destiny are and must be inseparable from theirs. Born heirs to the same natural rights--having a just claim to the exercise of the same conventional rights, so long as we are governed by the same laws let, us implore them by their respect for the past, and their love for the future, not to fetter our spirits or manacle our limbs with chains, "which neither they nor their fathers could bear," and which required ages of labour to dissolve.

We will appeal to them by their religion and republicanism not to make a foreign issue with us on the grounds of *condition*. We have marked their issue--and nailed our flag to their complexional standard, and under it we will rally, sink or swim--survive or perish we will be found fiercely combating the enemies of equal rights, and in favor of the laws of Providence.

But let us first charge home upon ourselves. We too have admitted on our platform this abominable doctrine of *condition*; we have been allured by false ideas, we want not only language to express our detestation of existing evils, but we need new terms for the vindication of our rights. We have been advocates of the doctrine that we must be elevated before we could expect to enjoy the privileges of citizenship; we can never approach nearer the white man than we now are while he possesses all the machinery of progress. We do now henceforth and forever discard it, and deny that in the true republican sense of the term that we need to be elevated before we are enfranchised. The Almighty having clothed us with the attributes of human nature, we are placed on an equality with the rest of mankind. The declaration of American Independence, and our own State's Bill of Rights ask no more. If we admit the *fatalism* that we need to be elevated before we are fitted to possess the rights and privileges of white men, we consequently acknowledge our inferiority in the scale of creation. Let us never attempt to erect the temple of freedom on such a sandy foundation. Let us reject every attempt to dethrone the dignity of our manhood so long as the spirits of freedom runs in our veins, and we feel within us the evidence of immortality.

Let us rest our cause on the republican standard of the revolutionary Fathers, while we knock at the doors of the constitution and demand an entrance. If we are asked what evidence we bring to sustain our qualifications for citizenship, we will offer them certificates of our BIRTH and NATIVITY. If we are denied admission, let the cause of our rejection be ascribed to our complexion. Then we shall have a fair view of the question at issue, then we shall be able to see (and our friends too) that it is not our impiety--our ignorance--our immorality, or our wicked customs and habits that places us without the pale of constitutional landmarks. But that it is our *complexion alone* which furnishes the apology. If we could by a single "feat" of nature change our complexion, every objection to our full exercise of constitutional privileges would be banished before to-morrow's sun. We therefore hope that our friends will cease to place any faith in the doctrine, that our religious, literary, and moral improvement will be the means of enfranchising us. We need all these much, for our spiritual, moral and intellectual improvement for the promotion of our present and future welfare.

But these are not constitutional requirements. The people of Pennsylvania, in their conventional capacity, did not set up such a test on which to base the rights of elective franchise. To have carried out such a principle would have disfranchised a portion of the whites, while it would have clothed thousands of our people with those very privileges of which they are now denied. We are not asking the voters of Pennsylvania to elevate us; they cannot do it. All we ask of them is, that they "take their feet off our necks," that we may stand free and erect like themsleves. We prescribe for them no form of government; all we desire is that they will practice their own professed principles. In our present form of government, the will of the people is the law of the land. It is therefore the rankest form of injustice and despotism to require of those whom they have *denied the exercise of their will* in the formation of those laws to yield implicit obedience to the same. All we ask of them to perform, they have sworn before high heaven to execute. We desire to disabuse the public mind with regard to a fatal error which has long been entertained by many gifted and philanthropic minds, *viz.* that our religious, moral, and intellectual elevation would secure us our political privileges. We aver that it will not; we can now produce sufficient samples in these virtues and acquirements to redeem the character of a world. Sodom would have been saved with a far less proportion. No, if we had colored men who could write like Paul, preach like Peter, pray like Aminadab, iron hearted prejudice would cry out he is *black*.

If our halls of science, the bar, and the forum, reverberated with the eloquence of Cicero[28] or Demosthenes,[29] or to come down to modern times, if they were capable of eclipsing those master spirits of the American Senate with the power of their genius--or possessed the wealth of Croesus[30] or a Girard,[31] the vulgar voice of the populace would still cry out they are a degraded people, *because* they are *black*. We are not among those who believe that neither religion, humanity or legislation can remove this *unholy prejudice* against our complexion. We know it to be vincible, and we feel assured that where true religion exists it cannot enter. Every human being, according to *Scripture*, who hates his brother without a cause, is totally destitute of the spirit of christianity. Our political elevation is more depending on the improvement of the white man's heart than on the colored man's mind; we need moral and intellectual cultivation as a means through which we may be able to enlist the advocacy of our friends and influence the minds of our opponents. Our present situation is a living commentary on the *principle* that governs American legislation, and controls American justice.

Finally, brethren, in conclusion we cannot part without again admonishing you that you must not fail to battle with the *demon* of *complexional* INTOLERANCE FIRST, and let the subject of our *condition* follow, for unless you pursue this course your labours will prove fruitless. In Massachusetts, Vermont, and Rhode Island they have slain this *monster*, and now they are enjoying the blessings of political equality. The avenues to industry, wealth, and power now being open to them as to others, they can construct the edifice of their own fortunes, and make their condition vie with that of the most favored class of citizens.

When we take a retrospective view of the past, we have reason to believe that the republican pride of the old Keystone State will excite her ambition to occupy the loftiest position in the temple of freedom. She has already in her legislative capacity erased from her statute books the last remains of domestic Slavery, she will not long suffer her fundamental code to be tarnished with a relic of political barbarism. Until then we must labour with an untiring devotion, making Liberty our watchword and the elective franchise our ruling idea. We must collect our people from their distracting factions, and cement the dismembered elements around one common standard which [will] *establish union*, and consolidate their strength, and the day will not be distant when we shall be clothed with the robe of citizenship, when the constitution of Pennsylvania like the SUN of *liberty* will send forth her refulgent rays of civil and political liberty on us as upon the rest of mankind.

                Wm. Whipper,
                Abram D. Shadd,
                J. J. Dickson,
                J. J. G. Bias,
                Robert Purvis,

M. W. Gibbes,
Samuel Van Brakle,
Committee.

CONSTITUTION

Article I.

The Name of this Association shall be "THE CITIZENS' UNION OF THE COMMONWEALTH OF PENNSYLVANIA."

Article II.

Its object shall be, to obtain for the colored people of Pennsylvania all the Rights and Immunities of Citizenship.

Article III.

It will endeavor to obtain these Rights and Immunities by holding PUBLIC MEETINGS, delivering LECTURES, circulating NEWSPAPERS and TRACTS, thereby producing such a change in PUBLIC OPINION as shall induce the LEGISLATURE when PETITIONED, and the VOTERS of the Commonwealth when presented therewith, to grant them.

Article IV.

Any person being eighteen years of age, and a citizen of Pennsylvania, or desirous of becoming a citizen, and subscribing to this Constitution, and paying into its TREASURY, or the Treasury of any of its AUXILIARIES, the sum of fifty cents annually, shall be a member of this Association.

Article V.

The annual instalment shall be paid on or before the first Monday of October in each year; and any member failing to pay it by that day shall not be allowed to vote in any of the doings of this association, or any of its Auxiliaries until it is paid.

Article VI.

County Associations, Auxiliary to this, may be formed in each of the several Counties of the State, and shall be entitled to a representation in the Annual Meeting of this Association, equal in number to the number of Senators and Representatives of such County in the State Legislature.

Article VII.

A certain portion of the funds of each Auxiliary shall be paid into the Treasury of this Association on or before the day of its Annual Meeting, otherwise the representatives of such Auxiliary shall not be entitled to vote in said Annual Meeting.

Article VIII.

The President, Vice President, Recording and Corresponding Secretaries, and Treasurer, and seven members chosen to that office, shall constitute the EXECUTIVE COMMITTEE, a majority of whom shall constitute a quorum.

Article IX.

The several Officers of this Association shall discharge their respective duties in the usual manner, and shall continue in office until their successors are elected.

Article X.

The Annual Meeting for the election of officers, hearing the annual Report of the Executive Committee, and transacting the business of the Association, shall be held on the second Wednesday in December in each year.

Article XI.

All Agents and Lecturers in the service of this association, shall be employed and directed in their labours, by the Executive Committee, and shall be accountable to it for the faithful discharge of their duty.

Article XII.

In view of the object of this association, and the means it will be enabled to command. It shall be the duty of the Executive Committee in the commencement of the discharge of their duties, to confine themselves to the publication of such papers, and the delivery of such lectures, as shall tend to possess the colored people of KNOWLEDGE, WEALTH and GOODNESS, and thus elevate them intellectually, morally, socially, and politically to the ranks of free and equal citizenship of the Commonwealth of Pennsylvania.

Article XIII.

Whenever undue sectional influences, in the doings of this Association, are apprehended by any two of its members, any number of members, from any one County, shall be entitled to no greater number of votes, than the number of Senators and Representatives of such County in the State Legislature.

Article XIV.

This Constitution may be altered or amended by a vote of a majority of the members present at the Annual Meeting.

Copy in the Historical Society of Pennsylvania and the Library Company of Philadelphia.

THE HARRISBURG DELEGATION, DECEMBER 18, 1848

Pursuant to arrangement, the colored citizens of Philadelphia, met in the Wesleyan Church, Lombard street, for the purpose of receiving the delegates from the Harrisburg Convention, the Rev. Wm. T. Catto in the Chair, and Joseph C. Moore, Secretary.

Prayer was offered by the Rev. Joshua P. B. Eddy. After the President had stated the object of the meeting, the Rev. Stephen Smith, one of the Delegates, addressed the assembly, stating that they, (ten in number,) in obedience to the request of their constituents, convened together in Harrisburg, in the Shakespeare Saloon, on the 13th instant, with some fifty-five other delegates from the various counties of the State.

By a special resolution of the Convention (he said) it was agreed that there be $5,000 raised to carry on the object for which they had met. The city and county of Philadelphia promised to raise $2,000 of the above-mentioned sum. He sustained the same, by offering a resolution to that effect, which was unanimously adopted.

Mr. J. Ware read some of the resolutions adopted by the Convention, and stated that the delegation from Philadelphia had been constituted the medium to bear our petition to the Legislature--appoint an agent or agents to canvass the State, and lay the claims of the disfranchised impartially before the people, both colored and white.

M. W. Gibbs, in a brief but eloquent speech, set forth the great necessity of raising the sum of $5,000 to promote the cause. He was followed by D. B. Bowser, who called upon the assembly to know if they would assist in the advancement of the enterprise. He received a hearty response from the audience; after which, in a brief and enthusiastic speech, showed the necessity of concerted and immediate action. J. J. G. Bias then made a few remarks, calling upon young and old, male and female, to lend their assistance, both physical, moral and pecuniary, to obtain our God-given rights. C. L. Remond followed, on the great advantage of having the elective franchise, and the great disadvantage of our disfranchised condition, concluding with a resolution that there be a committee of three appointed to make arrangements for a public meeting. George W. Goines, Peter Lester, and Rev. Stephen Smith, were appointed that committee; after which the meeting adjourned, to be reassembled at the discretion of the committee.

Wm. T. Catto, Pres't.
Joseph C. Moore, Secy.

Philadelphia, Dec. 18, 1848.

The North Star, February 2, 1849.

REFERENCE NOTES

1. James McCrummell was a well-known Philadelphia Negro and abolitionist. Along with Robert Purvis and James G. Barbadoes, he was among several black delegates present at the formation of the American Anti-Slavery Society in December 1833. He was also a founder of the Pennsylvania Anti-Slavery Society, established in 1837. Concerning McCrummell, a story is related that when the Female Anti-Slavery Society of Philadelphia was organized on December 14, 1833, it was discovered that the women lacked sufficient parliamentary experience to run the proceedings. Lucretia Mott, the Society's guiding spirit, later recalled that the assembled ladies then requested McCrummell, who was in the audience, for assistance.

2. William Whipper was an active black abolitionist. Along with Stephen Smith, mentioned above, he ran a prosperous lumber establishment at Columbia, Pennsylvania. Whipper played a prominent role in the Negro Convention Movement. He was instrumental in founding at Philadelphia in 1835 the American Moral Reform Society, a predominantly black group. A vigorous supporter of the temperance crusade among blacks, in 1834 Whipper opened a free labor and temperance grocery store next door to the Bethel A.M.E. Church in Philadelphia. A most efficient worker in the Underground Railroad, Whipper used his home to hide fugitive slaves, on one occasion almost risking the destruction of his lumber yard by fire because of this activity. A generous contributor to the antislavery cause, Whipper gave $1,000 dollars annually, over a thirteen-year period, to aid in the struggle against slavery.

3. Robert Purvis (1810-1898) was the son of a white South Carolina merchant and a Moorish-Jewish woman whose mother had been a slave. Independently wealthy and so light-skinned that he could have passed for white, he was educated in private schools in Philadelphia and finished his education at Amherst College. But he left college to devote himself to the antislavery movement and at the age of seventeen made his first public speech against slavery. A founder of the American Anti-Slavery Society, Purvis was a supporter of William Lloyd Garrison throughout the pre-Civil War era.

4. James J. G. Bias of Philadelphia was a noted black physician and clergyman. One of the key operators on the Underground Railroad, his home and bed were always available to slaves directed to him by the white abolitionist Charles Torrey. In addition to providing sleeping accommodations for his runaway charges, it was not unusual for Bias to give his overnight guests a quick medical check-up. A member and active worker in the Pennsylvania Anti-Slavery Society, Bias was also a founder of the Philadelphia Vigilance Committee, established in 1838, which assisted some three hundred slaves annually before passing out of existence in 1844.

5. Charles Lenox Remond (1810-1873) was an eloquent antislavery lecturer who served for many years as an agent of the American Anti-Slavery Society. Remond was the first abolitionist speaker to address large audiences. In 1840, he attended the World Anti-Slavery Convention in London. After spending

two years lecturing in Great Britain and Ireland, he returned to the United States in 1842 and became involved in the campaign to end segregation on the railroads of Massachusetts. In February 1842, he testified before a legislative committee of the Massachusetts House of Representatives that was then holding hearings on the issue. Segregation was finally abolished in April 1843. After this victory, Remond returned to his antislavery labors, becoming in the words of one historian (Benjamin Quarles, *Black Abolitionists* [New York, 1972], p. 131), "one of abolition's most effective speakers."

6. On February 24, 1848, the working class of Paris which had driven King Louis Phillipe from the Tuileries routed the Royalist deputies from the Chamber of the Palais Bourbon, and a Provisional Republican government was proclaimed by Alphonse Lamartine. Soon afterwards, owing to the insistence of the unemployed, the government founded the National Workshops under the direction of Louis Blanc.

7. The reference is to Sir Isaac Newton (1642-1727), English physicist, natural philosopher and mathematician and one of the greatest of English scientists, whose famous theory on the law of gravitation profoundly influenced the scientific thought of his day.

8. The reference is to John Locke (1632-1704), English philosopher and founder of British empiricism. Locke gained acclaim as a result of two distinguished works which appeared in 1690, *Essay Concerning Human Understanding* and *Two Treatises on Civil Government*, the latter of which in part argued in favor of the Glorious Revolution of 1688.

9. Francis Bacon (1561-1626) was the brilliant English philosopher, essayist, and statesman.

10. Charles Louis de Secondat Montesquieu (1689-1755) was the famous French jurist and philosopher. He gained acclaim with the publication of his greatest work, *The Spirit of the Laws*, a comparative study of three types of government--republic, monarchy and despotism. The book advanced the theory that climate and circumstances determine the form of government and that the powers of government should be separated and balanced.

11. Sir William Blackstone (1723-1780), the noted English jurist and professor of law at Oxford University, systematized the structure of English law, making it comparable to its Roman counterpart. His *Commentaries on the Law of England* (1765-1769) has undergone many reprintings and continues to this day to be the standard legal reference work for law students and practitioners alike.

12. The reference is to William Penn (1644-1718), a leading Quaker and the founder of Pennsylvania.

13. Philadelphians Benjamin Franklin, Benjamin Rush, Caspar Wistar and Anthony Benezet were active in the antislavery movement before and after the American Revolution, while New Jersey Quaker John Woolman (1720-1772) was a prominent crusader against slavery.

14. Robert Morris (1742-1798) was a leading Revolutionary patriot, active in the Pennsylvania Council of Safety, a member of the Continental Congress, and a signer of the Declaration of Independence.

15. James Wilson (1742-1798), Pennsylvania lawyer and revolutionary patriot, served in the Second Continental Congress and was a signer of the Declaration of Independence. Wilson later played a key role in the Pennsylvania fight for the ratification of the Constitution and served as an associate justice of the United States Supreme Court.

16. John Taylor (1753-1824) was an influential Virginian active in the American Revolutionary cause. Elected a delegate to the Continental Congress, Taylor also served in the Virginia House of Delegates and later joined with George Mason and others in opposing the new Constitution because it lacked a bill of rights. Taylor supported strongly a wider franchise, fairer representation and taxation, and strict construction of the Constitution, being an early exponent of States' rights and Southern consciousness.

17. The reference is to George Ross (1730-1779), Pennsylvania jurist, revolutionary patriot, and a signer of the Declaration of Independence.

18. John Adams (1735-1826) was the second president of the United States and a leading figure within the American Revolutionary cause, gaining prominence in 1765, when he attacked the Stamp Act of that year. Samuel Adams (1722-1803), a second cousin of John Adams, was a militant Revolutionary

agitator, organizer of the Sons of Liberty, member of both Continental Congresses, and a signer of the Declaration of Independence.

19. Thomas Paine (1737-1809) was a noted reformer, British by birth, who came to America and gained celebrity as author of the brilliant and incisive pamphlet *Common Sense*, which appeared early in 1776 and became an immediate best-seller, presenting in cogent terms the reasons why the colonies should declare their independence from England.

20. Elbridge Gerry (1744-1814) was a prominent revolutionary figure, born in Washington, D.C., educated at Harvard, and later elected to the Massachusetts General Court in 1772, becoming a member of its committee of correspondence. Gerry served in the Continental Congress and was a signer of the Declaration of Independence. He is perhaps remembered most for his "Gerrymander Bill," proposed in 1812 while he was governor of Massachusetts and designed specifically for the purpose of redistricting the state in such a way as to give his Republican Party more seats in the state senate than their actual numbers warranted.

21. The reference is to Stephen Hopkins (1707-1785), colonial governor of Rhode Island, member of the First and Second Continental Congresses, and a signer of the Declaration of Independence. Hopkins gained attention with the publication of his pamphlet, *The Rights of Colonies Examined*, which was reprinted widely throughout the colonies and in England and attacked such measures as the Sugar Act and the Stamp Act on the ground that direct taxation of an unconsenting people was tyrannous.

22. William Ellery (1727-1820) was a Rhode Island Revolutionary patriot and a signer of the Declaration of Independence. During the signing of that famous instrument, Ellery was said to have taken his position near the secretary of the gathering to observe the facial expressions of each delegate as they affixed their signatures to a document that might prove to be their death warrant. Ellery noted that they acted with "undaunted resolution."

23. James Forten (1766-1842) was born free in Philadelphia, served as a powder boy aboard a privateer during the Revolution, and invented a device for handling sails which earned him a fortune. Forten devoted much of his wealth to the campaign against slavery and discrimination against free blacks. He was also founder of the National Negro Convention movement.

24. George III (George William Frederick), 1738-1820, King of Great Britain and Ireland (1760-1820), ruled England during the period of the American Revolution. Noted for his secretiveness and obstinacy, his policies engendered widespread resentment and resistance throughout colonial America.

25. The reference is to Martin Luther (1483-1546), German leader of the Protestant Reformation.

26. Michael Servetus (1511-1553) was the eminent Spanish theologian and physician whose views on the Trinity provoked disapproval and condemnation by the adherents of both the Reformation and the Catholic Church. The publication of a book setting forth his ideas on Christianity led to his arrest and execution at Geneva, Switzerland, in 1553, largely on the testimony of another great Christian theologian, John Calvin.

27. The reference is to Robert Emmet (1778-1803), the militant Irish patriot, whose strong nationalist sympathies and dislike of the British resulted in an uprising led by him in the summer of 1803. The rebellion, however, soon degenerated into a brawl, and Emmet, who afterwards fled, was later captured, tried and hanged, gaining stature as a great hero of Irish patriots, largely on the basis of his stirring speech made from the scaffold.

28. Cicero (Marcus Tullius Cicero), 100 B.C.-43 B.C., greatest Roman orator, was famous also as a politician and philosopher.

29. Demosthenes (384?-322 B.C.), Greek orator, was generally considered the greatest of the Greek orators.

30. Croesus (560-546 B.C.) was a fabulously rich Lydian king of the sixth century B.C. whose name has become proverbial for great wealth.

31. Stephen Girard (1750-1831), the famous merchant, financier and philanthropist, was born in Bordeaux, France, and went to sea as a cabin boy in the French merchant marine. He later became a sea captain and a businessman of unusual acumen. Emigrating to Philadelphia in 1776, he engaged in a lucrative dry goods business. Girard soon expanded his interests into real estate, insurance and banking. During the War of 1812, he helped to avert a financial crisis by underwriting, with the aid of John Jacob Astor and David

Parish, most of a government war loan of 1813. At his death, he had willed over $6,000,000 for the establishment of Girard College, a school for orphaned white boys (subsequently integrated), which opened in 1848.

PROCEEDINGS OF THE STATE EQUAL RIGHT' CONVENTION, OF THE COLORED PEOPLE OF PENNSYLVANIA, HELD IN THE CITY OF HARRISBURG FEBRUARY 8th, 9th, and 10th, 1865, TOGETHER WITH A FEW OF THE ARGUMENTS PRESENTED SUGGESTING THE NECESSITY FOR HOLDING THE CONVENTION, AND AN ADDRESS OF THE COLORED STATE CONVENTION TO THE PEOPLE OF PENNSYLVANIA

To the members and friends of the Pennsylvania State Equal Rights' Convention

FELLOW CITIZENS--

The Committee, to whom was referred the matter of collecting, arranging and publishing the proceedings of the Convention, after having carefully revised and corrected the various documents placed in their hands by the Convention, would respectfully submit the following as their Report.

Yours fraternally,

Octavius V. Catto,
Alfred M. Green, } *Committee on Publication.*
Joseph C. Bustill,

PROCEEDINGS

In accordance with a call issued by the Pennsylvania State Equal Rights' League, the Convention was convened in the Union Wesleyan Church, Harrisburg, on Wednesday morning, February 8th, at 10 o'clock.

Mr. William Nesbitt of Altoona, Vice President of the State League, called the Convention to order, and by common consent, acted as its temporary Chairman, and Mr. Octavius V. Catto,[1] of Philadelphia, as Secretary.

By invitation of the Chairman, the Rev. John Price of Harrisburg, offered a prayer for the guidance and blessing of God during the deliberations of the Convention.

On motion of Mr. C. H. Vance, the Convention appointed the following gentlemen a Committee on Credentials:--

Charles H. Vance, *of Harrisburg*,
O. L. C. Hughes, *of Harrisburg*,
Moses Brown, *of Hollidaysburg*,
William Cooper, *of Philadelphia*,
James Davenger, *of Pittston*.

The first six seats across the front of the Church, were, on motion of Mr. A. M. Green, set apart for the accommodation of the members of the Convention.

On a motion of Mr. A. M. Green, Mr. David B. Bowser of Philadelphia was called upon to address the Convention while the Committee on Credentials were preparing their report.

Mr. Bowser proceeded to show the bright promises for the future which are everywhere now evident, and urged the importance of a strong and united effort for the purpose of securing our political rights throughout this Commonwealth. He hoped that from the proceedings of this Convention, the white citizens of the whole State would be made acquainted with the noble deeds and heroism of the Colored American; that we would make prominent the facts upon which we base our claims for equal and exact justice. The speaker enforced the necessity for organized action,--such, that when we return to our homes, every man shall feel it to be his duty to work earnestly and persistently for the furtherance of the great and glorious objects for which this Convention has been convened.

Mr. Daniel Williams of Hollidaysburg, was the next to address the Convention, on motion of Mr. R. M. Adger. He expressed himself as fully satisfied of the importance which attaches to the actions and proceedings of this body, and hoped that our actions would be harmonious and tend to the advancement of the cause of our people in this State.

On motion of Mr. D. D. Turner, Mr. John Q. Allen of Philadelphia, was called upon to make a few remarks. The gentleman spoke very briefly and hoped that the blood of the Negro, shed upon the fields of this rebellion, would prove sufficient to wash away the obstacles which prevent us from the enjoyment of our political rights.

Mr. J. J. Wright[2] of Wilkesbarre, was next called out, on motion of Mr. P. N. Judah. He believed that what we have come here to ask is, that there shall be restored to us, that which was unjustly wrested from us in 1838,--the right of Franchise. We have come to ask that our white fellow-citizens may act as though they believed in their own Declaration of Independence, and especially in its assertion, that all men are equal.

On motion of Mr. C. B. Gordon, Mr. Aaron Still of Reading, addressed the Convention. The speaker urged the importance of immediate action,--he thought that this was the opportune time, and that we should not allow the shedding of our brother's blood to be in vain. He maintained that there was some equivalent due the black man for his life and services, and that we should exert ourselves to receive it.

Rev. E. Weaver spoke next. The Reverend gentleman held forth earnestly upon the righteousness of the cause which called us together; he knew that the fact of our assembling had gone abroad over the State and urged that we proceed to business as wise and earnest men. He referred to the good which had resulted from the labors of John Brown,[3] Wendell Phillips, Charles Sumner[4] and the other champions of Liberty, and to the recent constitutional amendment abolishing Slavery,[5]--to the admission of John S. Rock[6] to practice in the Supreme Court, and declared it as his opinion that we were moving onward and our cause progressing.

The Committee appointed on Credentials made the following Report. This Roll includes all those subsequently reported from the Committee and those elected Honorary members by the Convention.

Pittsburgh

John Peck,	Equal Rights' League
George B. Vashon	" " "
A. J. Billows,	" " "
William H. Simpson,	" " "
A. W. Dunlap,	" " "

Philadelphia

Joseph C. Bustill,	Sixth District	Equal	Rights'	League	
Octavius V. Catto,	" "	"	"	"	
James R. Gordon,	" "	"	"	"	"
Alfred S. Cassey,	Fifth "	"	"	"	"
David D. Turner,	" "	"	"	"	"
William Cooper,	" "	"	"	"	"
James W. Purnell,	" "	"	"	"	"
Philip N. Judah,	" "	"	"	"	"
John Q. Allen,	Fourth "	"	"	"	

PENNSYLVANIA, 1865   141

Charles B. Gordon,   "   "   "   "   "
David B. Bowser,   Third   "   "   "   "
Redman Fauset,   "   "   "   "   "
Alfred Green,   "   State   "   "   "
Elisha Weaver,   "   "   "   "   "
William D. Forten,   Ladies' Union Association
William J. Alston,   Sanitary Com. St. Thomas' Church
Robert M. Adger,   Banneker Institute
George B. White,   "   "   "   "   "
James Prosser,   (honorary).
Joseph S. Campbell,   "
Matthias W. Johnson,   "
John C. Bowers,   Union League
Jesse E. Glasgow,   "   "
William Morris,   First District Equal Rights' League

                              Pittston

George W. Butler,   State Equal Rights' League
James Davenger,   State Equal Rights' League
James Green,   (honorary).
Decatur Blue,   "

                           Allegheny City

Benjamin F. Pulpress,
Samuel A. Neale,
H. B. Williamson,
George W. Dimey,
Edward R. Parker,

                              Harrisburg

Joseph A. Nelson,   State Equal Rights' League
John E. Price,
Charles H. Vance,
William M. Jones,
Martin Perry,
Curry Taylor,
B. J. Carter,   Baptist Church
Alex T. Harris,   Brotherly Love Lodge, O. F.
O. L. C. Hughes,
Thomas Early,   (honorary).
James Alexander,   "
Charles H. Cann,   "
George W. Saunders,   "

                              Birmingham

James Henry,   Equal Rights' League
Henry Jackson,   "   "   "

                               Altoona

William Nesbitt,   Equal Rights' League
Thomas B. Shorter,   "   "   "
John Alexander,   (honorary).
John H. Shorter,   "
George Hooper   "

                             Williamsport

Lewis Hill,   Equal Rights' League
Charles Bryan,   (honorary).
Charles H. Kelly,   "

Hollidaysburg

Daniel Williams,   Equal Rights' League
Moses Brown,   "   "   "
John Thomas,   (honorary).

Wilkesbarre

J. J. Wright,
Benjamin Wilson,   (honorary).

Bellefonte

John Welsh.   Equal Rights' League

Lewistown

Samuel Molston.   Equal Rights' League

Reading

Aaron L. Still.

Towanda

Solomon Cooper.

Huntingdon

J. G. Chaplain.

York

Merriman Cupit,   (honorary).

Mr. J. C. Bustill of Philadelphia, moved that a Committee of twelve be appointed to nominate permanent officers for the Convention.

Moved by Daniel Williams of Hollidaysburg, that the motion be so amended that the Committee shall consist of one delegate from each county now represented in the Convention.

The amendment was carried without debate, and the original motion as amended was then put and unanimously carried.

On motion of Mr. Hughes of Harrisburg, that the President appoint the Committee to nominate permanent officers, the President appointed the following:--

> Joseph C. Bustill, of *Philadelphia*,
> Samuel Molston, of *Mifflin county*,
> Lewis Hill, of *Lycoming county*,
> John C. Chaplain, of *Huntingdon county*,
> Daniel Williams, of *Blair county*,
> Aaron L. Still, of *Berks county*,
> John E. Price, of *Dauphin county*.
> William H. Simpson, of *Allegheny county*,
> J. J. Wright, of *Luzerne county*,
> John Weish, of *Centre county*.

The Committee retired for consultation, and in their absence Mr. Turner of Philadelphia, moved that a Committee of five be appointed to draft Rules for the government of the Body.

The motion was carried, and the Convention appointed the following as the Committee:--

> David B. Bowser,

PENNSYLVANIA, 1865 143

        David D. Turner,
        George B. Vashon, } 7
        Benjamin F. Pulpress,
        Moses Brown.

  Moved by Mr. Robert M. Adger, that when we adjourn, we adjourn to meet at 2 o'clock this afternoon. Carried.
  On motion of Mr. Bustill, the Convention then adjourned.

Afternoon Session.

  Pursuant to adjournment, the President, pro tempore, called the Convention to order at 2 o'clock.
  The Roll, as reported from the Committee on Credentials, was called, and the minutes of the morning session read and approved.
  Mr. Joseph C. Bustill, Chairman of the Committee on Permanent Organization, asked permission to make the following Report,--

        FOR PRESIDENT,

        Rev. John Peck, *of Pittsburg.*

        VICE-PRESIDENTS,

        Rev. Elisha Weaver, *Philadelphia,*
        Moses Brown, *Hollidaysburg,*
        O. L. C. Hughes, *Harrisburg,*
        James Davenger, *Pittston,*
        John Welsh, *Bellefonte,*
        William Nesbitt, *Altoona.*

        SECRETARIES,

        Octavius V. Catto, *Philadelphia,*
        A. T. Harris, *Harrisburg,*
        George B. Vashon, *Pittsburgh.*

  Mr. A. M. Green, moved that the name of Mr. Redman Fausett of Philadelphia, be substituted for that of Prof. Vashon on the list of Secretaries. Carried.
  The Report, as amended, was then unanimously adopted.
  The President elect then took the Chair, and the Convention and audience joined in singing:--

        Blow ye the trumpet, blow;

after which, the President, having delivered an earnest and feelingly eloquent prayer for the harmony and wisdom of the deliberations of the Convention, proceeded to acknowledge the honor conferred upon him by electing him to the position which he occupied, and gave it as his opinion that the present Convention had more reasons to hope for the success of the objects which it was convened to further, than any other ever held by the Colored people of this State. He believed firmly in the hand of Providence as seen in the shifting scenes through which we are now passing, and urged the members to lay aside all sectional feelings and proceed to the business before them, as one man, united in desire and united in action.
  On motion of Mr. A. M. Green, the following was unanimously adopted.
  Resolved, That the thanks of this Convention are due, and are hereby tendered to Messrs. William Nesbitt of Altoona, and Octavius V. Catto of Philadelphia, for the able and efficient manner in which they have respectively served this Body as temporary Chairman and Secretary.
  Mr. D. B. Bowser, Chairman of the Committee on Rules, made the following

Report

1st. There shall be two regular daily sessions of the Convention, and each opened with prayer.

The Morning Session shall commence at 9½ o'clock, A.M., and ajourn at 12½ o'clock, P.M.

The Afternoon Session shall commence at 2 o'clock, P.M., and adjourn at 5 o'clock, P.M.

2d. One-third of the enrolled members of the Convention shall constitute a quorum for the transaction of business.

3d. No member shall leave the Convention without permission from the President, and no member shall be recognized or motion received as before the Convention, unless the speaker or mover is at the time within the bar of the Convention.

4th. No member shall be allowed to speak more than twice upon the same question, unless by special consent of the Convention; and not longer than ten minutes the first, and five minutes the second time.

9th. Mathias' Manual shall govern the proceedings of the Body, in all cases for which provisions are not herein stated.

Appended to the Report was a Resolution for the discharge of the Committee, and on motion of Mr. D. D. Turner the Resolution was adopted.

Mr. R. M. Adger then moved the adoption of the Report as presented by the Committee. Carried.

The Convention, on motion of Mr. O. L. C. Hughes, appointed the following gentlemen as a Committee on Finance:

James R. Gordon,	John E. Price,
Joseph C. Bustill,	George Butler,
William H. Simpson.	

Mr. Redman Fausett moved that a Business Committee of seven be appointed. Carried.

The Committee was appointed by the Body and consisted of

George B. Vashon,	Alfred M. Green,
Daniel Williams,	Benjamin F. Pulpress,
David B. Bowser,	James Henry,
Joseph A. Nelson.	

Moved by Mr. Joseph C. Bustill, that all Resolutions for the consideration of this Convention shall be presented by or through the Business Committee.

Messrs. A. L. Still and William Nesbitt opposed the passage of the Resolution on the ground that it had the appearance of trammeling our action and not allowing that freedom among us which would insure harmony through fair play.

Mr. D. D. Turner urged the passage of the Resolution and argued against the assumption of the gentlemen who preceded him. He maintained that there was no disposition or intention to trammel, tie or gag;--but that such a rule was necessary to guard us against subjects of trifling importance over which much valuable time might be wasted.

Mr. E. Weaver believed the Resolution sufficiently proper in the spirit which prompted it, but thought for the sake of disarming even the appearance of unfairness, we might so amend it as to satisfy both sides of the question. He therefore moved as an amendment, "that all Resolutions be read before the Convention and then referred to the Business Committee." He thought, by this course, such Resolutions as the Business Committee deemed impolitic need not be returned to the Convention.

The amendment was then put and unanimously carried. The question was then taken upon the passage of the Resolution as amended and decided in the affirmative.

Mr. D. D. Turner moved that O. L. C. Hughes be appointed to secure an

American Flag, for the decoration of the President's desk. Carried.

On motion of Mr. P. N. Judah, the Rev. W. J. Alston of Philadelphia, was unanimously elected Chaplain of the Convention.

Mr. James R. Gordon moved the appointment of a Sergeant-at arms. Carried.

The Convention appointed Mr. George W. Saunders, of Harrisburg.

Mr. O. L. C. Hughes having secured the National Flag, was, on motion of Mr. M. Cupit, thanked for his services and discharged from further action in the matter.

Mr. James R. Gordon, Chairman of the Finance Committee, reported, that after due consideration, the Committee had concluded to recommend the Convention to pass the following Resolutions:

1st. That each enrolled member of the Convention be taxed two dollars.

2d. That a collection be raised at the close of each session, and that the proceeds from both enactments be disbursed to meet the expenses of the Convention.

The Report, on motion of Mr. A. S. Cassey, was adopted.

Mr. D. D. Turner offered a Resolution endorsing the action of the Pennsylvania delegation to the Syracuse Convention, in forming the basis of the State League of Pennsylvania, and moved the previous question, on its reference to the Business Committee.

The question,--"shall the previous question be taken?"--was decided affirmatively and the question then recurring on the reference of the Resolution, it was unanimously adopted.

Mr. Joseph C. Bustill then presented a series of Resolutions on the state of the country at large, which, on motion of Mr. A. S. Cassey, were referred to the Business Committee.

On motion of Mr. James R. Gordon, the members of the Convention were now requested to proceed at once to the payment of the two dollars tax as recommended by the Finance Committee.

Mr. J. J. Wright moved that Messrs. James Green, Decatur Blue and Benjamin Wilson be elected honorary members of the Convention. Carried. On motion of Mr. A. S. Cassey, Mr. Jas. Prosser, of Philadelphia, was elected an honorary member; and also Mr. Thos. Early, of Harrisburg, on motion of Mr. A. L. Still.

The hour of adjournment having arrived, Mr. A. T. Harris moved the suspension of the rule, and that the session be extended one half hour. Carried.

The half hour was passed in hearing the Report of the Committee on Evening meetings, and collecting the Finance Committee's tax.

After the expiration of the half hour extension, the President declared the Convention adjourned to meet this evening at $7\frac{1}{2}$ o'clock.

Evening Session.

A large and enthusiastic audience assembled in the Church at an early hour, and at $7\frac{1}{2}$ o'clock the President called the Convention to order.

Prayer was offered by the Chaplain, Rev. W. J. Alston. Sergeant-Major A. M. Green, in accordance with the report of the Committee on Evening meetings, was introduced as the first speaker.

The gentleman proceeded briefly and graphically to a review of the disabilities under which we have been laboring for years, and portrayed in eloquent and vivid language the promises which are now so evidently before us.

He then reviewed the efforts of the Colored man for the restoration of the Union, and reminded the audience of their unswerving and unexceptional loyalty throughout the entire struggle.

The address was frequently interrupted by applause.

Mr. Davis D. Turner was introduced and after a few patriotic remarks, asked to be excused, with the understanding that he would address the audience, if an opportunity were afforded, before the adjournment of the Convention.

Mr. A. M. Green said that the Hon. Morrow B. Lowry, Senator from Erie, (cheers) was in the house, and he was well assured that this assemblage would be highly gratified to hear a speech from so fearless and eloquent a defender of impartial liberty.

The audience immediately raised a shout of applause which was not abated until Mr. Lowry had ascended to the speaker's desk.

The President introduced the gentleman in a few appropriate remarks and Mr. Lowry said, that he had been "advised of the object which has called this highly creditable and large Convention of the most intelligent Colored men of the State,"--he had learned that the most important subject now agitating our minds, was the elective franchise;--and proceeded to point out the difficulty in the way of our immediate possession of this right, so justly due us.

"There is a provision in the Constitution of our State which allows its amendment, only once in five years, and you will remember that one year ago our Constitution was amended so that our soldiers in the field might vote as if at home, and hence we are at present prevented from making any other amendments for five years from the passage of the last." He thought, however, that the general government might propose amendments and in that case the Legislature could take immediate action thereon. Mr. Lowry claimed to be one of the first who argued for the arming of the negro, and his entering this struggle as a soldier.

He had said in the beginning of the war that "he would arm the blacks, put them in front and let the rebels shoot at their stolen property with stolen guns at the rate of a thousand dollars a shot."

For this expression he had been almost mobbed, and was waited upon by a committee and asked to define his position:--this he did not fail to do; in the course of which he went much further in the same direction, and much too to the discomfiture of said committee.

He would remind us that the Government would do nothing for us that it could possibly help; it never had, and never would.

"The Government needed your aid, and on this account you have received the little which to-night you enjoy."

He believed that the white loyalists. would be forced to give the colored man his rights;--"if we get those devilish rebels back, they and the foreign copperheads would put the loyalists in a minority, and to avoid this the negro would have to be enfranchised."

In conclusion he would urge the colored people "to educate themselves and their children, take care, by all means, of your children; educate and rear them properly, ask for what is right, and submit to nothing wrong."

The speech was received with great applause, and after its eloquent delivery, three hearty cheers were given for Senator Morrow B. Lowry, of Erie county.

Mr. O. L. C. Hughes, offered the following Resolution, and it was adopted with acclamation.

"*Resolved*, That we have listened with commingled feelings of pride and admiration to the very able and eloquent address of the Honorable Senator Lowry, and that we regard him as an unfaltering, indefatigable and fearless vindicator of the rights of the colored man."

The audience, accompanied by Mr. D. D. Turner at the Melodeon, then sang the John Brown song.

The Rev. William J. Alston was next called upon to address the meeting, but after a few well chosen words, asked to be excused for this evening.

Mr. John Q. Allen then took the stand and delivered a short and very acceptable speech. He believed that the white man had contempt for the condition of a slave, and hence his opinion of the colored man, who either is a slave, or descended from slaves.

Prof. George B. Vashon, made the closing speech; and by his eloquence, argument and truths, kept the closest attention of the vast assembly throughout the enitire delivery.

The benediction was pronounced by the President, and the Convention adjourned to meet to-morrow morning at 9½ o'clock.

SECOND DAY

Thursday Morning, February 9th.

Pursuant to adjournment, the Convention met at 9½ o'clock.

In the absence of the President, Vice-President E. Weaver called the Convention to order, and prayer was offered by the Chaplain.

The Roll was called and the minutes of the last session read and approved.

On motion of Mr. William Nesbitt, Mr. John Alexander, of Altoona, was made an honorary member of the Convention; also Mr. James Alexander, of Harrisburg, on motion of Mr. O. L. C. Hughes.

Mr. D. D. Turner moved that Messrs. Charles Bryan, M. W. Johnson and Joseph S. Campbell be elected honorary members. Carried.

Messrs. John Shorter and George Hooper, on motion of Mr. Moses Brown, and Mr. John Thomas, on motion of Mr. William Nesbitt, were elected honorary members.

The Business Committee, through their Chairman, Prof. George B. Vashon, made their first Report, consisting of a Declaration of Sentiment and the following Resolutions.

On motion of Mr. R. M. Adger, the Declaration of Sentiment was adopted. [See Appendix.]

Mr. O. L. C. Hughes moved that the Resolutions reported by the Committee be taken up separately. Carried.

The first of the series of Resolution was read, as follows:

Resolved, That we, the Pennsylvania State Equal Rights' Convention in Assembly met, do congratulate one another, the State League, and the friends of Equal Rights without regard to color throughout the State and country, upon the assembling of so large a number of delegates representing the feelings, sentiments and desires of our people upon this all important subject of Political Equality; and that we pledge our harmonious and energetic efforts in all our deliberations for the common good. Mr. Charles B. Gordon moved its adoption. Carried.

2. *Resolved,* That the Emancipation of the District of Columbia,[8] Maryland, Louisiana, Missouri[9] and Tennessee; the amendment of the Federal Constitution,[10] and its endorsement by various State Legislatures, including that of Pennsylvania; the admission of John S. Rock to the Supreme Court of the United States; and the progress of liberal sentiments everywhere manifest, are auspicious signs of the times, and demand our earnest and united efforts for the improvement of our moral, social and political condition. Adopted, on motion of Mr. B. F. Pulpress.

3. *Resolved,* That we, regarding the Elective Franchise as the all important subject for our deliberation and united action, insist upon the necessity of petitioning Congress and the Legislature to so alter and amend the laws as to give every native born colored citizen over the age of twenty-one, the right to vote, as fully as their white fellow citizens possess it. The Resolution was adopted, on motion of Mr. Joseph A. Nelson.

4. *Resolved,* That we are for measures and not for men, and will not permit friend or foe to retard the great movement now in operation, aiming to secure Equal Rights without regard to color; and that every man in the State be solicited to contribute one dollar a year to create a permanent fund to carry on this great movement. Adopted, on motion of Mr. William Nesbitt.

5. *Resolved,* That the present state of affairs demands of this Convention, which is the legitimate exponent of the sentiments of the colored people of this State, that it give all efforts looking toward their elevation to legal and political equality, and the entire recognition of their rights as men, citizens and soldiers, its unqualified approbation and support. And that of all the many efforts being put forth in the cause of humanity, we recognize none more commendable to the lovers of justice and christianity, than those of the "Ladies' Union Association" of Philadelphia, to which this Convention tender their warmest thanks, for untiring exertions in relieving the wants of our sick and wounded soldiers, whose suffering can only be imagined but never truly described; and that we pledge ourselves to use every influence within our power, to encourage and sustain these ladies in their laudable and benevolent enterprise.

Moved, by Mr. Joseph C. Bustill, that the Resolution be adopted.

Mr. O. C. Hughes moved to amend by inserting "and their auxiliaries," after the words "Ladies' Union Association of Philadelphia." Mr. Hughes argued earnestly for the amendment,--that other associations which had been working in the same good cause, might receive notice and encouragement at our hands.

Mr. Joseph C. Bustill raised the point that the amendment was not in order, as it destroyed the original intent of the Resolution.

After an animated discussion on Mr. Bustill's point of order, Mr. Hughes withdrew his amendment by common consent.

The question being now on the original resolution, Rev. W. J. Alston desired to make a few remarks in opposition to the passage of the Resolution in its present form. He said, that he was here, a member of this Convention, as a delegate from an Association in his Church. That Association was known as the Ladies' Sanitary Commission of St. Thomas Church, and had been working, and are now earnestly and persistently, in season and out of season, working for the alleviation of the sufferings of the sick and wounded soldiers.

They had commenced early in this good work, and had recently held one of the largest and most successful fairs ever held in Philadelphia, for this cause. Over twelve hundred dollars had been raised at this Fair, by these ladies, and he was deprived accidentally on his way to Harrisburg of a record of their deeds and a report of their workings which would satisfy any member of this body, that there was no association among us which has done, and is now doing more for the sick and wounded soldiers than the Ladies of this Commission. He thought the ladies ought to be included in this Resolution.

Mr. Wm. D. Forten, said that as he had written and presented this Resolution, which seems so to arouse us, he thought it proper to state a few facts in explanation of it. In the first place, this society, the "Ladies' Union Association," was independent of any other in the State, they were not as his friend Alston's society is, connected with, or auxiliary to a white Society. They were entirely free to dispose of their funds as pleased them best, and they were primarily organized for the purpose of relieving the needs of colored sick and wounded troops. Furthermore, this society had so far sympathized with the objects for which this Convention had been convened, that they had paid their ten dollars and joined the State League. He thought this Association alone should go through in this Resolution, and assured the Convention that their noble efforts in behalf of our Troops, merited any compliment we could give.

The Rev. E. Weaver, called for a second reading of the Resolution, after which Mr. James R. Gordon obtained the floor and opposed the passage of the Resolution. Mr. Gordon said, from what he knew personally, the Association represented by Rev. Alston had done nobly for the suffering heroes who had follen wounded and sick upon the field and in the camp. He was in favor of giving "honor to whom honor is due," and as both these societies, and others throughout the State had been engaged in this good work--he thought it unfair to notice one and ignore the others;--he would therefore offer an amendment, that after the title, "Ladies' Union Association," there be inserted, "Ladies' Sanitary Commission of St. Thomas Church," "Union Association of Harrisburg," and other similar associations throughout the State."

Rev. W. J. Alston, in favoring the passage of the amendment, wished it to be understood that he was only contending for the equality of these societies,--he did not desire the one to be in the least above the other--he desired a unanimity of action and harmony with respect to both.

Messrs. A. S. Cassey and Jesse E. Glasgow participated briefly in the discussion and Mr. D. D. Turner moved the previous question.

The President inquired if the previous question should be taken, and it was declared affirmatively.

The question, then being on the amendment offered by Mr. Gordon, it was adopted. The Resolution as amended, was then put upon its passage and carried.

Mr. Robert M. Adger read a Resolution in reference to the Banneker Literary Institute and similar Societies. On motion of Mr. Geo. B. White it was referred to the Business Committee.

Mr. J. J. Wright offered a Resolution in reference to colored teachers for colored schools. It was referred to the Business Committee on motion of Mr. M. Cupit.

A Resolution, thanking Charles Sumner, M. B. Lowry and others for their exertions in behalf of colored men's rights, was introduced by Mr. James W. Purnell, and on motion of Mr. William Cooper, referred to Business Committee.

Mr. A. M. Green moved that the Committee on Evening meetings be directed to invite the Hon. Messrs. Graham, Striker and Bingham to address the Convention this evening. Carried.

The President then declared the Convention adjourned until this afternoon at 2 o'clock.

Afternoon Session.

The Convention assembled at the appointed hour; the President in the Chair. Prayer was offered by the Rev. C. J. Carter, and the minutes read and approved.

Mr. O. L. C. Hughes offered a Resolution in reference to the formation of a State League. On motion of Mr. A. T. Harris it was referred to the Business Committee.

Rev. Elisha Weaver and John E. Price read, each a Resolution, which were both referred to the Business Committee.

Mr. Jackson, of Birmingham, desired to make a few remarks before the Convention, and was, on motion, permitted to speak.

The gentleman had come from opposite Pittsburgh, and had recently an interview with the Hon. Mr. Morehead, who had told him that it was best for the colored people to keep possession of their funds and not to expend them in efforts which at the present time would only prove fruitless.

Mr. Jackson was gratified to see that the Convention had proceeded thus far with so much harmony. He stated that the colored people of Birmingham had taken part in the celebration of President Lincoln's first inauguration, and were invited and expected to participate in his second inauguration. When asked by the copperheads, if they were voters--they answered, they were men.

Mr. B. F. Pulpress moved that the Secretary, on behalf of the Convention, extend an invitation to both branches of the Legislature, to attend this evening's session of the Convention. Carried.

Mr. James Alexander, on motion of Mr. A. T. Harris, was elected Assistant Sergeant-at-arms.

Mr. Moses Brown moved that a committee of three be appointed to wait on the Superintendents of Railroads and enquire what arrangements could be made to secure a reduction of fare to those members of the Convention who had paid full fare. Carried.

The President appointed Messrs. O. L. C. Hughes, Charles H. Vance and Thomas Early, the Committee.

The Business Committee, through their chairman, reported the following Resolutions, which, on motion of Mr. W. H. Simpson, were considered separately.

The following Resolution was read first:

Resolved, "That this Convention recognizing the importance of the moral and literary elements in a people's character, earnestly urge our young colored men to organize among themselves institutions tending to their intellectual and moral elevation." Adopted on motion of Mr. J. J. Wright.

The second Resolution, on motion of Mr. John Chaplain, was adopted, as follows:

Resolved, "That we regard with disdain, and question the loyalty of those members of the State Legislature who so strenuously opposed the ratification of the anti-slavery clause of the United States' Constitution, and all other matters which particularly pertain to the interests of the 50,000 loyal colored citizens of the State; and that we heartily thank the Hon. M. B. Lowry, of Erie County, for his manly and Christian stand in defence of the disfranchised portion of this Commonwealth, and particularly for his answer to the inquiry in reference to the elective franchise;--that he would give that right to the negro, as well as to the white man."

Resolution the third, presented by Mr. J. J. Wright, reads as follows:

Resolved, "That inasmuch as the School Law of Pennsylvania provides that where there are twenty children of African descent, a separate school shall be established for them; and as we know by experimental knowledge, that colored children make greater advancement under the charge of colored teachers than they do under white teachers, therefore we consider it to be our incumbent duty, as lovers of the advancement of our race, to see to it, that our schools are under the charge of colored teachers."

Mr. D. D. Turner opposed the Resolution in its present wording; he thought that as we came to this Convention to protest against proscription and prejudice, we ought to be very careful of the kind of Resolutions we passed.

Rev. Mr. Jones thought the matter under consideration had the tendency to produce ill effects on the welfare of our people--therefore he could not support the measure.

Mr. B. F. Pulpress, said the subject was ill advised and injurious in its operations--and he was, in consequence, opposed to its going out as the sentiment of this body.

Mr. John Q. Allen took the floor and spoke against the passing of the Resolution. He thought it had the appearance of that very distinction on account of color, against which we were all so ready to complain, and he would therefore offer as an amendment, that the Resolution be so worded as to include the clause,--"no discrimination on account of color ought to be made in the appointment of teachers for colored schools."

Rev. W. J. Alston thought the Resolution of Mr. Wright judicious and necessary, he was therefore opposed to the amendment. He said the wisdom of such a Resolution from this Convention, had been made evident to him by an experience of twelve years, and instanced the difference in appearance between the schools under white and those under colored teachers.

Mr. James R. Gordon spoke in opposition to the amendment and mentioned the particulars of an instance in which no such charity toward us was shown, as is provided for in this amendment. Mr. Gordon continued his remarks at length and with earnestness.

Mr. J. J. Wright advocated the passage of the original Resolution; he was unwilling to accept any such amendment as the one under consideration, and said that there was no use of our making any provision about literary qualifications, for white teachers sufficiently qualified could not be induced to take charge of colored schools. He was surprised to hear gentlemen of intelligence discussing this amendment favorably.

Mr. A. M. Green thought it disgraceful for colored men, particularly the Philadelphia delegation, to argue against such a Resolution as that presented by Mr. Wright. He thought it particularly so in their case, as they knew the shameful treatment which colored persons had received at the hands of the Board of School Controllers in Philadelphia. He also believed that these gentlemen from that city would be ashamed to meet their constituents after having opposed such a Resolution as the one under consideration.

Mr. D. B. Bowser was of the same opinion as the gentleman who had preceeded him, and said that he and others had tried for nine years to secure a colored teacher for a colored school in his section of Philadelphia, and that their efforts were without success. The gentleman instanced several cases of which he knew, in sustaining his position against the amendment, and for the Resolution.

The hour of adjournment having arrived, the rule was suspended and the session extended one-half hour, on motion of Rev. C. J. Carter.

Mr. John Alexander obtained the floor and spoke against the amendment. He thought the Resolution the right thing and at the right time, and would therefore vote for its passage.

The question on the amendment was then put and lost.

Mr. O. V. Catto thought that the Resolution offered by Mr. Wright was just and proper in the motive which prompted it and in the object toward which it looked, but he was of the opinion that while the spirit of the Resolution was right, the phraseology was such that it might be quoted as a document based on preferences for certain teachers merely on account of their color. He did not wish to turn his back on the fact that the colored man was the best teacher for colored children. He had long been of the belief that no white man could so well instruct colored children as could a colored teacher. This opinion he thought was not founded on any superior mental abilities of the one man over the other--he was of the belief that all men under similar circumstances were equal, and while he would vote in favor of the colored teacher as Mr. Wright's Resolution required, he would do it on principle and not from even the shadow of prejudice in favor of any particular color. The colored man, he believed was the better teacher because he had the welfare of the race more at heart, knowing that they rose or fell together, and because he would take more care to strengthen those faculties in which the white reace thought the colored child deficient.

As an amendment, he would therefore offer, in order to avoid all misunderstanding and place this body right before the people at large, that the

Resolution be so amended as to contain this clause:--"in the appointment of teachers for these schools, colored persons, their literary qualifications being sufficient, should recieve the preference; not by reason of their complexion, but because they are better qualified by conventional circumstances outside of the school-house."

Mr. A. M. Green then moved the previous question. The demand "shall the previous question be taken," was declared affirmatively, and the amendment unanimously adopted. The Resolution as amended was then carried, on motion of Mr. R. M. Adger.

The time having expired, the President declared the Convention adjourned to meet this evening at 7½ o'clock.

Evening Session.

At an hour long before the opening of the Convention, the Church was crowded to its utmost capacity, and at 7½ o'clock the President called the house to order. After singing a hymn, the Convention listened to an earnest and eloquent prayer from the Rev. W. J. Alston, Chaplain.

Mr. Davis D. Turner was then introduced by the President as the first speaker.

The gentlemen began by making evident the fact that we are a rising people and the times are changing in our favor. He believed that the struggle now going on in this country could not be ended unless colored men entered the war more numerously. He enumerated some of the signs of our advancement, and said these rapid and onward strides of freedom showed the development of a higher civilization: the fact that Hayti and Liberia are placed in the same category with other nations of the earth, the emancipation of several States and the District of Columbia, the amendment to the Constitution, and its being ratified by several Legislatures, are so many evidences of our progress, and urge upon us the necessity of united efforts. We should not falter by the way, but being determined, move steadily onward, allowing no dissentions, no party strifes, no chimerical schemes, nothing whatever, to swerve us for one moment from the line of duty. We would say "let the dead past bury the dead," keep pace with the age in which we live; then and only then, would we be doing our duty to God, to ourselves, and to our race. The speech was frequently interrupted by applause.

Prof. Geo. B. Vashon, now read a memorial to the Legislature of Pennsylvania, asking them to grant the colored man the elective franchise.

On motion of Mr. D. D. Turner, it was adopted, ordered to be printed, and distributed, one to each member of the Legislature, on behalf of this Convention. [See Appendix.]

The Hon. James L. Graham, of the State Senate, being in the house, was loudly called and he responded.

"We are living," said he, "in a great age, in the midst of a rebellion which has had no parallel in the world's history;--it is similar only to that which occurred in the fair fields of Eden." He had often been reminded through the phases of this rebellion, of the sentiment, that there is a "Divinity which shapes our ends;" and we ought to bow to-night, in reverence and thanks to that God above us, for His interposition in our affairs. "We have just begun the work, and you the colored people, have it in your hands to shape your own destiny. The time was, when the black man was looked upon as a chattel, bought and sold in the market place; but thank God a purer and brighter life has burst upon us, and the colored race may now elevate itself to a respectable place among the nations of the earth." "I am," said Mr. Graham, "no new man in the Anti-Slavery belief, twenty-two years ago I entered the field, and although told that I was too young to combat these strong prejudices, I have continued to this day.

"Look at the course of this rebellion, just so long as the administration hesitated to let the oppressed go free, just so long did our armies suffer defeat; but when God taught Abraham Lincoln to let them go free, and he did it, we began to conquer, and have gone on from victory to victory. Your disabilities as colored men will be removed, you will yet enter upon the enjoyment of equal rights, and from the fullness of my heart, I hope the day will soon come." The speech was eloquently delivered and at its conclusion, three cheers were given for Senator Graham of Allegheny County.

The Hon. Mr. Bingham, was next introduced by the President, and said that on the question of equal rights, he thought old Allegheny sound. He spoke in complimentary terms of the size and intelligence of the Convention and thought the memorial awhile ago read was an able and opportune paper. One of the members of the Legislature, in a conversation with him thought that should the question of extending the elective franchise to colored people, be presented to the people of the State, it would be lost by about one thousand against one. Mr. Bingham was, however, of the opinion that his county would do much better than that on the question.

He said that the strongest speech, he ever delivered in the Senate, was against that prejudice which endeavored to prevent colored men from presenting such a memorial as the one adopted here to-night. The gentleman proceeded at length to show the changes through which the American people were now passing, and adverted to the fact, that in the Dred Scott case, the Court having decided the man a slave, the Chief Justice went entirely out of the record to give an additional opinion on a subject not before them, and that now the Almighty has overturned him and all who sustained him. He advanced the belief that any man who four years ago would have said that the general government would interfere with slavery where it existed, would have been thought a fit subject for yonder lunatic asylum. But Providence had changed all of this, yes slavery was dead; there is no resurrection or human power that can raise this wrong again, or bind the chains around the black man as they existed four years ago to-night. He declared that this country was yet to be an asylum for all men, without regard to color or clime. Still, said he, "you must not hope to see prejudice entirely wiped out in your life time. I will not flatter you; that which had the growth of a century cannot die out in a year, and permit me in conclusion, to say that as long as I live no deed or word of mine shall ever be against the negro's enjoyment of every legal and political right." The address was received with great applause and three cheers given at its conclusion.

The vast audience, led by Mr. D. B. Bowser, and accompanied by Mr. D. D. Turner at the melodeon, then sang the John Brown hymn.

Prof. Geo. B. Vashon was called up and introduced by the President. The Professor said that he was not prepared to make a set speech and thought it best for the audience to excuse him, but as they insisted upon his saying something and as he thought no one could be present in such an assembly as this without feeling some degree of inspiration he would present such thoughts as naturally arose in his mind.

He said that we had come together in this Convention to present our claim for equal and impartial liberty, that principle of liberty which is instilled in every man at his birth, that spirit, which is common to every human breast, that freedom which is desired by all men, whether they be the fur-clad denizen of the polar regions or the swarthy children, blackened by the sun of the tropics. The sentiment, "that whatever interests mankind, as such interests me," was the sentiment uttered by a slave, and it makes an echo in the heart of every man to-day. It was that sentiment which brought the echo from Russia, England and all Europe.

The speaker said that the American people might become great and powerful,--they might be able to count the whole continent as theirs,--and see no inch of soil not dotted by villages or other marks of civilized life,--their scholars may look in their reach to the limit of human knowledge and become almost creative in their grasp of intellect,--but if their government be not founded and administered in justice and equity, if the people did not enjoy impartial liberty and equality before the law, there was nothing secure or permanent in this country.

He thought, if it were necessary, that we would come together every year until our complete enfranchisement were secured. If we should die while making the effort, let us remember the words of Byron,[11]

They never fail who die in a just cause.

But he believed we were nearing the good time when all men throughout the broad expanse of this country would enjoy equal legal and political privileges and immunities.

The address was eloquently delivered and listened to with the utmost attention by the vast audience, except when interrupted by applause.

Sergeant-Major A. M. Green was loudly called for and addressed the Convention as follows: He had endeavored last evening to present a legal argument in favor of our demands. Thus far, this evening's speeches have tended to show, upon moral principles and natural rights, the title of the colored man to liberty and equality before the law. I will, said he, throw aside these arguments and take those which God is pleased to be showing throughout the land in events now transpiring. He then presented the part which the colored American had taken, the suffering he had endured, and the labor he had performed in saving the government and institutions of this country.

He asserted that Daniel Webster had years ago said, that this anti-slavery principle would force itself into respect, and that he knew nothing in the Union which was secure against its advance. The speaker believed that the two principles admitted in the administration of our government are in direct opposition, they must conflict, slave and free labor are irreconcilable, and freedom has for years been making concessions to the slave power:--in the purchase of Louisiana[12] and Florida,[13] in waging the Mexican war,[14] in forming and repealing the Missouri Compromise[15] and in giving the Dred Scott decision, slavery had received what she demanded. But after a few years the conflict took another phase, and John Brown began it at Harper's Ferry, and it was now being continued in the midst of a sea of blood. He proceeded next to show the changes which had taken place in the character of the war, and said if Pennsylvania asked colored men to enlist in the United States service, let us ask Pennsylvania to grant us our rights. We have the common good in view and are willing to fight for equal rights and privileges. Colored men cannot now be asked to go south to free their brethren, Jefferson Davis[16] himself admits that slavery is dead; let us then demand another plea when we are invited to the field.

We ask that when the colored man returns from the field of battle, he will not be turned from your ballot box, your railroad cars, your hotels and schools, thereby renewing in the bosom of his white fellow soldier who has fought side by side with him, all the old prejudices which existed before the war. Let us demand that our pensions and back pay may not be so generally neglected as is the case west. Let our white fellow citizens remember that God will make fruitless all efforts for peace until we acknowledge that truth embodied in the principle of the Law of the Prophets,--"thou shalt love the Lord will all thy heart and thy neighbor as thyself," then shall we have a permanent and secure peace.

The speech was eloquently delivered and well received.

Mr. J. J. Wright was the next speaker. After thanking God for bringing upon the country this bloody rebellion as an exterminator of the barbarous system of American slavery, and acknowledging John Brown as the champion of freedom, and John C. Fremont as the man who cleared the way for Abraham Lincoln to walk in, he asked to be excused from making a speech as the evening was now so far spent.

Mr. Joseph C. Bustill, on behalf of the ladies of Harrisburg, invited the members of the Convention to attend a collation on to-morrow evening in the basement of this church.

The President, after the benediction, then declared the Convention adjourned till to-morrow morning at 9½ o'clock.

THIRD DAY

Morning Session, Friday, February 10th.

The President called the Convention to order upon the arrival of the morning hour, and prayer was offered by the Chaplain. The minutes of the previous afternoon's session were read and approved.

The Business Committee reported, through their Chairman, a series of Resolutions as follows:

1. *Resolved,* That we urge upon our people throughout the State, the necessity of using every exertion to secure real estate, and that we would urge upon our young men and women the desirability of obtaining a good

business education, and the great importance of making earnest endeavors to secure positions in which they may be practically engaged in some mercantile or mechanical pursuit. On motion of Mr. O. L. C. Hughes the Resolution was adopted.

2. *Resolved,* That we re-iterate the sentiment contained in the fifth Resolution adopted by the National Convention of Colored men, held in the city of Syracuse, N.Y., October 4th, 1864, viz.:--"that we extend the right hand of fellowship to the freedmen of the South, and express our warmest sympathy and our deep concern for their welfare, prosperity and happiness; and desire to exhort them to shape their course toward frugality, the accumulation of property, and above all, to leave untried no amount of effort and self denial to acquire knowledge, and to secure a vigorous moral and religious growth. We desire, further, to assure them of our co-operation and assistance; and that our efforts in their behalf be given without measure and be limited only by our capacity to give, work and act." On motion of R. M. Adger, the Resolution was adopted.

3. *Resolved,* That this Convention endorse the action of the delegates from this State to the late National Convention, in the preliminaries laid down by them, looking toward the formation of a State Equal Rights' League; and that the movement started by them receive our hearty co-operation and support. The Resolution was adopted on motion of Mr. Thomas Early.

4. *Whereas,* The National Convention of Colored men which assembled in the city of Syracuse, N.Y., October 4, 1864, organized a National Equal Rights' League, having for its objects the promotion of education, the encouragement of sound morality, the exemplification of temperance and frugality, the practice of economy and everything which pertains to well ordered and dignified life; and *whereas,* the National Equal Right's League so formed, have invited the co-operation of the several States, and recommended to them the formation of auxiliary Leagues to aid in furtherance of its objects, therefore,

Resolved, That we heartily endorse the action of the said National Convention, in the organization of an Equal Rights' League, approve the principles as adopted by that League, and will proceed to organize in this Convention, a State Equal Rights' League in accordance with its provisions. The Preamble and Resolution were recommended by the Business Committee to be indefinitely postponed.

Rev. Joseph A. Nelson moved, that in accordance with the Business Committee's recommendation, the whole subject be indefinitely postponed.

The motion was opposed by the Rev. C. J. Carter, and supported by Mr. A. M. Green, who stated that the State League which now exists, had already been sustained and endorsed by the Resolution previously passed.

On motion of Mr. P. N. Judah, the subject was laid on the table until the Report of the Finance Committee should be heard.

Mr. James R. Gordon, Chairman of Committee on Finance, then presented the following Report:

RECEIVED			PAID	
Feb. 8, Tax from Delegates,	$89.00		For Church Hire,	$50.00
" " Afternoon Collection,	4.36		" Erecting platform	2.50
" " Evening	10.71		" Stationery and Printing,	2.55
" 9, Morning Collection,	1.74		" Expenses of Traveling Agent,	47.00
" " Tax from Delegates,	46.00		" Printing Call and Appeal,	25.00
" " Afternoon Collection,	1.36		" Printing second Call,	7.50
" " Evening Collection	21.77		" Advertising Appointm's, Agt.	4.00
Total Receipts	$174.94			
" Paid out.	138.55			
Balance in hand,	36.39		Total Paid Out,	$138.00

Mr. P. N. Judah moved that the Report of the Finance Committee be adopted.

Mr. J. W. Purnell spoke in opposition to adopting the Report, as the expenses of the traveling agent have been paid out of their funds; he said this Convention appointed no such agent, and as he was appointed by the State League that body should pay him.

Mr. J. R. Gordon was in favor of the motion made by Mr. Judah, and said that as this Convention have enjoyed the benefits resulting from the labors of this agent, they are justly obligated to pay this bill.

Mr. Charles H. Vance followed in opposition to the adoption and said he would brand it as an imposition and would record his vote against it.

Mr. J. E. Glasgow hoped that we would continue in the harmony which so far has been with us, and that we would pay the bill and part in peace.

Mr. Daniel Williams spoke in favor of paying the bill, and urged that as our time was fast going, we ought to settle this question and proceed to other business.

Mr. J. W. Purnell urged that he was in favor of paying all the legitimate expenses of this Convention, but he could not see that this bill belonged to us at all.

Mr. A. M. Green rose to explain. He desired it to be understood that he was particularly interested in this question as he was here as a representative of the State League. He was also the agent referred to in this bill, and had travelled and published at his own expense, and as a member of this Convention he would be willing to pay five dollars from his own pocket to reimburse the State League for its outlay in getting up this Convention.

Mr. D. B. Bowser said he came here untrammelled by membership of the State League or any of her body, and he would urge that the harmony of this assembly should not be endangered by the small sum of forty-seven dollars. We have come here, said he, to legislate for the good of the people and the cause, let us then not waste time in this idle discussion, but accept the bill and pay it.

Mr. Redman Fausett was opposed to the adoption, he said, he too was untrammelled, having come from the same source as the gentleman who had just preceded him.

It was not the question of forty-seven dollars, that merited his opposition, it was the principle involved. He denied the right of the Finance Committee to spend the money of this body without their resolution to that effect. If we pay this bill, it will be acknowledging the right of the State League to govern this Convention, on these grounds he objected to its payment.

Mr. James R. Gordon said that it appeared from Mr. Fausett's remarks that the main objection seems to be to the words State League. The gentleman thought this bill ought to be paid to its proper source the State League or any other League.

Mr. Thomas Early was not opposed to the State League, he would be willing to pay every cent of the surplus funds of this Convention into the treasury of the League, although not a member of it.

Mr. James Prosser stated that he was no speaker, but was of the belief that if he were Sergeant-at-arms he would silence some of these members in one way or another.

Mr. D. D. Turner thought as the State League had taken all the preliminary expense of getting up the Convention, we ought to pay this bill without further quibbling.

The motion to adopt the report was then put and carried.

The following statement was made by Mr. James R. Gordon, Chairman of the Finance Committee. This entire Church was rented for the use of this Convention at a cost of fifty dollars, and the basement of the Church had been given, without the knowledge of this body, in order to hold an entertainment for raising money to pay the entrance to this Convention, of the Harrisburg Reserve delegation. The sale of refreshments had been held on Wednesday and Thursday evenings and this Convention had been deceived by the notice given from the desk, stating that the proceeds of the entertainment were for the sick and wounded soldiers.

After considerable debate and explanation the following resolution was presented by Mr. Jos. C. Bustill and unanimously adopted.

Resolved, That as the entire Church was under the control of this Convention, and used without their consent, the proceeds from these entertainments, after expenses, are paid, be, and are hereby donated to the Ladies Union Association of Harrisburg, for the benefit of sick and wounded soldiers.

Mr. Chas. H. Vance, of the Committee on Railroads, reported that all members who had paid full fare could, by presenting a certificate of membership, signed by the President and Secretary, receive the deduction necessary in each case. The report was received and the Committee discharged.

The hour of adjournment having arrived, the rules were suspended and a motion carried, that when we adjourn we adjourn *sine die*.

Mr. J. W. Purnell now called up the Resolution presented by Mr. O. L. C. Hughes in favor of forming from this Convention a State Equal Rights' League.

Prof. G. B. Vashon moved that the Resolution be indefinitely postponed. Carried.

5. *Resolved,* That the thanks of this Convention are due, and are hereby tendered to the Colored People's Union League of Philadelphia, for their untiring and successful exertions in regard to the removal of the odious and unjust proscription of certain railroad corporations in Philadelphia, in prohibiting colored persons from the use of their cars.[17] And that we hereby send our hearty congratulations to our brethren of the Union League and all others who have in any way aided in the enterprise, for their partial success in the undertaking, and that we pledge our countenance and co-operation in supporting their well begun and efficiently prosecuted labors.

Mr. J. E. Glasgow moved the adoption of the Resolution.

Mr. Redman Fausett, objected to the motion of Mr. Glasgow, on the ground that other similar organizations could claim mention in connection with the labors in which this Resolution gave the Union League such prominence. He mentioned the Civil, Social & Statistical Association of Philadelphia as equally active and effective in securing our privileges in the cars, and would, he said, offer an amendment to the Resolution, inserting the Civil, Social and Statistical Association, after the words "Union League."

Mr. A. M. Green remarked that this car question, was the special object had in view upon the organization of the Union League, and proceeded at some length to name the continued efforts which this League had made in the direction named in the Resolution. He was opposed to the passage of the amendment.

Rev. E. Weaver favored the amendment and spoke of some of the actions of the Civil, Social and Statistical Association in this car movement.

Rev. Wm. J. Alston followed in support of the amendment and said that the most influential meeting on the car question, ever held in Philadelphia, was under the auspices of the Civil, Social and Statistical Association.

Mr. D. B. Bowser answered the Rev. Alston and explained how the management of that great meeting went from the hands of the League to those of the Civil, Social and Statistical Association. He was opposed to the amendment presented by Mr. Fausett.

Mr. D. D. Turner moved the previous question, which being demanded was unanimously carried, and the amendment adopted.

The Resolution as amended was then put to the body and adopted.

6. *Resolved,* That in the event of the setting apart a day of Thanksgiving, as recommended by the Convention, all the Churches and Associations participating in the same, be, and are hereby requested to donate the proceeds of the same for the use and benefit of the Freedmen. The resolution was unanimously adopted on motion of Rev. C. J. Carter.

7. *Resolved,* That we are highly gratified at the exhibition of intellectual ability and business talent manifest in the columns of the *Christian Recorder*, a weekly paper published by a colored man (Rev. Elisha Weaver)[18] within the limits of our State; and that we therefore, cordially commend it to the patronage of every colored family therein. Adopted on motion of Mr. Samuel Molsen.

8. *Resolved,* That colored men should receive the same accommodation and meet the same treatment under all circumstances, as white men receive from colored men engaged in all manner of business, and that we will hereafter frown with contempt upon all proprietors of barber shops, restaurants and other places of business kept by colored men who exclude people of their own complexion from privileges they extend to white men.

Mr. H. Jackson, moved to adopt the Resolution and stated in favor of its passage, that much of the seeming prejudice against working and receiving accommodations in common with colored men, was only skin deep with white people. He said that there were under his supervision, colored and white men working harmoniously together.

Messrs. B. F. Pulpress and Wm. Cooper followed in favor of the Resolution, and Messrs. Wm. Nesbit and Moses Brown opposed it as ill advised and injudicious, assigning that men living and conducting business in Copperhead towns, where prejudice was very strong, could not, without destroying their business, accommodate white and colored men alike.

Mr. Geo. B. White did not agree with the gentlemen who had immediately preceded him, he knew from experience in his own profession, that of a barber, that this question could be successfully and squarely met, for he had been shaving colored and white in his place of business for years; said he, let us get right ourselves and then we may consistently ask others to do right.

Prof. G. B. Vashon moved to amend the Resolution by striking out "will hereafter frown with contempt," and insert, "cannot but regard as inconsistent and highly reprehensible the conduct of all proprietors."

The amendment and the Resolution as amended were then adopted.

9. *Resolved,* That we look with the deepest interest on the efforts which are now being made to secure us equal political rights, by the noblest and best spirits of the land, and that among them we name with feelings of gratitude, Wendell Phillips,[19] the true reformer, Charles Sumner, Henry Wilson,[20] Wm. D. Kelley[21] and others in Congress, Morrow B. Lowry and others of the Pennsylvania Legislature, who catching the inspiration of the hour, outstrip the old anti-slavery spirit which seems to rest satisfied with the prospect of securing our freedom; and further, that with feelings of sorrow we observe the attitude assumed by our long tried friend, Wm. Lloyd Garrison, on the subject of the colored man's franchise,[22] involving as it does, our dearest interest as citizens of this country, and that in his seeming determination to support and sustain the policy of Gen. Banks in his plan of reconstructing the States,[23] which excludes colored men from equal political privileges, is evinced an entire departure from the principles which we have always regarded as vital to the security of our best interests.

Mr. James R. Gordon moved that the Resolution be adopted.

Mr. D. D. Turner opposed the Resolution and proceeded to define the position of Mr. Garrison. He thought Wm. Lloyd Garrison was too old and well tried a friend to receive such consideration as this Resolution expressed, and he thought Mr. Garrison saw plainly, that as a people, we are progressing, and therefore willing to take up with such men and measures as would advance the cause, whether these men and measures were radical or not.

Mr. William D. Forten, who had presented the Resolution, contended for its passage. He said that Mr. Garrison and all his Resolutions were voted down in the Massachusetts Anti-Slavery Convention, and that he had denounced Frederick Douglass because he demanded the right of suffrage for the negro in the conditions of reconstruction. The Hovey Fund too had been withdrawn from the support of his paper, and Mr. Garrison to-day, said he, is at odds with the leading anti-slavery men of the nation.

Prof. George B. Vashon read the Resolutions which Mr. Garrison presented at the last meeting of the Massachusetts Anti-Slavery Society, favoring the disbanding of the Society on the ratification of the anti-slavery amendment to the Constitution of the United States.[24] He quoted from the remarks of Mr. Garrison on Banks, negro-suffrage, and in denunciation of Frederick Douglass' position "that freedom without the right of suffrage was a mere sham."

Mr. A. M. Green argued for the Resolution, and was of the opinion that Mr. Garrison's position against Mr. Douglass could not be otherwise than an evidence that he was either behind the times unknowingly or from a lack of effort to keep up with the events through which we are passing. He believed the right to vote belonged to every native born citizen in the country, and inquired why Mr. Garrison did not come out and put his finger on the objectionable features in General Banks' manner of reconstruction. He was not in favor of denouncing Garrison, but let us express our sorrow at what we believe to be a false position.

Mr. D. D. Turner said there are two classes of rights, one natural and the other conventional, and he thought the right to vote belonged to the latter class. His belief was, that the Anti-Slavery Society had been organized for a special purpose, the abolishment of Slavery, and when that object was achieved their work of course ceases.

Mr. William D. Forten stated, in answer to Mr. Turner, that the whole question before the Anti-Slavery Society, at the time referred to, was the reconstruction of Louisiana, and they could consistently have given expression to their objections to some of its features.

The Resolution was then adopted.

Prof. George B. Vashon, Chairman of Business Committee, presented an Address, which may be found in the Appendix, and the following Preamble and Resolutions. They were adopted on motion of Mr. William Cooper.

Whereas, A great and bloody civil war has been raging in this country for nearly four years, destructive of the peace, prosperity and happiness of the American people; and

Whereas, Every offer of compromise and all terms of peace suggested from the beginning of the contest have been utterly abortive, and have failed to secure even a short cessation of hostilities, for the purpose of reconstruction and compromise; and

Whereas, We have distinctly seen the arm of God made bare in leading the nation through this sea of blood to a higher civilization and a more holy and God-approved religion:--

1st. By the emancipation of the District of Columbia and all other territories of the United States from the dark barbarism of Slavery;

2d. By emancipating all escaping slaves, and fixing a penalty upon all officers who returned said slaves from our lines to their masters,[25]

3d. By emancipating the slaves of all States in rebellion, on the first of January, 1863;

4th. By revoking the infamous decision of the late incumbent of the Supreme Court of the United States, whereby colored men are declared citizens of the same;[26]

5th. By the enlistment of thousands of colored men in the army and navy of the United States,[27] thus practically setting beyond all doubt the opinion of Attorney-General Bates in regard to their citizenship, etc.;[28]

6th. By equalizing the pay and compensation of the U. S. Colored Troops, and providing for the freedom and security of their families;

7th. By the repeal of the Fugitive Slave Law;[29] the recent adoption of a new article in the Constitution forever prohibiting Slavery or Involuntary Servitude throughout the United States, and the endorsement of all these by an overwhelming vote of the people at the late Presidential election; all of which points with unerring certainty to the wisdom and power of God in subverting the power and contraverting the wicked machinations of the pro-slavery propagandists throughout the country; Therefore

Resolved, That it is the duty of the American people, viewed in the light of all past history and the Divine revelations, to recognize the mysterious hand of God in vindication of His own righteous will and in verification of the prophetic injunction, "to unloose the hands of wickedness, to undo the heavy burdens, and to let the oppressed go free, and that ye break every yoke," and, that a full and entire submission to these demands, is the only means left for a peaceful reconstruction of the Union, and the future peace and prosperity of the country.

Resolved, That the recent emancipation of Maryland, Missouri and other slave States, by the vote of the people of these States themselves, influenced alone by the force and power of these truths, is an example worthy of the imitation of the people of the free States in freeing the colored people from the prejudice and breaking the political yokes which shackle them in nearly every loyal State in the Union.

Resolved, That a Committee of three, consisting of Messrs.

Octavius V. Catto,   Alfred M. Green,
Joseph C. Bustill,

be appointed to revise, correct and publish the proccedings of this Convention for general distribution.

Resolved, That this Convention return its sincere thanks to its officers for the manner in which they have conducted its business, and to the citizens of Harrisburg who have so kindly and generally extended their countenance and hospitalities to the members during its session.

On motion of Mr. James R. Gordon the money in the hands of the Finance Committee was paid over to the publishing Committee, and the State League authorized to determine the number of minutes to be published and supervise their distribution.

After a few eloquent and feeling remarks from the President, on the solemnity of the occasion of our parting, and expressing the hope that our labors had not been in vain, the Convention, at 4 o'clock P.M., adjourned *sine die*.

        Attest,

                Octavius V. Catto,
                Redman Fausett,   Secretaries.
                Alex. T. Harris,

MASS MEETING
OF THE
STATE EQUAL RIGHTS' LEAGUE

Friday Evening, February 10th, 1865.

At an early hour the Church was crowded by the audience waiting for the organization of an ajourned meeting of the State Equal Rights' League.

Rev. John Peck, President of the League called the house to order at 7½ o'clock. After the singing of a hymn, the Rev. W. J. Alston offered an earnest prayer for the success of the League and the achievement of its aims.

Mr. A. M. Green then presented the following Preamble and Resolution, which upon motion of the Rev. Joseph A. Nelson, were unanimously adopted.

Whereas, The objects and aims of the State Equal Rights' League and the Equal Rights' Convention of the colored people of Pennsylvania, are one and identical; and Whereas, these objects are best promoted by a consolidation of all the interests of our people throughout the State, especially those now assembled in Convention; therefore,

Resolved, That the members of this Convention be declared members of the State Equal Rights' League, for one year, and that by a compliance with sections first and tenth of the constitution, they may continue their connection therewith as long as desired by the auxiliaries or subordinate organizations which they may be elected to represent.

Mr. Jos. C. Bustill read the Constitution of the State League as it [illegible] with Mr. Green's Resolution appended.

The Rev. W. J. Alston was the first speaker introduced, and began by stating that a short time ago the word colonization raised the tiger in him and made him feel like taking up the sword. But there had come over him a change, and he was now a colonizationist as it applied to the occupancy of the Southern States by the colored people. He saw through the freeing of Maryland the gate by which the whole 779,000 square miles of southern territory would be opened to the colored people. He urged upon the people unity, concord and action. The speech was well received and frequently applauded.

Mr. J. J. Wright spoke next. His opinion was that this Convention could very consistently preach the funeral sermon of slavery. He insisted that we should lose no time, or neglect no opportunity to show forth our rights and make plain the claims upon which we demand them, and he believed that our aims would be ultimately successful. The speech was replete with argument, wit and humor, and defied all attempts at our reporting it; the vast audience testified their appreciation of it by round after round of deafening applause.

Mr. Octavius V. Catto was then introduced and said that in the midst of these wildly excited times there were, at least occasional thoughts crowding upon us which like the flashes in the dark sky would light up some of the dark phases of the present crisis. He met the assertion of our inferiority by claiming that we had as many Frederick Douglasses as the whites had Sumners, as many Bannekers as they had Mitchells,[31] and as many Vashons as they had Anthons.[32] He was of the opinion that the political horizon is not clear while Banks is mis-constructing Louisiana, Germans commanding Germans, even Irishmen commanding Irishmen, and Negroes not allowed to command Negroes. He thought we should call without ceasing upon the clergy and all who follow them in communion to vindicate the principles of their profession; upon the

Press with its great influence; and upon Congress and the Administration to lend us their aid in a cause so just, so reasonable and so necessary, as the possession of equal rights without regard to color. And he believed that while our great armies moved on to victory the nation would move on to justice. The speech was frequently applauded.

Rev. Elisha Weaver addressed a few remarks to the assemblage, and urged the people to a union in their labors and the necessity of encouraging one another in business.

Mr. Joseph C. Bustill then, on behalf of the ladies of Harrisburg, reminded the delegates of the collation awaiting them in the basement of the Church. The meeting was then adjourned and dismissed with the benediction by the President. The vast assembly slowly, and with evident feelings and demonstrations of the deep interest which had been awakened in their minds, wended their way from the Church, presenting an interesting and encouraging spectacle.

APPENDIX

A FEW OF THE ARGUMENTS PRESENTED SUGGESTING THE NECESSITY FOR HOLDING THE CONVENTION

1st. It is the duty of any people who have grievances and wrongs to be redressed, to exercise themselves in their own behalf; and we would be unworthy of the notice or consideration of those to whom we appeal, if we possessed no energy, or intelligence, and refused to exert every faculty we possess, and embrace every opportunity within our reach to emancipate ourselves from disfranchisement in the State on the soil upon which we were born.

2d. The old proverb so often applied to us,

> Hereditary bondsmen, know ye not
> Who would be free themselves must strike the blow?

is most faithfully borne out in the more recent motto of the people of this country, that "self-reliance is the sure road to Independence;" and while we accept the application of the former, we feel in duty bound to adopt the practice of the latter, so far at least, as the means and opportunity are at hand.

3. We believe that no people have greater reason to complain, or have suffered greater and more frequent cruelties and injustice, or received less consideration for long and faithful services in promoting the general interests of the State, or have been more patient, law-abiding and discreet, than have been the colored people of the State of Pennsylvania.

4th. We, as a class, are not merely adopted or naturalized citizens of this State; our residence therein and our connection with the history thereof began with us, as with our forefathers, at the time of our birth. In the pursuits of manual labor and commercial enterprise, we began with the State itself; and from the time of the revolution, the noble defence of our frontier and the defeat at Red Bank of an enemy flushed with exultation at the prospect of the speedy fall of Pennsylvania's chief commercial city, we have ever been, to the interest and honor of our State, as true as the needle to the pole, never wavering, never changing, never deserting her cause, even when many of her most highly favored children have turned their backs upon her and united their destiny with that of her wayward sisters in rebellion.

5th. We, at one time, enjoyed our suffrages in this State, and met but little of the cruel prejudice that now meets us at every step we make in the direction of human progress. A prejudice barring against us the doors of your public libraries, of your colleges of science, of your popular lecture rooms, of your military academies, of your jury boxes, of your ballot boxes, of your churches, of your theatres, and even of your common street cars; and knowing all this to be the direct result of the defunct system of barbarism --American Slavery--we now ask that, as you have slain the cause with the rebellion, you give us security against the continuance of the effect, as manifested in the existence of these inhuman prejudices and prohibitions.

6th. While nearly every State in the Union is moving in the direction, not only of arming its colored population, but also of securing them their rights of citizenship, it is the duty of the people of Pennsylvania, she having sent more colored men than any two States to the field, to take such action as shall do justice to these soldiers and their friends, and at the same time do honor and credit to the State they represent.

7th. Our duty to the brave men who have represented us and you upon many a well contested field of mortal strife, our duty to the dear ones they have left behind, and to the glorious cause they serve, demand our earnest and uniting efforts towards procuring for ourselves and for them, full indemnity for the past, compensation for the present, and security for the future; and we believe that in so doing we cannot but have the approbation of all good men, and the support and direction of that arm and wisdom which are mightier than the power of man.

8th. With these views then we come to you, and we ask of you a calm and patient hearing, that when our cause is properly before you, we may rest assured that you will do your part earnestly and faithfully as christian men and women, who believe in the practice and exercise of virtue and piety, and in the common brotherhood of the human race.

ADDRESS OF THE COLORED STATE CONVENTION
TO THE PEOPLE OF PENNSYLVANIA

Fellow-Citizens:--

We, the colored people of Pennsylvania in Convention assembled at Harrisburg on the 8th, 9th and 10th of February, 1865, viewing the complex state and condition of affairs, and of public sentiment in our State, deem it our duty to present to you our grievances, our sufferings, and the outrages heaped upon us because of our helpless and disqualified position for self-defence, resulting, as we think we can prove, from no greater cause than our long and unjust political disfranchisement.

We do not come to you in the spirit of reproachfulness and denunciation; neither do we feel in pleading for equal rights without regard to complexional differences, that we are in the least degree selfish. Nor do we in any respect seek to lower the standard of refinement, intelligence or honor among the great and loyal people of the Commonwealth of Pennsylvania, by urging at this time these questions upon your consideration. On the contrary, we would view if possible, the brightest side of the picture we have to present, and give to our beloved State all honor and credit possible, in this hour of universal rejoicing over the rapid strides our great nation is taking in the direction of universal emancipation and equality before the law.

We would plead for an equality that would recognize all men as created equal, and endowed by their Creator with certain inalienable rights, among which are "life, liberty and the pursuit of happiness," believing that to secure these blessings governments were instituted among men, and that when they fail to secure, or seek to subvert these principles, they should no longer exist, but should become extinct or be so revolutionized as to promise these blessings, and not despotism as the recompense to their subjects for loyalty and devotion to the interests and prosperity of the State.

We believe that, in this country, to elevate the standard of political equality in favor of the one and only disfranchised portion of the inhabitants of the republic, is indeed but another word for securing to all the present and future population of the entire continent, those blessings of refinement, intelligence, and honor which having hung tremblingly in the balance of God's eternal truth, weighed and found wanting, are now passing through the fiery furnace of a fierce and bloody revolution.

We recognize, and most gratefully acknowledge the Old Keystone State as among the first to strike off the fetters of slavery from the shackled limbs of her colored people.[33] We turn with the most pleasant emotions to that day in the history of Pennsylvania, upon which the inscription upon the bell (still enshrined within the sacred temple of our liberty--Independence Hall) "proclaim liberty throughout all the land, unto all the inhabitants thereof," was the universal sentiment of the people of our State. We give full faith and credit to the sentiment advanced in the 9th article, 1st and 2d sections of our State Constitution, which declare

1st. That all men are born equally free and independent, and have certain inherent and indefatigable rights, among which are those of enjoying and defending life and liberty, of acquiring, possessing and protecting property and reputation, and of pursuing their own happiness.

2d. That all power is inherent in the people, and all free governments are founded on their authority, and instituted for their peace, safety and happiness. For the advancement of those ends, they have at all times, an inalienable and indefeasible right to alter, reform or abolish their government, in such a manner as they think proper.

We remember with feelings of both joy and sorrow, that the time once was, in the history of our State (before the encroaching spirit and domineering power of the slave oligarchy had subverted or controlled the pulpit, press and forum of almost every State in the Union) that all men were in reality recognized as entitled to the enjoyment of these indefeasible and inalienable rights. But through the dominant power of this crude and most barbarous institution, every right and every instinct, whether inherent or conventional, has been assailed and trampled under foot and crushed out of the black man whenever possible to reach him, over the broad expanse of our country. We have been hunted and driven from State to State, by the most cruel enactments, and have been abused, insulted, and disgraced wherever found, through and by the influence and power of that monster which having bloated itself by reveling in our blood and tears for more than three centuries upon the continent and adjacent islands, now rolls itself in defiant gluttony in the blood and treasure of your brightest and noblest youth and your unexampled prosperity of more than half a century.

We have borne our disfranchisement patiently. We have calmly submitted to the most wicked and outrageous treatment at the hands of persons, who, in the hour of National trial and State invasion, have deserted your cause, and even invited the enemy to your doors, and given him aid and comfort in the work of sacking your homes and murdering your children, brethren and fathers. We barely escaped the horrid massacre at Detroit, New York,[34] and other places, because of the active measures taken by the National government to protect us against our own irresponsible population of rebel sympathizers and those whom they had invited from other parts of the country to fan and feed the fire of rebellion, and inaugurate a counter revolution throughout the entire North.

The State authorities of Pennsylvania, with a loyal population of loyal colored people numbering a fraction less than sixty thousand, (60,000) through the cruel, proscriptive policy of our State Government toward her colored people, were as perfectly powerless for their own protection as for ours. In the day when the keepers of the house trembled, and strong men bowed themselves, when the doors were shut in the streets, and the sound of the grinding was low, and men rose up at the voice of the bird, and all the daughters of music were brought low,--when the foot of the rebel horde polluted and desecrated our soil, plundered our towns and villages, threatened our State Capitol, and loosed the silver cord of thousands of our best and bravest young men at Gettysburg, and men were afraid of that which was high, and the grasshopper had become a burden,--when, instead of the music of the organ and the church choir, our churches were turned into general recruiting offices, and drums and trumpets and the clash of swords greeted the ear, even then, so firm a hold had the power and influence of the accursed institution (that was pouring out the nation's blood in streams) upon the hearts of our people, and so infatuated were they by the seething, poisonous prejudice distilled by this despotic power and diffused throughout the land, that the colored people of the State, rushing by hundreds to the scene of danger and the field of death, were coldly denied the right to strike one blow even for their own defense or yours, under sanction and by authority of the State Government.

Now how does this action comport with section 21st, article 9th of our State Constitution which says, "the right of the citizens to bear arms in defence of themselves and the State, shall not be questioned?" It may be assumed that the word "*citizens*" shuts us out from this privilege, since some claim that we are not citizens, and not eligible to become so on account of color.

We would not insult you by attempting to argue before the world at this day and hour the barbarity of such a proposition. If such statutes have been passed they are contrary to the letter and spirit of our Constitutions, both State and Federal. It cannot be true that color renders us ineligible to bear arms and to exercise the right of suffrage.

Article 3d, section 1st, middle clause of our State Constitution reads thus, "but a citizen of the United States, who had previously been a qualified voter of this State, and removed therefrom and returned, and who shall have resided in the election district, and shall have paid taxes as aforesaid, shall be entitled to vote, after residing in the State six months." Now this is precisely the condition of hundreds of colored people of the State of Pennsylvania to-day. We deem it a work of supererogation to argue our right to citizenship in the United States. All things rise in proof of this now generally conceded opinion. The thousands of brethren in the army and navy fully recognized as citizen soldiers,--the sentence, "no person except a natural born citizen" found in article 2d, section 5th of our Federal Constitution, together with the opinion of Attorney General Bates, go so far in establishing this point beyond question, that we will not attempt to argue it. Equally clear is the fact that colored men have been qualified voters of this State, and in every sense filled the requirements of article 3d, section 1st of our Constitution. How then can it be affirmed, even by authority of our amended Constitution, that color is the bar to our eligibility to citizenship in this State?

And even if we concede the point here raised, for argument's sake, there is sufficient in article 9th, section 1st of our Constitution, to entitle us to bear arms in defense of ourselves and the State, and quite enough in section 3d of the same article, to entitle us to such alterations or reforms of our statute laws, or even of the Constitution itself, as shall secure to us the rights of full citizenship within the State, and perfect equality before the law.

But we repeat that all this is attributable to the firm power with which the despotic and controlling institution of slavery ruled the north on all questions touching the conditions and interests of their colored population. Having yielded every point demanded by the south, up to their treasonable seizure of the national property and murder of the national troops, the remuneration of Pennsylvania has been to be styled "mudsills," "cowardly yankee pimps," and to have their soil dishonored, and their people pillaged and murdered by these minions of the despotic system who, like ravenous wolves, have made our State their hunting ground for nearly three years.

We have never yet been secure in our persons, houses, papers and possessions, from unreasonable searches and seizures, as warranted to all persons under the State Constitution. When tried by accusation before our State Courts, it has been almost impossible to secure an impartial jury of the vicinage where persons of the opposite complexion are parties of the suit; and in no case can it be claimed that we are tried, and judgment rendered by our peers.

All these disadvantages have contributed to rivet the shackles of prejudice and political slavery upon us, and throw us upon the mercy of those who know no mercy even up to this very hour of national calamity and moral revolution. Since, then all this is attributable to the power and prejudice fostered and maintained as the direct result of slavery, why should it not now cease? Slavery is now dead. Maryland, Missouri, Tennessee, West Virginia, and even Old Kentucky will yet give the world a spectacle of wealth, prosperity and happiness under the new regime, well worthy of patronage by all their free sisters of the republic.

Slavery [is] dead throughout the land,--black men declared to be citizens of the United States, and marching by tens of thousands on field and flood against this monstrous rebellion, the common enemy of God and man--fighting, bleeding, dying in defense of our Constitution and the maintenance of our law. Can it be possible that loyal Pennsylvania will still suffer herself to be dishonored by refusing to acknowledge or to guarantee citizenship to those who have suffered so much, and still been foremost among her own sons in defending their country and the interests of the State against treason and rebellion? Is it not our duty to ask in the name of justice, in the name of humanity, in the name of those whose bones whiten the battle-fields of the south, that every bar to our political enfranchisement be now and forever removed? Do this, and all other evils and outrages will disappear as the dews of morning melt before the morning sun.

We have omitted many, very many acts of barbarity and inhuman aggressions made upon us by the dominant race (and which are as commonly perpetrated as though the laws of the land laid the obligation upon those who inflict them to do so) because we believe you are well aware of the facts yourselves, and because we believe that every sense of justice and honor stands out in vindication of our claims without further argument or encroachment upon your time. We have come together to consult and advise with each other upon these questions of vital interest to ourselves and our country, and having canvassed all the ground, we have concluded to present our desires, our hopes, our claims to justice, before you, and in the sincere anxiety of our hearts, we ask a calm and careful consideration of the whole subject of our disfranchisement, and our suffering originating therefrom; and having given it this, we have no doubt but that truth, justice, honor, and the security, prosperity and happiness of our State will aid you in arriving at such conclusions as shall vouchsafe to us those blessings so long denied us, and for which, above all other considerations, our Constitution and government were formed.

When, after continued refusals of both State and Federal authorities, it was found necessary to arm and muster the colored men of Pennsylvania as United States soldiers, we were urged to enlist, ignoring the question of pay, bounty, and every other consideration that was presented as an inducement to white men to enlist, because it was claimed that it was our duty, discarding all other considerations, to help our brethren of the south to their freedom. On this consideration, more than twelve thousand (12,000) men have been enlisted and sent from our State to swell the ranks of the Federal army. Many of these men are credited to the quota of this State under the several calls of the President. Pennsylvania still calls for colored men as volunteers to fill her quota in the late call. She asks her colored men now as before to assist her in the overthrow of the rebellion. But we answer, "what is our reward for it." We tell you now, as you told us at first, that pecuniary interests are of minor importance compared with freedom and our enfranchisement. We have the admission on all sides, that the question of slavery is settled. Slavery is dead to all intents and purposes. This is the admission of the confederate authorities themselves.

We have even seen and heard the representatives of slave States demanding, not only freedom but enfranchisement for their colored people, during the past year. Witness Maryland, Missouri, Tennessee and Louisiana, and mark the recent action of the State of Illinois in the repeal of her black laws. Have we not equal claims upon the people of our State? Can you ask us now to aid you to secure your own freedom and interests against the fearful assault made upon them, without promising us an equivalent equal to what you, by a vote of great significance, guaranteed to the soldiers during the past year?

Colored men are no longer fighting for the freedom of the slaves in the south. They are fighting for the Union, the Constitution and the enforcement of your laws; and we ask you, fellow-citizens, to see to it, that our rights and interests be regarded in this respect: that no more fear may be entertained of the overthrow of our National Government by the toleration of the plotters of treason, to the exclusion of true loyalists, and State interests made insecure by traitors in our midst armed with bullets and ballots to do us mischief, while our loyal colored people, as a measure of State policy are denied the use of both.

<u>MEMORIAL</u>
PRESENTED TO THE LEGISLATURE--FEBRUARY, 1865

*To the Honorable Senate and House of Representatives
of the State of Pennsylvania, in General
Assembly met*

Gentlemen:--

Your memorialists, Citizens of Pennsylvania, but disfranchised on account of their *color*,--having met in Convention to consider their grievances, would, in behalf of themselves and their fellows, reiterate the oft made *Appeal*, that you would do them justice.

In respectfully urging you thus to act, they would remind you that, at one time, men of Color were acknowledged as Citizens, under the Laws of Pennsylvania, and possessed all the political franchises which were enjoyed by their white Fellow Citizens. But nearly thirty years ago, the Supreme Court of the State, decided that this class of persons were not included in the term "Freemen," as it was employed in the Constitution of 1790;--that consequently they were not Citizens, and therefore had no legal title to the enjoyment of the elective franchise.

Subsequently, an amendment of the State Constitution debarred colored men from any claim to that privilege which they might base upon the wording of that document. Here then, was a blow aimed not at any immunity which they might enjoy as Citizens, but at the very citadel of their Citizenship itself. Now your memorialists are not insensible of the importance of this right of Citizenship.

They know how sacredly it has been prized by all Nations and in all ages. They are conscious, that it is now as ever, a Palladium conferring blessings upon the individual whom it shelters;--the sun of the political firmament, gilding every object with its beams, and spreading health and happiness with its rays. They therefore hold tenaciously to the position that they are Citizens of Pennsylvania, in spite of the Supreme Court's decision referred to, and of the amended Constitution; and they insist the more earnestly upon their Citizenship, in view of the fact, that their disfranchisement was based upon the assumption of their not being Citizens. Are they right or wrong in so doing? Let facts attested by our National records decide.

Your memorialists would premise that, if they are Citizens of the United States, they have a guarantee contained in Art. IV. Sec. 2d, of the Federal Constitution, that they are also Citizens of Pennsylvania. Now, in view of the opinion of Attorney General Bates, they are at present recognized in the former character; and, therefore, the latter one follows as a necessary consequence. Is that opinion regarded as unsound? Let it be judged of in the light of History. And to History your memorialists appeal, in order to establish the proposition that Free Colored persons were Citizens of the Union, prior to the year 1789; and that, as they were not declared to be otherwise by the Constitution then adopted, they are Citizens still. To substantiate this let us refer to the debates which took place in the Continental Congress, during the framing of the Articles of Confederation. On the 30th of October, 1777, while the motion in reference to the manner of adopting the Articles was pending, an amendment was proposed for the purpose of excluding Colored persons from taking part in that adoption. The Delegates from Virginia were the only ones who voted in favor of it, and they were afterwards instructed to vote for the Articles as they stood.

And again on the 13th of the following month, the 4th Article of the Confederation was proposed. It read as follows:-

"The better to secure and perpetuate mutual friendship and intercourse among the people of the different States in the Union; the free inhabitants of each of these States, paupers, vagabonds and fugitives from justice excepted, shall be entitled to all the privileges and immunities of free Citizens in the several States." The Delegates from South Carolina moved that the Article should be amended by the insertion of the word "White," before the word "inhabitants." This motion was lost, and the Article was then adopted by a unanimous vote. Here then were two recognitions of Colored persons as Citizens within fourteen days of each other, by the assembled representatives of the Union. This is proof positive that Colored Freemen enjoyed Citizenship under the Confederation. Where is the Article, in the present Constitution, that denies their claims? And in the absence of any such denial, what is more clear than the corollary that Colored men are still Citizens of the United States? The proposition thus sustained finds additional support in the language of various Congressional Laws enacted during the first half century of our National existence, wherein are contained either direct or indirect recognitions of the Citizenship of men of Color; and it is still farther substantiated by the explicit declaration of such men as Chancellor Kent, the profoundest legal authority of America, and as Alexander Hamilton[35] and Rufus King,[36] both of whom were members of the Convention that drafted the Federal Constitution, and who certainly ought to have known whether or not that instrument had branded Colored men as aliens. Now in view of all this concurrent testimony, your memorialists claim that they are Citizens of the United States, and by virtue of the guaranty of the Federal Constitution before alluded to, Citizens also of the State of Pennsylvania, that they have been unjustly dealt with in being deprived of the elective franchise upon the false assumption of their not being Citizens; and that a proper regard both for the honor of the Commonwealth, and for that consideration which in all true republics is ever due to the meanest Citizen, demands at your hands, the redress of this mighty wrong. They understand fully the importance of this right of suffrage,--the dearest treasure in the gift of any government,--the strongest weapon in the possession of the subject, repelling the approaches of despotism and guaranteeing the possession of all other immunities, a weapon that, in the expressive language of Whittier,

>executes a freeman's will,
>As lightning doth the will of God.

Now, to deny such a right to one class of Citizens, while it is accorded to another, without good reason for such a discrimination, is manifestly unjust and anti-republican. The present State Government is an aristocracy the more intolerable, because by it the insignia republican nobility are conferred upon the many, while they are withheld from the few. Your memorialists earnestly implore you to redress this state of things and to restore to them the rights wrongfully wrested from them. In advocacy of their claim, they insist upon their Citizenship. In the same advocacy, they would modestly and briefly remind you of the proofs of determined manhood and loyalty manifested by Colored men of Pennsylvania, during the course of the existing unholy rebellion, in defence both of the State and of the Union. Your State Capital was endangered. Straightway a band of Colored men rushed to its rescue. A Call for additional troops is issued; and soon twelve thousand black Pennsylvanians respond, and aid in filling up your quota.

There is no need to tell you how these men have comported themselves upon the embattled plain;--at Olustee, before Petersburg, and on other fiercely contested fields. Their general officers have already in many instances alas, lost life in behalf of a country they loved, and which they hoped would yet prove grateful.

Gentlemen, do not say that years must intervene before the wrong in question can be redressed,--that precedent is in the way of an immediate action in the premises. Remember, that your memorialists do not ask for favors. They claim rights. For the conferring of benefits, there may be another, and more convenient time, but

>for justice
>All place a temple and all seasons summer.

Then, let custom be disregarded, and "let justice be done though the heavens fall." Do this gentlemen, and your memorialists will ever pray.

Copy in the Historical Society of Pennsylvania and the Library Company of Philadelphia.

REFERENCE NOTES

1. Octavius V. Catto was a Philadelphia black leader who played a prominent role in the struggle of Pennsylvania Negroes to regain the suffrage after this right had been taken away from them in 1838. During the Civil War, Catto was commissioned a major within the infantry. He later became a high school principal and a firm equal rights advocate in Philadelphia. In 1871, along with several other blacks, he was killed by a mob of whites who sought to prevent them from voting, a right which had been recently guaranteed by the passage of the Fifteenth Amendment.
2. Jonathan Jasper Wright (1840-1885) was born of free black parents in Luzerne County, Pennsylvania. His father was a farmer. Wright received his

education at Lancaster University in Ithaca, New York, taught school for
several years, and then studied law in the offices of white lawyers. In 1865
the American Missionary Society sent Wright to Beaufort, South Carolina, to
organize schools for freedmen. He later played an important role during the
black Reconstruction period which followed, having been elected as the first
Negro to serve a full six-year term on the South Carolina State Supreme Court.
    3. John Brown (1800-1859) attacked the federal arsenal at Harpers
Ferry, Virginia, October 16, 1859, with the aim of fomenting a slave revolt
and eventually establishing a Negro republic in the mountains of Virginia.
Brown and his men captured the arsenal, but the next day a company of United
States Marines under Colonel Robert E. Lee assaulted the group, killed ten,
and took Brown prisoner. After a hurried trial, the wounded Brown was
sentenced to be hanged. Brown's bravery and dignity during the trial on the
scaffold moved millions of people to regard him as a hero. Among the Negro
people, he was considered a saint.
    4. Charles Sumner (1811-1874), United States senator from Massachusetts
(1851-1874), was the outstanding foe of slavery and champion of black rights
before and after the Civil War.
    5. The reference is to the Thirteenth Amendment, which was ratified in
December 1865.
    6. John S. Rock (1825-1866) was born in New Jersey of free parents and
subsequently became one of the outstanding leaders in the movement for equal
rights for black Americans in the North. His was a most unusual and brilliant
career. He became a teacher in the public schools during 1844-1848, and in
1849 he finished studying dentistry under Dr. Harbert Hubbard. In 1850 he
began practicing dentistry in Philadelphia, and in 1851 he received a silver
medal for the creation of artificial teeth and another silver medal for a
prize essay on temperance. In 1852, he graduated from the American Medical
College in Philadelphia, and the following year began the practice of medicine
and dentistry in Boston. He was admitted to practice law in Massachusetts in
1861 and on September 21 of that year received a commission from the governor
as justice of the peace for seven years for the city of Boston and County of
Suffolk. In Februaray 1865, presented by Charles Sumner as a candidate to
argue cases before the Supreme Court, Rock was sworn in by Chief Justice
Salmon P. Chase as the first Negro to be accredited as a Supreme Court lawyer.
    7. George B. Vashon, a graduate of Oberlin College, lawyer and poet,
held the professorship of belles lettres at Central College, in McGrawville,
New York.
    8. Slavery was abolished in the District of Columbia on April 16, 1862.
    9. On December 15, 1862, a bill was introduced in the House of Represen-
tatives to secure the abolition of slavery in Missouri, providing for the compensation of loyal persons who owned slaves. It was referred to the Select
Committee on Emancipation, and on January 6, 1863 it was reported back to the
House without amendment. It was speedily passed by the House, but in the
Senate the bill ran into considerable opposition, and finally a substitute
bill was adopted. This was taken up by the House on March 3, but it could
not be acted on until considered in the Committee of the Whole, which required
a two-thirds vote. The requisite vote could not be secured, and the bill was
lost in the House. Three years later, on January 11, 1865, an ordinance was
passed by a state convention in Missouri, abolishing slavery in the state,
immediately and unconditionally.
    10. The reference is to the Thirteenth Amendment, which provided: "Nei-
ther slavery nor involuntary servitude, save as a punishment for
crime . . . shall exist within the United States, or any place subject to
their jurisdiction." The amendment passed Congress in January 1865, and
secured ratification of the requisite three-fourths of the states in December
1865.
    11. The reference is to George Gordon Noel Byron (1788-1824), English
poet and fighter in the cause for Greek independence.
    12. The purchase of Louisiana from France in 1803 for $15,000,000 made
available a vast territory for the expansion of slavery.
    13. Florida was purchased by the United States from Spain in 1819.
    14. American-Mexican relations deteriorated after the annexation of Texas
in December 1845. American troops had moved into the territory claimed by
Mexico in July 1845, and when the Mexicans entered this territory, President

Polk requested a declaration of war, which Congress made on May 12, 1846. The war was basically the result of the drive by the slaveowners to acquire new land for cotton.

15. The Missouri Compromise of 1820 was passed by Congress to forestall the possibility of disunion between the North and South. Under it, all territory north of the line 36° 30', except Missouri, was to be barred to slavery. The Supreme Court, in the Dred Scott Decision of 1857, declared the Compromise unconstitutional, thus in theory giving slavery new land upon which to expand.

16. Jefferson Davis (1808-1889) was a congressman, senator, and later president of the Confederate States of America.

17. Most of Philadelphia's streetcars allowed Negroes to ride only on the front platform, and some refused to admit colored people at all. Under the leadership of William Still, Philadelphia's Negroes launched an attack on streetcar segregation in 1859, and it increased in scope and intensity during and immediately after the Civil War. Final victory against this discrimination was to come in 1867. For a discussion of racism in Philadelphia, see Philip S. Foner, "The Battle to End Discrimination against Negroes on Philadelphia Street Cars, Part I," *Pennsylvania History*, XL (July, 1973), 261-267.

18. The *Christian Recorder* was for many years the official weekly organ of the African Methodist Episcopal Church. Established in 1856, it was edited in 1865 by the Reverend Elisha Weaver.

19. Wendell Phillips (1811-1884), Boston-bred and Harvard-educated, was one of the greatest of the abolitionist leaders associated with William Lloyd Garrison. He fought against discrimination as well as against slavery.

20. Henry Wilson (1812-1875) was a U.S. senator from Massachusetts between 1855 and 1873. A leading opponent of slavery, he was one of the founders of the Republican party. In 1872 he was elected vice president of the United States on the Republican ticket with Grant as president.

21. William Darrah Kelley (1814-1890) was elected to Congress from Pennsylvania in 1861 and won re-election fourteen times. Always opposed to slavery, he broke with the Democratic Party and became one of the founders of the Republican organization.

22. The reference is to Garrison's defence of Lincoln's reconstruction policy in Louisiana. Discussion the question of Negro suffrage in relation to Reconstruction, Garrison wrote: "Chattels personal may be instantly translated from the auction-block into freemen, but when were they ever taken at the same time to the ballot-box, and invested with all political rights and immunities? According to the laws of development and progress it is not practicable. . . . Besides, I doubt whether he [the president] has the Constitutional right to decide this matter. Ever since the Government was organized, the right of suffrage has been determined by each State in the Union for itself, so that there is no uniformity in regard to it. . . ." (*Liberator*, Oct. 14, 1864).

23. Nathaniel P. Banks (1816-1894) was a congressman, governor of Massachusetts and Union soldier. On January 29, 1863, General Banks issued General Order No. 12 from New Orleans, which set up a system of sharecropping for the Negroes on a contract basis. The order assured employers that "all the conditions of continuous and faithful service, respectful deportment, correct discipline and perfect subordination" would be "enforced on the part of the Negroes by the officers of the Government." This system of labor was severely criticized by the abolitionists, and General Banks was accused of returning the Negroes to slavery.

24. Garrison took this position at the annual meeting of the American Anti-Slavery Society in May 1864. At the annual meeting in May 1865, he declared: "We organized expressly for the abolition of slavery; we called our Society an Anti-Slavery Society. The other work [Negro suffrage] was incidental. Now, I believe, slavery is abolished in this country, abolished constitutionally, abolished by a decree of this nation, never, never, never to be reversed, and, therefore, that it is ludicrous for us, a mere handful of people with little means, with no agents in the field, no longer separate, and swallowed up in the great ocean of popular feeling against slavery, to assume that we are of special importance, and that we ought not to dissolve."

Garrison resigned as president of the American Anti-Slavery Society at this meeting, after a vote to disband the organization was rejected. He was succeeded by Wendell Phillips, who kept the organization in full working until the ratification of the Fifteenth Amendment in 1870, giving the Negro the right to vote.

25. On March 31, 1862, President Lincoln signed a bill forbidding the army or the navy to return fugitive slaves. Any officer violating the law would "be discharged from service, and be forever ineligible to any appointment in the military or naval service of the United States." (See Henry Wilson, *History of the Rise and Fall of the Slave Power in America* [New York, 1877], III, 291ff.)

26. Since blacks did not officially become citizens of the United States until the passage in 1868 of the Fourteenth Amendment, this statement is probably in reference to the admission of John S. Rock (mentioned above), the noted Boston Negro, to practice before the Supreme Court in February 1865. His recognition as a lawyer in the highest tribunal of the land was *ipso facto* a tacit recognition of his citizenship in the United States.

27. Blacks were officially mustered into the Union forces in July 1862, when Congress authorized the president to employ Negro troops. Four months later, the "First South Carolina Volunteers," commanded by Colonel Thomas Wentworth Higginson of Massachusetts, was mustered into service. Lincoln's Proclamation of Emancipation, issued on January 1, 1863, announced that freed slaves would be received into the armed forces of the United States "to garrison forts, positions, stations, and to man vessels of all sorts in said services." Then finally, in early 1863, a bill passed the House of Representatives which authorized the president "to enroll, arm, equip and receive into the land and naval service of the United States such number of volunteers as he may deem useful to suppress the present rebellion." The Senate returned the bill to the House, refusing to pass it on the ground that it was unecessary because the president had such power under previous acts of Congress.

28. In an opinion rendered on November 29, 1862, Attorney-General Edward Bates (1793-1869) affirmed the citizenship of blacks in the United States.

29. The Fugitive Slave Law was repealed on June 28, 1864. See Stanley W. Campbell, *The Slave Catchers: Enforcement of the Fugitive Slave Law, 1850-1860* (New York, 1970), p. 194.

30. The reference is to Benjamin Banneker (1731-1806), the free Negro astronomer and mathematician of Maryland. In 1791, Banneker began to publish a series of almanacs that won wide recognition.

31. Ormsby MacKnight Mitchel (1809-1862), American astronomer and Union soldier, taught mathematics at West Point (1829-31) and later became professor of mathematics, natural philosophy, and astronomy at Cincinnati College, which later became part of the University of Cincinnati. In 1842 he secured the establishment of an observatory in Cincinnati and conducted important investigations. When the Civil War broke out, Mitchel was made a brigadier general of volunteers.

32. Charles Anthon (1797-1867), American classical scholar, entered Columbia College in 1811 and later graduated with high honors. In 1820, he was chosen adjunct professor of Greek and Latin and finally Jay professor of Greek language and literature, a position he occupied until his death. His numerous textbooks, replete with critical notes and scholarly commentary, went through several editions, and by the middle of the nineteenth century he stood preeminent as the leading classical authority in the United States.

33. In 1780, Pennsylvania became the first state to enact a program looking toward the gradual emancipation of her slaves, feeing men at the age of twenty-eight and women at the age of twenty-five.

34. The reference is to the Draft Riots in New York City, which began shortly after the drawing of conscription lots on July 13, 1863. The riots continued for four days during which a thousand casualties and $1,500,000 property losses were sustained. The mob, egged on by the Copperheads, attacked the Negro population. A number of Negroes were beaten to death, hanged to trees and lamp-posts, and burned as they hung. The Colored Orphan Asylum was sacked and burned. The rioting soon spread to other cities, of which Detroit was one.

35. Alexander Hamilton (1755-1804) was author of the *Federalist Papers* and secretary of the treasury under Washington.

36. As a delegate to the Continental Congress (1784-87), Rufus King

(1755-1827) helped draft the Ordinance of 1787, which excluded slavery from the Northwest Territory. At the Federal Constitutional Convention of 1787 he favored a strong central government and in 1789 was elected a senator from New York.

PROCEEDINGS OF THE INDIANA CONVENTIONS

INTRODUCTION

In her book *The Negro in Indiana before 1900* (Indianapolis, 1947), pages 144-147, Dr. Emma Lou Thornbrough makes reference to 1842, 1847, and 1851 Indiana conventions. We have the proceedings for the 1851 convention. Unfortunately, we have been unable to obtain the 1847 proceedings. As far as can be determined, there are also no extant proceedings covering the convention of 1842. The information included in our volume is drawn from a meeting called to consider the propriety of holding such a convention. Thornbrough's reference to the 1842 convention is also not to the proceedings itself but to the information we give. Since, however, the 1842 meeting called specific attention to the possibility of holding such a convention, which presumably assembled shortly thereafter, we have decided to include it in this volume.

The 1851 Indiana convention met on the very eve of an election which resulted in the disfranchisement of the Negro. Like most black conventions, this gathering touched upon the many concerns of the Negro community, including education, temperance, and economic enterprise, but the suffrage issue appeared uppermost in the minds of the delegates.

REPORT OF A MEETING OF THE COLORED CITIZENS OF INDIANA
JANUARY 17, 1842

A BLACK STORM BREWING

We learn by a "circular" printed at the Rat Journal office, and addressed to the "colored citizens of the State of Indiana," that the said "colored citizens," are about taking measures to hold a *State Convention at terre Haute*, for the purpose of appointing delegates to a *National Convention*. For what purpose the National Convention is to be held, unless it is to second John Q. Adams, and his Whig coadjutors in their attempt to dissolve the Union, we know not.[1] It may be that considering their success in the late Presidential campaign, through the influence of money, hard cider, debauchery and amalgamation, they hope to impose upon the country a "*colored*" *President*, should Clay's prospects appear slim, who would be "headed" easier than Captain Tyler.[2] We warn the lovers of the country to be on the look out for this new Whig movement.

That no misunderstanding may exist, we conclude to publish the circular just as we received it fresh from the Journal office. Here it is:

CIRCULAR

To the Colored Citizens of the State of Indiana

The friends of Philadelphia having called on the colored citizens of Indiana to co-operate with them in getting up a national convention, to be composed of colored representatives, elected and sent from the different States, our brethren of Madison in Jefferson county have honorably espoused the call. The deep interest and ardent philanthropy which led our afflicted brethren to such a train of considerations signalized the meeting held by the brethren of Madison, by whose kindness we were favored with a minute of said meeting.

Pursuant to the above, a meeting was held in the African M.E. Church, in Indianapolis, Marion county, Indiana, on the 17th of January, 1842, to take into consideration the propriety of getting up a State convention, which our Madison brethren had not taken into consideration. We regret that they did not consider the expediency of co-operation through the means of a State convention, and we wish the public to understand the whole subject.

Though we wish to be understood that we appreciate the manly proceedings of our Madison friends, we hope, nevertheless, that they will concur with us in getting up a State convention, and let the national delegates be then elected.

The meeting was called to order by J. G. Britton. Turner Roberts was called to the chair, and A. J. Overalls was appointed secretary. Prayer was then offered by Jesse White, beseeching the God of all goodness to accelerate our weak but willing faculties.

John G. Britton was then called on by the chairman to read the circular from Madison, and state the object of the meeting. He made some very appropriate remarks, and was followed by several other gentlemen.

On motion of J. G. Britton,

Resolved, That the different committees be appointed by the Chair, which was adopted.

On motion, *Resolved,* That a committee of three be appointed to draw up a statement of the business done at the present meeting and prepare resolutions for the next; which resulted in the appointment of Allen E. Graham, John G. Britton, and Jesse White to said committee.

Resolved, That we concur with our Madison friends in the fundamental doctrine as stated in their circular, to wit, that we believe no well informed colonizationist is a devoted friend to the moral elevation of the people of color.

On motion of J. G. Britton,

Resolved, That a committee of five be appointed to determine when and where the State Convention shall be held, and report the next meeting.

Willis Brown, O. Mifflin, A. Turner, O. Stuart, and J. Tucker, were appointed said committee.

On motion,

Resolved, That we do wholly and solely believe our friends, when they tell us the importance of a general union among our people.

J. White arose, and made some appropriate remarks on the subject of the resolution, and was followed by Mr. T. Roberts.

Resolved, That in our opinion meeting in State convention will be a great means of producing a general union among our people.

Resolved, That we invite all our friends to lend us their influence in getting up a general union among our people.

The meeting then adjourned to meet again at the same place, on the 21st instant.

   T. Roberts, Chairman.
  A. J. Overalls, Sec.

January 21, 1842.

The colored citizens met pursuant to adjournment.

The meeting being called to order, prayer was offered by the Rev. A. E. Graham.

It was moved by A. E. Graham that the Rev. T. Roberts be appointed Chairman and A. J. Overalls Secretary. Agreed to.

On motion of J. G. Britton, the proceedings of the former meeting were read by the Secretary.

The chairman then called upon the committee of five, appointed at the last meeting, to bring forward their report relative to the time and place of holding the convention, when

A. Turner, chairman of the committee, reported that, in the opinion of the committee, the first Monday in May next would be the most convenient time at which to hold the State convention, and the place Terre-Haute.

The report was accepted and the committee discharged.

On motion, the meeting resolved itself into a committee of the whole, for the purpose of electing a committee of three, to be called the central committee.

G. Britton, A. E. Graham, and V. Morgan were elected said committee.

On motion, it was *Resolved,* That it shall be the duty of the Central committee to correspond with our brethren throughout the State, and with the different committees which may be hereafter appointed.

The meeting then went into the election of delegates, which resulted in the choice of John G. Britton, John Crowder, A. E. Graham, T. Roberts, and N. Morgan.

On motion of J. G. Britton,

Resolved, That we will co-operate with our brethren in Philadelphia, by getting up a State convention, and appoint delegates to represent us.

After a warm and patriotic address from A. E. Graham, the meeting adjourned.

    T. Roberts, Chairman.
   A. J. Overalls, Secretary.

  P.S. Since our last meeting J. G. Britton received a letter from the colored friends of Terre-Haute. They have had a large meeting, and invite the friends to hold the convention at Terre-Haute. They have appointed a committee to prepare a room for the convention to meet in, and three delegates, and passed a resolution to entertain the delegates free of charge. We highly commend their liberality and patriotic spirit. They have also appointed J. G. Britton corresponding secretary for the State of Indiana.

Indiana State Sentinel, March 4, 1842.

REFERENCE NOTES

  1. In December 1838, the House of Representatives adopted a resolution by a vote of 194 to 6, declaring that Congress had no power over slavery in the states. John Quincy Adams, sixth president of the United States and later a member of Congress, opposed the resolution, arguing that in case of war the government could have power to abolish slavery in order that the nation might be saved. This position, viewed as radical by his detractors, helped to link him with the abolitionist agitators of the day, who some believed sought the dissolution of the Union.
  2. John Tyler (1790-1862), tenth president of the United States, was also governor of Virginia (1825-27) and a U.S. senator (1827-1836). At first a Jacksonian Democrat, he later gravitated to the Whig Party, joining its states' rights Southern wing, which differed with many of the nationalist policies associated with Henry Clay's leadership.

STATE CONVENTION OF THE PEOPLE OF COLOR OF THE STATE OF INDIANA
AUGUST 9, 1851

The State Convention of the People of Color of the State of Indiana met in the African M.E. Church, on Friday morning, 1st inst., at 9 o'clock, A.M., according to the call of the circular issued by the State Central Committee. The Convention was called to order by the chairman of the Committee, and prayer offered to the Throne of Grace by the Rev. John A. Warren; after which the credentials of the delegates from the several counties were called for, when the following were presented, J. G. Britton acting as President *pro tem.*, and W. J. Greenly, Secretary:

J. G. Britton, of Marion; J. Callihan, do.; T. Bushrod, do.; W. H. Manly, do.; P. B. Delany, do.; J. L. Johnson, do.

J. H. Bundy, of Vigo; W. H. Carter, do.; J. Mitchell, do.

Rev. J. Morgan, of Washington.

W. J. Greenly, of Floyd.

Rev. J. A. Warren, of Clark; Rev. W. Couzins, do.

Rev. W. Chandler, of Vigo; Rev. D. Johnson.

Rev. D. Dudly, Bartholomew.

Rev. J. J. Fitzgerald, of Jefferson; Rev. B. Crider, do.; Rev. Wm. Anderson, do.; Rev. S. Jones, do.

Rev. E. Weaver, of Vanderburgh, Posey, and Gibson.

Rev. J. M. Brown, of Ohio; J. B. Delany, do.

Mr. Blanks, of Michigan, and Mr. J. Merriwether, of Kentucky, were admitted to seats in the Convention.

On motion, a Committee of Organization was appointed by the Chair, as follows:

W. H. Carter, T. Bushrod, P. B. Delany, J. L. Johnson, Rev. J. Morgan.

The committee withdrew, and during their absence the Convention was addressed by the Rev. J. J. Fitzgerald, who gave his views very clearly. He spoke with much warmth and eloquence. The committee returned and reported as the result of their nomination, the following as permanent officers of the Convention:

John G. Britton of Marion, President; Rev. John Morgan of Washington, and D. N. McDowell, of Ripley, Vice Presidents; W. J. Greenly, of Floyd, and W. T. Boyd, of Madison, Secretaries; which nominations were confirmed by the Convention.

The President then took his seat, and after appointing Mr. J. Manly door-keeper, addressed the Convention as follows:

Gentlemen of the Convention: I am aware of the honor you have conferred upon me, in calling me to preside as chairman over this deliberate body of Colored Americans of the State of Indiana, now in Convention assembled, for the purpose of discussing subjects of a grave and important character.

Gentlemen, we have been called together at a period of great excitement; at a time when the whole State is in commotion, with regard to our race. For, on Monday next is the annual election, which, I have no doubt, for the best information that I can gain, will seal the destiny of the Colored Americans in this State by at least thirty thousand votes against us.[1] I believe that this Convention will produce a new epoch in the history of the Colored Americans of Indiana; and I truly regret that your choice has not devolved upon some one who, from his experience and knowledge of parliamentary rules, would be more able to discharge the duties required on this occasion. This is the second convention of any note I have had the privilege of meeting in, and the first time that I have ever been called to the chair, to preside over a body of such magnitude. Gentlemen, I would ask to be excused, were it not that I do not wish to be considered remiss in the performance of any duty assigned me by my fellow citizens, especially when our liberties are at stake. Without any further apology, I will impartially endeavor to discharge the duties devolving upon me, to the best of my ability. Gentlemen of the Convention, and fellow citizens, before I take my seat you will permit me to say to you, that there are several important subjects which I think will claim the undivided attention of this Convention. And as I shall be confined to the chair, during the sitting of this Convention, you will permit me to lay before you a few important subjects, which I had contemplated to introduce, for the consideration of this Convention. 1st. As Americans we are entitled to all the rights, privileges, and immunities of citizenship as other citizens, according to the letter and spirit of the Constitution of the United States. 2d. We are deprived of these inherent rights, set forth in the Declaration of Independence, and confirmed by the Constitution of the United States; they are taken from us and conferred upon foreigners that come into this country. 3d. Industry, Education, and Temperance should claim the undivided attention of each delegate in this Convention. 4th. The proposition of England to colored Americans of the United States to migrate to the Island of Jamaica, and the kind and friendly manner that we are received in Canada. 5th. The American colonization scheme, I do hope, will claim the special attention of this Convention, as it has been going the rounds of the public papers, that the colored people of Indiana had called a convention for the purpose of emigrating to Liberia. 6th, and lastly. The call for a National Convention; the time and place of holding it, and the propriety of electing delegates to represent the Colored Americans of Indiana, in said Convention.

With these remarks, gentlemen, I take my seat, hoping that the Great Creator of all mankind will bless our efforts on this important occasion.

Indiana State Journal, August 9, 1851.

REFERENCE NOTES

1. The reference is to the suffrage issue. Blacks in Indiana lost the franchise after the election in question.

PROCEEDINGS OF THE MICHIGAN CONVENTIONS

INTRODUCTION

The Michigan State Colored Convention held in Detroit, October 26-27, 1843, assembled for the purpose of taking into consideration the political status of blacks within the state. Like Negroes in most of the free states, Michigan blacks were denied the franchise. The convention denounced this deprivation. As one clause of the resolutions put it: "whereas we find ourselves existing in this State, (many native born), with no marks of criminality attached to our names as a class--no spots of immorality staining our characters--no charges of disloyalty dishonoring our birth-right; and *whereas* we yet find ourselves the subjects and not the objects of legislation, because we are prevented from giving an assenting or opposing voice in the periodic appointments of those who rule us." The convention also registered concern over the limited opportunities for black youth to enter occupations from which they could obtain a livelihood, especially the manual trades. It saw no solution for blacks through any schemes of emigration or colonization outside the limits of the United States, but stressed the need to cultivate good morals, to establish moral reform societies, and to inculcate habits of industry, thrift, education, and temperance among the Negro population.

MINUTES OF THE STATE CONVENTION, OF THE COLORED CITIZENS OF THE STATE OF MICHIGAN, HELD IN THE CITY OF DETROIT ON THE 26th & 27th OF OCTOBER, 1843, FOR THE PURPOSE OF CONSIDERING THEIR MORAL & POLITICAL CONDITION, AS CITIZENS OF THE STATE

THE CALL

Fellow Citizens:--

At a Public Mass Meeting, held in the city of Detroit, on the 19th of September, 1843, (Mr. Henry Jackson, chairman, and O. P. Hoyt, secretary,) for the purpose of considering the propriety of holding a State Convention of the oppressed citizens of this State; after mature deliberation, it was resolved, that a Convention of the Colored Citizens of the State of Michigan, be held in the city of Detroit, to commence its sessions on the 26th day of October next, at 10 o'clock, A.M. On motion, the following individuals were appointed a committee to prepare and issue the Call for a State Convention, viz.:--

Messrs. Wm. Lambert, Wm. C. Monroe, Henry Jackson, F. Delany, and O. P. Hoyt.

Dear Brethren:--Believing the time has come for us to be united in sentiment and action, and to speak out in our own defence upon the great cause of Human Liberty and Equal Rights: we call upon you to co-operate with us in this important movement that we are about to make. For as we are an oppressed people wishing to be free, we must evidently follow the examples of the oppressed nations that have preceded us: for history informs us that the liberties of an oppressed people are obtained only in proportion to their own exertions in their own cause. Therefore, in accordance with this truth, let us come up, and, like the oppressed people of England, Ireland and Scotland, band ourselves together and wage unceasing war against the high-handed wrongs of the hideous monster Tyranny. Come up, brethren, and rally under the banner of Freedom; for since our late National Convention, a new and a bright star has made its appearance in our dark horizon, and has attracted the attention of our oppressors, and caused many to cry out, Go on, thou genius of Liberty, go on! The friends of liberty throughout the civilized world has hailed it, and now stand cheering us to go on. Then, brethren, shall we not meet together, and consult how we may better our condition? Shall we not infuse into the minds of our young men, and posterity, a disposition to be free, and leave their present low and degraded employment, and endeavor to obtain mechanic arts, and follow agricultural pursuits? Shall we not meet together and endeavor to promote the cause of Education, Temperance, Industry, and Morality among our people; and by our correct, upright and manly stand in the defence of our liberties, prove to our oppressors, and the world, that we are determined to be free?

Yes! yes! let us assemble--let us come together, and pledge ourselves in the name of God and bleeding humanity and posterity, to organize, organize and organize, until the green-eyed monster Tyranny, shall be trampled under the feet of the oppressed, and Liberty and Equality shall embrace each other, and shall have scattered their blessings throughout the length and breadth of our land.

> Then, come, dear brethren,
> If we would be free,
> We must demand our Liberty,
> And strike the blow with all our might,
> For Liberty is the Balm of Life.

Wm. Lambert, Chairman of Com.

N.B. The above call, when issued, was signed by a large number of individuals besides the committee.

PROCEEDINGS OF THE CONVENTION

Pursuant to the preceding call, issued to the Colored Citizens of this State, through the Signal of Liberty, at Ann Arbor, and the *Daily Advertiser* of Detroit, urging said people to assemble at Detroit in Convention on the 26th day of October, for the purpose of taking into consideration their Political Standing as a People, and to adopt measures for the improvement of the same; the Fort Street Second Baptist Church was thrown open at an early hour on Thursday morning of the above date, and soon became the scene of the most spirited and manly meetings that have ever engaged the energies of our people in this state.

At 10 o'clock, A.M., about eleven delegates were assembled from the different counties of the State, together with twelve who were chosen in this city.

The Convention was called to order by the Rev. W. C. Monroe of Detroit, who moved the appointment of Wm. Lambert of Detroit, as Chairman *pro tem*.

On motion of Henry Jackson of the aforesaid place, W. R. Wilson of the same place, was appointed Sec'y.

Mr. Lambert, in taking the chair, remarked as follows:

Friends and Fellow-Citizens:--It is with great reluctance that I receive the honor that you have been pleased to confer upon me. Not that I wish to shrink from the duty I owe to my oppressed fellow citizens. But, because --besides my limited education, youth and inexperience--I have been deprived of that encouragement, aid and culture which we should have received to enable us to fulfill those noble designs for which the Great Author of the universe, created man. This is the reason why I so reluctantly receive the responsible station to which you have been pleased to call me. As this is the first time that we, the oppressed portion of the citizens of this State, have assembled in convention to consider our political condition, the eyes of the public are gazing upon us with great interest, to behold the course that we are about to pursue; many are waiting for an opportunity to belittle us, by taking the advantage of our inexperience, to use as a handle in argument to sustain them in their position of depriving us of those inalienable rights, which we have assembled to consider and deliberate upon; others are standing cheering us on, aiding and assisting us in the great cause of Human Liberty and Equal Rights; a subject with which Ireland is now threatening to revolutionize the combined powers of Great Britain--a subject that is now agitating the world. Yes, fellow citizens, we have convened to deliberate upon a subject which is now fast revolutionizing public opinion, and promises to extend human liberty and equal political rights to all the oppressed of these United States. Therefore it behooves us, as the representatives of the oppressed of this State, to act with that calm, cool, and brotherly affection, and unanimity of feeling, sentiment and action, which would be becoming to an oppressed people wishing to be free; for we are placed in a very responsible station, the future destiny of our people in this State for years yet to come, depends greatly upon our conduct here in convention assembled;--if our acts be good, they will give life, vigor and energy to the efforts of our friends who have enlisted in our cause, and will command honour and respect for our people and ourselves. Many of our oppressors who are now halting between the two opinions of right and expediency will flock to our standard and eagerly aid and assist us in promoting our cause, for which we have now assembled. But if our acts be bad, they will only be so many disparagements to be used in the mouths of our oppressors, to impede the progress of our political advancement, and in a great measure would palsy the soul and cripple all the powers of our people and their friends.

Therefore, let us by our upright, correct, and manly stand in defence of our Liberty, prove to our oppressors and the world, that we are deserving of our rights, and are determined to be free.

After Mr. Lambert's remarks, the Rev. Mr. Brooks was called upon to address the throne of grace.

On motion of Mr. Henry Jackson of Detroit,

Resolved, That a committee of five, consisting of M. J. Lightfoot and A. Derrick of Detroit, J. W. Brooks and A. Aray, of Pittsfield, and G. B. Blanks, of Marshall, be appointed by the Chair, as a committee to examine the credentials, and to make out a roll of this Convention. Adopted.

On motion of Richard Gordon, of Detroit,

Resolved, That all persons, favorable to the call of this Convention, and who have been sent under that call, to deliberate in the doings of this Convention, are requested to hand in their names and their credentials to the committee for examination. Adopted.

The committee after collecting the names and the credentials of all who had appeared as delegates, retired below, in the basement room, to make out the roll. After an absence of about fifteen minutes, they returned, and reported the following list, as the names of those who had been legally elected, and sent to participate in the transactions of the Convention.

The roll here given, stands as the one subsequently completed and used by the Convention, to wit:

Detroit--Rev. W. C. Monroe, Richard Gordon, Henry Jackson, William Dolerson, William Lambert, Willis R. Wilson, Alford Derrick, Madison J. Lightfoot, Robert Allen, George R. Sims, Henry Bibb, Othello P. Hoyt.

Jackson--Calvin Hackett, Henry Calvin.

Marshall--G. B. Blanks, A. R. West.

Washtenaw Co.--William Smith, W. Hardy, John Rigs, Nelson Ockry, Asher Aray, Rev. J. W. Brooks, Thomas Freeman of Ann Arbor.

The committee after reporting the above roll, also stated that eight other individuals of Detroit had appeared and handed in their credentials to the committee, and after a strict examination, was by them rejected, upon the consideration of their not having been elected by the mass of the people, but at a private meeting, called by themselves, after the regular delegates here reported, had been legally elected by the mass of the people of the city.

A dispute took place which occupied much time, and continued until the leader of those eight, who also claimed seats as delegates, had left the house. The Convention then resumed its business.

On motion of Mr. Dolerson.

Resolved, That a committee of three be appointed by the Chair to select from among the delegates, candidates for the regular officers of this Convention, the said committee to report forthwith. Adopted.

The chair appointed the following gentlemen, as said committee:-- Henry Jackson, Asher Aray, and Thomas Freeman.

The committee, after retiring, reported the following gentlemen who were unanimously elected, and took their seats as officers of the Convention:

> Rev. Wm. C. Monroe, *President.*
> Calvin Hackett, of Jackson, } Vice Presidents.
> J. W. Brooks, of Pittsfield, }
> Othello P. Hoyt, of Detroit, } Secretaries.
> Nelson Ockry, of Sharon, }

The Rev. Wm. C. Monroe, in assuming his station as President of the Convention, in his usual plain and impressive style, addressed the members in a brief but very appropriate manner.

After the President had taken his seat, and declared the Convention open for regular business, it was, on motion of Henry Bibb,[1]

Resolved, That the committee that was appointed to examine the credentials, and make out the roll, now be a standing committee, to take the names and examine the credentials of all who may hereafter appear as delegates. Adopted.

On motion of Wm. Lambert,

Resolved, That a committee of three be appointed by the President, to draft rules for the government of this Convention. Adopted.

The President appointed the following gentlemen as said committee: Henry Jackson, G. B. Blanks and Richard Gordon.

On motion of Wm. Lambert,

Resolved, That a committee of five be appointed by the President, to suggest in a becoming form, business for this Convention. Adopted.

The following gentlemen were appointed as the business committee:

Wm. Lambert, of Detroit, chairman, Asher Aray, of Pittsfield, Thomas Freeman, of Ann Arbor, William Hardy, of Pittsfield, Willis R. Wilson, of Detroit.

After adopting the preliminary arrangements, at 12 o'clock the Convention adjourned, to meet at 2 o'clock, P.M.

Thursday Afternoon.

The Convention assembled as per adjournment, and after singing a Liberty Song, (title, I am a Friend of Liberty,) was opened with prayer by J. W. Brooks.

The committee on Rules, then submitted the following report, which, on motion, was, as a whole, adopted.

Rules

1. Upon the appearance of a quorum, the President shall take the chair, and the Convention be called to order.
2. The minutes of the preceding session shall be read at the commencement of each meeting, at which time, mistakes, if any, shall be corrected.
3. The President shall decide all questions of order, subject to an appeal to the Convention.
4. All motions and addresses shall be made to the President, the member rising from his seat.
5. All motions (except of reference,) shall be submitted in writing.
6. All committees shall be nominated by the President, unless otherwise ordered by the Convention.
7. The previous question shall always be in order, and until decided, shall preclude all amendments and debate of the main question, and shall be put in this form, "Shall the main question be now put?"
8. No member shall be interrupted while speaking, except when out of order—when he shall be called to order by or through the President.
9. A motion to adjourn, shall always be in order, and shall be decided without debate.
10. No member shall speak more than twice on the same question, without leave, or over fifteen minutes at each time.
11. No motion shall be reconsidered at the same session at which it is passed.
12. No resolution, (except of reference,) shall be offered to the Convention, except it come through the business committee.
13. The sessions of the Convention shall commence at 10 o'clock in the morning, and 2 o'clock in the afternoon.

Henry Jackson, *Ch'n of Com.*

The Convention was now again interrupted by George W. Tucker, and one Almond Goff, who were the leaders of those eight individuals, who interrupted the Convention in the morning, and who in the afternoon declared that they would break up the Convention, unless they were admitted in as delegates. They thus continued to interrupt the Convention until near evening, when the city Marshal was sent for, who came, and after conversing with both parties, begged leave of the Convention to make a few remarks, and also to offer the following resolution, (which was the proposal of this Almond Goff.)

The yeas and nays was taken on the request, and the rule suspended, and the Marshal permitted to proceed, after which, the resolution, which read as follows, was offered by Wm. Lambert, chairman of business committee:

Resolved, That the claims of the two sets of city delegates, be left to the county delegation to decide, which set of delegates are entitled to seats. Adopted.

The Country delegation, after collecting the public papers containing the call for the convention, and the public meetings of the citizens at which the delegates were elected, retired below, in the business room, and returned and submitted through their chairman, Mr. J. W. Brooks, the following report, which settled the question at issue:

Report

The country delegation, to which was referred the claims of the two sets of city delegates, would now respectfully report which of the two are entitled to seats. After giving the subject a thorough investigation, we are convinced that the city has but one legitimate set of Delegates, and they are those who have already been enrolled upon the list and have taken their seats as delegates. The ground upon which we give this decision, is as follows:

On the 19th of September, we had our attention drawn by the *Signal of Liberty*, to a public meeting, held by the colored citizens of Detroit, of which Mr. Henry Jackson, was chairman, and O. P. Hoyt, secretary, and at which, a committee was appointed to issue a call for a State Convention, and as we were acquainted with the majority of that committee, we took a deep interest in reading the call, and resolved to throw down our farming utensils for a few days, and in obedience to the call, to assemble with our brethren, and consider and deliberate upon our moral, mental and political condition. We were again informed by the *Signal of Liberty*, the *Detroit Daily Advertiser*, and *Free Press*, of a public mass meeting, called by this same call committee, on October 16th, who were appointed at the first meeting to issue the call, and after they had done so, to call the citizens to elect their delegates and appoint committees to make preparation for the Convention. At that meeting, the regular city delegates were elected by ballot--committees were appointed to make all necessary arrangements, also to receive and provide quarters for the country delegates; money was also collected to defray the expense of printing the Liberty Songs, which we now behold scattered all over the house. Thus were we informed by the public papers of Detroit, of all the public meetings, and business transacted by our brethren here in the city, long before we left our homes; we were well informed who were the regular city delegates, and how elected, and who were the committee to receive us, and to make all necessary arrangements for the Convention. But of these other eight individuals, we had seen nothing, heard nothing, nor knew nothing of their existence, until we saw them here, declaring that they would break up the Convention, unless they were admitted to have a seat in it. A few minutes ago a paper was handed to us by one of the leaders of those eight, bearing the date of October 25th, which was yesterday, and in it, there was a meeting called by the leaders of these eight individuals, which was held on the 17th of October, the night after the regular mass meeting, at which the regular delegates were elected. Therefore, this is sufficient to show that these eight individuals have no right to seats in this convention, because they were not elected by the public, but a private meeting, called by themselves, after the regular delegates, which have been here reported, and are now in possession of their seats, had been legally elected by the mass of the people.

Therefore, we hope that no more time will be spent in this dispute, for we have thrown down our farming utensils, to attend this Convention, hoping to accomplish much good, and we now trust that the Convention will be permitted to resume its business.

On motion of Henry Jackson, the Convention adjourned to meet at 7 o'clock in the evening.

Thursday evening.

The Convention assembled as per adjournment, and was opened with prayer, by Mr. A. Aray. The minutes were read and approved.

The business committee reported by Wm. Lambert, their chairman, the following preamble and resolutions which, after being ably supported were unanimously adopted:

Whereas, We, the oppressed portion of this State, have been called upon by the deprivations experienced daily by our oppressed brethren and ourselves, to assemble in convention to consider and deliberate upon the cause of our being deprived of our rights as citizens of the State; and whereas we find ourselves existing in this State, (many native born,) with no marks of criminality attached to our names as a class--no spots of immorality staining our characters--no charges of disloyalty dishonoring our birthright; and *whereas* we yet find ourselves, the subjects and not the objects of legislation, because we are prevented from giving an assenting or opposing voice in the periodic appointments of those who rule us;

And *Whereas* we are thus made passive instruments of all laws, just or unjust, that may be enacted, to which we are bound to subscribe, even while we have no instrumentality, either in their formation or adoption;

And *Whereas* said laws in their operation, act upon us with destructive tendencies, by subjecting us to taxation without representation--by allowing us but a scanty and inadequate participation in the privileges of education --by shutting us out from the elective franchise, a right which invigorates the soul, and expands the mental power, and is the safe-guard of the liberty and prosperity of a free and independent people, and by being deprived of this right, we are virtually and manifestly shut out from the attainment of those resources of pecuniary and possessional emoluments, which an unshackled citizenship does always insure.

And *Whereas* for the same avowed proscriptions in the privileges of the government, did the fathers of the Revolution of 1776, declare these United States to be absolved from allegiance to the British crown, and established a republican form of government for their future protection, laying its foundation upon the broad platform of those noble principles set forth in the Declaration of Independence, which declares that "all men are born free and equal, and endowed by their Creator with inalienable rights, among which, are life, liberty, and the pursuit of happiness; That to secure these rights, governments are instituted among men, deriving their just power from the consent of the governed; that the people have a right to institute, alter or abolish forms of government whenever they fail to secure the ends for which they were established; that to enable all men to exercise their right to institute governments, they should enjoy the right of suffrage, that this right, is a natural right belonging to man, because he is a person and not a thing, an accountable being, and not a brute; that government is a trust to be executed for the benefit of all, that its legitimate ends are the preservation of peace, the establishment of justice, the punishment of crime and the security of rights;

And *Whereas* the fathers of the revolution pledged to each other their lives, their fortunes, and their sacred honors, for the maintenance of those noble republican principles, and thereupon established the Constitution of the United States, which guarantees to every State in the Union, a republican form of government, and expressly declares that the citizens of each state shall be entitled to all the privileges and immunities of citizens in the several states; and *whereas* the first three clauses in the first article of the Constitution of this State, (Michigan) expressly declares, 1st. That all political power is inherent in the people. 2d. Government is instituted for the protection, and benefit of the people, and that they have the right at all times to alter or reform the same, and to abolish one form of government and to establish another, whenever the public good requires it. 3d. No man or set of men are entitled to exclusive or separate privileges;

And *Whereas,* we, the oppressed, form a portion of the people of this State, and are deprived of all the rights and privileges guaranteed to the people;

Therefore, *be it Resolved by this Convention,* That we enter our solemn protest against the word "white," embodied in the first clause of the second article of the State Constitution, which provides for all white male citizens, the exclusive and separate privilege of the exercise of the elective franchise, of which we are deprived, and which is also contrary, and gives the lie to the third clause of the first article of said Constitution, which expressly declares that no man or set of men are entitled to exclusive or separate privileges.

Resolved, That as the long lost rights and privileges of an oppressed people are only gained in proportion as they act in their own cause, therefore it is our duty, here in convention assembled, to breathe out our sentiments without reserve against all political injustice.

Resolved, That this Convention declare it to be a violation of the Declaration of Independence, the Constitution of the United States, and not in accordance with a republican form of government--contrary to the first article of our State Constitution--injustice of the most aggravated character, either to deprive us of a just and legitimate participation in the rights and privileges of the State, or to make us bear the burdens, and submit to its enactments, when all its arrangements, plans, and purposes are framed and put into operation, utterly regardless of us, and which in their practical operation act upon us with a destructive tendency.

Resolved, That we the representatives of the oppressed of this State, will continue to write, publish, cry aloud and spare not, in opposition to all political injustice, and all legislation, violating the spirit of equality until the first and second articles of our State Constitution shall cease to conflict with each other and the blessings of Equal Political Liberty, shall have been extended to all men of whatever clime, language or nation within this State, and also the United States, which professes to be the land of the free, and an asylum for the oppressed of all nations.

Resolved, That the Declaration of Independence, is the text-book of this nation, and without its doctrines be maintained, our government is insecure.

[This last resolution above, called the President from his chair, who, in his able support of it, showed the many great causes that led the fathers of 1776 to make its avowal, and bleed and die in its defence. Among whom were many of *our* fathers, who were laid low in obtaining the liberty demanded by that noble declaration, and which we, as American citizens, ought now to enjoy. Therefore, it was our duty, if need be, to lay down our lives, in the maintenance of those noble principles avowed in the Declaration of Independence, for on them depends our political salvation.]

On motion of W. R. Wilson,

Resolved, That a committee of three be appointed by the President, to draw up an address to the State of Michigan, upon the political condition of our people. Adopted.

Wm. Lambert, Richard Gordon, and M. J. Lightfoot, were appointed said committee.

On motion of H. Jackson,

Resolved, That a finance committee be appointed by the President, to collect funds to defray the incidental expenses of the Convention. Adopted. H. Bibb, Wm. Dolerson and R. Allen, were appointed said committee.

On motion of A. Derrick,

Resolved, That a committee of three be appointed on printing. Adopted.

Wm. Lambert, Henry Jackson, and O. P. Hoyt, were appointed said committee.

On motion, adjourned to meet on the following morning, at 10 o'clock.

Friday Morning, Oct. 27.

The Convention met according to adjournment, and after singing several Liberty Songs, was opened with prayer, by Mr. Ockry. Minutes read and approved. The chairman of business committee, then reported the following resolutions from R. Allen, which, after being ably supported by R. Gordon, H. Bibb, and others, were unanimously adopted.

Resolved, That as a State Convention, we will exert our influence to the utmost, for the immediate abolition of American slavery, and the improvement of the condition of our colored people throughout the Union.

Resolved, That we believe State Conventions, composed of colored people who are deprived of their political rights, may do much towards ameliorating our own condition, and extending the blessings of liberty to our Southern brethren, who are the victims of American slavery.

Resolved, That we hold this to be a sound and essential principle of republican governments, to wit: That all men are entitled to enjoy equal civil and political privileges and that any act or measure of Government, calculated to create distinctions in political rights, is hostile to this principle, and shall ever receive our entire opposition.

Resolved, That we believe in the principles avowed by the fathers of the Revolution of 1776, and for which they shed their blood, and that by these principles we are willing to have our civil and political rights determined.

Resolved, That we are fully sensible of the benefits of general education and freedom of opinion in all matters civil and religious, that by every means in our power, we will extend the benefits of education to the colored children of this city and State, and will wage war against tyranny in every form, whether emanating from a crowned head abroad, or an overbearing aristocracy at home.

Resolved, That we, the colored citizens of Michigan, claim the name and rights of American citizens; that we find ourselves at home in a land professing civil and religious liberty, and yet we are most unjustly debarred of any voice in making those laws, to which we and our property are subject.

Resolved, That we will whisper in the ears of our white brethren, that the time is not far distant when they can no longer stifle in us that spirit of liberty which burst forth from the bosom of their ancestors and led them to bleed and die in its defence.

Resolved, That the colored citizens in every part of this State, be requested and urged to petition the Legislature of this State, year after year, until they extend to us those political rights and privileges which as American citizens we have a right to demand at their hands.

G. B. Blanks of Marshall offered the following resolutions through the business committee, which were unanimously adopted:

Resolved, That this Convention holds in remembrance, the name of Jabez M. Fitch, late of Marshall, State of Michigan, deceased, who exemplified in his practice, the sincerity of his professions in the cause of human rights --gave freely, of not only his money, but was willing to sacrifice (what most men prize more dearly,) his personal popularity, in his efforts to promote the welfare of his fellow beings.

Resolved, That while we reverence the names of *Wilberforce*[2] and *Clarkson,*[3] as the great champions in the cause of human liberty, we also appreciate the efforts of those among us in Michigan, who, actuated by the same good spirit, are willing to be called *Abolitionists*, despite the sneers and the ridicule of men, who profess to believe that "all men are born free and equal, and possessed of certain inalienable rights," but who, by their conduct, give the lie to their professions.

Resolved, That in the self-denying life and martyr death of *Lovejoy,*[4] we have the gratifying assurance that American Abolitionists are to be found who prove their faith by their works, and who are willing, if need be, to sacrifice worldly goods, and life itself, in the cause of the oppressed slave; and as the blood of the martyrs has heretofore proved to be the seed of the church, we trust the day is not far distant when the blood of Lovejoy may cry from the ground, and the millions now in slavery shall shout their jubilee song of deliverance from the bondage which oppresses them.

The following resolution of R. Gordon, after being supported by himself and others, was unanimously adopted.

Resolved, That our Government was instituted to mete out equal justice to all mankind; hence the tax on northern men to support slaveholders, is unjust, and therefore they having the largest proportion of representation should secure to themselves their lost rights, and show to the *slave-holders* that they will no longer submit to *dough-faceism.*[5]

The following resolution of H. Bibb, was ably supported by himself and others, and adopted.

Resolved, That we, the colored citizens of Michigan, be united in sentiment and action and never to consent to emigrate or be colonized from this, our native soil, while there exists one drop of African blood in bondage in these United States.

The following resolutions were offered through the business committee, by A. Derrick, and after being ably supported were adopted:

Resolved, That indolence is the parent of vice; it is a fact that cannot be denied, that the want of mental and manual employment often proves the incentive to vice which will infallibly produce misery, and so surely as the earth will bring forth noxion weeds when left uncultivated, so surely will one vice beget another, which, if not eradicated, will multiply to an alarming extent, until its victims become a pest to civil society, and a disgrace to mankind.

Resolved, That productive labor is the legitimate source of all our wealth, individual and National, and this labor is profitable to us as a nation.

The following resolution, by J. W. Brooks, was ably supported by John Riggs, and adopted:

Resolved, That *whereas* agriculture is the bone and sinew of our country: Therefore be it resolved, that we recommend it to our people as best calculated to promote their rise and progress in this State.

The following resolution by John Riggs, was ably supported by himself and others, and adopted:

Resolved, That *whereas,* for fourteen years, our cause has been agitated by our warm hearted white friends, yet we find ourselves the objects of oppression: Therefore be it *resolved,* that we awake to the importance of our own cause by united action for the promotion of literary institutions of our own, and encourage agriculture and mechanism among ourselves, and thereby establish a character which will do much to lighten the burdens of our suffering brethren in the South.

The following resolution was offered by O. P. Hoyt, through the business committee:

Resolved, That we recommend to our people throughout the State the great necessity of their using their utmost endeavors to procure education for their children, moral, mental, and political, that they may in due time be qualified to demand, and able to appreciate their rights, and thereby become good and useful citizens.

On motion of H. Jackson, *Resolved,* That a committee be appointed to report on the above resolution. Adopted.

The following gentlemen were appointed as said committee: Willis R. Wilson, Asher Aray, Alford Derrick.

On motion, adjourned to 2 o'clock, P.M.

Friday Afternoon.

After singing a Liberty Song the Convention was opened with prayer by J. Anderson. Minutes read and approved.

The business committee then reported the following resolutions from the following members, and which, after being ably supported were adopted:

The following resolution of Thomas Freeman, was ably supported and adopted.

Resolved, That the mechanical arts if practically adopted and carried into effect by us, would wear upon the prejudices of the community--put to silence the unworthy aspersions with which we are assailed,--overcome the obstacles now in our way, and lead us forth to the happy issue of our equal political rights.

The following resolutions of O. P. Hoyt, were ably discussed and adopted.

Resolved, That it is the duty of those among us, who are parents, to give their children trades, where circumstances will admit, it is therefore the duty of each and every one of us to give the preference and support, by patronage to those among us who are mechanics, and thereby enable them to support apprentices.

Resolved, That we, the colored citizens of this State (being well convinced that neglect is in a great measure the cause of degradation) form throughout the State, among our people, Moral Reform societies, the object of which shall be to cultivate good morals, and to instill into the minds of each other, habits of industry, and that said societies shall correspond with each other throughout the State, upon the great topics of education, temperance, morality, human liberty, and equal rights.

The Convention was here again interrupted by Almond Goff, the leader of those eight individuals who disturbed the Convention on the previous day. The President requested him to sit down and be silent, which he refused to do, and declared that no business should be done, unless he had a hand in it, he thus continued to disturb the Convention until the members seized hold of him and put him out of doors, after which, the city Marshal was sent for, who came and took him in custody and held him to bail for his appearance at the Mayor's court, to answer to the charge of disturbing the public peace.

The Convention was again permitted to resume its business. The following resolution of R. Gordon's, was called up, and after being ably discussed by J. Brooks, R. Gordon, and others, was adopted.

Resolved, That alcohol is not a product of creation, but regenerates after the life of the original is dead; therefore it is the mother of misery, the bane of society, and life-blood of oppression; for it dethrones the reason, stupefies the conscience, and hardens the heart; therefore the use of it is detrimental to an oppressed people.

On motion, adjourned until 7 o'clock in the evening.

Friday evening.

After singing a Liberty song, the convention was opened with prayer by Wm. Dolerson. Minutes read and approved.

The committee appointed to report on the subject of Education, submitted, through their chairman, Willis R. Wilson, the following report:

Mr. President, the committee on the subject of Education, after a short consideration, respectfully submit the following REPORT:

As Education is the great rampart in protecting Human Liberty, we should as an Oppressed People, encourage it to its fullest extent. As the ball of oppression is now about to burst, let us arouse to a sense of our duty. With our crippled minds we see the season of reflection has come. Therefore let us exert ourselves--let us cultivate our minds, and we may yet glean a rich harvest for ourselves and posterity. To do this, let us lay the corner stone with a mutual desire for a general diffusion of knowledge, based on the principles of Human Liberty and Equal Rights. By so doing, we will increase our individual happiness and prosperity, by improving the minds of our people, and elevating the standard of Liberty, raise ourselves up and take our stand with the well informed. Then let us be consolidated into one party, not sectarian, but the true Liberty and the Free-Knowledge-Dispensing Party. As our youths are coming up, it behooves us to put them on the right track, that they may not tread the paths of vice and misery. Let us arouse from our lethargy, and by an appeal to the liberal minded and generous hearted, we will retrieve that which has been kept from us by the unjust. Let the palladium of Liberty be sounded, let the voices of our parents, wives and children, be united with our own, and with one united and vigorous effort, raise ourselves from the state of disgraceful despondency into which we are plunged, and place ourselves on a level with our energetic rivals, by ingrafting into the minds of our youth, virtue and intelligence, which will in time to come, bring forth fruit pleasing to the eye, and which will cheer us in our declining years and cause them to bless our memory, when we are cold in the grave.

Therefore be it resolved, that we use our utmost endeavors to educate our children. WILLIS R. WILSON, ch'n of Com.

The above report, after being submitted, was unanimously adopted.

Wm. Lambert, chairman of the committee to draw up an Address to the State, then submitted the following report, which was received with great applause, and unanimously adopted.

Mr. President, the committee appointed to draw up an Address to the State would now respectfully report and submit the following address to your consideration:

AN ADDRESS TO THE CITIZENS OF THE STATE OF MICHIGAN

Fellow Citizens,--The State Convention of Colored citizens, assembled in Detroit, October 26th, and 27th, to consider their political condition, in behalf of their people in this State, would respectfully address you on a subject to them of the most vital importance.

We, the oppressed portion of this State, rejoice that we are the native born inhabitants of a country that professes to be the land of the free, and an asylum for the oppressed of all nations.

But yet we feel ourselves aggrieved, that we are deprived by injustice of those inalienable rights with which we are endowed by the Creator of the Universe, and incorporated and made sacred to every native born inhabitant of these United States, by the Declaration of the American Independence.

Therefore do we solemnly appeal to you for a just reason, why we should be deprived of our free born rights, which are guaranteed to us as native born Americans.

For we find ourselves existing in this State, with no marks of criminality attached to our names as a class, no spots of immorality staining our characters--no charges of disloyalty dishonoring our birth-right; yet we are prevented from being participants in those free-born rights and sympathies, that are bountifully guaranteed not only to common humanity of this State, but also to foreigners of whatever clime or language. We find ourselves the subjects and not the objects of legislation, because we are prevented from giving an assenting or opposing voice in the periodic appointment of those who rule us, and are made passive instruments of all laws, just or unjust, that may be enacted, to which we are bound to subscribe, even while we have no instrumentality, either in their formation or adoption, and which in their practical operation act upon us with destructive tendency. By subjecting us to taxation without representation, by allowing us but a scanty and inadequate participation in the privileges of education. For we are deprived of a just and equal participation in the educational privileges of the State, for which we are equally taxed to support.

By shutting us out from the exercise of the elective franchise, a right which invigorates the soul, and expands the mental powers, and is the safeguard of the liberty and prosperity of a free and independent people, and by being deprived of this right, we are virtually and manifestly shut out from the attainment of those resources of pecuniary and possessional emoluments, which an unshackled citizenship does always ensure. These proscriptions in the privileges of the State, we consider to be undemocratic, unjust, and not in accordance with the spirit and political institutions of our republican form of government, and contrary to the first article of our State Constitution, which in the first three clauses of said article, expressly declares that, 1st, All political power is inherent in the people. 2d, Government is instituted for the protection, security and benefit of the people, and they have the right at all times, to alter or reform the same, and to abolish one form of government and establish another, whenever the public good requires it. 3d, No man or set of men are entitled to exclusive or separate privileges. And as we, the oppressed form a portion of the people of the State, and are deprived of all the rights and privileges guaranteed to the people, therefore, we enter our solemn protest against the word white, embodied in the first clause of the second article of the aforesaid Constitution, which provides for all white male citizens, the exclusive and separate privilege of the exercise of the elective franchise, of which we are deprived, and which is also contrary, and gives the lie to the third clause of the first article of the Constitution, which so positively declares that "no man, or set of men are entitled to exclusive or separate privileges."

For the same here avowed proscriptions in the privileges of the government, did the fathers of the Revolution of 1776, declare these United States to be absolved from all allegiance to the British crown. They published as a justification, a declaration of rights, and an extensive list of grievances, and then established a republican form of government for their future protection, laying its foundation on the broad platform of those noble principles set forth in their Declaration of Independence; which so nobly declares that all men are born free and equal, and endowed by their Creator with inalienable rights, among which, are life, liberty, and the pursuit of happiness; that to secure these rights, governments are instituted amongst men, deriving their just powers from the consent of the governed; that the people are the only legitimate force of lawful political power, and that they have a right to institute, alter or abolish forms of government when they fail to secure the ends for which they were established; and that this right is inherent, inalienable and supreme.

That the definition of "the people," is all men; that to enable all men to exercise their right to institute government, they should enjoy the right of suffrage. That this right is a natural right, belonging to man, because he is a person and not a thing--an accountable being and not a brute. That government is a trust to be executed for the benefit of all; that its legitimate ends are the preservation of peace, the establishment of justice, the punishment of crime, and the security of rights. These principles declare eternal war against all political injustice. They condemn all Legislation violating the spirit of equality. They are the foundation of a true, and unproscriptive republican form of government and the correct guides in all political action.

For the maintenance of these noble republican principles, the fathers of the Revolution, pledged to each other their lives, their fortunes, and their sacred honors, and thereupon ordained and established the Constitution of these United States, which guarantees to every State in this Union a republican form of government, and explicitly declares that the citizens of each State shall be entitled to all the privileges and immunities of citizens in the several States. In accordance with these glorious republican principles, have we, year after year petitioned our State Legislature for the redress of grievances, and we have received from time to time but little or no attention.

In that declaration of fundamental principles, set forth by the fathers of '76, we fail to discover anything like a system of exclusion. No! there is not an expression, nor an implied sentiment to be found making a distinction in the rights and privileges of any class of American citizens. But on the contrary, its first infant breath, boldly proclaims that all men are born free and equal, and that consequently life, liberty, and the pursuit of happiness, are inherent in every individual, vested inalienably by natural birthright.

Had the declaration said that all "white men are born free and equal," then our ancestors would not have been deceived into the belief, that they were included as constituting a portion of the party, engaged in the strife against British oppression. Nor have given occasion to the observation of General La Fayette, when he visited this country, that, during the Revolution, the white and black soldiers fought and messed together without hesitation. The records of that period clearly prove that the blacks rushed forth to the conflict, and poured out their blood with as much bravery as their white fellow soldiers, in the attacks made upon what they then considered to be the common enemy. The testimony of Generals Washington, Green,[6] and many others, to the valor of our people in the time of our country's greatest peril, and danger, shines too conspicuous to be impeached by an enlightened individual.

Yes! fellow-citizens,--again in the War of 1812, our people were called upon to repel an invading foe from our soil. Regardless of the wrongs that had already been heaped upon them, they immediately rushed forth to the conflict; and under the command of General Jackson in the Southern Army, and especially at the battle of New Orleans, distinguished themselves as valiant soldiers, fighting in defence of their country's honor.[7] The splendid naval achievements, on Lakes Erie and Champlain, were owing, mostly, to the skill and prowess of Colored men. The fame of Perry was gained at the expense of the mangled bodies and bleeding veins of our disfranchised people. The blood of our fathers is mingled with the soil of every battle field and their bones have enriched the most productive lands of our country. Yes! in those ever-memorable battles which achieved the Independence, and maintained the honor of our country, *your* fathers and *ours*, fought side by side, many of both were laid low, bleeding and wallowing in their gore, which was the dear price they paid for the Independence of this, our beloved, country, that all their posterity might enjoy the blessings of Equal Liberty.

Therefore, we feel ourselves aggrieved, that the blessings obtained by the blood and toil of our fathers, are not administered as equally to us as to yourselves. We feel that our sufferings caused by our being deprived of our Political Rights, should call forth the sympathies of the whole human race, but more especially those of yourselves, among whom we dwell & who are the authors of our calamities. For you have trampled our Liberties in the dust, and thus standing with the iron-heel of Opression upon our heads, you bid us rise to a level with yourselves; and because we do not rise, you point the finger of scorn and contempt at us, and say, that we are an inferior race by nature. Yes! when all the avenues of privileged life have been closed against us, our hands bound with stationary fetters, our minds left to grope in the prison cell of impenetrable gloom, and our whole action regulated by constitutional law, and a perverse public sentiment, we have been tauntingly required to prove the dignity of our human nature, by disrobing ourselves of inferiority and exhibiting to the world, our profound scholars, distinguished philosophers, learned jurists, and eminent statesmen. The very expectation on which such a requisition is founded, to say the least, is unreasonable; for it is only when the seed is sown, that we can justly expect to reap. But yet we feel constrained to say, we present the curious and acknowledged credible spectacle of a people beinding under the weight of a galling proscription, who will not suffer by comparison with our more privileged fellow citizens of the same rank, either in religion, morality, industry or general information.

A spirit of intelligence pervades our entire population, keeping pace with the progressive spirit of the age, and the continual intellectual progress of the nation. There are but few families in which pen, ink and paper, and books, are not common and necessary commodities. If then, amidst all the difficulties with which we are surrounded, and privations we have suffered, we present an equal amount of intelligence with that class of our fellow citizens that have been so peculiarly favored, a very grave and dangerous question presents itself to the world, on the natural equality of man; and the best rule of logic, would place those who have oppressed us, in the scale of inferiority.

Our condition as a people in ancient times, was far from indicating intellectual or moral inferiority. For, we are informed by the writings of Herodotus,[8] Pindar,[9] Aeschylus[10] and many other ancient historians, that Egypt and Ethiopia held the most conspicuous places amongst the nations of the earth. Their princes were wealthy and powerful, and their people distinguished for their profound learning and wisdom. Two thousand years ago, people flocked from all parts of the known world, down into Africa, to receive instruction from those woolly haired and black skinned Ethiopians and Egyptians. Yes, even the proudest of the Grecian philosophers, historians and poets, among whom were Solon,[11] Pythagoras,[12] Plato,[13] Herodotus, Homer,[14] Lycurgus,[15] and many others, all went down into Africa, and set at the feet of our ancestors, and drank in wisdom, until they were taught in all the arts and sciences of those ancient African nations. The code of laws administered by Solon to the inhabitants of Athens, shows no inferiority of their black African tutors. The form of Government established by Lycurgus, to raise up the downtrodden Spartans, to become the dread and terror of all their neighboring Grecian states, shows no inferiority in the Governmental knowledge of his black African teachers. The song of Homer sung of Egypt's Thebes with her hundred gates of polished brass, her splendid architecture, her statues, her pyramids, and temples of sculptured marble, which were so gigantic and stupendous, that the very ruins are yet so tremendous, that they still impress the mind with such gigantic phantoms, that Napoleon's whole army (while in Africa) all suddenly stopped, and with one accord, stood in amazement, and clapped their hands with delight, over the ancient world's great Empress, on the Egyptian plain, which *three* thousand years ago,

> Spread her conquest over a thousand States,
> And poured her heroes through a hundred gates;
> Two hundred horsemen and two hundred cars,
> From each wide portal issued forth to the wars.

Under the African conqueror (Sesostris, King of Egypt,) who went forth and conquered the whole known world, leaving Ethiopian and Egyptian colonies behind him, to civilize and improve the condition of the nations that he had conquered. He also caused his own statue to be carved of marble and placed among them that the name of the Great Sesostris, the African Conqueror of the World, might ever be fresh in their memory who had left his countrymen among them, to raise them from ignorance and barbarism, to learning and civilization. We are assured on the personal evidence of Herodotus and Strabo[16] that the statues erected by this African leader still remained in their days (which was from Sesostris, a period of 860 years) and even that they were actually inspected by them in India, Syria, Palestine, Arabia, Media and

Assyria. The inscription which these proud monuments every where bore was to the following effect:

> Sesostris, king of kings and lord of lords, subdued this country by the power of his arms.

Herodotus also mentions that Sesostris founded the Kingdom of Colchis near Pontus and left a colony there; and we are informed by Apollonius Rhodius[17] that the posterity of the Egyptian governor subsisted at Ea, the capital of Colchis for many generations. The descendants of this military colony presenting the black complexion and woolly hair of Africa, were long distinguished from the natives of the district among whom they dwelt. And it is possible even at this day, to find among the Circassians, certain distinguished families, whose blood might be traced to the soldiers of Sesostris, and whose features still verify the traditional affinity which connects them with the ancient inhabitants of Egypt and Ethiopia. The great Assyrian empire of the once powerful Babylon and Nineveh, were once founded by Ethiopian colonies and peopled by blacks. Tyre and Carthage, the most industrious, welathy and polished states of their times, were also once founded by Ethiopians and Egyptian colonies and peopled by blacks, from the banks of the Nile, whose proud monuments are still spared by the hand of time, to be the wonder and admiration of the world, and which by their gigantic dimensions and exquisite workmanship, shows no inferiority of the wealth, power or wisdom of those ancient African nations.

The sun of civilization rose from the centre of Africa, and like the bright luminary of the celestial regions, it cast its light into the most remote corners of the earth, giving arts, sciences and intellectual improvement, to all that lay beneath its elevating rays.

Therefore, fellow citizens, proscribe us no longer, by holding us in a degraded light, on account of natural inferiority, but rather extend to us our free born right, the Elective Franchise, which invigorates the soul and expands the mental powers of a free and independent people. We then would be able to disrobe ourselves of inferiority, and prove to the world, that we are worthy of the name of American citizens. Therefore, we appeal to you to secure to us our political rights; for the enjoyment of those rights in a free country, is a stimulant to enterprise, a means of influence, and a source of respect; they send life, vigor and energy through the entire heart of a people; the want of them in a community is the cause of careless [illegible] intellectual inertness, and indolence. Yet many of us have sprung above all these depressing circumstances, and exerting ourselves with unwonted alacrity, by native industry, have accumulated property, for which we are now taxed and not represented. We are firm believers in the doctrines set forth in the Declaration of Independence. We are among those who believe that taxation, and representation, should go together. We acquiesce in the sentiment that Governments can only derive their just power from the consent of the governed. Therefore, we declare it to be a violation of the Declaration of Independence, the Constitution of the United States, and not in accordance with a republican form of Government, contrary to the 1st article of our State Constitution, and injustice of the most aggravated character, either to deprive us of a just and legitimate participation in the rights and privileges of the State, or to make us bear the burdens and submit to its enactments; when all its arrangements, plans and purposes are framed and put into operation utterly regardless of us, and which in their practical operation, act upon us with destructive tendency.

Therefore, Fellow Citizens,--the Colored Citizens of this State, through us, their representatives, respectfully and earnestly ask at your hands, the speedy adoption of such plans, and the formation of such measures as may secure to them their Equal Political Rights.

Wm. Lambert, *Ch'n of Com.*

On motion of H. Jackson, *Resolved* that the Convention tender their heartfelt thanks to Wm. Lambert, chairman of the committee, for so ably defending us, in his address to the State. Adopted.

On motion of H. Jackson, *Resolved*, that this Convention adjourn tonight at 10 o'clock. Adopted.

On motion of R. Gordon, *Resolved*, that this Convention appoint a State Corresponding Committee, whose duty it shall be to appoint Public Meetings, call future Conventions, and transact all public business for the colored Citizens of this State, until the next Convention. Adopted.

The following gentlemen were appointed said committee, viz: Wm. Lambert, Henry Jackson, Richard Gordon, Madison J. Lightfoot, of Detroit;--Asher Aray of Pittsfield, Washtenaw co.;--Calvin Hacket of Jackson, Jackson co.;--A. C. West of Marshall, Calhoun co.;--J. W. Brooks of Pittsfield, Washtenaw co.; --John Smith of Pontiac, Oakland co.;--Samuel Dickerson of_____ Lenawee co.; --Henry Powers of Grand Rapids, Kent co.;--Jefferson Fitzgerald of York, Washtenaw co.;--Thomas Freeman, Kalamazoo co.;--Washtenaw co.

On motion of R. Gordon, *Resolved*, that each member now come forward and plank down his dollar to the committee on printing, to pay for the printing of the minutes of this convention.

Mr. Gordon then very ardently supported this resolution to some length and to substantiate the sincerity of his remarks, he "planked down" his dollar, he then turned and very sarcastically appealed to the rest of the members to come up and do likewise. The members not wishing to be out-done, consequently came up and planked down their money; which, after being counted by the committee, was found to be $9 cash, with the names of nine individuals with their promises to pay.

The Finance Committee then reported, that the money collected during the sessions of the Convention, had been more than sufficient to cover the expense, by the sum of $2.35.

It was moved that the balance be placed in the hands of the committee on printing, to aid in publishing the proceedings. Carried.

The President then announced that there was no more business before us. The following resolutions were then offered, and on motion unanimously adopted.

Resolved, that we tender a vote of thanks to the trustees of this church for the free use of it.

Resolved, that we tender a vote of thanks to the President, for the impartial manner with which he has presided over our deliberations; to the Secretaries, for the willing manner in which they have performed their duties, and also to the Chairman of the business committee, for his faithfulness in furnishing business for the Convention; and to all the other officers, who have amply discharged their duties.

The President then rose from his seat, and very feelingly addressed the members to some length, upon the leading subjects that had occupied their deliberations, and at the close of his remarks, he expressed a sincere desire that the sentiments which had been so earnestly expressed in the Convention, and which were now about to be published to the world, might grow brighter and brighter in their memories, and by their practical operations prove the sincerity of their avowals.

After the President had thus concluded his remarks and taken his seat, it was, on motion of Henry Jackson, Resolved, that we now sing a Liberty Song, address the throne of Grace, and adjourn, *sine die.*

The members then led off, and the audience joined in the song, after which the closing prayer was made by Wm. Smith,

ADJOURNED.

Copy in the Schomburg Collection, New York Public Library; Copy in the Burton Historical Collection, Detroit Public Library.

REFERENCE NOTES

1. Henry Bibb (1815-1854) was born in Shelby County, Kentucky, the son of a slave mother and a white father. As a slave, he was sold at least six times as a result of his stubborn resistance to discipline. An early escape attempt with his wife and child was aborted, but he finally succeeded alone in 1837, passing in the process through Missouri, Ohio, and Michigan to Detroit. While an active participant in the statewide convention of Michigan

blacks, held at Detroit in 1843, he also, in the following year, vigorously spoke for and supported the candidate of the Liberty Party.

With the passage of the Fugitive Slave Law of 1850, which struck terror in the hearts of the free black community and sent thousands fleeing into Canada, Bibb formed a colonization society to aid in resettling his people there. In 1851, he established in Detroit a bi-monthly newspaper entitled *The Voice of the Fugitive*. His Refugee's Home Society, founded at Detroit in May 1851, sought through public grant or private purchase from the Canadian government sufficient land to be distributed to refugee blacks in twenty-five acre plots.

An active figure in the antislavery movement, Bibb helped form the Anti-Slavery Society of Canada in 1851 and, in 1852, was appointed a vice-president of the group. His *Narrative of the Life and Adventures of Henry Bibb* appeared in 1849. Frederick Douglass reviewed it and noted in the *North Star* (Aug. 17, 1849) that Bibb's work was "one of the most interesting and thrilling narratives of slavery ever laid before the American public. . . . We deem the work a most valuable acquisition to the anti-slavery cause, and we hope that it may be widely circulated throughout the country."

2. William Wilberforce (1759-1833), aroused to the antislavery cause by Thomas Clarkson, began to work in Parliament in 1787 to end the slave trade. The slave trade was abolished in 1807.

3. Thomas Clarkson (1760-1846), pioneer British abolitionist, was active for over sixty years with Granville Sharpe and Wilberforce in the battle against slavery and the slave trade.

4. In 1837, Elijah P. Lovejoy (1802-1837), a clergyman who had edited an antislavery paper in St. Louis, was forced to leave that city and carry on his work in Alton, Illinois. Here he organized the Illinois Anti-Slavery Society and edited the *Alton Observer*. Pro-slavery mobs destroyed one printing press after another, and, on November 7, 1837, the night after the third press was installed, the printing office was attacked and Lovejoy was killed while defending his property.

5. A northern politician over-anxious to please the South was called a "Dough-face." The term is believed to have been invented by John Randolph of Roanoke.

6. The reference is to Nathanael Greene (1742-1786), American Revolutionary general. He should be distinguished, however, from Christopher Greene, Revolutionary soldier, identified below.

7. On December 18, 1814, General Andrew Jackson issued the following proclamation to the free people of color:

"Soldiers! when on the banks of the Mobile I called you to take up arms, inviting you to partake the perils and glory of your *white* fellow citizens, I expected much from you; for I was not ignorant that you possessed qualities most formidable to an invading enemy. I knew with what fortitude you could endure hunger and thirst, and all the fatigues of a campaign.

"I knew well you loved your native country, and that you, as well as ourselves, had to defend what *man* holds dear--his parents, wife, children, and property. You have done more than I expected. In addition to the previous qualities I before knew you to possess, I found among you a noble enthusiasm which leads to the performance of great things.

"Soldiers! the President of the United States shall hear how praiseworthy was your conduct in the hour of danger, and the representatives of the American people will give you the praise your exploits entitle you to. Your General anticipates them in applauding your noble ardor. . . ." See Philip S. Foner, *The Life and Writings of Frederick Douglass* (New York, 1950), II, 265.

8. Herodotus (484?-425? B.C.), Greek historian, was called the father of history.

9. Pindar (518?-c.438 B.C.), Greek poet, was generally regarded as the greatest Greek lyric poet. He travelled widely throughout the ancient world, but lived principally at Thebes.

10. Aeschylus (525-456 B.C.), famous Greek writer of tragedy, was the predecessor of Sophocles and Euripides.

11. Solon (c. 639-c. 559 B.C.), Athenian statesman and founder of the Athenian democracy, is best known as a lawgiver and reformer.

12. Pythagoras (c. 582-c. 507 B.C.), pre-Socratic Greek philosopher and founder of the Pythagorean school. The Pythagoreans were influential mathematicians and geometricians, and the theorem that bears their name is witness to their influence on the initial part of Euclidean geometry.

13. Plato (427?-347? B.C.), famous Greek philosopher and disciple of Socrates, established his Academy at Athens, where he taught mathematics and philosophy until his death.

14. Homer was the famous Greek poet, author of the *Illiad* and *Odyssey*.

15. Lycurgus (c. 7th cent. B.C.?) is traditionally credited with founding the Spartan constitution. The earliest mention of him is in Herodotus. Nothing is known of his life--when he lived or if he was a real man, a god, or a mythical figure.

16. Strabo (c. 63 B.C.-c. 21 A.D.) was a Greek geographer and historian.

17. Apollonius Rhodius (3d cent. B.C.), epic poet of Alexandria and Rhodes, was also librarian at Alexandria.

PROCEEDINGS OF THE COLORED MEN'S CONVENTION
OF THE STATE OF MICHIGAN, HELD IN THE CITY OF DETROIT,
TUESDAY AND WEDNESDAY, SEPT. 12th AND 13th, '65,
WITH ACCOMPANYING DOCUMENTS
ALSO, THE CONSTITUTION OF THE EQUAL RIGHTS LEAGUE
OF THE STATE OF MICHIGAN

Report of the Committee on Publication

To the Members of the State Convention:
Gentlemen:--The undersigned, Committee on Publication, in submitting the result of their labors in arranging and correcting the Journal of the proceedings of the late State Convention of colored men, beg leave to state, that owing to the continued indisposition of the Secretary, they were unable to publish the proceedings at an earlier date. They have now the pleasure of submitting to your consideration the proceedings as corrected and revised by your committee.

                    Very respectfully, your obedient servants,
                            G. W. Lewis,
                            H. J. Lewis,
                            B. Dolbeare Paul,
                                  Com. on Publication.
Adrian, Oct. 23, 1865.

PROCEEDINGS OF THE COLORED MEN'S STATE CONVENTION
HELD IN THE CITY OF DETROIT,
SEPTEMBER 12th AND 13th, 1865

The State Convention of Colored men assembled in the 2d Baptist Church, in Detroit, Mich., Sept. 12th and 13th, at 12 o'clock, M. H. J. Lewis, Esq., of Hudson, called the Convention to order. B. Dolbeare Paul, of Detroit, read the call. G. W. Lewis, Esq., of Adrian, was chosen temporary Chairman, and James Richards, Esq., of Detroit, temporary Secretary. Prayer was offered by Mr. Grinton, of Marshall.

On motion of Mr. D. Roberts, of Adrian, the chairman appointed a committee on credentials, consisting of O. P. Anderson, of Battle Creek, Willis Washington, of Detroit, and S. W. Burton, of Hillsdale.

After the committee had retired, Mr. Paul, of Detroit, D. Roberts, of Adrian, J. W. Brooks, of Ann Arbor, and B. Grinton, of Marshall, in response to the chair, addressed the Convention upon the issues of the day, in an able and lucid manner.

The committee on credentials reported the names of delegates whose seats were not contested. The full list, as corrected, is as follows:

Hudson--H. J. Lewis.
Adrian--D. Roberts, G. W. Lewis.
Lenawee Co.--Robert Brown.
Hillsdale--W. W. Burton.
Ann Arbor--J. W. Brooks, A. Boyar.
Romeo, Macomb Co.--John Hackley.

Kalamazoo--Geo. Nichols.
Jackson--Wilberforce Johnson.
Coldwater--F. R. Jenkins.
Battle Creek--John J. Evans, O. P. Anderson.
Ypsilanti--S. Wells, A. Prichard.
Detroit--G. H. Parker, B. Dolbeare Paul, Willis Washington, J. D. Carter, T. J. Rice, Lewis Pierce, A. Burgess, Chas. Gillam, Thomas Nichols.
"Moral and Intellectual Union."--Wayne Co.--J. W. Henry, J. T. Lee, James Richards.
State at large--O. C. Wood.

Honorary Members

James Fields, M.D., Adrian.
Capt. Buckner, Hillsdale.
James Hill, Hillsdale.
R. L. Cullen, Detroit.
T. J. Martin, Dowagiac.
Isaac Burdine, Niles.
S. Fowler, Eaton Rapids.
Wm. Watts, St. Johns.

On montion of Mr. D. Roberts, of Adrian, the chair appointed the following:

Committee on Rules

H. J. Lewis, of Hudson, T. J. Rice, of Detroit, J. J. Evans, of Battle Creek.
On motion of J. J. Evans, of Battle Creek, the chair appointed the following:

Committee on Permanent Officers

J. D. Carter, of Detroit; D. Roberts, of Adrian; H. J. Lewis, of Hudson; F. R. Jenkins, of Coldwater; S. W. Burton, of Hillsdale; J. W. Brooks, of Ann Arbor; B. Brinton, of Marshall; J. Henry, of Detroit; Geo. Nichols, of Kalamazoo; J. J. Evans, of Battle Creek.
On motion of Mr. J. Henry, of Detroit, the following were appointed a

Finance Committee

T. J. Rice, of Detroit; J. D. Carter, of Detroit; R. Brown, of Lenawee Co.; A. Prichard, of Ypsilanti.
On motion of Mr. Anderson, of Battle Creek, the Convention appointed as

Business Committee

G. W. Lewis, of Adrian, Chairman.
O. P. Anderson, of Battle Creek; J. H. Parker, of Detroit; R. L. Cullen, of Detroit; T. J. Rice, of Detroit; S. W. Burton, of Hillsdale.
On motion of J. D. Carter, of Detroit, Dr. Fields was made an honorary member.
On motion of Mr. Paul, A. Prichard, of Ypsilanti, J. J. Martin, of Dowagiac and J. Burdine, of Niles, were made honorary members of the Convention.
On motion of D. Roberts, of Adrian, G. H. Parker, of Detroit, and O. P. Anderson, of Battle Creek, were appointed a committee to install the permanent officers of the Convention.
Mr. Carter, from the committee on Permanent Organization, reported the following gentlemen as permanent officers of the Convention:
President--Rev. J. W. Brooks, of Ann Arbor.
1st Vice President--H. J. Lewis, Hudson.
2d Vice President--Benjamin Grinton, of Marshall.

3d. Vice President--James Richards, of Detroit.
4th Vice President--Geo. Nichols, Kalamazoo.
Secretary--B. Dolbeare Paul, of Detroit.
1st Assistant Secretary--J. J. Evans, Battle Creek.
2d Assistant Secretary--C. H. Gillam, of Detroit.

The chairman, having been escorted to the chair, made an appropriate speech, thanking the Convention for the honor conferred upon him.

On motion of Mr. Roberts, of Adrian, a vote of thanks was accorded the retiring temporary officers, for the able manner in which they had conducted the business before the Convention, and the Convention adjourned to meet at 3 o'clock.

Afternoon Session, September 12th, 1865, 3 o'clock.

The Convention re-assembled at 3 o'clock. Roll called, a quorum present. Religious services were conducted by Rev. Mr. McIntosh, of the African Methodist Episcopal church. Minutes of morning session read and adopted.

Mr. Lewis, of Hudson, from the Committee on Rules, presented the following Report on Rules, which was, on motion, adopted.

Report on Rules

1st. There shall be three sessions of the convention daily. The convention shall meet at 9 o'clock A.M., and adjourn at 12 o'clock, M. The afternoon session of the convention shall meet at 3 o'clock, P.M., and adjourn at 5 o'clock, P.M.

2d. The majority of the members of the convention shall constitute a quorum for the transaction of business at either of its sessions.

3d. The rules of order as laid down in Channing's Manual shall be the standing rules of order of this convention in all points not herein provided for.

4th. No member shall be allowed to speak more than twice upon the same subject without special leave of the convention, and not longer than ten minutes each time.

Mr. Lewis, of Adrian, moved that Mr. Rice be relieved from the Finance Committee. Carried.

On motion of Mr. Prichard, of Ypsilanti, Mr. Washington was elected to fill vacancy. Mr. Hackley, of Macomb Co., was on motion of Mr. Henry, added to the committee.

Rev. Mr. McIntosh, having been requested to address the convention, declined making a speech, but stated that he desired to sit near the Secretary's stand, so that he might report the proceedings of the convention to the paper which he represented, the *Christian Recorder.*

The President called upon Mrs. M. A. Shadd Cary.[1] Mrs. Cary said she declined making a speech, but she would say, that so far as the object contemplated was concerned, she heartily desired to see it accomplished.

While the Business Committee were absent the Convention were entertained with very fine music by Miss Sherman, of Marshall, Miss Hattie Berry and Miss Josephine Warren, assisted by Messrs. Russell and Warren, of Cleveland.

Mr. Lewis, from the Business Committee, reported the following

Declaration of Sentiments

Whereas, For reasons to be hereinafter stated, we deem it expedient that the Equal Rights League of Colored People, established in January, the 25th, 1865, should be dissolved, and an association formed, to be known as the "Equal Rights League of Michigan," for reasons set forth in the following circular, issued August, A.D., 1865.

CIRCULAR

To The People of Color of the State of Michigan:

The State Equal Rights League, organized under and by virtue of the constitution of the National Equal Rights League, by the people, through their representatives in convention assembled, January 25th and 26th, respectively, 1865, having failed to meet the object for which it was instituted, the undersigned, members of the Equal Rights League for the State of Michigan, and others, do hereby call a mass convention of the colored people of the State, for the following, among other reasons, to-wit:

1st. That your representatives were not permitted to take part in the deliberations of the meeting of the Equal Rights League on the 1st day of August, as provided in the constitution.

2d. That the officers of the Bureau, at Detroit, did, without the consent of the Executive Board, or your representatives, set aside the constitution and institute another, which your representatives could not and did not adopt.

3d. That in defiance of the expressed will of your representatives, the said Bureau did, then and there, in the aforesaid meeting of the Equal Rights League, held in the Methodist church at Detroit, proceed to transact business for and in the name of the people, without the sanction, and in defiance of the expressed wish of your representatives, and that the said Bureau did futhermore elect representatives for the people, to represent the people in the National Equal Rights League meeting,[2] to be held in the city of Cleveland in September ensuing, under protest.

For these reasons, we the undersigned, members of the State Equal Rights League, and others, do hereby call a mass convention of the people of the State, to be held in the city of Detroit, on the twelfth day of September next, A.D., 1865, for the purpose of organizing another Equal Rights League, and for the purpose of obtaining an opinion of the people of the State. Therefore, be it

Resolved, That that portion of the officers of the State Bureau, located in the city of Detroit, who were instrumental in perpetrating such a gross outrage upon the people's rights, by first insulting and then excluding their representatives, and that too, without the sanction of law, merit our hearty disapproval.

Resolved, That the alteration of the constitution of the State League, in order to cater to the wishes of men whose only object is to rule, should meet with the reprobation and contempt of all honest men and women.

Resolved, That we, as legitimate members of the State Equal Rights League for the State of Michigan, do most solemnly enter our protest against this outrage, upon the principles of right and justice.

Resolved, That we, the people of the State of Michigan, in convention assembled, on this twelfth day of September, 1865, do hereby declare that all proceedings and doings of the former conventions, meetings, societies, and leagues, heretofore convened for the object contemplated, by the National Equal Rights League, null and void, and of no effect whatsoever.

Mr. Anderson moved to strike out the second resolution of the Declaration of Sentiments.

Mr. Lewis, of Hudson, said he thought the section ought to be modified, and proceeded to argue at length in defence of his position.

Mr. Rice, of Detroit, said that some gentlemen had been insulted, and if concessions were to be made it ought to come from the so-called Bureau.

Mr. Parker, of Detroit, said that he was decidedly opposed to any concessions being granted, if any overtures were to be made they should come from the other side. He had been informed that a prominent gentleman of this city had gone to the President of the so-called Bureau, and stated that he deprecated the course pursued by them, and he was sure that the people would not sanction their proceedings. The President replied, that he did not care for the people. Mr. Parker proceeded to relate the proceedings of the League on the first of August.

Mr. Lewis, of Hudson, argued against the section, and in favor of its being struck out.

Mr. Roberts, of Adrian, in an eloquent and forcible speech, urged the expediency of the resolution being struck out.

Mr. Lewis, of Adrian, said that he had conversed with the gentlemen of the Bureau, and they had stated that they did not intend to conciliate parties, but they were prepared to carry the matter to the National League. He was in favor of the report.

After considerable discussion, Mr. Washington moved the previous question, which, however, was withdrawn, and Messrs. Washington and Paul, of Detroit, proceeded to argue at length, the former in favor of the section being struck out, and the latter against its rejection. The question to strike out, being put, was carried, and the report, as amended, adopted. The Convention then adjourned to meet at half-past seven o'clock in the evening.

Evening Session.

The convention re-assembled; quorum present.

Religious services were conducted by Mr. Burton, of Hillsdale.

Mr. Anderson, from the Committee on Credentials, presented the names of Wilberforce Johnson, as a representative from Jackson, and Thos. Nichols, to be members of the Convention.

Mr. Cullen, of Detroit, proceeded to address the convention.

Mr. Cullen said: "I want you to understand that I am working for the people, and not for any aggrandizement of mine own. I want a unit of the people of Michigan. We have the question of equal rights to fight, which we have fought for years. The colored men of Michigan ought to be united." His motto was, "Procure our own Rights at home," then we could help our friends in Kentucky or elsewhere. He therefore moved the following resolution:

Resolved, That the members of the so-called Bureau of the Michigan State Equal Rights League be invited to participate in the proceedings of this Convention.

Mr. Roberts, of Adrain, supported the resolution.

Resolution lost.

Mr. Roberts, of Adrian, moved the following resolution:

Resolved, That any person or persons favorable to the object of this Convention, and for the good of the people of color of the State of Michigan, be invited to participate by laying down all party spirit, and conform to the rules by which, and the object for which we are here assembled.

Mr. Rice, of Detroit, rose to support the resolution. He had voted for Mr. Cullen's resolution. We could not ask equal rights from the whites, when we were unwilling to accord equal rights among ourselves. While he would stand upon his manhood, he was in favor of the resolution.

Mr. Washington, of Detroit, in reply, said he thought this Convention had assembled in accordance with the circular, to denounce the proceedings of the so-called Bureau. He was in favor of the gentlemen of the so-called Bureau coming here as individual members, but not as a State Bureau.

Mr. Cullen, of Detroit, said: "I understood from your proceedings to-day that you had done away with the State Bureau."

Mr. Roberts, of Adrian, said: "This resolution in my judgement I offer for the good of the people of the United States, as well as Michigan. We have said that we would not emigrate, but would remain here as long as our brethren were in bondage. Now they have been set free, and we are here for the purpose of uniting for the good of the cause. Our acts are for the good of the whole. All persons who have an interest in our welfare we invite to come here for the purpose of aiding the good cause. Our motives are pure."

Mr. Carter, of Detroit, said he was not here to parley with rebels. They had altered the constitution to suit themselves, regardless of the people, and so long as they held office in the so-called Bureau he could not act with them.

Mr. Parker, of Detroit, said they must bring forth fruit meet for repentance first, before we can receive them.

Mr. Cullen said, the most cowardly way to treat any one was to stab him in the dark. Now we are arguing against a set of men who are not here to defend themselves.

Mr. Parker--The gentlemen is a member of the City League. Have they ever given me a hearing?

Mr. Cullen--That is just the point. He was a peoples' man. Do you want to take this matter to the National League?

A Voice--(No, no.)

Mr. Parker--Who proposes to take it there?

Mr. Cullen--The delegates appointed by the Bureau will be in Cleveland, and their seats will no doubt be contested by you. What he wanted was that the Bureau should be admitted here the same as he.

MICHIGAN, 1865

Mr. Rice, of Detroit--He was in favor of the resolution.
Mr. Paul, of Detroit--Have any of the gentlemen applied for admission?
Mr. Rice--I am not aware that they have.
By request the Secretary read the resolution again, and
Mr. Rice moved to amend it by striking out the word "invite."
Mr. Roberts, of Adrian--I did not offer the resolution for contention. If we are not capable of acting for the people of the State, why there must be some great men here (Detroit.)
The amendment being put was carried.
Mr. Lewis, of Adrian, moved the following resolution:
Resolved, That this Convention appoint a committee of one to learn what concessions the so-called Bureau are willing to make, so as to effect a union, and report the result to this Convention in writing.
Mr. Cullen would support the resolution.
Resolution lost.
Mr. Anderson, of Battle Creek, moved "That we do now proceed to form a State Equal Rights League."
Mr. Carter, from the Finance Committee, made the following

Report on Finance

Your Committee on Finance would respectfully submit that they have received in contributions the sum of two hundred and seven dollars ($207.00) to meet the expenses of the Convention, and to qualify the delegates from the State Equal Rights League to seats in the National Equal Rights League. The committee desire to express their gratification at the generous manner in which the delegates have responded to the solicitation of your committee --which they view as another mark of the confidence reposed and interest felt in the objects contemplated by the Convention.

Mr. Lewis, of Adrian, moved that the report be received and adopted. Carried.
Mr. Anderson's resolution was then considered and adopted.
After some desultory conversation
Mr. Roberts, of Adrian, moved to refer the matter to the Business Committee, to report to-morrow morning at 9 o'clock. Carried.
Mr. Rice, of Detroit, moved that the Secretary be instructed to forward the proceedings for publication to the *Christian Recorder* and *Anglo-African*[3] of New York. Carried.
The Convention then adjourned until to-morrow morning at 9 o'clock.

Wednesday Morning, September 13th, 1865, 9 o'clock A.M.
The Convention re-assembled pursuant to adjournment, the President in the chair.
Prayer by the Rev. J. W. Brooks, of Ann Arbor. Minutes of preceding sessions read and adopted.
Mr. Anderson, from the Committee on Credentials, presented the names of S. Wells, of Ypsilanti, and O. C. Wood, of Detroit. Mr. Wells being qualified took his seat. Mr. Wood was admitted on motion of O. P. Anderson.
On motion, S. Fowler, of Eaton Rapids, and Wm. Watts, of St. John, were made honorary members of the Convention.
Mr. Parker, of Detroit, introduced the following resolution:
Resolved, That we point with exultation and pride to that epoch in history which records the noble, patriotic, philanthropic and humane deeds of our much beloved and ever to be praised late Chief Magistrate, Abraham Lincoln, who, though tardy, yet sure in the march to the prison house, there to unlock the door and let the poor slave go free. May his name be ever cherished in the memory of all impartial lovers of liberty until the last day of recorded time.
Mr. Roberts, of Adrian, moved to receive the resolution.
Mr. Anderson, of Battle Creek, moved to refer the resolution to the Business Committee. Lost.
Mr. Roberts moved that the resolution be adopted.
Mr. Lewis, from the Business Committee, presented the following report in regard to the organization of a League for this State.

Report

Whereas, For reasons stated in the curcular convening this mass Convention, and in the judgment of those who have responded to the call, they believe that the interest of the whole people whould be better subserved by organizing an Equal Rights League, to be known as the "Equal Rights League for the State of Michigan." Therefore

Resolved, That we proceed to organize an association to be called the State Equal Rights League for Michigan, having for its object the securing of the rights of the colored people of this State and United States, acting in harmony with the intentions of the National League.

Resolved, That we adopt for the government of the State Equal Rights League for the State of Michigan, so much of the constitution of the National Equal Rights League for the United States, held in the city of Syracuse, October 4th, 5th, 6th and 7th, 1864, as far as found adapted to the wants of the State League.

Resolved, That the officers of said League shall consist of a President, one Vice President from each county represented, Recording Secretary, Corresponding Secretary, Treasurer, and Executive Committee of 5 others.

The consideration of the resolutions of Mr. Parker, was resumed.

Mr. Johnson, of Jackson, offered an amendment, which was accepted, amending the resolution as follows:

Resolved, That we point with exultation and pride to that epoch in history which records the noble, patriotic, philanthropic and humane deeds of our much beloved and ever to be praised late Chief Magistrate, Abraham Lincoln, who, ever ready to favor human rights, was sure in his march to the prison house, there to unlock the door and let the poor slave free. May his name be ever cherished in the memory of all impartial lovers of liberty until the last day of recorded time.

The report of the Business Committee was then considered.

Mr. Washington moved that the report be adopted.

Mr. Roberts moved as an amendment that the report be considered and adopted by sections. Carried.

The report after some discussion was adopted.

Mr. Anderson, Battle Creek, offered the following resolution:

Resolved, That in the judgment of this Convention the policy of reconstruction, as developed by the present administration in restoring the seceded States to their former practical relations to the general government, is unwise, unfaithful to the colored American who has been faithful and self-sacrificing during the four years of desperate war, in which the existence of the unity of the nation trembled in the balance.[4] And that this Convention pledges itself to use all intelligent and legitimate means to reconstruct upon no basis other than the basis of Universal Suffrage.

Mr. Rice moved to accept the resolution. Carried.

Mr. Anderson moved its adoption.

Mr. Lewis, of Hudson, said he favored moderation. Although we had not been treated as we ought to have been, yet he thought it unwise to censure the administration. Its policy had been at all times not to admit that the Southern States had been out of the Union at any time.

Mr. Anderson, of Battle Creek, said that it had been shown by the President that he was in favor of our people only so far as it subserved his own interests. Mr. Anderson proceeded to speak at length, making a most eloquent and able speech.

Mr. Parker, of Detroit--I do not think Mr. Johnson is right upon this question. He has said that he is too old to change, and has referred to his former acts as an indication of what his policy will be hereafter.

Mr. Lewis, of Adrian, read in support of Mr. Parker's position a speech of Mr. Johnson's, made on the 11th of September.

Mr. Parker, resuming--He wanted it to be known throughout the Union that the black man is alive to that which is for his interest, and will submit no longer to his own degradation. He had become convinced that the elevation of the black man depended upon the black man.

Mr. Johnson, of Jackson, would support the resolution. Resolution adopted.

On motion of Mr. Paul, the resolution was ordered to be sent to the Hon. Chas. Sumner, Maj. Gen. B. F. Butler,[5] Wendell Phillips, Esq., and Mrs. Laura Haviland.

Mr. Rice, of Detroit offered the following:

Resolved, That in view of the many obstacles, difficulties, and embarrassments that our brethren the freedmen of the South have to encounter in their struggles from a state of slavery to that of liberty, causes our very hearts to burn within us. We assure them that we as their brethren--many of us have worn the same galling yoke--fully comprehend their position, and they have our united sympathies, believing that the day for equal rights and justice at home to all men is near.

On motion of Mr. Washington the resolution was received and considered, and on motion of Mr. Evans, of Battle Creek, adopted.

Mr. Washington, of Detroit, moved that the constitution be read and considered by sections.

Mr. Roberts, of Adrian, moved a substitute to the resolution, that a committee of three be appointed to revise and correct the constitution, and report to this convention. Substitute agreed to. The chair appointed Mr. Roberts, of Adrian, Paul, of Detroit, and J. D. Carter, of Detroit.

Mr. Paul moved that the committee have power to add to their number not to exceed two. Agreed to. The committee afterward added Messrs. Woods, of Detroit, and Johnson, of Jackson. On motion the convention adjourned until 3 o'clock.

Afternoon Session, September 13th, 1865, 3 o'clock.

The Convention re-assembled. Roll called and quorum present. Religious services were conducted by Mr. Grinton, of Marshall. Minutes read, corrected and adopted.

Mr. Roberts moved that the Convention appoint a committee on printing. Carried.

Mr. Roberts moved that G. W. Lewis, of Adrian, be chairman of the Printing Committee. Carried.

On motion of Mr. Parker, H. J. Lewis, of Hudson, was also appointed on the Printing Committee.

On motion of Mr. Roberts, Mr. Paul was added to the Printing Committee.

Mr. Rice, from the Business Committee, read the address to the people of the State of Michigan. Received and adopted.

Mr. Roberts, from the Committee on Constitution, reported, recommending the constitution of the National Equal Rights League, (with certain amendments to meet requirements of the State,) for the government of the Equal Rights League of Michigan. [Note--This was the constitution adopted in the January convention--Secretary.]

Mr. Parker moved that the report be received. Carried.

Mr. Rice moved that the constitution as read be adopted. Carried.

Mr. Anderson moved to reconsider the vote, which after considerable discussion was adopted.

Mr. Washington moved to adopt by sections. Carried.

Mr. Wells, of Ypsilanti, took exceptions to the last section, and asked for explanations, after which the constitution was adopted.

Some considerable discussion arose as to when the League should meet. Several gentlemen proposed September, and Mr. Parker proposed the 22d of February. The first Tuesday in September was at last agreed upon.

On motion of Mr. Lewis, of Adrian, the chair appointed Messrs. Rice, Anderson and Parker to nominate officers for the League.

On motion of Mr. Roberts the chair appointed Messrs. Roberts, Gillam and Parker a committee to nominate the representatives to the National Equal Rights League at Cleveland.

Mr. Rice, from the Committee on Officers, presented the following gentlemen as officers of the Equal Rights League for Michigan:

President--James Fields, Esq., M.D., of Adrian.
Recording Secretary--H. J. Lewis, of Hudson.
Corresponding Secretary--B. Dolbeare Paul, Detroit.
Treasurer--Geo. W. Lewis, of Adrian.

Executive Committee--T. J. Rice, Detroit; T. R. Jenkins, Coldwater, J. J. Evans, Battle Creek; Dr. Greenberry Cousins, Cass county.

Vice Presidents for Each County

J. W. Johnson, *Lenawee county.*
S. W. Burton, *Hillsdale county.*
A. Boyer, *Washtenaw county.*
John Hackley, *Macomb county.*
George Nichols, *Kalamazoo county.*
Wilberforce Johnson, *Jackson county.*
F. R. Jenkins, *Branch county.*
G. H. Parker, *Wayne county.*
Benjamin Grinton, *Calhoun county.*
S. Fowler, *Eaton county.*
I. Burdine, *Berrien county.*
T. J. Martin, *Cass county.*
William Watts, *Gratiot county.*

The report was received and adopted.

Mr. Roberts, from the Committee on Representatives, presented the names of the following gentlemen to represent the State Equal Rights League for Michigan in the National Equal Rights League:

B. Dolbeare Paul, Detroit; O. P. Anderson, Battle Creek; J. W. Johnson, Adrian.

The report was received and adopted.

A letter of congratulation was received from James Fields, Esq., M.D., President of Lenawee Co. League, read and ordered to be incorporated and printed in the minutes.

Mr. Johnson, of Jackson, offered the following resolution:

Resolved, That this Convention instruct its delegates, immediately on their return home, to organize city, town and county Leagues, subordinate to the State Equal Rights League. Carried.

Mr. Roberts, of Adrian, offered the following:

Resolved, That we, the members of this Convention, do tender a vote of thanks to the officers of this body for the gentlemanly and efficient manner in which they have discharged their duties. Carried.

A vote of thanks was accorded Mrs. Dales and the other ladies of the committee appointed to provide accommodations for the delegates.

On motion of Mr. Anderson, of Battle Creek, a vote of thanks was accorded Mr. Paul, of Detroit, Lewis of Adrian, and Parker, of Detroit, for the praiseworthy manner with which they had labored for the success of the League.

A subscription list was opened and the handsome sum of $207 raised within fifteen minutes to pay the expenses of the Convention, and the expenses of the representatives to the National League. (See Finance report.)

On motion of Mr. Roberts, of Adrian, the State Equal Rights League for Michigan adjourned to meet at Battle Creek, the first Tuesday in September, 1866.

B. Dolbeare Paul, Secretary.

ADDRESS OF THE CONVENTION

To the People of Color of the State of Michigan:

When the convention of colored men assembled in Syracuse, N.Y., October 4th, 5th, 6th, and 7th, 1864, the friends of impartial freedom rejoiced, because they felt that the days of tyranny and oppression were numbered.

Those among you who had the happiness to know and appreciate that assemblage of earnest representative men, coming up from Maine to Florida, who then and there inaugurated plans looking to the freedom and elevation of our entire race from the blighting and crushing effects of American slavery, felt renewed hope in the future, and under the leadership of such veterans of the anti-slavery army as Douglass, Garnet and others, pledged themselves to return to their homes to labor with renewed zeal for the dissemination of those great principles and labors laid down in that convention as the legitimate work for every member to perform during the recess of the convention.

Doubtless many of the representatives of the Northern, Southern and Western States, true to their pledges to their constituents at home, have labored faithfully to spread before their people the necessity and importance of the preliminary measures adopted at the convention, and have spared neither time or money thoroughly to canvass every county in their respective States.

All honor to such men who have labored to organize auxiliary Leagues, and strove to impress upon the mind of every colored citizen the vast importance of united action, in order to dispel the clouds that slavery and prejudice have cast upon our brethren in their native land. In this war between slavery and freedom there can be no neutrals.

The eternal principles of truth and liberty need and must have the united support of every man and woman throughout the land. Hence any failure by any colored community to develop the entire strength of every portion of a State where colored people's rights are withheld, or only partially granted, is a virtual abandonment of those rights without which life is a miserable blank.

In this connection it is a matter of painful regret that the State Equal Rights League established in January, 1865, has ceased to possess the confidence of the colored portion of the community, through an extraordinary use of power (not provided in the constitution,) on the part of that portion of the officers of the State Bureau residing in the city of Detroit. These gentlemen, without the knowledge or consent of the other members of the executive committee of the State Equal Rights League, ignored the existence of the constitution and provided another which deprived a majority of the members of the association of any participation in the proceedings of the meeting of the association on the first day of August, 1865.

The members of the association who had been thus treated, as well as a large portion of the people of color throughout the State, felt that they had been grossly misused--that their intelligence had been insulted by the very men in whom they had reposed the most implicit confidence, and selected in preference to all others to carry out their views as expressed in the constitution of the Equal Rights League. At the first annual meeting, on the first day of August, 1865, the acts of the gentlemen of the Bureau were severely criticized and condemned by the very men they had calculated would support them. But true to their preconcerted plan of policy, they refused to listen to words of warning, and still persisted in a course of conduct prejudicial to the best interests of the people. Having become sincerely imbued with an earnest desire to assist our brethren in their effort to procure for themselves "Equality before the Law," we have in convention assembled this 12th day of September, 1865, dissolved the State Equal Rights League of Michigan, wherein the rights and wishes of the colored people of the State shall be respected, and the object contemplated by the National Equal Rights League attained. It now remains for the people to say whether or not our efforts in their behalf shall be appreciated, and whether they are willing to assist us with their means to carry out the work so auspiciously begun. We have, as already stated, organized an association upon the basis of justice and right, wherein the wishes of the people may be more generally consulted and promoted. In presenting this address to you, we desire to impress upon your minds the importance of aiding the good work in which we are now engaged in your behalf. The great question of colored suffrage will occupy the minds and attention of the electors of this State in November, 1866, at which time they will be required to vote for or against the proposed amendment to the constitution. The Equal Rights League propose to employ agents to canvass the State in support of the proposed amendment. This will necessarily require a considerable amount of money, which can only be met by your generous and liberal contributions. A great work is before us. To you, "Colored men of Michigan," we look for support. Upon you we rely for sympathy and pecuniary assistance in the attainment of a principle of justice fraught with so much importance to you and us. Let us, then, act promptly and with energy.

Adrian, September 8th, 1865.

The "Lenawee County Equal Rights League," located in the City of Adrian, to the State Convention of Colored Men, Assembled in the City of Detroit, Send Greeting:

Fellow-Citizens:—Identified with you in all that is embraced in the objects contemplated by the Colored National Convention that assembled in Syracuse October 4th, 1865, permit me through our delegates, (whose appointment and proper credentials are herewith presented,) to assure you of the united and friendly interest felt by each and all of us as brothers working in the common cause of a loyal but oppressed people, determined henceforth to use all legal and peaceful means to secure the ends of a perfect equality before the law, that guarantees to all men the right to "Life, Liberty and the Pursuit of Happiness."

We pray that the blessing of Almighty God may rest upon your united labors while in convention, and that pursuing calm and deliberate means to ensure the ends proposed by our National League, you may be permitted to realize the momentous interests involved in the questions of the day, and the grand future, rapidly unfolding before the colored people of the United States, unlimited by mere geographical boundaries.

For and on behalf of the "Lenawee County Auxiliary League," permit me to subscribe myself,

Very respectfully, yours, &c.,

James Fields, President.

LENAWEE COUNTY LEAGUE
RESOLUTIONS ON THE FIFTH RESOLUTION OF THE NATIONAL CONVENTION

The Lenawee County League respectfully beg leave to lay before the members of the Michigan State Equal Rights League when assembled in convention at Detroit, the following views entertained by the majority of the members of the Lenawee County League, together with the why and wherefore they felt impelled to pass the resolution herein contained, founded on the perusal of a resolution contained on the 34th page of the National Convention minutes, and the 5th resolution in relation to the freedmen of the South, and our efforts in their behalf.

The advocates of the freedmen of the South maintain that the nominal freemen of the North and West, by the resolution above alluded to, have renewed their past pledge to labor for the freedmen's elevation by contributing educational facilities at the South, even if the elective franchise at the North be left to a more distant day.

Through the long night of slavery and oppression (say they) that has obscured the moral atmosphere of the colored race on this continent, the nominally free people of the North have strove to identify themselves with the four millions of bondmen and women of the South—resisting manfully pro-slavery pressure at the South, as well as its supple tool, prejudice against color at the North. Now protesting against the passage of oppressive and unjust enactments, both State and National, at the bidding of the slave power.

At times flying before the wrath of pro-slavery mobs; wrought up to frenzy by designing politicians and demagogues for their own base purposes; hunted like the partridge on the mountains, their manhood crushed and humbled in the dust; their homes desolated; the chastity of their wives and daughters violated—nay their very lives sacrificed in the very sanctuary of the living God.

Through all these horrors, and others still untold, have the free people of color passed in their Northern homes, still asserting their undying love for their brethren in Southern bonds, and their fixed resolve to maintain the principle of the universal brotherhood of man, irrespective of color or country, and that come weal or woe, come life or death, to labor and to wait for the entire civil and political liberty of themselves and brethren of the South.

This state of facts being conceded as to our past course, and in view of the present apparent lifting of the dark clouds that have so long delayed the rising beams of the "Sun of Liberty" on ourselves and our Southern brethren, shall we, *can* we, as an organized League, labor exclusively to obtain our elective franchise at the North, while contenting ourselves with the display of our *past* sympathy for the bondman of the South, leave him at such a crisis to seek his political rights alone, and without means to educate themselves and little ones? In a word, shall we leave our struggling brethren, just emerging from the prison house of bondage, to find their way to the temple of liberty as best they may?

The last clause of the fifth resolution referred to, we consider clear and explicit language, which, if it means anything, means our entire surrender of self, and a voluntary pledge to help the freedmen of the South in every possible way to obtain, if no more, at least equal privileges with ourselves, and thus go on unitedly to obtain equal privileges before the law.

The foregoing views and further discussion by the members generally of the County League being concluded, it was

Resolved, Unanimously, that apart from all proper and necessary expenditure for the maintenance and support of our organization and proper representation at our State and National Leagues, we will devote all other moneys received into our treasury in future in the redemption of our national pledge to the freedmen, as contained in the fifth resolution above quoted, and that our delegates to either State or National Leagues be instructed to confer with the several delegates at such conventions, as to the most feasible plan to direct all surplus funds of the Leagues in aid of the freedmen's educational and political advancement, as the first requisite to redeem our pledge as expressed in the last clause of the fifth resolution of the National League.

Adrian, Septembler 11, 1865.

CONSTITUTION OF THE STATE EQUAL RIGHTS LEAGUE FOR MICHIGAN

Preamble

Whereas, The purposes entertained by the callers of this Convention and those who have responded to that call, can be best promoted by a close union of all interested in the principles of justice and right sought to be established. Therefore,

Resolved, 1st, That we proceed to organize an association to be called the State Equal Rights League of the State of Michigan, with auxiliary and subordinate associations in the different counties of the State.

2d. That in the establishment of the Colored Men's State League, we do not seek to disorganize or in any way interfere with any existing society or institution of a benevolent or other character, but believing that the interest of colored men generally will be best subserved and advanced by a union of all our energies, and the use of all our means in a given direction, we therefore invoke the co-operation of such societies in the advancement of the object of the League.

Constitution

Sec. 1st. The objects of this League are to encourage sound morality, education, temperance, frugality and industry, and promote everything that pertains to a well ordered and dignified life; to obtain by appeals to the minds and consciences of the people of the State, or by legal process when possible, a recognition of the rights of the people of the State to citizenship.

Sec. 2d. The members of this Convention shall be constituted members of the State Equal Rights League for the first year. Hereafter such persons as shall be duly accredited representatives of the auxiliary associations hereinafter provided for, shall constitute its members. Provided, that no auxiliary society shall be entitled to more than one representative for each ten dollars contributed by such society, with an additional member for any amount over five dollars thus contributed. Provided, also, that any locality that shall not have population sufficient to form an auxiliary association, may be represented in the League by a delegate or delegates, by paying into the treasury of the State Equal Rights League three dollars for each delegate.

Sec. 3d. The officers shall be a President, one Vice President for each county represented in the convention, Recording and Corresponding Secretaries, Treasurer, and an Executive Committee consisting of the President, first and second Vice Presidents, Recording Secretary, and five other persons to be elected by the League at the same time with the other officers.

Sec. 4th. The President shall preside at all meetings of the League, and of the Executive Committee, see that all decrees of the League are duly executed, and perform such other duties as may be imposed by the League.

The Vice Presidents in the order of their election shall, in the absence of the President, perform his duties. The Recording Secretary shall duly record the proceedings of the League and Executive Committee, draw all orders on the Treasurer when directed by the proper authorities, receive all money paid to the League, pay the same to the Treasurer and take his receipts therefor, and the Treasurer sahll give two or more sureties for the due performance of his duties.

The Corresponding Secretary shall, under the guidance of the League and Executive Committee, conduct the correspondence of the League, receive from the agents of the League or other persons all documents of historical, statistical or general interest, and shall carefully preserve and tabulate such documents for the use of the League.

The Treasurer shall keep all moneys collected by the agents or contributed by the auxiliary Leagues. He shall report to the League annually, and to the Executive Committee whenever required, the condition of the treasury. He shall pay out money only upon order of the Executive Committee, and when properly signed by the President and Recording Secretary.

Sec. 5th. The Executive Committee shall establish an office in the city of Adrian, in which place they shall hold such sessions as may be necessary to promote the purposes of the League. They shall hire an agent or agents, who shall visit the different counties of the State accessible to them, and shall call the people of those counties together in convention or otherwise, and urge them to take the steps necessary to secure the rights and improvements for the attainment of which this League is formed. They shall encourage the publication of such documents as may be of advantage to our cause, and may at their discretion publish brief appeals, arguments or statements of facts which may have a tendency to promote the ends of the association. Provided, that such documents shall be furnished to the public at such rates as shall admit of their general distribution. They shall apportion among the auxiliary leagues, according to the number of members reported, the amounts which the League shall determine to raise, and shall urge upon the officers of such auxiliary societies a prompt response to such demand. They shall cause orders to be drawn on the Treasurer for the payment of such expenses as may be incurred in carrying out the purposes of the association. They shall make an annual report to the association of their labors, and shall recommend such improvements as may be suggested by their official experience.

Sec. 6th. The officers shall hold their offices for one year or until their successors are elected. The officers of the League may receive such compensation as may be determined by the Executive Committee.

Sec. 7th. Persons in the different counties friendly to the purposes of this League, may form county Leagues auxiliary to this, with such subordinate organizations as they may deem proper. Provided, that no distinction on account of color or sex shall be permitted in such auxiliary or subordinate associations. Such Leagues may at their discretion employ agents and issue such documents as they may deem conducive to the end for which this League is formed. They shall collect and pay into the treasury of the State Equal Rights League such sums as may be assessed upon them by a vote of the majority at any meeting, and shall co-operate with that association in all movements which it shall inaugurate for the accomplishment of the purposes for which it was formed.

Sec. 8th. The sessions of the State Equal Rights League shall be held annually on the first Tuesday in September, at 10 o'clock A.M., for the election of officers and the transaction of such other business as may be brought before it.

Sec. 9th. At any annual meeting of the State Equal Rights League this constitution may be altered or amended by a vote of a majority of the members present.

OFFICERS OF THE STATE E. R. LEAGUE

President

James Fields, Esq., M.D., of Adrian

Vice Presidents

J. W. Johnson--------------------------*Lenawee county.*
S. W. Burton---------------------------*Hillsdale county.*
A. Boyer-------------------------------*Washtenaw county.*
John Hackley---------------------------*Macomb county.*
George Nichols-------------------------*Kalamazoo county.*
Wilberforce Johnson--------------------*Jackson county.*
F. R. Jenkins--------------------------*Branch county.*
G. H. Parker---------------------------*Wayne county.*
Benjamin Grinton-----------------------*Calhoun county.*
S. Fowler------------------------------*Eaton county.*
I. Burdine-----------------------------*Berrien county.*
T. J. Martin---------------------------*Cass county.*
William Watts--------------------------*Gratiot county.*

Secretaries

Recording Secretary--H. J. Lewis, of *Hudson.*
Corresponding Secretary--B. Dolbeare Paul., *Detroit.*

Treasurer

George W. Lewis, of *Adrian.*

Executive Committee

T. J. Rice-----------------------------*Detroit.*
F. R. Jenkins--------------------------*Coldwater.*
J. J. Evans----------------------------*Battle Creek.*
Dr. Greenberry Cousins-----------------*Cass county.*

STATE BUREAU AT ADRIAN, MICH.

Copy in the Schomburg Collection, New York Public Library.

REFERENCE NOTES

1. Mary Ann Shadd Cary (1823-1893), daughter of black abolitionist Abraham D. Shadd of Wilmington, Delaware, was a militant crusader in the cause of black rights. After the passage of the Fugitive Slave Law of 1850, she settled in Windsor, West Canada, and became deeply involved in the political and educational life of a colony of United States blacks who had settled there. Establishing a school, she taught for over a decade and received assistance from the American Missionary Society, later becoming its agent to promote Negro education there. A pamphlet which she published, *Notes on Canada West*, sought to encourage black emigration to the province.

Between 1854 and 1856, she edited the *Provincial Freeman*, a weekly antislavery newspaper published at Chatham, Ontario. With the outbreak of the Civil War, she returned to the United States, was appointed a recruiting army officer by Governor Levi Morton of Indiana, and aided in the establishment of a regiment of black soldiers. Following the war, she settled in Washington, D.C., headed an American Missionary Society school, and in her late forties entered the newly founded law school of Howard University. She received her degree in 1870, becoming probably the first black woman lawyer in the United States.

2. The National Equal Rights League was formed in October 1864 at the National Convention of Colored Citizens of the United States, which convened in Syracuse, New York.

3. The *Anglo-African* was perhaps the most interesting periodical to be published by blacks in New York City. It was founded in January 1859 by Thomas Hamilton of Brooklyn. As a monthly it appeared regularly from January 1859 through February 1860. A weekly newspaper, known also as the *Anglo-African*, edited by Robert Hamilton, succeeded it and appeared intermittently until 1865.

4. The reference is to President Andrew Johnson's policy of Reconstruction. Johnson, who succeeded to the presidency in April 1865, had demonstrated his hatred of the Southern oligarchy by noting on one occasion that "treason should be made infamous and rebels should be punished." He at first denied amnesty to persons who had supported the Confederacy and whose taxable property was assessed at $20,000 or more. But soon he began to grant pardons to many of the leaders of the Confederacy. Johnson also had appointed "provisional governors" over several Southern states who had drawn up constitutions based on white male suffrage. Futhermore, from 1865 to 1866, Southern states had enacted statutes known as the "Black Codes" which reduced the freedmen to a condition very close to slavery. In order to pay off the prison charges and fines he was hired out. If a Negro quit work before his contract expired, he was arrested and imprisoned for a breach of contract and the reward to the person performing the arrest was deducted from his wages. Some of the codes also provided that if a Negro laborer left his employer he would "forfeit all wages to the time of abandonment." Johnson did nothing to reverse this reactionary state of affairs in the South.

5. Benjamin F. Butler (1818-1893) commanded the land forces in the capture of New Orleans by the Union Army in 1862 and was military commander of the city until removed and transferred to the Department of East Virginia. While in New Orleans, Butler earned the hatred of the Southern whites because of his use of black troops and his general policy that Negroes were entitled to equal rights.

PROCEEDINGS OF THE OHIO CONVENTIONS

INTRODUCTION

The State Convention of Colored Citizens of Ohio assembled at Columbus January 10-13, 1849, primarily to consider the operation of the state's notorious Black Laws, and called upon the legislature to vote their immediate repeal. Prominent at the convention were such influential Ohio black leaders as John Mercer Langston, Charles H. Langston, and William Howard Day.

During the debate on the colonization issue, John Mercer Langston spoke out sharply against a resolution opposing emigration. "I for one. . . ," he told the delegates, "am willing, dearly as I love my native land (a land which will not protect me however, to leave it, and go wherever I can be free. We have always drank too long the cup of bitterness and woe, and do gentlemen want to drink it any longer." Langston was convinced that blacks must "have a nationality, before we can become anybody," and he underscored that point by noting that "the very fact of our remaining in this country is humiliating, virtually acknowledging our inferiority to the white man."[1] Despite this appeal, the convention adopted a resolution pointing out emphatically that "we will never submit to the system of colonization to any part of the world, in or out of the United States; and we say once for all, to those soliciting us, that all their appeals to us are vain; our minds are made up to remain in the United States, and contend for our rights at all hazards."

While the Black Laws were the major issue at the second black state convention in Ohio (Columbus, January 9-12, 1850), one of the other major points raised was the feasibility of establishing a newspaper devoted to advancing the interests of blacks in the Mid-West. (The convention judged *The North Star*, published by Frederick Douglass in Rochester, New York, as strictly an eastern paper.) Some delegates felt that the newspaper proposed for the midwest could not be sustained primarily because blacks in Ohio did not have the financial means to keep it going. But John Mercer Langston dismissed this argument. He cited the fact that "colored men were becoming cultivated; that they were being educated; that they had poets, statesmen, reviewers, printers and philosophers, who could fathom Baconian Philosophy and solve Newtonian Problems; and who should have an outflow--a manifestation of their genius and talent." His argument this time prevailed. The Convention made plans to set up such a paper while, at the same time, reaffirming its support of the white *Ohio Standard* "as worthy of the confidence, encouragement and support of the colored citizens of Ohio and the Union."

The Ohio Convention of 1850 also established an association called the Ohio Colored American League, which would operate on an ongoing basis during the times the conventions were not sitting. The League was to press for the complete freedom and total enfranchisement of the colored people of the United States. County associations or leagues would also be set up throughout the state. The Ohio Convention of 1850 also laid plans for the appointment of six lecturers whose duties would be to canvass the state seeking public support in the battle against the Black Laws. One resolution also called for the legislature to appoint a superintendent of the colored schools in the state and recommended William H. Day for the post.

The 1851 State Convention of the Colored Citizens of Ohio revolved around the effects of the recently enacted, notorious Fugitive Slave Law. (Under the provisions of this act, passed by Congress on September 18, 1850, the Negro claimed as a fugitive by a master's affidavit presented before a United States judge or commissioner, was given no jury trial. Futhermore, the officials' fee was ten dollars if he found the black person to be a fugitive, five dollars if he did not. Only the testimony of a white man was accepted in determining the status of the Negro. In addition, all citizens were subject to call to assist in the prosecution of the statute.) Many blacks in the north now found themselves in a precarious position, subject--often upon false charges--to be thrown into slavery. The Ohio Convention condemned the law as, in the words of John Mercer Langston, "unworthy the name of law" and denounced any cooperation with the statute.

A heated and intense debate broke out at the convention over the question of whether or not the Constitution of the United States was a proslavery or antislavery instrument. It started when H. Ford Douglass introduced a resolution which asserted that no black person could consistently vote under the Constitution since it was a proslavery document. In defending his resolution, H. Ford Douglass echoed the usual Garrisonian arguments against any participation within the government, pointing to the three-fifths, the slave trade clauses, and provision for the return of fugitive slaves. William H. Day took issue with Douglass, arguing that even if the government acted as a proslavery agency, this did not justify a proslavery interpretation of the Constitution. Charles H. Langston, on the other hand, tried to strike a balance between the two opposing arguments. On the one hand, he agreed with Douglass that the Constitution was "made to foster and uphold that abominable, vampirish and bloody system of American slavery." Yet the fact that the Constitution was proslavery did not require blacks to reject the idea of voting under that document. "I would vote under the Constitution on the same principle, (circumstances being favorable,) that I would call on every slave from Maryland to Texas to arise and assert their *liberties* and cut their masters' throats if they attempt again to reduce them to slavery." His view prevailed.

Like the Ohio Convention held in 1850, the 1851 gathering again raised the issue of a press. It believed that 25,000 blacks within the State of Ohio were sufficient to sustain such a newspaper. Indeed, the name *Clarion of Freedom* was proposed for the new organ, and William Howard Day and Charles H. Langston were appointed to serve as editors once the paper was established.

The 1852 Convention of the Colored Freemen of Ohio, held in Cincinnati, January 14-19, 1852, reiterated its predecessors' opposition to the program of the American Colonization Society and overwhelmingly rejected the idea of mass emigration of black Americans. Two new resolutions were adopted. One condemned businessmen in the black community who discriminated against their own people in favor of white patronage. "A colored man who refuses to shave a colored man because he is colored," one resolution asserted, "is much worse than a white man who refuses to eat, drink, ride, walk or be educated with a colored man because he is colored, for the former is a party *de facto* to riveting chains around his own neck and the necks of his much injured race."

Another new policy was expressed in a resolution urging black men over the age of eighteen "to form themselves into independent military companies, when they cannot be admitted into white, to the end that they may acquire a finished military education, for the purpose of rendering efficient aid to this State or the United States in case of foreign invasion."

The feasibility of establishing a separate black press had still to be resolved. The convention regarded the idea of a black press as "the best and most speedy means to raise our people from the present stupor and cause them to see more clearly their critical situation." In line with this idea, the Report of the Select Committee on Press recommended that a fund of $1,000 be raised by the formation of a joint stock company, which would issue shares worth $50, half of which would be paid on or before the first day of June 1852. Instead of recommending that control of any paper established be placed under the supervisory control of two editors, a position recommended previously, the 1852 Convention recommended that a three-man editorial committee be set up, appointed by the stockholders and subject to their decisions.

A Committee on Church Action issued a report critical of the attitudes of the American church, arguing that the "majority of the Churches in the land" supported either directly or indirectly the institution of slavery, pointing out that such tendencies went contrary to the Gospel message "which brings deliverance to the captive." It coupled these strictures with another resolution which brought some colored churches to task which would not do all in their power "to discountenance slaveholding and slave-holding apologists," declaring that such conduct "shows a great want of self-respect, a want of intelligent devotion to their own cause, and deserves the disfellowship of all good men."

The 1852 Convention designated John Mercer Langston to prepare and submit a Memorial to the General Assembly of Ohio on behalf of the colored people of Ohio. The document was a compelling defense of the black man's right to the franchise. Langston recounted with convincing evidence the constitutional claims of blacks to the vote, pointing up the heroic services of black Americans in the Revolutionary War and the War of 1812. He underscored the fact that while every emigrant to these shores eventually received the full enjoyment of American citizenship, black Americans, despite their years of services to the nation, were outcasts in their own land. Langston also based the Negro's right to the suffrage on their status as taxpayers. "Nor is this fact," he argued, "to be regarded as a light and unimportant one. It will be seen at once that our tax is not of such insignificant account, since our real estate and personal property amount to more than five million dollars." He concluded on a telling note: "Since then it is a cardinal, a fundamental maxim of your political faith that taxation and representation are never to be sundered, but always go together; and since we are taxed in common with all others to meet the expenditures of the government, we respectfully submit, that we ought to have the advantages of a fair and impartial representation."

The vote was also the issue that led to the State Convention of Colored Men of Ohio, held in Columbus, January 16-18, 1856. Specifically, the Ohio blacks gathered to request the Ohio legislature to strike out the word *white* in the first section of the fifth article of its constitution relating to the qualifications of persons to vote.[2] Coupled with this demand, the convention asked the "repeal" of all laws and parts of laws "making complexional discriminations." Like earlier conventions which met in Ohio, this gathering also authorized the formation of a committee of three to look into the practicability of establishing a permanent press for blacks of the state. It also adopted a resolution calling for the establishment of Mechanic's Institutes, Agricultural Associations, and Education, Literary, Temperance, and Moral Reform Societies.

Although the notorious Ohio "Black Laws," which placed proscriptions upon the Negro people in the state in nearly every aspect of their daily life, had been largely repealed in 1849, a few remained. The 1857 State Convention of the Colored Men of Ohio, held in Columbus, January 21-23, 1857, called upon Ohio "not only to *repeal all* of the remaining Black Laws of this State, but to strike out the word WHITE from the Constitution wherever it occurs." The Convention set as its specific objective "to foster morals, discourage an ignorant ministry, encourage education, temperance, industry and economy among the colored people, and to seek the repeal of all laws which make distinction on account of color, by refusing colored persons admission into the public institutions of the State for the insane, blind, deaf and dumb, and especially to have the obnoxious feature in the Constitution erased which *prevents colored men from the rights of an election*." John I. Gaines, a delegate, struck home sharply in observing during the discussion of exclusion of blacks from all public institutions of the State: "We beg pardon, for there is one institution wherein we are admitted, but not on terms of equality--we mean the Penitentiary."

On the issue which had been most divisive in some circles of the black community--colonization,--the 1857 convention made clear its opposition to the "*agitation of colonization or emigration* in every shape and form, if it means the removal of the colored people in the States to the North, South, Central America, Canada or Africa, believing such *agitation* to be detrimental to the best interests of the race, and we do pledge ourselves to resist it, come from what quarter it may."

This position was reiterated at the 1858 Convention of the Colored Men of Ohio, held in Cincinnati, November 23-26, 1858. The fourth resolution, adopted overwhelmingly, declared: "*Resolved*, That we say to those who would induce us to emigrate to Africa or elsewhere, that the amount of labor and self-sacrifice required to establish a home in a foreign land, would if exercised here, redeem our native land from the grasp of slavery; therefore we are resolved to remain where we are, confident that 'truth is mighty and will prevail.'"

With remarkable prophetic insight, the 1858 Convention announced it was happy to note on the national scene "the declension of the Democratic Party in the North, and hope that its defeat presages the downfall of slavery, of which accursed system it has been a firm supporter."

By the time the Colored Men of Ohio met in Convention again, at Xenia, January 10-12, 1865, the end of slavery was in sight. The first resolution adopted by the meeting expressed in clarion tones where blacks now stood: "*Resolved*, That we are in favor of our Government and the Union, against all enemies, at home or abroad, that our fathers fought to establish, and will fight to maintain them; that we will not hesitate in the prompt performance of our duty to the nation in this, its dreadful hour of peril, but will prove with our blood that we deserve to be treated as American citizens."

Before the Convention adjourned, it adopted a "Constitution of the Ohio State Auxiliary Equal Rights League." This body was an outgrowth of the National Equal Rights League established by the National Convention of Colored Citizens of the United States, held at Syracuse, New York, October, 1864. It sought to maintain an ongoing effort to ensure black rights after the conventions were no longer in session. Located permanently in Cincinnati, the organization would employ a press "and such numbers of agents and lecturers as may be needed to carry out the objects of its creation . . . a recognition of the rights of the colored people of Ohio as American citizens."

REFERENCE NOTES

1. Langston reaffirmed his position on colonization at the Cincinnati Convention of Colored Citizens in 1852, when he spoke for nearly two hours in favor of hemispheric emigration, preferably to Canada and South America, where blacks would remain well within the orbit of the United States and could make common cause with their brethren in bonds in the South. By 1854, however, Langston was to make a complete about-face on the issue. At an emigration convention held by blacks during that year, he disappointed Martin R. Delany and many of his other listeners by declaring that he intended "to work out my destiny in Lorain County, Ohio." He had made these remarks two weeks before being admitted to the Ohio Bar, as one of the first black lawyers in the United States. Langston now felt assured that "success was certain for the colored man in common with the white man in the United States." Writing in 1856 at a state convention of his people which assembled at Columbus, Ohio, he affirmed "that we are not Africans but Americans, as much as any of your population. Here then is a great injustice done us, by refusing to acknowledge our right to the appellation of Americans, which is the only title we desire, and legislating for us as if we were aliens, and not bound to our country by the ties of affection which every human being must feel for his native land; which makes the Laplander prefer his snows and skins to the sunny skies and silken garb of Italy; which makes the colored American prefer the dear land of his birth, even though oppressed in it, to any other spot on earth." (William F. Cheek, "John Mercer Langston: Black Protest Leader and Abolitionist," *Civil War History*, June, 1970, p. 111. See also Floyd J. Miller, *The Search for a Black Nationality: Black Colonization and Emigration, 1787-1963* [Urbana, Ill., 1975].)

2. The section referred to read: "Every *white* male citizen of the United States, of the age of twenty-one years, who shall have been a resident of the State one year next preceding the election, and of the county, township, or ward in which he resides, such times as may be provided by law, shall have the qualifications of an elector, and be entitled to vote at all elections."

MINUTES AND ADDRESS OF THE STATE CONVENTION OF THE COLORED CITIZENS
OF OHIO, CONVENED AT COLUMBUS,
JANUARY 10th, 11th, 12th, & 13th, 1849

Call for the Convention as Reported in the North Star,
December 8, 1848

Cleveland, Sept. 11, 1848

  At a meeting of the Ohio Delegation attending the National Convention of Colored Freemen at Cleveland, Ohio, September 6th, Rev. S. P. Lewis of Zanesville, was called to the Chair, and W. H. Burnham appointed Secretary. J. L. Watson stated the objects of the meeting, after which, C. H. Langston,[1] J. L. Watson and John Malvin[2] were appointed to bring forward business for said meeting, when the committee reported as follows:
  Whereas, The peculiar circumstances under which the colored people of the United States are placed, demands immediate, constant and energetic action on our part, and
  Whereas, We believe that Conventions are pre-eminently calculated to enhance that action, Therefore,
  Resolved, That we, a portion of the Ohio Delegation to the National Convention, do earnestly call upon the State Central Committee to call a State Convention to assemble in the city of Columbus some time in January, 1849.
  Resolved, That we individually pledge ourselves to do all in our power to secure a full representation to said Convention.
  Resolved, That the proceedings of this meeting be published in the *True Democrat* and *Herald*, Cleveland, the *North Star*,[3] N.Y., and *Ohio Standard*, Columbus, and the *Globe*, of Cincinnati, and all other papers friendly to the elevation and improvement of the colored people in Ohio.
  On motion, J. L. Watson was appointed a Committee of one to secure and furnish each paper named a copy of the proceedings of the meeting.
      Rev. S. P. Lewis, Pres't.
    W. H. Burham, Sec'y.

  In accordance with the recommendation of the resolution adopted at this meeting, the State Central Committee have issued the following call:

CONVENTION OF COLORED CITIZENS

  A Mass Convention of the Colored Citizens of Ohio, will be held in Columbus, commencing January 10th, 1840. The object of this Convention is our elevation, moral, intellectual, and political. Encountering us in the first step of our march, stand Ohio's "Black Laws."[4] They must be repealed. It is true, stripped as we are of all political power, we have only a moral power over them, but it is only necessary to wield this power aright, and it is mighty to the pulling down of the strongholds of oppression and wrong.

Therefore, let us not be slothful, but diligent, doing all we have the ability to do; so that if we must be made longer to bleed beneath the cruel inflictions of ignorance, prejudice, and heathenish proscription, we may at least, amidst our sufferings, have this consolation--"That we have exerted ourselves to the uttermost to escape the bloody scourge."

TO THE COUNTY COMMITTEE.--You, gentlemen, are expected to co-operate with the Central Committee in bringing together, to form this Convention, a body of independent, fearless and talented men--men in whose hearts burns unquenchably the love of liberty; and who will permit no surmountable obstacle to work any intermission in their efforts to come at once into the most complete enjoyment of that liberty which they love. There are such men; and reasonable exertion will suffice to assemble them together. Hitherto, our Conventions have been made up of men who had received the suffrages, and been sent up by the authority of their constituents. Under that arrangement, there is reason to suspect that in very many instances those most thoroughly acquainted with our grievances, and the best qualified to remedy them, have from their faithfulness in reproving whatever evil they have seen prevailing in their respective communities, incurred the displeasure of their fellow-citizens, and been repudiated by them as busy-bodies, meddlers in other men's matters; while those who have stood by, cordially assenting to the shouts of the multitudes, knowing nothing about the interest of the people, and caring less, are sent up to do business for our oppressed people. In order that this, as well as other evils resulting from the old order of things, may be averted, we have proclaimed a Mass Convention, thus affording every man who feels the weight of the yoke, and is tired of wearing it, and has sufficient intelligence to contribute aught to remove it, a fair opportunity to do so.

       J. Poindexter,
       J. Booker,
       Wm. Ward,
       W. Dept,
       P. Litchford,
       A. M. Taylor,
       N. M. Copeland,
       Isaiah Redmar,
       E. Fields,
          State Central Com.

The North Star, December 8, 1848.

PROCEEDINGS

NAMES OF DELEGATES ENROLLED

Hamilton County

Elder Wallace Shelton,	James McGowan,
Charles M. Wilson,	Joseph Bennett.

Ross County

Dr. C. Henry Langston,	George R. Williams,
J. Mercer Langston,	John T. Ward.

Franklin County

Wm. Copeland,	T. Jefferson Goode,
Lorenzo Dow Taylor,	Robert B. Goode,
David Jenkins,	James Poindexter,
J. Monroe Cardozo,	Emanuel Butler,
Rev. John M. Brown,	Moses Redman,
John Booker,	J. William Lyons,
Frank Boyd,	Wm. Lyles,

      Peyton Shelton.

Muskingum County

W. Hurst Burnham.

Jackson County

N. Nooks.

Fayette County

John W. Mason,   Andrew Manly,
W. Mitchell.

Lorain County

Thomas Brown,   Walker B. Depp,
William Howard Day,   John Lane,
John Watson,   Marshall Bibbs,
Lawrence W. Minor.

Cuyahoga County

John L. Watson.

Richland County

James S. Thompson.

Pickaway County

T. J. Merritt.

Fairfield County

McPherson Turner,   Luke Matthews.

Union County

Madison Cunningham.

MINUTES

First Session, Wednesday Morning.

Pursuant to a call of the State Central Committee, for holding a Mass State Convention, the delegates to said Convention met in the "*Bethel Church*," in the city of Columbus, on Wednesday, Jan. 10th, at 9 o'clock, A.M.

The Convention was called to order by D. Jenkins, of Franklin, and was organized by appointing John T. Ward, of Ross county, Chairman pro tem., and W. Hurst Burnham of Muskingum county, Secretary pro tem.

On motion, a committee of eleven were appointed to nominate permanent officers for the Convention. During their absence the Convention was very agreeably entertained by eloquent and soul-stirring speeches from Messrs. J. M. Langston,[5] Day,[6] Depp, Brown, and Dr. C. H. Langston. The committee returned and reported the names of the following gentlemen as officers of the Convention: Dr. Charles H. Langston of Ross, President; John L. Watson of Cuyahoga, Thomas Brown of Lorain, J. S. Thompson of Richland, and N. Nooks of Jackson, Vice Presidents; Lawrence W. Minor of Lorain, Charles M. Wilson of Hamilton, and J. Monroe Cardozo of Franklin, Secretaries.

The President elect was then escorted to the chair by the President *pro tem.*, and on taking the chair made an appropriate address which was received with deafening shouts of applause.

On motion, a committee of nine were appointed to prepare business for the consideration of the Convention. The committee consisted of Messrs.

William H. Day, chairman, J. Mercer Langston, George R. Williams, David Jenkins, W. H. Burnham, Wallace Shelton, J. M. Brown, T. J. Merritt, and L. D. Taylor.

On motion, Rev. John M. Brown was appointed chaplain to the Convention.

A committee of three was appointed to prepare rules for the government of the Convention. The committee consisted of Messrs. Ward, Booker, and McGowan.

A committee on finance were then appointed consisting of Messrs. J. M. Cardozo, Wm. Copeland, and John L. Watson.

It was moved by D. Jenkins that a committee of seven be appointed to draft an address to the citizens of Ohio, which motion was laid on the table.

The Convention then adjourned until 2 o'clock, P.M.

Second Session, Wednesday Afternoon.

Convention met according to adjournment. President in the chair. Convention opened with prayer by the Chaplain.

The committee on rules for the government of the Convention not being ready to report, by suggestion of W. H. Day, the meeting was laid open for an interchange of views relative to the objects of the Convention. Elder Wallace Shelton was then called for. He came forward and expressed himself in a very pertinent and chaste speech.

The committee appointed for that purpose having arrived, reported rules for the government of the Convention.

Report was accepted, and adopted after striking out the hour of six and inserting five o'clock P.M. for adjournment. A motion was then made to insert 9½ o'clock, A.M., for meeting. Motion lost.

The business committee not being ready to report, Mr. Poindexter was called upon to address the Convention. He, excusing himself, moved that Mr. J. L. Watson address the Convention. After some reluctance, Mr. Watson came forward, and eloquently dwelt on the capacities of the colored freemen to elevate themselves. What a triumph they might achieve if their energies were but directed aright. Adverted to the so called Black Laws of this State. He spoke of the advantages that some sections of the State possessed over every other--the feeling of the whites towards their colored *fellow citizens.* Referred to the act of the Legislature last winter, making provisions for establishing schools wherever twenty colored children could be found. Condemned in strong terms the vote of Mr. Backus, the Senator from his district, because he voted in favor of the "*Bill.*" He wanted to know why there were so few of the Central Committee present. He thought that there was something wrong in the matter.

After taking his seat a song was called for, whereupon Messrs. Day, Watson of Cuyahoga, Watson of Lorain, and Minor came forward and sang "Freedom's Gathering," after which the chairman of the business committee reported a platform and resolutions.

On motion of L. Dow Taylor, it was determined to lay the platform on the table, and take up the resolutions one by one. The 1st resolution was taken up, discussed and adopted.

On motion a committee of three were appointed to secure the Hall of the House of Representatives, or some other suitable place for holding a public meeting. Committee consisted of Eli Nichols, Thomas Brown, and David Jenkins.

A motion was made by Elder Shelton that the committee be instructed to apply for the Hall on Thursday evening. Carried.

The 2d resolution was then taken up and adopted.

On motion of Mr. Jenkins, a committee of five were appointed to draft a petition to the Legislature for the repeal of the Black Laws. Committee consisted of Messrs. Poindexter, L. D. Taylor, T. J. Merritt, David Jenkins, and J. M. Brown.

The 3d resolution was then taken up, and after some discussion, it was moved that it be referred to a committee of three, consisting of Messrs. Watson of Cuyahoga, J. Mercer Langston, and Elder Shelton. Carried.

The 4th resolution was then taken up, and on motion of Mr. Copeland, it was laid on the table.

Mr. Taylor, from the committee on drafting a petition for the repeal of the black laws, reported the petition framed.

Mr. Copeland moved for an adjournment, which being waived,

Mr. Watson of Lorain, in accordance with the resolution passed by the Convention, "that the Convention hold public meetings every night during its session," moved the Convention now appoint speakers. On motion, Messrs. Watson of Cuyahoga and Shelton were appointed.

Mr. Copeland renewing his motion, Convention adjourned.

Third Session. Thursday Morning, Nine o'clock.

Convention met according to adjournment, President in the chair. The Convention was opened with prayer by the chaplain. The Secretary in making his report begged the indulgence of the Convention for its imperfections, owing to the unusual amount of business on hand.

During the reading of the report Mr. Jenkins moved that the report be amended by striking out the name of Eli Nichols from the committee on procuring the Hall, which was objected to by Messrs. Watson of Lorain, Watson of Cuyahoga, and Nooks. Dr. C. H. Langston, thought it was contrary to the genius and spirit which ought to characterize the Convention; was opposed to the appointment at first, thought we ought to show to the world that we were capable of doing our own business. Mr. Depp was opposed to the amendment and spoke fervently in favor of the Report as it was. After a discussion "in extenso," pro and con, by several gentlemen, the main question was put, which was, should Mr. Nichols' name be stricken off, which was carried. The Secretary finished reading the minutes of the last meeting, which were agreed to.

Third Resolution, which had been laid on the table from Wednesday afternoon, was taken up and after some discussion, adopted.

The fifth Resolution was then read and discussed by Messrs. Poindexter and Watson of Lorain.

Mr. Poindexter rather questioned the ability of the Convention to pass any measures which would really prove a benefit, thought it was better merely to recommend measures and not enforce them; he was apprehensive lest the Convention should pass measures which were not practicable.

Mr. Watson replied to Mr. Poindexter, did not believe in persuasion, but in enforced action.

Mr. Poindexter moved that the fourth resolution be altered so as to read, Resolved, that the Convention make it obligatory on its members to persuade men to put in practice the acts passed in the Convention, which alteration was carried.

Mr. J. M. Langston, from the committee, to which was referred the third resolution, reported, which after an amendment by Dr. C. H. Langston, adding to it the third and fourth sections of the act of '93, was adopted. On motion of Mr. Jenkins, a committee of three were appointed to draft a memorial to Congress, setting forth some of the disabilities of the law, which was carried. Committee consisted of Messrs. Jenkins, Day, and Dr. Charles H. Langston. It was moved by Mr. Taylor, that the memorial to Congress be signed by the Officers of the Convention. The chairman of the business committee reported further, a platform in accordance with that read on the first day. It was moved that the report of the committee be laid on the table, which was lost. It was moved that resolution 8th, appointing a committee of seven to write an address to the people of the State, be taken up, which was carried. It was moved that the house appoint four of the committee. The committee were Messrs. Day, C. H. Langston, Shelton, Jenkins, Brown, of Franklin, Watson, of Cuyahoga, and Thompson. It was moved by Mr. Brown of Franklin, and seconded, that a committee of three be appointed, whose duty it shall be to report the opinion of this Convention in regard to the observance of one day out of seven as the Lord's day. On motion of Mr. Jenkins, it was referred to the business committee.

The 6th Resolution was then read, pending which resolution, the Convention adjourned.

Fourth Session, Thursday Afternoon.

The Convention met according to adjournment, President in the chair. The Convention opened with prayer by the Chaplain. It was moved and carried, that the resolution pending from the morning session be taken up. The Chairman of the business committee here begged leave to introduce several additions to the resolutions.

Mr. Jenkins was opposed to the resolution, thought there were circumstances under which it would be beneficial to emigrate.

L. Dow Taylor rose to correct Mr. Jenkins, thought he did not understand the true import of the resolution. Mr. Jenkins did not stand corrected. He said he was in favor of a scheme whereby we all might move out of the United States. He said he thought "there was a great change going on in the minds of the people." He prayed God that it would go on faster. We never can be anything in the United States. Mr. J. said that, two years ago while traveling in the State of New York, he always had the benefit of two seats. "Why was it?" said he. So far as he was concerned, he would always be found battling for his people.

J. L. Watson of Cuyahoga, said he was in favor of the resolution, and he was ready and willing to contest every point with any and all of its friends. He said our *"Pilgrim Fathers,"* who first came to this country, were *not* colonized. "But what was it sir, that brought them here? Their indomitable love of liberty. Their unabated hatred to tyranny, and firm resolve to be freemen." "Go to Liberia," said Mr. W., "become President, Senator, Judge or what not. Come to this country and see how the founders of this scheme will treat you. I hope the resolution will pass."

Mr. Williams thought the resolution ought to be discussed with great care, as it affected not only this State, but every State in the Union. He said that he did not want to look up to the white man for every thing. "We must have [a] nationality. I am for going any where, so we can be an independent people."

Mr. Depp said he never would favor any scheme of colonization, he believed that God created all men free and equal. We have come here for our rights, and our rights we will have. His motto should be, *"Fight on, fight ever."*

Rev. J. S. Thompson said he was in favor of the resolution. The principle of it was correct. He hoped it would pass.

Mr. J. Mercer Langston, here addressed the Convention as follows:

"Mr. President, I regret exceedingly that this question has been forced upon the Convention. But trusting as we do, in the omnipotence of truth, we are willing and ready to 'battle on and battle ever.' The resolution goes against the emigration of the colored people, free and bond, of the United States. I for one, sir, am willing, dearly as I love my native land, (a land which will not protect me however,) to leave it, and go wherever I can be free. We have already drank too long the cup of bitterness and woe, and do gentlemen want to drink it any longer? The spirit of our people must be aroused, they must feel and act as men. Let them proclaim from hill-top and valley, the memorable sentence given birth to by a Roman slave, *'Homo sum atque nihil humani a me alienum puto.'"* The prejudices, he said, were strong in this country, against the colored man, and he was fearful that they would remain so. He thought we must have a nationality, before we can become anybody. "Why sir, the very fact of our remaining in this country, is humiliating, virtually acknowledging our inferiority to the white man; I hope sir, that gentlemen, will vote down the Resolution."

Mr. Wilson and several others took part in the discussion, but the Secretary being obliged to leave, can not report what they said.

It was moved by Mr. Williams that the resolution be referred to a committee of three, which was preceded by a motion to have it laid upon the table, which last motion was lost. Mr. Williams' motion then prevailed, and the resolution was referred to a committee consisting of the following gentlemen. Watson of Cuyahoga, J. Mercer Langston, and William H. Burnham.

The 21st resolution was then read, and discussion was going on when on motion, it was laid on the table, for the purpose of hearing a report from the chairman of the committee on obtaining the Hall of the House of Representatives. Mr. Jenkins then announced that the Hall had been obtained. The announcement was received with three hearty cheers. And on motion of Mr. Jenkins, Messrs J. L. Watson of Cuyahoga and Wm. H. Day were appointed to address the citizens in the Hall of the House, this evening. A resolution was then presented and adopted, that the officers of the Convention meet at this place at half past six o'clock and march in order to the State House.

The President then gave some instruction to the Financial Committee. On motion the 21st resolution was again taken up, pending which, the Convention adjourned.

Thursday Evening.

A meeting was held in the Hall of the House of Representatives and addressed by the appointees for the evening. Messrs. W. H. Day and J. L. Watson. [See extracts.]

At the close of the meeting the following resolutions were presented and passed:

Resolved, That we tender our thanks to the members of the House of Representatives for the use of this Hall.

Resolved, That we request our white fellow citizens to visit us in our Convention.

Fifth Session, Friday Morning.

Convention met according to adjournment. John L. Watson in the chair. Prayer by Rev. James S. Thompson.

The Secretary being absent, on motion the reading of the journal, was then taken up.

Mr. J. L. Watson of Cuyahoga took the stand. He remarked that he had said a great deal already. The resolution under consideration was of too much importance--had too much to do with the salvation, politically and morally, of his brethren in the South, to allow him to pass it by unnoticed. The Methodist denomination, as such, was opposed to us as a people. "Why sir, the brethren in whose house we now sit, dare not come out and defend their position."

Rev. J. M. Brown here arose to correct Mr. Watson. A dialogue took place between the two, much to the amusement of the Convention.

Mr. W. resumed his remarks. Said the Baptists were no better. He found them just as pro-slavery as the whites. He hoped the resolution would pass. Given as it was to rebuke them, he thought they would certainly profit by it.

Mr. Nooks followed him. Said he had heard a great deal said against the ministers. They had been severely handled, but not too much so. He himself belonged to that class. So strongly opposed were some professed Christians and so full of prejudice against us, that when the white brethren came to preach to their colored brethren, they generally came like "Nicodemus" in the night, and we thought they did us a great favor when they called us "friends" instead of brethren.

Rev. J. M. Brown next came forward to clear his denomination from the charge of being pro-slavery. After speaking at some length, he read a long article from the minutes of the last Conference of the A.M.E. Church, to prove his point.

He was followed by Elder Wallace Shelton, who warmly advocated the passage of the resolution. He spoke of the pro-slavery character of both churches. Said that he had been silenced by his [Baptists] church on account of his anti-slavery views. He was in favor of excluding, not *slaveholders* only, but their apologists; nay, more, he was in favor of excluding those who would fellowship with slaveholders or their abettors.

Mr. Poindexter was also in favor of the passage of the resolution.

Dr. Langston next followed. He also was in favor of the resolution when amended. Dr. Langston's amendment was, on motion, adopted.

Mr. Poindexter moved an amendment, which was adopted.

Elder Shelton again came forward, and supported the resolution.

Mr. Williams also sustained the resolution. During the remarks of this gentleman, Rev. J. S. Thompson rose to a point of order. He claimed that the gentleman was not speaking to the resolution. Chair decided the point not sustained. Mr. Williams in the course of his remarks was eloquent and earnest, evincing a thorough knowledge of his subject, and the repeated cheers with which the gentleman was greeted, plainly told how much the effort was appreciated.

Rev. J. M. Brown rose to reply, when the select committee of three to which was referred the 5th resolution, through J. Mercer Langston, reported the following

Majority Report

Whereas, the question of colonization in the United States, is being greatly agitated, and whereas, certain colored men, together with whites, in the United States, have taken a position relatively to the matter which we deem incorrect, detrimental and destructive to our interest; and whereas, we deem it expedient for us to define our position on this point, determined at any hazard whatever, never to submit to any scheme of colonization, in any part of the world, in or out of the United States, while a vestige of slavery lasts; therefore,

Resolved, That in the event of universal emancipation, taking our freed brother as our coadjutor and helper in the work, prompted by the spirit of the fathers of '76, and following the light of liberty yet flickering in our minds, we are willing, it being optional, to draw out from the American government, and form a separate and independent one, enacting our own laws and regualtions, trusting for success only in the God of Liberty and the Controller of human destiny.

All which is respectfully submitted.

J. Mercer Langston, } Committee.
W. Hurst Burnham,

Mr. J. L. Watson of Cuyahoga, dissenting from the report of the majority, begged leave to submit the following

Minority Report

Gentlemen of the Convention:

The undersigned, a minority of the committee to which was referred the following resolution, would respectfully recommend its adoption.

"*Resolved,* That we will never submit to the system of colonization to any part of the world, in or out of the United States; and we say, once for all, to those soliciting us, that all of their appeals to us are in vain. Our minds are made up to remain in the United States, and contend for our rights at all hazards."

All which is respectfully submitted.

J. L. Watson, Committee.

Rev. J. M. Brown resumed his remarks. Mr. Merritt here rose to a point of order. Point, violating the 11th of the standing rules of the Convention. Chair decided point not sustained.

The 21st resolution, then under consideration, was adopted.

On motion, W. H. Burnham and G. R. Williams were appointed to assist the Secretaries in making out reports of the proceedings of the Convention for publication in the *Daily Standard.*

On motion, the resolution relating to adjournment was then taken up. An amendment was offered by Mr. Williams that Convention adjourn to-morrow at two o'clock, P.M. Amendment lost.

Mr. Burnham moved that we adjourn to-morrow at two o'clock, A.M. Amendment adopted. The resolution as amended was then adopted.

The 9th, 10th, 11th and 12th were adopted.

The 13th resolution was then read, pending which Convention adjourned.

Sixth Session, Friday Afternoon.

Convention met, according to adjournment President in the chair. Convention opened with prayer by Elder Shelton. The journal was read, corrected, and approved.

13th resolution was then read and adopted.

25th resolution was passed, and the following gentlemen were appointed a State Central Committee: David Jenkins, James Poindexter, Lorenzo D. Taylor, Rev. John M. Brown of Franklin, Elder Wallace Shelton of Hamilton, Dr. C. Henry Langston of Ross, and John L. Watson of Cuyahoga.

The 7th resolution was read and adopted. After the nomination and declination of several gentlemen, Mr. D. Jenkins was appointed to canvass the State.

Mr. W. Howard Day moved that the subject be referred to a committee of three, to report at the evening session. Dr. C. Henry Langston, W. Howard Day, and J. Mercer Langston composed said committee.

28th resolution was read and adopted. In accordance therewith the following gentlemen were appointed Delegates to the next National Convention: Messrs. C. Henry Langston, W. Howard Day, John L. Watson, David Jenkins, Noah Nooks, Wallace Shelton, James S. Thompson, Thomas Brown, John M. Brown, J. Mercer Langston, James Poindexter, Charles M. Wilson, T. Jefferson Merritt, W. Hurst Burnham, Eli Moore, R. Hodge, John I. Gaines, John B. Lott, Mr. Bowles and George R. Williams.

14th, 15th and 16th resolutions were adopted. And W. H. Day, John L. Watson and David Jenkins were appointed a committee to raise funds, to fee lawyers for testing the validity of the School law.

On motion of Mr. Day, the minority report on the 6th resolution, was taken up and adopted.

Mr. J. Mercer Langston hoped the report of the minority would not be adopted. The gentleman in his private opinion is with us, but he is afraid to express himself. "But sir, if I have a private opinion I will speak it out. If you ask a white man whether you may associate with his daughter, or whether you may marry her, he will tell you, *no!* I want to separate myself from such a government. Gentlemen, if you go to Oberlin, *there* you will find a colored school, brought into existence on account of prejudice even *there*. Will any gentleman deny this?"

Mr. Day arose and said, "I deny it." Mr. L. asked for the proof. Mr. Day called on Mr. Thomas Brown, Vice President of the Convention, and one of the trustees of the school in question, and who had in his possession the original papers for founding the school. Mr. Brown arose, and was about to speak in denial of Mr. Langston's assertion, when Pres. Langston decided the whole matter out of order.

Mr. Watson of Cuyahoga said that the gentleman, (Mr. J. M. Langston,) had misrepresented him. He was not with him. He was opposed to colonization. He was unwilling that a single sentiment should emanate from him in favor of the scheme.

Elder Shelton said that there never was a nation situated like ourselves. "We are free-born Americans, but are robbed of our rights by our American-born brethren. A portion of us have the elective franchise, and exercising that right in common with others, love the soil upon which we were born. I would say to gentlemen, stay where you are, and never think of leaving this land as long as one chain is to be heard clanking, or the cry of millions is to be heard floating on every breeze." He felt that he but reiterated the sentiments that burned in every bosom present. "And when Hallelujah! Hallelujah! shall resound from every hill-top and vale, when the shouts of the ransomed shall be heard reverberating louder than the roar and din of conflicting elements, then gentlemen, I feel assured that you will never regret that you have remained in this country."

Mr. J. L. Watson of Cuyahoga, made some remarks, condemning in strong terms, the course of Messrs. Douglass and Delany in publishing what *they* call a report of the National Convention, but which in reality was only a synopsis furnished for the papers by the Secretaries. He condemned Mr. Malvin, the treasurer, for paying the money without the order of the Secretaries. He said it behooved us to correct men in high places as readily as them that are least among us, from the king on his throne down to the meanest peasant. It seemed Mr. Douglass had made Cleveland the only post office in Ohio, so far as distributing the (so called) report was concerned. [Roars of laughter.]

[At this point, Mr. Jenkins came in with much haste, and said he had just come from the Auditor's office. He was told that the colored people were taxed for the support of schools, whether there were any colored children in them or not. He said that he had just paid for the support of *white* children.

Mr. Poindexter said that we were before exempt from paying taxes for school purposes, but *now* we were not permitted to reap the benefit of the school fund. He said that Mr. Jenkins and himself had sought an interview with Mr. Blake, and he told them that the law that had taken the school tax off of them had been re-enacted, and the law as it now stands, takes money out of our pockets to school the other class—it would be better if the law had stood as it had been, for then, sir, we did stand some chance.]

The 17th, 18th, 24th and 22d resolutions were adopted. 31st resolution was read and adopted. 15th resolution was read, and a motion to lay it on the table by J. Mercer Langston, was lost. Resolution was adopted.

Convention adjourned to meet at half past six of the clock.

Evening Session.

Convention met according to adjournment. J. L. Watson of Cuyahoga in the chair. Convention opened with prayer by the Chaplain. Minutes read, corrected and approved. 19th resolution was, on motion, laid on the table. 20th resolution was read and adopted. Resolution was spoken to by Messrs. Poindexter, Brown of Lorain, and Shelton. The Chairman of the Business Committee reported the following resolution, submitted by Mrs. Jane P. Merritt.

Whereas we the ladies have been invited to attend the Convention, and have been deprived of a voice, which we the ladies deem wrong and shameful. Therefore,

Resolved, That we will attend no more after to-night, unless the privilege is granted.

Mr. Watson of Lorain advocated a resolution inviting the ladies to participate. Messrs. Burnham and Reynolds opposed. Resolution was finally adopted, inviting the ladies to share in the doings of the Convention. Resolutions 23rd, 27th, were then adopted.

On motion the declaration of sentiments was taken up, and the repeated calls for Mr. Day to speak thereto, brought this gentleman to the stand. If we could paint a sun-beam or picture the glowing colors of the rain-bow, then we might do justice to the gentleman's brilliant effort.

Mr. Eli Nichols, a white friend, rose to speak to the platform--he was opposed to it. Mr. Day answered him. On motion the resolution fixing the time of adjournment, was reconsidered, and the motion fixing the time for adjournment at one o'clock Saturday 13th was carried. On motion the treasurer of the Financial Committee was ordered to pay one dollar to Mr. Jenkins for publishing notices of the Convention, and also that to the Sexton of the church for fuel, lights, &c. Whereupon Day, Minor and Watson were called upon for a song. After singing "I dream of all things free," the Convention adjourned.

Sixth Session. Saturday, Forenoon.

Convention met according to adjournment. President in the chair. Convention opened with prayer by the Chaplain. Minutes read, corrected and approved. 30th resolution was read and after some discussion, pro and con, it was moved to strike out the names of Messrs. Hale[7] and Root,[8] and leave only Mr. Giddings.[9] Lost. On motion of Mr. Day, the name of the Hon. John G. Palfrey[10] was added. The 30th Resolution was carried. Messrs. Dr. Langston, J. Mercer Langston, John Watson of Lorain, George R. Williams, W. H. Burnham and Wm. H. Day, begged leave to enter their protests against the resolution. On motion the 30th was reconsidered and indefinitely postponed. The 26th, 28th, 29th, and 33rd, resolutions were severally read and adopted.

On motion, Messrs. Minor, Watson of Cuyahoga and Brown of Lorain, were appointed a committee to prepare a Constitution and By-Laws for the government of the Parent Anti-slavery Society to be organized at the next State Convention.

On motion, the Convention resolved itself into a committee of the whole, on the condition of the colored people in the state. W. Howard Day in the chair. The committee after spending some time in session, gathering statistics, etc. rose and Mr. Day reported to the Convention as follows:

That he had found that the Convention was composed of pastors of churches, school teachers, students, farmers, plasterers, house painters, sign and ornamental painters, glaziers, paper hangers, wheel-wrights, joiners, printers, barbers, independent barbers, (shave anybody, white or colored,) and Black-smiths.

On motion the following resolutions were adopted:

Resolved, That it shall be the duty of the statistical committee to report at the next Convention the number of colored inhabitants, their occupation, amount of taxes they pay, &c.

Resolved, That we hereby present our thanks to the Trustees for the use of this house for the deliberations of the Convention.

Resolved, That the thanks of this Convention be tendered to the officers for the able manner in which they have discharged their duties.

On motion Mr. Day was appointed a committee in connection with the Secretary, to publish the proceedings of the Convention. The following resolution was then read and adopted:

Resolved, That the printing of 500 copies of the proceedings of this Convention be given to Wm. H. Day of Lorain, and that he be requested to state the probable cost of such printing.

A song was here sung by the Ladies, which elicited much applause.

After giving three hearty cheers for "Liberty, Equality, and Fraternity," Convention adjourned.

Resolutions

The resolutions are not placed in the order in which they were acted upon, but more according to the subjects contemplated in each.

Declaration of Sentiments

Whereas, we the free colored people of the State of Ohio are cursed by the blighting influence of oppression in this professedly free State, to which many of us have fled for refuge and protection, and

Whereas, the history of the political world as well as the history of nations clearly shows that "who would be free, himself must strike the blow," and

Whereas, both the old and new worlds are shaken throughout their length and breadth, by the uprising of oppressed millions who are erecting firm foundations and stupendous platforms on which they may unitedly battle for that liberty which God has benignantly given to all his creatures, and which will be wrested from them only by vampire despots, therefore,

Resolved, That we adopt the following as our Declaration of Sentiments, as to State and National policy, and in harmony with these we will ever fight, until our rights are regained. It is our purpose,

I. To sternly resist, by all the means which the God of Nations has placed in our power, every form of oppression or proscription attempted to be imposed upon us, in consequence of our condition or color.

II. To acknowledge no enactment honored with the name of law, as binding upon us, the object of which is in any way to curtail the natural rights of man.

III. To give our earnest attention to the universal education of our people.

IV. To sustain the cause of Temperance in our midst, and advocate the formation of societies for its promotion.

V. To leave what are called menial occupations, and aspire to mechanical, agricultural and professional pursuits.

VI. To respect and love that as the religion of Jesus Christ, and that alone, which, in its practical bearings, is not excitement merely, but that which loves God, loves humanity, and thereby preaches deliverance to the captive, the opening of the prison-doors to them that are bound, and teaches us to do unto others as we would have them do to us.

Resolutions

1. *Resolved,* That the Convention appoint a committee of three to request the General Assembly of this State to allow a hearing from some member of the Convention before their body, respecting the disabilities of the colored people of Ohio.

2. *Resolved,* That we the colored citizens of Ohio, in Convention assembled, petition the Legislature now in session, to repeal all laws making distinction on account of color, and that we urge the duty of petitioning upon our brethren throughout the State.

3. *Resolved,* That we petition Congress to repeal all laws of the United States making distinction on account of color.

4. That to elevate ourselves as a people--to toss from our shoulders the dead weight in the way of our religious, political and social elevation, *concerted action* is necessary.

5. *Resolved,* That the Convention make it obligatory on its members to persuade men to put in practice the acts passed in the Convention.

6. *Resolved,* That we will never submit to the system of Colonization to any part of the world, in or out of the United States; and we say once for all, to those soliciting us, that all of their appeals to us are in vain; our minds are made up to remain in the United States, and contend for our rights at all hazards.

7. *Whereas,* we believe it necessary to enlighten the public mind in this State as to our condition, and

Whereas, the colored people need to be aroused and encouraged, and

Whereas, the living speaker is a powerful enginery to accomplish these ends, therefore

Resolved, That we recommend to the different towns and counties of the State, to create a fund to sustain and remunerate a colored man as Lecturer, to traverse the State for the purposes above named.

8. *Resolved,* That a committee of seven be appointed to prepare an Address to the People of this State, and report the same to this Convention as early as possible.

9. *Resolved,* That we the colored citizens of the State of Ohio, hereby declare that whereas the Constitution of our common country gives us citizenship, we hereby, each to each pledge ourselves to support the other in claiming our rights under that Constitution, and in having the laws oppressing us tested.

10. *Resolved,* That we hereby, now and forever refuse to vote for or support any man for office, who will not go for us and ours in common with others.

11. *Whereas,* we believe with the "Fathers of '76," that taxation and representation ought to go together.

Resolved, That we are very much in doubt about paying any tax upon which representation is based, until we are permitted to be represented.

12. *Resolved,* That we still adhere to the doctrine of urging the slave to leave immediately with his hoe on his shoulder, for a land of liberty, and would accordingly recommend that five hundred copies of Walker's Appeal,[11] and Henry H. Garnet's Address to the Slaves,[12] be obtained in the name of the Convention, and gratuitously circulated.

13. *Resolved,* That we urge all colored persons and their friends to keep a sharp lookout for men-thieves and their abettors, and warn them that no person claimed as a slave shall be taken from our midst without trouble.

14. *Resolved,* That we recommend to the colored inhabitants throughout this State, immediate and energetic action on their part, in aiding our brothers and sisters in fleeing from the prison-house of bondage to the land of freedom; and furthermore we declare that he who would not aid our brothers and sisters in this most glorious cause, should by every community be published to the world as a bitter enemy to the cause of justice and humanity.

15. *Resolved,* That the attempt to establish churches or schools for the benefit of colored persons EXCLUSIVELY, where we can enter either upon equal terms with the whites, is in our humble opinion reprehensible.

16. *Resolved,* That a committee of five be appointed to recommend a school system which may be used until school privileges are granted us in this State.

17. *Resolved,* That we hereby recommend to our people throughout the State to give their children mechanical trades, and encourage them to engage in the agricultural, professional and other elevating pursuits of the day. And futhermore,

Resolved, That every clergyman who feels the importance of this Resolution be hereby requested to read it or lecture upon it once to his congregation.

18. *Resolved,* That we establish a Parent Anti-Slavery Society at this Convention, and appoint State officers, and recommend County Societies as auxiliary to said Parent Society. [For want of time amended by appointing a committee of three to draft a Constitution for the government of a Parent Society--the committee to report at the next Convention.]

19. *Resolved,* That this Convention take measures to establish a Newspaper, in some of the towns in this State, which paper shall be the organ of the people.

20. *Resolved,* That the Conference of colored men or association that is afraid to speak out against the monster, SLAVERY, when they have an opportunity so to do, and while their own brethren are in bonds, is not only undeserving of our confidence, but deserving of our deepest reprobation. And we further believe that the man, be he white or colored, who wrapped in ecclesiastical dignity, shuts his pulpit against the claims of God's suffering poor, whether those claims be presented in the anti-slavery, temperance or other causes, is not unworthy only of the name of minister, but of the honored appellation, MAN.

21. *Resolved,* That we regard the conduct of that portion of our people who fellowship those men who treat them as things and not as men, or encourage those that do, and who will not encourage in their churches the elevation of the colored people, and who vote for men-stealers to fill the highest offices in the gift of the people, thereby tightening the chain upon three millions of our brethren in the South, as highly detrimental to our elevation, at war with the injunctions of the Bible, and contrary to the progressive light of the age.

22. *Resolved,* That we are determined to consider all colored men who do not treat other colored men on terms of perfect equality with the whites in all cases, as recreant to their dearest cause, and should be esteemed outcasts.

23. *Resolved,* That we consider the treatment of the "Ohio Stage Company" towards colored persons unjust--a species of slavery of the blackest die --emanating from the blackest hearts--therefore deserving the contempt and reprobation of every colored man and his true friend; and we further believe that the Stage Houses and other hotels in Ohio, that will not accommodate respectable colored persons, ought not to be patronized by our professed friends, where they know of other houses of different principles.

24. *Whereas* the ladies of England, Scotland, Ireland and France have made strenuous efforts in behalf of right, liberty and equality, in giving their burning rebuke to the God-defying institution of American Slavery, and protesting against the contemptible conduct of that miserable wretch, H. G. WARNER, in excluding from the Seminary in Rochester the child of the far-famed Frederick Douglass,[13] therefore

Resolved, That the conduct of those ladies and gentlemen in this respect has our hearty approbation and united concurrence, and we hail it as an omen of the time when the world of mankind will be engaged on the side of outraged and oppressed humanity.

25. *Resolved,* That a Central Committee of [illegible] four of them in Franklin County, be appointed, to call a State Convention whenever they in their judgment may deem it expedient.

26. *Resolved,* That the Central Committee be hereby instructed to call a Delegated and not a Mass Convention.

27. *Resolved,* That we hereby recommend that the next National Convention be held in Detroit, Mich., sometime in the year 1849.

28. *Resolved,* That the Convention elect twenty-three Delegates to attend the National Convention, provided that the National Convention be held before the next State Convention.

29. *Whereas* we believe in the principle that who would be free, himself must strike the blow; and

Whereas Liberty is comparatively worth nothing to the oppressed, without effort on their part, therefore

Resolved, That we recommend to our brethren throughout the Union, that they thanking their white friends for all action put forth in our behalf, pursue an independent course, relying only on the right of their cause and the God of Freedom.

30. *Resolved,* That the course of Messrs. Hale, Giddings, Root and others who have advocated our claims in the U.S. Congress, merits our sincere thanks and highest approbation.

31. *Resolved,* That we in our efforts for elevation, recognize no such word as FAIL.

32. *Resolved,* That we contemplate with joy the successful career of the *North Star*, thus far, and recommend that the colored people in particular and all friends of humanity in general, give it the best support in their power, until the ends for which it is designed shall have been accomplished.

33. <u>Whereas</u> there has been issued from the *North Star* office, Rochester, N.Y., an edition of pamphlets as the Report of the proceedings of the National Convention held at Cleveland, Sept. 6, 1848, but which is really merely a *Synopsis* of those proceedings, and

<u>Whereas</u> twenty-five dollars has been demanded from and paid by Mr. Malvin, the Treasurer of the Convention, for printing said Synopsis, and

<u>Whereas</u> said Synopsis was printed, and the money paid without any order from the Committee of Publication, therefore

Resolved, That we deem the publishing of said Synopsis under the circumstances as culpable, the Treasurer of the Convention responsible for the twenty-five dollars, and would recommend that the Secretaries of the National Convention be requested to act with the Secretaries of this Convention, to publish the minutes of each Convention together, and of course to ask for money from the National Convention Treasurer sufficient to pay for printing the National Convention Minutes.

TO THE CITIZENS OF OHO

In compliance with the vote of the above noticed Convention of your colored fellow citizens, the undersigned in their behalf essay to address you in brief upon the great topics in [which] we and you in this state are or ought to be interested.

The desire of universal man for liberty, you own acts when oppressed by Great Britain, the curse of the Black Laws in this State, and our appreciation of that curse, is our only apology for thus addressing you.

The intelligent and Christian among you admit that you and we have a common destiny. That we are children of the same great parent, and heirs of the same immortality. You admit that we are in the same government. That seventy-two years ago you helped to form it, announcing as its primal principle--all men are created equal--endowed by their Creator with certain inalienable rights--among which are life, liberty, and the pursuit of happiness --and that to secure these rights governments are instituted among men, deriving their just powers from the consent of the governed. You here asserted two important principles:--1st. That the object of legislation is to secure rights; and 2. That every one governed, is in the sense of giving or refusing consent, a legislator, and as an inference from these, you say, the government which does not respect these two principles is not just.

In accordance with these principles you framed a United States Constitution. This you claimed as supreme law, and in accordance with it in 1802 framed a constitution for this State. To the principles thus announced we heartily subscirbe. We believe them just and equitable. We believe they ought to be enforced as well for us as for you. *Our fathers* helped to rear this temple of Liberty. Their sons, we claim, ought to be inheritors of its blessings. We therefore beg leave to state to you our and your principles, and constrasting the enactments in this state against us, with these, state what ought to be our and your conclusions.

We believe not only that "liberty is the birth-right of all, and law its defence," but we believe also that *every human being* has rights in common, and that the meanest of those rights is legitimately beyond the reach of legislation, and higher than the claims of political expediency. Do you admit our belief as true? We believe in the fact, the "fixed and unalterable" fact "that *to secure these rights* governments are instituted among men deriving their just powers from the consent of the governed." This you have taught us. Ohio law is a violation of this principle. Now for the proof.

1st. We are unrepresented. The elective franchise, one of the dearest privileges of a free people, we are deprived of. For members of the Convention framing the Ohio Constitution, colored men voted without distinction. The question was raised in that Convention whether the colored man should still enjoy the elective franchise, and it was carried in the affirmative by a vote of 19 to 15. But ultimately, by a reconsideration, the casting vote of the

President decided it against us, and the illegitimate word "white" became a part of the Ohio State Constitution. We are thus by this one word, strange and inconsistent as it may seem, deprived of all the blessings which flow out from the "free consent of the governed." But,

2d. We are taxed, while we are unrepresented. You hire your Governor, Secretaries, Auditor and Treasurer, 108 Members of the General Assembly, together with the officers attached, and you filch our property to help pay them. You have built Asylums for the Blind, for the Deaf and Dumb, and for the Lunatic, together with Houses for the Poor, and you not only demand that we should help sustain them, equally with you, but deny us the benefits of them. Only last year Governor Bebb endeavored to place a colored child in the Asylum for the Deaf and Dumb, and the child was refused. Until within a short time, colored persons have not been permitted to enter the Lunatic Asylum, even as visitors, and yet colored persons are taxed for its support. We say then, these things are violations of the fundamental principles you yourselves, of your own accord, have laid down. Ohio law ought in this respect then to be a nullity.

Fellow Citizens--The 5th clause of 1st section of Article 2d, of the United States Constitution, recognizes the principle that *natural birth gives citizenship*. Article 4th, section 2d, and 1st clause, claims that the citizens of the each State, shall be entitled to all privileges and immunities of citizens of the several States; and the Ohio Bill of Rights, Article 8th, of the Ohio State Constitution, Section 1st, declares, that all men are born equally free and independent, and have certain, natural, inherent, and inalienable rights, among which are the enjoying and defending life and liberty, acquiring, possessing, and protecting property, and pursuing and obtaining happiness and safety: therefore we claim that the colored citizens in the State of Ohio have rights equal with the rest of her citizens. And we claim in addition that he who solemnly swears to support her Bill of Rights--swears to give to "all men," irrespective of any accidental distinction, "the certain natural, inherent and inalienable rights" therein specified.

Article 8th, Section 7th, Ohio State Constitution, announces--That all courts shall be open, and every person, for any injury done him in his lands, goods, person or reputation, shall have remedy, by the due course of law, and right and justice administered without denial or delay. We hold that the "testimony law," so called, is of this part of the Constitution, if of no other, a direct and shameful violation.

Article 4th, Section 1st, Articles of the Confederation, provides that "the better to secure and perpetuate mutual friendship and intercourse among the people of the different States in this Union, the free inhabitants of each of these States, paupers, vagabonds, and fugitives from justice excepted, shall be entitled to all privileges and immunities of free citizens in the several States; and the people of each State shall have free ingress and regress, to and from any other State, and shall enjoy therein all the privileges of trade and commerce, subject to the same duties, impositions and restrictions, as the inhabitants thereof respectively.

Says the law of Ohio, "No negro or mulatto person shall be permitted to emigrate into and settle within this State, unless such negro or mulatto persons shall, within twenty days thereafter, enter into bond with two or more freehold sureties, in the penal sum of five hundred dollars, before the clerk of the court of common pleas of the county in which such negro or mulatto may wish to reside, (to be approved by the clerk,) conditioned for the good behavior of such negro or mulatto, and moreover, to pay for the support of such person, in case he, she, or they should thereafter be found within any township in this State, unable to support themselves. And if any negro or mulatto person shall migrate into this state, and not comply with the provisions of this act, it shall be the duty of the overseers of the poor of the township where such negro or mulatto person may be found, to remove immediately such black or mulatto person, in the manner as required in the case of paupers."

We are neither "paupers, vagabonds, or fugitives from justice," therefore we hold this enactment to be in direct opposition to the spirit and principles of the Articles of Confederation of the thirty States of this Union.

Article 8, Section 25, State Constitution, says, that "no law shall be passed to prevent the poor in the several counties and townships within this

State, from an equal participation in the schools, academies, colleges, and universities within this State, which are endowed, in whole or in part, from the revenue arising from the donations made by the United States for the support of schools and colleges; and the doors of said schools, academies and universities, shall be open for the reception of scholars, students and teachers, of every grade, without any distinction or preference whatever, contrary to the intent for which the said donations were made." We hold that the actual exclusion of colored inhabitants from the benefit of the school fund is a violation of the principle here announced.

Permit us here to say a word to you on the effect of such a law.

1st. It encourages ignorance in your communities. To encourage ignorance is to encourage vice. The vicious character of uneducated communities, both in the direct and indirect influence, is seen the world over, and to prove it we need not to cite you to all past history. Therefore, even if the colored people of Ohio were aliens, your own interest would demand the extending educational privileges to them all; but here we are, born on your soil, and unless your own professed principles be a lie, entitled to all the rights and privileges of all others. Consequently, you are doubly bound to act for us as for yourselves.

2d. In children thus divided by law, the most Satanic hate is likely to be engendered. This, no one who has studied human nature will deny. This hate "grows with the growth and strengthens with the strength." What children are in the school room, they are when manhood has come over them, and what feeling the school-room fosters appears in after life in the shape of a monster called law.

But another thing. We ask what was the "intent for which the said donations were made?" Was it merely for men called "*white*?" We say no. Nor was it left a bone for quibblers by saying "*citizens*"--nay, verily, but for the "INHABITANTS." With all deference, we ask, who are they?

We wish those in authority to be at least consistent, either by wiping the black laws, (aye *black* enough to merit a birth place other than in the free soil of Ohio,) we say, either by wiping them from her statute book, or else by openly repudiating the free principles which she by agreement is bound to regard as her higher law.

But we appeal not to Constitutions alone. We convict you of inconsistencies by them. But we appeal in the name of Him who presides over the destinies of nations, to the principles of Right and Justice, existing and hoary in their age, long before Constitutions were known, or the Unites States nation born. We care not then, as far as the actual right is concerned, whether the Constitutions be leagues with death and agreements with hell or no. We appeal from them, (if they be such,) to a higher *judicature*.

Our moral and social elevation we speak of last, but not because we deem them of the least consequence. We speak to you of *political* privileges *first*, for which you is the entire political power. Still you can assist us in attaining a true moral and social position. We ask not that you remove the disabilities under which we labor merely because you pity us. We ask for no such sympathy. We ask for equal privileges, *not* because we would consider it a condescension on your part to grant them--but because we are MEN, and therefore entitled to all the privileges of other men in the same circumstances.

We ask that the "negro pew" in your churches be removed, and that *character* and not color be the basis of your treatment of colored men, both in those churches and in your families.

We ask for school privileges in common with others, for we pay school taxes in the same proportion.

We ask permission to send our deaf and dumb, our lunatic, blind, and poor to the asylums prepared for each.

We ask for the repeal of the odious enactments, requiring us to declare ourselves "paupers, vagabonds, or fugitives from justice," because we can "lawfully" remain in the State.

We ask that colored men be not obliged to brand themselves liars, in every case of testimony in "courts of justice" where a white person is a party.

We ask that the word "white" in the State Constitution be stricken out at once and forever, and of course that the privileges growing out of such striking out be restored to us.

We ask that we may be one people, bound together by one common tie, and sheltered by the same impartial law.

Citizens of Ohio--We have had put into our hands copies of a memorial to the General Assembly, signed by David Christy, Agent of the American Colonization Society, speaking of the increase of the colored people in the West, and especially in the State of Ohio. He urges their increase as a reason why the Legislature should furnish money to transport colored people from this State to "Ohio in Africa." We wish him 1st to show to candid minds, if he can, that the increase of the colored people in this State, is an evil. He basely hints that we are a nuisance in your midst, and gratuitously informs you that you thus consider us, and that therefore you do not intend to repeal your black enactments. We as gratuitously, and with a better right, inform you, that we independently but humbly beg leave to differ with Mr. Christy and the Colonization Society, and say, we believe you *do* mean to repeal the enactments against us, and also, that whether they are repealed or not, we mean, in the spirit of our resolution, here to remain amid the broken columns of our temple of liberty, and cry, "Repeal, Repeal, Repeal," until that repeal is granted.

To those in this State who have labored in our behalf, we tender our heartfelt thanks: we ask them still to labor; but while they labor we beseech them not to despise us. In the spirit of the heathen slave, and we hope as intelligently, we each say, "Homo sum, atque humani nihil a me alienum puto" --"I am a man, and I think that nothing is estranged from me which pertains to humanity"--and therefore entitled to all the privileges--moral, mental, political and social, to which other men attain. We ask for no more--no less privileges than ye yourselves would desire to enjoy under the same circumstances.

To the Colored Citizens of Ohio, we would echo the voice of the Convention and say, come out, as soon as possible, from situations called degrading --encourage education--be temperance men and women--resist every species of oppression--serve God and humanity. Let us go to work. In our Platform the principles of action are laid down. Let us study them--let us practice them --humbly--independently, and, devising means for sustaining them, thus inform our opposers that we are coming--coming for our rights--coming through the Constitution of our common country--coming through the law--and relying upon God and the justice of our cause, pledge ourselves never to cease our resistance to tyranny, whether it be in the *iron* manacles of the *slave*, or in the unjust *written* manacles for the *free*.

In behalf of the Convention,
Yours in bonds,
William Howard Day,
Charles Henry Langston,
Wallace Shelton,
David Jenkins,
John M. Brown,
John L. Watson,
James S. Thompson,
Committee.

STATISTICAL COMMITTEES

Hamilton

Elder Wallace Shelton,
Charles M. Wilson,
John I. Gaines.

Ross

George R. Williams.

Franklin

David Jenkins.

Brown

E. Cumberland.

Van Wert

Henry Taylor.

Licking

Moses Walker.

Muskingum
W. Hurst Burnham.

Jackson
N. Nooks.

Fayette
Andrew Manly.

Lorain
William H. Day.

Cuyahoga
John L. Watson.

Richland
James S. Thompson.

Pickaway
T. J. Merritt.

Fairfield
McPherson Turner

Union
Madison Cunningham.

Delaware
Samuel White, Jr.

Highland
John Taylor.

Stark
J. J. Walls.

Mercer
J. Bowles.

Erie
J. B. Lott.

Logan
Elisha Bird.

Belmont
A. Harper.

Jefferson
____ Walker.

Champaign
Lewis Adams.

Shelby
Enoch Shackler.

Montgomery
Thomas Jefferson.

Summit
William Bird.

Lake
Isaac Stanton.

Morgan
Epping Brown.

Green
Westley Roberts.

Marion
____ Kinney.

Gallia
Thomas Scott.

Clark
Harrison Little.

Pike
Washington Evings.

Knox
Otho Martin.

Wayne
S. H. Brown.

Scioto
William Cook.

Harrison
Thomas Steward.

EXTRACTS FROM NEWSPAPERS
REFERRING TO THE PUBLIC MEETING IN THE HALL OF THE
HOUSE OF REPRESENTATIVES, JAN. 11th, 1849

From the "Ohio Daily Standard."

Convention of Colored People

A Delegate Convention of the colored people of Ohio is now in session in this city. The convention is respectable in numbers and in talents, and their proceedings are conducted with ability, order, and decorum. Their object is to devise means for the repeal of the Black Laws of this State, the abolition of slavery, and the adoption of means for the improvement of their race. On Thursday evening, on motion of Dr. Townshend, the hall of the State House was opened for their accommodation. A large audience of both colored and white citizens were present. They were addressed by Mr. Day, a colored graduate from Oberlin, and by J. L. Watson of Cleveland. The speeches of both gentlemen exhibited much thought, and patriotic devotion to their country and race, and were listened to with perfect attention. Several songs were sung, and in good taste. We can not, and would not if we could, refrain from bidding God speed to the efforts of these oppressed people to elevate themselves and their race. The yielding of the use of the State House, and the attention of the audience, and their perfect good behavior, show a most cheering state of progress in the public mind.

Colored Men's Convention in Columbus

We can not fail to take a strong and lively interest in the series of Colored People's Conventions now being holden. The one at Cleveland, last September, was an era in the intellectual, social, and educational elevation of the colored people of our nation. Grave in its deliberations, prudent in its suggestions, animating and inspiring in its resolutions, dignified in its whole bearing, it served to give impulse to a mass of mind too long and too cruelly crushed, and also to give character before the world to their determined efforts for real improvement.

Another Convention has recently been called in Columbus, a brief account of which we transfer from the Columbus State Journal, of Jan. 13th.

Oberlin Evangelist.

"A Convention of the colored Freemen of the State of Ohio has been in session in this city for several days, and is numerously attended by intelligent, respectable men from all parts of the State. It was organized by the appointment of Charles H. Langston Esq. of Chillicothe, as President, with the usual number of Vice Presidents and Secretaries.

"On Thursday evening, pursuant to permission obtained for that purpose, the Convention met in the Hall of the House of Representatives. The meeting itself, aside from the unusually interesting nature of the exercises, is an incident in our history well worthy of reflection and remark. The colored man has been allowed to come up, without insult and without reproach--to enter into a place hitherto deemed sacred to the white man alone, and standing there to plead his right to be deemed a man and a brother, and to claim a community of interest in all that appertains to humanity--to say 'our God,' and to beg permission to say 'our country.'

"A prepared address was delivered by William H. Day, a young man from Oberlin, upon the subject of the grievances which the colored people of the United States--both in slavery and emancipation--suffer in comparison to those borne by the fathers of this Republic, under the rule of Great Britain, before the Revolution. The parallels drawn between the two cases were extremely striking and forcible, and for beauty of composition and propriety of delivery, the oration would bear a comparison with the labored efforts of men of far greater fame and far higher pretensions.

"After the close of Mr. Day's address the audience was agreeably entertained by a speech by John L. Watson of Cleveland. Mr. Watson announced himself a native-born citizen of Virginia--the land of Washington, and a 'self-

emancipated slave.' He thought that he might recommend himself and his
remarks to the Democrats present by the fact that he was born upon the same
soil, and had breathed the same air that blew over the same hills with
Thomas Jefferson. An emigrant from a sister State, he came here to beg as a
boon the bestowal upon him and those who were in his situation, of those
privileges which were freely granted as a right to the emigrant from Ireland
or from Germany. He went into an examination of the Black Laws--their constitutionality, and their legal and moral effect. They work, he said, degradation to the black and disgrace to the white man. If they are a dead letter,
why leave them as monuments of the barbarism of the past? If they are living
law, interpose to prevent the horrid injustice of which they may be the instruments in future.

The address was a strong and a good one, and was enlivened by sparks of
geniune wit, which elicited frequent and tumultuous applause. The speaker
himself was an evidence of what a soul can do, even under the pressure of
extraordinary difficulties. In his case it has made a man.

The meeting was enlivened by some fine singing, and was a model of all
that was decorous and respectable."

Let the gall's jade wince!
For the following precious bit, we are indebted to our friend, W. P. N.

From the *Cincinnati Gazette*, of February 2d.

"Even in the Capital the blacks have already assumed high airs. A friend
visited a meeting lately held in the Hall of Representatives, before the laws
were repealed in the House. He handed me the following:

"'Mr. Day, a black from the 'Reserve,' addressed the audience. In the
course of his remarks he arraigned the Governor and the people of the United
States, upon charges of the grossest tyranny and usurpation--comparing them
to the English previous to the Revolution. He found the white folks guilty,
and then enumerated the number of *rebels* (meaning the blacks) in the United
States, and what they could accomplish. They demanded their rights as did our
forefathers in the Declaration of Independence, and threatened rebellion
ultimately if it did not come.'

"In confirmation of this movement, your attention is invited to the
following circular, [what the circular is he does not say,] which was placed
on the desk of every member of both Houses. Sitting by an honorable Senator
yesterday afternoon, several of my Democratic friends had the kindness to send
me a copy with their compliments--I could not do less than pass them round.

"Observe with what arrogance a noble philanthropist is treated, Mr.
Christy, laboring only for the elevation of their race in the region allotted
to them by Providence--from which they were taken, and to which they must be
restored! Let them be kindly treated, well educated, and prepared for the
mission of civilizing those once as degraded as themselves. T."

Copy in the Pennsylvania State University Library.

STATE CONVENTION OF THE COLORED CITIZENS OF OHIO

As Reported in the North Star, January 26, 1849

We have received a letter from our friend Geo. B. Williams, enclosing the
following account from the *Ohio Standard* of the Convention recently held in
Columbus, O. Agitate! agitate! agitate!

A Convention of the Colored Freemen of the State of Ohio has been in
session in this city for several days, and is [sic] attended by intelligent
and respectable men from all parts of the State. It was organized on
Wednesday, in the Methodist Episcopal Church on Long street, by [illegible]
of Charles Langston Esq., of Chillocothe, as President, with the usual
[number] of Vice Presidents and Secretaries.

On Thursday evening, pursuant to permission obtained for the purpose, the
Convention met in the Hall of Representatives. The meeting itself, aside
from the unusually interesting nature of the exercises, is an incident well

worthy of reflection and remark. The colored man has been allowed to come up, without insult and without reproach--to enter into a place hitherto deemed sacred to the white man alone, and standing there, to plead the right to be deemed a man and a brother, and to claim a community of interest in all that appertains to humanity--to say "our God," and to beg permission to say "our country."

A prepared address was delivered by Wm. H. Day, a young man from Oberlin, upon the subject of grievances which the colored people of the United States, both in slavery and emancipated, suffer in comparison with those borne by the fathers of the Republic under the rule of Great Britain, before the Revolution. The parallels drawn between the two cases were extremely striking and forcible, and for beauty of composition and propriety of delivery, the oration could bear a comparison with the labored efforts of men of far greater fame and far higher pretensions.

At the close of Mr. Day's address, the audience was agreeably entertained by a speech from John M. Watson, of Cleveland. Mr. Watson announced himself as a native born citizen of Virginia, the land of Washington, and a "self-emancipated slave." He thought he might recommend himself and his remarks to the Democrats present, by the fact that he was born upon the same soil, and had breathed the air that blew over the same hills, with Thomas Jefferson. An emigrant from a sister State, he came here to beg as a boon the bestowal upon him and those who were in his situation, of those privileges which were freely granted as a right to the emigrant from Ireland or from Germany. He went into an examination of the black laws, there constitutionality, and their legal and moral effect. "They work," he said, "degradation to the black and disgrace to the white man. If they are a dead letter, why leave them as a monument of the barbarism of the past. If they are a living law, interpose to prevent the horrid injustice of which they may be made the instruments in future."

The address was a strong and a good one, and was enlivened by sparks of geniune wit, which elicited frequent and tumultuous applause. The speaker himself was an evidence of what a soul can do even under the pressure of extraordinary difficulties. In his case it has made a man.

The meeting was enlivened by some fine singing, and was a model of all that was decorous and respectable.

The North Star, January 26, 1849.

REFERENCE NOTES

1. Charles H. Langston (1817-1892) was a prominent Ohio black leader and abolitionist. Highly active in the Negro Convention movement of the 1850's, Langston later received considerable notoriety as a result of his role in the celebrated Oberlin-Wellington Rescue case. In September 1858, he joined the students of Oberlin College and citizens of the town in rescuing a recaptured fugitive slave, John Price, who was being held in the neighboring town of Wellington. Price was removed from custody and transported to Canada and freedom. Langston was the second to be tried for violating the law in the famous case, and he delivered a brilliant and moving speech in answer to the question of the judge why sentence should not be pronounced. His speech struck the court so favorably that even though he was sentenced to twenty days' imprisonment and fined $100 and costs amounting to $872.72, it was a much lighter sentence than that given to his white predecessor, whose actions were judged equally "criminal."

On one occasion, his well-known brother John Mercer Langston described Charles as follows: "He is widely known as a devoted and laborious advocate of the claims of the Negro to liberty and its attendant blessings. Discreet and farseeing, uncompromising and able, he has labored most efficiently in behalf of the slave and the disfranchised American."

2. John Malvin was an influential Negro leader and the owner and operator of a canal boat business in Cleveland, Ohio. On one occasion, Malvin used part of his earnings to ransom his father-in-law, Caleb Dorsey, from slavery. During the late 1830's, Malvin served as a traveling agent for the

Colored American. He also spearheaded the drive to promote education among his people, organizing in his native city the School Education Society. A fearless and diligent worker on the Underground Railroad, his canal boat was often used to convey escaping slaves to freedom.

3. Founded in 1847 by Frederick Douglass at Rochester, New York, the *North Star* became a leading antislavery newspaper.

4. In an editorial entitled "Ohio Black Laws" (the *North Star*, March 10, 1848), Frederick Douglass, the great Negro abolitionist, wrote: "In no State of this Union are to be found laws more cruel, unjust and atrocious, than those on the Statute Book of Ohio. An assembly of devils could not have enacted laws more infernal, and better fitted to promote crime, than that what are called the 'black laws' of that State." Among other provisions, the laws required Negroes entering the state to place a bond of five hundred dollars for good behavior with a state official. Ohio also excluded Negroes from public schools by law.

5. John Mercer Langston (1829-1897), a noted educator and abolitionist, was born a slave in Louisa County, Virginia. Langston was emancipated after the death of his father and owner and sent to Ohio where he attended school. He graduated from the literary department of Oberlin College in 1849 and from the theological department in 1852. He studied law and was admitted to the bar in 1854. In 1855, he became the first Negro elected to public office in the United States, when he won the post of township clerk in Brownhelm, Ohio. During the Civil War he was a recruiter for the famed Negro regiment of the Fifty-fourth and Fifty-fifth of Massachusetts and the Fifth of Ohio. He was dean of the law department of Howard University from 1869 to 1876. Langston served in Congress from September 23, 1890, to March 3, 1891, representing the Fourth District of Virginia. See, for example, John Mercer Langston, *From the Virginia Plantation to the National Capitol* (New York, 1894), *passim*. See also William F. Cheek, "John Mercer Langston: Black Protest Leader and Abolitionist," *Civil War History*, XVI (June, 1970), 101-120.

6. William Howard Day (1825-1900), a noted black editor, abolitionist and orator, was born in New York City. He received his preparatory training at Northhampton, and entered Oberlin College in 1843. Graduating in 1847, he achieved the unique distinction of being the only black man in his class of fifty. A person whom the *National Anti-Slavery Standard* (Dec. 31, 1853) described as "an educated gentleman of refined manners and winning address," Day played a prominent role in the antislavery movement, particularly in Ohio. His efforts led in part to the repeal of that states' notorious "Black Laws" in 1849.

For a time Day worked as a compositor, a clerk, and later an editor for the Cleveland *True Democrat*. In 1852, Day became editor of the *Aliened American*, a black newspaper which he established in Cleveland and which became the leading organ of blacks in the Midwest until it ceased publication in 1856. In 1857, due to ill health, Day went to Canada and, shortly thereafter, became a vigorous exponent of Canadian emigration, a position which owed its genesis to the passage of the Fugitive Slave Law of 1850. In 1859, he visited England, Ireland, and Scotland to raise money for the black settlement at Buxton, Canada, where he remained until the end of the Civil War.

7. The reference is to John P. Hale (1806-1873), an abolitionist senator from New Hampshire. The request to strike out his name from the resolution was probably owing in part to an incident which had occurred nearly one year before. Prompted by a mob attack in Washington on the *National Era*, the official weekly journal of the American and Foreign Anti-Slavery Society, a bill was introduced in the Senate by Hale on April 20, 1848, making that city liable for injuries inflicted by mobs on property in the District of Columbia. Some Negro leaders, like Frederick Douglass, complained that the bill made no reference to injuries to blacks.

8. Joseph M. Root was a member of Congress from Ohio.

9. Joshua Reed Giddings (1795-1864), an abolitionist, was for twenty years a militant antislavery congressman from the Western Reserve of Ohio.

10. John Gorham Palfrey (1796-1881), Unitarian clergyman, editor, historian, was a grandson of Maj. William Palfrey who was paymaster of the American forces in the Revolution. In 1842 and 1843 he was a member of the Massachusetts legislature and from 1847 to 1849 a member of Congress. Active also as a lecturer and abolitionist, he himself freed a few slaves, inherited

from his father, who had lived for a while in Louisiana.

11. David Walker (1785-1830) was the black author of a powerful tract, published in Boston at his own expense in 1829, called *Walker's Appeal, in Four Articles*, addressed to the "coloured citizens" of the world, but particularly to those of the United States. Walker called upon the Negro slaves to revolt and overthrow their oppressors.

12. In August 1843, Garnet attended the National Convention of Negro Citizens at Buffalo, New York, and delivered a militant speech calling for slave rebellions as the surest way to end slavery. It was the most radical speech by a black American during the antebellum period. The proposal stirred the delegates and failed by one vote of being adopted.

13. Refusing to accept Rochester, New York's, system of segregated public schools, Douglass in August 1848 arranged for his daughter Rosetta to attend Seward Seminary, a fashionable school for girls in that city. Shortly thereafter he left for a visit to Cleveland happy in the thought that his child "was about to enjoy advantages for improving her mind, and fitting her for a useful and honorable life." What was his rage to discover on his return that Rosetta had been isolated in a room by herself and was being taught separately. He promptly protested to the principal "against the cruelty and injustice of treating [my] child as a criminal on account of color." The principal weakly replied that the trustees of the school had objected to the admission of a Negro girl, and to overcome their prejudices by gradual stages had hit upon the idea of having the child taught separately until such time as she could be admitted to the regular classes.

Upon Douglass' protest, the principal of the school submitted the question of Rosetta's status to the pupils and then to their parents. None of the children objected to Rosetta sitting with them, but one parent, H. G. Warner, editor of the Rochester *Courier*, objected and the child was asked to leave the school. Douglass had already decided to withdraw his daughter from the seminary, but he did not permit the incident to pass over quietly. In a scathing letter to Warner, he promised that he would use all his powers to proclaim this "infamy" to the nation. The incident indeed attracted nationwide attention, for scores of newspapers reprinted his letter. See Philip S. Foner, *The Life and Writings of Frederick Douglass* (New York, 1950), I, 371-374.

MINUTES OF THE STATE CONVENTION, OF THE COLORED CITIZENS OF OHIO,
CONVENED AT COLUMBUS, JANUARY 9th, 10th, 11th, AND 12th, 1850

CONVENTION OF THE COLORED CITIZENS OF OHIO

MINUTES

First Session, Wednesday Morning.

Pursuant to a call of the STATE CENTRAL COMMITTEE, for holding a Delegate State Convention, the delegates to said Convention met in the *Bethel Church*, in the City of Columbus, on Wednesday, January 9th, at 10 o'clock, A.M.

The Convention was called to order by D. Jenkins, of Franklin County, and was organized by appointing L. D. Taylor, of Franklin, President pro tem., and C. A. Yancy, Secretary.

Prayer having been offered by the Rev. Mr. N. Nooks, the Convention proceeded to enrolled the names of the Delegates.

W. H. Day, of Lorain, introduced the following resolution:

Resolved, That persons present from their respective counties, who have credentials, and those who have been regularly elected, constitute this Convention.

Which resolution, after some discussion, was amended at the suggestion of D. Jenkins, as follows:

Resolved, That all persons present from counties not duly represented, and those who have been duly elected, constitute this Convention.

The following gentlemen were present to represent their respective counties:

Fairfield County--A. Strauder.
Lorain County--John Watson, W. H. Day, Thomas Brown, and C. Ross.
Morgan County--G. Hilton.
Champaign County--H. Ford, J. D. Pattison, L. Adams.
Madison County--J. Purnell.
Cuyahoga County--J. L. Watson, J. Mercer Langston, H. F. Douglass, Jas. Monroe Jones.
Jackson County--N. Nooks, A. Yancy, J. W. Stuart.
Gallia County--W. Stuart, J. Gee.
Logan County--K. Artis.
Pickaway County--D. S. Moss, G. Adams.
Warren County--F. Wilson.
Geauga County--H. Lott, Sr., H. Lott, Jr.
Erie County--J. J. Pearce.
Mercer County--S. Jones.
Clark County--N. Morgan, A. Dempsey, W. P. Morgan.
Greene County--J. W. Divine, J. H. Johnson.
Jefferson County--T. H. Dorsey, J. P. Underwood.

Seneca County--D. Roberts.
Muskingum County--W. H. Burnham.
Ross County--G. R. Williams, Dr. C. H. Langston.
Franklin County--J. Poindexter, D. Jenkins, L. D. Taylor, J. Booker, P. Letchford, W. S. Davis, J. M. Brown, T. Washington, T. J. Goode, J. H. Johnson, D. Hart, D. Trent, W. Copeland, J. Bennett, J. Freeland.
Licking County--Morgan Melton.
Highland County--J. W. Delany, J. Taylor.
Montgomery County--John Jackson, Thos. Jefferson.
Pike County--G. W. Evans.

D. Jenkins moved that a committee of one from each county represented, constitute a committee to nominate permanent officers for the Convention.

The committee having retired, the Convention was entertained by eloquent speeches from Messrs. H. F. Douglass[1] and Wm. H. Day.

The nominating committee having returned, reported through their chairman, C. H. Langston, the following gentlemen as officers for the Convention: J. L. Watson, President; L. D. Taylor, W. H. Burnham, John Watson of Lorain, and John Gee, Vice Presidents; and Jas. Monroe Jones, C. A. Yancy, K. Artis, and George R. Williams Secretaries. J. P. Underwood and J. D. Pattison were appointed Chaplains to the Convention.

W. H. Day moved that the report be adopted.

While the motion was pending, Wm. Copeland moved to amend report, by striking out the name of J. L. Watson from the list of permanent officers of the Convention. He said he thought that the young members of the Convention ought to be placed in office, in order that they might become acquainted with conventional affairs.

Mr. J. Mercer Langston then arose and made a most eloquent speech [in] favor of sustaining the original list of officers. He said that Mr. Watson was the "*wheel horse*" of the Reserve, and had devoted his time and talents in defense of the colored men of the States. He eulogized the manly conduct that had characterized Mr. W's whole life as an Anti-slavery Lecturer. He therefore thought the Convention ought to place him in the Chair, as a mark of respect to one who had so well deserved it.

The question on the adoption of the original report was called for, and the report was unanimously adopted.

Whereupon, Messrs. W. H. Day and G. Adams were appointed to escort the President Elect to the Chair. The President, on taking the chair, made a very appropriate address; which was received with shouts of applause from the members of the Convention.

On motion of L. D. Taylor, Jefferson's Manual was adopted as the [guide] for the Convention.

D. Jenkins moved that the Convention appoint a business committee, consisting of one from each county represented; Whereupon the following gentlemen were selected as a business committee: John Mercer Langston, of Cuyahoga; D. Jenkins, of Franklin; Dr. C. H. Langston, of Ross; T. H. Johnson, of Greene; John Gee, of Gallia; A. Strauder, of Fairfield; J. D. Pattison, of Champaign; Thos. Brown, of Lorain; F. Wilson, of Warren; J. J. Pearce, of Eric; J. Lott, of Geauga; D. L. Moss, of Pickaway; J. P. Underwood, of Jefferson; J. Purnell, of Madison; S. Jones, of Mercer; W. H. Burnham, of Muskingum; G. W. Evans, of Pike; N. Morgan, of Clark; G. Hilton, of Morgan.

It was then moved by L. D. Taylor, that W. H. Day, of Lorain, be Chairman of the Business Committee. Mr. Day asked to be excused on account of his being expected to report the daily proceedings of the Convention for the Cleveland *True Democrat* and other papers.

J. Mercer Langston was then chosen Chairman.

On motion of Dr. C. H. Langston, a Financial Committee consisting of three, was appointed. The following gentlemen composed the said committee: C. H. Langston, W. H. Burnham and J. Booker.

The Convention then adjourned to meet at 2 o'clock P.M.

Second Session, Wednesday Afternoon.

The President in the Chair. The Minutes of the morning were read, corrected and approved.

Calls were made for someone to address the Convention.

After several calls from the audience, W. H. Day rose and made some very interesting remarks. He concluded by reading a letter from a gentleman of high standing in the State, concerning the Convention of the Colored people of Ohio.

Mr. Adams, of Champaign, made some interesting remarks also. Mr. J. Watson, of Lorain, likewise addressed the Convention at some length.

Mr. J. L. Watson, of Cuyahoga, made a lengthy speech on his *happy escape* from slavery, and the necessity of all colored men saying and doing all they can to elevate themselves and liberate the slave.

The Business Committee having returned, reported through their Chairman, J. Mercer Langston, resolutions for the consideration of the Convention.

The Committee recommended the same declaration of sentiments adopted by the last Convention.

Dr. C. H. Langston moved that the resolutions be laid on the table, and taken up, one by one and discussed; which was carried.

The first, second and third resolutions were then taken up, and indefinitely postponed.

The fourth resolution being under discussion--Mr. Poindexter said he hoped that some gentleman would convince him of the truth of the resolution. He could not favor the resolution until he heard more from gentlemen who advanced it.

Mr. W. H. Day, upon being called for, remarked that, though he was in favor of the principle set forth in the resolution, and thought it could be demonstrated to be correct, yet he came to this Convention for one principal object--the securing for the colored man a vote in the State. The resolution seemed to him to detract the attention from the great end of the Convention. He would move the indefinite postponement of it. He felt more at liberty to do this, on account of the resolution being penned by his constituents; and, being about to make the motion, he yielded the floor to D. Jenkins, who said he was in favor of the resolution.

Mr. Burnham said he thought there was no necessity for adopting such a resolution.

Mr. Divine said he would go heart and hand for the resolution; and concluded with some pithy remarks.

Mr. Poindexter said he was misunderstood; he prayed as fervently for the downfall of slavery as any man. He said his wishes should not overrule his better judgment.

Dr. C. H. Langston moved that the resolution be laid on the table; which was carried. He then moved that rules be adopted for the government of the Convention, as to the time of meeting and adjourning.

Whereupon the Convention decided to meet at 9 o'clock A.M. and adjourn at 12 o'clock M.: and meet at 2 o'clock P.M., and adjourn at 5 o'clock P.M.

The hour of adjournment having arrived, the Convention adjourned to meet at 7 o'clock P.M.

Third Session, Wednesday Evening.

The President in the Chair. Rev. Mr. Underwood read a portion of the Scriptures.

The President arose, and made some remarks.

D. Jenkins moved that the Convention take up the fourth resolution for consideration.

After a spirited discussion between Messrs. Poindexter, J. M. Langston and others, Dr. C. H. Langston offered a resolution which was adopted. He moved that the Convention take up the resolution referring to the competency of persons from a distance, to participate in the Convention.

After some discussion, it was indefinitely postponed.

Dr. C. H. Langston moved that the Convention adopt a rule not to allow any gentleman to speak more than fifteen or thirty minutes at a time on any subject; which was adopted.

The hour of adjournment having arrived, the Convention then adjourned to meet on Thursday morning at 9 o'clock A.M.

Fourth Session, Thursday Morning.

The President in the Chair. Prayer having been offered by the Rev. J. D. Pattison, the Minutes of the preceding session were read, corrected and approved.

Mr. Copeland, of Franklin, raised the question of the legality of last night's proceedings.

The President decided that the proceedings of last evening were not the legitimate business of the Convention.

Mr. Douglass took an appeal from the decision of the Chair. The decision of the Chair was not sustained.

Mr. Artis asked to be excused from serving as one of the Secretaries, which was granted, and Dr. C. H. Langston was appointed in his place.

J. Mercer Langston, Chairman of the Business Committee, proceeded to lay before the Convention business for the order of the day.

A motion was made to lay the whole on the table, and dispose of the items one by one, which was carried.

Resolution 5th was then taken up, and after some discussion, the Convention appointed a committee to draft a Constitution.

The Committee consisted of the following gentlemen: W. H. Day, L. D. Taylor and T. Brown.

On motion of Dr. C. H. Langston, the 6th resolution was then taken up. Mr. H. F. Douglass presented the following amendment:

"That each County in the State be hereby requested to employ efficient men to canvass its respective districts and towns, as may be deemed best."

The vote being taken on the amendment, it was negatived--Yeas 8, Nays 46.

The original resolution was then adopted.

The 7th, 8th, 9th and 10th resolutions were taken up and adopted.

The hour of adjournment having arrived, the Convention adjourned to meet at 2 o'clock P.M.

Fifth Session, Thursday Afternoon.

The President in the Chair. Prayer having been offered by the Rev. Mr. Stewart--

The minutes of the preceding session were read, corrected and approved.

The 18th resolution being called for, Mr. Williams made an interesting speech; and, among other things, he said he thought that the colored people of the State amounted in number to 25,000, and were abundantly able to support an organ of their own; and they would do it if it was commenced upon a proper basis.

He remarked that the colored people of Cincinnati, for instance, were not awake to their true interest; for they supported the Pro-slavery Press in that city to an extent which was evidence to him that the Cincinnati people did not have their own elevation at heart as much as they ought to have.

Mr. Jenkins, of Franklin, also spoke in favor of the resolution; referred to the advantages of a paper devoted to the interest of the colored people of Ohio. He said that Ohio, with a population of twenty thousand, *could sustain* a newspaper devoted to their interest.

Mr. Burnham said that the Convention ought to appoint an Agent to collect funds to establish a newspaper--an organ strictly devoted to the interests of the colored people of the State. He thought the *North Star* was not "*the People's*" paper, but strictly an *Eastern* paper.

Mr. Lott said he thought the paper must "go down."

Mr. Divine said he was sorry to hear gentlemen predict the downfall of the contemplated paper.

J. Mercer Langston then arose and advocated the immediate establishment of an organ devoted to the interest of the colored people. He instanced the progress of the intellectual condition of the colored people. He thought the objections urged by those gentlemen who had just left the floor, groundless. He said the growing intelligence of the colored people demanded that a paper should be established. He said that the "North Star," edited by the *immortal* Douglass, had proved recreant to the assertion of its editor, at the Cleveland National Convention. He said further, that the "North Star" was the only paper in the United States conducted by a colored person, in whose columns it is *especially* desirable for us to be noticed; and *it* fails to notice the articles of western colored men. He also said that colored men were becoming cultivated; that they were being educated; that they possessed the germ of a peculiar literature; that they had poets, statesmen, reviewers, printers and philosophers, who could fathom Baconian Philosophy and solve Newtonian Problems; and who should have an outflow--a manifestation of their genius and their talent. He thought the "Christian Herald" was not the colored people's paper, but strictly a Methodist organ. He said the intellectual attainments of the colored people of Ohio, were not inferior to any in the Union.

Dr. C. H. Langston said he did not intend making a speech; but he wished to explain the whole matter, as to the former failures of newspapers. He said that *talk* would never support a paper. He thought that our people had to many old prejudices and predilections peculiar to slavery, and they were too frequently looking up to the "white man" for every thing.

J. M. Brown remarked, that he thought the gentleman from Cuyahoga, Mr. Langston, had been personal in his remarks concerning the Methodist denomination.

Mr. Nooks said, his feelings had suffered from the remarks made by Mr. Langston, from Cuyahoga.

Dr. C. H. Langston, moved that the resolution be laid on the table, which was carried. Dr. Langston then moved that a committee of three be appointed to devise means for sustaining the lecturers.

The following gentlemen were chosen for the said committee,--viz:

> J. L. Watson,
> C. H. Langston,
> J. Jackson.

Dr. C. H. Langston then moved that the 12th resolution be taken up again. He explained the reasons why the editors engaged in publishing newspapers for the colored people had failed formerly; he thought if men would use their purses more than their lips, the newspapers *"would live."*

The resolution was then adopted; a committee of seven being appointed by the convention, to fill up the blank in the resolution, composed of the following gentlemen,--viz:

> J. Mercer Langston,
> W. H. Day,
> D. Jenkins,
> C. H. Langston,
> G. R. Williams,
> W. H. Burnham,
> Wm. Copeland.

The 13th resolution was taken up, and on a motion for its adoption, an amendment was offered by W. H. Day, to add an address to the voters, and an other to the colored people; which was adopted.

A Committee of five to prepare the addresses, was then appointed by the Convention, consisting of the following gentlemen:

> W. P. Morgan,
> J. N. Stuart,
> W. H. Day,
> F. Wilson,
> J. W. Delany.

The 14th resolution was read. Calls were made for Speakers. W. H. Day was called for, he declined; but repeated calls brought the gentleman to the stand. He referred to the privileges enjoyed by the colored people of Massachusetts, and the manner by which they were gained. He referred to the suffrage question in the State of New York, and also the benevolent action of Gerrit Smith, in making three thousand voters. He thought the privileges of the colored men in New York, were not in so imminent danger as those of Ohio.

He thought we ought to act so as to be a model of the colored people in the surrounding States; he also referred to the principles laid down in the Constitution of the U. States. He said the people of Ohio must strike the word "*white*" out of the State Constitution, if they would be consistent. He said that the colored men in his own town were able to control the elections; that men now place "*Free Soil*" over the heads of their papers, to secure patronage; concluding his remarks, he thought the signs of the times gave full evidence that there was a "good time coming." The question being put, the resolution was unanimously adopted.

A petition was offered to permit certain persons to participate, and vote in the convention. The petition was, by the President, decided to be in opposition to the standing rules of the convention. An appeal was taken from the decision of the chair; and the chair was sustained.

The 15th resolution was called up. J. W. Stuart offered a substitute.

The 16th and 17th resolutions were read and adopted.

The 18th resolution, or the subject matter of the letter of L. N. Milnor, was referred to a committee of three, composed of the following gentlemen, viz:

C. H. Langston,
Wm. Copeland,
J. Gee.

The Chairman of the business committee announced that the first resolution in series (six) would be the order of the Evening Session.

Mr. W. H. Burnham offered a preamble and resolutions, setting forth the pro-slavery character of the Methodist denomination.

Jas. Monroe Jones moved that the preamble and resolutions be indefinitely postponed. While the motion was pending, a motion was carried for an adjournment to 7 o'clock, P.M.

A song was then called for, which was responded to with cheers.

Sixth Session, Thursday Evening.

President in the chair. Prayer having been offered by the Rev. Mr. Nooks, the convention proceeded to the business of the evening, namely, the Election of Lecturers. W. Copeland nominated W. H. Day, J. M. Langston, H. F. Douglass, D. Jenkins, Dr. C. H. Langston, speakers, to canvass the State. [The Secretary cannot tell how the motion was disposed of.]

Mr. D. Jenkins moved that the convention proceed to ballot for a suitable person to address the constitutional convention.

Messrs. W. H. Day and J. Mercer Langston were candidates for this office. The vote stood as follows:

For W. H. Day, 46, J. Mercer Langston, 6, C. H. Langston, 1. Mr. Day being called for, made some pithy remarks.

It was moved that the convention proceed to ballot for six Speakers to canvass the State.

Mr. Poindexter said he wished to examine this question with great care; that an important crisis had come upon us.

The question to reconsider, being put, was carried.

It was then moved to appoint a committee of five to select Speakers to canvass the State, which was withdrawn. It was moved that J. L. Watson, W. H. Day, Dr. C. H. Langston, J. M. Langston, be speakers. Mr. Langston declined; J. M. Brown and several others declined serving. Mr. Douglass was also nominated--motion was withdrawn. Mr. Sampson P. Lewis was chosen also. Mr. Divine declined. Jas. Monroe Jones also declined, but who, on further consideration, consented to serve. The lecturers then came forward and made some remarks. J. P. Underwood was chosen as one of the Speakers.

The resolution of Mr. Burnham was then taken up; and after some discussion, in which Messrs. Jas. M. Jones, J. M. Langston, and Mr. Burnham, participated, the main question was put, for its indefinite postponement, which was carried by a large majority.

The hour having arrived for an adjournment, the convention adjourned, to meet Friday Morning, 9 o'clock, A.M.

Seventh Session, Friday Morning.

President in the chair. Prayer was offered by Mr. Underwood. The minutes of the preceding session were laid over until the committee on business, could make a report. Resolution, No.____, was taken up and adopted.

The minutes were then read, corrected and approved.

Mr. Gee moved, that the minutes stand with the exclusion of Mr. Burnham's Preamble and Resolutions.

A discussion then arose, in which J. M. Langston, and others participated. J. L. Watson said, that if the delegates looked upon the subject as he did, they would think differently. Some confusion arose, and a point of order was raised.

J. L. Watson said that gentlemen ought not to impeach the chair in the exercise of his serious convictions.

J. Mercer Langston said, he did not wish to be misrepresented; he wished to be correctly reported before the people of the State of Ohio, and the delegates of the convention. He said he opposed the Methodist E. Conference, on the ground of their not being sufficiently anti-slavery.

J. M. Brown said, he did not wish to be reported at all; all knew his views very well. He thought it unkind to speak in such terms of his denomination, (the Methodist.)

Mr. Gee, then, with the consent of the convention, withdrew his motion, provided the subject was not agitated any more; and provided the minutes stand as reported by the Secretary.

On a motion of Dr. Langston, the minutes stood as they were read.

Mr. Jenkins announced that the members of the House of Representatives, in the Ohio Legislature, had passed a resolution, granting the Hall to the convention, by a vote of 51 to 17; which was received with applause.

Resolutions No. 19 and 20, were taken up and adopted.

On a motion, a new State Central Committee was appointed, consisting of the following gentlemen,--viz:

        D. Jenkins,
        J. M. Brown,
        W. Copeland,
        L. D. Taylor,
        John Booker,
        Jas. Poindexter,
        A. M. Taylor.

The 21st and 22d resolutions were taken up and adopted.

The 23d was taken up, and after some consideration, was referred to the Rev. J. M. Brown, for revision.

The 24th and 25th were also adopted.

Mr. J. M. Brown, then came forward, and reported the 23d resolution revised; the report was received and adopted.

The hour of adjournment having arrived, the convention adjourned to meet at 2 o'clock, P.M.

Eighth Session, Friday Afternoon.

President in the chair. Prayer was offered by the Rev. Mr. Underwood.

W. H. Day proposed a resolution appointing J. M. Langston, L. D. Taylor, and J. P. Underwood, as speakers in the evening, in the Hall of the House of Representatives. Being strongly urged to withdraw the resolution, he did so.

A resolution was brought forward to appoint W. H. Day, J. L. Watson, and J. M. Langston, to speak to the members of the Legislature this evening, Jan. 11th, 1850, at 6 o'clock; which resolution was adopted.

The minutes being called for, two of the secretaries were absent, and the proceedings could not be read. The resolution in relation to an adjournment was taken up, and after discussion, it was so amended that the convention adjourned at 6 o'clock, instead of 11 o'clock.

On motion, a committee of five was appointed to receive and disburse the funds which may be collected for the men to canvass the State. Messrs. J. Poindexter, Jenkins, C. H. Langston, J. Booker, and Wm. Copeland, were appointed said committee.

The select committee of seven appointed to take into consideration, the propriety of establishing a PAPER, reported through their chairman, J. M. Langston.

The committee appointed to draft a constitution for the league, reported through their chairman, W. H. Day, which was laid on the table.

On a motion, a select committee of five was appointed to revise and print the proceedings of the convention, consisting of the following gentlemen,--viz:

> D. Jenkins,
> C. H. Langston,
> G. R. Williams,
> Wm. Copeland,
> J. Mercer Langston.

On motion of D. Jenkins, the question to print the proceedings in pamphlet form, was reconsidered. He moved to amend it by inserting the *Ohio Standard*.

Mr. Douglass said, he was opposed to printing the proceedings in the *Ohio Standard*; he wished every man in the State should read them, so that they might see that we were not insensible to the demonstrations in favor of liberty, now shaking the entire nation. He further contended, that, if they were printed in pamphlet form, they would be more durable,--he would have them handed down to posterity as a lasting memento of the struggle for our rights.

J. J. Pearce,* said that he was in favor of pamphlet form, and that he wanted the people of this State to know what we are doing for ourselves.

Mr. Yancey then moved to amend the resolution by inserting "circular form," which motion was lost.

The question on printing in pamphlet form, was carried by the casting vote of the President.

The select committee on sustaining the speakers, reported through their chairman, C. H. Langston, a plan for dividing the various parts of the State. The report being under consideration--

On a motion of W. H. Day, the words "and no longer," were stricken out; the report was then adopted.

Mr. W. H. Day reported a constitution for the government of the League, which was then taken up and adopted.

CONSTITUTION

Whereas, three millions of our brethren and sisters are yet in bonds; and Whereas in the free States, the colored man is only nominally free: and Whereas, the elevation of the colored man must depend mainly upon himself; and believing, that by union, we can better attain the liberation of our brethren in bonds, and the elevation of the colored American, half-free, we hereby agree to form ourselves into a State Society, to be governed by the following articles:

1st. This Association shall be styled, The Ohio Colored American League.

2nd. Its object exclusively shall be to forward the objects contained in the Preamble, namely, the liberation of the slave and the elevation of the colored American, half free. And, laying aside all jealousy, we will "help the cause along" to the best of our ability.

3d. Any man or woman subscribing to the principles of this League, as above expressed, shall become a member, by paying into its treasury or the treasury of its auxiliaries, annually, not less than the sum of fifty cents.

4th. County Associations or Leagues, auxiliary to this, may be formed in each county of the State, and shall be entitled to a representation in the Annual Meeting of the Association.

5th. A certain portion of the funds of each Auxiliary, shall be paid into the Treasury of this League, on or before the day of its annual meeting; otherwise, the representatives of such Auxiliary shall not be entitled to vote in said Annual Meeting.

6th. The officers of this League shall be a President, two Vice Presidents, a Recording Secretary, Corresponding Secretary, and Treasurer, who, with seven chosen from the remaining members, shall constitute the Executive Committee, and shall all hold their offices one year, or until others are chosen.

7th. The duties of the President, Vice President, Secretaries and Treasurer, shall be those usually attaching to their respective titles, the Treasurer giving bonds in the sum of $500. The duties of the Executive Committee shall be, in the interim of the meetings of the League, to take charge of the particular and general interests of the League, be wide awake to promote them, either by helping the fugitive or otherwise--by encouraging or discouraging lecturers in the State, and to perform any duties which this League may reasonably and constitutionally impose upon them.

8th. The Annual Meetings of this League, for the election of officers, hearing the annual report of the Executive Committee and Treasurer, and transacting business for the Association, shall be held on the last Wednesday of October in each year.

9th. All Agents and Lecturers in the service of this League, shall be employed and directed in their labors, by the Executive Committee; and to them alone shall be accountable.

10th. Whenever undue sectional influences, in the doings of this League, are apprehended by any ten of its members, any number of members from any county shall be entitled to no greater number of votes than the number of representatives of such county in the State Legislature.

11th. This Constitution may be altered or amended, by a vote of two-thirds of the members present at the Annual Meeting.

The Officers of the League were then elected, which were as follows:

J. L. Watson, *President*.
J. Watson, *Vice President*.
Lewis Adams,   *do*.
John Mercer Langston, *Recording Secretary*.
William H. Day, *Corresponding Secretary*.
John Gee, *Treasurer*.
J. W. Stuart,
G. R. Williams,   *Executive Committee*.

The following gentlemen, appointed to receive the funds for Lecturers, were then voted a part of the Executive Committee of the Colored American League:

J. Poindexter, L. D. Taylor, D. Jenkins, C. H. Langston, and John Booker.

Mr. William H. Day informed the Convention that he was now in the employ of the "Oberlin Colored American League," and would have to be governed to a great extent by their decision, as to where he should go, and how long he should occupy the field. He stated this to avoid being misapprehended; but he thought the League for which he was acting would coincide in the decision and recommendation of the Convention.

A Letter was received from Mrs. Scurry. It was moved that it be inserted in the minutes of the Convention.

Mr. G. R. Williams moved that the resolution in relation to adjournment, be reconsidered, which was carried.

On motion, the Convention adjourned to meet in the Hall of the House of Representatives, at 7 o'clock, to listen to speeches from the gentlemen appointed for that occasion--Messrs, Day, Watson and Langston.

The Convention adjourned to meet on Saturday morning, at nine o'clock A.M.

Ninth Session, Saturday Morning.

The Convention met pursuant to adjournment. The President in the Chair. Prayer was offered by Elder Jones.

The reading of the Minutes of the preceding session was omitted.

The subject of the Press came up, and gentlemen were called on to subscribe what they would pay for the support of the paper.

A committee of one from each county, was appointed to make arrangements for the speakers, as they travelled through the various counties.

H. F. Douglass was appointed for Cuyahoga County, J. L. Watson for Lorain County. Afterwards it was agreed to leave the appointment to the State Central Committee.

A letter was then read from Henry Hurd, the substance of which was ordered to be inserted in the minutes of the Convention.

A motion was made that the Secretaries prepare the minutes for publication in the *Ohio Standard*; which was adopted.

A letter was read from Justin Holland, the substance of which was' ordered to be inserted in the minutes of the Convention.

On motion, D. Jenkins was appointed to ascertain the cost of publishing the proceeddings. Mr. Jenkins, having made an inquiry concerning the cost, said that the amount would be about thirty dollars, if no larger as to size and number of copies (500) than the proceedings of the last Convention.

The Financial Committee reported that they had collected $33.58 cents.

The report was received and adopted.

The Committee appointed to take into consideration L. W. Minor's letter, reported through their chairman, C. H. Langston, that, should there be any moneys left or received, after printing the proceedings of the Convention, the said money should be applied to the liquidating of the said claim.

Mr. Nichols, of Franklin, arose on permission of the Convention, and stated that there was no necessity of the colored people establishing an independent paper at this time, as the Editors of the *Ohio Standard* were willing to devote a part of their columns to the interest of the colored people of the State.

Mr. C. H. Langston asked, if the Editors were willing to change the name, so as to read, "Ohio Standard and Voice of the Oppressed?"

Mr. Nichols said he thought they would let that or any other name be over the columns devoted to their interest.

The report was adopted.

The Ladies attending the Convention proposed to defray the expenses of the house for the sitting of the Convention.

Whereupon, W. H. Day moved that the Convention tender their sincere thanks to them for their geniune patriotism.

A vote of thanks was also tendered to the Trustees of the A.M.E. Church.

L. D. Taylor then moved that the committee on the Press be instructed to confer with the Editors of the *Ohio Standard*, and make such arrangements as they may deem best; which was adopted.

The Convention having resolved itself into a Committee of the Whole, J. M. Langston in the Chair; the committee, after a few minutes sitting, arose and reported that the gentlemen on the old statistical committee were unable to report.

Whereupon a motion was then made that the same committee act for the ensuing year.

The following gentlemen were added to the old list:

Rev. Samuel Jones, *of Mercer County*.
John Jackson, *of Hamilton County*.
J. Purnell, *of Madison County*.
H. Ford, *of Champaign County*.
F. Wilson, *of Warren County*.
D. Roberts, *of Seneca County*.
T. Crawford, *of Delaware County*.

Dr. C. H. Langston offered the form of a petition to be presented to the Legislature; which was adopted.

It was voted to fill the blank, as to Superintendent for the Colored Schools, with the name of William H. Day.

The Convention then adjourned *sine die*.

Resolutions

The resolutions are not placed in the order in which they were acted upon, but more according to the subjects contemplated in each.

Declaration of Sentiments

Whereas, we the free colored people of the State of Ohio, are cursed by the blighting influence of oppression in this professedly free State, to which many of us have fled for refuge and protection; and whereas, the history of the political world, as well as the history of nations, clearly shows, that "who would be free, himself must strike the blow;" and whereas, both the old and new worlds are shaken throughout their length and breadth, by the uprising of oppressed millions who are erecting firm foundations and stupendous platforms, on which they may unitedly battle for that liberty which God has benignedly given to all his creatures, and which will be wrested from them only by vampire despots; therefore,

Resolved, That we adopt the following as our Declaration of sentiments, as to State and National policy, and in harmony with these we will ever fight, until our rights are regained. It is our purpose,

I. To sternly resist, by all the means which the God of Nations has placed in our power, every form of oppression or proscription attempted to be imposed upon us, in consequence of our condition or color.

II. To acknowledge no enactment honored with the name of law, as binding upon us, the object of which is in any way to curtail the natural rights of man.

III. To give our earnest attention to the universal education of our people.

IV. To sustain the cause of Temperance in our midst, and advocate the formation of societies for its promotion.

V. To leave what are called menial occupations, and aspire to mechanical, agricultural, and professional pursuits.

VI. To respect and love that, as the religion of Jesus Christ, and that alone, which in its practical bearings, is not excitement merely, but that which loves God, loves humanity, and thereby preaches deliverance to the captive, the opening of the prison-doors to them that are bound, and teaches us to do unto others as we would have them to do to us.

Resolutions

Resolved, 1. That all persons present during the Session of this convention, be hereby requested to participate in the discussion of the questions which may come before the convention.

Resolved, 2. That it is the duty of every colored man, to do every thing in his power, to secure to himself and brethren, their political rights.

Resolved, 3. That we re-affirm the great and unalterable doctrine, promulgated by the State convention of last winter, that we are men, and as such are entitled to all the privileges and immunities granted to other men, and that we will *fight and fight ever* until these privileges are *granted* to us.

Resolved, 4. That we hail the signs of the times, as clearly indicating the downfall of that monstrosity, and sum of all villainies, American Slavery; [amended as follows, by Dr. C. H. Langston.]

Resolved, That the signs of the times indicate, that slaveholders and their abettors, are determined at all hazards, to perpetuate forever, that monstrosity, "the sum of all villainies," American Slavery: regardless of the cries of their outraged victims or the agitations of christians and philanthropists.

Whereas, our 3,000,000 brethren and sisters are yet in bonds; and Whereas, in the Free States the colored man is only nominally free; and Whereas, the elevation of the colored man must depend mainly upon himself; Therefore--

Resolved, 5, That, for the sake of *united effort* in this respect, the business committee would recommend the formation of a State society for these ends alone, and the appointment, immediately, of a special committee, to draft for it a Constitution.

Whereas, the Elective Franchise is a right of inestimable value, and a liberty that the citizens of all well regulated governments should enjoy and cherish; and Whereas, it is of the highest importance that every one should be prompt and energetic in the acquirement and defense of all such natural and inalienable rights; and, Whereas, we are taxed without representation, and deprived without just cause, of enfranchisement, which is the birthright of humanity; and, Whereas, a Convention for amending the Constitution of the State is to be holden during the ensuing year; and believing that, by vigorous and energetic action, we may induce the Convention to alter the Constitution in such a manner as to give to all citizens of the State without discrimination, this heaven bestowed and inalienable right; and, Whereas, we believe that the best way, in which this result may be brought about, is by agitating the public mind in regard to our claims to all rights in common with other citizens, *and especially to the right of suffrage*; Therefore--

Resolved, 6. That we appoint and support six able and intelligent lecturers, whose duty it shall be to canvass the State forthwith, laying before the people the justice and propriety of securing to us our just and equitable right to vote as do other men according to their wishes and their choice.

Resolved, 7. That we instruct our lecturers to oppose before the electors of the State, the proposition to submit in a separate clause, the elective franchise, to the consideration and disposal of the people; unless as a last trial for the right we claim.

Resolved, 8. That the lecturers be employed until the Delegates to the Constitutional Convention be nominated and elected.

Resolved, 9. That a committee of three be appointed to consider and lay before the Convention a plan whereby the charges and expenses of the lecturers may be settled and defrayed.

Resolved, 10. That the Convention select a Speaker to address the Constitutional Convention touching the interests and claims of the colored people of the State.

Resolved, 11. That we deem the elective franchise and its associate privileges, of the highest importance to our happiness, and future prosperity, and our lawful birthright under the established principles of freedom, which are the true foundation of law in our common country, and that we will cordially co-operate in such systematic counsel and action as shall be deemed best suited to their attainment and full enjoyment.

Resolved, 12. That the Convention appoint a committee of seven to consider the propriety of establishing a paper devoted to the interests and claims of the colored people of the State, and that said committee, if they see fit, suggest a plan for its establishment and support.

Resolved, 13. That the Convention appoint a committee of five to prepare addresses to the voters and colored people of the State.

Whereas, there is no object so dear to a freeman as the right of suffrage, and that no man can be free without it; therefore,

Resolved, 14. That this Convention will make *that* the permanent object of their deliberations, and that they will show to the people of Ohio that they are capable of appreciating and sustaining that right.

Resolved, 15. That there be appointed by this Convention one man in every county to take the number of voters in his county, to make arrangements for public meetings, and to see that a fair tax is laid upon and paid by the people for the support of delegates to their Conventions; and that it be recommended to every community that they do what they can to make it obligatory upon every person who votes for a delegate, to help defray his expenses.

Resolved, 16. That the delegates be instructed to urge upon the people in their respective counties the propriety and necessity of forming auxiliaries to the Colored American League of this State; that, by that means they may secure a *union* politically and socially, among the oppressed of the State.

Resolved, 17. That the Convention recommend to our people not to employ incompetent teachers, nor such as cannot bear examination as district school teachers, nor such as do not sutain a good moral character.

Resolved, 18. That the merits of the letter of L. W. Miner to J. Mercer Langston, be considered by this Convention.

Resolved, 19. That a committee of one be appointed to confer with our friends in regard to obtaining the House of Representatives, in which to hold our Anti-Slavery meeting; and further, that D. Jenkins, Esq., constitute said committee.

Resolved, 20. That we recommend to our brethren throughout the State, the adoption of some plan by which to communicate with each other, and thus interest all in promoting a more complete system of education--obtaining a more solid and substantial acknowledgment of our political rights--and such measures as shall insure more rapidly the social elevation and civil freedom of our people.

Resolved, 21. That the delegates of this convention and others be requested to circulate in their respective counties a petition, asking for the abolition of the remaining *laws* of the State, making *distinction* on account of color--and that this petition be forwarded to the Legislature at its next session.

Resolved, 22. That the *Ohio Standard* of this City, is worthy the confidence, and that it should receive the encouragement and support of the colored citizens of Ohio, and of the Union.

Resolved, 23. That the Convention petition the Legislature to appoint a Superintendent of the colored schools of the State, and that we recommend W. H. Day, as the person.

Resolved, 24. That we tender our thanks to the Legislature of last winter, for what they did in repealing those odious Black Laws, that existed against us, and we pray their successors that they wipe out the remnant.

MR. W. H. BURNHAM'S PREAMBLE AND RESOLUTION

Whereas, The Methodist Conference of the colored Church has passed silently over the subject of American Slavery, and has by that means given sanction to an institution that tramples on the necks and liberties of three millions of human beings, and these very beings have the same hopes and fears, and are identified with these men who are saying nothing in behalf of their cause, by color and suffering, prejudice and wrong; and whereas, according to the words of the exponents of their faith and order, they are thus silent in order that they may extend their connection into Slave States, and thus have power over, and get money from the poor, worn, and heart broken slave; in this *unchristian* and *cruel* operation, they are keeping the slave from purchasing his liberty, and tightening the chain on his posterity yet unborn; and whereas they have established a newspaper entitled the *Christian Herald*, edited by one Rev. A. R. Green, which they deem too sacred to admit the subject of human rights in its columns, or they are too mean, pro-slavery, and time serving, to come up to the work and thus assist in "loosing the bands of *wickedness*, undoing the heavy *burthens*, and letting the oppressed go *free*, and breaking every *yoke*;" and whereas, we believe that this convention, being the assembled representatives of the colored people of the State, should speak out against all such monstrous *evils*; Therefore--

Resolved, That we recommend to the annual Ohio Conference, of colored people, to pass resolutions defining their position on the subject of slavery; and we further recommend that they enquire into the conduct of said A. R. Green, in prohibiting the discussion of slavery in his paper, and see if he acts in accordance with the instructions received at the general conference; and by so doing, they will show themselves on the side of *liberty*, and their oppressed and downtrodden brethren.

Report

The committee appointed to devise a plan for establishing a paper in the State in behalf of the colored people, having had the same under consideration; would respectfully report, as follows:--

That in their judgment, the peculiar condition of the colored people of the State imperiously demands that we establish such an organ, that we may talk to each other, and to the world.

We are brought to this conclusion from the following considerations:--

We are scattered over so large a territory, and while we have increasingly important interests, we have not a single paper of our own west of New York, and in those there, we do not consider ourselves properly represented, neither can we be fully represented in the papers edited at the west by our white friends, for we have interests peculiar to ourselves. This is our condition. But the establishment of a paper must depend upon the available means to sustain it. Among the 25,000 colored persons in the State, there certainly are sufficient to give it a handsome support, to say nothing of the thousands of our white friends in the State, who stand ready to-day to welcome such a periodical. In this connection, we would not forget the expected support of our western *brethren*, whose interests, like ours, need to be advocated.

Your committee would therefore respectfully recommend the adoption of the following plan for the establishment and support of a paper:

I. To find out from each person present interested, how much he or she will pledge, if it be needed to support the paper one year.

II. The appointment of a committee of nine from those who pledge money, the business of which committee shall be to manage the publishing and all the financial concerns of the paper.

III. The issuing immediately of a prospectus, to be circulated by the lecturers upon the suffrage question, for subscriptions, payable upon the receipt of the first number of the paper.

IV. Columbus, Franklin County, as the place for issuing the paper.

V. William H. Day, and Dr. C. H. Langston, Editors.

VI. The principles of the paper shall be the advocacy of the rights of the colored man, urging his liberty, and his moral, mental, social and political elevation.

VII. The name, "Voice of the Opressed."[2]

All which is respectfully submitted.

        J. M. Langston,
        Wm. H. Day,
        Wm. Copeland,
        Wm. H. Burnham,
        David Jenkins,
        Geo. R. Williams,
        Dr. C. H. Langston.

LETTER FROM JUSTIN HOLLAND

        Cleveland, Ohio, Jan. 5th, 1850.

Gentlemen of the Convention:--Dr. J. McCune Smith delivered an address to the members of the Legislature of New York, on the subject of removing the property qualifications, which applied to colored persons. So great was the array of statistics and facts, so conclusive were his arguments and deductions, and so successfully were they presented, that at the close, the meeting unanimously adopted four resolutions, the second of which reads as follows:

"*Resolved,* That the charge of ignorance which was urged in the convention of '27, as a reason to deprive a large class of our citizens of the privileges of the elective franchise is no longer tolerable; as their advancement in the arts and sciences, in intellectual and moral culture, does abundantly testify."

It seems to me, that something of this sort would do us good, if properly carried out. Let us by an overwhelming show of facts, deprive the trading politicians of even a decent excuse for further opposing our enfranchisement. Again sirs, the question of our enfranchisement, I think, should be settled by the convention to revise the Constitution. The proposition to submit it, in a separate clause to the people, no doubt originated in a desire to escape all odium that might arise from vindicating a measure that is daily receiving the condemnation of an enlarging number of citizens of the State. Would it not be well, sirs, to send men well qualified, to that convention--men having a knowledge of our history, furnished with ample statistics of our progress and present condition, to hold meetings between its sessions, and lay before the members of that convention our claims to political equality? I have but little faith in the honor and justice of the masses when they come to decide a question like this for us, swayed by their prejudices and the exaggerations of designing demagogues. Therefore I think every effort should be made to have it settled in the convention. The future quiet and progress of the State require it.

    Justin Holland.

LETTER FROM H. HURD

Carthagena, Mercer County,
Near New Bremen, Auglaize County, Jan. 1, 1850.

Gentlemen of the Convention: There are small hands as well as great ones which have to do with this subject, [the welfare of the colored people,] and among them, you are assembled to deliberate. With me it appears that we should be deliberative, mild and manly, in our decisions. The opinions of others must be respected. Our weapons should be inoffensive and our conclusions impartial, while we should vigorously prosecute them. We are a part of the citizens of Ohio, to the number of some twenty thousand, and our condition, though greatly bettered from what it was, is yet one of the worst for freemen; though the burthen has been removed to some extent; yet the yoke is not broken. The repeal of the Black Laws has not removed all our oppressions; yet we must approve of what is done, and appreciate the privileges we have, by properly enjoying them, while we petition the Authorities for equal laws in every respect. The enslavement of our colored brethren in the South, and the long oppression of the colored freemen of the North, may have (for reasons which we cannot comprehend!) induced a portion of those who now form the sovereignty, to draw such a conclusion as they allege, that we cannot rightly exercise the elective franchise or appreciate full political rights! This may answer as an excuse for them; but, let it be so or not; the great strides made, and which are still making, by the oppressed of all Europe, for Liberty, warn us not to be indolent, while the deep and goading abuses imposed on three millions of colored Americans in the South, with the prejudicial stigma it reflects upon us, imperatively demand of us to arise and plead our own cause, and prove to the oppressors that they are wrong. I believe that we have the ability, as it is our duty, and the mass must help the few who are willing to breast the storm. Guided by truth and shielded with facts, we must canvass the State and appeal to the philanthropy and calm reason of the people. Let us appeal to the sense of the Electors of Ohio, and make known our wants as citizens; and their votes will answer the question. Did not God make all the nations of the earth of one blood? Did not our Savior declare "all brethren?" Should we be then as one people? Surely if any person denies these things, he rejects the word of God and rebels against his designs. Will the Christian professors and republicans of Ohio do this? I hope not; but time will prove the truth. The Declaration of American Independence heralds to the world that "All men are born free and equal;" and the Constitution of Ohio does the same, and farther proclaims the rights of man.

When we ask for equal political rights, we know that God and Nature are with us. Then let us be honest in our advocacy, calm in our address, and unchangeable in our purpose.

Will any man of sense pretend to say that the colored freemen of Ohio cannot vote for officers as well as the German and Irish emigrants who never read the Constitution or Laws of the State? Can we not exercise our judgments as correctly as nine-tenths of the voters of Ohio? No one with ordinary sagacity can doubt it. We are not to be held in contempt because we are yellow or black, or because our condition may not be in every respect as it should be. Did not God make our colors? And did not our white brethren enslave our fathers and mothers, whom they bought and sold like the cattle of the fields? There are men, apparently in respectable standing, who have, through their blind prejudice, concocted a plan, by which they are in hopes to exile a large number of the colored citizens of this country, in the form of colonization. We should look upon such men as our worst enemies. For under a pretense of friendship for the colored people, they expect to accomplish their hellish intentions. "They are wolves in sheep's clothing." I claim that we are native Americans; and in America I intend to remain--equal laws, or no laws. Here we are, and here let us remain and plead our cause for justice.

I am your obedient servant,
Henry Hurd.

Copy in the Harvard University Library.

REFERENCE NOTES

1. H. Ford Douglass (1832-?) was a runaway slave who became a leading abolitionist orator in the Midwest. For a time he lent his voice to the cause of Negro emigration, on the American continent or elsewhere, owing to the harsh discrimination and proscription of his people. In 1853, Douglass edited the *Provincial Freeman*, a newspaper which appeared in Windsor, Canada West.

During the election campaign of 1860, he became an outspoken critic of the views and politics of Abraham Lincoln, believing him a supporter of white supremacy and an opponent of equality for blacks. With the outbreak of the war, however, Douglass, now a captain, along with Lieutenant W. D. Matthews, led an independent battery of black troops at Lawrence, Kansas. Like Frederick Douglass, H. Ford Douglass spelled his name with a double s. See, for example, Robert L. Harris, Jr., "H. Ford Douglas: Afro-American Antislavery Emigrationist," *Journal of Negro History*, LXII (July 1977), 217-234. Harris, as can be observed in the above article, used only a single s.

2. The paper in question was called the *Aliened American*, established in 1853 by William Howard Day and published in Cleveland.

MINUTES OF THE STATE CONVENTION, OF THE COLORED CITIZENS OF OHIO,
CONVENED AT COLUMBUS,
JAN. 15th, 16th, 17th AND 18th, 1851

CONVENTION OF THE COLORED CITIZENS OF OHIO

First Session--Wednesday Morning, Columbus, January 15, 1851.
The Convention of the Colored Citizens of the State of Ohio, Pursuant to the call of the State Central Committee, met in the City of Columbus, in the Second Baptist Church, at 10 o'clock A.M. The convention was called to order, by the Chairman of the State Central Committee, after which, on motion, L. D. Taylor Esq., of Franklin county, was appointed Chairman pro tem. By motion of Dr. C. H. Langston of Franklin county, W. H. Burnham, of Coshocton county, was appointed Secretary pro tem.
Prayer having been offered by the Rev. T. N. Stewart, the Convention proceeded to the enrolling of the names of the Delegates. The following gentlemen were present, to represent their respective counties.
Cuyahoga county--H. Ford Douglass.
Champaign county--H. H. Ford.
Ross county--J. Mercer Langston.
Jackson county--C. A. Yancy, Rev. T. N. Stewart.
Madison county--J. Purnell.
Clark county--Wm. Roberts, Wm. Lewis, Wm. Hope, Wm. P. Morgan.
Pickaway county--G. Stanup, Wm. Jackson.
Coshocton county--W. Hurst Burnham.
Franklin county--A. Barrett, John Booker, James Poindexter, L. D. Taylor, John Brown, D. Jenkins, J. Freeland, J. H. Johnson, John T. Ward, C. H. Langston.
Montgomery county--James Dunlap.
Logan county--Sterling Heathcock, William Walden.
Shelby county--J. Berde.
Muskingum county--J. McCarter Simpson.
Pike county--Thomas Haines.
Licking county--Jerome Stebot.
Seneca county--Felix Whitsill, Darius Roberts.
Fayette county--Mills Melton.
Lorain county--W. Howard Day.
Hamilton county--Joseph Henry Perkins, John I. Gaines, John Jackson, Lawrence W. Miner.
On motion of D. Jenkins Esq., of Franklin county, a committee of five were appointed on organization.
Committee,--Dr. Charles H. Langston, Charles A. Yancy Esq., H. Ford Douglass Esq., H. H. Ford and John Booker.
During the absence of the committee on organization, the Rev. T. N. Stewart, of Jackson and Gallia counties, entertained the Convention with a speech, followed by some remarks by the Rev. J. McCarter Simpson of Muskingum

county, during which time the committee on organization being ready to report, the gentleman gave way, the report was as follows:

For President, David Jenkins of Franklin county; for Vice Presidents, J. Mercer Langston of Ross, H. F. Douglass of Cuyahoga, H. H. Ford of Champaign, Wm. Roberts of Clark; for Secretaries, W. Hurst Burnham, Charles H. Langston; for Chaplain T. N. Stewart.

The President on taking the chair, spoke as follows:

"Gentlemen of the Convention, the honor you have conferred upon me is undeserved, and never before having the privilege, of occupying a position so responsible in your deliberations, I shall look to you for support in the faithful discharge of the arduous duty devolving on me, as President of this Convention. The object of this Convention, has already been stated by gentlemen who preceeded me, and it only remains for me to thank you for this token of your approbation.

"I have been battling for the last ten years in this State, for the attainment of the elective franchise, with what success I leave you to judge. I only claim for myself sincerity of purpose, the Emancipation of the Slave, and the Elevation of the Colored American, half free, has been the loftiest aspirations of my heart. For the attainment of this object, I have ever strove to be at my post, ready to march in any direction to meet a subtle foe. It is true that the 'Aldebarian of our hope,' is obscured and 'may not shine upon us for many days,' yet success is certain and victory sure, let us put our trust in him,

> Whose cause is ours,
> In conflict with unholy powers,
> We'll grasp the weapons he has given,
> The light, and truth, and love of Heaven.

"Gentlemen, again thanking you for the honor you have done me, I resume my seat."

On motion of L. D. Taylor, a committee of five were appointed, to report business for the Convention. The committee consisted of J. McCarter Simpson, chairman, L. D. Taylor, H. Ford Douglass, Wm. P. Morgan, and Sterling Heathcock.

On motion, a committee of three were appointed, on finance: John Booker, Chairman, Wm. Hope, H. H. Ford.

It was on motion of Doct. C. H. Langston, agreed that the Convention meet at 9 o'clock, take a recess at 12 M., re-assembling at half past 3 P.M., and adjourning at 5 P.M.

On motion it was resolved that Hamilton Campbell be admitted to a seat in the Convention, for the purpose of taking a report of the proceedings of the Convention, for publication in the daily papers of the city. Carried.

J. McCarter Simpson offered a resolution, that a committee of five be appointed to prepare anti-slavery music, for the opening and closing of each session of the Convention.

On motion of J. Mercer Langston, on the adoption of the above resolution, it was amended as follows, that J. McC. Simpson prepare music for the Convention. Carried.

On motion of Mr. Simpson, it was resolved that persons present from counties not represented and those who have been regularly delegated and have their credentials, shall constitute this Convention.

While the above was pending, the hour of 12 o'clock, M., arrived, and the session closed.

Afternoon Session.

The Convention met pursuant to adjournment. The President in the Chair. Prayer by the Chaplain. The question was on the adoption of Mr. Simpson's resolution.

After a full discussion it was unanimously adopted.

The Chairman of the business committee reported a preamble and resolutions.

On motion of C. A. Yancy, they were laid on the table to be taken up resolution by resolution.

On motion of H. F. Douglass it was resolved that the Convention hold evening sessions.

On motion of Doct. C. H. Langston, it was resolved that the members of this Convention be allowed to speak only twice to any one question, nor more than ten minutes each time, unless with the consent of the Convention.

Their being no question pending before the Convention the preamble and first resolution were called up.

And on motion of J. T. Ward, of Franklin, the preamble and first resolution was referred to a select committee on one, and Rev. James Poindexter appointed said committee.

The second resolution was then taken up, and on motion of L. D. Taylor, of Franklin, was referred to a select committee of one--Dr. C. H. Langston constituting the same.

The third resolution was taken up and adopted.

The 4th resolution, on motion of J. Mercer Langston, Esq., was made the order of the day for to-morrow, Jan. 16th, 1851.

On motion the 5th resolution was taken up and adopted.

On motion the 6th resolution was taken up, and during its consideration the hour of 5 o'clock P.M., having arrived, the session closed.

Evening Session.

The Convention met pursuant to adjournment. The first Vice President in the Chair. The 6th resolution was taken up and discussed, and was amended by motion of C. A. Yancy, as follows: That we strike out all after the word Resolved, and insert the following: That we hold it to be the imperative duty of every delegate who represents the people in our annual Conventions, to bring a full report of all the statistics in the district which he represents. Carried.

The 7th resolution was then taken up and adopted.

The 8th resolution was then taken up, and while it was pending, J. Mercer Langston offered a resolution as a substitute; and while it was pending, on motion of C. A. Yancy, the resolution and substitute were laid on the table.

The 9th resolution was then taken up, and while under consideration, Mr. Barrett, of Franklin, moved to amend as follows--That there be an agent in each Congressional District.

The 10th resolution was then taken up, and after being amended by the insertion of the word "American," was adopted unanimously.

The 11th resolution was indefinitely postponed.

The 12th resolution was taken up and carried.

The 13th resolution was then taken up and adopted.

On motion, the evening session closed by singing the song composed by J. McC. Simpson, entitled that "Liberia is not the place for me."

Morning Session, Columbus, Jan. 16th, 1851.

Convention met pursuant to adjournment. President in the Chair. Anti-slavery song by the Rev. J. McC Simpson. Prayer by Mr. William Hope. In the absence of the Secretary's report of the last meeting, the Convention proceeded to business.

On motion of Chas. A. Yancy, it was resolved that all persons from a distance have all the privileges of the Convention except that of voting.

On motion of Doct. C. H. Langston, it was resolved that no preceding Convention has any power to say who shall or shall not be delegates in a subsequent Convention, who are not elected delegates, which was referred to a select committee of one, L. D. Tayor constituting said committee.

The chairman of the business committee reported sundry resolutions--15th, 16th, 17th, 18th, and 19th.

Resolution No. 4, being the order of the day, was then taken up. W. Howard Day was then called on, but excused himself upon the ground of being disinclined to speak under existing circumstances.

After repeated calls, J. Mercer Langston spoke as follows:

"Mr. President and Gentlemen of the Convention!--No enactment ever given birth to by the American Congress has created so much dissatisfaction and excitement, as the Fugitive Slave Law of 1850. This is not to be wondered at when we remember that mankind are not entirely divested of their humanity, and that this enactment possesses neither the form nor the essence of true law, that it is a hideous deformity in the *garb* of law. Blackstone has justly recorded that real law commands what is right, and prohibits what is wrong. This enactment--unworthy the name of law--reverses this definition, by *prohibiting* what is *right,* and *commanding* what is *wrong.* Such is the outrage of this abomination of all abominations, upon the just and universally admitted principles of the common law. But it does not stop here. By it all the great bulwarks of Liberty are stricken down. It kills alike, the true spirit of the American Declaration of Independence, the Constitution, and the palladium of our liberties. It is unconstitutional for the following considerations:--It strips man of his manhood and liberty upon an ex parte trial; sets aside the constitutional guarantee of the writ of *Habeas Corpus,* which, under the constitution, can never be suspended, except in cases of rebellion or invasion; declares that the decision of the commissioner, the lowest judicial officer known to the law, upon the matter of personal liberty--the gravest subject that can be submitted to any tribunal, shall be final and conclusive; holds out a bribe in the shape of double fees, for a decree contrary to liberty and in favor of Human Slavery; forbids any enquiry into the facts of the case by confining it to the question of personal identity. Thus the law strikes down all the shields of liberty, by aiming to make a local crime a national sin.

On motion of Doct. C. H. Langston, the resolution was amended as follows: that a committee of three be appointed, to draft a petition to Congress, asking the unconditional repeal of said law, after which the resolution, as amended, was unanimously adopted.

The 14th resolution was taken up, considered, and adopted.

The 15th resolution was adopted.

The 16th resolution was adopted.

The 17th resolution was then taken up, and while pending, Mr. C. A. Yancy arose, and remarked as follows:

"Mr. Chairman:--I am constrained to oppose the resolution now before us, from the fact that I believe it will have a tendency to disunite the efforts of the colored people of this State. The resolution declares that we shall not countenance, support, or associate with any person, society, or church, unless we are satisfied that they are purely anti-slavery. Now, Mr. Chairman, I am not satisfied that *this Convention* is purely anti-slavery, notwithstanding it is composed of the literati of the colored men of the State, who should be purely anti-slavery. The majority may be, but I don't believe that it is purely so. Again: Whenever you interfere with the Church, you scatter discord, strife, and disunion among our people. So I think it inexpedient to pass such a resolution. Not because I think there is any society or church to sacred or profane for me to strike at if it restricts my liberties. Yet I think that the language of that resolution is too tenacious, and will fail to effect the object which it seems to aim at."

Thos. Harris, of Pike, was opposed.

J. H. Johnson, of Franklin was in favor of the passage of the resolution.

Mr. Douglass of Cuyahoga, offered the following amendment, "nor the Constitution of the United States."

Mr. Chas. H. Langston offered the following as a substitute for the whole:

Resolved, That we will not support any Church, unless we are convinced that it is anti-slavery.

In support of which he offered the following remarks: He did not think that the discussion of the resolution would tend to divide people--he wished it to be fully discussed. He did not think the church matters too sacred to be talked of. It does the church great injustice for gentlemen to say, that its character cannot be brought under review without creating hard feelings and divisions. If the Church possess any good, investigation will only tend to increase its brightness. I wish the Church separated from all other matters, and stand or fall upon its own merits. It has now reached its eighteen-hundredth year, and is certainly able to stand alone. I hope therefore the amendment will prevail.

The hour of 12 o'clock having arrived, the Convention took a recess.

Afternoon Session.

President in the Chair. Prayer by the Rev. J. McC. Simpson. The Chairman of the business committee reported 21, 22, 23, 24, and 25, resolutions.

On motion of C. A. Yancy, the resolutions reported by the committee were laid on the table, to be taken up one by one.

J. McC. Simpson presented from the Rev. E. Davis, of the A.M.E. Church, a petition asking the Convention to dispense with the evening sessions, and come up to the help of the Lord against the mighty. Petition referred to H. Ford Douglass, committee of one.

The 17th resolution was taken up being laid on the table by adjournment. H. Ford Douglass moved that the resolution be made the special order of the evening. Lost. The substitute of C. H. Langston was then discussed, and on motion of C. A. Yancy, the substitute was amended by putting before the word "church," "society." Mr. Taylor moved to amend the amendment, which was as follows: "That we do not allow any pro-slavery ministers to officiate in our churches." Mr. Yancy, on leave, withdrew his amendment, with the understanding that he would offer a separate resolution in reference to the societies.

While the motion was pending the yeas and nays being called, for, the vote stood yeas 28, nays 11.

On motion of H. Ford Douglass, That it is the opinion of this Convention, that no colored man can consistently vote under the United States Constitution, John Brown, of Franklin, moved its indefinite postponement, whereupon, Mr. H. F. Douglass arose, and made the following remarks:

Mr. Chairman--I am in favor of the adoption of the rsolutions. I hold, sir, that the Constitution of the United States is pro-slavery, considered so by those who framed it, and construed to that end ever since its adoption. It is well known that in 1787, in the Convention that framed the Constitution, there was considerable discussion on the subject of slavery. South Carolina and Georgia refused to come into the Union, without the Convention would allow the continuation of the Slave Trade for twenty years. According to the demands of these two States, the Convention submitted to that guilty contract, and declared that the Slave Trade should not be prohibited prior to 1808. Here we see them engrafting into the Constitution, a clause legalizing and protecting one of the vilest systems of wrong ever invented by the cupidity and avarice of man. And by virtue of that agreement, our citizens went to the shores of Africa, and there seized upon the rude barbarian, as he strolled unconscious of impending danger, amid his native forests, as free as the winds that beat on his native shores. Here, we see them dragging these bleeding victims to the slave ship by virtue of that instrument, compelling them to endure all the horrors of the "middle passage," until they arrived at this asylum of western Liberty, where they were doomed to perpetual chains. Now, I hold, in view of this fact, no colored man can consistently vote under the United States Constitution. That instrument also provides for the return of fugitive slaves. And, sir, one of the greatest lights now adorning the galxy of American Literature, declares that the "Fugitive Law" is in accordance with that stipulation;--a law unequaled in the worst days of Roman despotism, and unparalleled in the annals of heathen jurisprudence. You might search the pages of history in vain, to find a more striking exemplification of the compound of all villainies! It shrouds our country in blackness; every green spot in nature, is blighted and blasted by that withering Upas. Every monument of national greatness, erected to commemorate the virtuous and the good, whether its foundation rests upon the hallowed repositories that contain the ashes of the first martyrs in the cause of American Liberty, or lifts itself in solemn and majestic grandeur, from that sacred spot where the first great battle of the Revolution was fought, no matter how sacred the soil, whether fertilized by the blood of a Warren,[1] or signalized by the brilliant and daring feats of Marion![2] We are all, according to Congressional enactments, involved in the horrible system of human bondage; compelled, sir, by virtue of that instrument, to assist in the black and disgraceful avocation of re-capturing the American Hungarian, in his hurried flight from that worse than Russian or Austrian despotism, however much he may be inspired with that love of liberty which burns eternal in every human heart. Sir every man is inspired with a love of liberty--a deep and abiding love of liberty. I care not where he may dwell--whether amid the snows of the polar regions, or weltering beneath an African sun, or clanking his iron fetters in this free Republic--I care not how degraded the man--that Promethean spark still lives, and burns, in secret and brilliant grandeur, upon his inmost soul, and the iron-rust of slavery and uninterrupted despotism, can never extinguish it. Did not the American Congress, professing to be a constitutional body, after nine months' arduous and patriotic legislation, as Webster would have it, strike down in our persons, the writ of *Habeas Corpus*, and *Trial by Jury* --those great bulwarks of human freedom, baptized by the blood, and sustained by the patriotic exertions of our English ancestors.

The gentleman from Franklin, (Mr. Jenkins), alluded to the Free Soil candidate for Governor. "I will here state, that I had the pleasure, during the Gubernatorial campaign, to hear Mr. Smith make a speech in opposition to the 'Fugitive Law,' in which he remarked, that it was humiliating to him to acknowledge that our forefathers did make a guilty compromise with Slavery in order to form this Union; and so far as the validity of that agreement was concerned, he felt that it was not binding upon him as a man, and that he never would obey any law which conflicts with that higher law, that has its seat in the bosom of God, and utters its voice in the harmony of the world."

Mr. Douglass having taken his seat, Mr. Day of Lorain, obtained the floor, and addressing the President, in substance said:

I cannot sit still, while this resolution is pending, and by my silence acquiesce in it. For all who have known me for years past, know that to the principle of the resolution I am, on principle opposed. The remarks of the gentleman from Cuyahoga, (Mr. Douglass), it seems to me, partake of the error of many others who discuss this question, namely, of making the *construction* of the Constitution of the United States, the same as the Constitution itself. There is no dispute between us in regard to the pro-slavery action of this government, nor any doubt in our minds in regard to the aid which the Supreme Court of the United States has given to Slavery, and by their unjust and, according to their own rules, illegal decisions; but *that* is not the Constitutuion--they are not that under which I vote. We, most of us, profess to believe the Bible; but men have, from the Bible, attempted to justify the worst of iniquities. Do we, in such a case, discard the Bible, believing, as we do, that iniquities find no shield there?--or do we not rather discared the false opinions of mistaken men, in regard to it? As some one else says, if a judge make a wrong decision in an important case, shall we abolish the Court? Shall we not rather remove the *judge*, and put in his place one who will judge righteously? We all so decide. So in regard to the Constitution. In voting, with judges' decisions we have nothing to do. Our business is with the Constitution. If it says it was framed to "establish justice," it, of course, is opposed to injustice; it it says plainly no person shall be deprived of life, *liberty*, or property, without due process of law,"--I suppose it means it, and I shall avail myself of the benefit of it. Sir, coming up as I do, in the midst of three millions of men in chains, and five hundred thousands only half free, I consider every instrument precious which guarantees to me liberty. I consider the Constitution the foundation of American liberties, and wrapping myself in the flag of the nation, I would plant myself upon that Constitution, and using the weapons they have given me, I would appeal to the American people for the rights thus guaranteed.

Mr. Douglass replied by saying--

"The gentleman may wrap the stars and stripes of his country around him forty times, if possible, and with the Declaration of Independence in one hand, and the Constitution of our common country in the other, may seat himself under the shadow of the frowning monument of Bunker Hill, and if the slaveholder, under the Constitution, and with the 'Fugitive Bill,' don't find you, then there don't exist a Constitution."

"Yes," resumed Mr. Day, "and with the Constitution I will *find* the 'Fugitive Bill.' You will mark this,--the gentleman has assumed the same error as before, and has not attempted to reply to my argument. This is all I need now say."

Mr. C. H. Langston obtained the floor and spoke as follows:

Mr. President:--I do not intend to make a speech, but merely to define my position on this subject, as I consider it one of no ordinary importance.

I perfectly agree with the gentleman from Cuyahoga, (Mr. Douglass,) who presented this resolution, that the United States' Constitution is pro-slavery. It was made to foster and uphold that abominable, vampirish and bloody system of American slavery. The highest judicial tribunals of the country have so decided. Members, while in the Convention and on returning to their constituents, declared that Slavery was one of the interests sought to be protected by the Constitution. It was so understood and so administered all over the country. But whether the Constitution is pro-slavery, and whether colored men "can consistently vote under that Constitution," are two very distinct questions; and while I would answer the former in the affirmative, I would not, like the gentleman from Cuyahoga, answer the latter in the negative. I would vote under the United States Constitution on the same principle, (circumstances being favorable,) that I would call on every slave, from Maryland to Texas, to arise and assert their *liberties*, and cut their masters' throats if they attempt again to reduce them to slavery. Whether or not this principle is correct, an impartial posterity and the Judge of the Universe shall decide.

Sir, I have long since adopted as my God, the freedom of the colored people of the United States, and my religion, to do any thing that will effect that object,--however much it may differ from the precepts taught in the Bible, such as, "Whosoever shall smite thee on thy right cheek, turn to him the other also;" or "Love your enemies; bless them that course you, and pray for them that despitefully use you and persecute you." Those are the lessons taught us by the religion of our white brethren, when they are free and we are slaves; but when their enslavement is attempted, then, "Resistance to Tyranny is obedience to God." This doctrine is equally true in regard to colored men as white men. I hope, therefore, Mr. President, that the resolution will not be adopted, but that colored men will vote, or do anything else under the Constitution, that will aid in effecting our liberties, and in securing our political, religious and intellectual elevation.

During the remarks of other gentlemen, the hour of adjournment, 5 o'clock, P.M., the session closed with an anti-slavery song.

Evening Session.

President in the Chair, session opened with an Anti-slavery song, the resolution of Mr. Douglass, being under consideration at the adjournment, it was again called up, after some discussion. C. A. Yancy called the previous question, which, was carried, the main question was put, the yeas and nays being demanded, the vote stood as follows:

Yeas--H. F. Douglass, Wm. Jackson, 2.

Nays--T. N. Stewart, J. Parnell, H. H. Ford, C. A. Yancy, J. Mercer Langston, Wm. Lewis, G. Stanup, W. Hurst Burnham, James Dunlap, John Booker, L. D. Taylor, John Brown, C. H. Langston, J. Freeland, J. H. Johnson, James Poindexter, John T. Ward, Sterling Heathcock, J. Bird, Thomas Harris, Jerome Stebot, Felix Whitsill, Mills Melton, Levi Day, E. Whitsill, Wm. P. Morgan and President, 28.

C. H. Langston, reported on a resolution that was referred to him, which was adopted as amended. After which, James Poindexter reported a resolution, which was adopted as amended.

On motion of C. H. Langston, that there be a committee of three, to report an address to the Constitutional Convention, which is in session in the city of Cincinnati, and further, that W. H. Day be Chairman of said committee. On motion, it was resolved that C. A. Yancy and C. H. Langston, constitute said committee.

The 20th resolution was taken up and adopted.

The 21st resolution was taken up, and Mr. James Poindexter, moved to amend the resolution, by striking all out after the word resolved, and insert, that it is imperative on the colored people of Ohio to immediately establish schools under the Common School Law of 1849. W. H. Day, offered the following amendment or substitute to the foregoing, that they show their appreciation of the School Law of 1849, by establishing schools under it.

Mr. Brown of Franklin, moved to reconsider the 14th resolution.

While Mr. Brown's motion was pending, the Hamilton Delegation were announced to the Convention, and on presenting their credentials, they were permitted to taken seats. Joseph H. Perkins, John I. Gaines, John Jackson, Lawrence W. Minor.

The motion of Mr. Brown to reconsider prevailed.

On motion, the resolution was referred to a select committee of one, C. H. Langston constituting said committee.

The 17th resolution was taken up and adopted, the following gentlemen constituting said committee, H. Ford Douglass chairman, C. H. Langston, Wm. H. Day, J. Mercer Langston, D. Jenkins, James Poindexter. J. McCarter Simpson.

After which the Convention adjourned to Friday morning nine o'clock.

Morning Session, Columbus, Jan. 17th, 1851.

The First Vice President in the Chair. The Convention was opened by a portion of the 133d Psalm being read by the Rev. T. N. Stewart; J. I. Gaines of Hamilton, was called upon to address the Convention.

On motion of Mr. C. A. Yancy of Jackson, the resolution relating to Superintendants of Public Schools, and that a petition to that effect be laid before the Ohio Legislature now in session, was amended by striking out the second part, agreed to. The resolution reads as amended: Resolved, that the Convention petition the Ohio Legislature, to appoint a Colored Superintendant, to oversee the interests of the Colored District Schools. Passed as agreed to.

C. H. Langston, moved that the 21st resolution relating to a National Convention, be taken up. On motion of Mr. Perkins, it was referred back to the business committee for revision.

The 27th resolution was taken up, and on motion of L. D. Taylor of Franklin, it was laid on the table.

The 24th resolution came up for consideration, and was referred to a select committee of one, J. H. Perkins being the committee.

It was moved by W. H. Day, that the committee to whom was referred the 23d resolution on the press, be instructed to bring in a plan similar to the one of last winter. A letter from W. H. Day was read, and his resignation tendered, which was as follows:

Columbus, Jan. 1st, 1851.

To the State Convention of Colored Men, to be held in Columbus, Ohio, Jan. 15th, 1851.

GENTLEMEN:--The State Convention preceding this, very kindly nominated the undersigned, one of the Editors of the Newspaper entitled the "Voice of the Disfranchised," which paper it was then expected, would be started during last year. The undersigned has done what he consistently could, in connexion with others, to commence publishing said paper, and has held himself in readiness to assume the duties of the post assigned him; and Mr. C. H. Langston, the other Editor, has labored to the same end.

In view of important circumstances, effecting the interest of others as well as the interest of the undersigned, he cannot consistently remain in the position to which he was thus appointed, and hereby respectfully tenders his resignation, hoping that, if it be deemed necessary, another may be appointed in his stead, who may be better able to devote himself to the arduous duties of this position, although he claims for himself the praise that no one has been more willing.

Very Respectfully,
William H. Day.

On motion of C. H. Langston a select committee of one was appointed on statistics, and L. W. Miner constitute said committee, carried.

The 26th resolution was then taken up, and on motion of C. H. Langston, that it be amended by striking out, "most convenient point," and insert the words "Buffalo, New York," the amendment was agreed to, and the resolution adopted.

H. Ford Douglass, from the committee appointed to wait on the Governor, the Hon. R. Wood, reported the following answer:

Executive Office.

Columbus Jan. 17th, 1851.

Sir.--Your note came to hand this morning. It will suit my convenience, to receive your committee at three o'clock this afternoon, at my office.

Respectfully,
R. Wood.
H. Ford Douglass, Chairman.

The 28th resolution was taken up, and pending the motion to adopt, the hour of recess arrived and the session closed, J. Henry Perkins of Hamilton, having the floor.

Afternoon Session.

President in the chair; Prayer offered by W. Roberts. After which C. A. Yancy, offered a resolution with the names of persons who shall constitute the members of the State Central Committee for 1851. On motion of C. H. Langston, the resolution was referred to a select committee of three, which was as follows:--L. D. Taylor, C. H. Langston, and J. H. Perkins--carried, after which J. Mercer Langston, being select committee on the press, reported as follows:

Report

The committee appointed to devise a plan for establishing a paper in this State in behalf of the colored people, having had the same under consideration, would respectfully report, as follows:

It being admitted that the colored people of the United States are pledged before the world and in the face of Heaven to struggle manfully for advancement in civil and social life, it is clear that our own efforts must mainly, if not entirely, produce such advancement. And if we are to advance by our own efforts, (under the divine blessing,) we must use the means which will direct such efforts to a successful issue.

Of the means for the advancement of a people as we are, none are more available than a press. We struggle against opinions. Our warfare lies in the field of thought. Glorious struggle! Godlike warfare! In training our soldiers for the field--in marshaling our hosts for the fight--in leading the onset, and throughout the conflict, we need a Printing Press, because a printing press is the vehicle of thought--is a ruler of opinions.

That in our judgment, the peculiar conditon of the colored people of the State imperiously demands that we establish such an organ, that we may talk to each other, and to the world.

We are brought to this conclusion from the following considerations:

We are scattered over so large a territory, and while we have increasingly important interests, we have not a single paper of our own west of New York, and in those there, we do not consider ourselves properly represented, neither can we be fully represented in the papers edited at the west by our white friends, for we have interests peculiar to ourselves. This is our condition. But the establishment of a paper must depend upon the available means to sustain it. Among the 25,000 colored persons in the State, there certainly are sufficient to give it a handsome support, to say nothing of the thousands of our white friends in the State, who stand ready to-day to welcome such a periodical. In this connection, we would not forget the expected support of our western *brethren*, whose interests, like ours, need to be advocated.

Your committee would therefore respectfully recommend the adoption of the following plan for the establishment and support of a paper:

I. To find out from each person present interested, how much he or she will pledge, if it be needed, to support the paper one year.

II. The appointment of a committee of nine from those who pledge money, the business of which committee shall be to manage the publishing and all the financial concerns of the paper.

    III. That the editors be authorized and empowered to collect monies from the public, by voluntary contributions or otherwise, to purchase a press for the publication of said paper, which shall be their individual property, as an indemnity against losses sustained in its publication. When they have purchased the Press, they shall give security to said Committee of Nine for the publication of the paper for one year.

    IV. Columbus, Franklin county, as the place for issuing the paper.

    V. William H. Day, and Charles H. Langston, Editors; who are recommended as responsible men, to apply the funds collected to the object above mentioned.

    VI. The principles of the paper shall be the advocacy of the rights of the colored man, urging his liberty, and his moral, mental, social, and political elevation.

    VII. The name, "*Clarion of Freedom.*"

All of which is respectfully submitted.
J. Mercer Langston,
Committee.

Morning Session, Columbus, May 18th, 1851.

President in the Chair. Chaplain opened the Convention by reading a portion of the Scriptures.

It was moved by Mr. C. H. Langston, that each of the Delegates pledge himself to give whatever he can afford to establish a newspaper upon the plan stated in the foregoing report, which was agreed to. Mr. Roberts, of Seneca wished, to know to whom the Press would belong, when paid for. Pending this question, on motion of C. A. Yancy, said report was reconsidered, and on motion of D. Jenkins, after much deliberation it was indefinitely postponed.

At this stage of the proceedings, a communication was received from the following ladies of Columbus: Miss L. A. Stanton, Miss M. J. Hopkins, Mrs. L. M. Jenkins, Mrs. C. Hacley, Mrs. S. Mason, Mrs. S. P. Scurry, Miss L. Harper; pledging themselves to furnish means to publish the proceedings of this Convention.

On motion, the following gentlemen, J. McCarter Simpson, W. H. Day, C. H. Langston, were appointed to correspond with the leading colored citizens of the United States, touching the propriety of holding a National Convention, to be held at Buffalo, sometime in the year 1851.

The following gentlemen were appointed as State Central Committee for the ensuing year: J. I. Gaines, J. H. Perkins, J. Jackson of Hamilton county, W. H. Day of Lorain, D. Jenkins of Franklin.

On motion, the Convention adjourned *sine die*.

RESOLUTIONS

Preamble and Resolutions

1. Whereas, The first Section of the 4th Article of the Constitution of Ohio deprives every colored citizen of a free exercise of their inestimable right of the "Elective Franchise;" and whereas we are unprotected in person and property, in a so-called "*Free* and Independent" form of government; and whereas our social, political and religious rights are at the mercy of the law-makers of our land; therefore,

    Resolved, That we call upon, and earnestly pray the Constitutional Convention now assembled in Cincinnati to so alter said article as to give every citizen, irrespective of color, a right to say at the ballot box who shall make and execute the law by which he is governed.

2. Whereas, There still remains on the statute book of Ohio certain important restrictions and disabilities, founded only on the unjust and inhuman distinction of color, which laws tend greatly to degrade the Free Colored Citizens of the State, in attempting to annihilate the great principle of "Equal Rights" to all men as asserted in the Declaration of our American Independence; and whereas there are hard and unjust practices not lawful, tolerated in our State,--such as being prohibited the privilege of an inside seat in

the public Stage Coaches; also of the benefits of Colleges, Academies, and Seminaries; also of the Deaf and Dumb, Blind, and Lunatic Asylums, and Poor Houses,--therefore,

Resolved, That we look upon all those prohibitions as being unjust, and detrimental to the moral, intellectual and political elevation of the Colored people.

3. Whereas, Congress has recently passed a bill termed the "Fugitive Slave Law," evincing on its part a determination to degrade us by robbing us of the last vestige of human rights, to wit: Trial by jury, and Writ of Habeas Corpus--those great bulwarks of human freedom, defended by the hero's blood, and patriotic exertions of the wise and good of every age; therefore,

Resolved, That we look upon this bill as being more unjust than any law ever passed before, and look upon those who voted in favor of this fiendish enactment as being more despotic than the pagan edicts of Nero[3] or Caligula[4] --more cruel and Heaven-daring than any law makers that ever legislated, or practiced under heathen jurisprudence, even in the dark night of despotism that enshrouded France during her reign of terror.

4. *Resolved,* That we look upon the recent Fugitive Slave enactment as a hideous deformity in the garb of law--unconstitutional--opposed to the Institutions of the Free States--an outrage upon humanity--at war with the teachings of Christianity, and its place is first upon the catalogue of disgraceful, and abominable legislations that characterized the tyranny of Charles I., and we would urge upon the people the necessity of its immediate and unconditional repeal.

5. *Resolved,* That this Convention shall instruct each County in the State to send up to each State Convention held in the State hereafter, as correct a statistical list of the population, wealth, moral and literary attainments, agricultural and mechanical pursuits, &c., as can possibly be obtained.

6. Whereas, A combination of efforts is the only efficient way of elevating any people,

Resolved, That this Convention recommend to each County to appoint an Agent, whose duty it shall be to have the supervision of the County; to organize as many moral reform, and literary societies as he can, and to call county and other public meetings when circumstances demand it.

7. *Resolved,* That if the Convention would insert a clause providing that every colored man who owned three hundred dollars worth of taxable property shall be entitled to his citizenship, it would be the means of quickly making us an industrious people.

8. *Resolved,* That the delegates composing this Convention shall be requested to write out a report in as short a form as is expedient, giving the population, wealth and condition of their respective counties.

9. *Resolved,* That these Reports be published in the Minutes.

10. *Resolved,* We, as a people, occupy a peculiar position in society, which position subjects us to all manner of menial services,

Resolved, That we recommend our people to give their sons and daughters useful trades, so that they may leave the blacking rooms, horse stables, steamboats, washtubs and other menial employments; and we also recommend our people to put their children under colored mechanics whenever they can find any who are capable of giving such instructions.

11. Whereas, The people from time immemorial assembled in Conventions to make declarations of right, and to consult the best means of improvement, both social and political; and whereas our present condition loudly calls on us for such an assemblage, and such declarations; and whereas we believe that it is in our power to do much towards pulling down the strongholds of prejudice, and toward destroying its accursed and more powerful ally, American Slavery, we do therefore adopt the following Resolutions as our unflinching sentiments:

12. *Resolved,* That we are deeply interested in the elevation of our people, and will sacrifice our money, give our influence, and lay aside all sectarian and party principles for the accomplishment of our greatest good.

13. *Resolved,* That we will persevere in our efforts for self elevation. "Elevation!" shall be our motto, and if we perish, we will perish in the conflict.

14. *Resolved,* That we will neither support, countenance or associate with any person, society or church, unless we are convinced that they are purely Anti-Slavery.

15. *Resolved,* That we earnestly recommend the reconstruction of Temperance Societies among our people, in order that the morality of our youth may be secured, the overwhelming tide of intemperance may be stayed and the demoralizing holds of drunkenness and crime be broken up.

16. *Resolved,* That we are grateful for the school privileges we enjoy, and we do hope that our white fellow citizens will not so much degrade us as to take from us this great means of elevation, for we believe that we never can be good citizens without being educated; for immorality and crime are but the children of ignorance.

17. *Resolved,* That this Convention appoint a deputation to wait upon the Hon. Reuben Wood, Governor of this State, and respectfully request him to use his official influence in favor of the elective franchise being extended to the colored people in Ohio.

18. *Resolved,* That this Convention petition the Ohio Legislature to appoint an Agent to oversee the colored District Schools in this State.

19. *Resolved,* That this convention recommend to the colored people to hold annual Fairs, at which time and place men and women of all employments may exhibit specimens of the best product of their labors, best stock, &c.

20. *Resolved,* That each delegate present be requested to report their statistical list on Friday the 17th, at 2 o'clock.

21. *Resolved,* That this convention take into consideration the importance of calling a National Convention, to be held at the most convenient point in the U.S., sometime in 1851.

22. *Resolved,* That this convention recommend to the colored people in each free state to send up a petition to the National Convention, which petitions shall be sent to Queen Victoria, praying her Majesty never to consent to any proposal that may be made to have Canada annexed to the United States which may be hereafter designated.

23. *Resolved,* That a Corresponding Committee of three be appointed to correspond with the leading colored men in the U.S., for the purpose of determining the time of holding the National Convention.

24. *Resolved,* That our next State Convention be held in the city of Cincinnati, sometime in 1852, and that we appoint a State Central Committee, a majority of whom shall be located in said city.

25. *Resolved,* That this Convention recommend to the different colored Churches in the State, who do not hold monthly concerts of prayer in behalf of the slave, to immediately establish such concerts of prayer to be observed once a month, and not to forget in their private and public devotions to remember the slaves as bound with them.

Whereas, There still remains on the Statute Books of Ohio, important legal restrictions, and disabilities, founded on the unjust and inhuman distinctions of cast or complexion, which laws not only oppress and degrade the free colored citizens of the state of Ohio, but subvert and annihilate the great principles of "equal rights to all men," as laid down in our organic law, as the foundation of our political institutions.

Therefore, *Resolved,* That the laws which prohibit colored men from seats in the jury box, and the poor houses of the state, is tyrannical, infamous, unjust and oppressive, and ought therefore to be unconditionally repealed,

And Whereas, there are usuages and practices, founded on wicked and malicious prejudice, against an unoffending and loyal class of citizens, common in the state of Ohio, which operate greatly to our discomfort, annoyance and real injury, such as being prohibited comfortable seats in public stages, and other public conveyances, and being excluded from Colleges, Academies and Seminaries of learning, as well as from the benefits of the Deaf and Dumb Asylum of the state, and yet many of these Institutions are supported in part, by the taxes paid into the Treasury by colored men.

26. Whereas, the people have from time to time immemorial assembled in convention, to make declarations of rights and to consult the best means of improvement, both socially and politically, and whereas our present condition, loudly calls for such an assemblage, and believing that it is in our power to do a great work towards the pulling down of the strongholds of prejudice, and in destroying its accursed and more powerful ally, American

Slavery, we do therefore adopt the following resolutions, as our firm and unflinching sentiment.

1. *Resolved,* That past experience has proven that conventions, have done much towards our improvement and elevation.

2. *Resolved,* That we are opposed to the American Colonization Society, because its object is the expatriation of 600,000 defenceless free colored persons, which is cruel and unjust, and our opposition is deepened, when we consider that the greater part of the Churches and professed Christians in this country, are with that society, and are like that unprincipled and wicked minister of Ahashueras,[5] for neither their wealth, their literature, their successful experiment of self government, their world wide fame, nor even the atonement that was made on Calvary, avails them anything, so long as the Black Man has a place on the soil of America, to lay his head.

3. *Resolved,* That we look upon the recent fugitive slave enactment, as a hideous deformity in the garb of law; unconstitutional, opposed to the institutions of the free states, an outrage upon humanity, at war with the teachings of Christianity, and its place is first on the catalogue of disgraceful and abominable legislation, such as characterized the tyranny of Charles the 1st of England; and we would therefore urge upon the people, the necessity of its immediate and unconditional repeal.

Mr. C. A. Yancy offered the following resolutions, which were unanimously adopted:

Resolved, That the Convention return its thanks to the President for his faithful and impartial conduct while presiding over its deliberations.

Resolved, That the Convention return its thanks to the Trustees of this Chapel for the use of it during the sitting of the Convention.

ADDRESS

To the Constitutional Convention of the State of Ohio, now assembled

Gentlemen:

In behalf of the Colored Men of Ohio, in General Convention assembled, the undersigned have been appointed to present to you, a few things relating to the interest of the Colored Men of this State, and particularly in regard to amending the present Constitution, by striking out the word "white" in the fourth article, first section, thereby permitting colored men to exercise the Elective Franchise, with the same restrictions only, which are imposed upon you.

"HEAR US FOR OUR CAUSE."

Under an oath to support the Constitution of the United States, you are assembled to frame for the State of Ohio, her organic law. The United States Constitution, so says its preamble, was framed to support justice--therefore opposed to injustice, to promote domestic tranquility--therefore opposed to domestic turmoil; to promote the *general* welfare; and we need not tell you that the general welfare is not secured by "the greatest good to the greatest number, merely, but, in the language of the Hon. John Quincy Adams, by the greatest good to the whole." This is the *professed* end of all legislation; this is the *real* end of all *righteous legislation;* so much so, that it begins to be generally believed, that every law is, or ought to be, to use Mr. Webster's words, "a re-enactment of the law of God," or else, according to Mr. Seward,[6] to say nothing of Fortesque,[7] Coke,[8] Blackstone, Noyes,[9] Jenks and others, it is "null and void." "The reasonableness of law is the soul of law." "Statutes against fundamental morality are void." And a certain well known citizen of the United States, says--"law finds its home and its definition nowhere but in the bonds of an universal brotherhood, the claims of equality or equity, the demands of righteous legislation, and inalienable rights, identical with the principles of democracy and the genius of the Christian religion."

We ask, gentlemen, is not this the principle of all just government? As far as we admire the framework of any government, is not our admiration proportioned to the equality of its laws? When we see the Bey of Tunis abolishing slavery in his dominions, why is it that the universal conscience approves the deed? When Americans are rescued from the Algerines, why is it that the nation unites in the praise of those rescuing them? When the Autocrat of Russia lifts up with his own hand, the thousand serfs in his dominions, on to a half constructed platform of equality, why is that there is an acclaim in favor of the act, so far, around the world?[10] And why is it thrown in the scale of justice, to weigh against the oft-repeated terrors of his vindictiveness? Is it not because the universal conscience affirms this principle to be just, and the only principle to be exercised between man and man?

Our fathers of the revolution recognized this principle on the birth day of this nation, and proclaimed--"all men"--not a part of men--but "ALL men are created equal, endowed by their Creator with certain inalienable rights, among which are life, liberty, and the pursuit of happiness." To secure these *rights* said they, "governments were instituted among men, deriving their *just* powers from the consent of the governed." They here announced two important principles: First, That governments are instituted for the protection of the rights of--not of a set of men--but of the ALL men spoken of: And, Second, That the government which does not protect the rights of all men, is not just. And even now, North Carolina and Virginia vie with Connecticut and Rhode Island in claiming the honor of first making such a declaration. In accordance with it, colored men in N. Carolina, up till 1831, used the elective franchise in common with others. This, it seems to us, and this only, is in accordance with the spirit of free institutions, just like the democracy so eloquently described by Hon. Wm. Allen of our own State, "which asks nothing but what it concedes. And concedes nothing but what it demands. Destructive only to despotism, it is the sole conservator of liberty, labor, and property. It is the law of nature pervading the law of the land. "Yes,"--he glowingly continues, "that is a noble, magnanimous, sublime sentiment, which expands our affections, enlarges the circle of our sympathies, and elevates the soul of man, until claiming an equality with the best, he rejects as unworthy of his dignity, any political immunities over the humblest of his fellows." We respectfully represent to you, that the continuance of the word *"white"* in the Ohio State Constitution, by which we are deprived of the privilege of voting for men to make laws by which we are to be governed, is a violation of every principle thus announced.

It is also contrary to the governmental principles adopted practically in the law of nations, namely, that those born in a country are members of the body politic, on arriving at the requisite age, and on fulfilling the equal conditions imposed upon all. So that no accidental circumstance, like the color of the hair or the shape of the nose, has any power in reference to their rights.

Gentlemen: We have been taught by you to believe, that the United States' Constitution is the Supreme law of the land. The fifth clause 1st section, Article second, recognizes the principle that natural birth gives citizenship, otherwise, there seems to us to be no sense in the naturalization laws. Those of us, therefore, who were born in the United States, and reside in Ohio, *are citizens of Ohio*. If citizens of this State, entitled, by the United States' Constitution, to all the rights and immunities of citizens of the several States. The elective franchise being among these rights and immunities, we respectfully urge upon you our claim.

Says Chancellor Kent [Vol. II, p. 258, sec. 32,] "Citizens, under our Constitution and laws, mean free inhabitants born within the United States, or naturalized under the laws of Congress. If a slave, born in the United States, be manumitted, or otherwise lawfully discharged from bondage, or if a black man be born within the United States, and born free, he becomes thenceforward, a citizen." If Chancellor Kent be correct, we respectfully ask, where is the right to disfranchise us?

Said the Hon. Mr. Baldwin,[11] before the United States' Senate, "When the Constitution of the United States was framed, colored men voted in a majority of these States; they voted in the States of New York, in Pennsylvania, in Massachusetts, in Connecticut, Rhode Island, New Jersey, Delaware and North Carolina; and long after the adoption of the Constitution, they continued to vote in North Carolina, and Tennessee also. The Constitution of the United States makes no distinction of color. There is no word 'white' to be found in that instrument. All free people then stood upon the same platform in regard to their political rights, and were so recognized in most of the States of the Union. The free colored citizens of these States are as much entitled to the rights of citizenship, as are men of any other color or complexion whatever. To this day, in the State of Virginia, free colored persons, born in that State, are citizens."

The property of colored men, as in Ohio, had always been taxed to support government, and it was thought no more than right that they should enjoy that blessing of government, the twin brother of taxation, namely, representation. Accordingly, in New York, from 1777 to 1821, colored men were represented equally with others.

That colored men are citizens, is attested by the fact that in 1812-'15 colored men were drafted, in common with others for the war. In September 1814, General Andrew Jackson issued his proclamation to the free colored inhabitants of Louisiana, and told them, that "through a *mistaken policy* they had heretofore been deprived of a participation in the glorious struggle for national rights, in which our country was engaged," and told them that this should no longer exist. He appealed to them as "Sons of Freedom;"--as "Americans,"--"as fathers, husbands, and brothers," to enlist in behalf of all they held dear. Speaking to them of this land, he says,--"Your country;" and of the whites,--"Your white fellow citizens," and "countrymen." And when in December following, he addressed the free people of color, congratulating them upon the success of their arms, he said--"our brave citizens [no distinction as to color,] are united, and all contention has ceased among them. Their only dispute is, who shall win the prize of valor, or who the most glory, its noblest reward," showing an attachment to this government, such only as free citizens can give. We ask you, whether it is right to disfranchise a citizen, and if so, where is the power specified? Is it in the Declaration of American Independence? Is [it] in the Articles of Confederation? Is it in the Supreme Law of the land--the U. States' Constitution? Is it not contrary to justice--to law--to abstract and concrete right--to every principle of a free government?

It is also contrary to true political economy. In the State of Ohio, by the report of the Secretary of State made to you, there appears to be over twenty three thousand colored persons in Ohio, making about one eighty seventh of the whole population. We are here, and here lawfully, and we ask if it be true policy to exclude persons thus in your midst, from any participancy in these privileges, the enjoyment of which imposes upon those enjoying them, "correlative duties." Of course, if we have no protection, we owe no allegiance, the amount of allegiance, according to the arrangement of nations, being graduated by the rights guaranteed, and the protection afforded.

But, we repeat, colored men have participated in the struggles of this country, and have thereby helped to uphold it. Do you ask where? Let the waters of Lake Champlain, as they came crimsoned to the shore, answer. Let our old fathers' bones, mouldering in secluded grave-yards tell the tale. Ask the Black Rhode Island Regiment, of the gallant defence of Red Bank, where four hundred colored soldiers met and repulsed fifteen hundred Hessian mercenaries. Go with us to the attack on the American lines, near Croton river, 13th May, 1781. See Col. Green cut down and mortally wounded; but the sabres of the enemy reached him only through the bodies of his faithful guard of blacks. *Every one of them was slain.*[12] Go to the records of Congress, and you will find an act, recommending to South Carolina and Louisiana, the raising of three thousand troops who were to be rewarded by their freedom. Bring up the starving remembrance of Valley Forge, and the horrors of the Jersey prison ship. Colored men know of these, for they were there. In Champaign county, is a colored man who served with General Washington. In Ohio, are colored descendants of Revolutionary sires. In this Convention, pleading for right, were sons of men, who in 1812-'15, were drafted for the war, and faced with your fathers the storm of battle. And if history be correct, the first blood of the Revolution was that of a colored man.[13] We respectfully ask, have we not a just claim to the same rights with you?

Again, colored men are helping, through their taxes, to bear the burdens of the State, and we ask, shall they not be permitted to be represented? The property of the colored people of Ohio is now a matter of consequence. We take the liberty here to introduce some statistics in regard to the colored people of this State, most of which has been gathered by delegates to this Convention, a portion being attested by the County Auditors.

In returns from nineteen counties represented, we find the value of real estate and personal property belonging to colored persons in those counties, amounting to more than *three millions of dollars*. In thirteen of these counties we find a colored population of 13,213. In ten of these counties, we find twenty four schools reported as separate colored schools. In two counties of the nineteen, colored children attend schools with the whites.

Few statistics have been obtained, but we think the amount above specified, certainly demands at your hands some attention, so that while colored men bear cheerfully their part of the burdens of the State, they may have their part of the blessings.

What we have already presented, may perhaps, be deemed sufficient, but we beg leave to introduce here, an extract from a letter of the Secretary of State, Hon. Saml. Galloway, whose opportunity to know of what he affirmed, no one will question.[14] He is speaking of the progress of the colored people of Ohio, during ten years past, he says, "Now, (1849,) they have many and well conducted schools--they have teachers of respectable intellectual and moral qualifications--there are many who command general respect and confidence for integrity and intelligence;--they call and conduct conventions and associations of various kinds, with order and intelligence;--questions of general and proper interest have become with them topics of discussion and conversation--in a few words, the intellectual and moral tone of their being is ameliorated." We ask what more could be said?

The only objection which we deem it necessary now to notice, and one often urged against us, is--"the colored man would not profitably use the elective franchise, if it were granted him." We reply by offering a letter upon this point, from an observing and distinguished man:

"Washington, May 16, 1850.

"Dear Sir:--Your letter of the 6th inst. has been received. I reply to it cheerfully and with pleasure.

"It is my deliberate opinion, founded upon careful observation, that the Right of Suffrage is exercised by no citizen of the State of New York, more conscienciously, or more sincerely, or with more beneficial results to society, then it is by the Electors of African descent. I sincerely hope that the franchise will before long be extended as it justly ought, to this race who of all others need it most.

"I am very respectfully, your obedient servant,
William H. Seward."

We ask, Gentlemen, in conclusion, that you will place yourselves in our stead,--that you will candidly consider our claim, and as justice shall direct you, so to decide. In your hands, our destiny is placed. To you, therefore, we appeal. We look to you to

"TO GIVE US OUR RIGHTS--FOR WE ASK NOTHING MORE."

In Behalf of the State Convention,
We are Gentlemen,
Yours Very Respectfully,
William H. Day,
Charles H. Langston,
Charles A. Yancy.
Committee.

Copy in the Harvard University Library.

REFERENCE NOTES

1. Up till the eve of the war, Joseph Warren (1741-1775), American Revolutionary patriot and physician, played a prominent role in shaping public opinion in Massachusetts in support of the cause. While rallying the local

militia in the vicinity of Bunker Hill, he was shot dead by a British soldier on June 17, 1775.

2. Francis Marion (1732-1795) was an American Revolutionary War hero whose brilliant military exploits, particularly in the South, helped to turn the tide in favor of the patriot forces.

3. Nero (Nero Claudius Caesar) A.D. 37-A.D. 68. Roman emperor (A.D. 54-A.D. 68). This sadistic and infamous ruler murdered his mother and later his wife. In A.D. 64, he burned Rome and blamed the Christians, a growing and persecuted sect, for being responsible. According to Christian tradition his victims included St. Peter and St. Paul.

4. Caligula (Caius Caesar Germanicus) A.D. 12-A.D. 41. Roman emperor (A.D. 37-A.D. 41). When he was a small child with his parents on the Rhine he wore military boots, whence his nickname [*caligula*=little boots]. His name has become virtually synonymous for ruthless and cruel autocracy, and during his reign torture and execution became the order of the day.

5. Ahasuerus (519?-465 B.C.) is the Hebrew form of the name Xerxes, as used in the Bible. The Ahasuerus of Esther is probably Xerxes I, King of Persia (486-465 B.C.). His name in old Persian is Khshayarsha. In Esther (chapters 3-7), it is recorded that Haman, favored minister of Ahasuerus, commanded that all Jews be put to death. Esther the queen, interceded for her people, and Haman was hanged on the gallows he had set up for Mordecai.

6. William H. Seward, as mentioned above, was a noted American political leader and antislavery senator from New York. Seward opposed the Compromise of 1850, including the Fugitive Slave Bill. He upheld the principle of "Higher Law"--the law of God--under which slavery could never be justified.

7. The reference is to Sir John Fortescue (1394-1476), English jurist and chief justice of the Court of King's Bench from 1442 to 1460.

8. The reference is to Sir Edward Coke (1552-1634), eminent English jurist who served for a time in Parliament as solicitor general, speaker of the House of Commons and, finally, as chief justice of the King's Bench after 1613. While sitting on this tribunal, Coke gained fame as an ardent champion of common law against the encroachments of the royal prerogative and declared royal proclamations contrary to law null and void.

9. William Curtis Noyes (1805-1864) was an influential New York lawyer. Originally a Whig, he became a Republican upon the former's demise in 1856. As a staunch Republican, he publicly attacked the Kansas-Nebraska Bill and the Fugitive Slave Law of 1850.

10. Serfdom was finally abolished in Russia by the act of emancipation of February 19, 1861.

11. The reference is to Roger Sherman Baldwin (1793-1863), American lawyer, senator, governor of Connecticut and an organizer of the Republican Party. Baldwin was active in the movement for the abolition of slavery, making speeches on the subject at various times. On one occasion, he obtained a writ of *habeas corpus* for the release of a black man seized as a fugitive slave, who had escaped from the service of Henry Clay.

12. Christopher Greene (1737-1781), American Revolutionary soldier, headed a Rhode Island regiment of black troops recruited from slaves freed for patriotic service. In 1781, while commanding his lines at Points Bridge in Westchester County, New York, he was surprised by the enemy on May 14 and killed. His brave black soldiers heroically defended him until they were cut to pieces, the enemy reaching him over their dead bodies.

13. The reference is to Crispus Attucks (c. 1723-1770), a runaway slave, who was the first American to die in the American Revolution. He was one of five men killed in the Boston Massacre (March 5, 1770) and the first to die. He was canonized by black Americans of later generations.

14. Samuel Galloway (1811-1872), Ohio lawyer, educator and congressman, served as secretary of state of Ohio from 1843 to 1850 and was also in this capacity *ex-officio* superintendent of schools.

As a result of his Calvinistic educational tradition and his association with Horace Mann, he became an enthusiastic supporter of popular education. His reports to the legislature pointed up the deplorable conditions of the common schools of Ohio which brought about many substantial reforms. While antislavery in sentiments, he nevertheless allied himself with the Whig Party and served in Congress from 1854 to 1856.

PROCEEDINGS OF THE CONVENTION, OF THE COLORED FREEMEN OF OHIO,
HELD IN CINCINNATI, JANUARY 14, 15, 16, 17 AND 19, 1852

CENTRAL COMMITTEE FOR 1852

Wm. H. Day,   C. H. Langston,
Geo. Vosburgh,   D. Jenkins,
John Brown,   G. R. Williams,
R. Leach,   John I. Gaines.

PROCEEDINGS

Cincinnati, Wednesday Jan. 14th, 1852, 10 o'clock, A.M.
Pursuant to public notice by circulars and through the press, a large number of delegates convened at the Union Baptist Church. The Convention was called to order by D. Jenkins, of Franklin, and on his motion, C. H. Langston, of Franklin, was called to the Chair as President pro tem., and Henry Hurd appointed Secretary. On motion of D. Jenkins the delegates were requested to report their names to the Secretary by credentials or otherwise. The following gentlemen came forward and reported their names:

Butler County
J. E. Robbins,
S. D. Fox.
Gallia County
J. L. Ward
Montgomery County
Thos. Jefferson,
John Johnson.
Miami County
Robert Smith.
Warren County
Asa Pratt.
Seneca County
D. Roberts.
Mercer County
C. Hurd.
Ross County
G. R. Williams,
D. Williams.
Clark County
W. P. Morgan,
N. Morgan,
M. Roberts.

Champaign County
H. H. Ford.
Cuyahoga County
J. Brown,
W. H. Day,
G. Vosburgh,
R. Leach.
Franklin County
David Jenkins,
L. D. Taylor,
J. Booker,
H. Ford Douglass,
Hanson Johnson,
John Brown,
C. H. Langston.
Lorain County
John M. Langston.
Stark, Columbiana and Portage Counties
Wm. Pinn.
Erie County
G. J. Reynolds,
Lawrence G. Jackson.

Hamilton County
John I. Gaines,
H. P. Spears,
Isaac Wilson,
Wallace Shelton,
Lovell C. Flewellen,
John Liverpool,
Charles A. Rodgers,
W. R. Casey,
Joseph Fowler, Jr.,
Wm. Darnes,
W. M. Nelson,
Peter H. Clark,
George W. Brodie,
W. W. Watson,
John Jackson.

On motion of John I. Gaines, a committee of five, consisting of H. P. Spears, H. Hurd, John Booker, J. M. Langston and Wm. Pinn, were appointed to nominate permanent officers for the Convention. In the absence of the committee, the Convention was addressed by C. H. Langston, of Franklin, setting forth the importance of united action.

The committee on nomination reported as follows: President, John M. Langston of Lorain; Vice Presidents, John Booker of Franklin, Wm. Darnes of Hamilton, C. Yancy of Shelby; Secretaries, Henry Hurd of Mercer, P. H. Clark of Hamilton and W. M. Nelson of Hamilton. On taking the Chair the President addressed the Convention in substance as follows:

Gentlemen of the Convention:
The honor which you have conferred upon me was entirely unexpected. My inexperience and youth wholly precluded any such hope on my part. I thank you for the honor--indeed it is an honor in my humble opinion, greater than the honor done Millard Fillmore[1] by the American people, in calling him to the Presidency of this country. For in his position he is trammelled by an unjust public sentiment, a sentiment adverse to him or freedom. While the object of this Convention is, to oppose this public sentiment and further the cause of Liberty and Equality.

The subjects which we are to consider are of great importance. The education of our children--the Agricultural interests of our people--the temperance movement among us--the course which we are to pursue during our stay in this country and the plan of emigration which we shall adopt if we see fit to go out of this country, are matters for our most calm and deliberate consideration.

It is my sincere hope, that harmony and kind feeling will pervade the entire action of the Convention.

With indulgence and assistance, I hope to be able to discharge the duties imposed upon me by you, with impartiality and fairness. Again, gentlemen, I return my thanks.

A committee of five were then appointed to report business for the action of the Convention, consisting of John I. Gaines, C. H. Langston, C. A. Rodgers, J. L. Ward. On motion, W. H. Brisbane and J. V. Smith, were admitted to seats as reporters for the "Ohio Times" and "Cincinnati Gazette."

The following committees were on motion, appointed:
On Rules--L. D. Taylor, L. C. Flewellen, Rev. W. Shelton, Hanson Johnson and Rev. C. Yancy.
On Finance--W. W. Watson, W. R. Casey and G. W. Broady.
On Emigration--C. H. Langston, H. F. Douglass, P. H. Clark, L. C. Flewellen and L. D. Taylor.
On Address--D. Jenkins, C. H. Langston, H. F. Douglass, W. R. Casey and Rev. C. Yancy.
On Education--J. M. Langston, J. I. Gaines, C. H. Langston, W. W. Watson and W. H. Day.
On Agriculture--Henry Hurd, Wm. Pinn, A. Pratt, D. Roberts and Rev. C. Yancy.

On the Press--D. Jenkins, W. H. Day, H. F. Douglass, L. D. Taylor and P. H. Clark.

During the progress of the Convention letters were read from several distinguished citizens.

One from C. M. Clay,[2] Esq., which was pointed, eloquent, and manly; it was received with much applause. One from Hon. Horace Mann,[3] which constituted the main feature of the correspondence, it was able, argumentative and full of advice. It was received with a round of applause. One from Hon. Charles Durkee,[4] in every line of which could be seen the true philanthropist. One from Hon. B. F. Wade,[5] which was able, truthful and eloquent.

One from Hon. N. S. Townshend, which was able and practical. It was received with much applause. One from Hon. L. D. Campbell, which though earnest and frank, was nevertheless gloomy; it was received in silence and sadness. The letters will be found on the last pages, and we ask for them a careful perusal.

The subjects which enlisted most the attention of the Convention, were the resolutions in relation to Kossuth,[6] forming military companies, the case of Shadrach[7] the slave, and Emigration to some point on the American continent, and the one on church action. But the subjects which transcended all others in interest were those of Emigration and Colonization.

The discussion on Emigration commenced on one evening and was not terminated until the afternoon of the next day.

The principal speakers were J. M. Langston, of Oberlin, C. H. Langston, of Columbus, P. H. Clark, of Cincinnati, and H. F. Douglass, of Columbus, in favor of emigrating, and Wm. H. Day, of Cleveland, and John I. Gaines of Cincinnati in opposition.

The speeches were able and eloquent, pro and con, and created much interest in the community.

The final vote on African Colonization was complete, only two men in the whole body dared to record their vote in favor of the wicked system. On the subject of emigrating to some point on this continent *en masse*, (the colored people,) the vote stood 36 in opposition and 9 in its favor. This terminated the question which is at this hour absorbing the interest of the leading colored minds of this State. The interest taken in the Convention by the community, exceeded all anticipations. The large Baker street church was filled day and night and many had to go away for want of seats, and though the Convention lasted five days and four nights, the interest was not abated; and when the President announced that the body had adjourned *sine die*, three hearty and earnest cheers were given for GOD and LIBERTY.

Preamble and Resolutions

Whereas, a most cruel and bitter prejudice exists in the United States against the colored race--a prejudice unjust, unnatural, and opposed to the civilization of the age. And whereas, if this state of things is changed and the colored people assume their proper station, it must be by virtue of their own individual action, Therefore,

1. *Resolved,* That the colored people can do more to elevate themselves and break down the illiberal prejudice, which bears upon them as a millstone to blight their prospects, by an honest truthful effort, than can, or will be done, by any or all other agencies combined.

2. *Resolved,* That self-respect is a first and an essential element, for he who does not respect himself, no one else will respect him, and what is true of one is true of a nation.

3. *Resolved,* That they (the colored people) should aspire to be the equal of the "Saxon," equal in intelligence, wealth, enterprise, commerce, mechanism, arts and science.

4. *Resolved,* That the surest mode of being intelligent is to study the best Magazines, papers, authors, and in this way every one may be well posted up in the history, philosophy and literature of the times.

5. *Resolved,* That wealth may be acquired by industry and economy, and believing it to be the great lever of improvement, they, the colored people, should live within, not beyond their income, in order to attain it.

6. *Resolved,* That enterprise may be facilitated among us by two or more persons forming themselves into a company, and creating a fund from time to

time with this definite object in view, and we earnestly recommend the formation of such as soon as practicable.

7. *Resolved,* That they, the colored people, should not settle in large numbers in cities, but go to the country, cut down trees, split rails, and be farmers.

8. *Resolved,* That a colored man who refuses to shave a colored man because he is colored, is much worse than a white man who refuses to eat, drink, ride, walk or be educated with a colored man because he is colored, for the former is a party *de facto* to riveting chains around his own neck and the necks of his much injured race.

9. *Resolved,* That we are in favor of establishing a weekly journal in the State of Ohio, edited by a colored man, devoted to art, literature, morals, religion, and the political interest of the colored race.

10. *Resolved,* That we are in favor of the formation of a State Educational Society, the parent of which, to be located in Cincinnati or elsewhere, with branches for the purpose of establishing schools under the free school system of Ohio.

11. *Resolved,* That we are opposed soul and body to the African Colonization scheme.

12. *Resolved,* That the colored people of Ohio are loyal citizens and will defend the integrity and honor of the State when she shall have extended to her Sons, without respect to color, all the rights and immunities of American citizens.

13. *Resolved,* That we should unite ourselves in business transactions with the masses of the whites, so that the distinction of Irishmen, German, and African may be lost in the general appellation of American citizens.

14. *Resolved,* That this Convention recommend to all colored men in the State of Ohio, over the age of 18 years, to form themselves into independent military companies, when they cannot be admitted into white, to the end that they may acquire a finished military education, for the purpose of rendering efficient aid to this State or the United States in case of a foreign invasion.

15. *Resolved,* That we recommend the teaching of the German Language in our schools, believing that it will prove a great auxiliary to our cause.

16. *Resolved,* That so far as the formation of character is concerned, much depends upon temperance, and we pledge ourselves to do all in our power to promote the temperance reform.

17. *Resolved,* That we sympathize with the oppressed Hungarians and German Socialists in their efforts to throw off the yoke of despotism and reestablish their liberty, and that we hail Gottfried Kinkle and Louis Kossuth, and their representatives on this continent as the true apostles of European liberty.

18. *Resolved,* That we proffer to Kinkle and Kossuth our pecuniary means to aid them in their glorious struggle, and promise to them the same aid which our fathers gave in the American revolution at the battle of New Orleans, and to Bolivar[8] in the contest for Columbian independence.

19. *Resolved,* That tyranny in Russia, Austria and America, is the same and that tyrants throughout the world are united against the oppressed, and therefore the Russian Serf, the Hungarian Peasant, the American Slave and all other oppressed people, should unite against tyrants and despotism.

20. *Resolved,* That we sympathize deeply with the man *Shadrach*, of Boston, who fled from the American Fiery Furnace, to its contrast--the snows of Canada, with *Jerry*,[9] who at Syracuse was transported from the American "Babylon," where like Jeremiah of old, he had been taken captive--with the *men* at *Christiana*[10] who so honored a *Christian* name, by protecting their homes, and refusing to be made slaves; and have learned from their example that liberty is dearer than life, and eternal vigilance its only guarantee.

21. *Resolved,* In guarding our liberty, we will use the mildest means in our judgment, adequate to the end.

22. *Resolved,* That we look upon the law of God as being paramount to all human enactments and inasmuch as the fugitive slave law conflicts with that law, we believe it to be our duty to obey God rather than man, feed the hungry, clothe the naked and do all we can for the redemption of the slave.

23. *Resolved,* That to promote union, and render our action beneficial, we organize the State after the manner of the great political parties, with a

central committee in each county. And be it further resolved, that the President be empowered to appoint the committees for the several counties represented from the members present, and that the central committee be instructed to complete the organization as soon as possible.

24. *Resolved,* That the central committee for calling the next State Convention be requested to collect all the important facts in relation to the anti-slavery movements throughout the world and present the same in a tangible form at the next sitting of that body.

25. *Resolved,* That the next Convention be held in the city of Cleveland, Ohio, and that said city be restricted to ten delegates.

26. *Resolved,* That we claim our rights at the hands of this government, not only because we are native born American citizens, but because our ancestors and ourselves have contributed to the wealth, honor, liberty, prosperity and independence of this country.

Whereas, That in the person of the late Cornelius Burnet, we ever found a faithful and untiring friend of the oppressed, and in whose defence he has sacrificed his property and endangered his life, and that of his family. Therefore,

27. *Resolved,* That his services are held dear to every lover of liberty! And that we will assist in handing his name down to our latest posterity!

28. *Resolved,* That in order to perpetuate his memory in our hearts, we will contribute to the enterprise now in contemplation of erecting a monument to his memory.

29. *Resolved,* That this Convention return their thanks to the citizens of Cincinnati for their hospitality displayed in entertaining the delegates during their sojourn.

30. *Resolved,* That we hereby return our thanks to the President, Vice Presidents and Secretaries, for the faithful and impartial manner in which they discharged their duties.

31. *Resolved,* That we also tender our thanks to the trustees and congregation of the Union Baptist Church, for the use of their beautiful meeting house.

REPORTS OF THE SPECIAL COMMITTEES

Committee on Education

The importance of Education is fully admitted by the intelligent of all classes and conditions of mankind. None who witness the degradation of the ignorant, upon the one hand and the intelligent and refined character of the educated upon the other, can doubt the truthfulness of this admission. Education is indeed the glory of any people. It is the sure palladium of their Liberty--the positive evidence of their permanent and growing elevation. This has been the foundation of those governmental superstructures whose greatness is seen in the beautiful and judicious structure of their politics, their wise and comprehensive diplomacy and the durability of their institutions.

Especially, indeed, are the colored people of this State under many obligations to themselves and posterity to build up a permanent and efficient system of education among them. Our present situation demands united and energetic action in this particular. In the first place there is a great and growing demand for qualified teachers among us. In the second place as the people educate and improve themselves there will be a demand for intelligent ministers. Ministers who possess literary and scientific qualifications, and who take just and enlarged views of *truth*.

And in the third place we must be educated to meet the duties which are pressing themselves upon us from other quarters. We are to lend our aid in promoting the abolition of American Slavery, and in devising some judicious plan for the elevation of the half free of the northern States.

This State has extended to us some aid and we should avail ourselves of the proffered advantage.

We should strive to build convenient school houses and have them filled with well qualified teachers who possess the requisite intellectual and moral qualifications as well as a deep interest in the welfare of the communities --certainly none others should be employed among us.

We therefore recommend the colored people of Ohio to petition the Legislature for the privilege of electing a Superintendent to oversee the public schools of this State.

We also recommend the formation of an Association of the teachers of the colored schools in the State.

We further recommend that the free schools in the State be supported and encouraged in preference to all others, for upon them depend the education of the colored youth of Ohio.

All of which is respectfully submitted,

      J. M. Langston,
      P. H. Clark,
      J. I. Gaines,
      C. H. Langston,
      Wm. H. Day.

Report of Majority of the Committee on Emigration

The majority of the committee to whom was referred the subject of emigration, having given the subject all the consideration and attention which its importance demands and our limited time would allow would respectfully submit the following report:

1. *Resolved,* That we believe that the primary, secondary and ultimate object of the American Colonization Society, is the exportation of the free colored people from the United States, and thereby render the slave property more secure and valuable. We do, therefore, unconditionally, condemn the society and its advocates. Adopted.

2. *Resolved,* That in the voluntary emigration of the colored people of the United States, we see the only relief from the oppressions of the American people, and we believe that the concentration of the colored race at some point upon the continent, will react favorably upon the institution of slavery. Rejected.

3. *Resolved,* That we recommend a national convention of colored men to consider the subject, and appoint an agent who shall visit various portions of the western continent, with a view of determining the most suitable point for the settlement of our people, and the establishment of an independent nationality. Indefinitely postponed. Signed. C. H. Langston,
                    H. F. Douglass,
                     P. H. Clark.

                          Majority.

Minority Report on Emigration

1. *Resolved,* That it is not expedient for the free people of color of the United States to emigrate to any place out of these States while one slave is in chains.

2. *Resolved,* That we have not the means necessary to the accomplishment of the end, and had we them no nation has signified as yet a disposition to receive us as a body.

3. *Resolved,* That this is our native land--the land of our birth and inasmuch as birth gives citizenship according to the decision of the Supreme Court, it is our duty to contend for our rights as American citizens by all the moral and physical means which God has given us.

4. *Resolved,* That in consequence of these facts we recommend our people to remain in the United States. Adopted.

                 L. D. Taylor,
                 L. C. Flewellen.

The Report on Agriculture

Fellow Citizens:

Your committee to consider the Agricultural interests of colored citizens of Ohio, have considered the subject in haste and beg leave to Report:

That, they consider the employment of the farmer to be the most honorable and independent that colored persons can follow at this critical period, and they would recommend to our people, to leave the menial services of towns and cities, and

1st. Learn the science of agriculture by observing the manner that the best farms are conducted.

2d. To purchase books treating on agriculture and horticulture and the proper style of managing domestic affairs.

3d. We recommend as suitable works, Mrs. Lincoln's book on Botany, Cobbert's Gardener and the *Ohio Cultivator*, published at Columbus. Also, the *Ohio Farmer*, published at Cleveland.

4th. In order to get farms, either by purchase or otherwise, we recommend them to purchase, rent or lease the thousands of uncultivated acres of this State.

5th. To settle in numbers sufficiently large to be able to erect schools, churches and machinery, and thus enjoy the comforts of life; live, work and be happy in the land of their birth, where their fathers fought, bled and died, to establish a home in which their descendants might thus live.

6th. To attend the County and State Agricultural fairs; exhibit their fine stock, their fruits and manufactures and if possible claim the highest premiums.

Respectfully submitted,
H. Hurd, *Chairman*.

Report of the Select Committee on Press

It has been and still is an admitted fact that no people can be truly elevated or get beyond the dire and inhuman grasp of the oppressor without the means to enforce and encourage education, industry and morality--this is especially true in relation to the colored people of the west. The best and most speedy means to raise our people from their present stupor and cause them to see more clearly their critical situation, is the establishment and support of an efficient paper that shall advocate and encourage the cardinal principles of our elevation. Therefore,

Resolved, That immediate steps be taken by this Convention for the permanent establishment and support of such a paper.

We submit the following plan:

1st. That a fund of $1000 be raised by the formation of a joint stock company, each share of which shall be worth $50, half of which shall be paid on or before the first day of June 1852, to such person or persons as the committee may appoint; the balance by the 1st day of September, 1852.

2d. That an Agent be appointed to sell the stock and purchase a press.

3d. That it be edited and published by a committee of three, appointed by the stockholders and subject to their order.

4th. That the name and terms of the paper be left to the stockholders.

G. R. Williams,
W. H. Day,
C. H. Langston.

Statistical Report

Gentlemen of the Convention:

Your committee to whom was referred the subject of Statistics, beg leave to report the following:

In the statistics furnished me by the members from thirteen counties, I find that the colored people of those counties own in Real Estate, property which, according to the tax valuation amounts to $1,264,350. Of the personal properties and monies no account has been taken. In the opinion of the committee this is a very important matter and deserves to be taken into account at the next Convention. In the counties heard from there are 15 benevolent societies reported, all of which seem to be accomplishing an important mission. Some few of the counties have reported in regard to schools and educational movements, but as this has not been generally the case your committee make no report concerning them.

The Agricultural and mechanical interests of our people seems entirely to have been forgotten. As these two branches are those that in the opinion of the most enlightened statesmen are the most important and as in the struggle for elevation among us, we should not forget the main lever around which plays the beautiful machinery of government, therefore would your committee beg leave to submit the following:

Resolved, That the State Central Committee shall require and obtain in the couse of the year, full statistics from the county committees relating to the wealth, the educational, agricultural and mechanical interests of the colored people, and

Resolved, That the Central Committee shall report the same to the next State Convention.

All of which is respectfully submitted. Wm. R. Casey.
January 19, 1851.

Report of the Committee on Church Action

The select committee to whom was referred the resolution on church action, would respectfully report the following:

Resolved, That we believe the majority of the Churches in this land to support slave-holding, by holding their own brethren in bonds, or countenancing those who do--that the Gospel is one which brings deliverance to the captive, and that unless the Church places slave-holding on a level with man-stealing, and both on a par with theft, arson, or adultery, and discountenances them accordingly, she fails not only of her high mission, but in that essential characteristic given her when denominated by Jesus as the "Salt of the Earth."

Resolved, That any "Colored Church" which will not do all in its power to discountenance slave-holding and slave-holding apologists, shows a great want of self-respect, a want of intelligent devotion to their own cause, and deserves the disfellowship of all good men.

Resolved, That we hereby give our hearty God-speed to all those Churches and Associations, which, standing out from slavery and its influence, are striving for a pure Christianity. Adopted. Wm. H. Day,
Peter H. Clark,
Lovell C. Flewellen.

The act passed February 10, 1849, for the establishment of Schools for the education of colored children, being generally misunderstood, and in many cases, notoriously perverted; to the great injury of the cause of education among us, thus defeating the object of the framers of that act, the convention deemed it important, that the points sustained by the decision of the Court in Bank, in the case of the Directors of the Colored Common Schools, *vs.* the City of Cincinnati, should be placed before the people of the State, that they might be guided by it, in the formation of School Districts. They are as follows:

The act "to authorize the establishment of separate Schools for the education of colored children; and for other purposes," passed February 10, 1849, *"places colored youth, in Ohio, upon an equal footing with white youth, in respect to Common Schools; and if colored youth in any district, are excluded from Schools for white youth, in the manner indicated in the act, they are entitled to share pro rata with white youth in the Common School funds of such District."*

The "special tax for district purposes" referred to in the third section of the act, *"relates to special taxes for building and repairing School Houses, and the like assessed in particular Districts, and does not embrace general taxes levied on a City at large, and common to all Districts."*

In conformity with a resolution the President appointed the following committees:

Mercer County	Post Office Address
H. Hurd, J. Dover, Wm. P. Trust.	Chickasaw

	Post Office Address
Stark county	
Wm. Pinn, J. Palmer, Wm. Holliday.	Massilon.
Cuyahoga county	
Wm. H. Day, John Brown, George Vosburgh.	Cleveland.
Lorain county	
J. M. Langston, John Watson, John Copeland.	Oberlin.
Gallia county	
J. L. Ward, C. Yancy, John Gee.	Gallipolis.
Warren county	
Asa Pratt, J. Wilson, T. Benford.	Harveysburgh.
Butler county	
J. E. Robbins, S. D. Fox, J. Lewis.	Hamilton.
Montgomery county	
Thos. Jefferson, John Johnson, John Dunlap.	Dayton.
Clinton county	
A. Gregory, Cyrus King, Reuben Henaday.	Wilmington.
Green county	
Rev. J. Bowles, Jesse Devine, W. Roberts.	Xenia.
Pike county	
C. Harris, C. H. Lewis, C. Smith.	Piketon.
Belmont county	
P. Underwood, Alex. Harper.	Barnesville.

Lake county   Post Office Address

W. H. Burnham,   }
Isaac Stunton.   Painsville.

Jackson county

J. W. Stewart
Geo. Woods,   }   Berlin X. Roads.
Noah Newkes.

Logan county

Startling Heathcock,
J. Archer,   }   Bellefontaine.
K. Artist.

Darke county

Rev. J. Clemens,
Mr. Okay,   }   Palestine.
W. Clements.

Trumbull county

Wm. Jenkins.   }   Warren.

Highland county

Nelson Taylor,
Walker Delany,   }   Hillborough.
E. Cumberland.

Hamilton county

P. H. Clark,
J. I. Gaines,   }   Cincinnati.
W. R. Casey.

Ross county

G. R. Williams,
D. J. Williams,   }   Chillicothe.
R. R. Chancellor.

Franklin county

C. H. Langston,
D. Jenkins,   }   Columbus.
J. Booker.

Miami county

Robert Smith.   }   Piqua.

Clark county

W. P. Morgan,
Wm. Roberts,   }   Springfield.
Nelson Morgan.

Seneca county	Post Office Address
D. Roberts, W. A. Scott, F. Whetsell.	Tiffin.
Erie county	
G. J. Reynolds, John Winfield, John Brazier.	Sandusky City.
Champaign county	
H. H. Todd, P. Byrd, L. Adams.	Urbana.
Lawrence county	
G. Jackson, J. Critic, G. W. Bryant.	Burlington.

LETTERS

Burnet House, Cincinnati, December 16, 1851.

Gentlemen:--Your favor of yesterday, informing me of the proposed meeting of the Colored citizens of the State, to take "such measures as are best calculated to enhance the moral, social and political interests" of your people, is received. You do me no more than justice in saying I hold the cause of human rights "*sacred.*" The times also, are "auspicious" for the consideration of these things. For my part, as much as I sympathize with Hungary and her noble sons, I have just as much heart for the wrongs of Africa and her sons! I care nothing for that "*right*" which regards caste--nothing for that philanthropy which extends not to all men of all climes and all colors! If any nation in the Providence of God, happens to be poorer and weaker than another, so much the more does every generous heart feel their woes.

I have no faith in the permanent inferiority of nations! I think all history proves the opposite. Virtue, patience, energy, self-denial and an eternal purpose to improve, may place the African where the Saxon now is! whilst the opposite vices may degrade the Saxon below the African! I avoid no responsibility. My advice shall be given as freely as it is asked. Let it go for what it is worth. So far then, as "morals" are concerned, you will find the best guide in the Christian teachings. In that we all agree. Treating with contempt, all those false teachers of Christ, who recognize *caste* among nations, let us take more to our hearts those followers of our Savior, who honor God by the recognition of the Brotherhood of men! So far as "social" interests are concerned, my opinion is, that you have a long probation before you--so long as the slavery of your race exists in a portion of the Union, I regard social equality, even in the free States, as impossible. But then, as Burns has it, "a man's a man for all that." I would advise *universal education* as the first desideratum--rigid economy in *dress*, and all luxuries. The blacks should "get money." Let them go into the trades--become farmers--manufacturers--where capital and employment are wanting--let them combine, and thus diminish the expense of living, and increase their productive power. Action--action--action--must be the panacea for your present woes, and the "Sessame" of future regeneration. With regard to "political" rights, you must abide your time! I think nothing can be done at present by public resolves, &c. The best road to political elevation lies through the road of INDUSTRY and SELF-RESPECT, which will at last wear us into a generous magnanimity.

Above all, allow me, who am regarded (unjustly, though it be,) as a man of blood, to make *obedience to the laws* the first basis of all elevation, or, *even security!* After a while, if your oppressors do not knock off your chains, you will outgrow them! And may God defend the right! Your ob't serv't,

C. M. Clay.

Messrs. J. I. Gaines, John Jackson, and others, Com. &c.

Washington, December 31, 1851.

Gentlemen:--Your letter of the 17th inst, informed me that the colored people of Ohio propose to hold a State Convention at Cincinnati in the month of January ensuing, "to adopt such measures as are best calculated to enhance their moral, social and political interests," and you are pleased to ask my views "as regards the present position, and future prospects of the colored race in this country."

You submit to me a great problem. Its terms include the colored population alone. But I presume you would not exclude from contemplation the welfare of the white race, so far as that can be promoted by a full regard for the rights of the blacks. Fortunately, however, I believe there is no real conflict of interests between the races. The eternal laws of justice and right would promote the welfare of both. If either resists these laws, it will deserve, and must ultimately receive, an avenging retribution.

The "colored race of this country" now numbers nearly four millions of people. More than three-fourths of this number are in the lowest political and civil condition known to the human race. They are Slaves--a word that includes all woes and wrongs. They are denied all political rights. They are cut off from all civil rights. They can hold no property, but are themselves held as property. They have no marital or conjugal rights; no parental or filial rights; but husband and wife, parent and child, may be torn from each other, under the most agonizing of circumstances, and from the wickedest and meanest of motives--lust, cupidity, or revenge. The slave has no rights of reputation or character. He may be ridiculed, traduced, villified, to any extent, and without any possibility of redress. The laws of the Slave States, so far from securing to the slave any intellectual rights, absolutely build a wall of darkness around him, so that no ray of knowledge can illumine his soul, except such as the master desires for his own profit. In a land also, of professed Christianity, and among a people who call themselves Christian, the slave is without any moral or religious rights. His capabilities of virtue are developed only so far as virtue is profitable or convenient; and when his vices are supposed to be more profitable than his virtues, they only are cultivated. There is no such thing as religious freedom for the slave; for where there is no knowledge there can be no freedom. There is no such thing as free agency for a slave; for his body and limbs are at the control of his master, and his soul, in the blindness of its ignorance, is like any blind creature, under the dominion of its leaders. Thus, all the most precious and sacred relations of a human being to his fellow-beings, to nature and to God, are obliterated by slavery. True, it is said, that the institution of slavery permits the soul of the slave to be enlightened sufficiently to be saved, so that a wretched existence this side of the grave, may be followed by a happy one beyond it. But is this any thing more than saying, that it is impossible for the wickedness of man to send forward its cruelties into eternity, and there wholly to thwart and cancel the goodness of God.

The residue of the colored population of the United States, is in a condition vastly superior to that of the slaves, though still immeasurably below the position which they are entitled, and, as I believe, destined to fill.

Now, as one of the points of your letter regards the "future prospects of the race," it involves a consideration of the means which may be brought to bear upon those prospects, and to determine what they shall be.

I shall only attempt to throw out a few hints on this great subject.

In the first place, I think it neither probable nor desirable that the African race should die out, and leave that part of the earth to which they are native or indigenous, to the Caucasian or any other of the existing races. There are vegetable and animal races which we may lawfully desire to see supplanted by other kinds of vegetable or animal growths; nay, there are tribes of the human family, whose existence we may not wish to see continued, provided always, that they dwindle and reture in a natural way, and without the exercise of violence or injustice to expel them from the earth. But writers on the characteristics of the different races of men, ascribe to the African many of the most desirable qualities belonging to human nature. As compared to the Caucasian race, they are indeed, supposed to be less inventive, to have less power for mathematical analysis, and less adaptation for abstruse investigations generally, are less enterprising, less vigorous, and are less defiant of obstacles. But, on the other hand, there is great unanimity in according to them a more cheerful, joyous and companionable nature, greater fondness and capacity for music, a keener relish for whatever, in their present state of development, may be regarded as beauty, and more quick, enduring and exalted religious affections. The blacks, as a race, I believe to be less aggressive and predatory than the whites, more forgiving, and, *generally*, not capable of the white man's tenacity and terribleness of revenge. In fine, I suppose the almost universal opinion to be, that in intellect, the blacks are inferior to the whites; while in sentiment and affection, the whites are inferior to the blacks.

Under these natural conditions, may not the black develope as high a state of civilization as the whites? Or, what is perhaps the better question, may not independent nations of each race be greatly improved by the existence of independent nations of the other? I believe so.

I believe there is a band of territory around the earth on each side of the Equator, which belongs to the African race. Their Creator adapted their organization to its climate. The commotions of the earth have jostled many of them out of their place; but they will be restored to it when reason and justice shall succeed to the terrible guilt and passions that displaced them.

Under these circumstances, what endeavors shall the free colored population of the United States put forth, in order to improve the condition of themselves, their posterity, and their race?

It is almost too obvious for remark, that no nation or people can ever rise to prosperity, dignity, or power, without intelligence and virtue. These are the only means of individual or social elevation, and the end without the means, is impossible. Every colored man, therefore, who loves his children, or his kind, should be frugal, temperate, industrious and studious. He should abjure all ignoble ease, luxury or pleasure, and concentrate his efforts on the improvement of his family and his people. He should earn money that he may send his children to school and to the best schools; supply his house with books and all available means of knowledge, cultivate the refinement of manners which will help to gain him admission into intelligent society, inform himself of all his duties and fulfill them, and of all his rights and claim them--by no means forgetting the right of suffrage. Whenever any colored child evinces talent, his whole circle of acquaintance should take an interest in him. He should be educated for business, for any such mechanical trade that requires educated labor, for the professions, or for any department of life which he can fill with honor to himself, and with advantage to his fellows.

A condition, at present, nearly, or quite as indispensable to the elevation of the colored people, is the formation of communities by themselves. Scattered, or rather sprinkled, as they now are, among the whites, mostly engaged in occupations which are considered, (however unjustly,) to be subordinate and servile, the spirit of self-reliance and of an ambition for advancement, is fribbled out. At least, it is not nourished, and, like anything else without nourishment, it will not grow. Without a chance to rise to offices and stations of honor, trust or emolument, they must be far, very far, above the average of commen men, to qualify themselves for the discharge of duties, from whose honorable or lucrative performance they are debased. But, did they constitute a community by themselves, such, for instance, as a New England or an Ohio township, they they would rise from domestic labor and mere chance-service, from being ditchers and delvers, into farmers, mechanics, artisans, shop-keepers, printers, editors or professional men. Town officers, justices of the peace and candidates for those state offices which towns are authorized to elect, would be sought and found among themselves. The supply would follow the demand. The whites themselves, with all their education and their opportunities for improvement, by associating more or less with the most intelligent men, would never be able to carry on the affairs even of a municipal corporation, without some practice and training. They must go through with a period of pupilage, by observing the manner in which business is conducted, with a view to conducting it themselves. How difficult, then, for the colored population, in their present isolated and weakened condition, ever to rise, as a body, above a very low level of improvement. How painfully certain it is, under existing circumstances, that, as they are debarred from the opportunity and the ambition of making great progress, they are debased, also, from its possibility; and even what progress they do make, must be, with some extraordinary exceptions, *in the rear* of those among whom they live, and without any chance to pass by or overtake them, in the march of improvement. We may condemn the iniquity of this revolution, as vehemently as we please; but iniquity is a fact which a wise man takes into account as much as any other fact, and, in laying his plans for future action, he recognizes until he can remove it.

On these accounts, I have looked with great interest upon the colored settlements, or colonies, in Canada, in which the whites do not obstrude, and thrust aside the blacks, and seize upon all the posts of honor, and all the eligible and lucrative branches of business. As members of such communities, the blacks will be compelled to think for themselves, to act independently, and to qualify themselves and their children for the various offices and occupations which an independent community necessitates. Their minds will be forced into practical channels, they cannot run to a master or an employer every hour, to learn the order or the forms of business or how to execute work. They must judge, they must foresee, they must adopt means to ends. They must outgrow that most unnatural of relations, (altho' it still exists throughout the greater part of the world,)--that relation, I mean, in which one man furnishes muscles and another man brains. They must be brains unto themselves. Under such an unnatural relation, both the muscles and the brains are likely to be very poor articles. But the blacks will never be able to do these things for themselves, until they set themselves to doing them. A man might as well expect to learn to swim without going into the water.

As one of the consequences of these independent Canadian communities, I lately saw, with exceeding pleasure, that some colored people had been returned as jurors; because I recognized a germ of independence, of progress and of self-government.

Even to conduct the business of a society or a public assembly--a Lyceum, a Debating Club, or a Temperance meeting--is something. It tries the wings. It may only prepare to fly low; but even eagles fly low at first.

It is obvious, however, that even the management of public meetings, or of the affairs of a town in not enough. The colored people must open their eyes to a grander vision. They must qualify themselves for the responsibilities of self-government--to fill various offices, judicial, legislative and executive, of a State. For this purpose, they must, of course, have space, numbers and independence, and at least so much freedom from admixture with the whites, as will give them a fair chance in all the competitions for eligible and honorable stations.

And here, this topic indissolubly connects itself with another, namely, the conditions and prospects of the Slaves of this country, and the duty of the free colored population towards them.

That slavery is to continue always, it would be the grossest atheism to affirm. A belief in the existence of a just Governor of the Universe, includes a belief in the final and utter abolition of slavery. Not even this faith leaves the *means* and the *period* of emancipation unsettled.

Now, there are three modes of emancipation. The first is special and individual, as the emancipation of their slaves by patriotic and christian men who see both the impiety and impolicy of holding their fellow-beings in bondage, and the self-emancipation of the slave by escape from his chains.

Suppose, now, there were a prosperous and independent community of blacks in Jamaica, or in any other of the West India Islands, offering the equality and the dignity of free institutions to whomsoever of their African brethren would emigrate thither, would not numerous of the more benevolent and conscientious of the slaveholders give freedom to their slaves with the expectations and perhaps the means of their becoming citizens of such a government, and rising at once into the dignity of freemen. Not only so, but, with such a people in our neighborhood, would not thousands and thousands of the most healthy, intelligent and valuable slaves exercise that "inalienable right of life, liberty and the pursuit of happiness," which they are authorized by the law of Nature and of Nature's God, at any moment to enforce, by self-emancipation,--that is, escape. If the last census is to be relied on, about a thousand slaves escaped during the year that preceded its being taken. I have no doubt this is a great exaggeration; for many slaves who are charged with escaping to the north, are stolen and sent to the south. But suppose a thousand escaped into the bleak, and, to them, unnatural climate of Canada. Would not many times this number have exercised this unquestionable right, if there had been an asylum on the south side of the Union as accessible as that on the North? Suppose a free and independent Republic to exist in Jamaica or Cuba, with language, or even with laws and civil institutions like our own in which the hellish atrocities of our Fugitive Slave Law were unknown, and in which, therefore, the fugitive slave would be protected from his pretended owner, as we would now protect Kossuth and his glorious Hungarian compatriots from the clutch of Austria, what a glorious opportunity would this afford, from all southern ports and from the mouths of all the great southern rivers, to exercise this inextinguishable and indestructible right of self-emancipation.

I would not, however, be understood by this to commend or countenance the recently proposed plan of the authorities of Jamaica to import the colored people of the United States into that island, as indented apprentices, or laborers bound to service for a term of years. But, I would encourage and urge the migration of such of our more intelligent colored population, as have the means to buy land and become independent freeholders or proprietors. Real Estate, in Jamaica, is now at an immense discount. Making allowance for difference in fertility, land can be bought there almost as cheap as in any of the new States; and the purchaser can at once enter society on an equality with most of his neighbors. He can have all that any man ought to demand--a station according to his character, talents and attainments.

Another method of emancipation is by act of the Legislatures of the slave-holding States. Without fixing the time when this shall be done, it is not an improbable, nor, as I trust, a very future event, in regard to the northern tier of slave States. Few things would tend to hasten such a consummation more than the existence, in the law of all the world, of self-administered, successful governments by people of African lineage. Whether those governments should exist on the western coast of Africa, in the West Indian Archipelago, or elsewhere, the demonstration and influence would be the same. It would silence; it would annihilate that impious argument that slavery is a benefit to the slave. It would give full scope and encouragement to that bitter nature of the slave-holder, which, in spite of all his sophistries and his selfishness, is forever counselling him that it is a sin for man to claim property in man. It would bring the public opinion of nations to bear with irresistible force upon the institutions of slavery, and would put its voluntary upholders out of the pale of civilized men.

I would then adjure the free people of color to do whatever in them lies, to build up free colored communities, in whatever parts of the world may be most favorable to the communities themselves, and for re-acting upon their colored brethren in this country, I would invoke a missionary spirit among them. Nay, it is a higher than a missionary spirit. The missionary carries christianity among the heathen; but this enterprise would re-act upon heathenism in a land professed by christians. What a glorious change it would be in the condition and in the hopes of the world, so far as this question of slavery is concerned, if instead of our present debatings in Congress, whether we should establish a government line of steamers to the western coast of Africa, free and prosperous republics on that coast were debating whether they should not establish a government line of steamships to us. Would it not seem as though slavery in any place, could hardly co-exist with such a condition of the nations of the earth.

Let me here guard myself against mis-construction on one point. The idea of forcibly expelling the American born negro from the place of his birth and residence, and driving him out of the country against his will, is as abhorrent to my notions of justice and equality, as it can be to those of any one. The next most cruel thing to kidnapping a race of men, forcing them from their home and dooming them to slavery in a foreign land, would be the seizure of the descendants of that race, and driving them from the new home they had acquired. So great a crime as this second expatriation would be,

could hardly be conceived unless by a mind that had prepared itself for it
by participating in the commission of the first. My moral nature, therefore,
revolts, with an abhorrence which I cannot express, from those recommendations
of the governors of some of the southern States, who have proposed to expel
from their borders all free colored persons, under the terrible penalities of
fine, imprisonment and a subjugation to slavery of them and their descendants.
The proposition made last year, in the Senate of the United States, by a
Senator from Massachusetts, to appropriate the entire proceeds of the sales
of the public lands--estimated to be worth $200,000,000--to transport the
free colored population from the slave States, which would instantaneously
have set in motion the legislative and physical power of those states to
expel that population (and would have given the strongest guarantees for the
security and the perpetration of slavery among them,) from their homes, I regard as one of the most wicked ideas ever conceived by the human mind. And
I give it this bad eminence, in full recollection of the command of Herod to
murder all the Hebrew children under two years of age, of the persecution and
massacre of the Albigenses and Waldenses, and other culminating instances of
human wickedness.

But while I would oppose every form of force or intimidation to expel the
free colored people from the land of their nativity, I should rejoice beyond
measure to see great, intelligent and powerful African communities springing
up, wherever by their power or their proximity, they could encourage or succor
their enslaved brethren in this country. And I cannot see why the benevolent
and moral energy of the free colored people amongst us should not flow into
this channel.

There is one other means of emancipation--such as our revolutionary
fathers adopted against Great Britain, and such as Hungary has lately adopted
against Austria, not only with the justification, but with the approval of
the civilized world. For this there are two conditions: a sufficient degree
of oppression to authorize an appeal to force, and a chance, on the part of
the oppressed, of bettering their condition. The measure of the first condition is already full--heaped up--running over. The second condition will be
fulfilled, either when the slaves believe they can obtain their freedom by
force, or when they are so elevated and enlarged in their moral conceptions,
as to appreciate that glorious supplication of Patrick Henry, "Give me
liberty or give me death!"

It is most devoutly to be implored that God will save the slaveholders
from the madness of defying that vengeance that will assuredly be visited
upon them, if they continue much longer to act upon, or to advocate the
atheistic dogma that slavery is to be eternal. The very declaration that
slavery shall be eternal will give birth to the resolve that it shall not be
eternal! Hence, inevitable collision. And the ultimate result of collision
is as certain as the fulfillment of any natural law;--as certain as that gun
powder will explode on the application of fire, or that the generation of
steam, without vent, could convert the solid earth itself into another group
of asteroids. In such a collision, on one side is the power of man; on the
other side is the Omnipotence of God, "He that leadeth into captivity shall
go into captivity," saith the sure word of prophecy. "The Almighty hath no
attribute," says Mr. Jefferson, "which can take part with us in such a contest." However disastrous may be the result of the first, or the tenth, or
the hundredth struggle on the part of the slave; however many of the colored
Hancock's and Adams' of that revolution may be singled out for vengeance and
placed beyond the reach of pardon; however many Blums and Batthyasnies may
be massacred in cold blood, each death will be transfigured into a multitude
of more glorious lives, and for every drop of heroic blood which the earth
shall drink, it will send back an armed man.

Now, there are two things which, above and beyond all others, the Angel
of this Apocalypse will proclaim: first, a warning to the slave-Power, deep
and piercing as an afflatus of the Spirit of God, to escape this retribution,
by a voluntary and timely abandonment of its unholy domination, and second,
if the admonition is resisted, the inexorable and awful certainty of the doom
of that power.

Now this third method of emancipation, though infinitely to be deprecated, though to be accepted only in case the preceding methods fail to bring
relief, yet as an alternative to endless slavery, it is to be hoped for,

and *provided for*. And what provision can be so efficacious and toward, as that of establishing independent communities--in the West Indies, on the coast of Africa, or elsewhere,--which, should the great crisis ever arise, will be able to act for the freedom of their brethren in this country, as the laws of God may require. I say, as the *laws* of God, but ought I not rather to say, as the *example* of God may require; for did not He secure the emancipation of the children of Israel, by sinking their oppressors in the waters of the Red Sea? There was both justice and mercy in that dispensation. The pursuers only were destroyed, wives and children and those who did not participate in the guilt of the pursuit, were saved.

In considering this extreme aspect of the case of slavery, (never I trust to be realized, and certainly to be realized only as the last resort of outraged humanity,) we cannot refrain from seeing how vastly more efficacious for good would be the powers of the services of leading colored men, in a community of their own, than when scattered, and comparatively lost among people who have so little regard for their rights, as any existing community of whites now have. Frederick Douglass, Henry Bibb, Samuel R. Ward, William Crafts,[11] William Brown, surnamed Box,[12] and a score of others whom I might name, have talents that would adorn the highest stations in civilized society. Instead of making speeches they might be making laws. Instead of commanding the types of a newspaper press, they might be commanding armies and navies; and making those appreciate the weight of their power who will not regard the force of their logic and their humanity. Robert Purvis is a gentleman whose manners and education would become a court; yet now I suppose he cannot be so much as a constable or justice of the peace.

Do not these considerations, gentlemen, bear directly and strongly upon the great question, as your letter expresses it, "of the future prospects of the colored race in this country,"--that is, as I understand you, the colored race, both bond and free? I think they do. While, therefore, it is *our* duty to do whatever we can to ameliorate the condition of the colored people among us and especially to resist the pro-slavery action of ambitious politicians and of the general government, it is *your* duty to project some broad and comprehensive plan, and to devote all your energies to its execution, which shall look to the ultimate redemption and elevation, within the shortest practicable period, of your brethren in bondage, "in this country," and throughout the globe. Gird yourselves for this work. Seek for wealth as a means of education, advancement and influence; build yourselves up as far as possible into a condition of independence; let your hearts be penetrated with the moral and religious fervor which belongs to a good and a holy cause, and may God bless your endeavors.

Very truly, Yours, &c.   Horace Mann.

Messrs. John I. Gaines, Wm. H. Day,
John Jackson, and David Jenkins, } Central Committee.

Washington, Dec. 25th, '51.

Gentlemen:

I have the pleasure to acknowledge the receipt of your esteemed favor of the 17th, acquainting me of a Convention to be holden at Cincinnati the 14th of January by the colored people of Ohio, and asking my opinion as to their present position and future prospects in this country. The condition of this unfortunate class of our citizens is truly distressing and alarming. Like Joseph of old, they have been sold into bondage; but the same kind Parent that watched over and delivered him from Slavery, is alike mindful of them, and of their long-suffering and forbearnace. May they be patient and persevere a little while longer, when deliverance shall come. The slave will not only throw off his chains, but a great nation will be redeemed from worse than Jewish pride--the slavery of party, and enter upon its sublime mission of Christian Democracy, to regenerate the people and nations--not with the sword, but by the practical illustration of a humane and just government, carrying out those wise measures begun by the Fathers of the Revolution. The kidnapping law which disgraces our Federal Statute, is founded in supreme selfishness, and meant for evil, but God in his providence is overruling it for good. Its enormities are so palpable, as to startle and arrest the attention of that portion of community hitherto indifferent to the cause of suffering humanity. When the American people become fairly aroused in regard to the rights of man, there will remain no doubt about the final issue of the controversy now enlisting the attention of both countries. It rejoices my heart, gentlemen, to know that the colored race are becoming more active in asserting their rights. The Convention to which you allude, will result in good I cannot doubt, and materially aid the cause of emancipation. None can plead so eloquently and efficiently against tyranny and oppression as the victims of despotism themselves. Nevertheless, *all* should bear in mind that blessed injunction "remember those who are in bonds as being bound with them." You justly remarked that the people of the old world and of the new have taken up the problem of human rights, and are solving it for themselves. This is the surest indication of final success. Kossuth's present mission to the United States appears to my mind strikingly analogous to St. Paul's at Corinth, where he proclaimed, "He whom ye ignorantly worship, him declare I unto you." The very happy and forcible manner in which Kossuth elucidates the great principle of Justice, and the glorious doctrine of human Progress, cannot fail to produce a lasting and most beneficial effect on the mind and heart of the American people. The principle of Law which he elaborated so eloquently and powerfully to the New York Bar, ought to be indeliby impressed on every mind throughout the world. It is a great elementary principle which should be understood at the very threshold of moral and political investigation. I will here quote a few lines from the commencement of that speech:

"Let me say, as a member of your profession, in respect to my opinion about the system of codification as opposite to customary law; you have the great authority of Livingston,[13] and though it may be a piece of presumption for one to state a principle contrary to his, yet I would remark I differ from him. I confess I am no friend to codification. I am no friend to it because I am a friend to free and unresisted progress. It is an iron hand that hinders the circulation of intelligence, and fetters the development which freely must go on towards boundless perfection--*the destiny of humanity.* In conclusion, gentlemen, allow me to express my best wishes for your welfare, and for the cause you seek to promote."

Charles Durkee.

John I. Gaines and others, Central Committee.

Washington, Dec. 26th, 1851.

Messrs. Gaines, Day, Jenkins, and Jackson:
Gentlemen:--Yours of the 17th inst., is just received, and it gives me great pleasure to see our colored friends actively moving in so just and glorious an enterprise as stated in your letter. You have to encounter a most unjust and illiberal prejudice, which everybody knows, is all wrong; but it nevertheless, exists, and you must take things as they are, and not as they should be. The first thing, then, on your part, is to overcome this prejudice, by proving in your own persons that it is untrue and unfounded. In order to this, I would advise, as far as possible, that you should withdraw from all menial employments, form yourselves into communities by yourselves, when, by cultivating the soil, and practicing the mechanical arts, you will soon attain to independence, and thus situated you will have the means of educating your children, and bestowing upon them those advantages which they cannot, at present enjoy, while scattered about among the white people. They will thus acquire habits of self-respect and independence, and this will compel your white brethren to respect you: and I doubt not, soon convince them, that with equal opportunities, you are by no means their inferiors. I rejoice to see that the colored people have taken their own destinies into their own hands. This is the right way. All just men will sympathize with them, and aid them all in their power. But, after all, their ultimate emancipation, must depend upon themselves. Be temperate, industrious, and by all means in your power, promote among yourselves the cause of education, and the result cannot be doubtful. The color of the skin is nothing,--when was it ever known that virtue, industry and intelligence were not respected? When these results of your present most patriotic enterprise shall be realized, those who defame you most, will be the first to do you reverence.

I rejoice to see you organizing among yourselves, form one great brotherhood throughout the State, so that you can all co-operate to the same great end. And your property, power and importance will soon be felt and acknowledged--wealth and independence always command respect.

White people, while poor and ignorant, are no more respected than are you. I say again, color is nothing. When you have attained to intelligence and independence, you will soon be admitted to your social and political rights. Do not suppose, from what I have said, that I take all colored persons to be ignorant, far from it. I know many who will compare favorably with the best of the whites, but generally it is not so. Nor is this to be wondered at. You have labored under infinitely greater disadvantages. But it is to be your chief glory that you overcome these disadvantages. I feel, indeed, a deep interest in your Convention, and I have no doubt it will be of great advantage to your people. I hope you will meet together often, and take your own destiny into your own keeping. Rely on yourselves and you cannot fail. Of course, I have no definite plan of organization to recommend at present, but I should be pleased to hear from you often, and what course of operations the Central committee have in view.

Gentlemen, I have the honor to be most respectfully,

Yours, &c.,
B. F. Wade.

Messrs. John I. Gaines, W. H. Day, David Jenkins, and John Jackson, *Central Committee.*

Washington, January 8, 1852.

Messrs. John I. Gaines, John Jackson, and others--

Gentlemen: I received your letter of the 15th ultimo, asking my opinion of the "present position and future prospects of the colored race in this country."

It is an astonishing and lamentable fact, that in the nineteenth century, and in these United States, there should be found more than three millions of human beings in the condition of slaves, and almost half a million more who, if nominally free, are excluded from the most valued privileges of citizenship. Were the colored race incapable of anything better, or had they fallen into their present condition through any fault or choice of their own, some apology for keeping them in bondage might be attempted, but as no one imputes blame to them, or believes them incapable of intellectual and moral culture, and when they can only be kept in chains by the force of inhuman enactments which, in addition to all other wrongs, purposely consign them to ignorance and consequent degradation; we are compelled to say, there is no defence or apology for this system that can avail before High Heaven or an enlightened world. The evil consequences of slavery are almost as apparent upon the white race as upon the colored, and if the South suffers most there is no part of the North that does not reap some of its bitter fruits. It is an element of weakness and discord; it endangers our national existence by exposing us to foes from without and by exciting angry contentions at home; it is fatal to enterprise, industry and economy and therefore most injurious to national prosperity; it destroys the vitality and efficiency of the church, and saps the foundation of public and private morality. No evil existing in the country compares with it in magnitude, and therefore nothing to the same extent challenges the attention of the Christian or Statesman.

There may be some consolation in the reflection that perhaps the present condition of the colored race in this country is better, all things considered, than at any previous period since its introduction upon this continent. And it may also be said that the representatives of the race here are in advance of those who remained on the other side of the Atlantic. There are among you scholars, artists, mechanics, merchants, cultivators of the soil, and men of wealth and refinement who would be an honor to any race, and whose equals cannot now be found in the nations from which you were descended. I will not say that colored men in America are happier than those in Africa but they certainly have a larger capacity for happiness and this with a hope of a better future is something gained. Cruel and bitter has been your bondage and discipline but a Benevolent Providence has so overruled all as to compel some good to grow even out of evil.

That a brighter future awaits the colored race I confidently believe. The dreary night of slavery and oppression is wearing away, the day of universal liberty and brotherhood is already dawning upon the world, and every nation and every race will soon enjoy its glorious light. Whatever changes or revolutions add to the freedom and happiness of one portion of the human family, indirectly, perhaps, but certainly contribute to improve the condition of the rest of mankind. In all the triumphs of modern science and art, and in all the progress of the age, the colored race has a deep interest --they have suffered more than others, a greater change therefore awaits them and they may look forward with fonder hopes to the "good time coming."

As Anglo Saxons feel pleasure and pride an augur for themselves a glorious destiny from whatever is achieved by that race in any of its homes, so may the colored race draw encouragement and hope from whatever it is accomplishing in this or other countries. Every successful effort of individuals or of communities that serves to demonstrate the capabilities of your race will tend to disarm prejudice and ensure your respect. You have a deep interest in the personal success of each other, but a still deeper interest in the success of the experiments you are making as communities, whatever motives or causes have placed you in this country, in the West Indies, on the coast or in the interior of Africa, the necessity of mutual sympathy and co-operation is the same; success at one point will benefit all, failure any where will be equally widespread in its injury.

Whether your development as individuals and as a race will be best secured by being scattered over the whole country in immediate contact with other races, or by association as a separate community in some parts of it, or in the West Indies, or on the coast of Africa is a deeply interesting problem, the solution of which, if now difficult, may some day be pointed out more clearly by the finger of Providence, meanwhile I fully recognize the right of every human being to dwell in any part of God's earth where he may choose, and to enjoy there all the rights and blessings that pertain to humanity. I cannot believe that you are destined to be swallowed up and absorbed by any other race, neither can I for a moment believe that God has designed you to continue to be "hewers of wood and drawers of water" for other men. Your race has a noble destiny and its own measures of growth and happiness to fill and enjoy.

I rejoice that you meet to discuss all the questions that relate to your well being, and that some of you who have words of wisdom are ready to utter them. I rejoice that those of you who possess wealth are willing to lay it on the altar of liberty and progress. I rejoice also to know that so many of your people are striving to obtain that liberty and industrial education which will qualify them to discharge their duties to themselves and to society. You have friends of whose sympathy and assistance you may be assured, but after all you will not forget that God helps those only who help themselves. "Who would be free themselves must strike the blow." Your friend,

Norton S. Townshend.

House of Representatives, Washington, Jan. 5, '52.

Messrs. John I. Gaines, and others, Cen. Com., &c--

The courteous terms of your letter, of the 17th ult., asking my opinion "as regards the present position and future prospects of the colored race in this country," requires me at least to acknowledge its receipt.

I regard the "*present position*" of your race in this country, as infinitely worse than it was ten years ago. The States which were *then* preparing for gradual emancipation, are *now* endeavoring to extend, perpetuate and strengthen slavery! In others where the master *then* could teach a slave, he is *now* a criminal if he attempts to enlighten him! A vast amount of territory which was *then* free is *now* everlasting dedicated to slavery! The citizen of a free state could *then* speak a kind word to a fugitive for liberty without molestation; if he does so *now* he hazards an indictment and trial for treason! These are but a portion of the fruits (bitter as they may be to your people,) produced during the last ten years of this "age of progress and reform" through a war which cost our nation *two hundred and thirty millions* of dollars,[14] and an immense number of precious lives of her citizens. And I may add that all this has been accomplished in the face of the various party organizations which have professed to labor for different results.

I am "neither a prophet nor the son of a prophet," and from the lights of the past I confess I see nothing to justify a promise of much to your "*future prospects.*" We seem to have fallen on strange times. Instead of seeking to reform the great evil in our own land, and to fortify and make strong our own liberties, our people seem determined not merely to extend our institutions over "*the whole--the boundless* continent" here, but to reform the governments of the old world, "peaceably if they can--forcibly if they must." Whilst there exists this disposition to cut out this immense amount of work for "young America," candor compels me to say that my dim vision enables me to see nothing that is flattering to your "future prospects."

This is, however, a *coming future* when oppression may be over--when the principles of the *equality of men* will be enforced. You may hope for the glories of *that* future. You may strengthen your "prospects" for them by concentrating all your feeble powers to build up and sustain institutions of learning, which will disseminate knowledge, and thus increase your power which will purify and elevate the morals of your people, and dignify their character.

                Respectfully,   L. D. Campbell.

The following letter was sent to various persons, the replies to which will be found in the preceding pages.

                          Cincinnati, December 15, 1851.

Dear Sir:--The Colored people of Ohio will hold a Convention, in the City of Cincinnati, on the 14th day of January, 1852. The great object it has in view, is to adopt such measures, as are best calculated to enhance the moral, social, and political interest of the colored citizens of the State.

The times are auspicious for holding such a meeting. The people of the old and new world, have taken up the problem of human rights, and are solving it for themselves; and knowing the deep interest you have heretofore manifested in this SACRED CAUSE, is the only apology we have to offer, in asking you, your opinion as regards the present position and future prospects of the colored race in this country.

That we may receive an answer at an early day, is the ardent wish of
                            Sir, Yours very respectfully,
                            John I. Gaines,
                            William H. Day,   *Central Committee.*
                            David Jenkins,
                            John Jackson.

Copy in the Harvard University Library.

REFERENCE NOTES

1. Millard Fillmore (1800-1874), thirteenth president of the United States, signed the Fugitive Slave Act of 1850.
2. Cassius Marcellus Clay (1810-1903), American politician and abolitionist, was born in Madison County, Kentucky. Although his father was a wealthy and influential slaveholder, Clay had early developed a bitter hatred toward that institution. Educated at Yale, he later founded in 1845, at Lexington, Kentucky, the *True American*, an uncompromising antislavery journal which subsequently was published at Cincinnati after hostile citizens had boxed his printing equipment and shipped it there. During the Civil War, Clay was a close friend and advisor of Abraham Lincoln.
3. Horace Mann (1796-1859), educator and antislavery Whig member of Congress, was known as the "Father of the American Public School System" because of his work in reorganizing the entire public school system of Massachusetts.
4. Charles Durkee, an influential supporter of black rights, was a Republican senator from Wisconsin during the 1850's.
5. Benjamin Franklin Wade (1800-1878), antislavery senator from Ohio, served from 1851 to 1869. Wade was a Whig at first and then joined forces with the Republican Party. A vigorous and uncompromising supporter of black rights, he was associated with the Radical Republicans in Congress during and

after the Civil War and insisted that the Southern blacks be enfranchised and planter estates confiscated and distributed among blacks.

6. Louis Kossuth (1802-1894), Hungarian patriot and leader of the unsuccessful national revolt of 1849, disappointed American abolitionists because of his avoidance of the slavery issue while on tour of the United States in order to get maximum support for the cause of Hungarian independence. For Douglass' criticism of Kossuth, see "Letter to Kossuth," *Frederick Douglass' Paper*, Feb. 26, 1852, reprinted in Foner, *Life and Writings of Frederick Douglass*, II, 170-172.

7. In February 1851, Shadrach, a Negro waiter in Boston, was arrested and charged with having escaped from the South. Before the case was decided, a body of Negroes led by Lewis Hayden broke into the prison, seized Shadrach, and dispatched him to Canada.

8. Simon Bolivar (1783-1830), South American revolutionist, was called the Liberator. When the revolution against Spain broke out in 1810, he became a militant and enthusiastic patriot. With the subsequent independence of several South American states during the 1820's, Bolivar became the president of Greater Columbia and created Bolivia. In 1826 he expanded his vision of a united South America by calling the first Pan American Conference, which convened at Panama. While he failed in his attempts to bring about continental unity due to internal dissensions, petty jealousies, and fears of dictatorship which several republics thought he was trying to foster, he nevertheless is today considered the greatest of Latin American heroes.

9. The Jerry Rescue occurred at Syracuse, New York, on October 1, 1851. Gerrit Smith and other abolitionists forcibly rescued the fugitive slave Jerry McHenry, who had been seized and imprisoned by a deputy United States marshal, and helped him to escape to Canada and to freedom. A number of those involved in the rescue were arrested and tried.

10. In the early dawn of September 11, 1851, an attack was made on the home of William Parker, of Christiana, Pennsylvania, to arrest some fugitive slaves said to be hidden there. The Negroes in the neighborhood came to their defense, and a battle took place in which Edward Gorsuch, a Maryland slaveowner, was killed by Parker and Gorsuch's son was wounded. Parker escaped to Canada, assisted from Rochester by Frederick Douglass. Thirty-eight of the men involved in the battle, thirty-six Negroes and two whites were indicted for treason against the United States and brought to trial in Lancaster County Courthouse. Castner Hanway, a Quaker who had refused to assist in capturing the fugitives, was the first to be tried. The jury found Hanway not guilty, and the others were released. An old study of the Christiana Riot is W. U. Hensel, *The Christiana Riot and the Treason Trials of 1851* (Lancaster, Pa. 1911). But it has been superseded by Jonathan Katz, *Resistance at Christiana: The Fugitive Slave Rebellion, Christiana, Pennsylvania, September 11, 1851: A Documentary Account* (New York, 1974).

11. William and Ellen Craft were the famous black couple from Georgia who escaped from slavery by the ingenious method of her assuming the role of a slaveowner and he serving as her slave. After their escape, they lectured widely in the North and England.

12. The reference is to Henry "Box" Brown, a slave, who in 1856 was put in a box and shipped from Richmond to Philadelphia by way of the Adams Express Company. On arriving at the Anti-Slavery Office in Philadelphia, his sudden "resurrection" form his confinement created a sensation among the abolitionists and their sympathizers and gained new adherents to the cause.

13. The reference is to Edward Livingston (1764-1836), celebrated jurist, statesman and diplomat. In a long and brilliant career he served in Congress as a Jeffersonian Republican (1795-1801), was appointed a U.S. district attorney of New York (1801) and from 1801 to 1803 served as the elected Mayor of New York City. Financial difficulties drove him to New Orleans, where in 1803, he resumed the practice of law. Later he entered Louisiana politics, serving successively as a state legislator (1820), congressman (1822-1829), U.S. senator (1829-1831), and as President Jackson's Secretary of State (1833-1835). He gained enduring fame, however, as a codifier of laws, drafting in 1805 a code of procedure, which was adopted by the Louisiana legislature and was the first real law code in the United States. In 1825 he presented to the Louisiana legislature a comprehensive criminal code. Although not adopted by that body, it gained considerable acclaim abroad.

When finally published in 1833 it became a model for state penal codes in the United States. Elected as a member of the Academy of the Institute of France, Livingston was described by Sir Henry Maine as "the first legal genius of modern times."

  14. The reference is to the Mexican War, fought by the United States from 1846 to 1848.

MEMORIAL OF JOHN MERCER LANGSTON FOR COLORED PEOPLE OF OHIO TO
GENERAL ASSEMBLY OF THE STATE OF OHIO, JUNE, 1854

JOHN MERCER LANGSTON

This promising young man has recently won, for himself, the respect and gratitude of the colored citizens of the State of Ohio, by his able and manly efforts to secure for them the abrogation of everything in the organic law of that State, making a discrimination between its citizens on account of color. It is hardly necessary to state, in our columns, the fact that, without making any merit of it, Mr. Langston permits himself to be known as a member of the despised colored race. He is known also as having born a very distinguished part in the proceedings of the greatest Convention ever held in this country by the colored people. Mr. Langston is a farmer; and what he does in the way of philanthropy and patriotism, has the merit of being at his own expense; and he is, therefore, all the more entitled to the grateful respect and affection which we believe he largely enjoys among the colored people throughout the free states.

We take pleasure in laying before our readers the following, which sufficiently explains itself, being a report on the subject, from a Committee of the Ohio State Legislature:

Report of the Select Committee on Petitions and Memorials from colored persons, in Senate, April 19, 1854. Laid on the table and ordered to be printed

The committee to whom was referred sundry petitions and memorials, asking the political enfranchisement of the colored citizens of Ohio, has had the matter under consideration, and herewith submits a bill providing for an amendment of the constitution of the State, in accordance with the wishes of the petitioners, and accompany the same with the following

Report

The various reasons for extending the right of suffrage to colored persons are so ably set forth in the memorial of J. Mercer Langston, which was read to the Senate during the present session, and referred to this committee, that nothing further in the way of arguments seemed to be required. The committee therefore, adopts the language of that memorial and makes it a part of this report, and this course appears the more appropriate to the committee, inasmuch as Mr. Langston had been appointed by a State convention of colored people, to memorialize the General Assembly on this subject, he therefore, speaks by authority, and may be presumed to present the subject as it is understood and felt by the parties most interested. This report then is the plea of the colored citizens of Ohio, to their white fellow-citizens, and your committee unites with the disfranchised in begging that it may be impartially and candidly considered.

MEMORIAL OF J. MERCER LANGSTON

To the General Assembly of the State of Ohio

Your memorialist has been selected as the representative of the twenty-five thousand half freemen of Ohio, to ask your honorable body to the necessary and appropriate steps for striking from the organic law of this State, all those clauses which make discriminations on the ground of color.[1]

In doing this, we feel that we are but asking that the constitution of our State be made to reflect, in all its truthfulness and deep significance, the following living, breathing sentiment of the Declaration:--"We hold these truths to be self-evident, that all men are created free and equal, and endowed by their creator with certain inalienable rights, among which are life, liberty and the pursuit of happiness."

In doing this, we also feel that we but ask that the constitution of Ohio be made to harmonize with the genius and spirit of the constitution of the United States, which was ordained to establish justice and secure the blessings of liberty to the people of this country.

Nor are we unmindful of the fact that in making this request, we are asking your honorable body to take the first step towards making our government a democracy, which in the eloquent language of Hon. William Allen, "asks nothing but what it concedes, and concedes nothing but what it demands. Destructive only to despotism, it is the sole conservator of liberty, labor and property. It is the sentiment of freedom, of equal rights and equal obligations. It is the law of nature pervading the law of the land."

Since we present our memorial in the name of the Declaration, in the name of the constitution of the United States, the supreme law of the land, and in the name of genuine democracy, we are confident that you will consider it patiently and without prejudice.

What then, are the grounds upon which we claim the elective franchise?

In answering this question, we have to say, in the first place, that we are men. Nor is it necessary to enter upon an argument in support of so self-evident a proposition. We possess the physical, the intellectual and the attributes common to humanity. We have the same feelings, desires and aspirations that other men have; and we are capable of the same high intellectual and moral culture. As men then, we have rights, inherent rights, which civil society is bound to respect, nay, more, which civil society is bound to protect and defend. Prominent among those rights, and one which we deeply love and cherish, is the elective franchise. It is the privilege of saying who shall be our rulers, and what shall be the character of the laws under which we live. By none is this right, held in higher estimation than by the colored men. And those greatly mistake who think that we are contented without it. We are not. We know that it is one of our dearest rights. We feel that we ought to have it. We feel that civil society is under obligation to secure it to us, and protect us in its enjoyment. The first consideration that we offer, therefore, in favor of granting our claim, is the fact that it is a *dictate of justice and fair dealing*, between civil society and men living within its jurisdiction.

But it may be said in reply to this, that the elective franchise is not to be numbered among our inherent rights. It may be contended that the voting privilege is one of expedience. We, however, are not of this faith. We have no confidence in this principle. Self-government, in our opinion, is an inherent right. And without the privilege of saying who shall be the makers of our laws, who shall be their executors, and what shall be their general character, there can be no self-government. This was the view taken of the matter by the Fathers of the Republic. And it was upon this principle as enduring granite that they built up the free institutions of the land.

We could, with propriety, however, claim so much at your hands, if we were foreigners. But when it is remembered that we are native born inhabitants, and by our birth citizens, the consideration which has just been

offered, appears doubly significant, and therefore doubly forcible. It is
needless for us in grounding our claim to the elective franchise upon our
nativity, to remind you that it is a principle fully recognized by the constitution of the country, that natural birth gives citizenship, otherwise, our
naturalization laws are absurd and nonsensical. Says Chancellor Kent, in
confirmation of our view "citizens, under our constitution and laws, [means]
free inhabitants born within the United States, or naturalized under the laws
of Congress. If a slave, born in the United States, be manumitted, or otherwise lawfully discharged from bondage, or if a black man be born within the
United States, and born free, he becomes thenceforward a citizen." If Chancellor Kent's principle be correct, we may ask with some degree of force where
is the right to disfranchise us--where is the right to strip us of our citizenship? Said the Hon. Mr. Baldwin, in the U.S. Senate, "When the constitution of the United States was framed, colored men voted in a majority of these
States; they voted in the State of New York, in Pennsylvania, in Massachusetts, in Connecticut, Rhode Island, New Jersey, Delaware and North Carolina,
and long after the adoption of the constitution they continued to vote in
North Carolina and Tennessee also. The constitution of the United States
makes no distinction of color. There is no word 'white' to be found in that
instrument. All free people then stood upon the same platform in regard to
their political rights, and were so recognized in most of the States of the
Union. The free colored citizens of these States are so much entitled to the
rights of citizenship, as are men of any other color or complexion whatever.
To this day, in the State of Virginia, free colored persons born in that
State, are citizens."

But to deprive us of citizenship, is not only to outrage the well established principle of our political creed, that natural birth gives citizenship, but it is to trample in the dust that practically adopted principle in
the law of nations, to wit, that those born in a country become members of the
body politic on reaching the requisite age, and discharging the equal responsibilities imposed upon all. This is the principle which the nations of the
earth generally have seen fit to adopt. And as we hold this is the correct
principle. It is a dictate of reason and common sense. It is in accordance
with it, that we desire your honorable body to act in considering the propriety of enfranchising us.

We claim our enfranchisement also upon the ground *that we are patriotic*.
It is a fact that we love this country. We love her constitution, and we
love those free Institutions that might and ought to be built up all over this
land under its benign influence. Indeed at no time have we manifested for
this country any other spirit than that of deep abiding affection. And that
too when we have been outraged and abused most barbarously. In proof of our
patriotism it is only necessary to refer to our conduct in the revolutionary
contest and the war of 1812. It has been said, that those were times that
tried men's souls, and it is equally true that those were times that tried
men's patriotism. But in neither were we found wanting. Our course in those
struggles whether on land or sea, for we were in the campaigns under
Washington and Lafayette, and in the cruising under Decatur[2] and Barry,[3] was
marked by courage and heroic devotion. That our words may be fully attested
we beg leave to offer in this connection the opinions of several distinguished
American Statesmen.

Hon. Calvin Goddard, of Connecticut, states that, in the little circle
of his acquaintance, he was instrumental in securing, under the act of 1818,
the pensions of nineteen colored soldiers. "I can not," he says, "refrain
from mentioning an aged blackman, Primus Babcock, who proudly presented to me
an honorable discharge from service, during the war, dated at the close of it,
wholly in the hand writing of George Washington. Nor can I forget the expression of his feelings when informed after his discharge had been sent to
the war department that it could not be returned. At his request it was written for, as he seemed inclined to spurn the pension and claim the discharged."

"In Rhode Island," says Governor Eustis,[4] in an able speech against
slavery in Missouri in 1820, "the blacks formed an entire regiment and discharged their duty with zeal and fidelity. The gallant defense of Red Bank in
which the black regiment bore a part is among the proofs of their valor." The
glory of this defence in a very important sense belongs to the blacks. And it
has been pronounced the most heroic action of the war. Among the distinguish-

ing traits of this regiment was devotion to their leaders. Then on the 13th of May, 1781, the American forces were near Croton river; Col. Green, the commander, was cut down and fatally wounded; but the weapons of the enemy could only reach him through the bodies of his faithful black guards. They defended him till every one of them was killed.

The late Rev. Dr. Harris of Dunbarton, New Hampshire, a revolutionary veteran, in speaking of the perilous condition in which the regiment was placed, to which he belonged, and their brave and manly conduct, in the same connection makes honorable mention of a "regiment of the blacks in the same situation--a regiment of negroes fighting for our liberty and independence, not a white man among them but the officers--in the same dangerous and responsible position." "Had they been unfaithful," he says, "or given way before the enemy, all would have been lost. Three times in succession were they attacked with the most desperate fury by well disciplined and veteran troops, and three times did they successfully repel the assault, and thus, preserved an army. They fought thus through the war. They were brave and hardy troops."

Hon. Tristram Burgess, of Rhode Island in a speech delivered in Congress, in January 1828, said: "At the commencement of the Revolutionary War, Rhode Island had a number of slaves. A regiment of them were enlisted into the continental service, and no braver men met the enemy in battle; but not one of them was permitted to become a soldier until he had first been made a freeman."

The Hon. Charles Pinckney[5] of South Carolina, in a speech on the Missouri question made use of the following language: "They (the colored people) were in numerous instances the pioneers, and in all, the laborers of our armies. To their hands were owing the largest part of the fortifications raised for the protection of the country. Fort Monteriel gave, at an early period of the inexperience and untried valor of our citizens, immortality to the American arms. And in the Northern States numerous bodies of them enrolled and fought side by side with the whites in the battle of the Revolution." And in addition to all this, if history be true, the first man that fell in the Revolutionary War--the first man whose life and blood were yielded up in defence of the freedom of this country was a colored man. He died on the plains of Boston the first revolutionary martyr in the massacre of the 5th of March, 1770.[6]

Let us now see what the conduct of colored men was some forty years afterward. Said Martindale of New York, in Congress, on the 22d of January, 1828: "Slaves, or negroes who had been slaves, were enlisted as soldiers in the war of the revolution, and I myself saw a battalion of them, as fine martial looking men as I ever saw, attached to the northern army in the last war, on the march from Plattsburgh to Sackett's Harbor."

Said the Hon. Charles Miner of Pennsylvania, in Congress, on the 7th of February, 1828: "The African race make excellent soldiers. Large numbers of them were with Perry, and helped to gain the brilliant victory of Lake Erie. A whole battalion of them were distinguished for their orderly appearance."

In the constitutional convention of New York, held in 1821, Dr. Drake, the delegate from Delaware county, in speaking of the colored people of that State, said: "In your late war they contributed largely towards some of your most splendid victories. On Lake Erie and Champlain, when your fleets triumphed over a foe superior in numbers and engines of death, they were manned in a large proportion with men of color. And in this very House, in the fall of 1814, a bill passed receiving the approbation of all branches of your government, authorizing the Governor to accept the services of a corps of 2000 free people of color. Sir," he continues, "these were times which tried men's souls. In these times it was not sporting matter to bear arms. These were times when a man who shouldered his musket did not know but he bared his bosom to receive a death wound ere he laid it aside, and in those times these people were found as ready and as willing to volunteer in your services as any other. They were most compelled to go. They were not drafted. No! Your pride had placed them beyond your compulsory power. But there was no necessity for its exercise; they were volunteers; yes, they were volunteers to defend that country from the inroads and ravages of a ruthless and vindictive foe, which had treated them with insult, degradation, and slavery."

But I will not weary your patience, further than to quote the celebrated proclamation of General Jackson, in 1814, they are as follows:

HEAD QUARTERS, SEVENTH MILITARY DISTRICT, MOBILE,
Sept. 21, 1814

To the Free Colored Inhabitants of Louisiana

"Through a mistaken policy, you have been deprived of a participation in the glorious struggle for natural rights, in which our country is engaged. This no longer shall exist.

"As sons of freedom, you are now called upon to defend the most inestimable of blessings. As Americans, your country looks with confidence to her adopted children, for a valorous support, as a faithful return for the advantages enjoyed under her mild and equitable government. As fathers, husbands and brothers, you are summoned to rally around the standard of the Eagle, to defend all that is dear in existence.

"Your country, although calling for your exertions, does not wish you to engage in her cause without remunerating you for the services rendered. Your intelligent minds are not to be led away by false representations. Your love of honor would cause you to despise the man who should attempt to deceive you. With the sincerity of a soldier, and in the language of truth, I address you.

"To every noble hearted free man of color volunteering to serve during the present contest with Great Britain, and no longer, there will be paid the same bounty in money and land, now received by the white soldiers of the United States, namely, one hundred and twenty four dollars in money, and one hundred and sixty acres of land. The non-commissioned officers and privates will also be entitled to the same monthly pay, daily rations, and clothes furnished to any American soldier.

"On enrolling yourselves in companies, the Major General commanding will select officers for your government, from your white fellow citizens. Your non-commissioned officers will be appointed from among yourselves.

"Due regard will be paid to the feelings of freemen and soldiers. You will not by being associated with white men in the same corps, be exposed to improper comparisons, or unjust sarcasm. As a distinct, independent battalion or regiment, pursuing the path of glory, you will, undivided, receive, the applause of your countrymen.

"To assure you of the sincerity of my intentions, and my anxiety to engage your valuable services to our country, I have communicated my wishes to the Governor of Louisiana who is fully informed as to the manner of enrollments, and will give you every necessary information on the subject of this address.
  Signed,   ANDREW JACKSON,
    Major General commanding."

The second proclamation is one of the highest compliments that the General could have paid to his colored soldiers. This is his address:

"Soldiers!--When on the banks of the Mobile I called you to take up arms, inviting you to partake the perils and glory of your *white fellow citizens*, I expected much from you; for I was not ignorant that you possessed qualities most formidable to an invading enemy. I knew with what fortitude you could endure hunger and thirst, and all fatigues of a campaign. I knew well how *you loved your native country*, and that you as well as ourselves, had to defend what *man* holds dear,--his parents, wife, children, and property. *You have done more than I expected*. In addition to the previous qualities I before knew you to possess, I found among you a noble enthusiasm which leads to the performance of great things.

"Soldiers! The President of the United States shall hear how praiseworthy was your conduct in the hour of danger, and the representatives of the American people will give you the praise you exploits entitle you to. Your General anticipates them in applauding your noble ardor.

"The enemy approaches, his vessels cover our lakes, our brave citizens are united, and all contention has ceased among them. Their only dispute is, who shall win the prize of valor, or who the most glory, its noblest reward."
By order,
THOMAS BUTLER, Aid-de-camp.

Thus it is very evident that the glory and honor of the Revolution and the War of 1812, are to be shared with colored men of the country. And these facts will serve to answer the question "what right have the children of Africa to a homestead in the white man's country?" "Their rights," in the truthful language of John G. Whittier, "like that of their white fellow citizens dates back to the dread arbitrament of war. Their bones whiten in every stricken field of the Revolution; their feet tracked with blood the snow of Jersey; their toil built up every fortification south of the Potomac; they shared the famine and nakedness of Valley Forge, and the pestilential horrors of the old Jersey prison ship." Have we then no claim to an equal participation in the blessings which have grown out of the national independence, which we fought to establish? Is it right, is it just, is it generous, is it magnanimous to withhold from us those blessings and "starve our patriotism?" What foreigner, what Irish or German emigrant has ever given such evidences of deep devotion to your government? And yet you have taken pains to make special arrangement by which in due time they are to enter upon the full enjoyment of citizenship. To this arrangement we would not object. We simply ask that we who have given such strong and significant proofs of our love of this country and its laws, be clothed in the livery of free and independent citizens.

Another ground, upon which we claim a participation in the rights and privileges of citizenship, is the fact that we are tax payers--that we willingly bear the burdens imposed upon us by the State. Nor is this fact to be regarded as a light and unimportant one. It will be seen at once that our tax is not of such insignificant account, since our real estate and personal property amount to more than five millions of dollars. Taking it, however, at five millions, and making an estimate according to the rate of taxation, in Lorain county, where the rate of taxation is lower than it is in the average of the counties of the State, our annual tax would amount to $57,165.00. In some counties it would be at least one hundred thousand dollars. In order to illustrate and enforce this consideration still further, I will refer to the amount of property owned by the colored people in the city of Cincinnati, the largest place in the State; and the amount owned by them in Oberlin, one of the smallest places in the State. In Cincinnati the colored people are worth $700,000, which, according to the rate of taxation in that city, will make their taxes $11,550. In Oberlin, where are very few colored residents (only 135,) their property amounts to $98,000. Their taxes then, according to the rate of taxation in that place would be $1,519.00. With such facts as these before your eyes gentlemen, you cannot find it in your hearts to say, that we are an ie., worthless, degraded class of men, and do not deserve the privilege of voting. In this connection I would gladly refer to the circumstances of the colored people in other cities and villages, and especially to their circumstances in several of the farming districts of the State; in Chillicothe, Portsmouth, Zanesville, Columbus and Cleveland, and of their large and well cultivated farms in the Peepee district, the Piketon settlement, and the settlements in Jackson, Gallia, Brown, Highland, Miami, Shelby, and Mercer counties; but I must not enlarge.

Allow me, however, to add, that so far back as 1851, in the returns made from nineteen counties represented in a convention held in this city on the 15th of January, we find that the value of the real estate and personal property belonging to the colored people of those counties amounting to more than three millions of dollars. Since that time we have not been idle. We have been working day and night. Like our white friends we have been doing all we could to extend our borders, to increase our real estate, and add to our small stocks in cash. So that whereas one or two years ago we owned but one lot or farm, now we have two, three, four, and perhaps five. It is often said, that Americans are great lovers of money; and it is true. But it is no more true of white Americans than it is of black ones. Both classes love money, and both will go to the ends of the earth to get it. Since then, it is a cardinal, a fundamental maxim of your political faith, that taxation and representation are never to be saundered, but always go together; and since we are taxed in common with all others to meet the expenditures of the government, we respectfully submit, that we ought to have the advantages of a fair and impartial representation.

It is urged in reply to what we have presented however, "That we are an ignorant and degraded class, and would not use the elective franchise in an intelligent and manly manner if we had it." If this were true, it might be proper to withhold from us this right. But it is not true. It is doubly false. We are not more ignorant and degraded than other men. And here we would introduce the opinion of Hon. Samuel Galloway who had abundant opportunity for knowing what he affirmed to be true. In speaking of the progress that the colored people were making in his report of 1840, he said: "Now they have many and well conducted schools; they have teachers of respectable, intellectual and moral qualifications--there are many who command general respect and confidence for integrity and intelligence; they call and conduct conventions and associations of various kinds with order and intelligence; --questions of general and proper interest have become with them topics of discussion and conversation--in a few words, the intellectual and moral tone of their being is ameliorated!" What more could he have said, gentlemen, of the masses among the white people of the State?

As touching this point we would also submit the views of Hon. Wm. H. Seward as presented in the following letter:

Washington, May 16, 1854.

Dear Sir:--Your letter of the 6th inst. has been received. I reply to it cheerfully and with pleasure.

It is my deliberate opinion, founded upon careful observation, that the right of suffrage is exercised by no citizen of New York more conscientiously, or with more beneficial results to society, than it is by the electors of African descent. I sincerely hope that the franchise will before long be extended as it justly ought to this race, who of all others need it most.

I am very respectfully,
Your obedient servant,
William H. Seward.

Thus it will be seen, that in the estimation of such men--men who have bestowed some thought upon our condition and our conduct, that we are not after all so ignorant and degraded that we are incapable of exercising the elective franchise in an intelligent and manly manner.

Permit us to say in conclusion, then, in view of these considerations, we hold that it is unjust, and anti-democratic, impolitic and ungenerous to withhold from us the right of suffrage.

I behalf of the colored people,
J. Mercer Langston.

Frederick Douglass' Paper, June 16, 1854.

REFERENCE NOTES

1. John Mercer Langston had been commissioned to draw up this report by the Ohio Convention of Colored Freemen which met at Cincinnati in January 1852.
2. Stephen Decatur (1779-1820), American naval officer and son of the naval officer Stephen Decatur (1752-1808), gained fame in the War of 1812 by capturing the British frigate *Macedonian*. Then, in the so-called Algerine War of 1815, he used his squadron with decisiveness and vigor in forcing the dey of Algiers to sign a treaty which ended American tribute to Algeria.
3. John Barry (1745-1803), U.S. naval officer, was born in Wexford, Ireland. During the American Revolution, he commanded the brig *Lexington* when she captured (1776) the British tender *Edward*--first British vessel taken

by a commissioned American ship. Some consider him the foremost naval hero of the Revolution after John Paul Jones.

4. The reference is to William Eustis (1753-1825), U.S. government official and statesman. Eustis served as a surgeon in the patriot forces during the American Revolution and later served in Congress (1801-1805) as a Jeffersonian. Appointed secretary of war (1807) under Jefferson, he resigned in 1812 after charges of incompetency were brought against him for his handling the problems of the War of 1812. Eustis was U.S. minister to the Netherlands (1814-1818) and again a member (1820-1823) of the House of Representatives and governor (1823-1825) of Massachusetts.

5. Charles Pinckney (1757-1824), American statesman and governor of South Carolina, fought in the American Revolution and was taken prisoner in the British capture of Charleston (1780). As a delegate to the Federal Constitutional Convention of 1787, he submitted a plan for the Constitution whose broad outlines many believe had considerable influence on the final draft of the Constitution. From 1819 to 1821, Pinckney served as a member of the House of Representatives, where he made a celebrated speech against the Missouri Compromise.

6. The reference is to Crispus Attucks, identified above.

PROCEEDINGS OF THE STATE CONVENTION OF COLORED MEN, HELD IN THE CITY OF COLUMBUS, OHIO, JAN. 16th, 17th, & 18th, 1856

The Convention was called to order by the Chairman of the State Central Committee, and, on motion of John Booker, D. Jenkins was chosen President, pro tem., and John Booker appointed Secretary.

After reading the call for the Convention, on motion of P. H. Clark,[1] it was resolved that the delegates elected from Franklin county, and all gentlemen present from other parts of the State, who are willing to enroll their names and participate in our proceedings, be considered members of the Convention. The following gentlemen enrolled their names as delegates.

Lorain County

J. Mercer Langston, Solomon Grimes, J. H. Harris.

Franklin County

D. Jenkins, L. D. Taylor, C. H. Langston, John Booker, W. B. Ferguson, J. Poindexter, James Evans, Isham Martin, J. S. Ward, George Johnson.

Hamilton County

John I. Gaines, Peter H. Clark, George Johnson.

Jackson County

C. A. Yancy.

Highland County

Anderson Flinn, Granville Foster.

Ross County

D. E. James, C. D. Williams, J. A. Chancellor, J. H. Williams.

Pickaway County

Hinton Coles, Lewis Toles.

Champaign County

Lewis Adams, Henry Ford, John H. Williams, Francis Adams, George Reynolds,

Logan County

A. J. Scott, R. Heathcock, Wm. Walden.

Ashtabula County

H. T. Rankin.

Delaware County

U. D. Harris, J. Bruce, J. J. Williamson.

Greene County

James Lott.

Scioto County

John Miner.

Cuyahoga County

John Malvin.

The Committee on permanent organization reported the following gentlemen as officers of the Convention, which report was unanimously adopted:

President

John I. Gaines.

Vice Presidents

L. D. Taylor, C. H. Langston, A. Flinn, Thos. Benford, C. A. Yancy.

Secretaries

John Booker, Granville Foster, W. D. Harris.

The following committees were then appointed:

On Business

John M. Langston, C. A. Yancy, John Booker, Charles Williams, and John I. Gaines.

On State Organization

Messrs. P. H. Clark, Charles Williams, James Poindexter, John Booker, and A. J. Scott.

On Address

Messrs. Peter H. Clark, C. H. Langston, C. A. Yancy, D. Jenkins, John Williams, Solomon Grimes, and A. Flinn.

On Petitions

C. H. Langston, L. D. Taylor, D. Jenkins.

On Finance

D. Jenkins, G. Johnson, and J. H. Harris.

On Publication

C. H. Langston, John Booker, and D. Jenkins.

At the close of the last evening's exercises, Rev. Mr. Turban came forward and presented the Convention five dollars in behalf of the ladies of Bethel Church--in consequence of which the following resolution was unanimously adopted:

Resolved, That the thanks of the Convention are due, and are hereby tendered to the ladies of Bethel Church, for their liberal donation.

All the meetings of the Convention after the first, were large and enthusiastic. Every evening, the large and commodious City Hall was filled to its utmost capacity with anxious listeners, both white and colored.

The speeches made by Langston, Clark, Gaines, and others, were logical, pointed and eloquent, and were delivered with earnestness and great power.

The Committee on Business reported the following resolutions:

1. *Resolved,* That slavery is to be deeply deplored, because it is destructive of "whatsoever things are true, whatsoever things are honest, whatsoever things are just, whatsoever things are pure, whatsoever things are lovely, and whatsoever things are of good report."[2]

2. *Resolved,* That it may be appropriately characterized as the sum of all villainies, the perfection of all wickedness and outrage, the master-piece of all the devices which Satan has invented to alienate man from his brother man, and thereby destroy the happiness of the human family.

3. *Resolved,* That we regard all organizations, whose object is the maintenance of this stupendous system of wrong, as engaged in a crusade against our holy religion, against the pure principles of righteous civil government, against the spirit and tendency of geniune civilization, and against the tenderest and most important rights which belong to humanity.

4. *Resolved,* That we are compelled to believe, in view of its own pro-slavery and uncharitable action, in view of the inconsistent and unmanly conduct of its agents and leading members, that the professions made by the American Colonization Society, of promoting the abolition of slavery, are altogether delusive, and their pretensions of interest in behalf of the nominally free colored people of the country, hollow-hearted and contemptible.

5. *Resolved,* That we look upon the Society as the embodiment of the pro-slavery sentiment of the country; that its prime object is the perpetuity of slavery; and, while it is unworthy of our confidence and support, it should be despised and loathed by the friends of the slave, as a foul and filthy plague.

6. *Resolved,* That the great political party[3] which finds its head in Franklin Pierce,[4] and its pillars of support in Cass[5] and Douglas,[6] in Atchison[7] and Stringfellow,[8] has pledged itself to do the menial offices of slavery, to oppose all agitation of the question of Human Freedom, to make final the unconstitutional and inhuman Fugitive Slave Law, and to ignore all the great principles of justice which lie at the foundation of this government.

7. *Resolved,* That we pledge ourselves to each other and to the slave, to use all the means in our power to effect the overthrow of slavery and the destruction of American prejudice.

8. *Resolved,* That we do not despair of the attainment of this grand result; but, believing that God is the God of the oppressed, we are confident that in His own good time He will bring about our deliverance with the same mighty hand with which He led forth the children of Israel from Egyptian bondage.

9. *Resolved,* That unless we are greatly mistaken in respect to the indications of Providence, the day of our deliverance steadily draws nigh. May the God of the oppressed hasten its glad and joyous consummation.

10. *Resolved,* That while we rejoice in the death of the Whig party, once a strong ally of Despotism, in the waning influence of the Democratic party --the black-hearted apostle of American Slavery--we would welcome the inauguration of the Republican party, which, although it does not take so high anti-slavery ground as we could wish, demanding the immediate and unconditional abolition of slavery in the States as well as its eternal prohibition in the Territories belonging to the Federal Government, may do great service in the cause of Freedom, and the young, vigorous, and athletic defender of the Restrictive Policy.

11. *Resolved,* That we regard the great moral results which are coming to pass through the agency of the American Anti-Slavery Society, with unfeigned gratitude and thankfulness, and we will bid it a hearty Godspeed in its moral warfare against slavery and its audacious encroachments upon the rights of man.

12. *Resolved,* That we are opposed to all Caste, to all discrimination on account of complexion or birth-place, and in favor of the broadest Freedom consonant to just and impartial legislation.

13. *Resolved,* That, in the name of our manhood, in the name of justice and fair dealing, in the name of our nativity, in the name of the political axiom that Taxation and Representation are inseparable, and in the name of our loyalty and devotedness to our native land and her institutions, we demand the alteration and amendment of all clauses in our State Constitution making distinctions on the ground of color, as well as all laws and parts of laws making complexional differences.

14. *Resolved,* That we recommend to the Convention the appointment of a committee to prepare a petition to be presented to the Convention for signatures.

15. *Resolved,* That the political party that declares that there can be no law for slavery, is the real political party of freedom in the United States, and as such commends itself to the countenance and support of every colored man in the nation.

16. *Resolved,* That we recommend to the Convention the appointment of a committee of three, to prepare a petition to be presented to the Legislature, asking that honorable body to take the necessary steps to secure the alteration of the first Section of the ninth Article of the State Constitution, by striking out the word "white" from said section, and to repeal all laws and parts of laws making complexion discriminations; and we would also recommend that the members of this Convention be requested to circulate this petition for signatures, in their several districts, as soon as may be, and forward the same to the Legislature.

17. *Resolved,* That the Convention appoint a committee of five on State Organization; the object of this organization to be the arrangement of the debate in such way as to secure efficient and united anti-slavery action.

18. *Resolved,* That a committee of three be appointed to take into consideration, and report upon the propriety, necessity, and practicability, of establishing a permanent press, as the organ of the colored people of the State.

19. *Resolved,* That the establishment of Mechanics' Institutes, Agricultural Associations, Educational and Literary, Temperance and Moral Reform Societies, would tend to promote our social and domestic education.

Whereas, It appears, from proper information, that former Conventions had contracted with J. M. Langston and D. Jenkins, to perform certain public duties, in the discharge of which J. M. Langston expended thirty-three dollars, of which but five have been refunded, and D. Jenkins the sum of twenty-five dollars, therefore,

Resolved, That the delegates composing this Convention be requested to raise a fair proportion of said amounts, in their counties, and forward the same to a committee of three in the city of Columbus, who shall have charge of said funds, and who shall appropriate them to the satisfaction of said claims. We also recommend that the claims of John I. Gaines and Peter H. Clark, for thirty dollars, expended by them for printing the Minutes of the Convention of 1852, be allowed.

D. Jenkins, P. H. Clark, C. A. Yancy, were appointed that committee.

20. *Resolved,* That each Delegate present be requested to order a copy or copies of the *Ohio Columbian,* containing the proceedings of our Convention, and be requested to read such proceedings to their constituents, and urge them to carry out the recommendations therein contained.

21. *Resolved,* That Messrs. Clark, J. M. Langston, John I. Gaines, C. H. Langston, and L. D. Taylor, be appointed a committee to wait upon the Legislature now in session, asking a hearing concerning the grievances of which we complain.

22. *Resolved,* That this Convention return thanks to the City Council for the use of the City Hall; also to the officers of the Convention, for the manner in which they have performed their duties.

Plan of State Organization

The Committee on State Organization reported the following:

Whereas, The thorough organization and united effort of the Colored people of the State, is absolutely essential to the success of the struggle in which we are engaged for the acquisition of our rights, therefore, be it

Resolved, by the Colored people of Ohio in Convention assembled, That the State Central Committee shall consist of _____ members, to be elected annually; and the State Convention to be organized with a President, Secretary and Treasurer, to perform duties as hereinafter defined.

There shall be appointed by this Convention a Central Committee of five for each county here represented, to perform duties hereinafter provided, and to hold their office for one year, and until their successors shall be elected and qualified by the people of their respective counties.

The State Central Committee shall be empowered to employ an agent or agents to traverse the State, holding county conventions and township meetings of the colored people, to print and circulate memorials and petitions praying for relief from the oppressive laws under which we suffer, to collect in each county the statistics of wealth, education, mental and moral condition of the colored people of the State, and to raise funds for defraying the expense of said meetings, publications &c. And the Central Committee shall make out and publish an annual report, embodying all the statistics collected by said agents, the amount and mode of expenditure of all monies collected by them or their agents, and shall recommend such measures as they deem important to the welfare of the colored people of Ohio. And the agent or agents of the State Central Committees, shall report the amounts of money raised by them, quarterly, or oftener if required, to the State Central Committee. The county agents shall make monthly reports to the county committees.

Also, that the State Central Committee, and County Central Committees, shall, immediately on their organization, establish rules for the proper keeping of their accounts, the mode of disbursing their funds, and shall define the duties of their agents, and establish bylaws for the government of their own action.

The County Central Committees shall aid and assist the agents of the State Central Committee to hold county conventions, township meetings, &c., or shall, at their discretion, employ such competent persons as they may select, to lecture and circulate memorials and petitions, &c. in their counties, and shall take measures to have their counties represented in the annual meetings of the State Convention, and do all that lies in their power to advance the moral, mental, and financial condition of the colored people of the State.

That we proceed to raise the sum of three thousand dollars, to be expended by the State Central Committee for the before mentioned objects; and that the delegates be required to pledge themselves to raise, within their respective counties, a reasonable portion of said fund, and report the same to the Treasurer of the State Central Committee, who shall give bonds for the security of said funds.

ADDRESS

To the Senate and House of Representatives of the State of Ohio:

Gentlemen:--We, the disfranchised Colored Citizens of Ohio, assembled in General Convention, feeling deeply the grievous wrongs unjustly imposed upon us by the prohibitions implied in the first Section of the fifth Article of the Constitution of the State, and knowing the people have the right to assemble together, in a peaceful manner, to counsel for their common good, and petition the General Assembly for a redress of grievances; and, believing it to be a solemn duty we owe to ourselves, our posterity, and the honor and dignity of the free State of Ohio, to use every constitutional means which the law-makers of Ohio have left [in] our power, to remove from our necks the burdens too grievous to be borne; we do, therefore, most earnestly, in the name of our common humanity, in the name of the Declaration of Independence and the Bill of Rights of the State of Ohio, ask your Honorable Body to take the necessary constitutional steps to strike the word "white" from the section before referred to, and to all other places in which it occurs in the Constitution, and thereby abrogate the unwise and unjust distinction therein made between the citizens of the State on account of the accident of color. The section referred to is couched in the following language: "Art. V. Sec. I. Every *white* male citizen of the United States, of the age of twenty-one years, who shall have been a resident of the State one year next preceding the election, and of the county, township, or ward in which he resides, such times as may be provided by law, shall have the qualifications of an elector, and be entitled to vote at all elections."

The first reason we will assign for the removal of this odious word from the Constitution of a professedly free State, is, that we are MEN. This, to our minds, seems an all sufficient plea. Human rights are not to be graduated by the shades of color that tinge the cheeks of men. Any being, however low in the scale of civilization, that yet preserves the traits that serve to distinguish humanity from the brutes, is endowed with all rights that can be claimed by the most cultivated races of men.

That we are men, we will not insult your intelligence by attempting to prove. The most bitter revilers and oppressors of the race admit this, even in the enactments by which they wrong us. Statutes and ordinances are not necessary for the regulation and control of animals, but men, reasoning men, who can understand and obey, or plot to overthrow. The section of which we complain, by defining that *white* men may exercise the right of franchise, virtually admits that there are black men who are by the rule prohibited from voting. We ask any who doubt our manhood, Hath not the *negro* eyes? Hath not the *negro* hands, organs, dimensions, senses, affections, passions?--fed with the same food--hurt with the same weapons--subject to the same diseases --healed by the same means--warmed and cooled by the same summer and winter as the *white man* is? If you prick us, do we not bleed? If you tickle us, do we not laugh? If you poison us, do we not die?

We ask you to ponder the danger of circumscribing the great doctrines of human equality, which our fathers promulgated and defended at the cost of so much blood and treasure, to the narrow bounds of races or nations. All men are by nature equal, and have inalienable rights, or none have. We beg you to reflect how insecure your own and the liberties of your posterity would be by the admission of such a rule of construing the rights of men. Another nation or race may displace you, as you have displaced nations and races; and the injustice you teach, they may execute; perchance they may better the instruction. Remember, in your pride and power, 'That we are all children of one Father, and all ye are brethren.'

But the principles upon which our Government is founded, condemns the practice of excluding colored men from the advantages of the ballot box. To uphold the principle that taxation and representation should go together, the union between Great Britain and the American Colonies was broken, and a desolating war of seven years' duration was waged. As proof of the correctness of the principle, we have the declaration and actions of our fathers, and your own declarations. If the sentiment was so true in 1776, what new concatenation of circumstances has arisen to render it false in 1856? None whatever. It is one of those immutable truths that change not with time or circumstances. They are emanations from the eternal foundation of truth, which we all worship--the Deity Himself. Yet, in nearly every county of our State, colored tax payers are found, who are unrepresented, and can only be heard in your halls as a matter of favor. We are aware that difference of race is urged by our enemies as a reason for our disfranchisement; but we submit that we are not Africans, but Americans, as much so as any of your population. Here then is a great injustice done us, by refusing to acknowledge our right to the appellation of Americans, which is the only title we desire, and legislating for us as if we were aliens, and not bound to our country by the ties of affection which every human being must feel for his native land: which makes the Laplander prefer his snows and skins to the sunny skies and silken garb of Italy; which makes the colored American prefer the dear land of his birth, even though oppressed in it, to any other spot on earth.

But admit, for argument, that there is an irradicable difference between us and the whites of our land. That very difference unfits them to represent us. Our wants and feelings are unknown or unappreciated by them; nor can any one presume to represent us whom we have not aided to select. In our government, every citizen should be represented in the legislative councils, and this can only be attained by permitting each one a voice in the selection of representatives. No class of the white population would be willing to concede to any other class, however honest and enlightened, the custody of their rights. To demand such a thing, would be deemed monstrous: and the injustice is not lessened when the demand is made upon black men instead of white men.

Our want of intelligence is urged as a reason against our admission to equal citizenship. The assumption that we are ignorant is untrue; but, even if it were true, it really affords an argument for the removal of the disabilities that cramp our energies, destroy that feeling of self-respect, so essential to form the character of a good citizen. Give us the opportunity of elevating ourselves:--It can do you no harm, and may do us much good; and if we fail, upon us be the blame. We would bring to your recollection that by a decision of your Supreme Court, a large portion of our people are already in the possession of the elective franchise. These men are not above the average of colored men in intelligence or morals. They are educated under the same depressing social influences with the rest of us, and are no better fitted to exercise the rights of voting than their brethren. Yet, by an accident of color, they are enfranchised. What good reason can be adduced for permitting the father to vote and not the son, or the son and not the father, as is frequently the case? The most obtuse intellect can at once perceive the utter folly and injustice of such distinctions. But the folly and injustice is equally as great when the difference is made between white and colored men.

We are aware that it has been recently asserted by a high political personage, that this is a government of white men.[9] This we cannot admit. In addition to the arguments we have already advanced, touching the doctrine of the universality of human rights, we submit that the assertion casts an imputation upon the veracity and good faith of our fathers, who claimed the sympathy and aid of the world on the ground that they were contending for principles of universal application, and desired to found a government in which the doctrine of human equality would be reduced to practice.

The Bill of Rights of the State of Ohio sets forth "That all men are created equal and independent, and have inalienable rights, among which are enjoying and *defending* life and liberty, acquiring, possessing, and *protecting* property, and seeking and obtaining happiness and safety."

Now, admitted that we are men, how are we to *defend* and protect life, liberty, and property? The whites of the State, through the ballot-box, can do these things peacefully; but we, by the organic law of the State, are prevented from defending those precious rights by any other than violent means. For the same document that asserts our right to defend life, liberty and property, strips us of the power to do so otherwise than by violence. We ask you, gentlemen, in the name of justice, shall this stand as the judgement of the State of Ohio?

We are aware that deference to the opinions and institutions of the States tolerating slavery, to whom we are bound by the federal compact, may induce some to oppose this our application for equal rights. But those States, of all others, are the most tenacious of their rights as sovereign States, and reprobate all attempts to influence their domestic policy by the action of public opinion in other States. We pray you, therefore to do us justice; and, in doing right, imitate the independence they display in doing wrong. Our rights are as high and precious as theirs; and they can have no right to complain of any act of the people of Ohio, improving the condition of any class of her citizens.

We do not ask you to countenance any change destructive to your form of government. The principles we ask you to endorse are recognized by the wise and good of our own and other lands. It will be but the legitimate result of a proper appreciation of the Declaration of Independence and our Bill of Rights. Already five States of the Union have admitted colored men to vote; and we have yet to hear that the action has been followed by any other than beneficial results.

The arguments we have advanced are equally applicable to the statutory enactments which inflict such grievous disabilities upon us as a people.

The inestimable privilege and protection of a trial by a jury of our peers, we are deprived of, and to our great damage. Every legal gentleman in your body must be aware of the facility with which convictions are obtained against colored men.

Admission to your infirmaries and other benevolent institutions, is demanded by the spirit of the age. It is a shame to your civilization and humanity that decrepit age, the helplessly maimed, drivelling idiots and raving maniacs, are turned into the streets to die, as has been done in the metropolis of your State. In your public schools, too, needless and injurious distinctions are made. The duty of the State is the same to all her children. None are so insignificant as to be forgotten; none so important as to be preferred before others. The interests of the State demand that all should be educated alike.

In conclusion, we will call your attention to the duties incumbent on you as legislators—to pass such laws as will increase the happiness, prosperity and security of the people of the State; to remove all just causes of dissatisfaction.

Many may indulge the hope that the colored population is destined to pass away from your midst, and so refuse our prayer. But the hope is a delusion. We are a part of the American people, and we and our posterity will forever be a constituent part of your population. If we are deprived of education, of equal political privileges, still subjected to the same depressing influences under which we now suffer, the natural consequences will follow; and the State, for her planting injustice, will reap her harvest of sorrow and crime. She will contain within her limits a discontented population—dissatisfied, estranged—ready to welcome any revolution or invasion as a relief, for they can lose nothing and gain much. A contrary course of policy will enable us to keep step with our white fellow citizens in the march of improvement, disaffection will cease, and our noble State stand securely defended by the loving hearts of all her sons.

In behalf of the State Convention of colored men—

Peter H. Clark, Cha'n.

Charles Langston,
Charles A. Yancy;
D. Jenkins,
John Williams,
Solomon Grimes,   } Committee.
Anderson Flinn,
John M. Langston,
John I. Gaines,
L. D. Taylor,

The memorial was received and read, and referred to a select committee consisting of the following gentlemen: Messrs. Canfield, Brown, and Taylor of Geauga.

The following address was presented by Wm. Harris, in behalf of the Ladies' Anti-Slavery Society of Delaware:

Delaware, Ohio, 1855.

To the Convention of Disfranchised Citizens of Ohio:

Gentlemen:--Convened as you are in the Capital City of our State--a State great in wealth, power, and political influence, an avowed devotee of Freedom, and a constituent part of a Christian Democratic Confederacy--to concoct measures for obtaining those rights and immunities of which unjust legislation has deprived you, we offer this testimonial of our sympathy and interest in the cause in which you are engaged--a cause fraught with infinite importance--and also express our earnest hope that such determination and invincible courage may be evinced by you in assembly as are requisite to meet the exigencies of the times.

Truth, Justice and Mercy, marshaling their forces, sound the tocsin which summons the warrior in his burnished armor to the conflict against Error and Oppression. On earth's broad arena--through Time's revolving cycles--this warfare has been continuous; and now here, in this most brilliant star in the galaxy of nations, where Christianity and civilization, with their inestimable accompaniments and proclivities, have taken their abode and add their benign light to her stellate brightness--bands of her offspring, in very truth her own, despised, persecuted and crushed, assemble in scattered fragments to take the oath of fealty to Freedom, and swear eternal enmity to Oppression; to enter into a bond sacred and inviolable, ever to wage interminable intellectual and moral war against the demon, and to demand the restoration of their birthright, *Liberty*--kindred of Deity. Nor is the path to victory strewn with flowers; obstacles formidable, and apparently insurmountable, arise ominously before even the most hopeful and ardent.

As the Alpine avalanche sweeps tumultuously adown the mountain, overwhelming the peasant and his habitation, so the conglomeration of hatred and prejudice against our race, brought together by perceptible accumulation, augmented and fostered by religion and science united, sweeps with seeming irresistible power toward us, menacing complete annihilation. But, should these things exercise a retarding influence upon our progressive efforts? Let American religion teach adoration to the demon Slavery, whom it denominates God; at the end, the book of record will show its falsity or truth. Let scientific research produce elaborate expositions of the inferiority and mental idiosyncrasy of the colored race; one truth, the only essential truth, is uncontrovertible:--The Omnipotent, Omniscient God's glorious autograph --the seal of angels--is written on our brows, that immortal characteristic of Divinity--the rational, mysterious and inexplicable soul, animates our frames.

Then press on! Manhood's prerogatives are yours by Almighty fiat. These prerogatives American Republicanism, disregarding equity, humanity, and the fundamental principles of her national superstructure, has rendered a nonenity, while on her flag's transparencies and triumphal arches, stood beautifully those great, noble words: Liberty and Independence--Free Government--Church and State! And still they stand exponents of American character --her escutcheon wafts them on its star-spangled surface, to every clime --each ship load of emigrants from monarchical Europe, shout the words synonyma [sic] with Americans, their first paean in "the land of the free." Briery mountain, sparkling river, glassy lake, give back the echoes, soft and clear as if the melody was borrowed from the harps of angels. But strange incongruity! As the song of Freedom verberates and reverberates through the northern hills, and the lingering symphony quivers on the still air and then sinks away into silence, a low deep wail, heavy with anguish and despair, rises from the southern plains, and the clank of chains on human limbs mingles with the mournful cadence.

What to the toiling millions there, is this boasted liberty? What to us is this organic body--this ideal reduced to reality--this institution of the land?--a phantom, a shadowy and indistinct--a disembodied form, impalpable to our sense or touch. In the broad area of this Republic there is no spot, however small or isolated, where the colored man can exercise his God-given rights. Genius of America!--How art thou fallen, oh Lucifer, son of the morning! how art thou fallen!

In view of these things, it is self-evident, and above demonstration that we, as a people, have every incentive to labor for the redress of wrongs. On our native soil, consecrated to freedom, civil liberties are denied us, and we are by compulsion subject to an atrocious and criminal system of political tutelage deleterious to the interest of the entire colored race, and antagonistical to the political axioms of this Republic.

Intuitively then, we search for the panacea for the manifold ills which we suffer. One, and only one, exists; and when each individual among us realizes the absolute impossibility for him to perform any work of supererogation in the common cause, the appliances will prove its own efficacy; it is embodied in one potent word--ACTION. Let unanimity of action characterize us; let us reject the absurd phantasy of non-intervention; let us leave conservatism behind, and substitute a radical, utilitarian spirit; let us cultivate our moral and mental faculties, and labor to effect a general diffusion of knowledge, remembering that "ascendancy naturally and properly belongs to intellectual superiority." Let "Excelsior" be our watchword; it is the inspiration of all great deeds, and by the universal adoption of this policy we will soon stand triumphantly above that ignorance and weakness, of which slavery is the inevitable concomitant--will soon reach that apex of civilization and consequent power to which every earnest, impassioned soul aspires.

Continued and strenuous effort is the basis of all greatness, moral, intellectual, and civil. "Work, man," says Carlyle,[10] "work! work! thou hast all eternity to rest in."

To you, gentlemen, as representatives of the oppressed thousands of Ohio, we look hopefully. This convening is far from being nugatory or unimportant. "Agitation of thought is the beginning of truth," and, futher, more, by pursuing such a line of policy as you in your wisdom may deem expedient, *tending toward that paramount object*, the results may transcend those attending similar assemblies which have preceded it. True, you are numerically small; but the race is not always gained by the swift, nor the battle by the strong, and it has become a truism that greatness is the legitimate result of labor, diligence, and perseverance.

It was a Spartan mother's farewell to her son, "Brong home your shield or be brought upon it." To you we would say, be true, be courageous, be steadfast in the discharge of your duty. The citadel of Error must yield to the unshrinking phalanx of truth. In our fireside circles, in the seclusion of our closets, we kneel in tearful supplication in your behalf. As Christian wives, mothers and daughters, we invoke the blessing of the King, Eternal and Immortal, "who sitteth upon the circle of the earth, who made the heavens with all their host," to rest upon you, and we pledge ourselves to exert our influence unceasingly in the cause of Liberty and Humanity.

Again we say, be courageous; be steadfast; unfurl your banner to the breeze--let its folds float proudly over you, bearing the glorious inscription, broad and brilliant as the material universe: *"God and Liberty!"*

Sara G. Staley,
In behalf of the Delaware Ladies' Anti-Slavery Society.

The Committee on petitions reported the following:

We, the undersigned, citizens of_____county, respectfully but earnestly petition your honorable body, 1st. To immediately take the necessary constitutional steps to so alter or amend the Constitution of this State as to strike out the word "white" in the first Section of the fifth Article. 2d. To so alter or amend the first Section of the ninth Article of the Constitution as to strike out the word "white" in that Article. 3d. Also, to repeal all laws and parts of laws which make distinctions on account of color.

The Committee on Finance reported the following receipts and expenditures:

OHIO, 1856   315

                              RECEIPTS

From members of Convention. $24.75
   " Ladies A.M.E. Church. 5.00

Total. $29.75

                            EXPENDITURES

For Hall rent. $15.00
Expense of Central Committee. 6.75

Total. $21.75
Balance $8,00, which was paid to the Committee of Publication.

The following letters were received and ordered to be published:

                                        Peterboro' Dec. 27, 1855
   D. Jenkins, L. D. Taylor, J. Watson, J. Malvin, W. A. Scott, J.
Booker, W. H. Day--
                                        State Central Committee.
   Gentlemen:--I thank you for inviting me to attend your State Convention.
I wish I could attend it; but such is the state of my business, that I cannot.
   I suppose the object of your Convention is to promote the welfare of the
whole colored population of this country.
   For many years I have well nigh despaired of the peaceful, bloodless
abolition of American Slavery. Two things are lacking to secure such abolition. 1st. Entire *honesty* on the part of the abolitionists. 2d. *Self respect*
on the part of the free colored people.
   It is dishonesty in the abolitionists to admit that there can be law for
the enslavement of the American blacks--for they would admit no possibility
of law for the enslavement of the American whites.
   It is most painful and pitiable self-degradation, on the part of the
free colored people, to admit that there is, either inside or outside of the
Constitution, law--real, obligatory law--for the enslavement of their race.
They betray their destitution of true self-respect when they vote for men who
make such an admission, or when they unite with churches that make it, or
patronize free schools or school teachers that make it.
   Hoping that the proceedings of your Convention may be earnest, manly
and wise.
           I remain,
                    Your friend,
                         Gerrit Smith.

                                        Hall of Reps. U.S.
                                              Dec. 26, 1855
   Gentlemen:--I have received your kind invitation to attend the Convention of Colored men on the 16th January.
   It would give me pleasure to comply with your request; but you are aware
of the importance of the questions now pressed upon the consideration of
Congress. Of course it would be improper for me to leave my seat in this
body until the election of Speaker and disposal of some of the important
questions before us.
   I however feel a deep interest in the action of your Convention. There
can be no doubt among intelligent men, that knowledge is power. The more
our colored friends increase their intelligence, elevate their moral being,
the greater influence they will exert, and the sooner will they be admitted
to all the privileges which the whites possess.
   I know of no absurdity in morals or in politics more palpable than that
of making the complexion of a man the criterion of their moral or political
worth. While our colored friends should be constant in their demand for a
respectful consideration of their claims to the rights and privileges to

which their intelligence and moral worth entitle them; while they continue to do this, the philanthropists will of course use their influence to extend to the colored portion of our people equal rights and privileges.

Very truly,

J. R. Giddings.

D. Jenkins, L. D. Taylor, J. Watson, J. Malvin, W. A. Scott, W. H. Day.

STATE CENTRAL COMMITTEE

D. Jenkins,
C. H. Langston,
John Malvin,
Jonathan Underwood,
Isham Martin,
J. T. Ward,
P. H. Clark,
L. D. Taylor,
J. A. Chancellor.

In accordance with the resolutions adopted by the Convention, relative to the State Organization, the State Central Committee met on the 25th inst., and permanently organized by appointing D. Jenkins President, C. H. Langston Secretary, and John T. Ward Treasurer, all of the City of Columbus.

We do sincerely hope that every county will at once organize their county committees, and proceed to raise the money as recommended in the resolutions above referred to, and forward it to the State Central Committee.

Brethren, this is an *important crisis*. Let us go to work in earnest. If our rights are worth having, they are worth working for. We can only succeed by having MONEY.

D. Jenkins, Pres't.

C. H. Langston, Sec'y.

Copy in the Harvard University Library.

REFERENCE NOTES

1. Peter H. Clark, principal of the Colored High School in Cincinnati, Ohio, sat in many of the state and national black conventions during this period. Clark too was probably the first American Negro Socialist. See Philip S. Foner, "Peter H. Clark: Pioneer Black Socialist," *Journal of Ethnic Studies*, V (1977), 17-35 reprinted in Foner, *Essays in Afro-American History* (Philadelphia, 1978), pp. 154-177.

2. This quotation is taken in part from the Epistle of Paul the Apostle to the Philippians, chapter 4, verse 8.

3. The reference is to the Democratic Party, which had largely by this time become an apologist for slavery.

4. Franklin Pierce (1804-1869), New Hampshire Democrat and fourteenth President of the United States, was strongly identified with the pro-slavery interests of his party. His administration, though weak and ineffectual, provided many of the background issues and controversies that would later culminate in Civil War.

5. Lewis Cass (1782-1866), Democratic United States senator from Michigan in 1845-1848 and 1849-1857, supported strongly the Compromise of 1850, including the Fugitive Slave Law.

6. Stephen Arnold Douglas (1813-1861) was Democratic United States Senator from Illinois from 1847 to 1861. On January 4, 1854, he introduced his Nebraska Bill in the Senate. It would have permitted slavery in the Nebraska territory even though it was north of the 36° 30' line, thus repealing the Missouri Compromise, even though through "popular sovereignty" slavery might be kept out. It also provided that the Fugitive Slave Law of 1850 was to be applied to Nebraska.

7. David Rice Atchison (1807-1886), United States senator from Missouri from 1843 to 1855, played a prominent role in the passage of the Kansas-

Nebraska Bill and the repeal of the Missouri Compromise. He gained considerable notoriety for his part in the raids by the Missouri "border ruffians" into Kansas Territory in 1855-1856. During the Civil War, Atchison supported the Confederate cause.

    8. Dr. John H. Stringfellow (1819-1894) was born in Culpepper County, Virginia. Educated at the University of Pennsylvania, where he received his medical degree in 1845, he later became prominent in the Kansas controversy during the 1850's. Moving to the territory, he helped found the town of Atchison, edited the *Squatter Sovereign* and became speaker of the first territorial House of Representatives. During the Civil War he aided the Confederate cause.

    9. The reference is to Stephen Douglas, Democratic senator from Illinois, identified above.

    10. The reference is to Thomas Carlyle (1795-1881), English essayist and historian.

PROCEEDINGS OF THE STATE CONVENTION OF COLORED MEN OF THE
STATE OF OHIO, HELD IN THE CITY OF COLUMBUS,
JANUARY 21st, 22d & 23d, 1857

PREFACE

At the call of the Executive State Committee the Convention assembled in the City Hall, Wednesday morning, January 21st, at 9 o'clock, and continued three consecutive days and evenings, and adjourned on Friday night at 10½ o'clock, *sine die*, with three cheers for liberty and the progress of liberal sentiment in Ohio. Its objects were to foster morals, discourage an ignorant ministry, encourage education, temperance, industry and economy among the colored people, and to seek the repeal of all laws which make distinction on account of color, by refusing colored persons admission into the public institutions of the State for the insane, blind, deaf and dumb, and especially to have the obnoxious feature in the Constitution erased which prevents *colored men from the right of an election*. So noble a purpose ought to have enlisted the sympathy and active co-operation of the colored people in the whole State, but such I regret was not the fact, and instead of forty or fifty delegates we should have had five hundred deputies, resolute and firm, but not fanatical, but determined, though defeated every day in the year, to use all lawful means in their power to secure the immunities of an American citizen. But those who were present represented, in a fair proportion, the respectability, and I know the intelligence of the people. I was glad to see the interest taken in the meeting by the people of Columbus, especially the colored people. The weather was very cold, and the hall where the session was held was cold, but the ladies, God bless them! cheered us with their smiles, and wishes and approbation, and for which I thank them, not for myself alone, but for the millions with whom I am identified in suffering and wrong.

Among those who were conspicuous in Convention, were Peter H. Clark, of Hamilton, now assistant editor of "Frederick Douglass' Paper;" John Mercer Langston, a young and talented member of the Lorain bar; John Jones, a graduate of Oberlin College, and a promising young man; J. I. Gaines, a boat-store keeper of Cincinnati; Dr. Charles H. Langston, a teacher of a grammar school at Columbus; Thomas Goode, an enterprising mechanic of Cincinnati; Mr. David Jenkins, Mr. John Booker, Mr. Jno. Malvin, Mr. W. H. Burnham, and Mr. John Watson, of Lorain county. A great work is before these gentlemen. Not the making of a President, a Governor, or a member of the Supreme Bench, but to redeem from ridicule and contempt the religion, civilization and republicanism of America. Now, because a man is black, it is no reason why he should not kneel at the same altar, dine at the same table, ride in the same coach, be educated in the same school, and be buried, if he desires it, in the same graveyard, by the side of his anglo-American brother: and he who denies him the right, is either a heathen or a tyrant. But we are told that colored men are ignorant, and this is assigned as a reason why they should not vote. Are we any more ignorant than the thousands of foreigners who annually flood the country? Are we more ignorant than the thousands of poor white men in the States who can neither read nor write, as indicated by the census of 1850, and certain revelations made during the last campaign for President of the United States? Hon. Henry A. Wise,[1] the eccentric Governor of Virginia, boasted in a public speech that in his district there were but few newspapers and free schools, and of course but few men, comparatively speaking, who could either read or write; and I suppose those were the gentleman's constituents. And yet such persons are allowed to vote for Franklin Pierce or James Buchanan,[2] while an intelligent, educated and wealthy man of color is driven from the polls as though he were a dog. This monstrous injustice must be kept before the people, and since we have no organ to do it, no mouthpiece to tell our wrongs, we must avail ourselves of Conventions to spread the light. Long, then, may our annual meetings live! Long may they live to infuse a more catholic spirit, a more genial sentiment among the dominant class in Ohio towards the colored people!

PROCEEDINGS

Columbus, January 21, 1857.

Convention met as per call of the State Central Committee, in the City Hall.

Mr. Jenkins, of Franklin, called the house to order, and on his motion John Watson, of Lorain, was appointed temporary Chairman.

W. H. Burnham, of Cuyahoga, and J. A. Chancellor, were appointed temporary Secretaries.

On motion of W. P. Morgan, of Logan, a Committee of five was appointed on permanent organization. The Convention appointed the following gentlemen: J. M. Langston, of Lorain; Granville Foster, of Highland; W. P. Morgan, of Logan; D. S. Bruce, of Harrison, and David Barnett, of Pike.

After a few minutes absence, the Committee reported the following gentlemen permanent officers of the Convention:

President--John M. Langston.

Vice Presidents--John Watson, W. P. Morgan, W. W. Johnson, John Booker.

Secretaries--W. H. Burnham, Peter H. Clark, D. S. Bruce.

Business Committee--D. Jenkins, C. H. Langston, P. H. Clark, J. A. Chancellor, David Barnett, John I. Gaines, John Malvin.

Finance Committee--C. H. Langston, D. Jenkins, Jas. Evans.

When on motion of D. Jenkins, the report was adopted.

Whereupon the following gentlemen enrolled themselves as members of the Convention:

Lorain County.--J. M. Langston and John Watson.

Ross County.--J. A. Chancellor and C. D. Williams.

Hamilton County.--W. H. Fuller, Thomas J. Goode, W. H. Mann, Peter H. Clark, John I. Gaines and George W. Roots.

Pike County.--David Barnett.

Highland County.--Granville Foster.

Muskingum County.--Fenton M. Harper.

Logan County.--W. P. Morgan, W. Hocking, William Johnson, J. Archer, B. E. Heathcock, and W. P. Moxley.

Champaign County.--William Walden.

Harrison County.--D. S. Bruce and J. Manley.

Delaware County.--Washington Wooldredge.

Green County.--John C. Jones and W. H. Hanster.

Clark County.--Henry Washing and Robert Piles.

Wyandott County.--A. A. Allen.

Licking County.--Henry Lucas and William Henry.

Franklin County.--D. Jenkins, John Booker, Allen Johnson, Augustus Anderson, James E. Evans, C. H. Langston, Isham Martin and Wilman Milton.

Cuyahoga County.--W. Hurst Burnham, R. B. Leech and John Malvin.

The Business Committee reported the following resolutions, which were unanimously adopted:

Resolved, That, in the language of John Wesley, Slavery is the sum of all villainies, and ought to be resisted, even unto death.

Whereas, The accumulation of wealth has a great tendency to elevate any people, therefore

Resolved, That the Convention recommend to the colored people of this State to form in each county associations whose object shall be to unite the capital of our people for the purpose of buying real estate.

Resolved, That whereas a party favorable to the interests of the colored people, and of strong anti-slavery proclivities, is now in power in this State, therefore we most earnestly, yet respectfully, call upon them not only to *repeal all* of the remaining Black Laws of this State, but to strike out the word WHITE from the Constitution wherever it occurs.

Resolved, That we renew our recommendation to the colored people of the State of Ohio, to proceed at once in every town where it is practicable, and where they cannot be enrolled among the whites, to form a military company or companies for the study of Scott's military tactics, and to become more proficient in the use of arms.

Resolved, That all male inhabitants (white or colored) above the age of eighteen years, of good moral habits, and who have resided in the town or place where they may make application for membership, one year next preceding such application only, shall form a part of the company, and we pledge our influence everywhere and at all times to their support.

Resolved, That we hail with pride the company now at Cincinnati, under the title of the Attuck Blues, and we hope its star may never go down; that it may live to be of service to our State, our people and country.

Resolved, That we are opposed to the *agitation of colonization or emigration* in every shape and form, if it means the removal of the colored people in the States to the North, South, Central America, Canada or Africa, believing such *agitation* to be detrimental to the best interests of the race, and we do pledge ourselves to resist it, come from what quarter it may.

Resolved, That if any one desires to remove, and thinks by so doing he can better his or her condition, or that of his family, we recommend him to do so, but not to hazard the rights of those who choose to remain behind.

Resolved, That the utter impossibility of preaching the gospel of Christ in its full purity and power in most of the Southern States of this nation, renders it incumbent upon those in the Christian Church of America to withdraw all ministers and churches from that section, thus obeying the divine command:--"When they persecute you in one city flee ye unto another;" and thus bearing their strongest testimony against the unpardonable sin of American --Slavery--teaching the slaveholder that he is self-excommunicated by his persistence in that foul practice.

Resolved, That the General School Law of Ohio, by putting the education of the colored youth of those districts where they number less than thirty, at the mercy of any narrow minded creatures who may be prompted by their illiberal prejudices to object to their admission into the public schools of the neighborhood, afflicts a grievous wrong upon those children, and works a permanent injury to the interests of the State of Ohio by keeping a portion of her people in ignorance, and as colored men and citizens of Ohio we protest against the wrong.

Resolved, That we earnestly request our people to avail themselves of the educational facilities afforded by our State, to insist that the schools set apart for their especial use shall be properly graded and taught by competent teachers; to use well the advantages conceded and strive for more.

Resolved, That the Convention return thanks to the officers of the Convention for the impartial performance of their several duties.

Resolved, That the Convention return thanks to the City authorities of Columbus for granting us the free use of the City Hall.

Resolved, That the next State Convention be held in the city of Cincinnati, at a time designated by the State Central Committee.

Mr. John I. Gaines presented the following resolutions, which were unanimously adopted:

Resolved, That we have heard with deep sorrow of the demise, since our last annual meeting, of L. D. Taylor, Esq., of Columbus, Ohio, who has been in public life among us for many years, and a member of nearly every State Convention.

Resolved, That in the death of L. D. Taylor society has lost one of its best men, the colored people one of their most active and energetic members, and the poor slave a real friend.

Resolved, That a copy of the above resolutions be furnished by the Secretary to his bereaved family, and the same entered on the minutes of the Convention.

Pending the consideration of these resolutions, Messrs. C. H. Langston, D. Jenkins and James E. Evans in short speeches bore testimony to the high moral character and great usefulness of Mr. L. D. Taylor.

On motion of Mr. D. Jenkins, it was resolved that Mr. C. H. Langston be requested to furnish his remarks for publication with the proceedings of the Convention.

Mr. Langston spoke in substance as follows:

Mr. President, Ladies and Gentlemen:--I arise in obedience to a call of this Convention, to perform the solemn and melancholy duty of saying a few words on the life, labors and death of our departed brother and fellow laborer, Lorenzo Dow Taylor.

Although it is a painful task for us to dwell upon the death of the great and good, and to contemplate the loss which the world has sustained in their death, yet we may with profit, pleasure and delight meditate upon their goodness, their virtue and their benevolence, and hold up to ourselves those sublime characteristics as a burning light to lighten our pathway to usefulness and renown. For

> Lives of great men all remind us
> We can make our lives sublime,
> And departing leave behind us
> Foot-prints on the sand of time;
> Foot-prints that perhaps another
> Sailing o'er life's solemn main,
> A forlorn and shipwrecked brother,
> Seeing, shall take heart again.

Mr. Taylor was born in the western part of the State of Virginia, about the year 1815, and was therefore at the time of his death (April 25th, 1856,) about forty-one years of age. Of his early history I can say but little, for it is concealed in that black and impenetrable obscurity in which Slavery always seeks to envelope itself and its victims. Notwithstanding the same commonwealth which gave birth to the honored champions of human liberty, Washington, Henry and Jefferson, gave birth to Mr. Taylor, yet the latter was born a *Slave*. Although Henry had shouted, "Give me *liberty* or give me death," and Jefferson had declared that "all men are created *free* and *equal*," and Washington had led the hosts of *Liberty* from conquering unto conqueror, still in their native State, the galling fetters of the bleeding bondman were not broken, and the Old Dominion still produces its thousands of infant Slaves. Mr. Taylor, in his youth, was, of course, surrounded by all the blighting influences which crowd upon the fiendish institution of Slavery. His native State is remarkable for its pretended love of liberty, and its real love of despotism. It is renowned for its slaveholding, its slave-breeding and its slave-trading. It is famed for its ignorance and its odious laws, which forbid, under heavy penalties, the teaching of colored children to read their own names, the name of the God who made them, or of the sun which gives them light.

Under these degrading circumstances, and these odious and damning laws did our demised friend begin life, and in this deplorable and wretched condition spent many of his early years. By some unforeseen but kind providence he was emancipated from this state of thraldom--the relation of master and Slave being abrogated--and he joyfully removed with his parents to the free State of Ohio. He here commenced the cultivation of his mind, and having left the dominion of human Slavery, he had fondly hoped to enter the schools of learing unrestrained, and thereby prepare himself for future usefulness. But, alas! he was doomed to the saddest disappointment. In this free and otherwise liberal State he encountered a bulwark of prejudice more formidable than Alpine steeps--those mighty barriers which the hand of nature has lifted up as a limit to human ambition. This colossal mountain of negro hate, "rearing its lofty head to Heaven," bade defiance to every attempt to ascend its rugged cliffs. This pro-slavery spirit closed the doors of schools, colleges and seminaries, not only against Mr. Taylor, but against every colored man, woman and child in the State. This accursed prejudice became embodied in a code of enactments known as the "Black Laws of Ohio." At the very threshold of the State Mr. Taylor was met by this heathenising code, and denied a legal residence in the State, as well as every other immunity enjoyed by its citizens. By these laws, the public schools withheld from him their invaluable blessings. This adamantine wall of prejudice and negro hate propped and supported by statutary and constitutional enactments required an almost super-human energy and perseverance in a colored man to scale its summit, triumph over its power and influence, and rise to moral and intellectual eminence. L. D. Taylor did possess this energy and perseverance. He did triumph over these almost insurmountable obstacles, and rose to a high eminence of morality and intelligence.

As a father, Mr. Taylor was kind and indulgent, yet never forgetting the admonitions of Scripture, "Train up a child in the way he should go, and when he is old he will not depart from it." As a husband, his distinguishing characteristics were love and devotion. Being ever under the influence of these God-like traits of character, he made every sacrifice to render his family comfortable and happy, always remembering that "he who neglects to provide for those of his own household is worse than an infidel." As a citizen, his life and conduct were the purest exemplification of the deep and abiding faith which he possessed in that glorious and divine truth which says, "Righteousness exalteth a nation, but sin is a reproach to any people." As a scholar, he very far surpassed thousands whose opportunities for mental culture were much superior to his own. While he did not so much excel in the knowledge of letters, he seems to have fully appreciated the wise man's advice when he says, "Wisdom is the principle thing; therefore get wisdom, and with all thy getting get understanding." As a philanthropist and reformer, Mr. Taylor had those invaluable elements of character without which no reformatory enterprise can be pushed to a successful and speedy termination; namely, a fixed and unyielding determination, a "dauntless spirit," and an active and self-sacrificing energy. To convince him that any reform was in accordance with the immutable principles of rectitude, at once enlisted him in its support and advocacy, and when once engaged in any cause, his self-consistency, his inflexible will and his indefatigable exertions made him a mighty champion in its support. For twenty years Mr. Taylor was not only an active and untiring advocate of the cause of temperance, but a consistent temperance man having never been known to taste one drop of ardent spirits during that time. He was a barber, and as such was expected, in accordance with the prevalent as well as profitable custom, to follow his ordinary avocation on the Sabbath day. But so determined was he in his course of moral duty, that neither the prevalence nor the profit of the custom had any effect upon him. Although he did not belong to any religious organization, yet while men of high standing in the church were desecrating the Sabbath by pursuing their secular business on that day, Mr. Taylor might be seen surrounded by his family making his way to the church. In the anti-slavery reform he was always zealous and active, every remembering "those in bonds as being bound with them." The bleeding fugitive escaping from republican despotism to monarchial liberty, found in him a sincere and devoted friend and a ready and efficient helper.

The labors of Mr. Taylor, in the cause in which we are now engaged, must not be overlooked or forgotten. The moral, intellectual and political elevation of the colored people was a cause ever dear to his heart. He labored constantly and earnestly for its promotion.

This, I believe, is the first State Convention of colored men ever held in Ohio without his presence. He has always been with us in these efforts for self-elevation, and we have always been proud to honor him as one of our greatest benefactors. But he is gone. His warning voice will no more be heard in our assemblies, and while we are forced to grieve over the loss which his family, the cause of the slave and our own cause has sustained in the death of this great and good man, we are happy to know that he has so LIVED and so acted as not only to hand his name down to posterity with undying honor and unsullied fame, but has been admitted to that celestial habitation above, where he shall spend a glorious eternity in the immediate presence and favor of the great architect of the universe. Then while we are meditating upon his death, let us determine to imitate his life, and so be a blessing to the world, and an honor to our creator.

ADDRESS TO THE PEOPLE OF OHIO

Citizens of Ohio:--We address you in the name of the colored people in the State, (many of whom are natives) who have been deprived of their natural, civil and political rights, and all for no crime which is contrary to the spirit of the Constitution and your own Bill of Rights. "Hear us," citizens, "for our cause," while we present you facts in relation to the manner in which we have been oppressed, which ought to make your cheeks tingle with shame, especially when you remember it is done in the face of our Bibles, Missionary Societies and under the nose of the church. You say we are ignorant. If we are ignorant, you are the cause; if we are less educated and intelligent than you, the crime lies at your door. But we deny that we are more dishonest and more improvident than other classes of citizens, and those who assert to the contrary, the *onus probandi*, that is, the burden of proof, rests with them, and not with us.

In 1802, the old Constitution was adopted in convention, and here was the beginning of the enactments against the people of color, for prior to that day they voted, could hold office, and exercise the full right of franchise under the laws of the Territorial Legislature.

"In all elections," says that instrument, "all white male inhabitants above the age of twenty-one years, having resided in the State one year next preceding the election, and who have paid, or are charged with, a State or County tax, shall enjoy the right of an elector."

This clause, on first trial, was negatived by 19 to 15, but on reconsideration it was a tie, and the casting vote given in its favor by Edward Tiffin, Esq., who was the presiding officer. Thus our vote was taken from us by the inconsiderate will of one man. We trust he is in Heaven, but it is exceedingly questionable to say the most.

Now these gentlemen tacitly admit that there was a class of black inhabitants in the State above the age of twenty-one years, who had paid, or were charged with, a State or County tax, and therefore were entitled to vote, but they purposely kept them from it because they had the power. It reminds us of a circumstance which took place in a Southern city only a few weeks ago. A colored man was on trial for stealing, in the County Circuit Court of St. Louis, and the main witness against him was a white boy. Defendant's counsel asked him: "Boy, do you know the nature of an oath?" The witness replied: "Yes sir; to swear *agin the nigger!*"

So the gentlemen who framed the Constitution thought they were discharging their duty and filling the end and purpose of civil government by making a rule *agin the niggers*. That anti-negro clause has been transferred almost verbatim to the new Constitution, adopted March 10th, 1851, at Cincinnati. And for the sake of an enlightened civilization we would it were not there. Now, in Convention, where the latter passed and became the supreme law of the State, were 95 members, and among the number were the flowers of the Democratic and the old Whig parties, but only seven were found who were willing to restore the rights of an elector to colored men. The New Constitution substitutes the words or phrase, "every white male citizen of the United States," for white male inhabitants, and with this exception it is substantially the same. Now the Constitution of the United States recognizes but two classes of citizens, to-wit: Native and adopted.

Article 2d, section 51st, says: "No person except a natural born citizen, or a citizen of the United States at the time of the adoption of this Constitution, shall be eligible to the office of President, &c." Now, ninety-nine out of every hundred colored men now living in the United States were born in it. Hence the Convention of '51 is guilty of deliberately, *we will not say maliciously*, of depriving us of our birth-right, or a right which we acquired by being born on the soil, and the only right which gives a chance to the oft repeated declaration, "I am an American citizen." But we insist that the

State has no right to tax us and yet deny us representation, for taxation and representation go together, as man and wife, and you can no more separate them in point of fact, and according to the genius of our institutions, than you can annihilate matter, or obstruct the course of the Sun.

"My position," said Lord Chatham,[3] in the British House of Parliament, "is this: I repeat it; I will maintain it to my last hour, taxation and representation are inseparable. This position is founded on the laws of nature; it is more--it is of itself an eternal law of nature; for whatever is a man's own is absolutely his own; no man has a right to take it from him without his consent. Whoever attempts to do it, attempts an injury; whoever does it commits a robbery."

Patrick Henry, in the House of Burgesses in Virginia, declared, *in substance*, that the King, in giving his assent to the Colonies being taxed, had played the part of a tyrant, and reminded him that he might meet the fate of Charles the First. Indeed, citizens, the Revolution of '76 turned upon the single point that Great Britain had no right to bind her Colonies, to tax them and then deny them a voice in Parliament. The colonists were right, the people who sympathized with them were right, and every drop of blood shed was shed in a holy cause. It is then good American doctrine, and no one has a right to gainsay it.

You have no right, therefore, to deprive us of the elective franchise; he who does it, does a wrong; he who aids in doing it, or in retaining the anti-democratic feature in the Constitution, aids in retaining an abominable tyranny. But, fellow citizens, the word white works evil in other respects. No colored man (*as such*) can be a Governor, a Secretary of State, a Judge, a Lawyer, a Clerk, a Commissioner, Notary Public, a Magistrate, a Constable, or even a *nigger catcher*. He can fill no *political office* of trust or honor, or profit, under the Constitution. We read of a printer-boy who has risen to be an influential editor and a leader of the Democratic Party in the United States.[4] We read of a shoemaker, a mere driver of pegs in a boot, who is the legitimate successor of Daniel Webster in the Senate of the United States, and the champion of Free Soil, Free Speech and Free Men.[5] We read of the wagon boy of Ohio, who won golden opinions as an orator, worked his way into the Executive Chair of State, and then into the Cabinet of Ex-President Fillmore, and is now a distinguished member of the Cincinnati bar.[6] But no place of distinction is held out to the black man--no path of glory opened to his vision; he may thrive if he can; is at liberty to die, but is nowhere encouraged, fostered or protected. Is it just, is it politic, is it wise?

Fellow citizens, the word white prevents colored men from being enrolled in the militia. Article 9th, section 1st, holds the following language:

"All white male citizens, residents of the State, being eighteen years of age, and under the age of forty-five years, shall be enrolled in the militia, and perform military duty," &c. There it is in black and white: what think you of it, fellow citizens? No government on earth, save Democratic America, has a rule so despotic. In England, colored men are among her best soldiers; in France they are in the army and navy; in Russia they are in the camp and the field; in Turkey they form a part of her corps; in Brazil they are officers of the regular army, and of the corporation guards and militia.

Mr. S. S. Steward, of the United States Navy, saw in the latter country: "A squadron of dragoons, in a scarlet uniform, had just been placed in line on one side of the square; a mounted band, in huzzar dress, of the same color, was in attendance. I took a station for a moment near this. It was composed of sixteen performers; and in the number included every shade of complexion, from the blackest ebony of Africa, through demi, quarter, and demi-quarter blood, to the purely swarthy Portuguese and Brazillian, and the clear and white of the Saxon, with blue eyes and flaxen hair." The gallant Commodore thought that it was a very disgusting sight for an American, and doubtless it was, for we have no doubt he went into hysterics or had the rheumatism every hour. A time may come when the services of black soldiers will be needed, and when a general Jackson will call his black brethren to arms, as did the old hero in 1814, at the Battle of New Orleans, and we will not be found in the rear, but if there is any fighting to do, in the front of the battle. And yet men of such grit cannot comprise a part of the militia of Ohio. Shame!

Fellow Citizens, we invite your attention for a moment to the statutes which have been passed, infringing on our rights.

On the 5th of January, 1805, a law was passed regulating the condition of a legal residence of blacks and mulattoes. Who its author was, or where he lived, we are not advised; for if we where we would communicate the information for the benefit of the reading public; but one thing we do know, the bill was characterized by great barbarity. Here are a few specimens:

"Blacks or mulattoes shall first produce a fair certificate from some court within the United States, of his or her actual freedom." Failing to have or produce such certificate, any person who gave such an individual work was subject to a penalty of "not less than ten nor more than fifty dollars."

The 4th section says that if any resident shall harbor, secrete or feed "any black or mulatto person, the property of any person whatever, or in anywise hinder or prevent the lawful owner or owners from retaking and possessing his or her black or mulatto servant or servants, shall, on conviction therefore, be fined not less than fifty nor more than one hundred dollars."

So the General Assembly, by this act, constituted the people of Ohio an organized band of kidnappers. In 1807 this law was amended, and a black or mulatto person required, before he or she could obtain a legal residence in the State, to give bond and security in the sum of five hundred dollars for their good behavior; and they were also prevented in the same act from testifying in any case where a white person was a party concerned.

Now any jail bird, of a white skin or Saxon origin, could insult with impunity a colored lady, and if brought into Court to answer, all the prosecuting attorney would have to do would be to enter a *nolle prosequi*, and the case would be dismissed. We might give you many reminiscences of the workings of the testimony law, but we forbear; one instance will suffice for the present:

In the summer of of 1846-7, a colored man killed another in a melee at Cincinnati. The murderer was a quadroon, and the murdered man a pure black of the deepest African dye. The case came up for hearing in the Criminal Court of Hamilton County, and the witnesses were black and mulatto persons. The counsel for the defense objected to negro testimony against the prisoner, which was sustained, and the culprit went unwhipped of justice. George E. Pugh--now Senator Pugh[7]--was a counsellor in the case, and he planted himself from that hour against the law, and was a member of the Assembly when it was repealed, and voted for it. These laws were in force forty-two years, (1807 to 1849,) when they were repealed by a mixed Legislature of Whigs, Democrats and Free Soilers.

In 1831-2, acts were created for the relief [of] the poor in the several Counties of the State, and we confess that we cannot see how those laws and the amendatory acts passed since, strictly construed could or can deprive a lawful resident of the benefit of the Poor Fund; but, by some strange interpretation, colored persons have been and are excluded. We know something of the effects of this law, for some of us happened once to be on a committee to get certain persons of color in the Poor House of Hamilton County. We were debarred at every office door, and told by the gentlemen who held the keys that the law would not allow them to admit niggers, and that they would not do it. We turned from them more in sorrow than in anger; for we felt there was need of a *mission at Cincinnati*. Colored persons are excluded from all the public institutions of the State for the benefit of the insane, blind, deaf and dumb, and until recently they were not permitted to enter on a visit. We beg pardon, for there is one institution wherein we are admitted, but not on terms of equality--we mean the Penitentiary. No colored man can be a juryman. It is a principle of common law that a person charged with crime is entitled to a fair hearing by a jury of his peers. How can a colored person get such a hearing. Juryman generally have no association with him--no sympathy in common with him--and have been taught from infancy to hate and despise him. Doubtless if the poor slaves who have been slaughtered, quartered, their heads put on posts as a terror to their brethren in chains, *for a mere suspicion to rebel or revolt against unlawful authority*, could have been tried by a jury of their peers, not one out of the many would have suffered.

Hence, fellow citizens, we ask you to strike or cause to be stricken from the Constitution the word white wherever it occurs, and it occurs twice. We ask you to repeal the remnant of the *old black laws*, and in this we are certainly not asking too much. Justice, equity, humanity and the highest interest of the State, demand their immediate, instant and unconditional repeal. We ask it not as a favor, but as a right; for if you have a right to tax us for the benefit of the State, and this we do not deny, we have a right to demand of you protection, and if you deny us our plea, we say to you, "fie upon your law."

We ask it, in conclusion, because we are *men*--children of the same common parent--heirs of the same destiny--and like yourselves, our sweat has mingled with the soil and our means have been contributed freely to the development of the resources of our beloved State; and, therefore, whatever concerns her greatness, glory and expansion, concerns us.

Respectfully submitted in behalf of the Convention,

John I. Gaines.

ADDRESS

To the Legislature of Ohio:

In addressing you, as the law-makers of the State, we do not seek to be elaborate and elegant so much as to be simple and perspicuous. We seek to state the story of our wrongs in plain unvarnished phrase.

According to the 1st Section of Article 5th of the State Constitution, "Every *white male* citizen of the United States, of the age of twenty-one years, who shall have been a resident of the State one year next preceding the election, and of the county, township or ward in which he resides, such time as may be provided by law, shall have the qualifications of an elector, and shall be entitled to vote at all elections."

According to the 1st Section of the 9th Article of the same instrument, "All *white male* citizens, residents of this State, being eighteen years of age, and under the age of forty-five years, shall be enrolled in the militia and perform military duty in such manner, not incompatible with the Constitution of the United States, as may be prescribed by law."

According to the 3rd Section of the 62nd Chapter of the Revised Statutes of the State, "The Trustees of each township shall, on the second Tuesday of October next, (passed Feb. 9th, 1831,) and on the second Tuesday of October annually thereafter, select of good, judicious persons, having the *qualification of electors*, their apportionment of persons to be retained as jurors."

According to the 6th Section of the 86th Chapter of the Revised Statutes, it is also provided "That nothing in this act shall be so construed as to enable any *black* or *mulatto* person to gain a legal settlement in this State; provided, that nothing in this section shall be so construed as to prevent the directors of any country or city infirmary, in *their discretion*, from admitting any *black* or *mulatto* person into said infirmary." Passed March 1st, 1853. It is further provided by our State Statutes that no person shall gain admission to our Lunatic Asylums or benevolent institutions, who is not a "resident," that is, who has not gained "legal settlement" in the State. It will be perceived from these passages of the Constitution and Statutes, which we have quoted, that black and mulatto persons are not allowed, like other inhabitants of the State to enjoy the privileges and advantages of the Poor House, the Lunatic Asylums, and the comfortable and convenient homes provided by the State for the deaf and dumb and the blind. Nor are they allowed to act as jurors--to enjoy that inestimable right which every intelligent person holds in the highest consideration, namely, the privilege of being *tried by one's peers.* Nor can they become a part and parcel of the military strength of the State. They may be ever so patriotic--they may be ever so desirous to make an exhibition of their physical prowess in behalf of their State, when emergency demands, yet their patriotism is to be stained and their manly desires to be smothered and extinguished by legal imposition. They are also denied the right of suffrage--a right as inherent and inalienable as any other natural and indefeasible right. Such is our condition in Ohio. And it is to it that we ask your patient and candid attention, while we state the reasons upon which we demand the removal of these legal disabilities. It is in fact, however, but *one disability*. For let the word "white" be stricken from the Constitution, and black and mulatto persons come at once into the enjoyment of a full and complete legal equality; then the last vestige of the old barbarous and inhuman Black Laws will have been wiped out, and a new order of things instituted, whose peculiar and distinguished characteristics will be a democratic and Christian regard for the rights of all mankind, whatever their condition or complexion. What are the reasons, then, which we have to offer in favor of the erasure of the word "white" from the State Constitution? The Declaration of Independence, and the American definition of human freedom, declares that *all* men are created equal--that is, that all are equally endowed with natural and inherent rights. These rights are not *created by Constitutions*, nor are they *uncreated by Constitutions*. Their existence is not dependent upon the curl of a man's hair, the projection of his lips, the color of his skin, or the clime in which he had his birth. They are a constituent element of manhood--whether that manhood be found encased in ebony or ivory. And it is the natural and peculiar function of government not to destroy these rights, but to guard and defend them. When government fails to perform this function, its acts become unjust, anti-democratic and cruel. And then it becomes the duty of the law-making power of the State to alter and amend the laws in such a manner as to secure equal and exact justice to every inhabitant. In the name of the manhood of black and mulatto persons, then,--in the name of his inherent rights, which are inseparable from that manhood--and in the name of the true function of government, we ask the amendment of the Constitution.

In this first consideration, it will be perceived that we have assumed the manhood of black and mulatto persons. This we have done, because, at this late day, after so much has been done by the colored people of the State and Nation to educate, refine and elevate ourselves, so that we may be useful in our day and generation, to ourselves and mankind, we suppose that no one of moderate intelligence would question our humanity and manhood. But if there are persons who still would question our mental and moral capacities, and, therefore, our membership of the human family, we need only call the attention of such to the fact, that we have among us persons who are distinguished for their enterprise and attainments as doctors of medicine, those who are skillful and successful as attorneys and counsellors at law, and still another class whose industry and learning, whose devotedness and piety make them acceptable and influential as ministers of the Gospel. Indeed, not many years ago, a German University of Heidelberg, did itself and the colored people of the United States the honor to confer upon one of our number, in consideration of his scholarship and Christian bearing, the doctrinate of divinity.[8] Nor is this all that can be said in this direction. We have among us poets, orators and authors whose genius, eloquence and learning place them among the *savans* of this country. When we read the poetry of Whittier, all aglow with the radiance of divine inspiration--the historical pages of Bryant,[9] enlivened and beautified by a rich dramatic style--the speeches of Webster, whose manly sentiments and beautiful expression render them acceptable and captivating, let us not forget the effusions of Whitfield,[10] the historical productions of Nell,[11] and the burning and masterly eloquence of Douglass. Nor are we without mathematical and mechanical ingenuity. There are colored men who have done themselves great credit and the State great service by their mathematical and mechanical genius. These achievements of a mathematical and mechanical, a literary and scientific sort, to which allusion has been made are but the results of primitive, original fundamental faculties which belong to our nature, and which establish beyond decent cavil our unity and identity with the human family. Indeed, there is no argument in favor of the unity of the human race so strong and impregnable as this one from a psychological standpoint. Under existing circumstances we make no apology for this episode in favor of our manhood.

The second consideration which we have to offer in favor of the amendment of the State Constitution, is the fact that caste legislation--legislation founded upon accidental or complexional differences--is contrary to the drift and meaning of the United States Constitution. We find no word white in that instrument. It regards every man *as a man*, whether his skin be white or black, and as the possessor of rights which civil society ought to respect and protect. Indeed, it is stated in the preamble that it was ordained and established to "secure the blessings of liberty to ourselves and our posterity." And, among the miscellaneous provisions, the second section reads: "The citizens of each State shall be entitled to all privileges and immunities of citizens in the several States." In spite of this clause in the United States Constitution, however, the colored sojourner who comes into our State from Massachusetts, although he is a full-grown citizen of that State, is compelled to suffer in consequence of the odious complexional discrimination found in our State Constitution. It is not only contrary to the philosophy of the declaration and the drift and meaning of the United States Constitution to make such distinctions, but it is contrary to the ancient and well-established policy of the fathers of the Republic. So that Judge Phelimon Bliss,[12] is right when he says: "There is nothing in the principles of our government, or in its traditions, that will justify for a moment the denial of the elective franchise on account of color. The Declaration of Independence nor the Constitution of the United States make no such distinctions, but avow principles and objects entirely inconsistent with them. The original revolutionary constitutions of nearly all the States, made colored persons electors, and it was not till a race arose that knew not Joseph, a race that has changed the whole policy of the Government from an enfranchising to an enslavery, from a propagandism of free labor to a propagandism of slavery, that the old States began to disfranchise on account of color or descent." He continues: "As I can see no sound reason, no justice or propriety in the new policy, neither can I see any benefit resulting from it. I therefore prefer the policy of the Fathers." More than this, all such legislation is contrary to the fundamental principles of morality and natural justice, and according to every tenet of legal hermenutics, is null and void, and the courts ought to so construe them.

But in addition to the consideration which have already been advanced in favor of our enfranchisement, there are others of a little different character, to which we would call your attention. The first of these is the fact that we are native-born inhabitants, and therefore, citizens. This is no newfangled doctrine of our making, nor is it the teaching of a hair-brained fanatic. This is a well established principle of the law of Nature. It is a principle fully recognized and endorsed by all standard writers on law. Indeed, Chancellor Kent endorses this doctrine most fully when he says, "Citizens, under our Constitution and laws, mean free inhabitants, born within the United States or naturalized under the laws of Congress. If a slave, born *in* the United States, be manumitted, or otherwise legally discharged from bondage, or, if a black man be born within the United States, and born free, he becomes thenceforward a citizen." And it is an element of the creed of every political party and politician in America, that nativity gives citizenship. Why then deny us, who are native-born inhabitants, the elective franchise?

In the next place, we are *tax-payers*. We willingly do what we can towards bearing the burthens and expenses of the Government. We aid in building Poor Houses, Lunatic Asylums, edifices for the accommodation of the deaf and dumb and the blind; and we are not without a *property interest* in the beautiful and magnificent State House, the simplicity of whose construction, whose durability of material, and whose massive proportions are the admiration and pride of us all. And we make very great account of this consideration of our paying taxes; for it is a principle that is held in the highest estimation by every American who respects and reverences the teachings of the Fathers of the Republic. They declared that *taxation* and *representation* are *inseparable*. And to the support and maintenance of this doctrine they pledged their lives, their property and their sacred honors. Though weak in numbers, in commercial and financial resources, and without the prestige of a great national representation and the strong alliances of friendly powers, they came through an eight years contest, hard and bloody, with victory, glorious victory, perched upon every banner! All honor to their names! They fought in defence of a catholic and a world-wide principle, that has application to every human being, whether born in Europe, Asia, Africa or America. The Fathers of this country were right, then, when they enunciated the doctrine that, when a man pays taxes, he is, by law, by right and by justice entitled to representation --and ought to have the privilege of saying what shall be the legislation respecting taxation. Nor must any one suppose that our tax is of insignificant account, for be it known to every one that the colored men of Ohio are worth to-day over *seven millions of dollars worth of property!* In the city of Cincinnati they are owners of nearly a million of dollars in personal property and real estate, and in Columbus they pay tax upon about three hundred thousand dollars, and in Cleveland upon four hundred thousand. In many of the farming districts of the State, also, such as those in Jackson, Pike and Highland Counties, the colored men are owners of large farms, which, in many instances, are well stocked and cultivated according [to] the most approved methods of modern agriculture. Reference might be made to other portions of the State in which colored men are in comfortable and prospering circumstances; but there is no need of this. If our tax were but a mere trifle, the principle would be the same. We ask, then, that you endorse in your legislative decrees the doctrine of the Fathers in regard to this matter. It is hardly necessary for us, in considering this subject, to remind you that our rights in this country date back "to the dread arbitrament of war." Every one well read in the History of the Revolutionary War and the War of 1812, knows the part colored men played in those contests. He knows that they stood cheek by jowl with the white men of the country in every battle. He knows that the granite shaft of Bunker Hill was erected to commemorate the valor, the courage and the heroic devotion of the colored soldiers as well as the white. Like white men colored men in this country, with truthfulness and pride can boast,

> For God's inalienable rights to man
> Our Father's fought and bled;
> So glorious were the rights secured,
> The sons revere the dead

We have always shown ourselves patriotic and loyal subjects. And in the name of our patriotism, our loyalty and heroic devotion to the country, we make our demand for complete legal equality.

It is fit, in this connection, that your attention be called to the fact that while this vague and indefinite word "white" remains in the State Constitution, we are without a *jury trial*. We are not tried, as already stated, by our peers; but we are tried by men whose hearts are full of prejudice against us. Therefore, in nine cases out of ten we are not dealt with impartially in the courts of justice. So strong, indeed, is this prejudice against us, in many localities of the State, that lawyers, in presenting the causes of colored clients, are compelled to beseech the court and the jury not to allow the color of their skins to damage their claims. This is not right. The privilege of being tried by an impartial jury is, and ought to be, held in the highest estimation by every person, for it is one of the strong bulwarks of our rights. We demand the amendment of the Constitution, then, for the consideration that, since we have not the qualifications of electors we cannot act as jurors, and therefore are not tried by our equals, but by those who claim to be our superiors, and who, in almost every case, prejudge our cause.

In the name of the Declaration of Independence, the Constitution of the United States, the ancient policy of the Fathers of the Republic, the well-established doctrine that nativity gives citizenship, that taxation and representation are inseparable, in the name of our patriotism and loyal bearing towards the country in a trying hour, as well as the principle that every person ought to be tried by his peers, we ask the erasure of the word "white" from the State Constitution. What sound reason can be offered against this procedure? It is safe for us to say that there is none. There is nothing in the State Constitution against it. The Bill of rights of the State is altogether on our side. Nor can any one justly claim that we ought not to be made citizens, because of our ignorance and want of mental attainments. Through the influence of our common schools and our religious organizations, our mental condition has been greatly ameliorated within the last fifteen or twenty years. So that, if the objection founded upon our ignorance was ever good for anything, if is now wholly worthless. In our literary qualifications, we compare favorably with other inhabitants of this commonwealth.

Let us assure you, then, in conclusion, that no unjust and oppressive legislation shall ever drive us from this State. We are here, and here we intend to remain. Our position is as fixed and immovable as the pillars of this great State. Your history and your destiny shall be ours. And while cruel and despotic statutes disgrace our State legislation, we will express, in every possible manner, our dissatisfaction and disapproval of them.

John Mercer Langston,
*Chairman of the Committee
in behalf of the Convention.*

Copy in the Harvard University Library.

REFERENCE NOTES

1. Henry Alexander Wise (1806-1876) was a Virginia congressman, governor and confederate general. Wise served in the House of Representatives from 1833 to 1844 and was governor of Virginia from 1856 to 1860. He was the chief antagonist of John Quincy Adams in his effort to repeal the "Gag Law" against antislavery petitions and figured prominently in John Brown's raid on Harper's Ferry, which occurred during his administration.

2. James Buchanan (1791-1868), fifteenth president of the United States, held office on the eve of secession and civil war.

3. This address erroneously attributes to Lord Chatham the statement that "taxation and representation are inseparable." Actually, Charles Pratt, First Earl of Camden or Lord Camden (1714-1794), made the quoted remarks on the floor of Parliament on February 24, 1766. Lord Camden was an English jurist and chief justice of the Court of Common Pleas. Later, while in the House of Lords, he denounced the government's policy toward the American colonies and opposed the taxes imposed on the colonists.

William Pitt (1700-1778) served as prime minister during the French and Indian Wars (1756-1763) and became First Earl of Chatham or Lord Chatham in 1766.

4. The reference is probably to James Brooks (1810-1873), editor of the Whig *New York Express*, a conservative commercial daily in New York City. He was elected to Congress in 1848, serving two terms as a Whig. Becoming a Democrat in the 1850's, he supported Buchanan in 1856 and in 1864 again won election to Congress, serving continually until his death.

5. The reference is to Henry Wilson (1812-1875), identified above.

6. The reference is to Thomas Corwin (1794-1865), senator and governor of Ohio, also became secretary of the treasury in 1850, during Millard Fillmore's presidency. His canvass as governor in 1840 made him famous as a campaign orator.

7. George Ellis Pugh (1822-1876) was a Democratic senator from Ohio from 1854 to 1860. On the eve of secession, he urged acceptance of the Crittenden Compromise as a means of preventing civil war.

8. The reference is to the Reverend James W. C. Pennington, of New York City, identified above.

9. William Cullen Bryant (1794-1878), American poet and newspaper editor, practiced law briefly as a young man but became editor of the *New York Evening Post* in 1826, a position which he occupied until his death.

10. James M. Whitfield, black poet and advocate of emigration of black Americans, was well known in antislavery circles for his odes, which were generally read at the annual August 1 celebrations of West India Emancipation.

11. William C. Nell (1816-1874), a noted black writer, was born in Boston, the son of William G. and Louisa M. Nell. Nell attended the schools in Boston which had been established for colored children in 1820. He subsequently graduated with honors from the Smith School of Grammar, opened in 1835.

Connected with Garrison's *Liberator* for many years, Nell won fame as an orator and also as one of the first black historians in the United States. He began collecting Negro historical data and produced in 1852 the study *Services of Colored Americans in the Wars of 1776 and 1812*, followed four years later by *Colored Patriots of the American Revolution*, to which Harriet Beecher Stowe wrote an introduction. But it was his leadership in the desegregation campaign in Boston's schools which won Nell his greatest fame. Under his direction, Negroes in Boston deluged the Massachusetts Legislature with petitions demanding the abolition of separate schools and had the black children taught privately until in 1855 a law was enacted requiring public schools in the state to admit students without regard to color.

During 1851, Nell served as a correspondent for Frederick Douglass' *North Star*, and in 1861 he was appointed by Boston postmaster John G. Palfrey as one of his clerks, becoming the first black man to hold a post under the federal government.

12. Phelimon Bliss (1813-1889), Ohio jurist and congressman, was born in North Canton, Connecticut. He attended Oneida Institute in upstate New York and later emigrated to Elyria, Ohio, where he began the practice of law. A Whig by political persuasion, his strong antislavery views carried him into the Free-Soil Party in 1848 and later into the Republican Party. In 1854 he was elected to Congress from a formerly Democratic district and was re-elected in 1856.

PROCEEDINGS OF A CONVENTION OF THE COLORED MEN OF OHIO. HELD
IN THE CITY OF CINCINNATI, ON THE
23d, 24th, 25th and 26th DAYS OF NOVEMBER, 1858

PROCEEDINGS OF A CONVENTION OF THE COLORED MEN OF OHIO

November 23d, 1858.
PURSUANT to a call from the State Central Committee, a Convention of the colored men of Ohio, assembled in the Union Baptist Church, in the city of Cincinnati, Tuesday morning November 23, 1858.
John I. Gaines, chairman of the State Central Committee, called the Convention to order; whereupon John Booker was called to the chair, and Wm. E. Ambush chosen secretary.
Charles H. Langston moved that the Convention be opened with prayer. Rev. Wallace Shelton then addressed the throne of grace. Messrs Wm. H. Fuller, John Malvin, J. D. Harris, Jesse Devine, A. Redman, John Galley and A. N. Freeman, were appointed a committee to nominate permanent officers for the Convention. During the absence of the committee. [sic] Messrs. D. Jenkins, P. H. Clark, C. H. Langston and John I. Gaines, were appointed a Committee on Finance, Peter H. Clark, John I. Gaines, John M. Langston, J. D. Harris, John Booker, E. P. Walker, and Jesse Devine, were appointed a committee to report business for the consideration of the Convention.
The Convention agreed to meet at 9 o'clock A.M. and 2 P.M., taking a recess at 12 and at 5 o'clock.
The evening sessions to begin at 7 and close at 10 o'clock.
The Committee on permanent officers, reported the following names, viz:
For *President*, Charles H. Langston.
" *Vice Presidents*, A. M. Sumner, John Malvin, A. Redman.
For *Secretaries*, Wm. D. Goff, L. M. Troy, J. D. Harris.
For *Chaplain*, Rev. Wallace Shelton.
The Convention confirmed the nominations unanimously. W. D. Goff having declined, Wm. E. Ambush was elected in his place. On motion of J. D. Harris, Horace Morris was added to the corps of secretaries. Peter H. Clark moved that a committee of three be appointed to prepare a plan for a permanent organization of the colored people of Ohio. The chairman named John M. Langston, John Booker and John Malvin, the committee; when the Convention took a recess.

Afternoon Session.
President in the chair. Minutes read and approved. Committee on Finance reported that "Each delegate be requested to pay fifty cents on enrolling his name." Adopted. On motion it was agreed, that only the morning sessions be opened with prayer.
Mr. J. M. Langston moved, that Mr. Isaiah Mitchell be invited to participate in the deliberations of the Convention. The Business Committee through their chairman, Peter H. Clark, then reported the following resolutions,

which were received and laid on the table for the consideration of the Convention.

Whereas, The right to assemble and petition for a redress of grievances, is one of the few rights let to the colored people of the United States, therefore, we, the colored people of Ohio, deem it fit to represent to our fellow citizens the disabilities under which we labor, and for which we seek redress.

We have to complain that, in a country professing to realize in its Government, the grand principles of the Declaration of 1776, millions of our brethren are publicly sold, like beasts in the shambles, that they are robbed of their earnings, denied the control of their children, forbidden to protect the chastity of their wives and daughters, debarred an education and the free exercise of their religion; and if they escape by flight from so horrible a condition, they may be hunted like beasts from city to city, and dragged back to the hell from which they had fled--the Government which should protect them, prostituting its powers to aid the villains who hunt them.

Notwithstanding the rights and immunities of the citizens of the several States, are guaranteed to citizens of all the States, we can not visit large portions of our country in pursuit of health, business or pleasure, without danger of being sold into perpetual slavery, the shores of neighboring States being more inhospitable, than the bleakest or most savage shore that excites the mariner's dread.

To crown all, the highest tribunal of the land, solemnly denies that the great principles of Liberty and Equality which are the boast of our nation, were intended to apply to us and our unfortunate brethren, the slaves.[1] It decides the colored American sailor, or traveler, can receive no protection from his Government; that the National Courts are closed to us; that we have fewer rights in our own native country than aliens, for the aliens may claim and receive justice, from the tribunal before which we may not appear as suitors.

Futhermore, in our own State of Ohio, while we are permitted a partial freedom, we are subjected to iniquitous and burdensome legislation. We are refused the right to vote; we are refused a fair trial by jury; we are refused participation in the emoluments and honors of office; we are denied equal education; those of us who are reduced to pauperism, or afflicted with lunacy, are thrust into the cells of the felon's jail, all of which is unjust, tending to destroy those sentiments of self-respect, enterprise and patriotism, which it would be wisdom to foster in the people of the State. Therefore be it

Resolved (1), That if it is the province of governments to protect their subjects against unjust seizures and imprisonment, violence, robbery, murder, rape and incest; if they should encourage and sustain industry, marriage, the parental relation, education and religion; if it is their duty to honor God by respecting and protecting the rights of humanity, then should the American government immediately and unconditionally abolish that essence of infernalisms--American Slavery.

Resolved (2), That if the Dred Scott dictum be a true exposition of the law of the land, then are the founders of the American Republic convicted by their descendants of base hypocrisy, and colored men are absolved from all allegiance to a government which withdraws all protection.

Resolved (3), That we rejoice at the declension of the Democratic Party in the North, and hope that its defeat presages the downfall of Slavery, of which accursed system it has been a firm supporter.

Resolved (4), That we say to those who would induce us to emigrate to Africa or elsewhere, that the amount of labor and self-sacrifice required to establish a home in a foreign land, would if exercised here, redeem our native land from the grasp of slavery; therefore we are resolved to remain where we are, confident that "truth is mighty and will prevail."

Resolved (5), That we recommend to our people, in addition to the education they are so generally seeking to give their children, to train them in habits of useful industry.

Resolved (6), That a combination of labor and capital will in every field of enterprise, be our true policy. Combination stores of every kind, combination work-shops, and combination farms, will, if every where established, greatly increase our wealth; and with it our power.

Resolved (7), That a State which taxes a portion of its inhabitants without allowing them a representation, excludes them from offices of honor and trust, refuses them an impartial trial by Jury, refuses an equal education to their youth, disparages their patriotism by refusing to enroll them in her militia, allows them to be hunted through her cities, confined in her jails, and dragged thence to hopeless slavery, consigns their lunatics and paupers to the common jail, forfeit her claim to be called Christian or Republican.

Resolved (8), That in the vigorous and unceasing exercise of the rights of petition, we recognize a potent instrument of elevation, and we recommend the people of every city and school district to petition the Legislature to repeal all such laws, and to take the proper steps to expunge from the Constitution all traces of distinction on account of color.

Resolved (9), That a committee of three be appointed to prepare a petition for general circulation.

On motion the first resolution was taken up. Mr. Gaines desired gentlemen who thought that the American government has power to abolish Slavery, to show in what part of the Constitution that power is granted.

Peter H. Clark explained, that the term government in the resolution, was meant to apply to the people of the United States, who having the supreme power, can if they wish, alter or abolish all laws or constitutions, that stand between the slave and his freedom. Other gentlemen thought, that if there was power given in the Constitution to enforce its objects as set forth in the preamble, then was there sufficient power granted to abolish Slavery. Mr. A. Redman moved to table the resolution. Lost. The resolution was then adopted.

The second and third resolutions were specially ordered for the evening session.

Miss F. E. Watkins[2] was requested to take part in the Convention.

Wm. D. Goff and David Jenkins, were appointed to invite reporters for the press, to attend the sessions of the Convention.

Recess till 7 P.M.

Evening Session.

President in the chair. Minutes read, corrected and approved.

Mr. D. Jenkins, saw in the decline of the Democratic party, and rise of the Republican, omens of hope for the colored people.

Mr. John M. Langston said, "The Democratic party had always been the abettors of Slavery; it was now declining, for the people were opposed to Slavery, and willing to trample the fugitive act under foot, as they had recently done at Wellington.[3]

So fond are the Democrats of Slavery, that they had legislated off the statute book of the State, all laws against kidnapping. He hated the Democratic party because it was pro-slavery. He exhorted his friends to oppose by every means in their power, that party. The people were killing it every where, through the North, and he was glad to know it. His motto was, "the Democratic party must be destroyed."

Peter H. Clark did not consider his rights any safer with Republicans than with Democrats. He believed Slavery would be more secure with the Republicans than with Democrats. The Republicans were aiming to become national, and were therefore conservative.

William J. Watkins, believed that the Democratic party was the great foe to the colored man; the Republicans of New York had done something for the colored man, and he verily believed, would do more. The great aim in the late contest, was to kill the Democratic party, and they had done that.

The second and third resolutions were adopted when the Convention adjourned.

Wednesday, Nov. 24th.

Convention met. President in the chair. Prayer by Rev. Wallace Shelton. Minutes read and approved.

Fourth resolution read, and on motion of E. P. Walker, made the special order of the evening session. Fifth resolution read, and on motion of David Jenkins, adopted. Sixth resolution read, and on motion of R. G. Ball, adopted. Seventh resolution read. Considerable discussion was had upon this resolution. A portion of the members did not feel justified in denying the

Christian character of the State. Others feared the resolution conveyed a covert attack upon religion. Rev. Wallace Shelton thought that if to love impartial justice and mercy was an attribute of a Christian State, then a State against which such charges as were made in the resolution could lie, was surely not a Christian State.

Several gentlemen arose to ask whether they had met to discuss theological or political subjects. The previous question was finally ordered, when the resolution was adopted. On motion of J. H. Gurley, the eighth resolution was adopted. Ninth resolution read. John Brown moved to strike out the word *two* after the word prepare. Agreed to.

T. J. Goode moved to amend thus "that there be a committee of three" instead of the State Central Committee. Agreed to; and Thos. J. Goode, John I. Gaines and E. P. Walker were appointed that committee.

E. P. Walker offered the following:

Resolved, That Hayti sets the colored people of this country an example of proper independence; and that, that government is doing more for the upbuilding of the black race, than all other instrumentalities proposed or controlled by colored men.

Pending the discussion on this resolution, the Convention took a recess.

Afternoon Session.

Convention met--President in the Chair. Minutes read and approved.

Discussion on Mr. Walker's resolution was resumed. Messrs. J. D. Harris, T. J. Goode, and E. P. Walker participating. On motion, the resolution was indefinitely postponed. Messrs. Wm. H. Day and Wm. J. Watkins were, on motion of Mr. Wm. E. Ambush, invited to participate in the deliberations of the Convention. Pending the adoption of the preamble to resolutions, Mr. Wm. H. Day addressed the Convention, when he concluded, the preamble was adopted.

The Committee on permanent organization, reported a Constitution for a State Anti-Slavery Society, and accompanying resolutions. On motion of Chas. H. Langston, it was discussed by sections. On motion, so much of the preamble as declares "We do hereby agree to form ourselves into a State Anti-Slavery Society," was adopted.

Articles 1, 2, 3, were then adopted. Article 4 was read, and pending its passage, the Convention took a recess.

Evening Session.

Convention--President in the Chair. Minutes read and approved. The 4th resolution of the Business Committee's report being the special order, several ineffectual attempts to postpone, lay on the table, etc., were made. Mr. J. H. Gurley exhorted the people to either emigrate or concentrate their strength at some point or points in the United States. Mr. John Booker was opposed to emigration singly or *en masse*. What we want is numbers. He believed the language of the resolution to be truthful. To establish a respectable footing elsewhere, would require energy, fortitude, self-sacrifice, and these qualities, if exercised here in a corresponding degree, would accomplish all we desired. Mr. J. D. Harris proposed to show that we had numbers on the continent, sufficient, if concentrated, to force freedom and respect from our oppressors. Mr. Fuller thought emigration, as a panacea for the ills that afflict us, was an unmitigated humbug. Mr. E. P. Walker, at some length and with considerable ability, proceeded to argue, that the Cotton, Sugar, and Coffee growing regions of the world, belonged to the colored race, and that the nation or nations which produced those articles, must necessarily control the commerce of the world. Here then, was the path opened by Providence for our elevation. Let us concentrate upon the West Indies, upon Central America, where by our superior intelligence and energy, we would wield a wide influence, and many years would not pass away before we would have the world at our feet.

Mr. Day had years before, standing on the same spot, opposed the scheme of emigration, and after having become an emigrant himself, he returned to still resist it. He knew that labor and self-sacrifice were required to make a home in a foreign land; and when our minds were made up to endure that amount of labor--make such sacrifices as were essential to founding a home elsewhere--then we would be prepared to achieve our rights at home, and the necessity for emigration would be removed. Resolution adopted. Adjourned.

Thursday, Nov. 25th. 1858.

President Langston called Convention to order at 9 o'clock. Prayer by Rev. H. J. Andrews. Minutes read and approved.

Article 4th of the Constitution of the Anti-Slavery Society taken up. The amendment offered by P. H. Clark being decided out of order, the motion for adoption was put and passed. Article 5 read, and on motion of P. H. Clark, laid on the table. D. Jenkins moved that the resolution to establish a State Anti-Slavery Society be reconsidered, which was agreed to. Peter H. Clark, desired the Convention to pause before they added another to the long list of failed Anti-Slavery Societies, State Organizations, etc. If any lesson at all was to be learned from the past, it was that the people would not support such movements. The thing to be done was to get the colored people themselves, interested in their own welfare, and then would be time for the organization of societies, to operate upon Slavery in the South, or caste in our own State. Other gentlemen thought such a society the best instrument that could be devised to arouse the colored people from their torpor. The plan would succeed, especially if the churches became interested.

Mr. Josephus Fowler obtained the floor, when the Chair announced the hour for the noon recess.

Afternoon Session.

Convention met, President in the Chair. Minutes read and approved. Mr. Josephus Fowler spoke in favor of the establishment of the society. "We must do or die." Mr. Peter Harbison followed on the same side. Mr. J. D. Harris demanded the previous question--not succeeding, a general expression of feeling favorable to the formation of a society was had. Messrs. J. H. Gurley, T. J. Goode, T. Gross, John Johnson, John F. James, and L. C. Flewellyn, participating. The resolution was then adopted. Articles 5, 6, 7, 8, 9, 10, 11, 12, 13, with the preamble and resolutions appended, were then adopted.

John M. Langston offered the following resolutions, moving that they be the special order for the evening session:

1st. *Resolved,* That in the name of our humanity, in the name of our nativity, in the name of our love of our country, in the name of the old Revolutionary doctrine, that taxation and Representation ought not to be separated, in the name of justice and good policy, and in the Declaration of Independence and the United States Constitution, we demand of the people and government of the State of Ohio the repeal of all laws that make complexional discriminations, and full equality before the law. That we will continue to agitate this subject before the people, to circulate petitions on it among the people, and memorialize the Legislature in regard to it, till our State government becomes a true democracy, conservative of equal and impartial liberty.

2d. *Resolved,* That we tender to the noble men of Lorain county who rescued John Price from the bloody hands of a heartless slaveholder, and ruffian Duputy U.S. Marshal and his mercenary posse, our most hearty sympathy and grateful thanks, for their manly, brave and Christian conduct in that rescue; and that we pledge them our sacred honor that whenever the opportunity comes, we will imitate their worthy example.

3d. *Resolved,* That while we love law and order, while we venerate the Declaration of Independence, and the Constitution of the United States, and while we are ready to support and defend that system of government which finds its foundation in these great documents of freedom; that we trample the Fugitive Slave Law and the dicta of the Dred Scott decision beneath our feet, as huge outrages, not only upon the Declaration of Independence and Constitution of the United States, but upon humanity itself.

John F. James moved that this Convention recommend Chillicothe as the next place of meeting. E. P. Walker moved to strike out Chillicothe and insert Toledo. David Jenkins moved to insert Cleveland instead of Toledo. D. Jenkins asked leave to withdraw his amendment. E. P. Walker's amendment was lost. Josephus Fowler moved to insert Dayton. Lost. Original motion adopted. John F. James was selected as Chairman of the State Central Committee, the other members of which were John Williams, John R. Bowles and Joseph Ogelsby, of Chillicothe, John I. Gaines of Cincinnati, John Burke, of Columbus, O. S. B. Wall, of Oberlin.

On motion of P. H. Clark, those having statistics in charge were directed to hand them over to the Publication Committee.

On motion of P. H. Clark the Finance Committee were instructed to pay the balance remaining in their hands after defraying the expenses of the Convention, to the Publication Committee.

On motion of D. Jenkins, the Committee were instructed to print five hundred copies, and distribute them equally among the members of the Convention.

On motion of John M. Langston, the morning hour of the Friday session was devoted to perfecting the organization of the Anti-Slavery Society.

President appointed Peter H. Clark, I. M. Troy and John I. Gaines members of the Publishing Committee.

Committee on form of petition reported a form, which was adopted. Recess.

Evening Session.

Convention met. President in the chair. Minutes read and approved. Special order taken up. T. J. Goode moved that the resolutions be adopted singly. Agreed to. Messrs. W. J. Watkins, John M. Langston, and Wm. H. Day reviewed with severity the action of the American people in regard to the colored race, and advocated the right and duty of resistance by force of arms, when it was feasible.

John I. Gaines deprecated such advice to a weak, enslaved and ignorant people, with whom resistance, with any hope of success, was impossible. Adjourned.

Friday, Nov. 26th, 1858.

Convention met. President in the chair. Prayer by Mr. James Johnson. Minutes read and approved.

John M. Langston moved that the members of the Convention be constituted members of the Ohio Anti-Slavery Society.

On motion of Wm. Darnes, Peter H. Clark, John H. Gurley, David Jenkins, John F. James and J. D. Harris were appointed a Committee to nominate officers for the society.

Committee on Nominations reported for President, John M. Langston; Vice President, John Malvin; Recording Secretary, Chas. H. Langston; Corresponding Secretary, Horace Morris; Treasurer, J. C. Oliver; Executive Committee, J. Williams, D. Crosby, D. Jenkins, John I. Gaines, T. J. Goode, E. P. Walker, C. M. Richardson. Report received. The Convention ordered the name of Joseph Williams of Cleveland to be stricken out and that of J. J. Williamson of Delaware was substituted. After some debate, the report was referred to the committee.

On motion of John M. Langston,--C. H. Langston, D. Jenkins, John M. Langston, Miss Frances Ellen Watkins and Peter H. Clark were appointed a committee to raise the five hundred dollars contemplated in the resolutions appended to the Constitution.

Committee to nominate the officers for the Anti-Slavery Society reported the names of E. P. Walker, J. D. Harris, John I. Gaines, D. Jenkins, and Jesse Devine, for the Executive Committee. Approved.

Afternoon Session.

Convention met. President in the chair. Minutes read and approved. On motion of D. Jenkins the members from each county nominated a committee to solicit donations for, and collect pledges to the Ohio Anti-slavery Society. (See committees on page 25.)

Resolutions offered by Mr. John M. Langston were then taken up, and on motion of Mr. Darnes, the word *ask* was substituted for *demand*, in the 1st resolution. The 1st, 2nd, and 3d resolutions were then adopted.

On motion of John I. Gaines, the resolution selecting Chillicothe as the next place of meeting, was reconsidered. Toledo was then substituted for Chillicothe. The State Central Committee was then re-organized, and E. P. Walker, J. C. Greener, George W. Tucker, Wm. Merritt, of Toledo, and John I. Gaines, G. J. Reynolds, and Wm. Munson, were constituted that committee.

Mr. A. Redman moved a vote of thanks to the citizens of Cincinnati for the hospitable spirit they had evinced. Adopted. A vote of thanks was then passed to the officers of the Convention, for their zeal and fidelity, as shown in the performance of their duties. When the Convention adjourned.

LIST OF DELEGATES

John M. Langston, Chas. H. Langston, J. H. Gurley, I. Mitchell, of Lorain Co.

E. P. Walker, of Lucas Co.

J. C. Oliver, John Malvin, Wm. E. Ambush, J. D. Harris, Wm. Munson, of Cuyahoga Co.

John Booker, David Jenkins, A. Redman, John Brown, of Franklin Co.

Jesse Devine, Horace Morris, John C. Gally, Louis Overton, of Greene Co.

Wallace Shelton, James Johnson, H. Parram, R. G. Ball, I. M. Troy, L. C. Flewellen, Jesse Fossett, Peter Harbison, C. F. Buckner, Phillip Tolliver, Thos. J. Goode, John I. Gaines, Wm. D. Goff, A. M. Sumner, W. H. Mann, Wm. H. Fuller, P. B. Furguson, Wm. Darnes, George Peterson, J. A. Bowman, R. Conrad, Capt. J. Hawkins, R. Debaptiste, Josephus Fowler, Jr., A. V. Thompson, of Hamilton Co.

T. Gross, A. N. Freeman, of Brown Co.

H. J. Andrews, V. Moore, of Clermont Co.

John F. James, of Ross Co.

Alfred J. Anderson, Alexander Proctor, of Butler county.

Asa Pratt, of Warren Co.

J. J. Williamson, of Delaware Co.

CONSTITUTION OF THE OHIO STATE ANTI-SLAVERY SOCIETY

Believing that, by united and concentrated action, on our part, we can do much toward securing the immediate and unconditional abolition of American Slavery and the removal of the legal and social disabilities under which we suffer in the State of Ohio, and in the United States: And also, believing that such united and concentrated action can be secured in our State, through the instrumentality of a State Anti-Slavery Organization: Therefore, we do hereby agree to form ourselves into a State Anti-Slavery Society, to be governed by the following

Constitution

Art. 1. This Association shall be called the Ohio State Anti-Slavery Society.

Art. 2. The object of this Society shall be, to secure by political and moral means, so far as may be, the immediate and unconditional abolition of American Slavery, and the repeal of all the laws and parts of laws, State and National, that make distinctions on account of color.

Art. 3. To accomplish this object, the Society shall establish its Head Quarters permanently in the city of Cleveland, Cuyahoga Co., Ohio. There it shall have its office and business rooms. It shall also employ such numbers of Agents and Lecturers as may be needed to carry out the object of its creation.

Art. 4. Any man or woman may become a member of this Society, by subscribing to its principles as above expressed, and by making such contributions to its funds as he or she may be able.

Art. 5. The officers of this Society shall be: a President, Vice President, Recording Secretary, Corresponding Secretary and Treasurer, who shall hold their offices one year, or until their successors are chosen; and who, with five persons chosen from the remaining members of the Society, shall constitute an Executive Board.

Art. 6. It shall be the duty of the President to preside at all meetings of the Society and the Executive Board. In his absence these duties shall be discharged by the Vice President. It shall be the duty of the Recording

Secretary to keep a full and complete record of the doings of the Society and the Executive Board, which record shall be open to the inspection of the members of the Society at all times. And it shall be the further duty of the Recording Secretary to keep all the books and papers belonging to the Society and Executive Board at the office of the Society in Cleveland. And it shall also be the further duty of the Recording Secretary to take charge of, and keep in good order, the office and business rooms of the Society. For the performance of these duties the Recording Secretary shall receive such compensation as the Executive Board may determine.

The duties of the Corresponding Secretary and Treasurer shall be such as usually attach to such titles; the Treasurer giving bonds for the proper disbursement of all funds that may come into his hand, in the sum of one thousand ($1,000) dollars, and making report to the Executive Board of all moneys received by him, and expended under its order, at its quarterly meetings. And it shall be the duty of the Executive Board to take charge of the particular and general interests of the Society, and to make such needful rules and regulations for the accomplishment of the object of the Society as sound discretion and necessity may dictate. And it shall be the further duty of the Executive Board to make an annual report of all its doings to the Society at its annual meetings.

Art. 7. The annual meetings of the Society for the election of officers, hearing the Annual Report of the Executive Board, and transacting other business for the Society, shall be held in such places as the Executive Board may determine, on the first Monday of January in each year, after 1859.

Art. 8. The Executive Board shall hold its first meeting at Cleveland, on the first Monday in February next, and quarterly meetings thereafter at said city; at each of which it shall receive reports from its Agents and Lecturers in regard to all they have done, and all moneys collected; which reports shall be preserved by the Recording Secretary. It shall also be the duty of the Executive Board at each quarterly meeting to settle in full with its Agents and Lecturers.

Art. 9. All Agents and Lecturers in the service of the Society shall be employed and directed in their labors by the Executive Board, and to the Board alone shall be accountable.

Art. 10. The Executive Board shall receive for their services at each quarterly meeting (each quarterly meeting to be not longer than three days in its sittings), one dollar per day, and necessary traveling expenses.

Art. 11. All moneys in the hands of the Treasurer shall be drawn on the order of the Executive Board, attested by the Recording Secretary.

Art. 12. A majority of the Executive Board shall constitute a *quorum* for doing all business pertaining to the interests of the Society.

Art. 13. This Constitution may be altered or amended by a vote of two-thirds of the members of the Society, at any annual meeting.

In order that the funds necessary to put this organization in operation may be raised by the first Monday of February next, at which time the Executive Board will hold their first meeting, your Committee would recommend the adoption of the following resolutions:

1st. *Resolved,* That the Convention appoint five persons, who shall proceed immediately to raise five hundred dollars, by holding meetings in this State, and receiving donations for the benefit of the Society, and that said persons report their doings to the Executive Board of this Society, at its first meeting, and pay over to the Treasurer of the Society all funds by them collected.

2d. *Resolved,* That we recommend to the Executive Board, that they pay said persons just and reasonable compensation for their said services.

JOHN M. LANGSTON, Pres't.
John Malvin, Vice Pres't.

Chas. H. Langston, Rec. Sec'y.
Horace Morris, Cor. Sec'y.
J. D. Harris, E. P. Walker, John I. Gaines, D. Jenkins, Jesse Devine, Ex. Committee.

SIGNERS TO THE CONSTITUTION

The persons whose names follow, have paid the sum opposite their names, to be used for the purposes of the Society:

James C. Oliver, 50 cents; John Malvin, $1; Wm. E. Ambush, $1; John Booker, $1; David Jenkins, $1; John Brown, $1; A. Redman, $1; Horace Morris, $1; Louis Overton, $1; John C. Galley, $3; Jas. Johnson, $1; Jesse Collins, $1; Thos. Doram, $1; Edward Goodwin, $5; George Williamson, $1; J. J. Williamson, $1; Chas. H. Langston, $1; John Johnson, $1; Abram Fiddler, 50 cents; Cash, 50 cents; Brown, 75 cents; Cash, 25 cents; Cash, 25 cents; Miss Virginia C. Tilley, $1.

The persons whose names follow have pledged the sum opposite their names, to be paid before the first of February, for the purposes of the Society:

John Malvin, $2; William E. Ambush, $4; J. D. Harris, $1; Wm. Munson, $1; Jesse Devine, $1; E. P. Walker, $1; Jas. Johnson, $1; I. M. Troy, $1; Peter Harbison, $1; Thomas J. Goode, $1; John I. Gaines, $1; A. M. Sumner, $1; Wm. H. Fuller, $1; P. B. Ferguson, $1; Wm. Darnes, $1; John Jackson, $2; Robt. Troy, $1; Lewis Tilford, $2; Josephus Fowler, Jr., $1; Peter H. Clark, $5; Ant. Freeman, $1; W. E. Alston, $2, Jernegan, $1; James Scott, $5; J. J. Williamson, $1; I. Mitchell, $2; Chas. H. Langston, $4; John H. Gurley, $3; John M. Langston, $10; W. H. Day, $10; Wm. J. Watkins, $10; Frances E. Watkins, $10; A. Fiddler, $1; J. D. Young, $1; P. F. Fossett, $1; Mrs. Fossett, $1; G. T. Butler, $1; Miss Josephine Darnes, $1; Mrs. Mary Anne Aray, $1; Mrs. Eveline Cooper, $1; Miss Amelia Williams, $1; Miss Josephine Turner, $1; Mrs. Mary Gibson, $1. Mrs. A. E. Lewis and Jane Jackson, of get up a Fair or Levee for the benefit of the Society.

FORM OF PETITION

To the Honorable the General Assembly of the State of Ohio:

Your petitioners, citizens of_____County, State of Ohio, respectfully ask your honorable body to take the steps necessary to strike, from the Constitution, the word "white," wherever it occurs; and to repeal all laws, or parts of laws, making distinction on account of color or race.

And your petitioners will ever pray, etc.

To advance the objects proposed in the pan of organization, and in obedience to the first resolution, the following persons were named a committee to raise five hundred dollars:

C. H. Langston,   D. Jenkins,
Frances E. Watkins,   J. M. Langston,
         Peter H. Clark.

To these were added the following committees, whose duties are to hold meetings in their respective counties, and to make private solicitation for donations, and to collect pledges made to the treasury of the Ohio Anti-Slavery Society:

Cuyahoga County.--C. W. Richardson, Wm. Slade, David Crosby, Mrs. Parker, Mrs. T. H. Morris, Mrs. J. Moor, Mrs. Wm. Munson, Mrs. A. J. Davis.

Clermont County.--Rev. H. J. Andrews, V. R. Moor, O. T. B. Nickens, Mrs. E. Webster, Miss Alphea Austin, Miss V. Harding, Miss C. Coleman.

Delaware County.--J. J. Williamson, F. D. Merritt, Jas. Kizer, Miss D. Stanley, Miss D. A. Williamson, Miss H. Crawford, Miss V. Scurry, Mrs. C. Harris.

Franklin County.--D. Jenkins, J. T. Ward, Mrs. C. Hackley, Mrs. A. Redman, Mrs. M. Buckner, Miss M. J. Hopkins, Miss S. Davis.

Hamilton County.--P. H. Clark, T. J. Goode, Josephus Fowler, Mrs. A. E. Lewis, Mrs. E. Cooper, Mrs. M. A. Aray, Mrs. Jane Jackson.

Lorain County.--John Watson, O. S. B. Wall, J. M. Langston, Miss S. Wall, Mrs. Watson, Mrs. Campton.

Lucas County.--E. P. Walker, Wm. H. Merritt, Charles Ellis, Mrs. Wm. H. Merritt, Mrs. M. J. Ellis, Mrs. E. P. Walker, Mrs. O. Jacobs, Mrs. Wm. Cornish.

Greene County.--Wesley Roberts, Washington Bryant, Chas. W. Sweet, Mrs. E. Bryant, Mrs. Nancy Ruddles, Mrs. Wm. Hunster.

Ross County.--John F. James, C. D. Williams, J. A. Chancellor, Catherine Harris, H. B. Roberts, A. E. Nickens, Elizabeth Isaacs.

Montgomery County.--Allen Henson, Thos. Davis, John Johnson, Miss Ellen Sneed, Miss H. Broady, Miss V. Ball.

State Central Committee

Elias P. Walker, J. C. Greener, G. W. Tucker, W. H. Merritt, Toledo; C. J. Reynolds, Sandusky; John I. Gaines, Cincinnati; Wm. Munson, Cleveland.

Copy in the Harvard University Library.

REFERENCE NOTES

1. The reference is to the Dred Scott decision of 1857, identified above.
2. Frances Ellen Watkins (1825-1911), Negro authoress and lecturer, was born in Baltimore, Maryland. Miss Watkins was the niece of the Reverend William Watkins, by whom she was raised and educated. Her first collection of poetry and prose, entitled *Forest Leaves* was published in 1845. Then, in 1854, appeared another volume of verse, *Poems on Miscellaneous Subjects.* Active in the antislavery movement, she delivered her first lecture, "Education and the Elevation of the Colored Race," in 1854 in New Bedford, Massachusetts. After this, she lectured extensively throughout the North. She was married to Fenton Harper in Cincinnati in 1860, and lived with him on a farm near Columbus, Ohio, until his death in 1864, when whe resumed her lecturing. The closing years of her life were spent in Philadelphia.
3. The reference is to the famous Oberlin-Wellington Rescue case of September 13, 1858. On that day, John Price, a black man, living in Oberlin, Ohio, was arrested by a deputy United States marshal and his assistant and two Kentuckians who claimed him as a runaway slave from Kentucky. Removed to Wellington, Ohio, which was a station on the Cleveland and Columbus railroad, he was temporarily detained in a tavern preparatory to his journey back to Kentucky. News spread quickly of his arrest, however, and soon a crowd of people from both Oberlin and Wellington gathered and demanded that Price be freed. Fearful that a violent incident might ensue, his captors freed him and he was quickly led to safety.
    The thirty-seven people implicated in the rescue were indicted by a United States grand jury on December 6. Most of those charged were from Oberlin, a few from Wellington. By pre-arrangement, however, pending prosecutions against most of those indicted were dropped. Among those who were convicted was Charles H. Langston, a prominent Ohio Negro leader. He was let off with a small fine and a few days imprisonment, however, after he had swayed the court in a brilliant and moving speech in his defense.

PROCEEDINGS OF A CONVENTION OF THE COLORED MEN OF OHIO, HELD IN XENIA ON THE 10th, 11th AND 12th DAYS OF JANUARY, 1865; WITH THE CONSTITUTION OF THE OHIO EQUAL RIGHTS LEAGUE

PROCEEDINGS OF A CONVENTION OF THE COLORED MEN OF OHIO

Tuesday, January 10, 1865--10 A.M.

The Convention met in the First Baptist Church.

David Jenkins, of Columbus, called the house to order.

On motion, Elder Jas. Poindexter, of Columbus, was chosen Chairman of the temporary organization, and J. A. Thompson, of the same place, Secretary.

Messrs. J. McSimpson, Rev. J. T. Ward, and J. M. Devine were appointed a Committee on Credentials.

During the absence of the committee, Messrs. Jenkins, Poindexter and others made brief speeches.

On motion, the following gentlemen were appointed to nominate officers for a permanent organization: J. T. Ward, Rev. J. A. Warren, Eld. G. W. Bryant, Wesley Gassoway, Henry Hurd, H. Ford, Rev. J. M. Devine, George W. Wilson, and Benjamin Hudson.

On motion of D. Jenkins, the rules of the National Convention, held at Syracuse, N.Y., October 4th, 1864, were adopted as the rules of order of this Convention.

By amendment, it was voted to hold night sessions from 7 to 10 each evening.

Afternoon Session.

Rev. J. A. Warren opened the session with prayer. Elder James Poindexter in the chair. Minutes read and approved.

Committee on permanent organization reported as follows:

Elder James Poindexter, President; David Jenkins, Rev. J. A. Warren, Rev. E. Davis, F. D. Merritt, J. McSimpson, Vice Presidents; G. G. Collins, First Secretary; J. A. Thompson, Second Secretary; Rev. Jesse Devine, Chaplain.

On motion, the report of the committee was adopted and discharged.

On motion of Mr. David Jenkins, Messrs. Samuel Troy, Jr., J. D. Betts, and J. H. Johnson were appointed a Finance Committee.

On motion, it was resolved to appoint a Business Committee of nine; afterwards the number was increased to thirteen.

The following gentlemen were appointed that committee, viz: Messrs. A. J. Anderson, D. Jenkins, John Booker, E. C. Jackson, R. J. Robinson, Rev. H. J. Young, Rev. John A. Warren, H. Ford, Rev. J. Miller, Dr. J. McSimpson, Henry Hurd, A. N. Redman, J. C. Abney.

Mr. Robinson offered the following resolution:

Resolved, That the Convention will appoint a committee of one or more, to labor with the General Assembly, for the repeal of the laws which disfranchise the colored citizens of Ohio, and that the said committee be paid a salary of one dollar per day and expenses, and that the said services be rendered immediately on the adjournment of this Convention, and that the money to pay for the same be raised at once by subscription.

Referred to the Business Committee.

On motion of Mr. David Jenkins, gentlemen present from counties not otherwise represented, were invited to seats in the Convention.

On motion, it was further resolved that gentlemen present from other States be invited to participate in the proceedings as honorary members.

Prof. Murray, of Pennsylvania, returned thanks for the honor conferred upon him, and introduced Mr. Robert Hamilton, of the *Anglo-African*, who sung, "When Slavery dies there'll be Freedom, &c."

The Business Committee reported resolutions, reading:

"*Resolved*, That we are in favor of our government, against all its enemies," &c.

Another, recommending the *Anglo-African*, *Christian Recorder* and *Colored Citizen*[1] to the patronage of the people, and a series of five, commencing:

"*Resolved*, That, in the opinion of this Convention, the day is at hand when that unmitigated horror; that crime against God and humanity; that sum of all villainies; that hell-born and heaven-defying institution, of American slavery, known and hated by all men, shall cease to exist in the United States," &c.

The first two resolutions were adopted, and the first three of the last series. Pending the consideration of the remainder, the Convention adjourned, by the arrival of the appointed hour.

Evening Session.

President Poindexter in the chair. Minutes read and approved.

The consideration of the resolutions introduced by the Business Committee was resumed. On motion, the remaining resolutions of the series were adopted.

On motion of Mr. A. J. Anderson, the Convention resolved itself into a committee of the whole, Mr. David Jenkins in the chair.

A portion of the address of the National Convention to the people of the United States, was read by Elder James Poindexter.

It was moved that so much of the address as had been read by Mr. Poindexter, be adopted as the sense of this Convention. Laid on the table.

Mr. Henry Hurd read the draft of a petition to the Legislature, praying for the removal of disabilities on account of color. Referred to the Business Committee.

Mr. John Booker offered the following:

Resolved, That it is the opinion of this Convention that the colored man or woman who will not do for a colored person, the circumstances being the same, what they would do for a white person, is unworthy of our respect or confidence.

After considerable discussion the resolution was adopted.

Eld. Rufus Conrad and Mr. Peter H. Clark were, on motion, added to the Business Committee.

The motion to adopt a portion of the address of the National to the people of the United States, was taken from the table. Pending its consideration, the hour for adjournment arrived.

Morning Session, January 11th, 1865.

Vice President Jenkins in the chair. Prayer by Rev. J. A. Warren. Minutes read and approved.

The committee of the whole arose and reported progress.

On motion of Mr. A. J. Anderson, all unsettled questions were referred to the Business Committee.

Mr. A. N. Redman moved that M. David Jenkins be appointed an agent to press the claims of the colored man upon the Legislature. Laid on the table.

The Business Committee reported the following:

Resolved, That we proceed to organize a League, auxilliary to the National Equal Rights League. Laid on the table.

On motion of Mr. J. A. Thompson, the Convention resolved itself into a committee of the whole.

Mr. Thompson offered a resolution requiring the government to retaliate upon rebel prisoners the outrages inflicted upon colored soldiers.

The committee then arose and reported progress. The resolution offered by Mr. Thompson was then adopted. The resolution concerning the formation of a State League was taken from the table and adopted.

The Business Committee reported resolutions thanking Mr. David Jenkins for his services in procuring the passage of certain laws; declaring that the safety of the Republic demands that equal political rights be guaranteed to all in the territories and reorganized States; claiming promotion for colored troops; instructing the Executive Committee to prepare a digest of the laws of the State relating to colored schools, and publish them for the benefit of parties interested; recommending the printing of the address of the National Convention, &c.

On motion of Mr. P. H. Clark, the report was laid on the table until the afternoon session.

Adjourned.

Afternoon Session.

President in the chair. Minutes read and approved. Resolutions reported by the Business Committee were taken from the table. After some discussion they were adopted.

On motion of Mr. P. H. Clark, it was resolved to tax each member one dollar, to defray the expenses of the Convention. The total amount paid was $64.10, a portion being contributed by the audience.

Mr. Kinney, of Zanesville, presented his credentials. Messrs. J. McSimpson and W. Gassoway denied his right to a seat, he not having been elected by the general meeting of the citizens, at which they received their appointment. The Convention decided that, under the call, he was entitled to a seat.

Rev. J. A. Warren moved a resolution appointing a committee to arrange for a lecture by Mr. J. M. Langston on the evening of the 12th of January, the proceeds to be applied to sending papers to the colored soldiers. Adopted.

Messrs. J. A. Warren, E. Davis, and G. W. Bryant were appointed that committee.

Convention resolved into a committee of the whole, Mr. David Jenkins in the chair.

Elder James Poindexter read the draft of a preamble and constitution of an auxiliary Leage.

On motion of Mr. J. M. Langston the organization of a League was made the special order of the evening session.

Adjourned.

Evening Session.

M. David Jenkins in the chair. Minutes read and approved.

The special order being the consideration of the preamble and constitution of an auxiliary League, it was voted to consider the subject section by section.

Leave was granted Mr. J. M. Langston to read and explain the constitution of the National Equal Rights League.

On motion of Mr. P. H. Clark, the night session was extended one hour.

The committee then resumed the consideration of the special order. Article one and two were adopted. The blank in the third article was then filled by inserting Cincinnati. It was then adopted. The remaining articles and the preamble were then adopted seriatim, when the committee arose and reported the Preamble and Constitution of the Ohio State Auxiliary Equal Rights League, which was adopted by the Convention.

On motion of Mr. J. M. Langston, Messrs. P. H. Clark and Jackson M. Moore were appointed a Publishing and Revising Committee, and all monies remaining in the hands of the Financial Committee of the Convention were ordered to be placed in their hands, to defray the expense of publishing and distributing the minutes.

On motion of Mr. G. G. Collins, it was

Resolved, That the League, when organized, shall be incorporated.

On motion, article five of the Constitution was reconsidered.

On motion, it was resolved to insert in the article "and qualified" after the word "chosen." The article thus amended was adopted.

President

Peter H. Clark. . . . . .Hamilton County.

Vice President

David Jenkins. . . . . Franklin County.

Recording Secretary

John P. Sampson. . . . . Hamilton County.

Corresponding Secretary

John Booker. . . . . Franklin County.

Treasurer

Rufus Conrad . . . . Hamilton County.

Executive Committee

A. J. Anderson . . . . Butler County.
J. T. Ward. . . . . .Franklin County.
J. M. Moore. . . . . Hamilton County
J. A. Shorter. . . . . Hamilton County
J. H. Scott. . . . . Lorain County.
    Adjourned.

Morning Session, January 12th, 1865.

Mr. David Jenkins in the chair. Prayer by Rev. H. J. Young. Minutes read and approved.

A motion was offered to adjourn at 11 o'clock--amended by substituting 4 o'clock. The whole subject was then laid on the table.

The resolution reported from the Business Committee and adopted by the Convention, ordering the publication of the school law, was, on motion, reconsidered. Mr. J. M. Langston read, by request, the parts of the school law relating to colored schools.

The resolution was amended by striking out the words "all legal rights and privileges guaranteed by the State," and inserting "all laws and parts of laws referring to colored children." The resolution as amended was then adopted.

Dr. J. McSimpson offered a resolution for the appointment of a committee to ascertain the number of colored men from Ohio in regiments formed out of the State; the number of killed, wounded, captured, &c. The resolution was adopted, and Dr. J. McSimpson, Messrs. J. T. Ward, and J. M. Langston were appointed that committee.

Mr. J. H. Williams, of Chillicothe, offered a resolution requesting each member of the Convention to procure signers to a petition praying the Legislature to remove all disabilities on account of color. Adopted.

Mr. E. C. Jackson here requested the permission of the Convention to read an important item of news just received. Leave was granted. He then proceeded to read the dispatch announcing the action of the Missouri State Convention by which slavery was forever abolished in that State. The Convention received the news with loud and prolonged cheering.

Rev. J. A. Warren moved that the Convention sing a doxology, which was amended, on motion of Mr. J. M. Langston, that after singing Rev. John A. Warren shall offer a prayer of thanksgiving to Almighty God. Adopted.

After singing the doxology, and the prayer by the Rev. John A. Warren, the Convention resumed the consideration of business.

It was then resolved that after Mr. Langston's lecture in the evening the meeting be turned into a celebration of the glorious event, the announcement of which had caused so much joy.

On motion, the Secretary was directed to record the manner in which the convention received the news of emancipation in Missouri, and that a copy of the proceedings of this body be sent to each colored church in St. Louis.

Mr. Williams, of Gallia, offered a resolution expressive of the feelings of the Convention concerning the auspicious event, which was unanimously adopted.

Mr. Charles A. Yancy offered a series of resolutions recognizing the Divine Power in the ordering of this war, asserting the duty of colored men to yield unwavering support to the government, and proposing petitions to the authorities for the confiscation of the property of all colored men who evade their duty in this crisis. The resolutions were adopted.

On motion, the Publishing Committee was instructed to suppress all conflicting or synonymous resolutions.

Mr. J. H. Williams, of Chillicothe, offered a resolution commending Wilberforce University,[2] Albany Enterprise Academy, Oberlin College and Iberia College, which was adopted.

Mr. Ward moved that one thousand copies of the minutes be printed. Carried.

On motion, it was resolved to place the sum realized from Mr. Langston's lecture in the hands of Elder G. W. Bryant, to be held subject to the order of the editors of those papers for whose benefit it is intended.

On motion, it was resolved that the members of this Convention shall constitute the members of the Ohio State Auxiliary Equal Rights League for the first year.

Mr. Jackson, of Greene, moved that General Butler's farewell address to the colored soldiers in the army of the James be published with the minutes.

On motion of Dr. J. McSimpson, a resolution of thanks to General Butler was adopted.

Adjourned.

Afternoon Session.

President in the chair. Minutes read and approved.

Mr. Washington, of Franklin, offered a resolution condemning substitute brokers. Adopted.

On motion of Mr. Gassoway, of Muskingum County, the resolution offered by Mr. Yancy, concerning the confiscation of the property of colored men who evade their duty to the government, was reconsidered. The resolution was then indefinitely postponed.

Mr. Washington, of Franklin, offered a resolution recommending Mr. David Jenkins to the Executive Committee of the Equal Rights League as a suitable person to act as agent of the League. Adopted.

Rev. J. A. Warren offered a resolution of congratulation and advice to our brethren of the South, who are just emerging from the night of slavery. Adopted.

On motion of Rev. John A. Warren, the Convention adopted a resolution thanking the congregation of the Baptist Chruch, and the citizens of Xenia, for their kind treatment; also the officers of the Convention, for the manner in which they have performed their duties.

On motion, the Secretary was permitted to read the minutes of the entire day before the adjournment.

The Finance Committee reported the receipt of $22.99; expended $18.00; balance $4.99.

A vote of thanks to Messrs. Robert Hamilton and J. P. Sampson, editors of the *Anglo-African* and *Colored Citizen*, was adopted, when the Convention adjourned.

LIST OF DELEGATES

Champaigne County

Rev. Henry A. Jackson. . . . . .Urbanna.
Henry Ford.   "

OHIO, 1865   347

Clark County

Frank Boyd. Springfield.
Rev. Jesse M. Devine. . . . .   "
B. K. Sampson. . . . .   "
J. J. Whetsell. . . . .   "
A. J. Gordon. . . . . Yellow Springs.

Greene County

John Cousins. . . . . Xenia.
Rev. E. D. Davis. . . . .   "
Samuel Troy, Jr. . . . .   "
Elder G. W. Bryant. . . . .   "
Cyrus Viney. . . . .   "
Thomas D. Tucker. . . . .   "
Demby Roberts. . . . . .Xenia Wilberforce Institute.
E. C. Jackson. . . . .   "   "

Cuyahoga County

Rev. J. A. Warren. . . . . .Cleveland.

Mercer County

H. Hurd. . . . . .Carthagena via Celina.

Pickaway County

Benjamin Hudson. . . . . .Circleville.

Lorain County

J. M. Langston. . . . . Oberlin.
J. H. Scott. . . . .   "
G. G. Collins. . . . .   "
R. J. Robinson. . . . . Wellington.

Butler County

A. J. Anderson. . . . . Hamilton.

Warren County

J. C. Abney. . . . . .Lebanon.

Lucas County

Rev. H. J. Young. . . . . Toledo.

Franklin County

D. Jenkins. Columbus.
Elder James Poindexter. . . . .   "
John Booker. . . . .   "
J. H. Roney. . . . .   "
J. A. Thompson. . . . .   "
T. J. Washington. . . . .   "
J. H. Johnson. . . . .   "
J. T. Ward. . . . .   "

Montgomery County

S. Peters. . . . . Dayton.

Muskingum County

Wesley Gassoway. . . . . Zanesville.
Dr. J. McSimpson . . . .   "
W. R. Kinney . . . . Putnam.

Shelby County

A. N. Redman . . . . Dinsmore P.O.
J. D. Betts. Anna P.O.

Delaware County

F. D. Merrit . . . . Delaware.
E. R. Conrad . . . .   "

Miami County

Joshua Smith . . . . Troy.
Rev. J. P. Wilson. . . . . Piqua.
G. W. Wilson . . . .   "
Rev. John Miller . . . .   "
R. O. Smith.   "

Ross County

John H. Williams . . . . Chillicothe.

Hamilton County

P. H. Clark. Cincinnati.
Jackson M. Moore . . . .   "
John P. Sampson. . . . .   "
Rev. Rufus Conrad. . . . .   "
Rev. J. A. Shorter . . . .   "

Athens County

John T. Berry. . . . . Lee P.O.

Gallia County

Elder Henry Williams . . . . Gallipolis.

Jackson County

Charles A. Yancy . . . . Berlin X. Roads.

Meigs County

H. Coles . . . . Pomeroy.

Clinton County

Solomon Day. Martinsville.

Washington County

G. W. Harrison . . . . Harmar.

Honorary Members

Robert Hamilton. . . . . .184 Church Street, New York City.

W. D. Jones. . . . . Chatham, C.W.
P. H. Murray . . . . Reading, Pennsylvania.

RESOLUTIONS ADOPTED BY THE CONVENTION

1. *Resolved,* That we are in favor of our Government and the Union, against all enemies, at home or abroad, that our fathers fought to establish, and we will fight to maintain them; that we will not hesitate in the prompt performance of our duty to the nation in this, its dreadful hour of peril, but will prove with our blood that we deserve to be treated as American citizens.

2. *Resolved,* That in the opinion of this Convention the day is near at hand, when that unmitigated horror, that crime against God and humanity, that sum of all villainies, that hell-born, heaven-defying institution, American slavery, hated of men everywhere, will cease to exist in the United States.

3. *Resolved,* That we hail the event with joy and thanksgiving, as turning a bright page in the history of progressive civilization, a triumph of just principles, a practical assertion of the fundamental truths laid down in the great charter of Republican liberty, the Declaration of Independence.

4. *Resolved,* That while we rejoice in its overthrow as a system, there are serious reasons to fear that we will, in another form, remain its victims so long as we are helpless subjects of arbitrary legislation; and having been pronounced citizens by the judicial advisers of the Government; having been taxed for its support, required to hazard and sacrifice our lives in its defense, we do, therefore, solemnly ask, in the name of justice, that there shall remain no laws, State or National, making distinction on account of color.

5. *Resolved,* That the safety of the Republic demands that, in the Territories, in the rebel States, when reorganized, and throughout the entire nation, colored men shall exercise the elective franchise, and be otherwise fully clothed with the rights of American citizens.

6. *Resolved,* That there still remain upon the statute books of Ohio, laws unjustly making distinction on account of color, and we earnestly protest against them, and demand of our Legislature the laws be purified, and made to conform to the requirements of Republican justice.

7. *Resolved,* That we view with pride, the generous ardor of our fellow-citizens, men of color, who have rushed to the standard of their country, and have, in so many bloody fights, maintained the honor of their race, their State and their country.

8. *Resolved,* That justice demands that the path of promotion should be opened to them, and that they should have the same incentive to honorable exertion as are presented to the white soldier.

9. *Resolved,* That we extend to our newly emancipated brothers and sisters of the South, just emerging from their night of slavery, our right hand of fellowship and most cordial God-speed, and advise them to enter upon their new and free life with an earnest determination to cultivate among themselves education, temperance, frugality and morality, together with all other things "that pertain to a well ordered and dignified life," and we pledge to these, our brothers and sisters, a constant and manly endeavor, on our part, to secure to them, and ourselves, complete freedom and enfranchisement in this, our native land and under American laws.

10. *Resolved,* That we do also advise our newly emancipated brothers and sisters who have lived together as husbands and wives, according to slave-holding usages, while slaves, as soon as practicable to be married according to law, and thus legalize their marriage and legitimate their children.

Whereas, It is the opinion of the Convention that it is through the Divine Agency that the present war is thrust upon the American Government, as a just retribution for its insults to justice and its inhumanity to the colored people of the United States, and

Whereas, We believe it to be the duty of every colored man to yield a cheerful obedience to that Divine Agency, and

Whereas, We are convinced that it can be most effectually complied with by giving the Union Army service and support, therefore

11. *Resolved,* That in our petitions to the authorities of the Government, asking all the rights of American citizens, that we do not mean to include such as have illegally evaded, or refused in any way, to assist the Federal Army to subdue the rebellion.

12. *Resolved,* That we hail with joy the emancipation of slaves in the State of Missouri, and also the re-election of Abraham Lincoln,[3] and the installation of S. P. Chase as the Chief Justice of the United States Supreme Court.[4]

13. *Resolved,* That as fathers and brothers of the brave colored troops in the Army of the James, this Convention express our deepest gratitude to Major General Butler for his fatherly and impartial treatment of the colored soldiers under his command.

14. *Resolved,* That it is the opinion of this Convention that the colored man or woman who will not do for a colored person, the circumstances being the same, what they would do for a white person, is unworthy of our respect and confidence.

<u>Whereas</u>, Many of our rural districts are not thoroughly informed as to their rights and privileges under the State school laws, and

<u>Whereas</u>, In many cases said districts are deliberately deprived of said rights by Boards of Education; therefore be it

15. *Resolved,* That the executive Board shall compile, in a circular all laws and parts of laws bearing on the educational interests of the colored people of Ohio, and circulate the same where needed.

16. *Resolved,* That this Convention, in view of its very high appreciation of the conduct of our brothers in arms, feel called upon to inquire of the General Government what direct action, if any, has yet been taken to release our brave soldiers and sailors now prisoners in the hands of rebels. And that we ask of the authorities prompt retaliation for any wrongs done them.[5]

17. *Resolved,* That we appoint a committee of three persons, whose duty it shall be to ascertain the number of men from the State of Ohio who are filling regiments credited to other States; also the number of such men who have been killed, wounded or captured by the enemy, and for the sake of such killed, wounded or captured soldiers, or their families, seek to have the bounty pay or pension due them paid to them, and, if possible, to have such men credited to the State of Ohio.

18. <u>Whereas</u>, We believe great injustice has been done to colored recruits and substitutes by colored and white bounty brokers, acting as recruiting agents, who practice deception upon them, and take advantage of their ignorance, we feel that such men are not worthy of our confidence and respect, and they meet our most hearty disapprobation.

19. *Resolved,* That the delegates of this Convention be and they are hereby requested to use, in their several localities, their best endeavors to procure signatures to petitions asking the Legislature of this State to adopt such measures as will secure the repeal of all laws making distinctions on account of color; said petitions to be first forwarded to the President of the League at Cincinnati.

20. *Resolved,* That we view with pride and heartily indorse the efforts of the gentlemen composing the Faculties and Executive Boards of the Wilberforce University at Xenia, O.; the Albany Enterprise at Albany, O.; the Oberlin College at Oberlin, Lorain Co., O.; and the Iberia College in Morrow Co., O., to develop the intellectual powers of our youth, and for opening a field for the honorable employment of those powers.

21. *Resolved,* That we recommend to the patronage of the colored people of the State of Ohio, as the best family periodicals, the *Anglo-African*, *Christian Recorder*, and *Colored Citizen*.

22. *Resolved,* That this Convention return thanks to D. Jenkins, Esq., for his untiring efforts to effect the passage of the law securing to the families of our brave soldiers and sailors their rights, and also the passage of an amendment to the school law.

23. *Resolved,* That we do most respectfully recommend to the Executive Board of the State Equal Right's League, as a suitable person to act as an agent on behalf of the colored people of this State, with members of our State Legislature, to secure our rights according to law, David Jenkins, Esq., of Columbus, Ohio.

24. *Resolved,* That we recommend the Executive Committee of the State Rights League to print, for general circulation, the address of the National Convention to the people of the United States, if their funds will permit.

25. *Resolved,* That the members of the Convention, who assembled in Xenia on the 10th of January, 1865, in the First Baptist Church, return their hearty and sincere thanks to the citizens of Xenia and the members of said Church, for the hospitable manner in which they have been entertained; also that we heartily thank the officers of our Convention for the manner in which they have performed their duties.

CONSTITUTION OF THE OHIO STATE AUXILIARY EQUAL RIGHTS LEAGUE

Preamble

Believing that by united action on our part, we can do much to encourage sound morality, education, temperance, frugality and industry among the people, and promote everything to a well-ordered and dignified life; that we can obtain, by appeals to the minds and consciences of the American people, or by legal process, when necessary, a recognition of the rights of the colored people of Ohio as American citizens; and believing, also, that such united action can be secured in our State, through the instrumentality of a State organization; therefore, we hereby agree to form ourselves into a State Equal Rights League, and to be governed by the following

Constitution

Art. 1st. This Association shall be called The Ohio State Auxiliary Equal Rights League.

Art. 2nd. The object of this League shall be to secure, by political and moral means as far as may be, the repeal of all laws and parts of laws, State and National, that make distinctions on account of color.

Art. 3d. To accomplish this object the Society shall establish its headquarters permanently in the city of Cincinnati, Ohio. There it shall have its office and business rooms. It shall also employ the press and such numbers of agents and lecturers as may be needed to carry out the objects of its creation.

Art. 4th. Any person may become a member of this League, by subscribing to its principles as above expressed, and by making such contributions to its funds as he or she may be able. Church organizations, societies and schools may become auxiliary on the same conditions, and shall be entitled to send delegates to the annual meetings of the League.

Art. 5th. The officers of the League shall be, a President, Vice President, Recording Secretary, Corresponding Secretary, and Treasurer, who shall hold their offices one year, or until their successors are chosen and qualified, and who, with five persons chosen from the remaining members of the League, shall constitute an Executive Board.

Art. 6th. It shall be the duty of the President to preside at all meetings of the League and the Executive Board. In his absence, these duties shall be performed by the Vice President. It shall be the duty of the Recording Secretary to keep a full and complete record of the doings of the League and of the Executive Board, which record shall be open to the inspection of the members of the League at all times. It shall be the further duty of the Recording Secretary to keep all the books and papers belonging to the League at the office in Cincinnati. And it shall further be the duty of the Recording Secretary to take charge of and keep in good order the offices and business rooms of the League. For the performance of these duties, the Recording Secretary shall receive such compensation as the Executive Board may determine.

The duties of the Corresponding Secretary and Treasurer shall be such as usually attach to such offices. The Treasurer shall give bonds in the sum of one thousand dollars ($1,000), as security for the proper disbursement of all funds that may come into his hands, and shall make a report to the Executive Board of all moneys received by him and expended under its order, at its quarterly meetings.

It shall be the duty of the Executive Board to take charge of the particular and general interests of the League, and make such needful rules and regulations for the accomplishment of the object of the League, as sound discretion and necessity shall dictate. It shall be the further duty of the Executive Board to make an annual report of its doings to the League at its annual meetings.

Art. 7th. The annual meetings of the League, for the election of officers, hearing the Annual Report of the Executive Board, and transactions of other business of the League, shall be held in such places as the Executive Board may determine on the first Monday of January in each year, after 1865.

Art. 8th. The Executive Board shall hold its first meeting at Cincinnati on the first Monday in February next, and quarterly meetings thereafter at said city, at each of which it shall receive reports from its agents and lecturers in regard to all they have done, and all moneys collected; which reports shall be preserved by the Recording Secretary. It shall also be the duty of the Executive Board at each quarterly meeting, to settle in full with its agents and lecturers.

Art. 9th. All agents and lecturers, and agents in the service of the League shall be employed and directed in their labors by the Executive Board, and to the Board alone shall be accountable.

Art. 10th. The Executive Board shall receive for their services at each quarterly meeting, said meetings not to consume more than three days in its sittings, one dollar per day, and necessary traveling expenses.

Art. 11th. A majority of the Executive Board shall constitute a quorum for doing business pertaining to the League.

Art. 12. This Constitution may be altered or amended by a vote of two-thirds of the members of the League, at any annual meeting.

OFFICERS OF THE LEAGUE

Peter H. Clark. . . . .*President*.
David Jenkins . . . . *Vice President*.
John Booker . . . . *Corresponding Secretary*.
John P. Sampson . . . . *Recording Secretary*.
Rufus Conrad. *Treasurer*.

Executive Committee

A. J. Anderson, J. M. Moore, J. T. Ward, J. A. Shorter, J. H. Scott.

FAREWELL ADDRESS

of Major-General Benjamin F. Butler to the Colored Troops of the Army of the James

In this army you have been treated not as laborers, but as soldiers. You have shown yourselves worthy of the uniforms you wear. The best officers of the Union seek to command you.

Your bravery has won the admiration even of those who would be your masters.

Your patriotism, fidelity, and courage have illustrated the best qualities of manhood.

With the bayonets you have unlocked the iron-gates of prejudice, opening new fields of freedom, liberty and equality--of right to yourselves and your race forever.

Comrades of the Army of the James, I bid you farewell, Farewell!

Benj. F. Butler, Major General.

Copy in the Harvard University Library.

REFERENCE NOTES

1. The *Colored Citizen* was a weekly newspaper published in Cincinnati, Ohio, by the Reverend Thomas Woodson.
2. Wilberforce University, founded in 1856 at Xenia, Ohio, was an institution established for the education of black youth.
3. Lincoln was re-elected president in 1864.
4. Senator, governor of Ohio, secretary of the treasury in Lincoln's cabinet and chief justice of the U.S. Supreme Court (1864-1873), Salmon P. Chase (1808-1873) was a staunch defender of black rights. In May 1865, Chase began an extended Southern tour to investigate conditons in the states lately in rebellion. At Charleston, South Carolina, and elsewhere he addressed audiences of blacks, advocating Negro suffrage.
5. The statement that "we ask of the authorities prompt retaliation for any wrongs" done the black soldier while in rebel hands was probably a reaction to the Fort Pillow Massacre, which occurred on April 18, 1864. After the federal troops holding the fort, 262 of whom were colored soldiers of the 6th U.S. Heavy Artillery, surrendered to Confederate troops led by General N. B. Forrest, an indiscriminate massacre of the Negroes followed. Men were shot, pinioned to the ground with bayonets, clubbed to death while dying of wounds, and burned alive. The brutal massacre aroused tremendous indignation in the country and throughout the world.

INDEX

Abney, J. C., 342
Abolitionists, 25, 36, 41, 44, 51, 52-53, 76, 88, 239-40
Abyssinian Baptist Church, 24
Adams, Anne V., 43
Adams, John, 125, 136
Adams, John Quincy, 173, 175, 269, 390
Adams, Lewis, 249
Adams, Samuel, 125, 136-37
Addresses, of Black State Conventions, 15-23, 27-30, 32-36, 39-41, 54-55, 86-87, 112-15, 123-25, 126-32, 161-66, 190-94, 200-01, 206-08, 269-72, 310-12, 323-30
Address to Slaves (Garnet), 229, 240
Adger, Robert M., 144, 147, 151, 154
Aeschylus, 193, 196
Africa, 65-69, 193, 320, 333
African Emigration movement, 24, 65-69, 84
African Free Schools, 23, 24, 36
African Methodist Episcopal Church, xi, 168, 173, 176, 200, 224
African Methodist Episcopal Zion Church, 26
African slave trade, 196
Ahasuerus, 269, 273
Albany Enterprise Academy, 346, 350
Albany Vigilance Committee, 76
Aliened American, 239, 256
Alexander, James, 147, 149
Alexander, John, 147, 150
Allen, John Q., 140, 150
Allen, Richard, xi
Allen, Robert, 183, 187
Allen, William, 298
Allen, William G., 24, 77
Alston, Rev. William J., 145, 146, 148, 150, 151, 159
Alton Observer, 196
Ambush, Wm. E., 332, 335
American Anti-Slavery Society, 24, 25-26, 44, 45, 51, 118, 135, 157, 168-69, 308
American and Foreign Anti-Slavery Society, 24, 36, 239
American Colonization Society, xi, 3, 47, 52, 59, 60, 65-69, 77, 84, 86-87, 215, 234, 269
American Missionary Society, 167, 211
American Negro Academy, 24
American Reform Board of Disfranchised Commissioners, xii
American Revolution, 186, 187, 188, 191, 192
American Seamen's Friend Society, 36
American Society for Colonizing the Free People of Colour. See American Colonization Society.
Anderson, A. J., 342, 343, 345, 352
Anderson, Henry, 110, 116
Anderson, O. P., 198, 199, 201, 202, 203, 204, 205, 206
Anderson, Rev. Wm., 176
Anglo-African, 212, 343, 346, 350

Annexation of Texas, xii
Anthon, Charles, 159, 169
Anthony, John P., 13
Anti-Slavery Society of Canada, 196
Appolonius, Rhodius, 194, 197
Aray, Asher, 183, 184, 185, 189, 195
Archer, Rev. Armstrong, 5, 8
Articles of Confederation, 39-40, 165, 271
Artis, K., 241, 244
Ashmun, Jehudi, 65, 77
Astor, John Jacob, 137
Atchinson, David Rice, 307, 316-17
Athens, 193
Attendance, at Black State Conventions, 318
Attucks, Crispus, 271, 273, 303, 304
Austin, William M., 116

Babcock, Primus, 299
Bacon, Francis, 124, 136
Bailey, Dr., 53
Baker, George M., 116
Baker, James, 43
Baldwin, Roger Sherman, 270, 273
Ballou, Adin, 51
Baltimore, George H., 5, 8, 13
Banks, Nathaniel P., 157, 168
Banneker, Benjamin, 159, 169
Baptists, 224
Barbadoes, James G., 135
Barrett, A., 258, 259
Barrett, Owen A., 116
Barry, John, 299, 303
Bates, Edward, 158, 163, 165, 169
Battle, of Brandywine, 76; of Bunker Hill, 67, 273, 329; of Lake Champlain, 21, 26, 27, 40, 67, 192, 300; of Lake Erie, 21, 26, 27, 40, 192, 300; of New Orleans, 41, 192, 196, 271, 277, 301-02, 324; of Plattsburgh, 21; of Red Bank, 67; of Sacketts Harbor, 21
Bell, Howard H., xv
Bell, Joseph, 91
Bell, Philip H., 83, 84, 88, 90, 96
Beman, Amos G., 55, 56, 58, 62, 63, 64, 73
Beman, Jehiel C., 76
Benevolent Societies, xv
Benezet, Anthony, 124, 136
Benford, James, 116
Bennett, Joseph, 219, 242
Bethesda Congregational Church, 25
Betts, J. D., 342
Bias, J. J. G., 104, 119, 121, 122, 125, 132, 135
Bibb, Henry, 183, 187, 188, 195-96, 290
Bibbs, Marshall, 220
Bible, 44, 78
Bill of Rights, 311, 312, 323, 327
Bird, J., 263
Bishop, Edward H., 55

Black Abolitionists, 36, 41, 51, 52, 76, 84-85, 97, 117, 135, 195-96, 239
Black barbers, 157, 277
Black Brigade of Rhode Island, 40, 271, 273, 299-300
Black businessmen, 85, 117, 118, 238-39, 310
Black churches, 19, 24, 25, 26, 155, 168, 173, 176, 182, 200, 253, 278, 351
"Black Codes," 212
Black Congressmen, 239
Black dentists, 167
Black doctors, 51, 121, 167, 206, 211
Black educators, 151, 152, 166, 167, 169, 211
Black historians, 330-31
Black journalists, 318
"Black Laws," xi, 214, 216, 218, 221, 228, 229, 231-32, 236, 237, 238, 239, 253, 254, 268, 320, 322, 324, 325-26, 326-27, 333, 336, 340, 342-43, 350
Black lawyers, 167, 212
Black poets, 330, 341
Black press, 156, 214, 215-16, 230, 264, 346
Black public officials, 97, 118, 167, 239
Black scientists, 169
Black soldiers, 146, 158, 164, 165, 169, 352
Black teachers, 149-51, 318
Black women, xiv, 28, 43, 100, 147, 153-54, 200, 211-12, 227, 228, 250, 266, 307, 313-14, 318, 340, 341
Black State Conventions, Addresses, xvi-xviii, 15-23, 27-30, 32-36, 39-41, 54-55, 86-87, 112-16, 123-25, 126-32, 161-66, 190-94, 200-01, 206-08, 269-72, 310-12, 323-30; attendance, 318; call for productive labor for blacks, 188-89, 228; call for repeal of "Black Laws," 216, 218, 221, 228, 229, 231-33, 236, 237, 238, 253, 268, 320, 324, 325-26, 326-27, 333, 336, 340, 342-43, 350; calls for, 181-82, 218-19; circulars, 200-01; composition, 6, 227; condemn segregation, 230; constitutions, 133-34; controversies over delegates, 184-85, 189-90, 200-01, 202-03, 207; debate in over use of force in resistance, 337; debate in whether Constitution anti-slavery or pro-slavery, 215, 261-63; endorse temperance, 59, 109, 114, 167, 190, 228, 251, 268, 277; eulogies at, 321-23; favor black literary institutions, 189; favor farming for blacks, 189, 228, 276-77, 279-80, 281; favor teaching blacks trades, 189, 229, 267; first, 2; format, xvi; issues stressed at, xv-xvi; memorials, 164-66, 297-303; on press, 109, 110, 114, 156, 214, 215-16, 230; on restrictions on employment for blacks, 3; on taxes, 113; oppose colonization, 2-3, 80, 88, 202, 214, 215, 216-17, 223, 225, 335; oppose Dred Scott decision, 333, 336; oppose emigration, 2-3, 14, 47, 54, 60, 61, 65-69, 84, 86-87, 180; oppose Fugitive Slave Law, 72-73, 267, 269, 336; petitions, 10-12, 26, 31, 75, 109, 297-303, 308, 314, 336, 340, 350; position on Reconstruction, 204, 205; praise Abolitionists, 188; praise Abraham Lincoln, 203, 204; press comments on, 236-38; protest restrictions on black suffrage, 2-3, 9-13, 15-23, 24-30, 31-36, 37-41, 54, 57, 69-72, 75, 78, 89-90, 100-01, 104, 106-07, 113, 121, 123-25, 172, 176-77, 180, 186-88, 190-94, 207-08, 209, 216, 229, 231-32, 243, 245-46, 251-52, 254, 255, 258, 266-67, 269-72, 297, 298-303, 318-19, 323-24, 326-30; recommend county conventions, 115-16; significance, xv; stand against slavery, 187-88, 229, 251, 253, 255, 268, 278, 307, 308, 319, 334, 343, 349; stand on education, 54, 57, 73-75, 109, 113-14, 149-51, 153, 187, 190, 214-15, 226, 229, 230, 232-33, 263-64, 268, 272, 277, 278-79, 281, 334, 345, 350; stand on Republican Party, 4; statistical reports, 280-81; urge farming for blacks, 109-10, 114-15; urge former slaves to enter marriage, 349
Blacks, arrested for no cause, 28-29; as citizens of the United States, 158, 169; demands for productive labor for, 188-89; discrimination against, 36, 46, 154, 156, 168; in public schools, 30; plays by, 41; restrictions on employment of, 3; role in Civil War, 146, 164, 165, 256, 349-50, 352; role in War for Independence, 40-41, 67, 92, 216, 271, 299-300, 302, 324, 329; role in War of 1812, 21, 41, 67, 75, 192, 216, 271, 299-302, 324, 329; suffrage restrictions on, 104, 106-07, 113, 121, 123-25, 126-32, 146, 147, 151, 152, 160-66, 172, 176-77, 186-88, 190-94, 207-08, 209, 216, 229, 231-32, 243, 245-46, 251-52, 254, 255, 258, 266-67, 269-72, 297-303; urged to form military companies, 320
Blackstone, William, 124, 136
Blanc, Louis, 136

INDEX

Blanks, G. B., 183, 184, 188
Bliss, Philimon, 328, 331
Blue, Decatur, 145
Boler, Rev. G. W., 116
Bolivar, Simon, 277, 295
Bonds, for blacks, 232
Booker, John, 219, 221, 242, 247, 249, 257, 258, 263, 274, 275, 318, 332, 335, 342, 343, 345, 352
"Border Ruffians," 96, 97, 98, 316-17
Boston, Uriah, 9, 10, 12, 13, 14, 80, 89
Boston Female Anti-Slavery Society, 51
Boston Massacre, 273, 303, 304
Bouck, Governor, 33
Bourman, Benj., 89
Bowels, John R., 336
Bowers, John C., 119, 121, 122
Bowser, David B., 134, 144, 152
Boyar, John, 198
Boyd, Frank, 219
Boyd, W. T., 176
Brinton, B., 199
Britton, John G., 173, 174, 175, 176
Brodie, George W., 275
Brooks, Rev. J. W., 183, 184, 185, 189, 190, 195, 198, 199, 203
Brooks, James, 324, 330
Brown, Caroline, 43
Brown, George, 88
Brown, J. E., 83
Brown, J. M., 176
Brown, John (of Harper's Ferry), 140 146, 152, 153, 330
Brown, John (of Ohio Convention), 258, 261, 263, 264, 274
Brown, Rev. John M., 219, 221, 222, 223, 225, 226, 227, 234, 242, 245, 246, 247
Brown, Moses, 139, 147, 157
Brown, Robert, 198, 199
Brown, Thomas, 220, 221, 226, 241, 244
Brown, Thomas A., 106, 107, 108, 110
Brown, William, 290
Brown, William ("Box"), 290, 295
Brown, William Wells, 37-38, 41
Brown, Willis, 174
Bruce, Samuel, Jr., 110
Bruce, Samuel, Sr., 116
Bryan, Charles, 147
Bryans, Richard, 110
Bryant, G. W., 342, 344, 346
Bryant, William Cullen, 327, 330
Buchanan, James, 319, 330
Buchanan, Thomas, 65, 77
Bundy, J. H., 176
Burdine, Isaac, 199, 211
Burdine, J., 199, 206, 211
Burgess, A., 199
Burgess, Tristram, 300
Burke, John, 336
Burleigh, Wm. H., 43
Burnet, Cornelius, 278
Burnham, W. Hurst, 218, 220, 223, 225, 226, 227, 241, 242, 244, 245, 246, 247, 254
Burton, Henry, 116
Burton, S. W., 198, 199, 202, 206, 211
Bushrod, T., 176
Bustill, Joseph C., 139, 144, 145, 147, 148, 155, 158, 160
Butler, Benjamin F., xiv, 205, 212, 346, 350, 352
Butler, Emmanuel, 219
Butler, George, 144
Butler, Thomas, 41
Butler, Wm., 99

Calder, Benjamin P., 116
Caligula, 267, 273
Callihan, J., 176
Calls, for Black State Conventions, 181-82, 218-19
Calorn, Henry, 183
Campbell, Joseph S., 147
Campbell, L. D., 276, 293-94
Canaan Academy, 24
Canada, xi, 24, 44, 177, 196, 211, 239, 256, 268, 320
Canada West, 118
Cardozo, J. Monroe, 219, 220, 221
Carlyle, Thomas, 314, 317
Carney, Daniel, 106
Carter, Rev. C. J., 154, 156
Carter, J. D., 199, 202, 203
Carter, W. H., 176
Cary, Mary Ann Shadd, 118, 200, 214
Casey, W. R., 275, 281
Cass, Lewis, 307, 316
Cassey, A. S., 145, 148
Catholics, 130
Catto, Octavius V., 139, 150, 158, 166
Catto, Rev. Wm. T., 134, 135, 139
Central College, 24, 74-75, 76-77
Chancellor, J. A., 316
Chandler, Rev. W., 176
Chaplin, William L., 2-3, 43, 44, 47, 48, 49, 50
"Chaplin Committee, The," 43, 44, 51
Charles I, 78
Chase, Salmon P., 167, 350, 353
Chester, Rev. John, 9
Chidester, Richard, 110, 116
Christian Herald, 245, 253
Christian Recorder, 156, 168, 200, 343
Christiana Riot, 277, 295
Churches, and slavery, 216, 224, 260, 281
Cicero, Marcus Tullius, 132, 137
Circulars, of Black State Conventions, 200-01
Civil, Social and Statistical Association of Philadelphia, 156
Civil War, role of blacks in, xiv, 117, 146, 158, 164, 165, 169

256, 345, 349-50, 352; treatment of black prisoners, 343-44
Clarion of Freedom, 215, 266
Clark, Edward V., 83, 85, 88
Clark, George W., 44
Clark, Peter H., 275, 276, 279, 281, 305, 307, 308, 309, 312, 316, 318, 332, 334, 336, 337, 340, 343, 344, 345, 352
Clarkson, Thomas, 196
Clay, Cassius M., 276, 284-85, 294
Clay, Henry, 65, 77, 172, 175, 273
Clayton, C. T., 110
Cleveland, C. D., 44
Cleveland *True Democrat*, 242
Clinton, DeWitt, 27, 30
Clotel, or the President's Daughter, 41
Coke, Sir Edward, 269, 273
Collins, G. G., 342, 344
Collins, James, 88
Collins, Rev. Leonard, 107, 108, 109, 110, 111
Collins, Rev. Samuel, 116
Colonization, favored, 214, 217, 223, 234, 276, 279, 285-90, 293, 330, 335; Black State Conventions oppose, xi-xii, 3, 14, 47, 54, 59, 60, 61, 65-69, 84, 86-87, 180, 188, 202, 214, 215, 216-17, 223, 225, 228, 259, 269, 276, 277, 279, 307, 320, 333, 335
Colored American, 7, 25, 36, 84, 110, 118, 239
Colored American League, 249, 252
Colored Citizen, 343, 346, 350, 353
Colored Patriots of the American Revolution, 330
Colored People's Union League of Philadelphia, 156
Colored Schools, 149-51
Commentaries on the American Law, 77
Communipaw, 36
Compromise of 1850, 52, 93, 273
Confederacy, 317
Conrad, Rufus, 343, 345, 352
Constitution of the United States, 22, 51, 72, 89, 95, 100, 101, 136, 165, 186, 194, 260, 261-63, 270-71, 298, 323, 327-28, 329, 336
Constitutional Convention, 304
Continental Congress, 30, 137, 169
Cooper, William, 139, 148, 157, 158
Copeland, N. M., 219, 225
Copeland, Wm., 219, 221, 242, 244, 245, 246, 247, 248, 254
Copperheads, 149, 157
Cornish, Rev. Samuel E., 87, 118
Corwin, Thomas, 324, 330
County Conventions, 115-16
County Equal Rights Leagues, 208-09
Cousins, Dr. Greenberry, 206, 211
Couzins, Rev. W., 176
Craft, Ellen, 290, 295
Craft, William, 290, 295

Crawford, T., 250
Cresson, Elliott, 65, 77
Crider, Rev. B., 176
Crimean War, 98
Crittenden Compromise, 330
Croesus, 132, 137
Crosby, D., 337
Cross, Martin, 55, 88
Crowder, John, 174
Crummell, Alexander, 5, 9, 10, 12, 13, 14, 23-24
Crummell, Henry R., 9, 12
Cuba, 94
Cullen, R. L., 199, 202, 203
Cunningham, Madison, 220
Curtis, John, 107, 116
Cutler, Benjamin, 55, 57, 58, 60, 63, 69

Daniels, John, 24
Darnes, Wm., 275, 337
Davenger, James, 139
Davenport, John, 72, 78
Davis, Rev. E., 342, 344
Davis, Edward M., 44, 45, 51-52, 123
Davis, James H., 89
Davis, Jefferson, 153, 168
Davis, W. S., 242
Day, William Howard, 214, 215, 220, 221, 222, 223, 226, 227, 228, 236, 237, 238, 239, 241, 242, 243, 244, 245-46, 248, 249, 256, 335, 337
Debating societies, 19
Decatur, Stephen, 299, 303
Declaration of Independence, xviii, 12, 22, 30, 39, 48, 54, 71, 72, 89, 93, 100, 136, 137, 186, 187, 191, 192, 194, 208, 237, 255, 260, 262, 271, 298, 312, 327, 328, 329, 333, 336, 349
Declaration of Sentiments, 228, 251
Delany, F., 181
Delany, J. W., 242, 245
Delany, Martin R., 106, 108, 109, 110, 117, 121, 217, 226
Delany, P. B. (or J. B.), 176
Dell, Joseph, 88
Democratic Party, 24, 32, 39, 75, 93, 94, 307, 308, 316, 334
Demosthenes, 132, 137
Dempsey, A., 241
Depp, Walker B., 219, 220, 222, 223
Detroit Daily Advertiser, 185
Detroit Free Press, 185
Devine, Rev. Jesse, 332, 342
Dickens, David, 116
Dickerson, Samuel, 195
Dickson, Isaac J., 121, 122, 125, 132
"Diet of Worms," 130
District of Columbia, abolition of slavery in, xiv, 104, 151, 158,

167; slavery in, 42, 49
Divine, J. W., 241, 242, 244, 246, 337, 339
Dolerson, William, 183, 187, 189
Dorris, Charles, 110
Dorsey, T. H., 241
Douge, Francis H., 55, 56, 64
Dougee, Michael, 9, 13
"Dough-face," 188, 196
Douglas, Stephen A., 307, 316, 317
Douglass, Frederick, xviii, xix, 31, 43, 76, 89, 90, 91, 96, 97, 157, 159, 196, 204, 206, 226, 239, 240, 290, 295, 327, 331
Douglass, H. Ford, 215, 241, 244, 246, 248, 250, 255, 257, 258, 259, 261-62, 263, 264, 265, 275, 276, 279
Douglass, Rosetta, 239, 240
Dover, J., 281
Downing, George T., 87
Draft Riots, 162, 169
Drayton, Daniel, 49, 50, 53
Dudley, Rev. D., 176
Duffin, James W., 5, 8, 9, 10, 12, 13, 37, 79, 80, 82, 84, 92, 96, 99, 100, 101
Dunbar, Ambrose, 10, 13
Dunlap, James, 258, 263
Durkee, Charles, 44, 276, 290-91, 294
Duterte, F. A., 121, 123

Early, Thomas, 121, 145, 149, 155
Eddy, Rev. Joshua P. B., 134
Education, Black State Conventions stand on, 54, 57, 73-75, 109, 113-14, 149-51, 153, 189, 190, 214-15, 226, 229, 230, 232-33, 263-64, 277, 278-79, 281, 320, 334, 345, 350
Egypt, 193-94
Election of 1860, 256
Ellery, William, 125, 137
Emancipation Proclamation, 158, 169
Emancipator, 51, 52, 56
Emigration, Black State Conventions oppose, 188, 202, 214, 215, 216-17, 223, 225, 234, 269-72, 276, 277, 279, 307, 320, 333, 335
Emmet, Robert, 130, 137
Employment for blacks, 3
England, 196
Ennis, Jacob, 55
Equal Rights League, 200, 204
Erie Canal, 30
Ethiopia, 194
Eulogies, at Black State Conventions, 321-23
Eustis, William, 299, 304
Evans, G. W., 242
Evans, James E., 321
Evans, John J., 199, 200, 206, 211

Farlen, Rev. U. C., 96
Farming, urged for blacks, 109-10, 114-15, 189, 228, 276-77, 279-80, 281

Fausett, Redman, 155, 156, 159
Female Anti-Slavery Society of Philadelphia, 135
Fields, E., 219
Fields, James, 99, 205, 206, 208, 211
Fifteenth Amendment, 166, 169
Fillmore, Millard, 53, 275, 294, 324, 330
First Colored Presbyterian Church, 24
Fitch, Jabez M., 188
Fitzgerald, Rev. J. J., 176
Fitzgerald, Jefferson, 195
Flewellen, Lovell C., 275, 279, 281, 336
Flinn, Anderson, 312
Florida, 153, 167
Foote, Charles C., 44, 52
Ford, H. H., 250, 252, 258, 263, 274, 342
Forrest, N. B., 353
Fort Pillow Massacre, 353
Forten, James, xii, 128, 129, 137
Forten, William D., 148, 158
Fortescue, Sir John, 273
Fowler, Joseph, Jr., 275, 336
Fowler, Josephus, 336
Fowler, S., 199, 203, 206, 211
Fox, S. D., 274
Francis, Abner H., 5, 8, 9, 10, 13
Francis, R., 32
Frederick Douglass' Paper, 36, 59, 76, 82, 84, 97, 100, 318
Freedom of Speech, 94-95
"Freedom's Gathering," 221
Freeland, J., 242, 258, 263
Freeman, A. N., 332
Freeman, Edward, 55
Freeman, Thomas, 183, 184, 189, 195
Fremont, John C., 153
Free Produce, 50
Free Soil, 246
Free Soil Party, 50, 53, 93, 97, 262, 331
French Revolution of 1848, 124, 136
Fugitive Slave Act of 1850, xv, 26, 41, 43-50, 52, 54-55, 57, 61, 72-73, 75-76, 95-96, 158, 196, 214, 215, 239, 259-60, 267, 273, 288, 295, 307, 334, 336, 341
Fugitive Slave Law Convention, xvi, 43-53
Fuller, Wm. H., 332, 355
Fulton, Robert, 30

"Gag Law," 330
"Gag Rule," 75
Gaines, John I., 216, 226, 258, 264, 266, 274, 275, 276, 279, 294, 308, 309, 312, 318, 320, 326, 332, 334, 335, 337, 339
Galbreath, George, 106, 121
Galley, John, 332
Galloway, Samuel, 272, 273, 303

Gardiner, Wm. C., 55, 58, 69
Gardner, George, 106, 116
Gardner, Wm. 89
Garnet, Rev. Henry Highland, xii, 3, 5, 6, 9, 10, 13, 23, 24, 33, 100, 101, 206, 229, 240
Garrison, William Lloyd, xii, 25, 51, 52-53, 117, 135, 168-69
Garrisonianism, xii, xix
Garrisonians, 36, 215
Gassoway, Wesley, 342, 344, 345
Gee, John, 241, 242, 246, 247, 249
George III, 130, 137
German language, 277
German Socialists, 277
Gerry, Elbridge, 125, 137
"Gerrymander Bill," 137
Gibbs, Jacob, 88
Gibbs, Jonathan C., 89, 90, 91, 96, 99
Gibbs, M. W., 121, 122, 126, 133, 134
Gibson, Alfred, 116
Giddings, Joshua Reed, 44, 227, 239, 315-16
Gilbert, Theodosia, 43
Gillam, Chas. H., 199, 200
Girard College, 138
Girard, Stephen, 137
Glasgow, Jesse E., 148, 155, 156
Goff, Almond, 184, 189
Goff, Wm. D., 334
Goffe, William, 78
Goines, George W., 119, 122, 135
Goode, Robert B., 219
Goode, T. Jefferson, 219, 242, 318, 335, 336, 337
Goodell, William, 43, 47, 51
Gordon, Charles B., 140, 147
Gordon, James R., 144, 145, 148, 154, 155, 157
Gordon, Richard, 183, 184, 187, 188, 189, 195
Gordon, Robert, 110
Gradual Emancipation, 24, 76, 161, 169
Graham, Rev. Allen E., 174, 175
Graham, James L., 151
Grant, T. E., 37
Greeks, 196-97
Greeley, Horace, 76, 94, 97
Green, A. R., 253
Green, Alfred M., 139, 144, 145, 148, 150, 151, 153, 156, 158
Green, James, 145
Greene, Christopher, 196, 271
Greene, Nathanael, 192, 196
Greener, J. C., 337
Greenly, W. J., 176
Griffin, R. A., 91
Grimes, Solomon, 312
Grinton, Benjamin, 198, 199, 206, 211
Gross, T., 336
Grosvenor, Cyrus P., 44
Gurley, J. H., 335, 337
Gurley, Ralph Randolph, 65, 77

Hackett, Calvin, 183, 195
Hackley, John, 198, 200, 206
Haines, Thomas, 258
Haiti, xiv, 3, 69, 77, 151, 335
Hale, John P., 227, 239
Hall, Daniel, 55
Hall, Rev. Eli N., 8, 9, 55, 56, 58, 61, 63, 64, 75
Hall, Jas., 83
Hamilton, Alexander, 165, 169
Hamilton, Robert, 212, 343, 346
Hamilton, Thomas, 212
Harbison, Peter, 336
Hardy, William, 183, 184
Harper, Frances Ellen Watkins. *See* Watkins, Frances Ellen.
Harper's Ferry, 153, 330
Harris, Alex. T., 149, 159
Harris, Horace, 339
Harris, J. D., 332, 335, 336, 337
Harris, Thomas, 260, 263
Harris, Wm., 313
Hart, D., 242
Harvard University, 239
Hasper, Lloyd, 55
Hathaway, Joseph Comstock, 43, 44, 51
Hathaway, Phebe, 43
Haviland, Laura, 205
Hawkins, Robert L., 116
Hayden, Lewis, 295
Heathcock, Sterling, 257, 258, 263
Henry, J. W., 199
Henry, James, 144
Henry, Patrick, 289, 321, 324
Herodotus, 193, 196
Hicks, Rev. Henry, 55, 56, 58, 60, 62, 63, 64, 75, 87
Higginson, Colonel Thomas Wentworth, 169
"Higher Law Doctrine," 72, 273, 277
Hill, James, 199
Hilton, G., 10, 241
History of the Colony in Liberia from December, 1821 to 1823, 77
Hodge, R., 226
Holland, Justin, 250, 254
Holly, J. C., 84
Homer, 193, 197
Hooper, George, 147
Hope, Wm., 257, 258
Hopkins, Stephens, 125, 137
Hornbeck, Peter, 88
Howard University, 212
Hoyt, Othello P., 181, 185, 187, 189
Hudson, Benjamin, 342
Hughes, O. L. C., 139, 144, 145, 146, 149, 154
Hungarians, 277
Hungary, 288, 289
Hunt, Washington, 76, 86, 87
Hurd, Henry, 250, 255, 274, 275, 280, 281, 342, 343

INDEX

Iberia College, 346, 350
Impartial Citizen, 59, 76
Independence Hall, 124, 125
Indiana, suffrage restrictions in on blacks, 172, 176-77
"Industrial School," 81
Institute for Colored Youth (Philadelphia), 24
Ireland, 130, 137, 182
Iverson, G., 91

Jackson, Andrew, 41, 192, 196, 271, 301-02, 324
Jackson, E. C., 342, 345
Jackson, Francis, 44, 51
Jackson, Henry, 157, 181, 183, 184, 185, 187, 189, 194, 195
Jackson, James C., 43
Jackson, John, 242, 245, 250, 258, 264, 266, 275
Jackson, Lawrence G., 274
Jackson, Lewis, 88
Jackson, P. L., 106, 107, 110
Jackson, Wm., 257, 263
Jacksonian Democrats, 175
Jamaica, 177, 287-88
James, John F., 336, 337
James, Rev. Thomas, 9
Jay, John, 22, 26, 30
Jay, Peter Augustus, 30
Jay, William, 30
Jay's Treaty, 26
Jefferson, Thomas, 30, 237, 242, 274, 289, 304, 321
Jenkins, David, 219, 221, 222, 223, 225, 226, 234, 241, 242, 243, 244, 245, 246, 247, 248, 250, 252, 254, 257, 258, 262, 264, 266, 274, 275, 276, 294, 308, 309, 312, 316, 318, 321, 332, 334, 336, 337, 339, 340, 342, 343, 344, 345, 350, 352
Jenkins, F. R., 199, 206, 211
Jenkins, T. R., 206
Jennings, Thomas L., 88
Jerry Rescue, 277, 295
Jews, 29, 130, 273
Johnson, Abr'm, 55
Johnson, Andrew, 212
Johnson, G. W., 44
Johnson, Hanson, 274, 275
Johnson, Henry, 55, 58
Johnson, Hiram, 55, 56, 58, 59, 60, 61, 63, 64, 72
Johnson, J. H., 241, 242, 257, 260, 263
Johnson, J. L., 176
Johnson, J. W., 206
Johnson, James P., 55, 58, 64, 73
Johnson, Jane, 97-98
Johnson, John, 336
Johnson, M. W., 147
Johnson, Reverdy, 53
Johnson, Rev. Samuel, 109, 110, 116
Johnson, Wilberforce, 199, 203, 204, 211

Johnson, William F., 55, 57, 58, 60, 61, 62, 63, 64
Johnson, William P., 5, 6, 33, 34
Jones, Daniel, 13
Jones, Jas. Monroe, 241, 246, 249
Jones, John, 88, 318
Jones, Matthew, 116
Jones, Rev. Samuel, 176, 241, 250
Jones, Rev. Wm., 55, 60, 61, 121
Judah, P. M., 140, 145, 154, 155
Julian, George W., 44, 52

Kane, Judge John K., 98
Kansas, 96, 97, 98
Kansas, Black State Conventions in, xvii-xviii
Kansas-Nebraska Act, 77, 98, 273, 316
Kelley, William Darrah, 157, 168
Kent, James, 71, 77, 270, 299, 328
Kentucky, 93
Kerndey, R. D., 92
King, Rufus, 165, 169-70
King's College, 30
Kinkle, Gottfried, 277

Ladies' Anti-Slavery Society of Delaware, 313-14
Ladies' Sanitary Commission of St. Thomas Church, 148
Ladies' Union Association of Philadelphia, 147, 148
Lafayette, Marquis de, 59, 76, 192
Lamartine, Alphonse, 136
Lambert, Wm., 181, 182, 183, 184, 185, 186, 187, 190, 194
Lane, John, 220
Langston, Charles H., 214, 215, 218, 219, 222, 223, 225, 226, 227, 236, 237, 242, 243, 244, 245, 246, 247, 248, 249, 250, 251, 254, 257, 258, 259, 260, 263, 264, 265, 266, 272, 274, 275, 276, 279, 280, 307, 309, 312, 316, 318, 321-23, 332, 335, 337, 339, 340 341
Langston, John Mercer, 97, 214, 215, 216, 217, 219, 222, 223, 225, 226, 227, 238, 239, 241, 242, 243, 244-45, 246, 247, 248, 249, 250, 252, 254, 257, 258, 259-60, 263, 265, 266, 274, 275, 276, 279, 297-303, 308, 309, 312, 318, 330, 332, 334, 337, 339, 340, 344, 345
Lawson, George W., 44
Leach, R., 274
Lee, J. T., 199
Lemoyne, F. Julius, 47, 52
"Letter to the American Slaves from those who have fled from American Slavery," 44-50
Levere, G. C., 99
Lewis, Abraham D., 107, 108, 109

110, 116
Lewis, George W., 198, 199, 200, 201, 203, 204, 205, 211
Lewis, H. J., 198, 199, 200, 205, 211
Lewis, James, 88
Lewis, Rev. Sampson P., 218, 246
Lewis, Wm., 257, 263
Liberator, xii, 25, 36, 330
Liberia, xi, xiv, 3, 65, 67, 68, 69, 77, 151, 259
Liberia, 77
Liberian Agricultural and Emigration Society, 86, 87
Liberty League, 51
Liberty Party, 2, 25, 32, 44, 45, 47, 48, 51, 52, 53, 97, 196
Liberty Songs, 184, 185, 187, 189, 190, 227
Liberty Street Negro Presbyterian Church, xii
Lightfoot, Madison J., 183, 187, 195
Lincoln, Abraham, 149, 151, 153, 158, 168, 169, 203, 204, 256, 294, 350, 353
Lincoln's Reconstruction Plan, 168
Litchford, P. V., 219, 242
Literary institutions, favored for blacks, 189
Literary societies, 19
Liverpool, John, 275
Livingston, Edward, 29, 295
Livingston, Robert, 30
Locke, John, 124, 136
Loguen, Jermain W., 12, 26, 43, 44, 79, 81, 82, 84, 88, 91
Lord Chatham, 324, 330
Lord Granville, 95
Lott, H., Jr., 241
Lott, H., Sr., 241, 244
Lott, John B., 226
Louisiana, Reconstruction in, 158
Louisiana Purchase, 30, 153, 167
Lovejoy, Elijah P., 188, 196
Lowry, Morrow B., 145, 146, 148, 149, 157
Luther, Martin, 130, 137
Lycurgus, 193, 197
Lyles, Wm., 219

McAlfrey, Lewis, 110
McCrummell, James, 104, 121, 135
M'Curdy, Nathaniel, 108, 110, 112, 116
McDonough, D. K., 80, 81, 82, 84
McDowell, D. N., 176
McGoway, James, 219
McGrawville College, 62, 76-77
McHenry, Jerry, 295
McIntyre, Wm. P., 55, 56, 58, 60, 61, 62, 63, 64, 75, 99
McSimpson, Dr. J., 342, 344, 345
Mahorney, Joseph H., 107
Malvin, John, 218, 231, 238-39, 316, 318, 337, 359
Manley, Andrew, 220

Manly, J., 176
Manly, W. H., 176
Mann, Horace, 273, 276, 285-90, 294
Manual Training Schools, xiv
Marion, Francis, 261, 273
Markley, J. F., 122
Mars, Rev. J. N., 9, 12
Marshall, John, 116
Martin, Charles S., 5, 7, 13
Martin, Isham, 316
Martin, T. J., 199, 206, 211
Mason, George, 136
Mason, John W., 220
Massachusetts, battle in to end segregated schools, 330-31; blacks right to vote in, 29
Massachusetts Abolition Society, 53
Massachusetts Anti-Slavery Society, 51, 57
Mathews, E. H., 92, 96
Mathews, Luke, 220
Mathews, Wm. W., 83, 99
Matthews, W. D., 256
May, Rev. Samuel J., 43, 44, 50-51
Melton, Morgan, 242
Memorials, of Black State Conventions, 164-66, 297-303
"Men of Color to Arms," 118
Merrit, F. D., 342
Merrit, T. Jefferson, 220, 221, 225, 226
Merriweather, J., 176
Methodist Church, 247
Methodist Conference, 253
Methodists, 224
Mexican War, 123, 153, 167-68, 293, 296
Michigan, suffrage restrictions on blacks in, 180, 186-87, 190-94
Military companies, 320
Military education, 277
Militia, blacks discriminated against in, 324
Miller, Charles D., 43
Miller, Rev. J., 342
Mills, Melton, 258, 263
Miner, Charles, 40, 42, 300
Miner, Lawrence W. (or Minor, Lawrence W.), 220, 227, 250, 252, 258, 264
Missouri, Black State Conventions in, xvii-xviii
Missouri, slavery abolished in, 158, 167, 345-46
Missouri Compromise, 70-71, 153, 168, 316
Mitchel, Ormsby MacKnight, 159, 169
Mitchell, Isaiah, 332
Mitchell, J., 176
Mitchell, John, 116
Molston, Samuel, 121
Monroe, James, 75
Monroe, Rev. Wm. C., 181, 182, 183

Montesquieu, Charles Louis de Secondat, 124, 136
Moore, Benjamin, 119, 122
Moore, Eli, 226
Moore, Jackson M., 344, 345, 352
Moore, Joseph C., 135
Moral Reform societies, 189
Morel, Junius C., 61, 76, 79, 80, 81, 82, 84
Morgan, Edwin D., 76, 101
Morgan, Rev. John, 176
Morgan N., 174, 241, 274
Morgan V., 174
Morgan, Wm. P., 241, 245, 257, 258, 263, 274
Morris, Horace, 337, 339
Morris, Robert, 97, 124, 136
Morton, Levi P., 211
Moss, D. S., 241
Mott, Lucretia, 52, 135
Mowers, W. F., 99
Munson, Wm., 337
Myers, Stephen, 13, 55, 56, 58, 59, 60, 61, 62, 75, 76, 89, 91, 92
Mystery, The, 117

Napoleon Bonaparte, 193
Narrative of the Life and Adventures of Henry Bibb, 196
National Anti-Slavery Standard, xii, 7, 15, 24, 25, 51, 239
National Council of Colored People, 3
National Equal Rights' League, 54, 200-01, 212, 217, 343
National Era, 53, 239
National League of Colored People, xix-xx
National Negro Congress, 137
National Negro Conventions, xi-xvi, xix-xx, 2, 3, 14, 21, 24, 76, 84, 154, 206-07, 217, 351
National Reformed Convention of the Colored People, xii
National Reformer, xii
National Workshops, 136
Needham, James, 110
Negro in Indiana before 1900, The, 173
"Negro-pews," 46, 50, 233
Negro suffrage, and Reconstruction, 157-58, 168
Nell, William C., xii, 327, 330
Nelson, Joseph A., 147
Nelson, Rev. Joseph A., 144, 147, 154
Nelson, Lewis H., 82, 83, 84, 88
Nelson, W. M., 275
Nero, 267, 273
Nesbitt, William, 139, 144, 147, 157
New Haven, xii
Newit, Joseph, 89
Newton, Isaac, 124, 136
New York, Constitution, 22
New York, gradual emancipation law in, 24, 26; restrictions in on black suffrage, 2, 8-9, 15-17, 25, 27-30, 31-36, 37-41, 54, 57, 69-72, 75, 78, 89-90, 91, 100-01, 254
New York City Colonization Society, 77
New York *Express*, 62, 76, 330
New York General Theological Seminary, 23
New York State Council of Colored People, 79-84
New York State Suffrage Association, 76, 92, 96
New York *Tribune*, xiv, 60, 68, 76, 97
New York Vigilance Committee, 24, 25, 26, 52
Nichols, Eli, 221, 227
Nichols, George, 199, 200, 206
Nichols, Thomas, 199, 202
Non-Resistance, 45
Nooks, Noah, 220, 223, 226, 241, 245, 246
Norris, Thomas, 106, 107, 110, 116
North Star, 117, 214, 231, 239, 244, 331
Notes on Canada West, 211
Noyes, William Curtis, 269, 273

Oberlin College, 167, 226, 239, 249, 318, 346, 350
Oberlin-Wellington Rescue, 238, 334, 336, 341
Ockry, Nelson, 183
Olgesby, Joseph, 336
Ohio, Black Laws in. *See* Black Laws.
Ohio, restrictions in on suffrage for blacks, 216, 229, 231-32, 243, 245-46, 251-52, 254, 255, 258, 266-67, 269-72, 297-303, 308, 310-12, 318-19, 323-24, 326-30
Ohio Colored American League, 214, 248-49
Ohio Colored American League, Constitution, 248-49
Ohio *Columbian*, 309
Ohio Conference, 253
"Ohio in Africa," 234
"Ohio Stage Company," 230
Ohio *Standard*, 214, 248, 253
Ohio *Standard and Voice of the Oppressed*, 250
Ohio State Anti-Slavery Society, Constitution, 338-40
Ohio State Auxiliary Equal Rights League, 346, 351-52
Ohio State Equal Rights League, 217
Oliver, J. C., 337
Olney, Frederick, 5, 8,
Ordinance of 1787, 170
Overalls, A. J., 173, 174, 175

Pacific Appeal, 85
Paine, Charles, 8
Paine, Thomas, 125, 137

Palfrey, John G., 227, 239, 331
Pan American Conference, 295
Parent Anti-Slavery Society, 229
Parish, David, 138
Parker, Edward R., 107
Parker, G. H., 199, 201, 202, 204, 206, 211
Parker, George W., 116
Parker, William, 295
Pattison, J. D., 242, 244
Paul, B. Dolbeare, 198, 199, 200, 202, 203, 205, 206, 211
Pearce, J. J., 241, 248
Pearl, 53
Peck, David J., 104, 119, 121, 122
Peck, John, 106, 107, 108, 109, 116, 117, 122
Penn, William, 124, 136
Pennington, Rev. James W. C., xii, 81, 84, 87, 88, 327, 330
Pennsylvania, suffrage restrictions in on blacks, 104, 106-07, 113, 121, 123-25, 126-32, 146, 147, 151, 152, 160-66
Perkins, Joseph Henry, 258, 264, 266
Perry, Oliver Hazard, 21, 26, 192
Petitions of Black State Conventions, 10-12, 26, 31, 75, 109, 297-303, 308, 314, 336, 340, 350
Philadelphia, colored schools in, 149-51; street car discrimination in against blacks, 156, 168
Phillipe, Louis, 136
Phillips, Wendell, 140, 157, 168, 169, 205
Phoenix Societies, xi, xii
Pierce, Franklin, 307, 316, 319
Pierce, Lewis, 199
Pinckney, Charles, 300, 304
Pindar, 193, 196
Pinn, Wm., 274, 275
Pinney, Rev. John B., 65, 77
Pitt, William, 330
Plato, 193, 197
Poindexter, James, 219, 221, 222, 223, 225, 226, 227, 241, 243, 246, 247, 249, 258, 263, 264, 342, 343, 344
Polk, James K., 168
Popular Sovereignty, 316
Porter, William, 108, 112
Powell, Aaron M., 25
Powell, William P., 34, 36
Powers, Henry, 195
Powers, Jeremiah, 33, 36, 87
Pratt, Asa, 274
Pratt, Charles, 330
Press, Black State Conventions on, 109, 110, 114, 156, 214, 215-16, 230, 253-54
Price, John E., 144, 149
Prichard, A., 199, 200
Prince, John, 238, 336, 341
Prosser, James, 145, 155
Protestant Reformation, 137
Proudfit, Rev. Alexander, 65, 77

Provincial Freeman, 211, 256
Public Schools, 30
Pugh, George Ellis, 325, 330
Pulpress, Benjamin F., 57, 144, 149, 150
Purnell, J., 241, 250, 257
Purnell, James W., 148, 155, 156
Purvis, Robert, xii, 26, 104, 119, 121, 122, 126, 132, 135
Putnam, Lewis H., 87
Pythagoras, 193, 197

Quakers, 51, 52, 136
Queen Victoria, 268

Radical Abolitionist, 51
Radical Abolitionist Convention, 36
Radical Abolitionist Party, 101
Radical Republicans, 294-95
Railroads, segregation on, 136
Randolph, James W., 89
Randolph, John, 196
Ray, Rev. Charles Bennett, 5, 7, 8, 9, 10, 14, 25, 32, 43, 64, 81, 82, 91, 108, 118
Ray, P. W., 92
Ray, Dr. Peter, 88
Raymond, Rev. John T., 5, 15, 24
Reason, Charles L., 5, 8, 9, 13, 14, 23, 24, 25, 77
Reason, Patrick H., 5, 8, 9, 10, 12, 13, 25
Reconstruction, Johnson Policy of, 212; Negro suffrage and, 157-58, 204; position of Black State Conventions on, 204, 205
Redman, A. N., 342, 343
Redman, Isaiah, 219
Redman, Moses, 219
Reed, Young, 116
Refugee's Home Society, 196
Remond, Charles Lenox, 121, 135
Republican Party, 4, 76, 77, 121, 168, 273, 294, 308, 331
Resistance, by force of arms advocated, 337
Reynolds, G. J., 227, 274, 337
Rice, Fordyce, 43
Rice, J. T., 198, 199, 200, 201, 202, 203, 204, 205, 206, 211
Rich, Wm., 55, 56, 58, 64, 72, 79, 80, 82, 84, 89, 96, 97, 99, 100
Richards, Benjamin, 116
Richards, Charles, 110, 116
Richards, James, 198, 199, 200
Richardson, C. M., 337
Riggs, John (or Rigs, John), 183, 189
Riots, 51
Robbins, J. E., 274
Roberts, Darius, 198, 199, 200, 201, 202, 203, 204, 205, 242, 250, 258, 274, 275
Roberts, M., 274
Roberts, Turner, 173, 174, 175

INDEX

Roberts, Wm., 257, 258, 265, 266
Robinson, Primus, 55
Robinson, R. J., 342
Robinson, Samuel, 116
Robinson, Thomas S., 107, 108, 112
Rock, John S., 104, 140, 147, 167, 169
Rodgers, Charles A., 275
Rodgers, Elimus P., 5, 6, 8, 9, 10, 13
Rogers, Nathaniel P., 51
Root, Joseph M., 227, 239
Ross, C., 241
Ross, George, 125, 136
Ruggles, David B., xii, 24, 26, 52
Rush, Benjamin, 124, 136
Rush, Rev. Christopher, xi
Russia, serfdom abolished in, 270, 273

Sampson, John P., 345, 346, 352
Sayres, Captain, 49, 50, 53
Schermerhorn, Jacob, 88
School Education Society, 239
Scott, J. H., 345, 352
Seminole Indians, 77
Servetus, Michael, 130, 137
Services of Colored Americans in the Wars of 1776 and 1812, 330
Seth, C. Edward, 55, 56, 58, 60, 61, 62, 64, 69
Seward, William H., 37-38, 41-42, 51, 269, 272, 273, 303
Shadd, Abraham D., 110, 118, 119, 121, 122, 125, 211
Sharecropping, 168
Sharp, Rev. James, 9, 10
Sharpe, Granville, 196
Shelton, Peyton, 219
Shelton, Wallace, 221, 223, 225, 226, 227, 234, 275, 332, 334, 335
Shiloh Presbyterian Church, 24
Shorter, J. A., 345, 352
Shorter, John, 147
Siebert, Wilbur H., 118
Signal of Liberty, 185
Simonds, J. J., 90
Simons, J. J., 88
Simpson, J. McCarter, 257, 258, 259, 260, 261, 264, 266
Simpson, William H., 144
Sims, George R., 183
Slater, A. B., 83
Slaveholding Party, 93-96
Slavery, abolished in District of Columbia, 151, 158, 167; abolished in Maryland, 158; abolished in Missouri, 158, 167, 345-46; abolished in the United States, 150, 151, 158, 167; Black State Conventions condemn, 187-88, 229, 251, 253, 255, 268, 278, 307, 308, 319, 334, 343, 349; churches and, 216, 224, 260, 281; death of, 163
Smith, Alfred, 116
Smith, Gerrit, xix, 36, 43, 44, 47, 51, 59, 77, 100, 101, 245, 295, 315
Smith, J. W. B., 79, 80, 81, 82, 84, 88, 96
Smith, Dr. James McCune, 2, 33, 34, 36, 254
Smith, John, 195
Smith, Joseph, 88
Smith, Robert, 274
Smith, Rev. Stephen, 104, 110, 118, 119, 121, 122, 134, 135
Smith, William, 183, 195
Smith, Wm. R., 43, 44
Society of Friends, 29
Solon, 193, 196
Sommerset, James, 78, 126
Sommerset case, 78, 126
Sons of Liberty, 137
Spartans, 193, 197, 314
Spears, H. P., 275
Springstead, Mary, 43
Springsteel, John, 55
Squatter Sovereignty, 317
Staley, Sara G., 314
Stamp Act, 136
Stanley, Abraham, 55
Stanton, Frederick Perry, 67, 77
Stanup, G., 257, 263
State Central Committee, Ohio, 309
State Equal Rights Conventions, 104-05
State Equal Rights League, 154, 159-61, 207, 350
Statistical Reports, of Black State Conventions, 280-81
Stebot, Jerome, 258, 263
Stephens, Alexander H., 3, 151
Steward, Austin, 5, 10, 14, 24, 37
Stewart, Barbary Anna, 91
Stewart, Rev. T. N., 257, 258, 263, 264
Still, A. L., 144, 145
Still, Aaron, 140
Still, John Nelson, (or Stills, John Nelson), 55, 56, 58, 59, 60, 61, 62, 63, 73, 75, 83, 88
Still, William, 168
Storum, J. H., 83
Stowe, Harriet Beecher, 330
Strauder, A., 241
Stringfellow, Dr. John H., 307, 317
Stuart, J. W., 241, 245, 246, 249
Stuart, Moses, 46, 52
Stuart, O., 114
Stuart, W., 241
Sugar Act, 137
Sumner, Charles, xiv, 53, 140, 148, 159, 167, 205
Symonds, J. T., 99

Taney, Roger B., 100, 101
Tappan, Benjamin, 25
Tappan, Lewis, 25, 51
Taylor, A. M., 219, 247
Taylor, J., 242

Taylor, John, 124, 136
Taylor, Lorenzo Dow, 219, 221, 225, 241, 242, 244, 247, 249, 250, 257, 258, 259, 263, 274, 275, 276, 279, 312, 316, 320-23
Taxes, 113
Telegraph, 59
Temperance, Black State Conventions endorse, 109, 114, 167, 190, 228, 251, 268
Templeton, John N., 106, 107, 108, 110, 112
Thirteenth Amendment, 140, 149, 151, 167
Thomas, H. K., 37
Thomas, John, 47
Thompson, Francis, 88, 96, 99
Thompson, J. A., 342, 343
Thompson, Rev. James S., 220, 222, 223, 224, 226, 234
Thomson, Wm., 121
Thornbrough, Emma Lou, 172
Toombs, Robert, 3, 51
Topp, William H., 5, 13, 14, 23, 24, 55, 56, 58, 60, 61, 62, 63, 64, 75, 79, 80, 82, 84
Torrey, Charles T., 49, 50, 52-53, 135
Townsend, J. H., 99
Townshend, Norton S., 276, 292-93
Trades, Black State Conventions favor for blacks, 189, 229, 267
Travelling Agents, 110
Trent, D., 242
Triffin, Edward, 323
Troy, Samuel, Jr., 343
True American, 294
Trust, Wm. P., 281
Tucker, George W., 184, 337
Tucker, J., 174
Turner, A., 174
Turner, David D., 140, 144, 145, 147, 148, 151, 155, 156, 157
Turner, McPherson, 220
Tyler, John, 173, 175
Tyson, Wm., 83

Uncle Tom's Cabin, xix
Underground Railroad, 26, 50, 97, 118, 135, 239
Underwood, J. P., 241, 242, 243, 246, 247, 316
Union Army, 52
Union Baptist Church, 278
University of Glasgow, 36

Valley Forge, 303
Van Brakle, Samuel, 120, 121, 122, 126, 133
Van De Zee, Peter, 60
Van Hussen, Chauncey, 88
Van Vranken, F., 55
Vance, Charles H., 139, 149, 156
Vandeveer, Peter, 60
Vashon, George B., 144, 146, 147, 151, 152, 156, 157, 158, 167
Vashon, Halson, 107, 108, 116
Vashon, John B., xii, 82, 104, 106, 107, 109, 110, 111, 116, 117, 121, 122, 123
Vidal, Ulysses B., 34, 36
Vigilance Committee, 52
Villiers, John Julius Le Moyne de, 52
Voice of Freedom, 76
Voice of the Disfranchised, 264
Voice of the Fugitive, The, 196
Vosburgh, Geo., 274

Wade, Benjamin Franklin, 276, 291-92, 294
Walden, William, 258
Walker, David, 229, 240
Walker, E. P., 332, 334, 335, 336, 337
Walker's Appeal, 229, 240
Wall, O. S. B., 337
Wallace, Elder, 219
War for Independence, 40-41, 192, 216, 271, 299-302, 329
War of 1812, 21, 26, 75, 137-38, 192, 216, 271, 299-302, 324, 329
Ward, J. L., 274
Ward, John T., 219, 221, 258, 263, 275, 316, 342, 345
Ward, Samuel Ringgold, 43, 51, 59
Ward, Wm., 219
Ware, Isaiah, 121
Warner, H. G., 240
Warren, Rev. John A., 76, 342, 344, 345, 346
Warren, Joseph, 76, 342, 344, 345, 346
Washington, Augustus, 60
Washington, George, 192, 299
Washington, T., 242, 346
Washington, Willis, 198, 199, 200, 202, 204, 205
Watkins, Frances Ellen, 334, 337, 340, 341
Watkins, William J., 89, 91, 99, 100, 101, 334, 335, 337, 341
Watson, Isaiah, 116
Watson, John, 241, 243, 249
Watson, John L., 218, 220, 221, 222, 223, 225, 226, 227, 234, 236-37, 238, 241, 242, 243, 246, 247, 250
Watson, W. W., 275
Watts, William, 203, 206, 211
Weaver, Rev. Elisha, 144, 148, 149, 156, 160, 168, 176
Webb, William, 110
Webster, Daniel, 46, 52, 94, 159, 324
Weekly Advocate, 84, 118
Weir, George, 80
Weir, George Jr., 64
Weir, Isaiah C., 104, 119, 122
Wells, Samuel, 43, 199, 203, 205

Wendell, John, 5, 8
Wesley, John, 319
Wesleyan University, 25, 76
West, A. R., 183, 195
West India Emancipation, 330
Whalley, Edward, 78
Wheaton, Chas., A., 43, 44
Wheeler, John W., 97
Whig Party, 2, 6, 25, 32, 39, 87, 93, 173, 175, 273, 308
White, Geo. B., 177
White, Jesse, 174
Whitfield, James M., 327, 330
Whitsill, Felix, 258, 263
Whittier, John G., 44, 51, 302
Wilberforce, William, 188, 196
Wilberforce Settlement, 24
Wilberforce University, 346, 350, 353
Williams, A., 6
Williams, Daniel, 140, 144, 155
Williams, Geo. B., 237
Williams, George R., 223, 225, 226, 242, 244, 245, 248, 249, 254, 274, 280
Williams, Henry, 55
Williams, J. H., 345, 346
Williams, John, 312, 336, 337
Williams, John F., 121
Williams, Rev. Peter, Jr., xi–xii
Williams, Rev. Samuel, 107, 108, 110, 116
Williamson, Passmore, 96, 97
Wilson, Benjamin, 145
Wilson, Charles M., 219, 220, 223, 226
Wilson, F., 241, 245, 250
Wilson, George W., 342
Wilson, Henry, 157, 168, 324, 330
Wilson, Isaac, 275
Wilson, James, 125, 136
Wilson, William J., 79, 80, 82, 84, 88, 96
Wilson, Willis R., 183, 184, 186, 189, 190
Wise, Henry A., 319, 330
Wistar, Caspar, 124, 136
Wolf, John, 121, 123
Wolf, John G., 121
Woman's rights, xix, 51, 52, 91, 180
Women. *See* Black Women
Wood, O. C., 199, 203
Woodson, Rev. Lewis, 106, 108, 110, 112, 116, 117, 121
Woolman, John, 124, 136
World Anti-Slavery Convention, 135-36
Wright, Jonathan Jasper, 140, 149, 150, 153, 166-67
Wright, R. P. G., 5, 13
Wright, Richard, 55, 56, 58, 59, 60, 72, 89, 96
Wright, T. T., 148
Wright, Rev. Theodore S., xi, 5, 8, 9, 10, 15, 24, 32, 51

Yancey, Charles A., 241, 248, 251, 259, 260, 261, 263
Yancy, A., 241
Young, Rev. H. J., 342
Youngs, James, 55

Zion Baptist Church (New York City), 24
Zuille, John J., 5, 23, 88